図解 英単語イメージ辞典

An Illustrated Dictionary of Common English Words

政村 秀實
Masamura Hidemi

Paulus Pimomo
英文校閲

大修館書店

はしがき

　絵本のような英語の辞典をつくってみたいという思いが編集部と通じ合い，本書への取り組みが始まりました．すべての見出し語 (1416 語) にその語義イメージを描き出すこと (一語一絵)．これが本書の大きな特徴です．英語の語義のコア (芯) となる意味合いを描き出し，学習者の語彙獲得の助けになることをもくろんだのです．とはいえ，本書で扱う英単語の多くは抽象的な意味を持っているので，各単語のイメージを図や絵に描き出すのは容易ではありませんでした．著者の原画をたたき台にして，イラストレーター，編集部にアイディア，アドバイスを得てようやく完成した次第です．しかし，本書の図や絵が各語義を表すものとして固定的に存在するわけでないことはいうまでもありません．

　さて，図や絵を読み取るときは，原義または語源から説き起こした簡明な意味の変遷を先に頭に入れ，図や絵に目をやるのがいいかと思います．語義の視覚化は容易ではないと申しましたが，語義の言葉による説明と図や絵のイメージとが，すっきりとつながるもの，あまり結びつかないもの，中には絵解きに苦労するものがあるかと思います．まずは，そのようなイメージの揺らぎをとらえながら，絵本をめくる感触あるいは感覚で図や絵を楽しんでもらいたいと思います．楽しむことでイメージが膨らみ，これまでに習得したはずの語義を改めて理解し，語彙をさらに増やしていくことに役立てば幸いです．

　語義イメージをとらえやすくするために，単語の原義または語源から現代の語義に至る過程をできるだけ簡潔に示し，随所に，発音やつづり字の持つ音感を記しています．さらに，約 1800 語の派生語 (派)・関連語 (関) は，原義や語源を同じくする語を，イメージが湧きやすいもの，頻度の高いものに絞って載せています．情報を網羅することを目指すよりも，語義のコアに迫るには説明が簡潔であるべきだと考えました．

　用例は，語義のコアを頼りに場面がイメージできる文をフルセンテンスで載せ

ています.様々な実際の場面に現れる内容に絞り,文中の見出し語の置き換え表現を数多く提示しています.英語で置き換えることにより見出し語の理解がさらに深まることでしょう.文中の[＝　　]の表現は,「記号が施されている箇所から置き換えが可能であることを示しています.例えば,Living「*above all else*[＝first of all] should be fun. は,Living above all else should be fun. とも Living first of all should be fun. ともいえるということです.「記号がない場合は,[＝　　]の直前の一語と置き換えてください.

　語義イメージの描出には,イラストレーターのひろせさかえさんに大変な工夫・努力をいただき,英文校閲をお願いした Paulus Pimomo 教授(Central Washington University)には,語義イメージ獲得への協力も得ることができました.また,構成・編集に際しては大修館書店編集部の五十嵐靖彦さんとランゲージアーツ言語教育研究所の武田優子さんの心からのご尽力をいただきました.上記の四氏に深甚の感謝を捧げます.本書が読者の方々の所期の目的達成のための十分な助けになるこを祈っています.

2017 年　晩秋　　著者

［図解］英単語イメージ辞典

a /ə/

語源は〈one（一つの）〉である．a は〈一つの〉の意味合いをもつが，one とは異なる概念である．例えば，"a boy" と発想したときの "boy" は話者の〈頭の中に描かれる一般的な boy〉であって，そこにいる一人の boy のことではない．"a" がつくとその名詞は〈不特定多数のたまたまの〉という意味合いになる．

They bought *a* house five years ago. The house is now being redecorated.　彼らは5年前に家を買った．その家は今，改装中だ．《a house：いわゆる家，the house：買った家》．　▶redecorate「改装する」〔← re（再び）decorate（飾る）〕；「(家を) 改修する」は renovate で，カタカナ語「リフォーム」にあたる reform は使わない．

He wears *a* beard.　彼はあごひげを生やしている．《a beard：いわゆるあごひげ》▶「彼はあごひげを伸ばし放題にしている」の場合は〈彼のあごひげ〉と特定されるので He lets *his* beard grow freely. となる．

able /éɪbl/

原義は〈持つことができる〉である．**持つ，つかむ《具体的》→力がある《抽象的》**．able は have や hold と語源的に同系のことばである．日本語でも「技術を持っている」，「こつをつかむ→〜できるようになる」などという．
派 ability（能力）　関 enable（可能にする）

Some animals ⌈*are able to* [=have the *ability* to] predict earthquakes.　動物の中には地震を予知できるものがいる．

He is an *able* pianist with nimble fingers.　彼は指さばきの軽快な有能なピアニストだ．　▶a nimble-fingered person「手先の器用な人」

about /əbáut/

語源は〈ab（側に）out（外）〉である．**対象のまわりに物や意識が存在する**ことを表す．周りにある→ほぼ近くにある→そろそろ，～のころ．カタカナ語では「大雑把」の意で「アバウトな表現」などというが，about にこの意はない．

I am *about* halfway through the book.　その本を半分ばかり読んだところだ．

What is his lecture *about*? ＝What is he going to lecture *about*?　彼は何について講演するの？《～について》　▶lecture＝give a lecture

He lives somewhere *about* [＝around] here.　彼はこのあたりに住んでいる．《～のあたりに》

Dirty clothes were scattered *about* [＝around] on the floor.　汚れた衣服が床のあちこちに散らかっていた．《～のあちこちに》

I *was about to* call you.　ちょうど電話しようと思っていたところよ．《そろそろ～する》　▶電話しようと思っていた相手から電話があった時に返す常套文句．

---

above /əbʌ́v/

語源は〈ab（外に）ove（越えて）〉である．**対象がある基準となるものより上に位置する状態・上位に位置する様子**．対象と基準との間には間隔がある．つづりに over が潜んでいる．

We are (at) 650 ⌈meters *above* sea level [＝meters high from the surface of the sea].　ここは海抜 650 メートルだ．

We watched fireworks burst *above* us in the sky.　頭上で花火が開くのを見た．

I am *above* [＝better than] average in school.　私の成績は平均より上だ．

Living ⌈*above all else* [＝first of all] should be fun.　生きることは，何はさておき面白くなければならない．

abroad /əbrɔ́ːd/

語源は〈a (ヘ) broad (広い)〉である. 昔は広い所といえば「屋外」, それが現代では「海外」になった.

The writer is popular both at home and *abroad*.　あの作家は国内および海外で人気がある.

Granma has never traveled *abroad* [=overseas].　おばあちゃんは海外旅行をしたことがない.

---

absent /形 ǽbsənt, 動 æbsént/

absent

語源は〈ab (離れて) sent (居る)〉である. **離れて＋存在する→しかるべき場に居ない《不在・欠席》→しかるべき場に存在しない《欠落》.** 主体が本来存在すべき場から離れているイメージ. 学生なら授業中なのに自宅にいたり, 映画館にいたりといった図が連想される.
派 absence (不在) ; absentee (欠席者, 不在者)
関 present (存在する) (←目の前に＋居る)

He ⌈was *absent* [=*absented* himself]⌉ from work.　彼は欠勤した.

She wore an *absent* expression.　彼女はうつろな表情をしていた.

Darkness is an *absence* of light.　闇とは光がない〔←不在である〕ことである.

Absence makes the heart grow fonder.　会えなくなる〔←いないこと〕と恋心は募るもの.

My grandfather seems to be somewhat *absent-minded* [=forgetful]; he often leaves his keys in the lock of the front door.　おじいさんはどうも忘れっぽい. よく玄関の錠に鍵を差し込んだままにしている.

absolute /ǽbsəlùːt/

語源は〈ab (離れて) solute (解かれた)〉である。**躊躇(ちゅうちょ)や疑いから解き放たれている→つべこべ言わず全面的に→絶対的に**.
派 absolutely (絶対に)

He places *absolute* [=complete] trust in his surgeon.　彼は主治医に全幅の信頼を寄せている．

She has *absolute* faith in the afterlife.　彼女は死後の世界があると絶対的に信じている．

"Do you come with me?" "*Absolutely*!"　「一緒に行く？」「もちろん」

"May I use your dad's car?" "*Absolutely* not [=No way]!"　「君のお父さんの車借りていい？」「絶対だめだよ！」

abuse /名 əbjúːs, 動 əbjúːz/

語源は〈ab (外れて) use (使う)〉である．**常軌を外れた使用とは文字通り「悪用・乱用」である**．

The boy had been *abused* by his father for a long time.　その少年は父親から長い間虐待を受けていた．

The child showed signs of physical *abuse*.　その子は身体的虐待を受けている兆候があった．

The governor was driven into resignation after he was accused of *abusing* his power.　知事は職権の乱用の咎(とが)で辞任に追い込まれた．

accept /əksépt/

語源は〈ac(を)cept(取る)〉である. **申し出・意見・詫びなどを快く,あるいは仕方なく受け入れる**.
派 acceptable(受け入れられる); acceptance(受諾)

Tom readily *accepted* our invitation to dinner.　トムはディナーの招待を快く受けてくれた. ▶readily＝willingly

An old driver hit my car and *accepted* his responsibility for the accident.　老齢の運転手が僕の車に衝突したが,事故の責任を取ってくれた.

Smoking used to be a socially *acceptable* practice.　喫煙は社会的に許される習慣だった.

I got a letter of *acceptance* [＝admission] from Hokkaido University.　北海道大学から入学許可書が届いた.

---

access /ǽksəs/

語源は〈ac(へ)cess(行く)〉である. **目的の場へ近づくこと→接近・出入り・利用すること→情報にたどり着く**.
派 accessible(利用できる)

This hotel ⌈provides *easy access* [＝is conveniently located] to the terminal.　このホテルからターミナル駅へすぐ行ける. ▶provide ～＝give ～

The program helps you *access* [＝*get access to*] the data you want more quickly.　このプログラムを使うと必要なデータにこれまでよりも早くたどり着ける.

Community facilities should be ⌈wheelchair *accessible* [＝*accessible* by wheelchair].　公共の施設は車椅子の利用ができるようになっているべきだ.
▶a *wheelchair-accessible* toilet「車椅子で利用できるトイレ」

accident /ˈæksədənt/

語源は〈ac（に）cident（落ちる）〉である．**降りかかってくる→偶然→災難**．古来，人の運命は星による，つまり天から降りかかるものと信じられてきた．
派 accidental（思いがけない）　関 incident（事件）

My brother had a car *accident* while traveling to work.　兄は通勤途上，車の事故に遭った．

Success doesn't happen *by accident* [＝by chance]. It often takes hard work.　成功は偶然生まれるものではない．たいてい懸命な努力を要するものだ．

accord /əˈkɔːrd/

語源は〈ac（へ）cord（心）〉である．**一方が他方と心を合わせる→一方が他方と調和する，一致する**．
派 accordingly（それに応じて）

His account doesn't *accord* [＝go] *with* the facts.　彼の説明は事実と一致していない．

According to a survey, [A survey says] 25 % of Japanese single women fear that they may look older than their actual age.　ある調査によれば，日本の独身女性の25％は実年齢よりも老けて見えるのではないかと恐れているそうだ．　▶according to ～「～によれば」〔←～の情報に添えば〕

When your business is low, you must adjust your expenditure *accordingly*.　商売が不振な時はそれに応じて出費を控えないといけない．

account /əkáunt/

語源は〈ac (を) count (数える)〉である．**金を数える《勘定》→目の前の状況をきちんと数え上げる→考慮する《考慮・評価》→説明する《説明・根拠》**．
派 accountable (説明責任がある)；accountancy (会計, 経理)；accountant (会計士, 経理士)
関 count (数える)

You have to open a bank *account* as soon as possible after your move.　引っ越し後, できるだけ早く銀行口座を開く必要がありますよ.

According to an eyewitness *account*, the victim was shot to death by a soldier.　目撃者の証言によれば, 犠牲者は兵士に射殺されたということだ.

I need software for keeping our *family accounts*.　家計簿をつけるためのソフトが欲しい.　▶software は数えられない名詞

Drinking water while doing exercise used to be *accounted* [= considered] ineffective.　運動中に水分を摂ることは無意味だと考えられていた.
▶ineffective=useless

accuse /əkjú:z/

語源は〈ac (を) cuse (責める)〉である．**人をひどく責める→非難する→告訴する**．-cuse は〈糾(きゅう)(＝問い責める)〉なので音の響きからも〈追及・問責〉の意味合いが感じられる．
関 excuse (免除する)〔←外す＋責める〕

There are plenty of people who have been falsely *accused*.　(無実なのに) 誤って告訴される人が多くいる.

She *accused* her boss *of* [brought her boss to trial for] sexual harassment.　彼女は上司をセクハラで訴えた.

The reporter was *accused* of [=was charged with] libeling the president in a magazine article.　その記者は, 雑誌記事で大統領の名誉を傷つけたとして告訴された.　▶libel /láibl/「(人) を中傷する」

The witness identified the *accused* [=the suspect].　目撃者は容疑者を本人に間違いないと証言した.　▶the+accused (形容詞)「告訴された人 (たち)」

achieve /ətʃíːv/

語源は〈a (へ) chieve (達する)〉である. **取り組む対象の頂へ到達する→〜を成し遂げる**.
派 achievement (達成, 業績)
関 chief (チーフ)〔←組織の頂にいる人〕

The campaign for disarmament failed to *achieve* its objectives. 軍縮キャンペーンはその目標を達成できなかった.

I have *achieved* what I set out to do. 僕は掲げた目標を成し遂げた. ▶set out=plan

I felt a great sense of *achievement* when I finished the marathon. マラソンを完走して大きな達成感があった.

across /əkrɔ́ːs/

語源は〈a (に) cross (十字)〉である. **(十字に) 横切って→①ある場を横切って《線的横断》. ②ある場の全体を横切って《面的横断》**. クロス (cross) は十字で, 十字とは ― と｜が互いに横切った文字である.

As the traffic was busy, we *ran across* the road. 道路は車が多かったので急いで渡った.《線的横断》

The trunk measures 18 inches *across* [=in diameter]. 幹は差し渡し18インチです.《線的横断》 ▶measure 〜「寸法は〜である」

I want to get this message *across* to as many people as possible. このメッセージをできるだけ多くの人に伝えたい.《線的横断》 ▶get 〜 across to ...「〜を…に伝える」

There are about 80,000 shrines *across* [=throughout] Japan. 日本国中に約8万の神社がある.《面的横断》

act /ǽkt/

act

原義は〈行う〉である. **do** が〈する〉なら **act** は〈(あえて) 行う〉の意味合い. 名詞では〈(単発の) 行為〉についていう.
派 active (活動的な); activity (活動); activist (活動家); actor (俳優)

You had better *act* soon enough if you want to be employed. 雇って欲しいのならすぐに行動しないとだめだよ.

The court found that the police officer *acted* properly when attacked. 裁判所は, 警官は正当防衛だったと判決した.

No more changes will be made to this schedule unless「there is *an act of God* [something beyond our control happens]. 想定外のことがない限り, この予定にこれ以上の変更はありません.

Mr. Yamada will be *acting* [=interim] manager until a new manager is named. 山田氏が新しい支配人が任命されるまで代理の支配人を務める.

---

action /ǽkʃən/

action

語源は〈act (行う) ion (こと)〉である. **act (行為) が連続したり繰り返されたりする時, action (行動) になる.** act+act+act ...=action といえる.

What *action* should be taken if child abuse is suspected? 幼児虐待の疑いがある時はどう対処すべきですか.

The government is slow to *take action* on issues like poverty and unemployment. 政府は貧困や失業といった問題に対応するのが遅い. ▶take action「行動を起こす」

Now, how do you put your plans into *action* [=practice]? では, どのようにしてその案を実行に移すのですか. ▶put ~ into action「~を実行に移す」

actual /ǽktʃuəl/

actual

語源は〈actu (実際) al (の)〉である．**外見とは違って実際の，本当の**．
派 actually（本当のところは，実際は）

Susan appears to be in her late teens, but 「her *actual* age is twenty-five [＝she is *actually* twenty-five]．　スーザンは十代後半に見えるが，実際の年齢は 25 だ．　▶ be in one's teens「十代である」

Dad complained that his computer wouldn't boot up, but *actually* the cable was unplugged.　父さんはパソコンが立ち上がらないとぶつぶつ言っていたけど，実はケーブルが外れていたのよ．　▶ boot up [＝start up] a computer; be plugged「プラグが差し込んである」

add /ǽd/

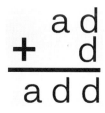

語源は〈ad (へ) d (置く)〉である．**既にあるもの（行為・ことば・物・数など）に新しく付け加える**．
派 addition（追加）; additional（追加の）; additive（添加物）

I want to *add* some words to what he said.　彼の発言に少し付け加えたい．

In addition to [＝Besides] being good for the environment, solar power systems cost you less in the end.　太陽光発電システムは環境によいうえに，コストも結局は安くなる．　▶ power「電力・エネルギー」

You'll have to 「pay *additional* fees for *additional* channels [＝pay an extra fee for every channel you wish to *add*]．　受信チャンネルを増やせば，追加料金を払わないといけない．

The foods we produce are 「all *additive free* [＝all free from artificial *additives*]．　我々の生産する食品はすべて，人工添加物が入っていません．

address /ədrés/

語源は〈ad(へ) dress(引く)〉である.〈**〜の方向へ引く**〉から, ①**声を〜へ向けて話す**. ②**郵便を〜へ向けて送る；住所**. dr- には〈引く〉の意味合いがある.
関 dress(正装する)〔←すそを引いて整える〕；drive(運転する)

He *addressed* [=made an *address* to] the UN on climate change.　彼は国連で気候変動について演説した.

Applications must be *addressed* [=directed] to the personnel division.　願書は人事部宛て送付のこと.　▶personnel「人事の」

What's your email *address*?　あなたのEメールアドレスは？

The arrested man was unemployed and had no fixed *address* [=adobe].　逮捕された男は無職で住所不定であった.

---

admit /ədmít/

語源は〈ad(へ) mit(送る)〉である.　①**提示や意見を納得して心の中へ送り込む→〜であると認める**. ②**資格を認めて入場させる**.
派 admission(入学者選抜)
関 mission(任務)〔←送り出す〕

You're right. I have to *admit*.　君の言うとおりだよ. 認めるよ.

She finally *admitted* her mistake.　彼女はやっと自分の間違いを認めた.

Tattooed persons are not *admitted* to the swimming pool.　刺青(いれずみ)の人はプールへの入場はできない.

You can apply for *admission* [=enrollment] in our college online.
私どもの大学への出願はEメールでできます.

advance /ədvǽns/

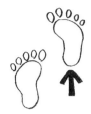

語源は〈ad (へ) vance (前へ進む)〉である．**前へ出る→前進する→予定の時期を早める**．
派 advancement (進歩); advanced (上級の)
関 advantage (利点)

Our team *advanced* to [=reached] the quarterfinals.　わがチームは準々決勝へ進出した．　▶semifinals「準決勝」; finals「決勝戦」

Rooms are limited, so you need to book *in advance* [=beforehand].　部屋数には限りがあるので前もって予約が必要です．　▶book「予約する」

Technological *advancements* [=developments] are taking place at a breathtaking pace.　技術の進歩が驚くべき速さで起こっている．　▶breathtaking「はっとさせるような」

The dictionary is for intermediate to *advanced* learners.　この辞書は中級～上級者向けです．

advantage /ədvǽntɪdʒ/

advantage

語源は〈advant (前にいる) age (状態)〉である．**他者より目標に近い位置にいること→他よりも有利な条件下にいること**．
派 advantageous (有利な)　関 advance (発展, 進歩)

This method has a couple of *advantages* over conventional treatments.　この方法は従来の治療法に比べて優れた点がいくつかある．　▶over「～より優れて」

If you go on a business trip to Hawaii, you could *take advantage of* the opportunity and spend an extra day or two on vacation.　仕事でハワイへ行くのであれば，その機会を利用して1日か2日休暇を過ごすことができるだろう．

Which is more *advantageous* [=favorable], leasing or purchasing?　リースするのと購入するのとではどちらが有利ですか．　▶lease「賃借りする」

advice /ədváis/

advice

語源は〈ad (を) vice (観察すること)〉である．**観察に基づいて意見をする→助言する；助言．**
派 advise /ədváiz/ (助言する)　関 visit (見舞う)

I want to give you some *advice* [=*advise* you] about it.　その件についてちょっと助言したいと思います．　▶数えられない名詞なので an advice は不可．

I started walking on my doctor's *advice* [=recommendation].　医者の勧めに従ってウォーキングを始めた．

The patient was *advised* not to drink alcohol.　患者は酒を控えるよう言われた．

---

affair /əféər/

語源は〈af (を) fair (すること)〉である．**世間の関心を呼ぶような事柄・事件．**

Young people in rich societies may take little interest in political *affairs* [=matters].　豊かな社会の若者は政治情勢にはあまり関心をもたない傾向がある．

I am very happy with the current *state of affairs* [=things].　僕は現状に満足している．　▶a state of affairs「状況」

Anne seems to be *having an affair* with her boss.　アンは上司と不倫関係にあるようだ．　▶have *a love affair*=have a sexual relationship「性的関係にある」の遠回しの表現．

affect /əfékt/

語源は〈af (を) fect (つくる)〉である．**物事が他へ働きかける→悪い影響を与える**．
関 effect (影響, 効果)

The cold weather will *affect* [=damage] the crops.　この寒気は農作物に害を及ぼすだろう．

Some websites contain viruses which will *affect* [=damage] the data on your computers.　サイトの中にはパソコンのデータを壊すウイルスを含んでいるものがある．

afford /əfɔ́:rd/

語源は〈af (へ) ford (前進する)〉である．**(少しの踏ん張りで) 〜できる→少しの努力で目的とするものを獲得できる**．
派 affordable (手ごろな) 〔←買おうと思えば十分買える値段である〕

We cannot *afford* a lawyer.　(資金がないので) 弁護士は雇えない．

I can't *afford* to go to the movies because I have to prepare for the exams next week.　僕は来週, 試験があるので映画に行けない．

We provide quality products at「an *affordable* [=a reasonable] price.　わが社は良質の製品を廉価で提供している．

afraid /əfréɪd/

語源は〈a (で) fraid (恐怖)〉である. **怖がって→恐れて→心配して→不都合を心配して**. 特に I'm afraid ... は「あいにく…です; 申し訳ないけど…です」の意でよく使う.

My boy *is afraid* [=scared] *of* being in dark places. うちの息子は暗い所にいるのを怖がる.

I'm afraid it will rain tomorrow. あいにく, 明日は雨のようです.

I'm afraid we are too late. 残念だけど, もう間に合わないよ.

I'm afraid [=sorry to have to say] that you must take off your shoes here. 申し訳ないけど, ここでは靴を脱いでいただかないといけないのです.

"Do you know anything about cars?" "*I'm afraid not.*" 「車のこと分かる?」「悪いけど, 分からないわ」 ▶例えば, エンジンがかからない時の問答.

---

after /ǽftər/

語源は〈af=off (離れて) ter (もっと)〉である. **(時間的・位置的に) 〜の後ろに→前から受け継いで《継承》→前を求めて《追求》**. -er は比較級.

I will meet you *after* work. 仕事が終わってからお会いします.

New Guinea is the second largest island in the world, *after* [=*next to*] Greenland. ニューギニアはグリーンランドに次ぐ世界第二の大きな島だ.

Kate「*takes after* [=*resembles*] her mother both in looks and in attitudes. ケイトは顔も態度も母親に似ている. ▶take after 〜「〜を受け継ぐ」

The store clerk *ran after* a shoplifter. 店員は万引き犯を追いかけた.

After you.=*Go ahead.* お先にどうぞ.

I decided to quit the job *after all*. やはり仕事を辞めることにした. ▶after all「結局」〔←いろいろ考慮した後に〕

again /əgén/

語源は〈a (で) gain (反対)〉である. **(反対向きに→元に返って) →再び**.

It won't [=I'll never let it] happen *again*. こんなことは二度と起こしません.

Tom was soon well *again* and was able to resume his work. トムはすぐに (また) 元気になって仕事を再開できた.

I deleted an email by mistake and had to start *all over again*. メールを誤って消してしまったので, もう一度始めから書き直すはめになった.

"The Prime Minister's speech was completely empty." "*You can say that again*!" 「首相の演説はまったく内容がなかったよ」「全くその通りだよ!」〔←言える, 言える!〕

against /əgénst/

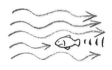

語源は〈a (へ) gainst (反対)〉である. **〜に反対して→〜に備えて→〜と向かい合って**.

The detective bravely fought *against* crime and corruption. 刑事は勇敢に犯罪や汚職と戦った.

I ⌈received an inoculation [=had a shot] *against* flu. 流感 (予防の) 接種を受けた. ▶inoculate「予防接種をする」

Marie stood with her back *against* her car. マリーは車に背をもたせかけて立っていた.

age /éɪdʒ/

原義は〈年齢〉である．**人や物事が生まれてからの年数，ある時期・時代．動詞では，人が歳月を積み重ねる→老化する，物が歳月を積み重ねる→熟成する．**

Daniel is twenty years of *age*. He began to smoke at *age* [=at the *age* of] seventeen.　ダニエルはいま20歳だが，17歳の時に喫煙を始めた．

School-age kids need to get outside and play every day.　学齢期の子どもは毎日，戸外で遊ぶべきだ．

My father seems to have *aged* [=grown old] and lost weight recently.　父は近ごろ老けて痩せてきたように見える．

As we *age* [=get older], our skin also *ages* [=gets old] slowly.　年をとるにつれ，肌も徐々に老化する．

The wine is *aged* for three years in barrels.　このワインは3年物だ．

agent /éɪdʒənt/

語源は〈age（行う）ent（者）〉である．**ある行為をする者→権限を与えられて代理で行う人→代理人・代理店．**
派 agency（代理業, 代理店）

Did you buy your tickets direct from the airline or through an *agent*?　チケットは航空会社から直接買ったの，それとも代理店を通して買ったの？

She works for an advertising *agency*.　彼女は広告代理店で働いている．

ago /əgóu/

語源は〈a (へ) go (行く)〉である. **現時点を基準としてどれほど過去へ go (さかのぼる) かをいう.** ago は元来 agone とつづっていた.

He left an agricultural college in Hokkaido 20 years *ago*.　彼は北海道にある農業大学を 20 年前に卒業した.

It was five years *ago* that you and I first met.　私たちが初めて会ったのは 5 年前だったね.

agree /əgríː/

語源は〈a (で) gree (心地よい)〉である. 相手に対して**心地よく思う→賛成する→一致する, 性に合う.**
派 agreement (賛成); disagreement (不賛成)

I totally *agree*. =I couldn't *agree* with you more.　大賛成です.〔←これ以上に賛成することはしようと思ってもできない〕　▶I totally *disagree*. =I couldn't *agree* with you less.「大反対だ」

Milk doesn't *agree* with me.　牛乳を飲むとお腹が下る.〔←体に合わない〕

City life does not *agree with* me at all.　都会での生活は僕には全然なじまない.

There are both *agreements* and *disagreements* about nuclear power plants.　原発については賛否両論がある.

ahead /əhéd/

語源は〈a(に)head(頭)〉である. **先頭の方に→前方に→(時間的に)先に.**

Keep an eye on the road *ahead* and other cars around you.　道路の前方と周りの車にちゃんと目を注ぎなさい.

Go ahead with your question.　どうぞ質問を始めてください.　▶中断していた行為を「続けてください」の意にもなる.

The project has been successfully completed *ahead* of schedule.　プロジェクトは予定より早く完成した.

aid /éɪd/

語源は〈a(へ)id(助け)〉である. **援助の手を差し伸べる.**
派 unaided(援助のない)

The scholarship *aided* me in continuing my education in college. = *With the aid of* the scholarship, I was able to continue my education in college.　奨学金のお陰で大学でも学ぶことができた.

Mercury, Venus, Mars, Jupiter and Saturn can be seen with *unaided* [=naked] eye.　水星, 金星, 火星, 木星, 土星は肉眼で見える.

aim /éɪm/

原義は〈目星を付ける〉である． **武器で狙いを付ける→目標を目指す；目標**．
派 aimlessly（あてもなく）　関 estimate（見積もる）

The masked man *aimed* his gun at me and said, "Shut up."　覆面をした男は銃を私に向けて「声を出すな」と言った．　▶mask「仮面を付ける」

He quickly regained his balance, *took aim*, and fired.　彼は素早く態勢を立て直して，狙いを付け発射した．　▶take aim「狙いを定める」

I often surf *aimlessly* [＝with no particular *aim*] from one site to another.　あてもなくサイトをあれこれ巡ることがよくある．　▶surf「あちこちサイトを巡る」（サーファーがあちこちの適当な波を見つけて波乗りをする様子に見立てた表現）

air /éər/

原義は〈空気〉である．**空気→（周りの）空気，雰囲気；（空気に当てる）→風に当てる，風を通す→空中に放つ→放送する**．
派 airy（風通しのよい）

Open the window and let the fresh *air* in.　窓を開けていい空気を入れよう．

She「*assumed an air of innocence* [＝pretended as if she knew nothing about it], saying "Why? What have I done?"　彼女は知らないふりをして「なぜ？　私が何をしたの．」と聞いてきた．　▶assume「〜の態度を取る」；innocence「無知」

We use balconies to *air* futons and dry clothes.　ふとんを干したり衣類を乾かしたりするのにバルコニーを使う．

Do they *air* the game?　その試合は放送されるの？　▶they は〈放送局従事者〉を漠然と指している．

all /ɔːl/

all　all

① (数えられるがその一つ一つを意識することなく) いきなり全体を総括的に捉える. ②「数えられないものをすっぽりまとめて全部」の意.

All (the) students passed.　全学生が合格した.　▶同じ状況でも各人を意識して描くと, *Every* student passed. ((どの学生も) みんな合格した) となる.

All the apples on the tree looked ripe enough to eat.　その木のリンゴはみなもう熟れて食べられそうだった.

I had to *stay up all night* to prepare for the examination.　試験のために徹夜しなければいけなかった.

He lost *all* his money in gambling.　彼はギャンブルで持ち金を全て失った.

The directions were *all* wrong.　指示はみな, とんでもない誤りだった.　▶形容詞を強調する：all right など.

---

allow /əláu/

語源は〈al (へ) low (場所に置く)〉である. **人が他者をある場所へ通す→望む「ところ」へ通してやる→受け入れる→〜を許す→〜を認める.**
派 allowance (手当, 許容量)

I'm sorry, but ⌈smoking is not *allowed* [＝you are not *allowed* to smoke] here.　ここでは禁煙ですよ.

Do you *allow* your kids to play games online openly?　子どもに自由にネットのゲームをさせているの?

I'm on a diet but I *allow myself* an occasional piece of cake.　ダイエット中だけど, ときどきケーキは食べるのよ.

almost /ɔ́ːlmoust/

almost

語源は〈all（すべて）most（大多数）〉である．**①ある状態がほとんど九分どおり完成する様子．②ある行為がもう少しで完結する様子**．

We've been married for *almost* [=*nearly*] 20 years now.　私たちは結婚してもうすぐ20年になる．

The pain is *almost* gone.　痛みはほとんどなくなった．

"Is this OK?" "*Almost*."　「これでいい？」「ほぼね」

Marie *almost* wept when she heard the news.　マリーはその知らせを聞いて泣きそうになった．

I *almost* missed the last train.　終電に乗り遅れるところだった．

alone /əlóun/

語源は〈all（まったく）one（一つ）〉である．**他から離れてまったく一人である→ひとりで，ただそれだけで**．物理的に単独であることをいい，寂しさは含意されない．

My grandpa lives *alone* [=by himself].　おじいちゃんはひとりで暮らしている．

We were *alone* on the beach.　浜辺には私たちだけだった．　▶主体は一人に限らない．

Don't *leave* the children *alone* in the kitchen. It is full of dangers.
子どもたちを台所に放っておいてはだめだよ．危険がいっぱいだから．　▶leave＋人＋alone「（人）をひとりにしておく」

along /əlɔ́ːŋ/

語源は〈a（に）long（長く）〉である．**物理的に相対する側面に沿って，心理的に相対する人と（衝突することなく）添って．**
関 belong（あるべき所にある）

We sailed northward *along* the coast of the main island of Japan.　本州の沿岸を北へ向けて航行した．

I don't *get along with* my wife in many ways.　妻とはいろいろな面で気が合わない．　▶get along with＋人「（人）と仲がよい」

already /ɔːlrédi/

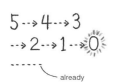

語源は〈all（まったく）ready（準備ができた）〉である．**基準時までに，ある状態・動作がすっかり完了している様子．**

"Would you like another beer?" "I've got enough *already*, thank you."　「ビールもう一杯いかがですか」「もう十分いただきました」

I can't believe it is *already* the end of the year.　もう年の瀬だとは信じがたいよ．

alternative /ɔːltə́ːrnətiv/

語源は〈alternate(入れ替わる)ive(べき)〉である. **ある目的に到達するために本来の方法の代わりとなり得るもの(他の選択肢)**. 富士山の頂上をめざす場合, まずは吉田ルートを考えるとき, 御殿場, 富士宮, 須走の各ルートは an alternative となる.

派 alternate(代わりの); alternatively(その代わりに)

Would you suggest any *alternative* approach [=any other approach than this]?　他のやり方はありませんか.

There are some *alternatives* to do it.　それをする方法は他にいくつかある.
▶an alternative「代替, 選択肢」

among /əmʌ́ŋ/

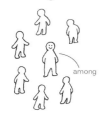

語源は〈a(で)mong(混ざって)〉である. **人や物に囲まれている→〜の間で; 〜の中で**. 通例, 囲むものは三者以上である.

The author is popular *among* young readers.　この作家は若い読者に人気がある.

Decide *among yourselves* who will do what.　誰が何をするかあなたたちで決めなさい.　▶among oneself「お互いの間で」

Most important *among* the town's problems is the lack of health facilities.　その町のいくつかの問題でとりわけ重要なのは医療機関が十分でないことだ.

amount /əmáʊnt/

語源は〈a (へ) mount (山となる)〉である．**積み重なって山となる→合計〜になる**．つづりに mountain (山) や mount (登る) が潜んでいる．

The average working hours per week *amounted* [=added up] *to* 48 hours.　週当たりの平均労働時間は 48 時間になった．

Here the average *amount* of precipitation is 800 mm per year.　当地の年間平均降水量は 800 ミリだ．　▶precipitation /prɪsìpɪtéɪʃən/＝rainfall

analogue /ǽnəlɔːg/

analogue　digital

語源は〈ana (添って) logue (表現)〉である．アナログ**とは現実に添ってそのまま表現する→同じ形に描く方式**をいう．アナログ時計 (analogue watch) は，時の流れを針の動きで表現し，デジタル時計 (digital watch) は時の流れを数字で表示する．analog ともつづる．
派 analogy (類似, 共通点)

My father belongs to the *analogue* generation, having never touched a computer.　父はアナログ世代の人間で，コンピュータに触ったことがない．

The optical functions are readily explained *by analogy with* the camera.　目の機能はカメラに見立てるとうまく説明できる．　▶by analogy with 〜「〜との類推によって」

analysis /ənǽləsɪs/

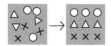

語源は〈ana(沿って)lysis(ほどくこと)〉である。**区分に沿って分け離すこと→説明や理解のために現象を分けて明らかにすること(分析)**.
派 analyst(分析者);analyze(分析する)
関 psychoanalysis(精神分析)

We did an *analysis* of the collected data.　収集したデータを分析した.
Scientists *analyzed* samples of soil taken from the contaminated area.
科学者たちは汚染地域から採取された土壌を分析した.

ancestor /ǽnsestər/

語源は〈an=ante(前に)cestor(行った者)〉である.
先に逝った者,先祖.通例,祖父母より前の世代の人についていう.先祖を個々に捉える時は ancestor, 集合的に捉える時は ancestry という.

Where are your *ancestors* from?　あなたの先祖はどこの出身ですか.
Scientists believe all modern humans share common *ancestors* in Africa.　科学者は,現代人はみなアフリカの祖先から発していると信じている.
Donald Trump is an American ⌈of German *ancestry* [=who is German by *ancestry*]. ドナルド・トランプはドイツ系のアメリカ人です.

anniversary /ænəvə́ːrsəri/

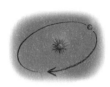

語源は〈anni(年の)versary(巡り)〉である. **年の巡り→周年→(周年)記念日**.
関 annual(毎年の)

Yokohama commemorated the 150th *anniversary* of the opening of its port in 2009.　横浜は開港150周年を2009年に祝った.

The couple celebrated their 25th *anniversary*.　夫妻は結婚25周年を祝った.

announce /ənáuns/

語源は〈an(へ)nounce(告げる)〉である. **一般の人々に伝える・知らせる→公表する**. カタカナ語のアナウンスは「放送」を連想するが, announceからは「口頭・声」が連想される.
派 announcement(公表, 通知)

The former prime minister *announced* his retirement from politics.　元総理は政界からの引退を表明した.

The roosters crowed to *announce* the dawn.　雄鶏が鳴いて夜明けを告げた.　▶crow「コケコッコーと鳴く」

Both leaders made an *announcement* that a trade agreement was finally reached after a long discussion.　両首脳は論議を尽くした末に貿易協定が成立したと発表した.

annual /ǽnjuəl/

語源は〈annu=year (年) al (の)〉である. **1年に一度起こる→毎年の, 例年の**. 名詞用法では「年報, 年鑑, 一年草」の意.
派 annually (毎年)
関 anniversary (〔毎年の〕記念日)

The employers can take paid *annual* leave. 従業員は年次有給休暇が取れる. ▶paid leave「有給休暇」

Pansies are *annual*; they grow and die within one year. パンジーは一年草で, 一年の内に成長し枯れる. ▶perennial「多年草」

another /ənʌ́ðər/

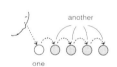

語源は〈an (一つ) other (他の)〉である. 同一種のものがいくつかある時, 話し手が**任意の一つに注目すると, それを one と認識する**. one が決まると同時に, **他の残りは others となる. others の一つひとつは an other, つまり another となる**.

I want to have *another* [=one more] child. もう一人子どもが欲しいわ. ▶この文脈では2人目か3, 4人目かは不明.

How would you say this in *another* way? これを別の表現で言うとどうなりますか.

We will tell you about it *another* time. その件についてはまたの機会に話します.

Do you believe ⌈there is *another* life after this [=in life after death]? あの世があることを信じますか.

answer /ǽnsər/

語源は〈an＝against（対して）swer（誓う）〉である．**問いかけや要求に対して誠実に反応する→返答する，応える；返答，解決策**．つづりに swear（誓う）が潜んでいる．

Would you *answer* the phone? 電話に出てくれませんか．〔←呼び出し音に対する反応〕

Her prayers were *answered*. 彼女の祈りは叶えられた．

There is no single *answer to* this question. この問いに対する答えは一つだけではない．

I think the *answer* to poverty is better education. 貧困の解決にはよりよい教育が必要だと思う．

anxious /ǽŋkʃəs/

語源は〈anxi（締めつけた）ous（ような）〉である．**息の詰まるような→はらはら，どきどき，いらいら**．
派 anxiously（不安そうに）；anxiety（不安）

The newly appointed captain was *anxious* [=worried] *about* whether he can live up to their expectations. 新しく選ばれた主将はチームの期待に応えられるかどうか不安に思った． ▶ live up to one's expectations「人の期待に応える」

She stopped and「cast an *anxious* look around [=looked *anxiously* around]． 彼女は立ち止まり不安そうに周りに目をやった．

Her *anxiety* grew as all of her phone calls to her husband were not answered. いくら夫に電話しても返答がないので彼女は不安が募った．

any /éni/

語源は〈an=one（どの一つ）y（でも）〉である．**あれでも，これでも→どれでも**．雲をつかむような，捉えどころのなさが感覚される：肯定文なら〈どれでも，誰でも〉，否定文なら〈何も，誰も，少しも〉，疑問文なら〈何か，誰か，何ほどか〉の意味合いになる．

Live your life *any* way you like.　自分の好きなように生きなさい．

It doesn't make *any* difference.　これでは少しも変わり映えがしないよ．

Do you have *any* role models?　誰か模範になる人がいますか． ▶a role model「生き方の手本となる人」

apart /əpá:rt/

語源は〈a（て）part（分ける）〉である．**位置や時間が離れて，別々に**．つづりに part（分ける）が潜んでいる．
派 apartment（アパート）
関 apartheid（人種隔離政策〔アパルトヘイト〕）

The couple have been living *apart* [=separately] for several months now.　あの夫婦はもう数か月別居している．

My sister and I are 6 years *apart*.　姉と私は6歳離れています．

Asparagus needs little attention「*apart from* [=except for] occasional weeding.　アスパラガスはときどき雑草を取ってやる以外はほとんど世話がかからない． ▶apart from ～「～は別として」；weed「雑草を抜く」

apology /əpάːlədʒi/

語源は〈apo=away(離れる)logy(ことば)〉である.
不都合・不始末から逃れるためのことば→詫び.
派 apologize(詫びる)

The minister「made a public *apology* [=*apologized to* the public] *for* his slip of the tongue. 大臣は国民に失言を詫びた. ▶apologize to+人+for+行為「(人)に(行為)を詫びる」

appeal /əpíːl/

語源は〈ap(へ)peal(追い立てる)〉である.**ことばで追い立てる→相手に訴える→雰囲気・内容が相手に訴える**. つづりに peal(とどろき)が潜んでいる.

The police are *appealing for* information regarding a missing boy from the park. 警察は公園で姿が見えなくなった少年に関する情報提供を呼びかけている. ▶appeal for ~「~を強く求める」

The defendant *appealed to* a higher court to review the judgment reached in a lower court. 被告は下級裁判所の判決を再審するために上訴した.

If fishing doesn't「*appeal to* [=interest] you, you can certainly enjoy other types of recreation in the area. 魚釣りに興味が湧かなくても,この地域では他のレクレーションがきっと楽しめます. ▶appeal to+人「(人)の興味をそそる」

appear /əpíər/

語源は〈ap (へ) pear (目に映る)〉である．**姿が目に入ってくる→姿が〜のように目に映る→物事が〜のように思われる**．
派 appearance (外観)

The moon *appeared* [=came out] occasionally between the clouds.　月が雲間からときどき顔を出した．

The commentator *appears* on television almost every day.　あの評論家はほとんど毎日テレビに出ている．

When questioned, she *appeared* [=looked] very upset and confused.　尋問を受けると彼女はとても取り乱した様子だった．

We are liable to be deceived by *appearances* [=looks].　私たちは外見に惑わされがちだ．

---

apply /əplái/

語源は〈ap (へ) ply (重ねる，添える)〉である．**物事を遂行するために必要なものを注ぎ込む〔←添える〕→適用する**．pl- は〈重ねる，添える〉の意味合い：plus (加える), plural (複数)
関 reply (返答する)

I *applied* [=put on] ointment to the sunburn.　日焼けに軟こうを塗った．

Can we *apply* the rule *to* the case?　その規則はこの件に適用できますか．

She successfully *applied for* a job at the restaurant.　彼女はレストランの仕事に応募して採用された．　▶apply for 〜「〜に志願する」〔←〜へ向けて身を投じる〕; apply (oneself) for 〜が意識下にある．

appoint /əpɔ́ɪnt/

語源は〈ap (へ) point (点を指す)〉である. **一点を指し示す→人を名指す《任命》→場所・時を指定する《指定・予約》**.

派 appointment ([面会・受診などの] 予約)

It made sense to *appoint* David to take over the job.　デビッドにその仕事の後任を命じたのは賢明であった. ▶make sense「意味を成す」[←理にかなう]

When I showed up at the *appointed* place and time, he wasn't around.　約束の場所へ時間通りに行ったが, 彼の姿はなかった. ▶show up「姿を現す」

Can I *make an appointment* for tomorrow at 5 pm?　明日午後5時に予約できますか.

appreciate /əpríːʃièɪt/

語源は〈ap (へ) preciate (値をつける)〉である. **物事の価値が上がる→物事のよさが分かる→他者の行為の価値が分かる, 有り難く思う**.「価値が分かる→有難く思う」の展開は, 日本語「有難い」が「在り難い→存在が稀である→希少価値がある→有難く思う」と展開するのと発想が似ている.

派 appreciation (値上がり, 鑑賞, 感謝)

We don't *appreciate* [＝know the value of] our health until we lose it.　健康の価値は病気になってはじめて分かるものだ.

We would *appreciate* any information regarding the incident.　この事件に関するどんな情報でもお知らせくだされば幸いです.

I don't *appreciate* wines.　私はワインの味が分からない.

I *appreciate* your concern, but honestly, I'm fine.　ご心配くださってありがとう. でも, けっこう元気にしています.

We say "arigato" to show our *appreciation*.　感謝を表すために"ありがとう"と言います.

approach /əpróutʃ/

語源は〈ap (へ) proach (近づく)〉である．**ある場所・目的・問題 (解決) へ近づく・迫る**．

I wonder how I should *approach* [=tackle] the problem. その問題にどう取り組んだらいいだろう．

I was *approached* by the Mayor to serve as his adviser. 市長から顧問になってくれないかと折衝があった．

As fall *approached*, the colors in the woods began to change. 秋が近づくと森の色が変わり始めた．

When I *approached*, the kids stopped whispering. 私が近づくと子どもたちはひそひそ話をやめた． ▶whisper「ひそひそ話す」

approve /əprúːv/

語源は〈ap (へ) prove (よいとみなす)〉である．**提案・行為をそれでよいと判断する→承認する**．つづりに prove (証明する) が潜んでいる．
派 approval (承認)

My parents don't 「*approve of* [=think well of] my miniskirts. 両親は私のミニスカートをよく思っていない．

They need to gain the government *approval* [=agreement] to establish a new department. 新規に学部を設けるためには政府の認可を得ることが必要だ．

appoint, appreciate, approach, approve

area /éəriə/

原義は〈空き地・中庭〉である. **広がる場所を区切った地域・区域及びその面積**.
関 arena (競技場)

The people living ⌈in the *area* [=in the neighborhood] are very friendly and cheerful.　このあたりの住人はとても親しみやすくて陽気だ.

What is the *area* of your farm? =How big is your farm?　農場の面積はどれほどですか.

It is about 500 square meters in *area*.　面積はだいたい 500 平方メートルだ.

What is the surface *area* of the cube?　この立方体の表面積はいくらですか.

argue /á:rgju:/

原義は〈ことばで事の次第をはっきりさせる〉こと. **発言が一方向なら〈主張する〉, 双方向なら〈激しく議論する・口論する〉となる**. discussion は〈種々の論の提示による話し合い〉の意味合い.
派 argument (主張, 議論, 口論)

Many *argue* that religion causes many problems in the world.
宗教は世界の多くの問題を引き起こしていると主張する人が多い.

They are *arguing* [=having *arguments*] over which party is to blame for the current economic crisis.　彼らは, どちらの政党が今の経済危機の元凶となっているか言い争っている.　▶over=about ; be to blame for 〜「〜の責任がある」

arm /ɑ́ːrm/

原義は〈(胴体とつながっている) 腕〉である. **腕→(腕に抱える) 武器→武装する**.

関 disarm (武装解除する); disarmament (軍縮)

Those who are prone to backaches shouldn't carry a heavy load in their *arms*. 腰痛になりやすい人は重いものを腕に抱えないほうがいい. ▶ be prone to 〜「〜に陥りやすい」

My father was often seen sitting in a chair *with his arms crossed*. 父はよく腕組みして椅子に腰掛けていた. ▶ cross one's arms「腕を組む」

Should Japan ⌈*arm* itself [=be *armed*]⌋ with nuclear weapons? 日本は核武装すべきだろうか.

around /əráund/

語源は〈a=on (に) round (周り)〉である. **①あるものの周りにぐるりと存在する様子. ②あるものの周りをぐるりと回転する様子. ③あるものとの正対 (まともに向き合うこと) を避けて周辺を回る様子.**

There are always dogs wandering *around* the house. その家の周りをいつも犬がうろついている.

I usually leave school *around* 5 pm. 私はたいてい5時ごろ下校する.

She turned *around* and walked away angrily. 彼女はくるりと背を向けて怒って歩いて行った.

There is no getting *around* the problem. その問題は避けて通れない.
▶ get around 〜「〜を回避する」

arrange /əréɪndʒ/

arrange

語源は〈ar（へ）range（揃える）〉である．**ばらばらのものを順序よく並べて活用するのに好都合な状態にする**．つづりに range（連なる，並行する）が潜んでいる．
派 arrangement（配列，手配）
関 mountain range（山脈）

I learned how to *arrange* flowers in a vase. 花器に花を生ける方法を覚えた．

We have *arranged* [＝planned] a welcome party for newcomers. 新人たちの歓迎会を計画した．

The staff is busy working on an *arrangement for* the conference. 職員は大会のための準備に懸命に取り組んでいる．

arrest /ərést/

語源は〈ar（を）rest（止める）〉である．**動きを止める→①犯人の自由な活動を止めること；逮捕する．②発作が心臓の活動を止めること**．つづりに rest（休める）が潜んでいる．

He was ⌈*arrested for* document forgery [＝caught forging documents]. 彼は文書偽造罪で逮捕された．

The patient had a cardiac *arrest* [＝The patient's heart stopped beating] during surgery. 患者は手術中に心臓停止に陥った． ▶cardiac arrest「心停止」

arrive /əráɪv/

語源は〈ar (へ) rive=river (川岸)〉である.**(川岸へ着く)→向こうからこちらへ着く**. 話者の目は到着地側にある. 類語 reach は〈こちらから向こうへ着く〉の意味合い. arrive の到着地は話者側にあるので必ずしも示さなくても分かるが, reach の目的地は無数に考えられるので到達地点を示す必要がある.
派 arrival (到着)

The packet has *arrived* [=been delivered to us] in good condition. 小包は無事届きましたよ.

Our first baby is due to *arrive* in July. =We are going to have our first baby in July. 初めての赤ちゃんが7月に生まれます.

What is the *arrival* time of the flight from NYC? =When does the flight from NYC *arrive*? ニューヨークからの便は何時着ですか.

art /ά:rt/

原義に〈つなぐ〉のニュアンスがある.**(つなぐ)→個々をつないで形にする→技術→芸術**. 絵画は一筆一筆のタッチの組み合わせ, 音楽は一音一音の音色の組み合わせ, 詩歌は一語一語の組み合わせで生まれる.

I teach *art* at an elementary school. 私は小学校で美術を教えている.

She practiced 「*the art of* walking [=how to walk]」 in high heels for the beauty contest. 彼女は美人コンテストに備えて, ハイヒールを履いて歩き方を練習した. ▶the art of ~ 「~の技術」

She learned karate—*the art of* self-defense. 彼女は護身術である空手を習った.

article /άːrtɪkl/

語源は〈arti (つなぎ) cle (小さい) →関節〉である. **全体を構成する個々のもの**. ① **(書籍の中の) 記事**. ② **(法律の中の) 条項**. ③ **(物品の中の) 品物, 一品**.

In this issue, there appears a frightening *article* [=report] about global warming.　この号に地球温暖化に関する驚愕の記事が出ている.

The ninth *article* of the constitution renounces any war in any form.　憲法第 9 条はあらゆる形のあらゆる戦争を放棄している.

Sara needs to buy some household *articles* [=items] like furniture and dishes to live away from her parents.　サラは両親と離れて暮らすために, 家具や食器など新しく家庭用品を買わないといけない.

ask /ǽsk/

語源は〈求める〉である. ①**助けを求める《依頼》**. ②**情報を求める《質問》**. -sk の音に〈追求, 求め〉が感じられる：seek (求める)

I would like to *ask* your cooperation in filling out this questionnaire.　このアンケートに (記入して) ご協力をお願いしたいと思います.

The interviewer ⌈*asked* me [=questioned me about] what I studied in college.　面接官は大学で何を学んだか聞いてきた.

Don't ask me!　知らないよ！〔←私なんかに聞かないで〕

The novel is pretty boring *if ⌈you ask me* [=if you want to know what I really think].　僕に言わせれば, この小説はひどくつまらないよ.

aspect /ǽspekt/

aspect

語源は〈a(ヘ) spect(目をやる)〉である. **視線を投げた所の様子→目に映る様相**. 一つの物事にさまざまな様相(aspect)があるのは, 視線は物事の全面(360度)を一瞥(いちべつ)できないからといえる.

What *aspect* of the job do you find the most difficult? その仕事のどういった面が一番難しいですか.

How we interact with others affects every *aspect* of our lives. 他人とどうつき合うかは生活のいろいろな面に影響を与える.

assemble /əsémbl/

語源は〈as(ヘ) semble(一緒にする)〉である. ①**ばらばらな部品を集める・組み立てる**. ②**散在する人を集める, 集まる**.
派 assembly(議会)

I learned how to *assemble* [=put together] a computer in college. 大学でコンピュータの組み立て方を学んだ.

Thousands of fans had *assembled* [=gathered] in downtown Yokohama to watch the final game on massive screen. 何千人ものファンが巨大スクリーンで決勝戦を見るために横浜の中心街に集まった.

assess /əsés/

語源は〈as（ヘ）sess（座る）〉である.**（裁判席に座って刑の査定にあたる）→じっくり評価対象の価値・質・能力を査定する**.
派 assessment（評価, 査定）

He sits on a committee to *assess* [=evaluate] the value of commercial land.　彼は商業用地の地価を査定する委員会に顔を連ねている.
▶この例文は〈sit（座る）〉と〈assess（査定する）〉の原義を図らずも語っている.

asset /ǽset/

語源は〈as（で）set（十分な）→担保に値する十分な資産〉**①財産, 資産　②強味, とりえ**. 日本語でも「健康だけが私の財産（＝とりえ）です」などという. satisfy（満足させる）と語源的に関連がある.

The company has closed with more liabilities than *assets*.　その会社は資産を上回る負債を抱えて倒産した.　▶assets and liabilities「資産と負債」

This wooded park is a great *asset* for the neighborhood.　この緑豊かな公園はこの地域にとって大きな財産です.

Your health is your most valuable *asset* [=possession].　健康が私の一番のとりえだ.

assist /əsíst/

assist

語源は〈as(へ)sist(立つ)〉である.**仕事に携わっている人のそばに立って支える,手を添える,手助けする,援助する**.
派 assistance(援助);assistant(補佐役)

Marie sometimes *assists* [=helps] her son with his homework.
マリーはときどき息子の宿題を手伝ってやります.

He has completed the thesis with the *assistance* [=the help] of a couple of friends.　彼は何人かの友達の助けを得て論文を仕上げた.

---

associate /əsóuʃièıt/

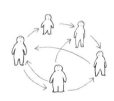

語源は〈as(へ)sociate(交わる)〉である.**①(考えが考えに交わる)→連想する,関連づける.②(人と人が交わる)→交流する,関連する**.
派 association(交わり,協会)
関 society(人の交わる社会)

What do you *associate* ⌈with Hokkaido [=Hokkaido *with*]?　北海道っていうと何を連想しますか.

I still *associate* [=socialize] *with* the people I used to work with.
昔の同僚と今も付き合っている.

He flatly denied any *association* [=connection] *with* the drug dealers.　その麻薬業者とは全く関係がないと彼はきっぱり否定した.

The barbers in the town formed an *association* [=a union] to protect their interests.　町の理容師たちは権益を守るために組合を結成した.

assume /əs(j)úːm/

語源は〈as (へ) sume (取る)〉である．**①態度を取る．②任務・責任を取る．③考えを取る，〜であると想定する・仮定する．**
派 assumption (想定, 装うこと)
関 presume (推定する)〔←前もって＋取る〕

That Nobel prize winner never ⌜*assumes* an air of superiority [=puts on airs]⌝.　あのノーベル賞受賞者はえらぶった態度を取らない．

When will the new President *assume* [=take] office?　新大統領はいつ就任しますか．

One should *assume* [=be ready for] the worst at all times.　人はいつも最悪の事態を想定しておくべきだ．

Assuming that the theory is true, what conclusions do you draw from it? =Let's *assume* the theory is true. What conclusions do you draw from it?　その論が本当だと仮定して，そこからどういう結論になりますか．

at /ət/

原義は〈ある一点へ〉である．**注目する領域 (場所・時間・状態・行動など) を一点に絞り込む．**

You should arrive *at* the airport *at* least two hours before your scheduled departure.　少なくとも出発予定時間の2時間前までに，空港にお越しください．

I can't give you any more information *at* the moment.　今のところ，情報はこれだけです．

Has Ken graduated, or is he still *at* college?　ケンは卒業したの，それともまだ在学中なの？

She was delighted *at* the results of the examination.　彼女は試験の結果に満足した．

atmosphere /ǽtməsfìər/

語源は〈atmos（水蒸気）sphere（球）〉である. **①地球を覆う水蒸気のかたまり→大気. ②人や場所の周りの空気・雰囲気.**
派 atmospheric（大気の）

The *atmosphere* [＝A layer of air] surrounds the earth. 大気が地球を覆っている.

I really like the restaurant—nice *atmosphere* and great food. このレストランはとても気に入っているよ. 雰囲気はいいし料理も最高だ.

attack /ətǽk/

語源は〈at（へ）tack（杭, 鋲を打つ）〉である. 鋲を打ち込む→**①武器・細菌などで攻撃する；攻撃, 発作. ②言葉で攻撃する（非難する）.**

A journalist was badly *attacked* by a group of thugs. 報道記者が暴漢の連中に襲われて, ひどいけがを負った. ▶a thug /θʌ́g/「暴漢」

This virus *attacks* [＝affects] the central nervous system. このウイルスは中枢神経組織を冒す.

My father suddenly had a *heart attack* while taking a bath. 父は入浴中に心臓発作を起こした.

The government's policy on the economy was badly *attacked* in the media. 政府の経済政策はマスコミにひどくたたかれた.

attempt /ətémpt/

語源は〈at (へ) tempt (試す)〉である．**試してみる→難事を企てる**．試み・企てが未遂，未完になるニュアンスがある．
派 attempted (未遂の)

The firm's *attempt* to overcome the economic crisis ended in failure. ＝The firm unsuccessfully *attempted* to overcome the economic crisis.　会社は経済危機を乗り越えようとしたが功を奏さなかった．

The man was arrested for arson and *attempted* murder.　男は放火と殺人未遂のかどで逮捕された．

attend /əténd/

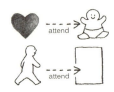

語源は〈at (へ) tend (伸ばす)〉である．① (足を伸ばす) →出席する．② (気持ちを〜へ伸ばす) →気持ちを〜へ向ける→〜に注意する→〜に付き添う，〜の世話をする．
派 attendance (出席)；attention (関心, 注意, 注目)；attentive (注意深い)；unattended (関心をもたれていない, 放置された)　関 extend (広げる)

Last night I *attended* [＝went to] an outdoor concert.　昨夜，野外コンサートを聴きに行った．

The workshop was well *attended* with over 120 participants.　講習会は120人余りの参加者があり盛況だった．

Tom's *attendance* at work is regular.　トムはいつもちゃんと出勤している．

Never *leave* your child *unattended* in a motor vehicle.　車の中に子どもを放っておいたらだめですよ．

The teacher is *attentive to* her children's needs and wishes.　その先生は生徒たちの困ったことや求めることに気を配っている．

attitude /ǽtət(j)ùːd/

語源は〈atti (〜に対する) tude (様子)〉である．**物事・事態に向き合う時に取る姿勢・態度**．

The boss was frustrated and had an aggressive *attitude* toward his staff.　部長は不機嫌で部下に対して高圧的な態度を取った．

In general Japanese *attitude* towards dress is conservative.　一般的に日本人は服装に対する姿勢が保守的だ．　▶dress は〈服装〉の意で，数えられない名詞．

attract /ətrǽkt/

語源は〈at (へ) tract (引く)〉である．**物を引きつける→人や動物の関心・興味を引きつける**．
派 attractive (魅力的な)；attraction (魅力, 魅力的なもの)　関 tractor (トラクター) (←牽引車)

President Barack Obama's inaugural address *attracted* worldwide attention.　バラク・オバマ大統領の就任演説は世界中の関心を集めた．

Lavender *attracts* wide range of bees.　ラベンダーはいろいろなハチを引きつける．

Sara is *attractive* in her own way.　サラには彼女なりの魅力がある．

There are many great tourist *attractions* in Kyoto. =Kyoto has a number of things that *attract* the tourists.　京都には旅行者を引きつける多くのものがある．

audience /ɔ́:diəns/

audience

語源は〈audi（聞く）ence（こと）〉，原義は〈耳からの情報を得る人〉である．**(発信・情報を受け止める人)→聴衆，観衆，読者．** audi- は根源にさかのぼると，〈知覚する〉の意があるので，audience が耳だけ（観衆）でなく，目を通した行為者（読者）をも指すのは理に適っている．
関 audio equipment（オーディオ機器）

The film attracted a ⌈large *audience* [=number of viewers]． この映画は多くの観衆を呼び込んだ．

His writings ⌈reached a wide *audience* [=were widely read] during the sixties through Penguin Books． 彼の著作物はペンギンブックスを通じて1960年代に多くの読者に読まれた．

authority /əθɔ́:rəti/

語源は〈author（創始者）ity（であること）〉である．創始者は命令・決断を下す権限をもつので**具体的には〈権威者〉，抽象的にはその〈権威〉**の意．
派 authorize（権限を与える）
関 author（著者）〔← auth=originate（創る）or（人）〕

Those students stood up against ⌈state *authority* [=the *authority* of the state]． 学生たちは国家権力に立ち向かった．

Steve is an *authority* [=an expert] on troubleshooting computer problems． スティーブはコンピュータの問題を解決する専門家だ．

I'm not *authorized* [=in a position] to answer the question on behalf of the company． 私には会社を代表してその質問に回答する権限がありません．

automatic /ɔːtəmǽtɪk/

語源は〈auto(自動で) matic(動くような)〉である. ①**機械が自動的に動く**. ②**生物が無意識に行動する, 自然に行動する**. 日本語の「自動的」は機械などに使うが, 英語では生物の無意識な動きについてもいう.
派 automatically (自動的に, 自然に)

We are going to install an *automatic* garage door. 車庫のシャッターを自動にするつもりだ.

I wake up *automatically* [=naturally] shortly after dawn. 僕は夜が明けるとまもなく自然に目が覚めます.

Normally you breathe *automatically* [=without thinking about it]. 普段, 人は無意識に呼吸をする.

available /əvéɪləbl/

語源は〈avail(価値) able(なり得る)〉である. **価値を生み出せる**→①**(価値のある)物を手に入れて使える**. ②**(価値ある)物事を利用できる**. ③**(能力をもつ)人の都合がつく**. 物や人の存在は活用することによって初めて価値が生じ, 活用しなければ「宝の持ち腐れ」になる.
関 value (価値)

The book is now *available* at bookstores nationwide. その本は今, 全国の書店で発売になっている.

Taxis are readily *available* once you exit the station. 駅を出たらすぐにタクシーはつかまりますよ.

Is anyone *available* to tutor my kid in piano? 子どものピアノの個人教師をしてくれる人はいませんか.

average /ǽvərɪdʒ/

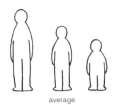
average

原義〈運送中の商品の損害 avarie（フランス語）を運送依頼者と運送者側が平均に負担したこと〉に由来する．**平均の；平均，標準；平均〜となる**．

He is above *average* for an amateur golfer.　彼はアマチュアのゴルファーとしては平均以上だ．

The *average* age of those attending is 35 years.　参加者の平均年齢は35歳だ．

We *averaged* 70 kilometers per hour driving from Sendai to Tokyo. ＝We drove at an *average* speed of 70 kilometers per hour from Sendai to Tokyo.　仙台から東京まで平均時速70キロで走行した．

avoid /əvɔ́ɪd/

語源は〈a＝out（外に）void（空）〉である．**嫌なものを目の前から無くする→嫌なものから距離をとる→嫌なものを遠ざける**．
派 avoidable（避けられる）; unavoidable（避けられない）

Errors ⌈cannot be *avoided* [＝are unavoidable] but they should be traced and reduced to a minimum.　ミスは避けられないものだが，原因を突きとめて最小限に食い止めなければならない．　▶trace「（原因や経緯）をたどる」; reduce 〜 to a minimum「〜を最小限に食い止める」

award /əwɔ́:rd/

語源は〈a (しっかり) ward (観察する)〉である. **(じっくり観察して評価を与える)→賞や賠償金を与える**.

Murakami Ryu was *awarded* the Akutagawa prize for his debut work.　村上龍はデビュー作で芥川賞を受賞した.

Her claim was successful and she was *awarded* $95,000 compensation.　彼女の訴訟は首尾よく9万5000ドルの補償金を得た.

---

aware /əwéər/

語源は〈a (しっかり) ware (見張っている)〉である. **周りの状況に感づいている《感覚的》→物事・状況の意義・性格について分かっている《知覚的》**.
派 awareness (認識)

I was *aware* that my parents were not completely satisfied with my decision.　私は,両親が私の決断に必ずしも満足していないことに感づいていた.

You smoke a lot. Are you *aware* of the dangers of smoking?　君はよくたばこを吸うね. 喫煙の危険性について知っているの?

away /əwéɪ/

away

語源〈a=on（〜の状態に）way（あちら）〉である．ある場所から**①離れていく様子《動的：さっと，さくさくと》．②離れている様子《静的：離れている，不在である》**．

She frowned at me and walked *away*.　彼女はふくれっ面を見せて出て行った．

He talked *away*〔＝on and on〕without any inhibition.　彼は何はばかることなくしゃべり続けた．

The secretary typed *away* on the keyboard.　秘書はキーボードにさくさくと打ち込んだ．

The hotel is two blocks *away* from the station.　ホテルは駅から2ブロックの〔←離れた〕ところにあります．

My husband has been *away* on a business trip to China.　夫は中国へ商用で出かけています．

---

back /bǽk/

原義は〈背中〉である．**背面→裏側→後部**．副詞用法では**後ろへ**，動詞用法では，**後ずさりする，（後ろから）支える**．
関 background（背景）

The man's hands were tied *behind his back*.　男の手は後ろ手に縛られていた．

Can you float, lying *on your back*?　あおむけになって水に浮くことできる？
▶ on one's stomach＝face down「うつ伏せで」

Don't talk *behind my back*!　陰で私の悪口を言わないで！

This project is *backed* by the government.＝This is a *government-backed* project.　これは政府支援の事業です．

baggage /bǽgɪdʒ/

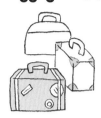

語源は〈bag（袋）age（集まった状態）〉である．**bag＋bag＋bag＝手荷物**．bag を集合的に捉えているので複数形にはならない．数を意識する時は，two pieces of baggage（手荷物2個）のようにいう．

I recommend traveling ⌈with little *baggage* [＝*light*]．　荷物は少なくして旅するほうがいいよ．

Keep your eye on your *baggage* [＝Don't leave your *baggage* unattended] at all times while traveling．　旅行中は常に手荷物から目を離さないようにしてください．　▶keep one's eye on ～＝keep an eye on ～「～に監視の目を注ぐ」

balance /bǽləns/

語源は〈ba＝bi（二つの）lance（皿）〉である．**(二つの皿)→天秤→バランス，平衡→残高**．バランス（平衡）をとるとき，常に〈差，残余〉が意識されるので，差額→残りの意味が生まれる．
派 balanced（偏りのない）

I lost (my) *balance* and fell．　バランスを失って転んだ．

I have to ⌈get my *work-life balance* right [＝*balance* work and family life]．　仕事と家庭生活のバランスをとらないといけない．

I have a *balance* [＝a deposit] of ¥50,000 in my bank．　5万円の預金がある．〔←残高5万円〕

A ¥20,000 deposit is required when ordering, and the *balance* [＝the remainder] is due on delivery．　注文時に2万円の手付け金が必要です．残金は配達時にお支払いいただきます．　▶due＝payable「支払うべき」

ban /bǽn/

原義は〈布告する〉である．**(布告する)→禁止令を出す**，**禁止する；禁止**．音が〈バンと威嚇する〉イメージ．
関 banish（追放する）

Many communities have *banned* [=prohibited] smoking in public places.　多くの社会で公共の場での喫煙を禁止している．

The school lifted its cell phone *ban* [=prohibition] on students.
学校は生徒の携帯の持ち込みを解禁した．　▶lift [=remove] a ban「解禁する」

bank /bǽŋk/

原義は〈台〉である．① **(土台)→土手→堤**．② **(勘定台)→両替商→銀行**．防波堤の堤と銀行のカウンターとは相似形である．
派 banker（銀行員）；banking（銀行業務）
関 bench（ベンチ）；bankrupt（破産した）

Willows line the both *banks* of the river.　柳が川の両岸に沿って並んでいる．　▶line「～に沿って並ぶ」

Make it a priority upon your arrival to open an account with a *bank*.
何はさておき到着次第，現地の銀行に口座を開きなさい．

bankrupt /bæŋkrʌpt/

語源は〈bank（台）rupt（崩壊）〉である．**土台が崩れる→台無しになる→破綻している；破産させる**．日本語の「台無し」と発想が似ている．rupt- には〈割れる・壊れる〉の意味がある：bankruptcy（破産），rupture（破壊），corrupt（堕落する）
派 bankruptcy（破産） 関 bank（土手）

His restaurant seems to be ⌈going *bankrupt* [＝into *bankruptcy*]．彼のレストランは破綻しそうだ．

The Global Economic Panic *bankrupted* hundreds of banks and companies． 世界経済恐慌によって何百もの銀行や会社が倒産した．

bar /bá:r/

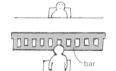

原義は〈棒〉である．**棒→（裁判席と被告席の仕切り棒のある）法廷，（棒を組んだカウンターで酒を供する）酒場**．棒は〈障害・拘束・基準〉の象徴．
関 embarrass（当惑させる）

He had been ⌈*behind bars* [＝in prison] for six years． 彼は6年間刑務所暮らしだった．《bar＝鉄格子》

He passed the national *bar* examination． 彼は国の司法試験にパスした．《bar＝弁護士業》

The company sets a very high *bar* [＝standard] for the people they recruit． その会社は採用の基準がとても高い．《bar＝飛び越えるべき棒》

Being a woman is no longer a *bar* [＝a barrier] to promotion in most professions． 女性であることがもはやたいていの専門職で昇進上の障害とはならない．《bar＝行く手をふさぐ棒》

bare /béər/

原義は〈むき出しの〉である．**通常はあるべき覆いがない状態**．副詞形 barely は，〈bare（むき出し）ly（状態で）〉→むき出し状態で→**(付帯物を除いて) 芯だけの状態で→かろうじて〜である**．
関 barren（不毛の）〔←大地がむき出し状態〕

The girl ⌈had *bare* feet [＝was *bare-footed*] and was bleeding on her legs.　少女は裸足で脚から血を流していた．

The soldier spoke the *bare* [＝naked] truth about his life in the army.　兵士は軍隊生活についてあからさまに語った．

He arrived home exhausted and *barely* capable of showering before collapsing on his bed.　彼は疲れ切って帰り，シャワーを何とか済ませるとベッドに倒れこんだ．

---

barrier /bériər/

原義は〈bar（棒）を組んだもの〉である．**通行・進展を妨げる壁，障害**．つづりに潜んでいる bar（棒）は〈ボウ害〉の象徴．

The Great Wall of China was a barrier to block invading forces from entering.　万里の長城は外敵の侵入を阻む障壁であった．

The city plans to build a *barrier-free* society for disabled persons in the region.　市は地域の障害者のためにバリアフリーの社会を築くことを計画している．　▶barrier-free「障壁のない」

base /béɪs/

原義は〈踏み台〉である.**土台→基礎→根拠；〜に基づく**.
関 basement（地階）

A river ran along the *base* [=the foot] of the mountain.　山のふもとに沿って川が流れていた.

The statue stands on a square stone *base* [=a stone pedestal].　像は石でできた四角い台座の上に立っている.　▶pedestal「台座」

The *base* [=The foundation] of Australian economy rests on its abundant natural resources.　オーストラリアの経済は豊かな天然資源に基盤を置いている.

He writes crime novels *based* on actual cases.　彼は実際の事件に基づいた犯罪小説を書いている.

---

basin /béɪsn/

原義は〈窪み〉である.**①窪地→水溜り→盆地→流域**.**②窪地→水溜め→洗面器→洗面台**.窪みに水が溜まるのは自然の理.

The Amazon *Basin* [=Valley] is the home to sixty percent of the planet's remaining tropical rainforests.　アマゾン川の流域には地球に残る熱帯雨林の60％が自生している.

Mom brought me a towel and *a basin of* water to wash my hands.　手を洗うため母はタオルと洗面器一杯の水を持って来てくれた.

bat /bǽt/

原義は〈棒〉である．**バット→バットでボールを打つ**．コウモリ (bat) の意は翼をバタバタと動かす特徴に由来．
関 battle (戦闘)〔←打ち合い〕; beat (打つ)

Ohtani of the Nippon Ham Fighters *bats* left-handed and throws right-handed.　日本ハムファイターズの大谷選手は右投げ, 左打ちだ．

The Red Sox are ⌈*batting* first [=first *at bat*].　レッドソックスが先攻だ．
cf. The Yankees are *fielding first*.「ヤンキースが後攻だ」

He is ⌈as blind as a *bat* [=completely blind].　彼は全盲だ．

bay /béɪ/

原義は〈奥まったところ〉である．**入江; ほえる, うなる**．入り江とオオカミや犬が太い声でうなる時の開口部の形は相似形．

Haneda airport is located on the shore of *the Bay of* Tokyo.　羽田空港は東京湾に接している．

Terrorist attacks have been *held at bay* by the FBI.　FBI によってテロリストの攻撃は抑え込まれている．　▶hold ～ at bay「～を追い詰める」

Why do dogs *bay* at the moon?　なぜ犬は月に向かってほえるの？

bear /béər/

原義は〈運ぶ〉である．①運ぶ→付帯する→支える→耐える．②運ぶ→生む→実をつける．
関 burden（重圧をかける）

The bridge was too weak to *bear* [=support] the weight of heavy traffic. その橋は激しい交通の重量に耐えられなかった．

We have to *bear* the unbearable until we come into a better situation. 我々は状況がよくなるまで耐えがたきを耐えなくてはならない．

I was *born* and brought up in Hiroshima until I was eighteen. 僕は18歳まで広島で生まれ育った．

His untiring efforts *bore* fruit. 彼の不屈の努力が実った．

Many of the plants don't *bear* [=produce] flowers in the shade. 日陰では花がつかない植物が多い．

beard /bíərd/

beard　mustache　whiskers

原義は〈あごひげ〉である．**あごひげ**, **口ひげ**, **ほおひげ**．それぞれ図のように区別していうが，単に「ひげ」はbeardを使う傾向がある．ネコやトラなどの口ひげはwhiskersという．

My brother began to wear a *beard*. 兄はひげを生やし始めた．

He lets his *beard* grow freely. 彼はあごひげを伸ばし放題にしている．

bearing /béəriŋ/

語源は〈bear (支える・運ぶ) ing (こと)〉である. 身の支え, 運び→態度, 振る舞い→周囲との関係→方角.

Diet has a profound *bearing* [=effect] on your health.　何を食べるかは健康に深く関係する.

Those issues arising in such a faraway country have no *bearing* on our lives.　あんな遠くの国の問題なんかは僕たちの生活には関係ないよ.

I *lost my bearings* after taking the wrong exit.　出口を間違えたので方角が分からなくなった.　▶ lose one's bearings (to one's surroundings)「(周りの環境との) 関係を見失う→方向感覚を失う」.

beat /bíːt/

原義は〈たたく〉である. たたく→繰り返したたく→相手を打ち負かす→不都合を追い払う.
関 bat (バット)

Through the night a violent storm of rain and wind *beat* on my tent.　夜通しひどい風雨がテントに激しく打ちつけていた.

In one way or another men don't like 「being *beaten* by [=losing to] women.　何かにつけて男は女に負けるのを嫌うものだ.

The victim was *beaten* to death by a group of men.　被害者は数人の男たちに殴り殺された.

I usually leave home early to *beat* [=avoid] the traffic.　渋滞を避けるためにいつも早めに家を出る.

become /bikʌ́m/

語源は〈be (へ) come (来る)〉である．**〜へ来る→〜になる** (＝come to be)，**ちゃんと来る→ぴたっと来る→似合う**．

A good player doesn't always *become* a good coach. 優れた選手が優れた監督になるとは限らない．

Life has *become* faster and more complex than it has ever been. 生活はかつてないほど速く，複雑になっている．

I wonder what has *become* of Mr. Brown. It's already two months since he disappeared into the bush. ブラウン氏はどうなっているのだろう．彼が雲隠れしてからもう 2 か月になるよ． ▶disappear into the bush「雲隠れする」

I think short hair ⌈is very *becoming* [＝looks well] *on* you. 短髪があなたにはとても似合うと思うよ．

before /bifɔ́ːr/

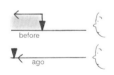

語源は〈be＝by (に) fore (前)〉である．**〜より前に**《時間的》→**〜より前方に**《位置的》→**〜より優先して**《重要性》．

I've heard the story *before*. その話は以前聞いたことがある． ▶before (now) が意識下にある．

You've only got a couple of weeks *before* the deadline. 締め切りまでに 2, 3 週間しかないよ．

I don't like speaking *before* an audience. 人前で話すのは苦手だ．

Lots of business people have been forced to put their careers *before* their family lives. 家庭よりも仕事を優先せざるを得ないビジネスマンが多い．
▶put A before B「B より A を優先する」

begin /bɪgín/

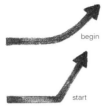

原義は〈始まる〉である. 類義語 start(始まる, 踏み出す)に較べると, 〈**自然に始まる, 気負いなく始める**〉の意味合いが強い.
派 beginning(始まり)

When does your new school year *begin*? 新学期はいつ始まるの?

I want to start investing but have no idea where to *begin*. 投資を始めたいのだけどどこから手をつけたらいいのか分からない.

This will be no easy road but everything must have a *beginning*. この仕事は多難だが何事も一歩からだよ.

Beginnings are necessarily small. 最初は何でも必然的にささいなものだ.

behalf /bɪhǽf/

語源は〈be=by(そばに) half(片側)〉である. **(傍らに立つ)** →支援, 味方, 利益. 常に成句 on [in] behalf of(〜のために, 〜を代表して)の形で使われる.

My father does lots of volunteer activities ⌈*on behalf of* [=for] the local community. 父は地域のためにボランティアでたくさんの活動をしている.

I would like to say thank you *on behalf of* the group. グループを代表して謝辞を述べたいと思います.

behave /bɪhéɪv/

語源は〈be(しっかり)have(持つ)〉である.**しっかりと態度を持つ→ちゃんとした振る舞いをする**.日本語の「身持ち(品行)」と発想が似ている.have は〈〜の行動をとる〉の意がある:have a walk(散歩する),have a care(用心する),have a thought(思いつく),have a fight(喧嘩する).
派 behavior(行為,(自然の)活動・作用)

My husband cannot control his anger; he *behaves* like a child. 夫は怒ったら抑えがきかなくなって,子どもみたいな振る舞いをする.

Behave yourself in class and not disrupt other students' learning. 教室では行儀よくして他の生徒達の勉強のじゃまをしないようにしなさい.

This volcano has a gentle eruptive *behavior* today, but in the past it had been very explosive. この火山の噴火活動は現在では穏やかだが,昔は噴火が激しかった.

---

behind /bɪhάɪnd/

語源は〈be(へ)hind(後ろ)〉である.**〜の後ろに位置している→〜より遅れている→〜より劣っている**.位置という具象で時間や優劣という抽象を表すのはどの言語にも共通している.
関 hind leg(後ろ脚);hinder(邪魔をする)〔←後ろに追いやる〕

I don't like when you criticize others *behind their backs*. 陰で人の悪口を言うのは嫌だよ.

Grandpa *left* his denture *behind* at the hotel. おじいちゃんはホテルに入れ歯を忘れてきちゃった.

The game began ten minutes ⌜*behind schedule* [=later than it was scheduled]. 試合は予定の開始時間より10分遅れて始まった.

You can tell just by looking at their out of date equipment that the company is well *behind the times*. 使っている古い機器を見れば,この会社がいかに時代遅れか一目瞭然だよ.

being /bíːŋ/

being

語源は〈be (ある, いる) ing (状態)〉である. **存在していること, ある状態であること.**

I hate myself for *being* fat.　自分は太っているから嫌なの.

Just your *being* here is enough for me.　あなたがここにいてくれるだけでいい.

What is the probability of the next one *being* a girl again?　次の子がまた女である確率はどれほどですか.

When and where「did Islam *come into being*? [=*was* Islam *born*?]　イスラム教はいつどこで生まれた〔←存在するようになった〕のですか.

believe /bəlíːv/

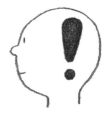

語源は〈be (強く) lieve (好む)〉である. **(〜を好きだと思う) → (理屈なしに) 〜をよいと思う→〜を本当だと思う.** 人は mind (頭) で think (考える) する, heart (心) で believe (信じる) するといえる.
派 belief (確信, 信仰); unbelievable (信じ難い, 〔信じ難いほどに〕 すばらしい)

Don't *believe* rumors until you can confirm them to be true.　自分で確認できないのにうわさを信じちゃだめだよ.

Do you *believe in* heaven and life after death?　天国や死後の世界の存在を信じますか.

My grandma *believes in* traditional herbal medicine.　祖母は漢方療法をいいものだと信じている.

I can't *believe* how fast our little boy is growing! It's *unbelievable* [=amazing]!　かわいい息子の成長は信じられないほど早いわよ. 素晴らしいわ!

belong /bəlɔ́ːŋ/

語源は〈be(強意) long(〜に添う)〉である. **(あるべきところ)にしっかり添う→〜に属する**.
派 belongings(持ち物, 所持品)
関 along(〜に沿って)

Does the copyright of these illustrations *belong to* the publisher or the artist?　これらのイラストの版権は, 出版社それとも画家にあるのですか.

People used to have a strong sense of *belonging to* their communities.
昔, 人々は地域への強い帰属意識をもっていたものだ.

Don't leave cash or other expensive *belongings* [=goods] in your hotel room.　現金とその他の貴重品は, ホテルの部屋に置いたままで出かけないでください.　▶one's belongings「持ち運べる程度の所持品」

below /bɪlóu/

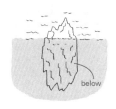

語源は〈be(に) low(下)〉である. **ある基準より下に位置する→〜より劣っている**.

The sun has already gone *below* the horizon.　太陽はもう地平線下に沈んだ.

He is paralyzed *below* the waist.　彼は下半身が麻痺している.

The river widens *below* this point.　川はここから(下流へ)広くなっている.

For details, *see below*.　詳しくは下記をご参照ください.

From here, you can see the whole town *below*.　ここから町全体が眼下に見える.

The rice crop was ⌈*below* average [=worse than usual] this year.
今年はコメの出来が平均以下だった.

being, believe, belong, below

belt /bélt/

原義は〈ベルト〉である.**(帯状の広がり)→地帯**；ベルトで締める, ベルトで打つ.

The driver was thrown out of the car because he wasn't wearing his *seatbelt*.　運転者はシートベルトを締めていなかったので, 車外に投げ出された.

This area is a commuter *belt* for Tokyo. ＝This area is a commuter town for people who work in Tokyo.　この地域は東京のベッドタウン〔←東京へ通勤する人たちの居住地帯〕です.

She always wears her raincoat, *belted* at the waist.　彼女はいつも腰のところにベルトをしてレインコートを着る.

bend /bénd/

原義は〈弓を引く (bend a bow)〉である.**(弓をしならせる)→物を曲げる→体を曲げる**.

She *bent down* to pick up a needle off the floor.　彼女はかがんで床から針を拾い上げた.

He *bent* his head and apologized.　彼は頭を下げて謝った.

Light *bends* as it passes from air to water.　光は空中から水へ入るとき屈折する.

We may *bend the truth* so as not to hurt others.　人を傷つけないために真実を偽っていうこともある.　▶bend the truth「真実を曲げる」

beneath /biníːθ/

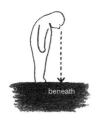

語源は〈be=by (に) neath (下)〉である. **〜のすぐ下に**. やや堅い響きがあるので話し言葉では under を使うほうが多い. -neath は, オランダの通称 Netherlands (←低い国土) のつづりにも潜んでいる.

Hippos can see above the water while their bodies are *beneath* [=under] it.　カバは体を水面下に沈めたままで水面上を見ることができる.

When I went outside without shoes on, the grass felt cool *beneath* [=under] my feet.　裸足で外に出てみると, 足の裏に芝生が冷たく感じられた.

benefit /bénəfɪt/

語源は〈bene (良い) fit (つくる)〉である. **(ある存在・状況に対してよいことを生み出す)→役立つ→利益を与える；利益, 恩恵, 保険金**.
派 beneficial (有益な)

We have ⌈*benefited* a great deal [=gotten a great deal of *benefit*]⌋ from his involvement with our project.　彼がプロジェクトに加わってくれたのでとても助かっている.

Name some *benefits* that you can gain from reading.　読書から得られる効用をいくつか挙げてごらん.　▶name「名前を挙げて言う」

You can receive unemployment *benefits* for up to six months if you are eligible.　条件を満たせば, 6か月を上限に失業保険金がもらえます.

beside /bɪsáɪd/

語源は〈be=by（に）side（側）〉である．**あるもののそばに→（本来のあり方から）それて．**

When I grow old, I want to live *beside* the sea.　年を取ったら海のそばで暮したい．

We would like to sit *beside* [=next to] each other.　（席の予約を依頼する時に）隣り合わせの席にお願いします．

Your complaint seems *beside* [=off] *the point*.　あなたの苦情は的をはずれているようですよ．

She was *beside herself* with passion for her lover and hungrily kissed him.　彼女は情欲で夢中になってむさぼるように恋人にキスをした．　▶ be beside oneself「我を忘れている」

besides /bɪsáɪdz/

語源は〈beside（そば）s（に）〉である．**(〜のそばに)→〜に加えて→その上に，さらに．**　beside に副詞的意味を持つ s がついている．

What else do you do online *besides* [=other than] blogging?　君はブログの他にネットでは何をしますか．

Besides [=In addition to] that, her physical condition has been so bad.　それに加えて，彼女の体調はひどく悪かった．

betray /bɪtréɪ/

betray

語源は〈be(強め) tray(手渡す)〉である．**内密にすべきことを相手にもらしてしまう**．
派 betrayal（裏切り）
関 traitor（裏切り者）〔←渡す＋者〕

He was accused of *betraying* his country by disclosing military secrets.　彼は軍事機密を漏えいして国を裏切ったかどで訴えられた．

Her true feelings were *betrayed* [=let out] by the word uttered by chance.　思わずすべらしたことばで彼女の本心が露呈した．

between /bɪtwíːn/

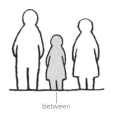
between

語源は〈be＝by(に) tween＝twos(二つ)〉である．**位置的・時間的に二つのものの間にある様子**．

What is the distance *between* the Earth *and* the Sun?　地球と太陽の間の距離はどれほどですか．

Avoid eating *between* meals!　間食はだめだよ！

This is just *between you and me*.　このことは二人だけの内緒だよ．

"Is David Arab or Indian?" "He looks like something *in between*."
「デビッドはアラブ人だろうかインド人だろうか？」「どちらとも言えない風貌だよ」
▶ in between「中間に」

beyond /biɑ́:nd/

語源は〈be (に) yond (向こう)〉である．**ある基準を越えて (位置的・時間的・質的に) 向こう側にある**．

Don't stand *beyond* the yellow line.　黄色い線の内側でお待ちください．
▶ JR 駅のプラットホームでの警告の英訳．

His presentation was ⌈*beyond* my expectations [＝better than I had hoped]．　彼の発表は思ったよりよかった．

The authenticity of the signature is *beyond* question.　この署名が本物であることは疑いがない．

We felt the situation had become hopeless and *beyond* our control.　事態は絶望的で，自分たちの手に負えない状態になってしまったと思った．

bias /báɪəs/

語源は〈bi (二筋) as (交差して)〉である．**筋交いになっている→斜めになっている→見方に偏りがある；偏見**．
派 biased (偏向している)

Your father seems to ⌈*have a bias* [＝be *biased*] *against* those who are without education.　君の親父さんは学歴のない人に偏見があるように見える．

The newspaper ⌈*has a bias* [＝is *biased*] in favor of the ruling party.　その新聞は与党寄りである．

All news is more or less *biased*.　報道はみな何らかの色がついているものだ．

bicycle /báɪsəkl/

語源は〈bi (二) cycle (輪)→ two-wheeled vehicle〉である．**自転車；自転車に乗る**．動詞では cycle や bike のほうが普通．日本語の「バイク」は motorbike という．
関 encyclopedia (百科事典)〔←周りのすべてに関する教本〈en (〜の) cyclo (周り全般) pedia (教育)〉〕

Let's go for a *bicycle* [=a bike] ride! サイクリングに出かけよう！
I ⌈ride a *bicycle* [=cycle] to work. 僕は自転車通勤をしている．

bid /bíd/

原義は〈強く言う〉である．**公言する→買値を申し出る；入札**．b- は破裂音なので発言者の気持ちの強さが感じられる．
派 bidding (入札)；bidder (入札者)

How much should we *bid* for the house? その家にいくらで入札したらいいだろうか．

The *bidding* will start at around ¥5,000,000. 入札は 500 万円あたりから始まるだろう．

The property will go to the highest *bidder* subject to a minimum price being attained. 最低入札額がクリアされる限り，最高額の入札者に物件は売られる． ▶subject to 〜「〜を条件として」

big /bíg/

原義は〈大きい，力がある〉である．規模や量が大きい様子を**感情的・感覚的に捉える時は big，冷静・客観的に捉える時は large** を使う．big は，力がある→質・内容が大きい（立派である）の意味でも多用される．

You're a *big* boy now and should know better.　もう子どもじゃないのだからもっとしっかりしなきゃだめよ．

He is a *big* man in industry.　彼は産業界の大物だ．

The manager is a guy with a *big* heart who leads by example.　部長は模範を示して引っ張っていく度量のある人だ．　▶lead (others) by example= practice what one preaches「範を垂れる」〔←範を示して他者を引っ張る，有言実行する〕

Jim is always talking *big* about himself and his achievements.　ジムはいつも自分の事や業績についてほらを吹いている．　▶talk big「威張って言う」

---

bilingual /baɪlíŋgwəl/

語源は〈bi（二）lingual（言語の）〉である．**二つの言語を使用している，二つの言語が話せるさま**．ラテン語 lingua は tongue「舌」の意．

We need help from someone who ⌈is *bilingual* in Italian and English [=speaks both Italian and English fluently]⌋.　イタリア語と英語の両方が自由に話せる人の助けがいる．

bill /bíl/

原義は〈(押印された)文書,紙片〉である.**(支払いの金額が書かれた紙片)→勘定書,請求書;(通貨額の書かれた紙片)→紙幣;(案文の書かれた紙片)→法案**.

Bill [=Check], please.　勘定をお願いします.

How much is your monthly cell phone *bill*?　携帯電話の料金は月いくら払うの?

When will the *bill* come into force [=effect]?　その法案はいつから施行されるの?　▶come into force「効力が発生する」

bind /báind/

原義は〈縛る〉である.**(二つのものを一つに)縛る→つなぐ,拘束する**.
派 binding (拘束力のある)　関 band (結束する)

The wrestler had his head ⌜*bound* with a bandage [=bandaged] to stop bleeding.　レスラーは止血のために頭に包帯を巻いていた.

These are just guidelines for you to refer to and they don't *bind* you to anything.　これらは単に参考にしてもらうガイドラインですから,何も拘束するものではありません.　▶refer to 〜「〜を参照する」

The troubles we had shared *bound* us much closer together.　共通の悩みを抱えていたので互いの絆がうんと深まった.

Oral agreements are less *binding* [=restrictive] than written agreements.　口約束は文書による約束よりも拘束力が弱い.

bit /bít/

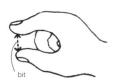

語源は〈かみ (bite) 取られた一片〉である. **ひとかじり→ちょっと**. つづりに bite (かじる) が潜んでいる.

I'm feeling *a bit* [=a little] tired.　ちょっと疲れてきたよ.　▶a bit「(副詞的に) ちょっと」

Let me give you *a bit of* advice.　少しアドバイスさせてください.

Susie hasn't changed *a bit* since she was in college.　スージーは大学時代からちっとも変わってないよ.

Her books are awesome; I'm *not a bit* surprised about her success.　彼女の書くものは素晴らしいよ. だから彼女の成功にはちっとも驚かないよ.

bite /báit/

原義は〈かむ〉である. **かみつく, 虫が刺す, 魚が餌に食いつく, 苦痛を与える; かむこと, 刺し傷, ひとかじり**.

Don't *bite* your nails.　爪をかむな.

A woman jogger was *bitten* by a dog.　女性のジョガーが犬にかみつかれた.

I got *bitten* by mosquitoes. =I had mosquito *bites*.　蚊に刺されたよ.

Tell me what's *biting* [=bothering] you.　何で困っているの.

Can I *have a bite*?　一口食べさせてくれる?

I think I tried to「*bite off more than I could chew* [=do more than I could] with this project.　この企画で僕は実力以上のことをやろうとしたように思う.　▶bite off more than you can chew「無理をする」

bitter /bítər/

原義は〈刺すように苦い〉である．**舌を刺すように苦い→心身を刺すように辛らつな・つらい**．つづりの中にbite（刺す）が潜んでいる．
派 bitterly（痛烈に）；bitterness（苦々しさ）

They had a *bitter* argument about which was to blame for the accident.　彼らはどちらに事故の原因があるかについて激しく言い争った．
▶ to blame for 〜＝to be blamed for 〜「〜のとがめを受ける，〜の原因となる」

Losing the championship was a *bitter*「pill to swallow ［＝thing to go through］for the team that was used to winning every year.　毎年常勝であったチームにとって選手権に敗れることは苦い経験であった．　▶ swallow a bitter pill「辛酸をなめる」

blame /bléɪm/

blame

原義は〈冒瀆（ぼうとく）する〉である．**人を名指して非難する**．bla- は破裂音なので罵声・叱責を浴びせるイメージが生まれる．
関 blaspheme（冒瀆する）

The police *blamed* the explosion on terrorists.　警察は爆破事件をテロリストの仕業であると非難した．

The manager *blamed*「us for the session's failure ［＝the session's failure on us］without criticizing himself.　幹事は自分のことは棚に上げて会合が失敗したのは我々のせいだと責めた．

bit, bite, bitter, blame　075

blank /blǽŋk/

原義は〈真っ白〉である．**真っ白→空白，空欄→うつろ；真っ白な，うつろな**．日本人も「頭が真っ白になる→うつろになる」と発想する．

May I have a *blank* sheet of paper? 白紙を一枚いただけますか．

You need to prepare a *blank* recordable CD for writing the updated data. 更新データの書き込みには生の CD を用意する必要がありますよ．

My mind went blank and I forgot what I was going to say. 頭が真っ白になって話そうと思っていたことが思い出せなかった． ▶ one's mind goes blank「頭が真っ白になる」

She gave me a *blank* look. 彼女は無表情で僕を見た．

---

blind /bláɪnd/

原義は〈まぶしくて目がくらむ〉である．**目がくらむ→目が見えない；目をくらませる**．
関 color-blind（色盲）

He ⌈went *blind* [=lost his eyesight] in one eye. 彼は片目が見えなくなった．

He was *blind* to the reality of the situation. 彼は現状が分かっていない．

The little boy was in the car's *blind spot* and was almost run over. 幼い男の子は車の死角にいて，すんでのところで轢(ひ)かれるところだった．

Oncoming car lights often *blind* [=dazzle] us. 対向車のライトに目がくらむことがよくある．

block /blá:k/

原義は〈丸太〉である. **丸太→ひとかたまりの石, ブロック→ひとかたまりの街区, ブロック；(石や丸太は) 通行をふさぐ→遂行の邪魔をする.**

We built a partition wall between us and the neighbor with concrete *blocks*.　隣との仕切り塀をコンクリートブロックで作った.

The parking place is two *blocks* away.　駐車場は2ブロック先にあります.

Blood clots *block* [=prevent] the flow of blood and can cause strokes.　血栓は血流を妨害し卒中を起こすことがある.

What is *blocking* [=obstructing] the negotiation between the two countries?　何が両国の交渉の進展を妨害しているの？

blood /blʌ́d/

原義は〈噴き出る液〉である. **血液**. bl- は〈噴出〉をイメージさせるが, 動詞の bleed「出血する」や bloom「花(が咲く)」についても同様である.
派 bloody (血まみれの)　関 bloom (花が咲く)

My *blood group* [=type] is O.　ぼくの血液型はOです.

Your *blood pressure* varies at different times of the day.　血圧は一日の時間によって異なる.

Your nose is *bleeding*. =You are *bleeding* from the nose.　鼻血が出ているよ.

The victim was stabbed and *bled to death*.　被害者は刺されて出血多量で死んだ.

bloom /blúːm/

原義は〈つぼみがぽっと開く〉である.**花が咲く；花が咲いている；花**. bl- は〈噴出・つぼむ〉をイメージさせる. 花壇の花, 色鮮やかな花など鑑賞の対象になる花についていう.
関 blood（血液）；blossom（花, 開花する）

Roses are *blooming* [=in *bloom*] at the garden. 庭ではバラが咲いている.
Daffodil *blooms* [=flowers] in early spring. タンポポは早春に咲く.
The cherry trees are ⌈*in full bloom* [=at their best]. 桜が満開である.

blossom /blάːsəm/

原義は〈木々の花がぱ〜っと開く〉である.**花が咲きつつある；木々の花が咲いている；花**. bl- は〈噴出・つぼむ〉をイメージさせる.
関 bloom（花が咲く）

The orange [cherry/apple] trees are *blossoming*. オレンジ[桜／リンゴ]の花が咲き始めている. ▶日本語では「木が咲く」とはいわない.
The *ume blossom* has come out early this year. 今年は梅の花が早く咲いた.

blow /blóu/

原義は〈息を吹きつける〉である. **風が起こる, 吹き飛ぶ；打撃**. bl- は〈噴出〉をイメージさせる.

The wind was *blowing* all day long.　風が一日中吹いていた.

The fuse *blew out* due to the overload.　電気の使い過ぎでヒューズが飛んだ.　▶overload「過多の電流を流すこと」

Do you *blow your nose* into a handkerchief or tissue?　鼻をかむ時, ハンカチかティシューを使いますか.　▶日本語で「鼻をかむ」は手の描写, 英語 blow one's nose は息の描写.

The airplane accident was a severe *blow* [=damage] to the tourist industry.　その飛行機事故は旅行業界にとって非常な痛手であった.

board /bɔ́ːrd/

原義は〈板〉である.**（板）→食卓→食事；会議卓→委員会；甲板→（船・電車・バス・飛行機などに）乗り込む**.

I prefer a plastic *cutting board* because it is easy to clean.　洗いやすいのでプラスチック製のまな板のほうが好きだ.

The principal immediately reported the incident to *the board of education*.　学校長はその事件を直ちに教育委員会へ報告した.

How many people were *on board* when the ship sank?　船が沈没した時, 何人乗船していたのですか.

Tickets must be bought before *boarding*; you cannot buy them from the driver.　切符は乗車前に買わないといけません. 運転手から買うことはできませんから.

boast /bóust/

原義は〈威張る〉である．①**人が自分のことを威張る→自慢する**．②**地域が地域のことを誇る**．

John *boasted*「that he was [＝about his being] the best player in the team. ジョンはチームで一番の選手だと自慢した．

I say this not to *boast* but simply to state a fact. 私がこう言うのは自慢するためではなくただ事実を述べるためです．

This is hardly a story to *boast* about. これは少しも自慢になる話ではない．

This city *boasts* a number of parks and gardens for residents and visitors to relax and enjoy themselves in. 当市は，住民や旅行者が憩うことのできるたくさんの公園や庭園があることを誇りにしている．

body /bá:di/

原義は〈ふっくらした樽(たる)〉である．樽は内容物を含む容器であることから，**(天然の水を含む容器である) 海，湖，池**→**(骨・肉・体液の容器である) 人体，死体**．その内容物は**かたまり**，**一団**，**本体**となる．bo- は〈ふくらみ〉のイメージがある．

What is the largest organ in the human *body*? 人体の中で一番大きな器官は何ですか．

The victim's family was called to identify the *body*. 被害者の家族が死体の身元確認のために呼ばれた．

I prefer swimming in natural *bodies of water* like oceans, lakes and rivers. 僕は海や湖や川など自然の水域で泳ぐ方が好きだ． ▶a natural body of water で連想されるのは〈海，湖，池，川〉である．

A large *body of* people became an uncontrollable mob. たくさんの人の一団が手に負えない暴徒と化した．

boil /bɔ́il/

原義は〈熱湯がぶくぶく泡立つ〉である. **沸騰する→湯を沸かす→湯を沸かせて(食材を)煮る**.
派 boiler (ボイラー, 給湯器)

At what temperature does water *boil*?　水は何度で沸騰しますか.
The water began to *boil*.　湯が沸騰し始めた.
Boil the water for tea, please.　お茶を入れるから湯を沸かしてちょうだい.
"How should we cook the potatoes?" "Let's *boil* them, shall we?"
「ジャガイモはどう料理しようか」「煮ましょうよ」

bomb /bá:m/

原義は〈ボーンという爆発音〉をなぞったもの. **爆弾→爆撃する**.
派 bombard (攻撃を浴びせる); bombardment (爆撃)
関 boom (とどろく, 響く)

A time *bomb* planted in the car exploded near the embassy.　大使館の近くで車に仕掛けられた時限爆弾が爆発した.　▶ plant a time bomb「時限爆弾を仕掛ける」

In 1945, Tokyo ⌈*was* heavily *bombed*[＝suffered heavy *bombardment*] and much of the city was burned to the ground.　1945年に東京は大空襲を受け, 町は広域にわたって焼け落ちた.

Enthusiastic audience *bombarded*[＝attacked] the speaker with questions.　熱心な聴衆は講師に質問を浴びせた.

bond /bάːnd/

原義は〈ひも, 帯〉である. **(つなぐ)** 絆(きずな) → **(結ぶ) 契約** → **(換金を約束する) 債券**.
関 bind (縛る); band (帯)

Ordeals they suffer may strengthen the *bond* [=ties] between family members.　試練に出くわすと家族間の絆は強まることが多い. ties は「つながり, 絆」の意味では複数形が通例.

A government or company issues a *bond* to borrow money from investors.　政府や会社は投資者から金を借りるために債券を発行する.

---

book /búk/

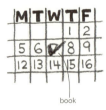
book

語源は〈boc=beech (ブナの木)〉である. **帳面→本; 帳面に記入する→予約する**. 紙の前はブナの木の皮に文字を記していた. 日本でも用紙の前身は植物の葉や木の板であった. モチ科の植物の葉の裏に引っかいて文字を記したので「葉書き」という.
派 booking (ブッキング, 予約)

The author writes *books* for a young adult audience.　この作家は若い読者層向けの本を書く.　▶audience「(集合的に) 読者」

You can *book* [=reserve] a hotel room online.　インターネットでホテルを予約できます.

All our flights are fully *booked* [=reserved] until the end of the week.　当社の飛行便は週末まで全席予約済みです.

We have to *keep* the *books* so as to record our profits and expenses.　収入と支出の記録をするために簿記をつけないといけない.　▶bookkeeping は発音してみると「ブッキ」→「簿記」となる!

boom /bú:m/

原義は〈ボーンというとどろきの音〉をなぞったもの. **とどろく→勢いがつく→ブームになる；ブーム, 大流行.** bo- は〈ふくらみ〉のイメージがある.
関 bomb（爆弾）

Cycling to work has been *booming* in recent years.　自転車通勤が近年ブームになっている.

There has been 「*a boom* in construction ［＝a construction *boom*］ since Tokyo was chosen to host the 2020 Olympic Games.　東京が2020年のオリンピック開催国に選ばれたので建設ブームが起こっている.

boost /bú:st/

語源は〈boo (m)（ボーンという音）＋ (hoi) st（持ち上げる)〉である. **物事を後押しして勢いづける.**
派 booster（増幅器）

This victory *boosted* ［＝raised］ my morale for the next competition.　この勝利は次の試合への士気を高めてくれた.

We should take more steps to *boost* the sales.　売り上げを伸ばすためにさらなる策を講じなければならない.

border /bɔ́:rdər/

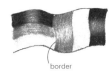
border

原義は〈板の縁(ふち)〉である. **縁→他と境を接する；境界**.
関 borderline（境界線）

Austria ⌈*borders on* [=*shares the border with*]⌉ Italy.　オーストリアはイタリアと国境を接している.

Mount Asama ⌈forms the *border* [=lies on the *border*]⌉ between Nagano-ken and Gunma-ken.　浅間山は長野・群馬両県にまたがっている.

What the association is ⌈doing *borders on* crime [=on the *borderline* between crime and non-crime]⌉.　この協会のやっていることは犯罪すれすれだよ.　▶border on ～「～も同然である」

---

bore /bɔ́:r/

原義は〈穴を開ける〉である. **気分に穴を開ける→退屈させる；退屈させるもの**. bore a hole（穴を開ける）と a hole in one's heart（心の空洞）の両表現は bore の語義理解のヒントになる.
派 boredom（退屈）；boring（つまらない）

His lecture ⌈*bored* me [=was *boring*]⌉.　彼の講演は退屈だった.
That movie was a real *bore*.　あの映画はほんとうにつまらなかった.
I'm going crazy with *boredom*.　退屈で気が狂いそうだ.
He drinks to cope with *boredom*.　彼は退屈を紛らわすために酒を飲む.
▶cope with ～「～を処理する, 対応する」

born /bɔ́ːrn/

原義は〈生まれた〉である．**生まれた→生まれながらの→天性の**．

My brother was "a *born* artist [=*born to be* an artist]. He had been drawing and painting ever since childhood.　弟は生まれながらの画家だった．子どものころからずっと絵を描いていた．

John is *a born loser* who had a breakdown and left his pregnant fiancée on his wedding day.　ジョンは本当にだめなやつで，結婚式の日にノイローゼになって身重の婚約者と別れたんだ．　▶a born loser「いつも失敗・敗北ばかりするだめな人」

Long-distance runners are not *born*, they are created over time.　長距離ランナーは，素質ではなく，時間をかけて生み出されるものだ．　▶over time「長い時間を経て」

borrow /báːrou/

原義は〈借りる〉である．**①具体物（金品）を borrow する時，返却を条件とするので無料である．②抽象概念（アイディア・文言など）を borrow する時，対象の移動が起こらないので返却の必要がなく，〈拝借〉になる．**

Graduate students may *borrow* [=check out] up to 15 books for 30 days.　大学院生は15冊まで30日間借り出せます．

Japanese has *borrowed* a considerable number of words from English.　日本語は英語から多くの単語を借用している．

The school *borrowed* [=employed] Dewey's educational theory for planning a new curriculum.　この学校はデューイの教育理論を新カリキュラム作成に取り入れた．

boss /bɔ́ːs/

原義は〈主人・雇い主〉である．**組織の長**．日本語でボスは親分といったニュアンスがあるが，boss は男女参画社会では女性についても使う．
派 bossy（横柄な）

My wife is the *boss* in our family; she controls all the money and makes most decisions.　わが家を仕切るのは妻で，金のやりくりをはじめ，ほとんどの決定を下す．

The store manager *bosses* us *around*.　店長は私たちをあごで使う．

The director is very *bossy* and likes to get his own way in everything.　部長は横柄で，なんでも自分の考えを通そうとする．　▶ get one's own way「我を通す」

both /bóuθ/

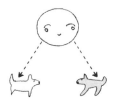

原義は〈両方〉である．**二者を前にして，その両方へ同時に意識を注ぐ時，both（どちらも→両方とも）という．**
bo- は〈両方向への意識の広がり〉が感じられる．

Both are [＝They are *both*] all right.　両方とも OK だよ．

Most designer products are *both* beautiful *and* functional.　たいていのブランド品は美しくて機能性がよい．

I fell and broke *both* of my ankles.　転んで両足首を骨折した．

Both of the parents [＝*Both* parents] were tall.　両親とも背が高かった．
▶二者のうちのどちらかの一つに意識を注ぐときは either という：Do you want to come on "Thursday or Friday?" "*Either* day is fine for me."（「木曜日，それとも金曜日に来られますか」「私はどちらの日でも OK です」）

bother /bá:ðər/

原義は〈騒音で悩む〉である．**精神の集中・精神の安定を妨げる**．名詞用法では「ちょっとした悩みの種」の意．

Don't let it *bother* you ... it's just a game, right?　そのことで悩むな，ゲームに過ぎないんだから，そうだろ？　▶bother+人「(人)を悩ませる」

My right ear has been *bothering* me for several weeks now.　右耳の変調にもう数週間悩まされています．

Heaven or hell is just a notion. I don't think it is worth *bothering* about.　天国や地獄というのは単なる概念上のことだよ．悩むことはないよ．〔←悩む価値があるとは考えない〕

If going to the ticket office is a *bother*, just get it online.　チケット売り場へ出向くのが面倒なら，ネットで買いなさいよ．

bottom /bá:təm/

原義は〈地面〉である．**物の上部から見た時に一番低い面（底）**．
派 bottomless（底なしの）　関 bottom line（要点）

The plane crashed, sank, and lies on the *bottom* [＝bed] of the ocean with everyone on board.　飛行機は墜落し，沈み，乗客全員を乗せたまま海底に横たわっている．

Bob was hopeless at school, and was (the) *bottom* of the class for every subject.　ボブは学業はさっぱりで，どの学科もクラスでビリだった．

However good the plan is, *the bottom line* is your enthusiasm to put it into practice.　いかに構想がよくても，重要なのは構想を実践に移す情熱だ．
▶〈bottom（底）line（行）〉→帳簿の末尾（帳尻）→最終の収益→つまるところ，要点，肝心なこと

bow /báu/

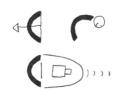

原義は〈曲がり〉である. **(曲がり)→弓→(弦楽器の)弓；(船首部の曲がり)→船首→船の先頭部；(身体を曲げて)おじぎする**.
関 elbow（肘）; rainbow（虹）

He drew a *bow*, aimed and let the arrow fly.　彼は弓を引き, 狙いを付けて発射した.

The ship turned her *bow* to the south and headed for the Cape of Good Hope.　船はへさきを南へ向け喜望峰を目指した.　▶ship は女性代名詞で受けることが多い.

We *bow* to show respect to others.　私たちは他人に敬意を表するために頭を下げる.

bowel /báuəl/

原義は〈ソーセージ〉である. **くねくねしている腸**. 通例, bowels と複数形になるのは, 腸は the small bowel [＝intestine]（小腸）+the large bowel [＝intestine]（大腸）であるから. bo- に〈膨らみ〉, -wel に〈曲がり, くねくね〉が感じられる.

I「get loose *bowels*［＝get diarrhea］after drinking milk.　牛乳を飲むと下痢をする.

I felt the sudden urge to have a *bowel movement*.　急に便意を催した.

With so much stress, I「was not able to move my *bowel*［＝didn't have a *bowel movement*］for three days when normally I do it every day.　ひどいストレスで, 普通なら毎日ある便通が 3 日もなかった.

brace /bréɪs/

原義は〈抱きしめる〉である. **腕で絞める→締める→(腕を両脇に締めて)身構える, 気を引き締める；ブレイス**.
関 embrace (抱き込む)〔←中に＋腕〕; bracelet (ブレスレット)

I have to *brace myself* for another exam next week.　来週, もう一つ試験があるので気を締めてかからなくちゃ.

I used to wear *braces* to straighten my teeth.　歯並びをよくするためにブレイス (歯列矯正器) をつけていた.

He is wearing a *neck brace* to help decrease the pain caused by the accident.　彼は, 事故が原因の痛みを和らげるためにネックブレイス (頚椎 (けいつい) 固定具) をしている.

brain /bréɪn/

原義は〈額 (ひたい)〉である. **思考や感覚をつかさどる器官 (脳)**.

She has a good *brain* and a good heart.　彼女は頭がよくて心の優しい人だ.

She is blessed with beauty and *brains*.　彼女は才色兼備だ.

He is suffering from a *brain tumor*.　彼は脳腫瘍を患っている.

branch /bræntʃ/

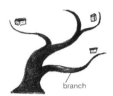

原義は〈(胴体に対する)足〉である．**(本体から枝分かれしている)枝・支流・支店**．branch (枝) がさらに二つに分枝すると twig (小枝← two と関連がある) になる．

You sometimes have to prune the *branches* of those trees.　ときどき木の枝を刈り込まないといけませんよ．

Does your company have *branches* in other countries?　貴社は外国にも支社がありますか．

This brook is a *branch* that falls into the Ishikari River.　この小川は石狩川に注ぐ支流です．

brand /brænd/

原義は〈焼印を入れる〉である．**家畜に焼印を押す，悪人に烙印(らくいん)を押す→製品に銘柄を入れる；銘柄，商標**．
関 bread (パン) 〔←焼く〕

Many *branded* Galileo as a dangerous heretic in his day.　当時，多くの人はガリレオを危険な異端者として烙印を押した．

Which *brand* of detergent do you recommend?　洗剤はどこの銘柄がいいですか．

If the clothes look cute, *brand* names mean nothing to me.　衣服は可愛ければ，銘柄は関係ないわ．

break /bréɪk/

原義は〈破壊する〉である．**安定した一つのものに突然力を加えて破壊・分離する→平静を破壊する→変化を突発させる；一休み．**
関 breakfast（朝食）〔←断食（fast）を中止させる（break）〕

I *broke* the glass [=The glass *broke*] when I dropped it on the floor. コップを床に落として割ってしまった．

My dad fell off a ladder and *broke* his hip. 父ははしごから落ちて，腰の骨を折った．

The peal of thunder *broke* the silence. 雷鳴が静寂を破った．

Let's *break* [=take a *break*] for lunch. 休憩して食事にしましょう． ▶a break「休憩」〔←仕事の連続の中断〕

---

breath /bréθ/

原義は〈息を吐き出す〉である．**呼吸．**元来は〈呼気だけ〉を意味していた．
派 breathe（呼吸する）

Take a deep *breath* [=*Breathe* deeply] when you're nervous. 緊張している時は，深呼吸しなさい．

He finished the draft *at a breath* overnight. 彼は原稿を一晩で一気に書き上げた．

Breathe in [=inhale] deeply and ⌈*breathe* out [=exhale] slowly. 深く吸ってゆっくり吐きなさい．

breed /bríːd/

原義は〈(動物が) 子を産む〉である. **(動物が) 子を産む→ (人が人為的に) 品種をつくる；品種, 種類**. bre- は〈噴出・生み出し〉のイメージ.
派 breeder (ブリーダー, 畜産家)

He *breeds* [＝is a *breeder* of] racehorses in Hokkaido.　彼は北海道で競走馬を飼育している.

What *breed* [＝kind] of dog is the smartest?　犬の中でいちばん頭のいい品種は何ですか.

breeze /bríːz/

原義は〈ひんやりした海からの風〉である. **そよそよと吹く風**. 動詞用法では, そよ風の連想から〈すいすい進む→物事を難なくこなす〉の意がある. 類義語 wind は「そよ風」から「強風」までを指すことができる.
派 breezy (そよ風の吹く)

Palm trees were swaying in the *breeze*.　ヤシの木がそよ風に揺れていた.

The Giants *breezed through* the first round of playoffs with a 10-3 win.　ジャイアンツはプレーオフの初戦を 10 対 3 で楽勝した.

It's *breezy* today.　今日は少し風がある.　▶It's windy today.「今日は風が強い」

bribe /bráɪb/

原義は〈パン〉である.**(パンを施す)→不正な施し→袖の下から密かに贈る金品(賄賂)**;賄賂を贈る.
派 bribery(収賄行為)

Is it a crime to「give a *bribe* to [=*bribe*] government officials? 役人に金品を贈るのは犯罪ですか.

The officer was dismissed on a charge of *bribery* [=accepting *bribes*]. 警官は収賄のかどで免職になった.

bridge /brídʒ/

原義は〈梁(はり)〉である.橋梁(きょうりょう)は,**双方をつなぐ,相違・隔たりを埋める**役割をする.

You have to cross over the railway *bridge* to the other platform. 反対側のプラットホームへは陸橋を渡ってください.

Japan's technology is leading the world in building *bridges*. 架橋技術で日本は世界をリードしている.

I want to work as a *bridge* between Japan and Malaysia in the future. 将来,日本とマレーシアの懸け橋として働きたい.

How can we *bridge* the generation gap between parents and children? どうしたら親子の世代間ギャップが埋められますか.

bright /bráit/

原義は〈輝く〉である. **輝く→明るい→（頭が）明敏な, 利口な.**

The sun of Southern California was dazzlingly *bright*.　南カルフォルニアの太陽はまぶしいほど明るかった．

The moonlight was *bright* enough to help me see the path that leads to my house.　月明かりが明るくてわが家への道がよく見えた．

I think there is a *bright* future for electric vehicles.　電気自動車の前途は明るいと思う．

The boy's very *bright* [＝smart].　その少年はとても利口だ．　▶bright は通例, 子どもの頭のよさについていう．「利口」も同様に子どもに対して使われる．

brim /brím/

brim

原義は〈端〉である. **容器の縁, 帽子のつば.** 動詞用法では, **中味が縁までいっぱいになる（あふれる）**.

Wear sunglasses and a wide *brim* [＝*brimmed*] hat when in the strong sun.　強い日差しの中ではサングラスと広い縁の帽子をかぶりなさい．

When greeting a friend, I usually touch the *brim* of my hat.　友だちにあいさつするとき, 私はたいてい, 帽子のつばに手を触れる．

The newly formed government seems to be *brimming* [＝filled] with confidence and enthusiasm to bring about a change.　新政権は変革をもたらす自信と情熱にあふれているように見える．

bring /bríŋ/

原義は〈物を持ってくる〉である．**向こうからこちらへ物を持ってくる，人や動物を連れてくる→物事をもたらす．**

I hope Santa *brings* me what I asked for.　サンタさんがお願いした物，持ってきてくれるといいな．

May I *bring* some friends to the party.　パーティーに友だちを連れてっていい？

Gandi made every effort to *bring* peace to the region.　ガンジーは地球に平和をもたらすために尽力した．

brink /bríŋk/

原義は〈崖っぷち〉である．**①一歩後退すると滑落する場所・状態にあること．②一歩進めば新天地へ行ける場所・状態にあること．**

Koalas are *on the brink* [=verge] *of* extinction in Queensland.　コアラはクイーンズランドでは絶滅の危機に瀕している．

If I am *on the brink of* losing my temper, I always try slowly counting to ten.　怒りが爆発しそうになったら，ゆっくり1から10まで数えるようにしている．

His business is *on the brink of* great success.　彼の商売はブレイク寸前だ．　▶on the brink of+〈不都合な事〉が多いが，この例のように〈肯定的な事柄〉にも使われる．

brisk /brísk/

原義は〈活発な〉である．①**活動がきびきび，てきぱきしている．**②**天気がひんやりしてさわやかである．**
派 briskly（元気よく）

My grandmother still walks ⌈at a *brisk* pace [=*briskly*]．　ぼくの祖母はまださっさと歩いている．

Small cars are selling ⌈at a *brisk* pace [=briskly]．　小型車の売れ行きが順調だ．

It was *brisk* [=cold and fresh] this morning．　今朝はひんやりとしていた．

brittle /brítl/

原義は〈砕けやすい〉である．**硬いが弾力性に欠けてもろい状態・性質．**

Bones may become *brittle* after menopause．　閉経すると骨はもろくなりがちだ．　▶brittle-bone disease「骨そしょう症」

Grandma's diary has yellowed and turned *brittle* with age．　おばあちゃんの日記は年月を経て黄ばんで，ぼろぼろになっていた．

broad /brɔ́:d/

原義は〈(大地の) 広がり〉である． **広々としている→広範な→満ち満ちた；広げる**．
派 broaden (広げる)；broadly (大ざっぱに)

She was tall and stately, with *broad* shoulders and an elegant waist. 彼女は長身で堂々としており，肩幅が広くて腰回りが上品だった．

The lawmaker tackles *broad* issues such as boosting early education, border security, and tax cuts. この議員は早期教育の促進，国境警備，減税など広範囲の問題に取り組んでいる．

The attack happened in *broad daylight* on a busy street. 襲撃は真っ昼間の繁華街で起こった．

He *broadened* [=widened] his horizons by reading numerous books. 彼は多くの本を読んで視野を広げた．

broadcast /brɔ́:dkæst/

語源は〈broad (広く) cast (投げる)〉である． **情報を伝播する，テレビやラジオで放送する**．
派 broadcaster (キャスター，解説者)
関 cast (投げる)；forecast (予測する)

NHK began television *broadcasting* [=*broadcasts*] in 1953. NHKは1953年にテレビ放送を開始した．

The proceedings of the Diet are being *broadcast* on NHK television. 国会審議の様子がNHKテレビで中継されている．

Don't *broadcast* the fact that I was fired. 僕が首になったことは内緒にしてね．

browse /bráuz/

原義は〈動物が若芽をあちこちと探してかじり食う〉である．**面白そうな情報を求めて本やネット上などであちこち拾い読みをしたり，いろいろな催しなどを見たりして回る．**

派 browser（ブラウザー〔ウェブサイトを閲覧するためのソフト〕）

I use a mobile phone that can *browse* the Web.　ネット検索ができる携帯電話を使っている．

My brother was *browsing* (through) the "wanted" ads in the newspaper, looking for a job.　兄は仕事を探すために新聞の求人広告に目を走らせていた．

I like *browsing* [＝wandering around] local museums, art galleries, and antique shops.　地域の博物館，画廊，古美術店などを見て回るのが好きだ．

bubble /bʌ́bl/

語源は〈bub（あぶく）le（繰り返し）〉である．**ぶくぶく；ぶくぶくと音を立てる→あぶく，泡→見かけは活動的だがすぐに消えるもの．**

The girl blew *bubbles* into water through a straw.　女の子はストローに息を吹き込んで水中にぶくぶくあぶくをつくった．

Kids like blowing *bubbles*.　子どもはシャボン玉を吹くのが好きだ．

The kettle began to *bubble*.　やかんの湯が沸き始めた．

When the *bubble* finally burst, hundreds of people lost their jobs.　バブル景気がはじけると何百人もの人が職を失った．

bud /bʌ́d/

原義は〈つぼみ〉である．**つぼみ（←袋状（bag）で小さく固まっている）；芽吹く, 育む**．

The apple trees are *budding* [=*in bud*] and a few more days of warm sunshine will cause them to burst open into fragrant blossoms.　リンゴの木が芽吹いており，もう数日暖かい日があればいっせいに芳しい花が開くでしょう．

War zones like Yemen or Syria serve as incubators for *budding* terrorists.　イエメンやシリアのような戦争地帯はテロリストを育む培養器の役割をしている．

I think we should *nip* the problem *in the bud*.　この問題が大きくならないうちに未然に防ぐ〔←つぼみのときに摘み取る〕べきだと思う．

---

budget /bʌ́dʒət/

原義は〈小さな皮袋（bag）→財布〉である．**財布の中身→予算**．

Make sure you stay within your household *budget*.　家計の予算を超えないように注意しなさい．

What is the average *budget* for a family of four?　4人家族の平均的予算はいくらですか．

The city is going to make huge *budget* cuts for the coming year.　市は来年度予算の大幅削減をする．

build /bíld/

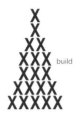
build

原義は〈家を建てる〉である．**①材料を組み合わせて具体物を組み立てる．②能力や状況など（目に見えないもの）をこつこつ築き上げる**．
派 building（建物）；builder（建築業者）

How many years did it take to *build* the Bay Bridge?　ベイブリッジの建設には何年かかりましたか．

Swallows *build* their nests under the eaves of my house every year.　ツバメが毎年，軒下に巣を作る．

We want to *build* a better relationship.　もっと良好な関係を築きたい．

burden /báːrdn/

原義は〈荷物〉である．**負担となる義務や困難なこと；重圧をかける**．-u- は〈圧迫〉のイメージがある．
関 bear（重荷を担う）

Carrying the *burden* [＝the weight] of the head of the department is not an easy task.　部長の重責を果たしていくのは容易なことではない．

The captain has the *burden* [＝the responsibility] of explaining how the collision occurred.　船長はどのようにして衝突が起こったのか説明する責任がある．

Don't unduly *burden* yourself with too many responsibilities.　たくさんの責任を引き受けて不当に自分を追い込まないようにしなさい．

burn /bə́ːrn/

原義は〈焼く〉である．①炎を上げて燃える．②高熱で対象物に変質を起こす〈焦がす，焼く〉．

Clothing and paper were *burning* in the parking lot.　駐車場で衣類や紙が燃えていた．

Do not eat or drink anything that is very hot. You could *burn* your tongue.　熱いものを飲んだり食べたりしないで．舌をやけどしてしまいますよ．

Someone's *burnt* a hole in the carpet.　誰かがカーペットに焦げ穴をつくっているわ．

Jogging helps you *burn* calories and lose weight.　ジョギングするとカロリーが燃焼して減量に役立つ．

burst /bə́ːrst/

原義は〈破裂する〉である．**溜まっている物質や感情が飽和状態になり，容器を突き破って一気に噴出する．**

The dam *burst* after days of heavy rain, destroying lots of houses and farms.　連日の豪雨でダムが決壊して多くの家や農場を破壊した．

The children *burst into tears* on hearing of the death of their puppy.　子どもたちは子犬が死んだと聞いてわっと泣き出した．　▶burst into 〜「急に〜し始める」：burst into flames（一気に燃え上がる）

bury /béri/

原義は〈埋める〉である．**物を覆って隠す，物を土中に埋める，死体を埋葬する．**
派 burial（埋葬）

The little girl smiled shyly and *buried* her face in the curtain.　幼い少女は恥ずかしそうに笑ってカーテンに顔を隠した．

A worker was *buried* alive by falling bricks and stones.　作業員が落ちてきたレンガや石で生き埋めになった．

My father was *buried* in the town's cemetery.　父は町の共同墓地に埋葬された．

business /bíznəs/

語源は〈busy（携わっている）ness（状態）〉である．**人が成すべきことに取り組んでいる状態→製造，商売，取引き，事業，営業．**
派 busy（忙しい）

My father is away on *business*.　父は出張している〔←仕事でいない〕．

Are you planning on doing *business* in China?　中国で商売をするつもりですか．

He started a small food *business*〔＝company〕in Fukuoka.　彼は福岡で小さな食品会社を始めた．▶ここでは business は可算名詞．

Small *businesses* are hard hit by the recession.　中小企業は不況の影響でひどく苦しんでいる．

A lot of companies went out of *business* during the economic recession.　経済不況の間に多くの会社が倒産した．

busy /bízi/

原義は〈忙しい・ふさがっている〉である．①**手がふさがっている《多忙・従事》**．②**場所がふさがっている〈混雑〉**．-u- は〈圧迫〉のイメージ．
派 business（仕事，事業，会社）

I'm going to be *busy* today.　今日は忙しくなりそうだ．

I have been too *busy* to enjoy even my weekends.　忙しくて週末も楽しめないよ．

This store is always *busy* [＝crowded] on weekends.　この店は，週末はいつもにぎわっている．

I found the bathroom was *busy*.　トイレは空いていなかった．

The old road has become less *busy*.　旧道は交通量が少なくなった．

buy /bái/

原義は〈買う〉である．**金を払って物品を得る，他者に（食事・酒を）おごる；買い物**．
派 buyer（買い手，仕入れ係）

I *bought* ⌈him dinner [＝dinner for him].　彼に食事をおごった．

He decided to *buy* time at the price of lower income.　収入は少なくなるが，時間を買うことを決めた．

This computer was a great *buy*; it has been running for over five years with no problems.　このパソコンはいい買い物だったよ．もう5年以上も故障なしでさくさくと動いている．

by /baɪ/

原義は〈そばにいる〉である.**(そばに限定する)→〜で限る, 〜で区切る**.

My teacher came and stood *by* me.　先生が来てわたしのそばに立った.《場所の限定》

His mental breakdown was caused *by* overwork.　彼は過労でうつ病になった.《原因の限定》

You have to hand in your report *by* 5 pm on Friday.　レポートは金曜日の午後5時までに提出しなくてはいけない.《期日時間の限定》

The horse I bet on won *by* a head.　賭けた馬が首の差で勝った.《長さの限定》

---

calculate /kǽlkjəlèɪt/

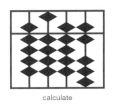

calculate

原義は〈小石(calculus=pebble)を使って数える〉である.**数える→計算する**.原初,人が石を使って計算したことは想像に難くない.
派 calculation(計算)

How can you *calculate* [=measure] the force of gravity on the moon?　月の重力はどのようにして測れますか.

The Happiness index is *calculated* [=measured] using surveys of workplace satisfaction and the number of days of leave taken.　この幸福指数は職場の満足度と休暇の日数を調査して計算されている.

You must be able to make simple *calculations* in your mind.　簡単な計算は暗算できないといけない.　▶in one's mind「頭の中で」

calf /kǽf/

原義は〈ふっくらしたお腹〉である．**大型動物の子**〔←いずれもふっくら感がある〕，**ふくらはぎ**〔←ふっくら＋脛(はぎ)〕

A mother whale and her *calf* were seen swimming off the coast of Muroto.　母クジラと子クジラが室戸沖を泳いでいるのが見えた．

I often get a cramp in my *calves* when swimming.　僕は泳いでいるとよくふくらはぎがつる．　▶get［＝have］a cramp「筋肉がつる」

call /kɔ́ːl/

原義は〈声をかける（呼ぶ）〉である．**声をかける→玄関で声をかける（訪問する）→（電話で）声をかける；（～を）～と呼ぶ，～と宣する**．

A stranger *called* to me from across the street.　見知らぬ人が通りの向こう側から私に声をかけてきた．

I often *call* on my grandparents after school.　放課後，よく祖父母の家に立ち寄る．

Call me tomorrow.　明日，お電話ください．

What are you going to *call* your new dog?　新しい犬は何という名前にするの？

The ball was clearly on the line but the referee *called* it "out."　ボールは明らかにライン上に落ちたが，審判はアウトを宣告した．

calm /káːm/

calm

原義は〈真っ昼間の静けさ〉である．万象の活動が止まって**静かな**，動揺がなく**穏やかである**．人里離れた田舎では，酷暑の昼間はし～んとした雰囲気（＝森閑）がある．

Good leaders should know how to stay *calm* [=even-tempered] in difficult times.　よい指導者は困難な時に冷静でいられる人でないといけない．

The city gradually returned to *calm* [=quiet] after a very hard election campaign.　激しい選挙戦が終わって街は元のように平穏になってきた．

After a storm comes a *calm*.　《諺》嵐の後には平穏がくるものだ．

camouflage /kǽməflàːʒ/

原義は〈欺く〉である．**偽装・迷彩で敵の目を欺く；偽装**．

Hundreds of soldiers dressed in *camouflage* gathered to pay their respects to the victims.　何百人もの迷彩服を着た兵士たちが，犠牲者たちに敬意を表するために集まった．

Chameleons change colors to *camouflage* [=disguise] themselves even while they are sleeping.　カメレオンは寝ている時でもカムフラージュする〔←擬態のために色を変える〕．

camp /kǽmp/

camp

原義は〈野原〉である．(戦時の連想は) 野営・そのテント，宿舎，収容所；野営する．(平和時の連想は) 湖畔のキャンプ・そのテント，小屋；キャンプする．

During World War II, many Japanese-Americans were put into concentration *camps*.　第二次世界大戦時，多くの日系アメリカ人が強制収容所に入れられた．

We ⌈made *camp* [=*camped*] on an uninhabited island off Shimane last summer.　去年の夏，島根沖の無人島でキャンプした．

---

can /kǽn/, could /kúd/

原義は〈知っている〉である。知っている (知識がある) →〜出来る (能力・許可) →〜であり得る (可能性)
関 canny (抜け目のない) 〔←よく心得ている〕

Can [=*Could*] you call back later?　後で折り返して電話してもらえますか．
▶could (仮定法) は「丁寧さ・控えめ」が加わる．

She *can* speak Korean.　彼女は韓国語が話せる．　▶canの語源「知っている」を色濃く語っている：can=know how to speak

Accidents *can* happen to anyone.　事故は誰にでも起こり得る．

She *could* [=was able to] read before she started kindergarten.　彼女は幼稚園へ上がる前から文字が読めた．

You're a good swimmer; you *could* swim across the river.　君は泳ぎがうまいから，向こう岸まで泳いで渡れるよ．　▶could「やろうとすればできるだろう」

cancel /kǽnsl/

原義は〈格子状に線を引く〉である.**(文言に × 印を入れて) 約束・計画を取り消す**.
派 cancellation (取り消し)

I had to *cancel* [=call off] lunch with friends because I was not feeling well.　気分が悪かったので，友人とのランチの約束を取り消さねばならなかった.

All the flights were *cancelled* due to poor weather conditions.　天候不良のため全便がキャンセルになった.

---

cancer /kǽnsər/

cancer

語源は〈蟹(かに)〉である. がん組織の血管が浮き出たような様態がカニの甲羅の模様や脚の形態に似ていることに由来する.
関 Cancer (蟹座)

What percentage of smokers develop lung *cancer*?　喫煙者のうち何パーセントが肺がんになりますか.

Cancer may spread to other parts of the body.　がんは他の器官へ転移しがちである.

Cancer is a disease in which cells grow uncontrollably and form tumors.　がんは細胞がやたら増殖して腫瘍を形成する病気だ.

candidate /kǽndədèɪt/

原義は〈白衣を着た人〉である．ローマ時代，公職の候補者は清廉潔白を象徴する白衣を着て選挙活動をしたことに由来する．**候補者→志願者→〜になりそうな人**．
関 candid（率直な）〔←腹が白い〕; candle（ろうそく）〔←白く輝く〕

Ten *candidates* vied for three seats on the board.　理事会の3つの席を10人の候補者が争った．　▶vie＝compete「競う」

Do you know how many *candidates* applied for the position?　この職の志願者は何人か知っていますか．

People who are overweight are most likely *candidates* for diabetes.　太りすぎの人は糖尿病のいちばんの予備軍だ．

cap /kǽp/

語源は〈頭〉である．**(頭にかぶせる) 帽子→(容器にかぶせる) キャップ (ふた)**．
関 cape（岬）〔← headland〕; captain（船長, 主将）〔←頭（かしら）〕; capable（有能な）

Please take off your *caps* in the classroom unless you have a medical reason to keep them on.　医療上の理由がなければ，教室では帽子を脱いでください．

The *cap* won't come off.　ふたが取れないよ．

Put the *cap* back on the coke or it'll go flat!　コーラのふたを締めてよ，気が抜けちゃうから．

capable /kéɪpəbl/

語源は〈cap(つかむ)able(出来る)〉である.**(つかみ取れる)→器が大きくて取り込める→素質がある**.
派 capability(能力)
関 cap(帽子)〔←頭をつかむ〕; capture(つかみ取る); capacity(容量, 能力)

With excellent facilities, our company is *capable* of producing more than 3,000 vehicles per month.　優れた設備を備えたわが社は, 月産3000台を超す車を生産できる.

My father is old and weak and he is not *capable* of taking care of himself.　父は高齢で病弱のため身の回りのことができない.

I'm perfectly *capable* of doing it myself, thank you.　大丈夫, 自分でちゃんとできます, (お申し出)ありがとう.

Mr. Suzuki is a very *capable* [＝skilled] architect.　鈴木氏はとても有能な建築家だ.

---

capacity /kəpǽsəti/

語源は〈capaci(広い)ty(状態)〉である.**物事を受け入れる器, 容量, 器量**.
関 capable(能力がある)

The *capacity* of the tank is 32 cubic meters.　このタンクの容量は32立方メートルです.

How big is the *capacity* of the hard disk?　このハードディスクの容量はいくらですか.

Aerobic exercise helps you improve the air *capacity* of your lung.　有酸素運動は肺活量の増進に役立つ.

The hall reached its *capacity* of 2,000 half an hour before the show started.　会場はショーの始まる30分前に2000人の定員いっぱいになった.

capital /kǽpətl/

語源は〈capit (頭) al (の)〉である．**首都 (頭の位置を占める都市)，大文字 (頭の位置を占める文字)，元金・資金 (頭の位置を占める金)．**
派 capitalism (資本主義)；capitalist (資本家，資本主義者)；capitalize (大文字で書く)

"What is the *capital* of Mexico?" "It's Mexico City." 「メキシコの首都はどこですか」「メキシコ市だよ」

The title of your paper should be written in CAPITAL LETTERS. 論文のタイトルは大文字で書くこと．

How much *capital* do you need to start the business? その商売を始めるのにいくらの元金が必要ですか．

I think his crime deserves *capital punishment*. 彼の罪は死刑〔←頭をはねる刑〕に値すると思う．

---

capture /kǽptʃər/

capture

原義は〈捕える〉である．**力を尽くして・工夫をこらして獲得する，(比喩的に) 人の気持ちをつかむ．** cap- は〈つかむ〉の意味合いがある．
関 capable (有能な)；escape (逃げる)

They managed to *capture* the monkey that ran away from the circus. サーカスから逃げ出したサルをやっと捕まえた．

Ryo Ishikawa *captured* much attention from the Japanese media as he debuted in the British Open. 石川遼選手は全英オープンにデビューした時，日本のメディアから大きな注目を浴びた．

capable, capacity, capital, capture

care /kéər/

原義は〈気遣う〉である．**気持ちを配る→心配，用心，世話；気持ちが向かう→好む**《否定・疑問・条件文で》．
派 careful（注意深い）
関 cure（治療）；secure（安全な）

Drive slowly and with *care* on snowy roads.　雪道は慎重にゆっくり運転しなさい．

Take good *care* of yourself.　お大事に．

Would you ⌜*care for* [＝like] another cup of coffee?　コーヒーもう一杯いかがですか．

I do*n't care for* rock music.　ロックミュージックはあまり好きじゃない．

career /kəríər/

原義は〈荷馬車の行く道〉である．**(車の走る道)→人の歩む道→経歴，職業，仕事**．つづりに car（車）が潜んでいる．

He started his *career* as an actor when he was 20 years old.　彼は20歳の時に俳優としての道を歩き始めた．

She decided to seek a *career* abroad, despite her family's disapproval.　彼女は家族の反対を押し切って，外国で仕事を探すことを決めた．

Sadaharu Oh hit 868 homers in his *career*.　王貞治は通算868本の本塁打を打っている．

careful /kéərfl/

語源は〈care(用心)ful(満ちた)〉である．**用心深い・注意深い**．
派 carefully(用心深く，念入りに)；careless(注意を欠いている)；carefree(心配・責任がなくて開放的である)

My mother is a *careful* shopper and has no regrets with her purchases.　母は慎重に買い物をするので買ったものを後悔することがない．

Tom is very *careless* about what he says; he does not care if he may hurt someone.　トムは発言がどうも不用意だ．誰かを傷つけてしまうかもって思いもしないんだ．

My wife is *carefree* about what is happening in the world.　妻は世事には無頓着だ．

---

carry /kéri/

carry

原義は〈(荷車で)運ぶ〉である．①行為者が目的物を持って移動すると〈運ぶ・携行する〉．②行為者が静止していると〈支える〉．③行為者が「物事を運ぶ」と〈運営する・扱う〉．つづりに car(運搬車)が潜んでいる．
派 carrier(輸送会社，病原菌保有者)

USB sticks are very convenient for *carrying* around data.　USB メモリーはデータの持ち歩きにとても便利だ．

The ferry *carries* passengers and cargo between New York City and Staten Island.　このフェリーはニューヨークとスタテン島の間で乗客と貨物を運ぶ．

Four wooden corner pillars *carry* [=*support*] the weight of the whole temple.　四隅の木柱がお寺の全重量を支えている．

This paper *carries* a weekly book review on Sunday.　この新聞は日曜日に週刊書評欄を掲載している．

case /kéɪs/

原義は〈降りかかってくる〉である.**(降りかかってくる)要件・事件・場合；(降りかかってくる)病状・病人**.降りかかってくる非日常の典型が〈事件の発生と発病〉である.
関 cast（投げる）; chance（機会）; casual（気軽な）; occasion（時, 場合）

In most *cases*, I don't answer personal questions about my family.　たいていの場合, 家族のプライバシーに関する質問には答えません.

This is not true with every *case*, though.　これがすべての場合に当てはまるわけではありません.

The evidence was too weak to continue the *case*.　証拠に根拠がないので裁判が継続できなかった.

HIV *cases* are still growing in that area.　あの地域ではHIVの患者が依然増加している.

---

cash /kǽʃ/

原義は〈投げ入れた金庫の中の金〉である.**現金；現金に換える**.
関 cast（投げる）

The store accepts only *cash*, not credit cards or checks.　この店では現金払いのみで, クレジットカードや小切手は使えません.

When you ask to *cash* a check, a bank gives you the written amount in bills and coins.　小切手の換金を依頼すると, 銀行は提示額を紙幣と硬貨に換えてくれる.

cast /kæst/

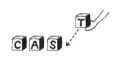

原義は〈目標へ向けて投げかける〉である．**視線を投げかける，票を投げ入れる→役を投げ渡す（役を振る）**．
関 broadcast（放送する）〔←広く＋投げる〕；case（事例）

She *cast* a doubtful *glance* at the man who stood behind her.　彼女は背後に立った男に疑わしい視線を投げた．　▶ cast a glance at ～「～をちらっと見る」

I am wondering which party I should 「*cast my vote* for ［＝vote for］．どの党に投票するか迷っているの．　▶ cast a vote ［＝ballot］「投票する」

Brad Pitt was *cast* in the lead role of Titanic.　ブラッド・ピットはタイタニックで主役を演じた．

casual /kǽʒuəl/

casual　　formal

語源は〈casu＝case（降ってくる）al（ような）〉である．**（起こってくる（←降ってくる）ことに任せて）構えない・気張らない・普段のままの**．
派 casually（カジュアルに，気軽に）
関 case（事件）〔←降って湧く〕

The students are allowed to attend school in *casual* ［＝everyday］ wear.　ここの学生は普段着で通学できる．　▶招待状に *Dress casual.* とあれば You don't have to dress up.（平服でおいでください）の意．

Dick is too *casual* about his life; he often changes his address and job.　ディックは生活に節度がない．しょっちゅう住所や仕事を変えている．

catch /kǽtʃ/

原義は〈捕まえる〉である． ① **(追いかけて) 捕まえる《意図的》**② **(ある状況に) 捕まる・陥る《偶然》**

How many fish did you *catch*?　何匹釣れた？

I failed to *catch* the last bus home.　帰りの最終バスに乗り遅れた．

I seem to have *caught* the flu.　どうもインフルエンザに感染したみたい．

The car chased by police crashed into a pole and *caught fire*.　警察の追跡を受けた車が電柱に衝突して火を噴いた．

We *got caught* in pouring rain on the way back.　帰る途中，土砂降りにあった．

The man *was caught* driving「drunk [=under the influence of alcohol].　男は飲酒運転で捕まった．

category /kǽtəgɔ̀:ri/

語源は〈cata (名づけて) gory (集める)〉である．**名をつけて同じものを集める→同じ種類のものを入れる枠・項目**．
派 categorize (項目別に分ける)

What are the age *categories* [=groups] of the race?　そのレースはどういう年齢部門になっていますか．

The books are divided into various *categories* such as fiction, nonfiction, history, science, arts, and so on.　本は小説，ノンフィクション，歴史，科学，芸術，などいろいろな分野に分けられている．

Scientists *categorize* [=classify] animals and plants by their properties.　科学者は動植物をその特徴によって分類する．

cattle /kǽtl/

原義は〈財産〉である．**牛，家畜牛**．中世には所有する家畜牛（cows, bulls）の頭数が財産（property）の量の指標であった．集合的に複数扱い．

A person's wealth used to be determined by the number of *cattle* he owned.　昔は人の財産は持っている牛の数で評価していた．

We saw *cattle* grazing peacefully on the farm fields.　牛が牧場でのどかに草をはんでいた．

How many head of *cattle* does the farmer have?　あの酪農家は何頭の牛を飼っていますか．　▶例えば，20頭の牛は twenty (head of) cattle という．

cause /kɔ́:z/

原義は〈原因〉である．**ある事が誘因となって別のことを引き起こす（原因）；ある目的が行動を引き起こす（大義）**．

What *causes* [＝What is the *cause* of] global warming?　地球温暖化の原因は何ですか．

Gandhi dedicated his whole life to the *cause* of India's independence.　ガンジーはインドの独立のために生涯を捧げた．

The relation between *cause and effect* of the change is not immediately determined.　この変化の因果関係はすぐには明らかにならない．

cavity /kǽvəti/

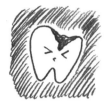

語源は〈cavi(洞穴)ty(状態)〉である. **空洞のある歯**→**虫歯**. cav- は〈中空(中が空っぽ)〉のイメージ.
関 cave(洞窟)

My wife never had a *cavity* before she got pregnant.　妻は妊娠するまでは虫歯が一つもなかった.

I have to get a *cavity* filled. ＝I have a *cavity* that needs to be filled.　虫歯に詰め物をしてもらわなければいけないわ.

The virus enters through nasal or *oral cavities*.　このウイルスは鼻腔や口腔から入る.

cease /síːs/

原義は〈行く〉である. **(行く)→徐々になくなる→やむ**. go の〈行く→なくなる〉と同じ発想.
関 ceasefire(休戦)〔←発砲をやめる〕; deceased(亡くなった)

The rain fortunately *ceased* [＝let up] before I started.　雨は運よく出発前にやんだ.

Height *ceases* [＝stops] to increase in late adolescence.　身長の伸びは青年期後半に止まる.

If you leave noodles uneaten for a while, they *cease* to be tasty.　麺類はすぐに食べないと味が悪くなる.

celebrate /séləbrèɪt/

語源は〈celebr(誉れ高く) ate (する)〉である. **褒めたたえる→祝う**.
派 celebration (祝賀会); celebrity (有名人) 〔←誉を与えられた人〕

His store *celebrated* [=held *a celebration* commemorating] its 10th anniversary last year.　彼の店は去年, 創業 10 周年を祝った.

Tadao Ando is an internationally *celebrated* [=famed] architect.　安藤忠雄は国際的に有名な建築家だ.

Koichi Tanaka became *a celebrity* [=a big name] after he won the Nobel Prize in Chemistry in 2002.　田中耕一氏は, 2002 年にノーベル化学賞を得て有名人になった.

cell /sél/

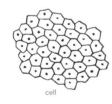

cell

原義は〈小部屋〉である. **壁に囲まれた部屋, 独房, 蜂の巣穴・細胞膜に囲まれた細胞**. cel- には〈くるっと囲む〉イメージがある.
派 cellar (地下貯蔵庫)　関 cell phone (携帯電話)

Abnormal *cell* growth develops into cancer.　細胞が異常に成長すると癌になる.

The suspect was put in a *cell* with only one blanket.　容疑者は毛布 1 枚だけで独房に監禁された.

Cell phones have become essential for our lives.　携帯電話は私たちの生活に必須なものとなった.　▶携帯電話を a cell phone というのは, 地域を区分けして各区画 (セル) に無線基地局を設ける通信サービスを行う方式だからである.

center /séntər/

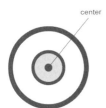

原義は〈円の中心点〉である. **(人が集まる) センター, 中央, (活動・関心の集まる) 中心**. 人や人の関心や活動が中心へ集まるのは自然の理.
派 central (中心の)

My wife goes to a yoga class at a community *center*.　妻はコミュニティーセンターのヨーガ教室に通っている.

She is the type who always has to be the *center* of attention.　彼女はいつも注目の的でないと気が済まない性分だ.

The Tone River flows through the *center* of the Kanto Plain.　利根川は関東平野の中心部を流れている.

centigrade /séntəgrèɪd/

語源は〈centi (100) grade (段階)〉である. **百段階に分けた目盛り→摂氏で計る温度数**.
関 centimeter (センチメーター)〔← centi (100) meter〕; centipede (ムカデ (百足))〔← centi (100) pede (足)〕; century (世紀)〔← 100 年〕

Keep your room temperature at around 18 degrees *centigrade*.　室温は摂氏 18 度位に保ちなさい.

Here, winter temperatures can drop to minus 20 degrees *centigrade*.　当地では, 冬は摂氏マイナス 20 度になることがある.

ceremony /sérəmòuni/

原義は〈宗教儀式〉である.**（結婚式などの）お祝い儀式**,**（儀式での作法）形式的な振る舞い**.

When and where is the *ceremony* going to be held? 式はいつどこであるの?

The wedding *ceremony* went on without a hitch. 結婚式は無事に終わった. ▶without a hitch「滞りなく」

Please sit down and make yourself comfortable. We do*n't stand on ceremony* here. 座ってくつろいでください. ここはかしこまる場ではありませんから.

certain /sə́ːrtn/

語源は〈cert（確かな）ain（である）〉である. **客観的に見て〜であると判断できる；（明言しないが）あるちゃんとした, しかるべく**. 類義語 sure は〈主観的確信〉の意味合いが強い.
派 certainly（確かに, もちろん）；certainty（確かなこと）

It is *certain* that the new government will fail unless it controls inflation. インフレを抑制できないと新政権が失敗するのは目に見えている. ▶この文で, it is sure ... といわないのは, it の〈客観性〉と sure の〈主観性〉が違和感を生むから.

There are things that you cannot understand until you have reached a *certain* age. ある程度の年齢になってみなければわからないこともある.

chair /tʃéər/

原義は〈豪華ないす〉である．**会長，議長；議長を務める**．中世では，深々と座れるいすは権威の象徴であった．
関 chairperson（議長，座長，司会者，会長）

He is the *chair* [=the chairman] of the board of education.　彼は教育委員会の会長だ．

Who will take the *chair* after him?　彼の後，誰がその職につくのですか．
▶the chair「（議長・会長・市長・学部長などの）職」

She has been *chairing* political debates on TV for many years.　彼女はテレビの政治討論会の司会を長年務めている．

challenge /tʃælindʒ/

原義は〈非難する〉である．**あえて異議を唱える→難事に挑む；物事が人に難題を与える**．
派 challenging（やりがいのある）

There were some scientists who *challenged* Einstein's theory of relativity.　アインシュタインの重力の法則に疑問を呈した科学者が何人かいた．

I'm mathematically *challenged* and don't know how to figure out the average speed of a car.　僕は数学が苦手で，車の平均速度の計算のしかたがわかりません．　▶be challenged は〈挑戦を受ける→こなすには努力が要る→容易でない→苦手である〉と展開している．

Leaning a foreign language is *challenging* and rewarding.　外国語の習得は難しいがやりがいがある（得るものが多い）．

chance /tʃǽns/

原義は〈降ってくる〉である. **物事がたまたま降りかかってくる→偶然, 運, 成り行き, 機会, 可能性**. カタカナ語の「チャンス(好機)」とは大きく異なる概念である.
関 case (出来事)

There's a *chance* of injury in any sport. どんなスポーツでも怪我をする可能性がある.

Being overweight may raise the *chance* [=the risk] of a stroke. 太っていると卒中の危険が高まる.

I will *take a chance* and tell him my situation. 思い切って事情を彼に話してみよう.

I ⌈*chanced upon* him [=met him *by chance*] at a coffee shop. 喫茶店で彼に偶然出会った.

---

change /tʃéɪndʒ/

原義は〈交換する〉である. **物が入れ替わる, 物事の内容が変化する;変化, 釣り銭**.
派 changeable (変わりやすい)
関 exchange (交換する)

The trees began to *change colors*. 木々の紅葉が始まった.

My hometown has *changed* a lot since I was a kid. 故郷の町は子どものころとはずいぶん変わった.

A number of significant *changes* have taken place since the turn of the century. 今世紀になって重要な変革がいろいろと起こった.

Always carry small *change* [=coins]; no bus drivers appreciate large notes. 小銭をいつも携帯しなさい. 万札を喜ぶ運転手はいないからね.

channel /tʃǽnl/

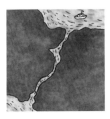

語源は〈canal(水路)el(小さな)〉である. **水路, 経路；道筋→海の水路 (海峡)；電波の経路 (チャンネル)**.
関 canal (運河)

The bridge passes over the Naruto *channel* [=strait] known for its tidal whirlpools.　この橋は渦潮で有名な鳴門海峡の上にかかっている.

We enjoyed a romantic gondola tour through the *channels* [=canals] in Venice.　ヴェニスの運河でロマンチックなゴンドラの旅を楽しんだ.

What *channel* is the game on?　何チャンネルでその試合の放送があるの.

chaos /kéɪɑːs/

原義は〈ガス体のような混沌(こんとん)〉である. **混沌, 混乱, 無秩序**. gas (ガス) は chaos からの造形語.
派 chaotic (混沌とした)

A theory states that the universe began in a state of total confusion called *Chaos*.　ある理論では，宇宙はカオスと呼ばれる全くの混沌から始まったと述べている.

The collapse of the mega-bank led to worldwide economic *chaos* [=confusion].　メガバンクが破綻したために，世界中が経済的混乱に陥った.

character /kǽrəktər/

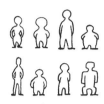
character

原義は〈刻印〉である. **文字や姿の刻彫→（くっきり目立つ）→記号・特徴・人物**.
派 characteristic（特質, 固有の）; characterize（〜の特徴を述べる）

Her *character* is very introverted. 彼女はひどく内向的な性格だ.

Every *character* is influenced by heredity and environment. 人の性格はすべて遺伝と環境の影響を受けている.

We use Chinese *characters* and phonetic *characters* in our writing. 私たちは漢字と音標文字（ひらがな, カタカナ）を使って書く.

Hayao Miyazaki's animation captures audience with very unique *characters* such as Mononoke-hime, Totoro and Ponyo. 宮崎駿のアニメは, もののけ姫, トトロ, ポニョなどのとてもユニークな登場人物で観客を魅了している.

---

charge /tʃɑ́ːrdʒ/

charge

原義は〈積み荷を車に詰め込む〉である. **電気を詰め込む；充電, 負担・責任を負わせる；経費, 負担, 責任**.
つづりに cargo（積み荷）が潜んでいる.
関 discharge（排出する）

This electric car travels up to 200 kilo-meters on a single *charge*. この電気自動車は一回の充電で 200 キロ走れる.

The shipping *charge* for these items is free. ＝We *charge* you nothing for shipping these items. これらの品物は送料無料です.

We will send replacements *free of charge*. 取替え品は無料でお送りします.

He was ⌈*charged* with [＝accused of] committing lewd acts on a mentally handicapped girl. 彼は知的障害の少女にわいせつ行為を働いたかどで訴えられた.

chase /tʃéɪs/

原義は〈追いかける〉である．**逃げるもの・欲しいものを追いかける**．
関 purchase（購入する）

Tom *chases* Jerry and the two engage in comical battles.　トムはジェリーを追っかけて，滑稽なけんかをしている．

We *chased* the snake *away* from the yard with a stick.　ヘビを棒で庭から追い出した．

He has been *chasing* [＝pursuing] his dream of becoming a comedian.　彼はお笑い芸人になる夢を追いかけている．

cheap /tʃíːp/

原義は〈格安品〉である．**値段が安い→品質が安っぽい**．
派 cheaply（安く，安上がりで）

This computer is inexpensive but not *cheap*.　このパソコン安いけど品質は悪くないよ．

You could buy the same item *cheaper* at online stores.　ネット通販なら同じ品を格安で買えるよ．

Many European and American companies have been exploiting *cheap* labor in developing countries.　多くの欧米の企業が発展途上国の低賃金労働者を巧妙に利用している．

He used to write *cheap* novels for a living.　彼は食うために安っぽい小説を書いていた．

cheat /tʃíːt/

原義は〈だます〉である．**我欲のためにひそかに他者をだます**．

The insurance salesman *cheated* an aged woman out of her fortune. その保険外交員は老女をだまして財産を横取りした．

He has admitted ⌈*cheating* on [=being unfaithful to] his wife and children. 彼は妻と子どもたちを裏切ったことを認めた．

I got caught *cheating* on my final exam. 期末試験でカンニングが見つかってしまった．

check /tʃék/

原義は〈王手！（チェスで）敵の自由な動きを止める〉である．**相手の自由な動きをいったん止める**．〔←整合性を確認したり，素性を照合したりすることができる；暴走を止められる〕

Check your composition with someone who speaks English. 英語を話せる人に文章を見てもらいなさい．

He couldn't *check* [=hold] his anger any longer and yelled. 彼は怒りを抑え切れなくなってわめいた．

Urgent measures are needed to *check* [=stop] the spread of a new strain of the flu. 新型インフルエンザのまん延を止めるために早急な対策が必要である．

cheer /tʃíər/

原義は〈元気な表情〉である．**明るい表情・言葉は人を元気づける→声援する；声援，喝采．**
派 cheerful（元気いっぱいの）

Which side do you *cheer* [=root] for?　あなたはどちらの応援をするの．

I had a bad day today and your words really *cheered* me *up*.　今日は散々だったけど，君のことばですっかり元気になったよ．

When you're down, what do you do to *cheer* yourself *up*?　落ち込んだ時，どうやって立ち直るの．

chest /tʃést/

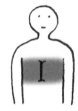

原義は〈箱〉である．**箱→（中が空洞）→胸，肺．**

I keep all my clothes in the *chest* of drawers.　衣類は全部，たんすに入れている．　▶a chest of drawers「たんす」〔← drawer（引き出し）が組み込まれた chest（箱）〕

He is tall and big around the *chest*.　彼は背が高くて胸回りが大きい．

The patient complained of *chest* pain while coughing hard.　患者は激しく咳き込みながら胸の痛みを訴えた．

chicken /tʃíkɪn/

a chicken　　chicken

語源は〈chick（雄鶏）en（小さな）〉である．**ひよこ→鶏**（にわとり）**→鶏肉**．

You should always keep *chicken* in the fridge until you're ready to cook it.　鶏肉は料理する時まで必ず冷蔵庫に保存しておかないとだめですよ．
▶chicken（鶏肉）は不可算名詞．〔←形が不定形〕

My grandma used to keep *chickens* in the yard.　祖母は庭で鶏を飼っていた．　▶chicken（鶏）は可算名詞．〔←形が定形〕

---

chief /tʃiːf/

原義は〈頭（かしら）〉である．**組織のリーダー**．
派 chiefly（主として）
関 chef（コック長，コック）；achieve（成し遂げる）

I am currently the *chief* [＝the head] of the accounting section.　今は会計課の課長をしている．

The police *chief* for London's financial district warned that terrorists will likely strike the capital's biggest business area.　ロンドンの金融街の警察署長は，テロリストが首都の最大のビジネス街を攻撃するだろうと警告を発した．

The *Chief* Justice of Japan is chosen by the cabinet and appointed by the emperor.　最高裁長官は内閣で選ばれ天皇によって任命される．

chill /tʃíl/

原義は〈冷やす〉である. **物を冷やす，大気が冷える；冷気.**
派 chilly (肌寒い)

Beer tastes better when it is *chilled*.　ビールは冷やしたほうがうまい.

The cold, wet wind *chilled* us to the bone.　寒くて湿った風で骨まで冷えた.

The sun has set and the air is beginning to *chill*.　日が落ちて空気が冷たくなってきた.

There was a *chill* in the air [＝It was *chilly*] this morning.　今朝は肌寒かった.

I had a *chill* last night and went to bed early.　昨晩は悪寒がしたので早く寝た.

chip /tʃíp/

原義は〈切れ端〉である. **かけら→小片，欠け跡・欠け傷；欠ける.**

The teacup ⌈is *chipped* [＝has a *chip*]⌋ on the rim.　紅茶のカップの縁が欠けている.

My daughter fell and *chipped* [＝broke off] her front tooth.　娘が転んで前歯を欠いてしまった.

I cannot stop eating potato *chips* once I have a bite.　ポテトチップスは食べ始めたらやめられなくなる.

chirp /tʃə́ːrp/

原義は〈チュチュ, チッチッ, チロチロのような鳴き声（擬音）〉である. **(虫や小鳥などが) 鳴く, さえずる.**

I like hearing birds *chirping* [=singing] in the woods.　小鳥が森で鳴いているのを聞くのが好きだ.

Crickets started *chirping* [=singing] in unison in the backyard.　コオロギが裏庭でいっせいに鳴き始めた.

Sparrows are *chirping* [=twittering] in bushes.　スズメが草むらで鳴いている.

choke /tʃóuk/

原義は〈声を詰まらせる（むせぶ）〉である. **声を詰まらせる→息を詰まらせる→窒息させる.**

His voice *choked* with emotion.　彼は感極まって声を詰まらせた.

"Mochi" is very sticky, so be careful not to *choke* it.　餅は粘り気があるので,（喉に）詰めないように注意しなさい.

choose /tʃúːz/

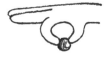

原義は〈気持ち(感覚)で選ぶ〉である. **選択肢の中から好きなものを選ぶ**. 類義語 select は〈考えて慎重に選び取る〉イメージ.
派 choice (選択)

We *chose and bought* a red car.　赤い車を買った.

My dad *chose* his career *over* us.　父さんは私たち家族よりも仕事を優先した.

Which do you *choose*?　どれを選ぶ?

There are many *options to choose* from.　選択肢はいろいろあります.

He *had no choice* but *to* resign.　彼は辞任するほか道はなかった.

You ⌈*have a choice* [=may choose] between Western food and Japanese food for breakfast.　朝食は洋食と和食のどちらかが選べます.

---

clan /klǽn/

原義は〈クルッとまとまる〉である. **まとまった一族・一門**. cl- は〈固まり〉のイメージがある.

The members of his *clan* have a strong spirit of unity.　彼の一族は強い団結心がある.

With the defeat of the Hojo *clan*, Hideyoshi was the virtual ruler of Japan.　北条氏一族の没落に伴って, 秀吉は事実上の日本の支配者となった.

clap /klæp/

原義は〈手をパンと合わせる(擬音)〉である. **賛同を表したり,注目を促したりするために拍手する.**

All those who support the proposal, please *clap* your hands.　提案に賛成の方は拍手願います.

The audience began *clap* along to her song.　聴衆は彼女の歌に合わせて手拍子をし始めた.

The teacher *clapped* her hands, calling for the students' attention.　先生は生徒たちの注意を促すために手をたたいた.

clash /klæʃ/

原義は〈カチャンとぶつかる(擬音)〉である. **人や人の考えが互いに衝突する.** clash によって形状の破壊は起こらない. 類義語 crash は〈砕ける〉, crush は〈つぶれる〉

Hundreds of protesters *clashed* with police.　何百人もの抗議者が警察ともみ合った.

Until a few centuries ago, science and religion were never thought to *clash* with each other.　数世紀前までは,科学と宗教が矛盾するとは少しも考えられなかった.

class /klǽs/

原義は〈同質のものをまとめたもの〉である．**質別にまとめると階級・等級，生徒をまとめて教えると組・クラス・授業**．cl- は〈クルッとまとめる〉のイメージ．
派 classify（分類する）
関 classic（一流の，古典の）〔←最高級としてまとめられる階級〕

You can work through college by taking *classes* at night.　夜間，授業を受けて働きながら大学を卒業できますよ．

There is always some conflict between the ruling and working *classes*.　支配者階級と労働者階級の間にはいつも何らかの衝突があるものだ．

Moby-Dick is a *classic* novel written by American author Herman Melville.　「白鯨」はアメリカのハーマン・メルビルによって書かれた古典的小説だ．

clean /klíːn/

原義は〈きれい〉である．**汚れがなくて清潔である；きれいにする**．
派 cleaner（清掃員，洗剤，掃除機）

You should always keep your teeth *clean*.　歯をいつも清潔に保ちなさい．

Clean [=Brush] your teeth after each meal.　毎食後，歯を磨きなさい．

Will you *clean* the table?　テーブルを拭いてくれますか．　▶clear the table「テーブルの上の物を片付ける」

I'm going to *clean* the windows this morning.　今朝は窓磨きをするつもりだ．

clear /klíər/

原義は〈透き通っている〉である. **透き通っている→はっきりしている→見通しがきく；通りをよくする→不要な物を取り除く→必要な空間をつくる**.
派 clearly（明らかに，はっきりと）
関 declare（宣言する）

Mount Fuji can be seen from here on a *clear* day.　晴れた日にはここから富士山が見える.

It is *clear* [=certain] that he is involved in the incident.　彼がその事件に関与しているのは明らかだ.

Keep the aisle *clear* of all objects.　通路には物を置かないでください.

The settlers *cleared* the forests for agriculture and livestock production.　移植者たちは農業と畜産のために森林を伐採した.

client /kláɪənt/

原義は〈寄りかかる人〉である. **弁護士に頼る人→依頼人，顧客**. cli- は〈傾き→寄りかかる〉イメージ.

The lawyer advised his *client* not to sign the contract.　弁護士は依頼人に契約書に署名しないように忠告した.

Clients of our internet service are supposed to pay fees in advance.　このインターネットサービスの顧客は使用料を前もって支払うことになっている.

cliff /klíf/

原義は〈波に"えグリ"取られた場所〉である．**絶壁**, **崖**.

The leopard went to the edge of a *cliff* and jumped over into the sea.　ヒョウは崖の縁まで来ると海へ飛び込んだ．

The bank is teetering on the *cliff* [=brink] of bankruptcy.　この銀行は破綻の瀬戸際にある．　▶teeter「ぐらつく」

climate /kláɪmət/

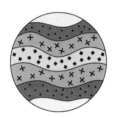

原義は〈傾き〉である．**天気の"傾"向→気候**, **風土**, **雰囲気**．ギリシアの地学者が大地の太陽に対する傾きが各地の気候を生じると考えたことに由来する．cli- は〈傾き〉の意．

What is the *climate* like in the desert?　砂漠はどんな気候ですか．

How is the *climate* going to change in the future?　将来，気候はどのように変わりますか．

Many human industrial activities affect global *climate*.　さまざまな人間の産業活動が地球の気候に影響を与えている．

climax /kláɪmæks/

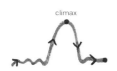

原義は〈傾斜の頂〉である．**昇りきったところ→絶頂，最高潮**．cli- は〈傾き〉の意．
派 anticlimax（あっけない結末）〔←反＋絶頂〕

The *climax* of the film was very touching.　この映画のクライマックス（山場）はとても感動的だった．

When you really look forward to something, it's often an *anticlimax* [＝a disappointment] when it actually happens.　期待していることが，現実になるとがっかりすることがよくあるものだ．

climb /kláɪm/

原義は〈しがみつく〉である．**よじ登る→苦労して登る→（ツタなどが）はい上がる→（太陽などが）昇る→（値段などが）上がる**．cli- は〈くっつく〉のイメージ．

My grandpa *climbed* the stone steps leading up to the shrine without any help.　祖父は神社への石段を何の手助けもなく上った．

She managed to *climb down* the rope-ladder.　彼女はやっとのことで縄ばしごを伝い降りた．

Ivy *climbs over* walls and tree trunks.　ツタは壁や木の幹をはい上がる．

We saw the full moon slowly ⌈*climb up* [＝go up]⌋ into the sky.　満月がゆっくりと空へ昇っていった．

Our costs have *climbed* [＝increased] gradually in the last few years.　ここ数年，生活費が徐々に高騰している．

cliff, climate, climax, climb

close /[動] klóuz, [名形] klóus/

原義は〈閉じる〉である.**(おもむろに) 閉じる→両端を近づける→近接する**. cl- は〈閉じる〉のイメージ.
[派] closed (閉じた, 非公開の); closely (密接に)
[関] conclude (締めくくる)

He *closed* the Bible and began to pray.　彼は聖書を閉じて祈り始めた.

Keep the curtains *closed* to prevent the sunlight from coming in during the day.　日中は日が差し込まないようにカーテンを閉めておきなさい.

They live very *close* to a beautiful beach.　彼らは美しい浜辺の近くに住んでいる.

I'm not as *close* with her as I used to be.　彼女とは昔ほど親しくしていない.　▶close「親しい」〔←近しい〕

---

clot /klá:t/

原義は〈固まる〉である.**血液が凝固する**. cl- は〈グルッと固まる〉の意味合い.
[関] clod (土の固まり)

Thick blood is likely to *clot* and clog blood vessels.　どろどろの血液は固まって血管を詰まらせることが多い.

If a blood *clot* happens in a blood vessel going to the brain, it can cause a stroke.　脳に通じる血管に血栓が起こると, 卒中になる.

cloth /klɔ́ːθ/

原義は〈布〉である．**cloth（布）から clothes（服）を作る**．clothes＋clothes＋clothes＋... → clothing（衣類）

The *cloth* is soft to the touch.　この生地は肌触りが柔らかい．

I like wearing loose-fitting *clothing* [＝clothes]．　ゆったりした服装が好きだ．

Kate is choosy about her *clothes*, taking a long time to decide what to wear each day.　ケイトは着るものにうるさくて，毎日何を着るかに時間をかける．

Like food and shelter, *clothing* is a basic human need.　食料や住居と同じく，衣類は人間の基本的必需品だ．　▶food, clothing, and shelter「衣食住」

---

cloud /kláud/

原義は〈固まり〉である．**(空に固まって浮かぶ) 雲；曇らせる**．cl- は〈クルッとした固まり〉のイメージ．
派 cloudy（曇った，曇りの）

I saw white *clouds* floating high in the sky.　白雲が空高く浮かんでいた．

When Bill heard the results, his face *clouded* [＝turned gloomy] with disappointment.　結果を知らされると，ビルの顔は落胆して曇った．

Your emotions can *cloud* [＝confuse] your decision.　感情の高ぶりが正しい判断を鈍らせることがある．

cloudy /kláudi/

語源は〈cloud(雲)y(がかかった)〉である.**曇っている**.空模様は〈名詞+y〉で表す:rainy(雨模様の),snowy(雪の降る),sunny(日差しのある),thundery(雷が来そうな)
派 cloud(雲)

It was sunny in the morning but *cloudy* right now.　午前中は晴れていたけど,今は曇っています.

Kanto area will be mostly *cloudy* with a chance of showers in the afternoon.　関東地方は概ね曇りで,午後には小雨があるかも知れません.　▶天気予報の言い回し.

clue /klú:/

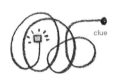

原義は〈(クッと丸まった)糸玉〉である.**グルグル巻きの糸玉をほどいて解決に至る→解決の糸口**.cl- は〈固まり〉のイメージ.

I haven't got a *clue* to what is wrong with my computer.　コンピュータのどこが悪いのか分からなかった.〔←解決方法が得られなかった〕

I have no idea. Give me a *clue* [=a hint]!　全然分かんないよ.ヒント出してよ.　▶なぞなぞ問答の場面.

cold /kóuld/

原義は〈寒い〉である．**温度が低い，身体が冷たい，物が冷たい，人の気持ちが冷たい (冷淡)**．
派 coldly (冷たく，冷淡に)

Drink your coffee before it gets *cold*.　冷めないうちにコーヒーをお飲みなさい．

I decided to stay away from the race because I felt *cold*.　寒気がしていたのでレースを棄権することにした．

My mother-in-law has been *cold* and mean to me in many ways.　義母はいろいろと私に冷たくて意地悪なのよ．

He got very wet in the rain and caught *a cold*.　彼は雨でずぶぬれになり風邪を引いた．

collapse /kəlǽps/

語源は〈col (一緒に) lapse (滑り落ちる)〉である．**持ちこたえられなくなってガクッと崩れる；一気の崩壊，卒倒**．-lapse は〈滑る〉の意味合い．

Thousands of people were trapped under *collapsed* buildings after a powerful earthquake.　強大な地震で何千人も崩壊した建物の下に閉じ込められた．

A tennis player *collapsed* [=fell down] during the match from sunstroke.　テニスの選手が試合中に日射病で倒れた．

colleague /káːliːg/

語源は〈col (一緒に) league (任命された)〉である. **共に仕事する人→職場の同僚**.

I often go out for a drink with my *colleagues* [=coworkers] after work. 仕事が終わってから同僚とよく飲みに出かけます.

Nancy is respected for her significant knowledge by her *colleagues*. ナンシーは博識なので同僚から一目置かれている.

collect /kəlékt/

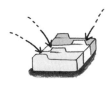

語源は〈col (一緒に) lect (選ぶ)〉である. **選んで集める→収集する**.
派 collection (収集); collector (収集家)
関 elect (選挙する)〔←出す+選ぶ〕

He *collects* rare and old maps for pleasure. 彼は珍しい古地図を趣味で収集している.

Over 50,000 signatures for a referendum have been *collected*. 住民投票を求める5万以上もの署名が集まった. ▶referendum /rèfəréndəm/「住民投票」

collide /kəláɪd/

collide

語源は〈col(一緒に) lide (打ちつける)〉である．**双方がぶつかり合う→衝突する**．一方が静止状態の衝突は crash という．
派 collision (衝突)

A taxi ⌈nearly *collided* [=had a near *collision*]⌉ with an ambulance. タクシーが救急車と衝突しそうになった．

Young people's values may *collide* with those of elderly people. 若者の価値観は年輩者の価値観と衝突することがよくある．

come /kám/

原義は〈来る〉である．**来る→人が姿を現す→物事が現れる，事が存在・発生する**．〈来る→発生・出現〉のように展開するのは，日本語でも「事件」や「事柄」のことを「出"来"事」ということからも連想できる．go は〈姿の出現〉，対照語 go は〈姿の消失〉の意味合い．

"What time shall I *come*?" "Well, *come* around noon. Your friends are welcome too." 「何時に行けばいい？」「えっと，正午ごろ来て．友だちを連れて来てもいいよ」

Our baby *came* [=was born] earlier than we had expected. 赤ちゃんは思っていたより早く生まれた．

"Dinner's ready, Tom." "I'm coming." 「トム，食事できたよ」「すぐ行きます」 ▶come は〈食事の場に現れる〉の意となる．

This dress *comes* [=is available] in different colors. このドレスは色違いもございます．

colleague, collect, collide, come

comfortable /kʌ́mftəbl/

語源は〈com(とても) fort(強い) able(状態である)〉である. **(不快がなくて)心地よい；(自信があって)心地よい**.〈とても強い〉と不安から解放される,〈実力がある〉と試合などが楽しめる.
派 comfort(快適さ)；comfortably(心地よく)

This bed is *comfortable* to sleep on.　このベッドは(クッションがよいので)寝心地がよい.

I don't feel *comfortable* being with someone who is very talkative.　ひどくおしゃべりの人といるとくつろがない.

I am not *comfortable* making a speech in a formal setting.　あらたまった場でスピーチするのが苦手だ.

command /kəmǽnd/

語源は〈com(強く) mand(任す)〉である. **命ずる→責任を負わせる→任せきる→意のままにする**.
派 commander(指揮官)　関 demand(要求する)

The officer *commanded* [=ordered] his men to open fire.　将校は兵士たちに発砲を命じた.

The presenter *commanded* the full attention of all the audience during the lecture.　発表者は講義の間じゅう,聴衆の全注目を引きつけた.

A lookout on the northern slopes of the hill *commands* a good view across the plains.　丘陵の北斜面にある展望台から平野の向こうまですばらしい景色が見晴らせる.

She has an impressive *command* of the English language.　彼女は英語がすばらしく自由に操れる.

comment /ká:ment/

語源は〈com (しっかり) ment (考える)〉である. **ある事柄について (よく考えた) 意見・説明・論評；よく考えて意見を言う**.
派 commentary (評論)；commentator (解説者)
関 mental (知的な)；mention (述べる)

May I have your *comment on* the issue? =How would you *comment* on the issue? この件についての見解をお聞かせください.

He made bitter *comments* [=commented bitterly] on the government's new educational policy. 彼は政府の新しい教育政策について辛らつな批評をした.

I wish to add some *comments* on the proposal. その提案について説明を少し付け加えたいのですが.

commercial /kəmə́:rʃəl/

語源は〈commerce (商業) ial (の)〉である. **商業上の・商売上の；(商品の宣伝をする) コマーシャル**.
派 commerce (商業)

Commercial whaling has been banned since 1986. 商業捕鯨は 1986 年以来禁止されている.

I hate clustering *commercials* [=ads] between programs. 番組が変わる時の連続するコマーシャルが嫌いだ. ▶cluster「群れになる」

commit /kəmít/

語源は〈com(強いて)mit(送る)〉である.**(強いてある場所・状態へ)追い込む・送り込む**.
派 commitment(〔自分を縛りつける〕約束・責任;〔自分を追い込む〕献身)

Don't *commit* [=push] yourself to rash promises.　軽率な約束〔←約束の状態に追い込む〕をしたらだめですよ.　▶rash=hasty「早まった」

The store manager ⌈*committed* suicide [=killed himself] in despair over his failure in business.　店長は商売の失敗をはかなんで自殺した〔←自殺へ追い込んだ〕.

committee /kəmíti/

語源は〈commit(送り込み)ee(された人)〉である.**他を代表して送り込まれた人たちの)委員会,(集合的に)委員**.「委員」とは〈委ねられた+員〔←人〕〉のことで, 日本語も発想が同じ.

He was elected a member of the International Olympic *Committee*.
彼は国際オリンピック委員会の委員に選出された.

When does the next *committee* meet? =When is the next *committee* meeting?　次の委員会はいつですか.

The local government has just set up a *committee* to study recycling.
地元の役所はリサイクルを研究する委員会を立ち上げた.

common /kɑ́:mən/

語源は〈com（共に）mon（行き交う）〉である．**（互いに行き交う）→よく出会う→よく見かける**．

関 communicate（情報を交換し合う）; communication（情報交換）; communism（共産主義）; community（〔同じ地域で暮らす人々の〕地域社会）

Food allergies among children are「increasingly *common*［＝on the rise］in Japan.　日本では子どもの食物アレルギーがだんだん増えている．

Is it *common* to get headaches during pregnancy?　妊娠中に頭痛がするのはよくあることですか．

I don't have much in *common* with my husband in terms of favorite foods.　夫とは食べ物の好みがあまり合わないのよ．　▶have much in common「共通点が多くある」; in terms of 〜「〜の点で」

company /kʌ́mpəni/

語源は〈com（一緒に）pany（パンを食べる人たち）〉である．**（同じ釜の飯を食った）仲間**；**（行動を共にする）付き合い**；**（同士の集まる）会社**．スペイン語では「パン（bread）」を pan という．

My husband works for an advertising *company* that makes these catalogs.　夫はこのようなカタログをつくる広告会社に勤めている．

I really enjoyed「your *company*［＝being with you］today.　今日はご一緒してとても楽しかったわ．

My boy is shy in the *company* of strangers.　息子は初めての人と一緒にいるのが苦手だ．　▶be in the company of 〜「〜と一緒にいる」

compare /kəmpéər/

語源は〈com(一緒に) pare(並べる)〉である. **二つの似たものを並べて相違点を調べる**.
派 comparable(比較可能な); comparative(比較による); comparison(比較)
関 pair(一対)

Retailers should always *compare* their prices *with* those of their competitors. 商人は自分たちの付け値と競争相手の付け値をいつも比較しないといけない. ▶compare A with B「AとBを比較する」

I hate being *compared with* other people. 他人と較べられることが嫌いだ.

compete /kəmpíːt/

語源は〈com(共に) pete(求める)〉である. **あるものを求めて互いに競い合う**.
派 competent(競う能力がある); competition(競争); competitive(競争的な); competitor(競争相手)
関 petition(請願); appetite(欲求)

Six figure skaters are *competing* for two remaining Olympic spots. 6人のフィギュアスケーターがオリンピックの残り二つの出場枠を目指して競っている. ▶compete for ~「~を求めて争う」

No one can *compete with* him in throwing a fast ball. 速球で彼にかなう人はいない. ▶compete with ~「~と競合する」

I think I'm not a very *competitive* man by nature. 僕は性来, 人と競うのがあまり好きじゃないように思う.

complain /kəmpléɪn/

語源は〈com (ひどく) plain (嘆く)〉である. **(苦痛を) 口に出して言う, (不満を) 口に出して訴える.**
派 complaint (不平)

Betty *complained* that she was terribly abused by her husband.
ベティは夫からひどい虐待を受けたと訴えた. ▶complain that ...「…ということを訴える」

My mother *complained* of neck pain after her car was rear-ended.
母は追突されたために, 首の痛みを訴えた. ▶complain of ~「~の症状を訴える」

Complaints arose from the residents that the planned tower would be an eyesore. 建設予定のタワーは景観を害するという不満が住民の間から出た.

complete /kəmplíːt/

語源は〈com (すっかり) plete (満たす)〉である. **すっかり満たす；欠けや不十分がなく完全である.**
派 completely (完全に)

The Tokugawa family had taken *complete* [=total] control over the whole of Japan. 徳川家は日本全土の完全な支配権を握っていた.

My life wouldn't be *complete* without music. 私の生活に音楽は欠かせない〔←音楽を欠いては完全でない〕.

Bob managed to *complete* [=finish] his paper before the deadline.
ボブは締切日までに論文をようやく完成させた.

complex /kɑ̀:mpléks/

語源は〈com（一緒に）plex（織り込む）〉である．**多種多様な部分を重ね合わせる→複雑である；集合体**．
ple- は〈重なり〉の意味合い：simple（簡単な）〔←同じ＋重なり〕
派 complexity（複雑さ）

Global warming is too *complex* an issue to be viewed from just one side. 　地球の温暖化は単に一面的に見ることのできない複雑な問題だ．

We live in a housing *complex* recently developed in the suburbs of Sendai. 　私たちは仙台の郊外に最近できた団地に住んでいます．

We saw many apartment *complexes* along the national highway. 　国道沿いにたくさんのアパート群が見えた．

You shouldn't have an inferiority *complex* about your academic background. 　自分の学歴に劣等感をもつことはないよ．　▶劣等 (inferiority) の感情が意識の深層に織り込まれて (complex) いる．

---

compose /kəmpóuz/

語源は〈com（一緒に）pose（置く）〉である．**バラバラなものを組み合わせて作る→（音符を並べて）作曲する；（ことばを並べて）作文する；（散漫な気分をまとめて）落ち着かせる**．
派 composition（〔組み立てられた〕曲，文，性格）；composer（作曲家）；composure（落ち着き）
関 pose（姿勢をとる）

Water is *composed* [=made up] of hydrogen and oxygen. 　水は水素と酸素から出来ている．

She *composes* [=writes] her own lyrics and music as well. 　彼女は自分で作詞作曲をする．

He breathed deeply, trying to *compose himself*. 　彼は落ち着こうとして深呼吸をした．

compromise /ká:prəmàɪz/

語源は〈com(共に) pro(前に) mise(送る)〉である. **双方が共に調停者を送り出す→歩み寄る,折れ合う→(折れ合うと 100%ではなくなるので) 完全を損なう**.
関 promise (約束する)〔←前に+ことばを送る〕

You should learn how to *compromise*; it is always better to bend a little than break a good relationship. 相手と折れ合う術(すべ)を覚えなさい, よい関係を壊すより, 少しだけ折れるほうがいつもいいに決まっているのだから.

Smoking impacts every cell in the body and over time will *compromise* your health. 喫煙は体の全細胞に影響を及ぼし, やがては健康を損ねることになる.

compulsory /kəmpʌ́lsəri/

語源は〈com(強く) pulsory(押しつけるような)〉である. **権威や法律が人に行動を押しつけるような**.
関 compel (強要する)〔←強く+押す〕

Doing military service is *compulsory* [=obligatory] for all men in South Korea. 兵役に服するのは韓国のすべての男性にとって義務である.

Wearing your seatbelt is *compulsory* [=mandatory] in Japan. 日本ではシートベルトの着用が義務付けられている.

concede /kənsíːd/

語源は〈con（一緒に）cede（行く）〉である．**自己の主張を抑えて相手に合わせて行く→譲歩する→負けを認める**．
派 concession（譲歩，容認）

The manager *conceded* [=admitted] that he had been wrong about his selling strategy. 支配人は自分の販売戦略が間違っていたことを認めた．

The candidate finally *conceded* [=accepted] defeat after a recount of the ballots. 数え直しで票数が決定すると，その候補者はようやく敗北を認めた．

concept /kάːnsept/

語源は〈con（しっかり）cept（つかみ取ること）〉である．**ある事柄のさまざまの現象・諸相から中心となる考えをつかみ出したもの→概念・コンセプト**．
派 conception（考え方）; conceptual（概念の）
関 conceive（思いつく）

"What is the *concept* [=the idea] of democracy?" "Well, there is little agreement on the details of the *concept*." 「民主主義の理念とは何ですか」「そうですね，この理念の細かな点についてはさまざまな意見があります」

The Copernican theory completely changed our *concept* [=view] of the universe. コペルニクスの地動説は我々の宇宙観を完全に覆した．
▶ Copernican /koupə́ːrnɪkən/

concern /kənsə́ːrn/

語源は〈con(しっかり)cern(分ける)〉である.**(しっかり見分ける)→強く関わる(関心・関係)→心配させる(心配・不安)**.
派 concerned(心配して)
関 discern(見分ける)〔←離す+分ける〕

There is growing *concern* about the safety of Chinese food products.
中国産の食品の安全性に関して懸念が高まっている.

Many people are *concerned* [=It *concerns* many people] that the pension system is not sustainable in the future. 現在の年金制度は将来破綻するのではないかと多くの人が不安を持っている.

I am now *less concerned* about my looks than when I was young.
若いころに比べると自分の容貌が気にならなくなった.

---

concise /kənsáıs/

$E=mc^2$

語源は〈con(ちゃんと)cise(切った)〉である.**(無駄・余分を切り捨てて)すっきりしている**.
派 concisely(簡潔に)
関 precise(きっかりの);decide(決める)

You have to make your reports and other documents more *concise* and consistent. 報告書やその他の文書を書くときは,もう少し簡潔に筋の通ったものにしなさい.

Her presentation was *concise* [=to the point] and easy to follow.
彼女の発表は簡潔で理解しやすかった.

conclude /kənklúːd/

語源は〈con (しっかり) clude (くくる)〉である. **あれこれの考え・意見をまとめて締めくくる**. cl- は〈閉じる〉のイメージ.
派 conclusion (結論)
関 include (含む)〔←中に+くくる〕; close (閉じる)

The President *concluded* [=ended] his speech by saying: "we have the power to make the world we seek."　大統領は演説を「我々は我々の求める世界をつくる力をもっているのです」と言って締めくくった.

The philosopher came to the *conclusion* that life is meaningless.
その哲学者は結局, 人生に意味は無いと悟った.〔←という結論に達した〕

condition /kəndíʃən/

語源は〈con (一緒に) dition (話すこと)〉である. **(話題となる) 条件・状態・体調・病状**.
関 diction (言い回し)

Would you check the *condition* [=the operating state] of my computer?　僕のパソコンの調子を診てもらえますか.

Hundreds of thousands of quake victims are living in terrible *conditions*.　何十万もの地震の被災者は悲惨な状態で生活している.

The patient has been in stable *condition* without any signs of disorder after the surgery.　患者は手術後, 不調の症状がまったくなく安定した状態にある.

confess /kənfés/

語源は〈con（強いて）fess（しゃべる）〉である．**秘めていることをあえてしゃべる→白状する**．fess- は〈息の破裂〉をなぞっている．
派 confession（告白）　関 profess（公言する）〔←前で＋話す〕；professor（教授）〔←人前で＋話をする人〕

He *confessed* [＝admitted] that he had made a false document.　彼は偽りの文書をつくったと告白した．

"Would you send me an email?" "I *confess* [＝I have to say] I don't know how to use a computer."　「e メールくれますか」「実はパソコンの使い方を知らないのです」

---

confidence /kάːnfədəns/

語源は〈confide（強く信じる）ence（こと）〉である．**(他者への信頼) 信用．(自己への信頼) 自信**．
派 confident（〔自己の考え・能力に〕自信がある）

Our captain seems to have lost *confidence* in his ability to lead the team.　主将はチームを率いていく自信をなくしているようだ．

He was honest and worked hard to gain the *confidence* of his coworkers.　彼はまじめに働いたので同僚から信頼された．

I am *confident* [＝sure] that things will come out right in time.　状況はやがてよくなると確信している．

confirm /kənfə́:rm/

語源は〈con(しっかり)firm(固める)〉である. **不明瞭なことをはっきりさせる→確かめる**.
派 confirmation(確認)
関 affirm(断言する); firm(固める)

Although my uncle didn't smoke, a biopsy *confirmed* that he had lung cancer. 叔父はたばこを吸わないが, 生体組織検査で肺がんであることがはっきりした.

I called to *confirm* my appointment with the attorney before I left. 出かける前に弁護士との約束を電話で確認した.

conflict /ká:nflıkt/

語源は〈con(互いに)flict(打ちつける)〉である. **互いに打ち合う→衝突する・争う; 衝突**. -flict は〈(刀で)振り(フリ)かかる〉イメージ.
関 inflict(打撲を負わせる); afflict(苦しめる)

Darwin's theory of evolution *conflicted* [=clashed] *with* the religious views of his time. ダーウィンの進化論は当時の宗教観と衝突した.

James is so rude and reckless that he is *in* constant *conflict with* his colleagues. ジェームズは無作法で奔放なので同僚といつも衝突している. ▶in conflict with+人「(人)と対立して」

confront /kənfrʌ́nt/

語源は〈con(〜に)front(向き合う)〉である. **苦境・難事に向き合う→対処すべく直面する・立ち向かう**. 元来, front には「額(ひたい)」の意があった.
派 confrontation(衝突)

We have to *confront* the global climate change squarely. 世界的な気候変化にしっかりと向き合わないといけない.

This issue could lead to a military *confrontation between* the superpowers. この問題は列強間の軍事的衝突を引き起こすことになりかねない.

confuse /kənfjúːz/

語源は〈con(一緒に)fuse(混ぜる)〉である. **さまざまの情報を頭に混ぜ込む→混乱させる**. con- は〈混〉と語呂合わせできる.
派 confusing(紛らわしい);confusion(混乱)
関 refuse(拒む)〔←反+混ざる〕

There are many who ⌈*confuse* themselves [=are *confused*] *with* too much information from very many sources. 多くの情報源から得られる情報過多で混乱している人が多い.

Some traffic signs are very *confusing* [=misleading]. 交通標識の中にはとても紛らわしいものがある.

The airport has been thrown into *confusion* after the explosion of a time bomb. 時限爆弾の爆発によって空港は混乱に陥った.

congratulation /kəngrædʒəléɪʃən/

語源は〈con (一緒に) gratulation (喜び)〉である. **喜び合うこと，祝うこと**.
派 congratulate (祝う)　関 gratitude (感謝)

Congratulations on your new house! ＝I *congratulate* you *on* your new house!　新築，おめでとう.　▶Congratulations!「おめでとう！」と呼びかける時は，祝福の気持ちを幾重にも込めて，常に複数形でいう．簡単に Congrats! ともいう．

We chatted about how difficult the project had been, and *congratulated* each other *on* our successful completion.　私たちはこのプロジェクトがどんなに難しかったかを語り，うまく完成したことを互いに喜び合った．

connect /kənékt/

語源は〈con (一緒に) nect (つなぐ)〉である. **二つのものをつなぎ合わせる**.
派 connection (関係)；disconnect (つながりを切る)

The ferry *connects* [＝links] the mainland *to* Itsukushima island in about 10 minutes.　このフェリーは本土と厳島を10分ほどで結んでいる．

There was no physical evidence to *connect* [＝link] the suspect *with* the crime.　容疑者と犯罪を結び付ける物的証拠はなかった．

My computer didn't boot up, because the plug was somehow *disconnected*.　どういうわけかプラグがはずれていたので，パソコンが立ち上がらなかった．

conscious /kάːnʃəs/

語源は〈con (強く) sci (知って) ous (いる)〉である. **よく認識している→気にかかる**.
派 consciousness (意識); self-conscious (自意識過剰な)
関 conscience (〔善悪の区別がつく〕良心)

Kate is overly *conscious* [=*self-conscious*] about her appearance.
ケイトは外見を気にしすぎる.

Most people feel 「a guilty *conscience* [=guilty] about the harm they have done to others. たいていの人は他人に被害を与えると悪いことをした〔←良心のとがめを感じる〕と思うものだ.

The patient began to regain *consciousness* as the anesthetic wore off.
麻酔が切れてくると患者は意識が戻り始めた. ▶wear off「(薬などの) 効き目がなくなる」

---

consequence /kάːnsəkwèns/

語源は〈con (一緒に) sequence (追うようにやって来るもの)〉である. **(行動に続いて起こる) 結果→ (結果は) 重要**.
派 consequently (その結果) 関 sequence (連続)

If you do not follow the advice, you must be prepared to accept the *consequences* [=the outcome] of your decision. もし忠告に従わないのであれば, (どうなろうとも) 判断の結果を受け入れる覚悟が必要ですよ.

One's academic background is of no *consequence* [=importance] as long as one is enthusiastic and has a sense of purpose. 情熱と目的意識があれば, 学歴は問題ではない.

conservative /kənsə́ːrvətɪv/

語源は〈con(しっかり)serve(保つ)tive(ような)〉である。**変化を嫌って現状を保つような→変化を避けて控えめである**。
派 conservation(保存,保護);conserve(保存する)

He is decidedly *conservative* [=traditional] in his views on social issues.　彼は社会的問題に対する見方が非常に保守的だ。

You should wear a *conservative* [=conventional] suit to a job interview.　就職の面接には地味なスーツのほうがいいですよ。

consider /kənsídər/

語源は〈con(しっかり)sider(星を見る)〉である。**(じっくり見て)あれこれ考慮する→(じっくり考慮して)〜だと考える**。昔,人は星を観察して吉凶を占った。
派 consideration(考慮);considerable(かなりの);considerate(思いやりのある)　関 desire(強く望む)

Have you *considered* the possibility that maintenance costs can be very high.　維持費が高額になる可能性があることを考慮しましたか。

The planning desk hesitated, *considering* the soaring cost of production.　企画課は制作費の高騰を考えてゴーサインをためらった。

You're old enough to *consider* leaving home.　あなたはもう自活する(実家を出る)ことを考えてもいい年ごろだよ。

Do you *consider* yourself a happy person?　自分を幸せだと思いますか。

consist /kənsíst/

語源は〈con (一緒に) sist (立つ)〉である．**〜で成り立つ．**

派 consistency (一貫性); consistent (首尾一貫している)〔←しっかり＋立っている〕; consistently (一貫して)

The Japanese archipelago *consists* [＝is made up] *of* four main islands and thousands of smaller ones.　日本列島は4つの主要な島と何千もの小さな島でできている．

His argument is *consistent* [＝coherent and logical] throughout.　彼の主張は始めから終わりまで首尾一貫している．

constant /ká:nstənt/

語源は〈con (しっかり) stant (立ち続ける)〉である．**しっかり立って倒れない→そのままの状態であり続ける．**

派 constantly (絶えず); stand (じっと立つ)

A cruising aircraft flies at a *constant* [＝steady] speed and altitude.　巡航中の飛行機は一定の速度と高度で飛ぶ．

You should make *constant* [＝continuous] efforts to achieve this objective.　この目的を達成するには絶えまない努力をしないといけないよ．

consult /kənsʌ́lt/

語源は〈con (〜に) sult (相談に行く)〉である. **人と相談する, 辞書・辞典を参照する**.
派 consultant (顧問); consultation (協議)

When making a big decision I usually *consult* [=seek advice from] my parents.　大きな決断をする時は, たいてい親と相談する.

Every time I come across a new word, I try to guess what it means before *consulting* [=looking it up in] a dictionary.　未知の語に出会った時はいつも, 辞書を参照する前に意味を推測するようにしている.

consume /kəns(j)úːm/

語源は〈con (すっかり) sume (取る)〉である. **取り尽くす→使い果たす→消耗する**.
派 consumer (消費者); consumption (消費)

How many calories does an average marathon runner *consume* [=burn] in a race?　平均的なマラソンランナーは1レースで何カロリー消費しますか.

If you *consume* [=take] too much salt, you are likely to suffer from high blood pressure.　塩分を取りすぎると高血圧になりやすい.

contact /kɑ́ːntækt/

語源は〈con(一緒に)tact(触れる)〉である. **人が他者と接触する；付き合い**.
関 tact(如才なさ)〔←接触の要領〕

We will *contact* [=notify] you as soon as we are ready to place our order.　注文の用意ができしだい連絡します.

Who should we *contact* [=get in touch with] in case of emergency?
非常の時は誰に連絡すればいいのですか.

The boy ran away from home and has not been in *contact with* his family for many days.　少年は家出して何日も家族との連絡を取っていない.

Modern children should ⌈be more in *contact with* [=get closer to] nature.　現代っ子はもっと自然に親しむべきだ.

---

contain /kəntéin/

語源は〈con(しっかり)tain(つかむ)〉である. 包むように中に封じ込める.
派 container(容器)

The head is the part of the body that *contains* [=holds] the brain.
頭は脳を内蔵している部位である.

Our products do not *contain* any preservatives or additives.　私どもの食品は防腐剤や添加物を少しも含んでいません.

Schools have taken measures to *contain* [=control] the spread of flu.
学校はインフルエンザのまん延を封じ込める対策を講じた.

Our kids couldn't ⌈*contain* their excitement [=help but show their excitement] at seeing the Eiffel Tower.　エッフェル塔を見て子どもたちは思わず歓声を上げた〔←興奮を抑え込むことができなかった〕.

context /káːntekst/

語源は〈con(一緒に) text(織り込む)〉である. **ことばの織り込み《文脈・前後関係》；状況の織り込み《背景, 付帯状況》.**
関 text(原文)〔←織り込んだことば〕；textile(布地)

It is important to look at things in their *context*; for example, your advice for a child should be different with a single parent from one for a child with both parents.　物事はその背景を考えに入れて見ることが大切だ. 例えば, 片親の生徒へのアドバイスは両親のいる生徒へのアドバイスとは違ってくるはずだ.

You can guess, in most cases, the meaning of a new word from the *context*.　たいていの場合, 前後関係から知らない単語の意味を推測できるものだよ.

continue /kəntínjuː/

語源は〈con(一緒に) tinue(保つ) **(前後をつなぐ)**→ **切らずに続ける, わずかな間を置いて同じことを続ける.**
派 continual(断続的な)；continuous(連続的な)；continuity(連続性)
関 continent(大陸)〔←陸がうねるように続く〕

She *continued* to work, even as her health weakened.　彼女は体調が悪い時でも仕事を続けた.

The search for the victims will be *continued* as soon as the weather improves.　遭難者の捜索は, 天候が回復しだい再開される.

Due to *continued* low temperatures, all the crops failed.　低温続きのために, 作物が軒並み不作だった.

contract /kɑ́:ntrækt/

語源は〈con(一緒に)tract(引く)〉である. **(双方を引き寄せて)契約する, (両側が引き合って)収縮する, (引き合って)接触感染する.**
派 contractor(請負人)

He is *contracted* to work 40 hours a week.　彼は週40時間働く契約をしている.

Most substances *contract* [=shrink] as they cool.　ほとんどの物質は冷えると縮む.

There are many patients who *contracted* hepatitis through blood transfusions from those already infected.　保菌者からの輸血によって肝炎に感染した患者が多くいる.

contrary /kɑ́:ntrèri/

語源は〈contra(反対)ry(の)〉である. **(性質・方向・意味が)それとは反対の.**
関 contradict(矛盾することを言う)〔←反対+言う〕; counter(反論する)

It is difficult to imagine a *contrary* [=an opposite] case.　逆の事例は想像しがたい.

Contrary to what is commonly thought, slightly overweight people live longer than normal weight people.　一般に考えられていることとは違って, 少し肥満気味の人のほうが正常の体重の人よりも長生きする.

We need to accept his testimony, unless there is evidence ⌈*to the contrary* [=that contradicts his explanation].　それとは反対の証拠がない限り, 彼の証言を受け入れなければならない.

contrast /kάːntræst/

語源は〈contra（反対に）st（立つ）〉である. **対比・対照をなす；対比・対照**.
関 stand（立つ）

The new manager's leadership ⌈sharply *contrasts* him from [=forms a sharp contrast with] his predecessor who was too soft on his staff. 新部長の統率力は，部下に甘かった前任者とは非常に対照的だ.

The snowy peaks of the Tateyama mountain range make a stunning *contrast* against the clear blue skies. 立山連峰の雪の峰々が真っ青な空を背景に見事な対照を成している.

How do you adjust the tint *contrast* [=brightness] of the computer screen? パソコンの画面の輝度はどう調節したらいいの？

contribute /kəntríbjuːt/

語源は〈con（一緒に）tribute（捧げる）〉である. **（努力・金を）与える；（要因を）与える**.
派 contribution（貢献，寄付）　関 tribute（貢ぎ物）；distribute（分配する）〔←分けて＋与える〕

The mayor has ⌈*contributed* greatly [=made a great *contribution*] to the improvement of public health and sanitation of the city. 市長は市の公衆衛生の改善に大いに貢献した.

He didn't really *contribute* much to the game. 彼はその試合ではほとんどチームに貢献できなかった.

Dental cavities may ⌈*contribute to* [=lead to] bad breath. 虫歯は口臭の原因になることがよくある.

control /kəntróul/

語源は〈cont=contra(対照して)rol=roll(帳簿)〉である．**帳簿と照らし合わせて管理する→支配する→抑える；管理，支配，制御**．
派 controller(管理者)

The driver lost *control* of his car on a bend and crashed into a utility pole.　運転手は，カーブで車の制御ができなくなって電柱に突っ込んだ．

The new teacher has no *control* over her class.　今度の先生はクラスの統制ができていない〔←生徒へのにらみが効かない〕．

Don't worry about things that ⌈you can't *control* [=are beyond your *control*].　自分ではどうしようもないことを思い煩わないようにしなさい．

You must practice birth *control* during treatment.　治療中は避妊をしないといけませんよ．

controversy /ká:ntrəvə̀:rsi/

語源は〈contro(反対へ)vercy(向かうこと)〉である．**反目する意見→意見が対立する論争**．
派 controversial(論争を引き起こす)

There is a lot of *controversy* over cell phone use in school.　学校でのスマートフォンの使用に関して多くの議論がある．

The relocation of an American air base on Okinawa ⌈caused much *controversy* [=became highly *controversial*] among local people.　沖縄のアメリカ空軍基地の移設は地元民の間で大きな論争を引き起こした．

convenient /kənvíːnjənt/

語源は〈con (一緒に) venient (来るような)〉である. **双方が一緒に来る→条件がぴったり合って好都合である**.
派 convenience (好都合)
関 convention (大会・会議)〔←一緒に＋来る・集まる〕

You can come and see us when it ⌈is *convenient* for you [＝suits you]. いつでもいいから〔←あなたの都合がいい時に〕遊びに来ていいよ.

Please stop by my office ⌈at your earliest *convenience* [＝as soon as possible]. ご都合がつきしだい, 事務所にお立ち寄りください.

conversation /kàːnvərséɪʃən/

語源は〈con (互いに) versation (ことばを向け合うこと)〉である. **声を互いに交わす→会話**.
派 converse (会話する)

We cycled side by side to *converse*. 僕たちは並んで自転車に乗って会話をした.

I don't know how to start a *conversation* with a stranger. 初めての人とは会話の糸口がつかめないわ.

convince /kənvíns/

語源は〈con(強く)vince(言い負かす)〉である．**相手を説き伏せる，事のありようを納得させる**．西洋文化は言論に勝ち負けの評価を付与する：win over(説得する)，win the case(勝訴する)，lose an argument(論争に負ける)，debate(討論する)〔←強く＋打つ〕，convict(有罪とする)〔←強く＋有罪を説き伏せる〕

You need to *convince* the interviewer of your ability and passion. 面接官に君の能力と情熱をちゃんと分からせないとだめだよ．

She was still half *convinced* by her husband's argument. 彼女は夫の言い分にまだ納得しかねていた．

Some people are so *convinced* they're always right that they don't bother to listen to others. 自分がいつも正しいと思い込んで，他人の意見に耳を貸そうとしない人がいるものだ．

OK, I'll give it a try. You've *convinced* me. 分かった，やってみるわ．あなたには負けたわ〔←あなたは私を説き伏せた〕．

cook /kúk/

原義は〈熱を加えて食材を料理する〉である．**食材を焼く，煮る，茹でる；料理人**．cook の方法は，① hot liquids(湯・汁)によるもの，例えば boil(煮る)と② dry heat(直火)によるもの，例えば bake(焼く)に大別される．
派 cooker(調理器具)
関 cookie(クッキー)〔←焼き上げた菓子〕

My mother is a good *cook*. ＝My mother *cooks* well. 母は料理が上手です．

Cooking may cause the loss of some valuable nutrients, like vitamin C. 加熱するとビタミンCのような大切な栄養素を失う場合がある．

I live alone in an apartment and *cook* for myself all the time. 私はアパートに一人で住んでおり，いつも自炊している．

How long and at what temperature should I *cook* chicken in the oven? 鶏肉はオーブンでどのくらい何度で焼いたらいいの．

Eggs can be eaten raw or *cooked*. 卵は生でもゆでても食べられる．

cool /kúːl/

原義は〈冷たい〉である．**冷たい→涼しい，冷静な→かっこいい**．
派 cooler（保冷容器，クーラー）; coolly（冷静に）

Keep medicines in a *cool* and dark place.　薬は冷暗所に保管しなさい．

Try to 「keep your *cool* [=stay calm] during an argument.　議論の時は冷静を保つようになさい．

Lots of teenagers start smoking just to be *cool*.　気取って〔←かっこよさを求めて〕タバコを吸い始める若者が多い．

Driving a sports car makes you look *cool*.　スポーツカーの運転はかっこよく見える．

---

cope /kóup/

原義は〈打ち砕く〉である．**難事をこなす**．日本語の「こなす」も〈砕いて粉にする→処理する〉と展開している．
関 coup（政変）〔←政府を砕く〕

Coping [=Dealing] *with* ever-increasing medical bills is frustrating.
高騰する医療費をやり繰りするのは気をいらいらさせる．

I wonder if my son can *cope* [=deal] *with* living in Tokyo on such a low salary.　息子はあんな安月給で東京で暮らして行けるのだろうか．

copy /kɑ́:pi/

語源は〈co（強く）opy（豊富にする）〉である．**原典を増やす→複写する；(複写印刷された) 書籍などの冊, 部**．

関 copious（たくさんの，豊富な）；copyright（版権）〔←原典を複写する権利〕

Before the invention of printing, books had to be *copied* by hand.　印刷術の発明以前は，本は手で書き写さないといけなかった．

All words and photos are protected by *copyright*; please do not use or *copy* them without permission.　文章も写真もすべて版権により保護されています：無許可の使用を禁じます．

I found the book very interesting and bought three *copies* for my friends.　その本はとてもおもしろかったので，友達のために3冊買った．

corner /kɔ́:rnər/

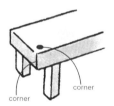

原義は〈角（つの）〉である．**角（かど）→角（すみ）；角（すみ）に追いやる→窮地に追い込む**．漢字「角」は「つの」「かど」「すみ」と読める．英語では角（つの）は horn という．

My son fell and hit his head on the *corner* of the bed.　息子が転んでベッドの角で頭を打った．

The police officer lost sight of the man after he turned the *corner*.　警官は男が角を曲がるとその姿を見失った．

The painter put his signature in the bottom right-hand *corner* of the picture.　画家は絵の右下隅に自分のサインをした．

The man was eventually *cornered* by police and fatally shot himself.　男は警察に追いつめられると，自分に発砲して自殺した．

correct /kərékt/

語源は〈cor（一緒に）rect（直す）〉である。**正しいものとつき合わせて直す**。rect-は〈直〉のイメージ：rectangle（長方形）〔←直角〕，rectum（直腸）
派 correction（訂正）；correctly（正確に）
関 direct（指導する）

Please *correct* my understanding if it's wrong.　私の解釈が間違っていたら訂正してください．

Your answers are all *correct*!　君の答えは全部正解だよ！

If the theory of global warming is *correct*, we need to use less fossil fuels.　もし地球温暖化の説が正しいなら，我々は化石燃料の使用を減らす必要がある．

Mark your *corrections* using a red pen so they will stand out.　訂正個所は目立つように赤ペンで記しなさい．

---

corrupt /kərʌ́pt/

語源は〈cor=com（強く）rupt（壊す）〉である．**人を道徳的，倫理的に堕落させる**．汚職・賄賂の匂いがする語．
派 corruption（汚職）　関 rupture（破壊）

The former mayor was *corrupted* by the desire for money and power.　前市長は金と権力への欲望で身を持ち崩した．

He was arrested on charges of perjury and *corruption*.　彼は偽証と汚職の廉（かど）で逮捕された．

cost /kɔ́:st/

語源は〈co（共に）st＝stand（起こる）〉である．**物の購入・サービスの受益には支払いが伴う；災難・被害には犠牲・損害が伴う．**
派 costly（膨大な金のかかる）

My dad had to have an emergency operation that *cost* him about 100,000 yen.　父は緊急手術が必要になって，費用が約 10 万円かかった．

Driving at more than double the speed limit *cost* the woman her driving license.　速度制限を 2 倍も超えていたので，その女性は免停を食らった．

Rafael Nadal underwent an operation on his elbow that will *cost* him the rest of the season.　ラファエル・ナダル選手は肘の手術をしたが，今シーズンの残り試合を全部棒に振ることになるだろう．

---

cough /kɔ́:f/

原義は〈せき込む（擬音）〉である．**せきをする，せき払いをする；せき．** 日本語でも，せきをなぞって「コンコン」と似た擬音を使う．

Cover your mouth when you ⌈*cough* or sneeze [＝have a *cough* or sneeze]．　せきやくしゃみをする時は口を覆いなさい．

He stood up, *coughed* and started his speech.　彼は起立し，せき払いをしてスピーチを始めた．

count /káunt/

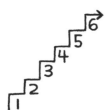

原義は〈数える〉である．**勘定する→勘定に入れる，考慮する→重要である**．
派 countable（数えられる）　関 account（説明する）

Can you *count* from 1 to 10 in French?　フランス語で 1 から 10 まで数えられますか．

I *count* my calories so that I will maintain a healthy weight.　健康的な体重を維持するためにカロリーを計算している．

If you can't finish the test within the allotted time, questions that are not answered will be *counted* as wrong answers.　制限時間内でやり残した問題は不正解とみなされる．

It's not quantity but quality that *counts* [＝matters]．　大切なのは量より質だ．

---

counter /káuntər/

原義は〈反対の〉である．**〜とは逆の；反論・反撃する**．
関 contrary（逆の）; country（国，田舎）; encounter（出くわす）

What he argues runs *counter* [＝contrary] to common sense.　彼の主張は常識に反している．

"I could say the same thing about you," she *countered*.　「あなたについても同じことが言えますよ」と彼女は言い返した．

counterpart /káʊntərpɑ̀ːrt/

語源は〈counter（相対する）part（役割）〉である．**他の場で同じ役割をする人，他のやり方で同じ役割をする物や事柄**．

Japanese Foreign Minister held talks respectively with his *counterparts* of France, China and India.　日本の外相は個別に，フランス，中国，インドの各外相と会談をもった．

Is an electric signature as valid as its handwritten *counterpart*?　電子署名は手書きの署名と同じ効力がありますか．

country /kʌ́ntri/

原義は〈向こうに（counter）広がる土地〉である．**広々とした土地→田舎，田園地帯→国土→国**．
関 counter（反対の）

Japan is considered as one of the safest *countries* in the world.　日本は世界で最も安全な国の一つと考えられている．

He owns a farm of sixty acres in the *country* [=countryside].　彼は田舎に60エーカーの農場を持っている．

The Olympic champion returned to his home *country* as a national hero.　オリンピックのゴールドメダリストは国のヒーローとして凱旋帰国した．

couple /kʌ́pl/

語源は〈cou(一緒に)ple(重ねる・つなぐ)〉である. **一対, 一組；夫婦, カップル**.
関 copulate(交尾する)

A young *couple* with a child moved in next door.　子どもが一人いる若夫婦が隣に越してきた.

I enjoy watching TV for a *couple* of hours in the evening.　夜, テレビを2, 3時間見ます.　▶a couple of 〜は, 厳密には「二つの〜」であるが,「2, 3の〜」の意味合いになる.

courage /kə́ːridʒ/

語源は〈cour(心)age(〜の状態)〉である. **困難・危険に心を決めて向かう状態→勇気**.
派 courageous(勇気ある)　関 cordial(心を込めた)

He has always faced challenges with *courage* and determination.　彼はいつも困難事に敢然〔←勇気と根性で〕と立ち向かった.　▶challenges=difficulties

Robert *plucked up the courage* to ask a woman out he had been attracted to for a long time.　ロバートは, 長い間憧れていた女性に勇気を出してデートを申し込んだ.

course /kɔ́ːrs/

語源は〈走ること〉である.**(移動・進行しながらたどる道筋)→物事が進行する筋道, 過程, (学びの) 課程.**

What and how many *courses* do you need to take to become a pharmacist?　薬剤師になるにはどういう課程をいくつ取る必要がありますか.

The grief for the loss of your dog will lessen in the *course* of time [=lessen as time goes by].　愛犬を失った悲しみは, 時が経てば〔←時の流れの中で〕薄くなるものだ.

You just have to *let it run its course* as there's no way to stop aging.　老化は避けられないので自然の成り行きに任せるほかないよ.

---

court /kɔ́ːrt/

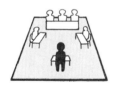

原義は〈中庭〉である.**(囲まれた) 庭→(囲まれた) 法廷・裁判所→(テニスなどの) コート.**

There are always events going on in the center *court* of the shopping mall.　ショッピングモールの中央広場ではいつもイベントをやっている.

She is an emotional player and often shows her frustrations with the referee's calls on the *court*.　彼女は感情が表に出る選手なので, 審判の判定に対していらいらする気持ちをコート上で見せることがよくある.

The city decided to take the case to a district *court*.　市はその問題を地方裁判所へ持ち込むことにした.

cover /kÁvər/

語源は〈c (クルッと) over (覆う)〉である. **覆う→かばう, 守る, (対象の範囲として) 扱う, 補う**.
関 discover (発見する)

What proportion of the Earth's surface is *covered* by water?　地球の表面の何割が海に覆われていますか.

The insurance policy does not *cover* damage caused by normal wear and tear.　この保険では，通常の使用による劣化は補償の限りではありません〔←補償の対象としません〕.

This article *covers* what you should know about cancer and its treatment.　この論文は，がんとその治療に関して知っておくべきことを扱っている.

---

crack /krǽk/

原義は〈ひび割れる音 (擬音)〉である. **(ガチャン，バリバリッと) 割れる；ひび割れ**.
派 cracker (クラッカー，爆竹)

Walnut shells are hard to *crack*.　クルミの殻は割れにくい.

Your password is kind of easy to *crack* [=be *cracked*]; you'd better change it to a more complicated one.　君のパスワードはどうも簡単に分かってしまう．もっと複雑にしたほうがいいよ.

We have to repair the *cracks* in the wall.　壁のひび割れを修繕する必要がある.

crash /kræʃ/

原義は〈ガチャンという衝突音（擬音）〉である．**動いている物体が静止している物体に衝突してガチャンと砕ける**．
関 crush（押しつぶす）

The train *crashed* into a truck that was stuck at a railroad crossing. 列車が踏切で立ち往生しているトラックに激突した．

A pile of books on the desk ⌈*crashed* to the floor [＝fell to the floor with a crash]． 机に積んだ本の山がドサッと床に崩れ落ちた．

create /kriéɪt/

原義は〈生み出す〉である．**無から有を生み出す・つくり出す**．cr- は〈増加・盛り上がり〉のイメージ：increase（増す）〔←中に＋増える〕，crest（頂上）〔←上りつめた位置〕，crescent（上限の月，三日月）〔←徐々に大きくなる〕，crescendo（(音楽)クレッシェンド）〔←だんだん強く〕 派 creation（創造）；creative（創造的な）；creature（生物）〔←神の創造物〕

The universe was *created* with the Big Bang about 15 billion years ago. 宇宙は約150億年前にビッグバンとともに誕生した．

We need to *create* more job opportunities, particularly for young people. とくに若者が仕事に就ける機会をもっとつくらないといけない．

crime /kráɪm/

原義は〈判決する〉である. **(法律上の) 犯罪行為**, **悪事**.
派 criminal (犯罪の)

It is a *crime* to neglect or abuse your children.　自分の子どもの世話の放棄や虐待は犯罪になる.

Any *crime* should be punished by the law.　どんな犯罪も法律の裁きを受けなければならない.

There is no proof that the defendant committed the *crime* for which he is being tried.　被告が訴えられている罪を犯した証拠はない.

crisis /kráɪsɪs/

原義は〈分かれ目〉である. **(どちらに転ぶかの) 分かれ目**, **分岐点**, **重大局面**→**危機**. cr- は〈曲がり・分岐〉のイメージ.
派 critical (重大な)

The company managed to survive the global financial *crisis* with minimal losses.　この会社は最低限の損失で世界的金融危機を乗り切った.

Do you have any friends you can turn to in times of *crisis* [= trouble]?　困ったときに頼れる友人がいますか.

critical /krítɪkl/

語源は〈critic(分かれ目)al(となる)〉である. **(局面を左右する)重大な, (分析する)批評の, (悪いと分析する)批判的な.** cr- は〈曲がり・分け目〉のイメージ.
派 crisis(危機);critic(評論家)

It is *critical* [=very important] to gain a good reputation among the customers for the success of this business. この商売がうまくいくには顧客の評判を得ることがとても大切だ.

He has been in a *critical* [=grave] condition for the past few days. 彼はここ数日,危篤状態にある.

There are many people who are *critical* of [=disapprove] a five-day school week. 学校5日制に批判的な人が多くいる.

---

criticize /krítəsàɪz/

語源は〈critic(分かれ目)ize(とする)〉である. **(悪いと判断して)相手への不満を口に出して責める.**
派 critical(批判的な);criticism(批評;批判)

Members of opposition parties harshly *criticized* the prime minister, claiming that the government failed to fulfill the people's expectations. 野党議員は,政府は国民の期待に応えていないとして首相を厳しく批判した.

She *criticized* herself *for* not preparing well for the examination. 彼女は試験のための準備を十分にしなかった自分を責めた.

crop /krá:p/

原義は〈丸まった頭〉である．**土の上に頭をもたげる（キャベツ・ブロッコリーなどの）農作物**．
関 group（集団）

The main *crops* [=agricultural products] in the district are rice and wheat.　当地方の主な農産物は米と小麦です．

Warm weather is good for crops [=agricultural plants] in general.　温暖な気候はたいていの農作物によい．

Thanks to the good weather, we can expect *a good crop* of apples this year.　好天のおかげで，今年はリンゴの豊作が期待できる．

---

cross /kró:s/

原義は〈横切る〉である．**一つのものが他方を横切る・交差する，十字を切る**．
派 crossing（交差点，横断歩道）　関 the Southern Cross（南十字星）; cross-examination（反対尋問）

He has a dream to *cross* the Tsugaru Channel by swimming [=to swim across the Tsugaru Channel].　彼は津軽海峡を泳いで渡る夢を持っている．

She knelt, *crossed* herself, and prayed.　彼女はひざまずいて（胸の前で）十字を切って祈った．

You may *cross* a broken white line to change lanes.　白の破線は横切って走路の変更ができる．　▶a solid white line「白の実線」

The president *crossed his arms* and began to think about the strategy for the next stage.　社長は腕を組んで次の段階の戦略を考え始めた．

crowd /kráud/

原義は〈押し込める〉である．**(押し込まれたような) 人込み；群がる→押し寄せる**．cr- は〈押しつけ・曲げ〉の意味合い．
派 crowded（混雑した）

He lost sight of his wife and son in the *crowd*.　彼は人込みで妻と息子を見失った．

Crowds of people began making their way to the Capitol.　大勢の人たちが議事堂に向かって歩き始めた．

A lot of fans *crowded* around the singer asking for his autograph.　多くのファンがサインを求めて歌手の周りに群がった．

The bus was so *crowded* that we had to stand in the aisle.　バスはとても込んでいたので通路に立っていなければならなかった．　▶aisle /áɪl/

crush /kláʃ/

原義は〈かみくだく〉である．**グシャッとつぶす**．cr- は〈押しつけ・曲げ〉の意味合い．
関 crash（壊れる）

Peel and *crush* [=mash] the garlic and add to the dish.　ニンニクの皮をむいてつぶして料理に加えなさい．

We saw a car *crushed* between two trucks at an intersection.　交差点で2台のトラックに挟まれてつぶれている車を見た．

cry /krάɪ/

原義は〈叫ぶ〉である. **泣き叫ぶ→泣く→涙を流す**.

I feel like *crying*, when I'm alone, for no particular reason.　一人になると，なんだか泣きたくなる.

The movie is so touching; I *cry* [=shed tears] every time I see it.　この映画はとても感動的で，見るたびに涙が出る.

culture /kʌ́ltʃər/

語源は〈cult (耕された) ure (もの)〉である. **(社会の中で耕され，練り上げられて生まれる) 文化，(頭の中で耕され，練り上げられる) 教養**.
派 cultural (文化の); cultured (教養のある)
関 agriculture (農業)〔←土+耕作〕

What is seen as beautiful and valuable varies from *culture* to *culture*.　何が美しくて価値があるかは文化によって異なる.

She is a person of *culture* [=a cultured person].　彼女は教養のある人だ.

cure /kjúər/

原義は〈世話をする (care)〉である．**病状の手当てをして治す；治療**．
関 care（世話）

Stomach cancer can now be *cured*, if detected and treated early enough.　胃がんは今では初期に発見，治療をすれば治る．

Is there a natural *cure* [＝remedy] for hypertension?　高血圧の自然療法はありますか．

current /kə́:rənt/

原義は〈流れ〉である．**(空気・電気・水・時の) 流れ；現時の，現行の**．
派 currently（現在は）　関 occur（起こる）

The circuit supplies *current* to the engine.　この電気回路がエンジンに電流を供給している．

We saw salmon swimming against the *current* as they made their way to the spawning areas.　産卵場所へ向かうサケが流れに逆らって泳いでいるのを見た．

How old is your *current* computer?　今使っているパソコンはいつ買ったの？

I'm *currently* [＝presently] living in Okinawa.　今，沖縄に住んでいます．

curse /kə́ːrs/

原義は〈怒り〉である.**かっとなってちぇっと言う；(ののしりたくなるような) 厄介なこと**.
関 cuss (〔嫌な〕野郎)

Being called out on strikes, the batter *cursed* [=swore] at the umpire. 見逃しの三振をとられて，バッターは審判に悪態をついた．

Long life can be a *curse*, not a blessing, when one can't live without putting others to a lot of trouble. 他者にひどく迷惑を掛けてしまうのであれば，長寿は恵みではなく厄介なものとなる．

curtail /kərtéɪl/

語源は〈cur (短く) tail (切る)〉である.**切り落とす**.
関 tailor (仕立て屋)〔←裁断する人〕

The government has sharply *curtailed* [=reduced] subsidies for colleges and universities. 政府は大学への補助金を大幅に削減した．

I think it's deplorable that freedom of speech has been *curtailed* [=limited] in quite a lot of countries. 多くの国で表現の自由が制限されているのは遺憾なことだと思う．

custom /kʌ́stəm/

語源は〈cu (一緒に) stom (慣れる)〉である．**皆が行う社会的慣習，風習，習わし，いつも行う個人的習慣．**
派 customs (関税) 〔←習わしとしての税〕; customer (顧客) 〔←いつもの客〕; customize (カスタマイズする) 〔←顧客の使い方に合うように設定する〕; customary (習慣的な)

In general, tipping is not「a *custom* [=*customary*] in Japan.　一般的に日本ではチップを出す習慣はない．

As is her *custom* while traveling, Mary wrote postcards to herself as reminders of her experiences abroad.　旅行の時のいつもの習慣で、メアリーは外国での経験の思い出のために自分宛てのはがきを書いた．

---

cut /kʌ́t/

原義は〈切る〉である．**刃物などで切る，切り取る，短縮する．**
関 shortcut (近道)

I've *cut* my finger with the kitchen knife.　包丁で指を切ってしまった．

She had *cut* her wrists to get rid of the emotional pain.　彼女は精神的苦しみから逃れるためにリストカットした．

How shall I *cut* your hair, sir?　どのように髪を切りましょうか．

We *cut through* the park to school.　僕たちは公園を通り抜けて学校へ行く．

cute /kjúːt/

原義は〈利発な((a) cute)〉である．**キューと心を打つような→かわい〜ぃ**．
関 acute（鋭い）

There is nothing as *cute* [=sweet] as a sleeping baby.　眠っている赤ちゃんほどかわいらしいものはないわ．　▶成人女性を cute と形容すると〈未成熟な〉イメージを伴う．

The young couple moved in a *cute* little house.　若夫婦は小さいすてきな家に引っ越した．

damage /dǽmɪdʒ/

原義は〈だめ (damn)〉である．**機能・価値をだめにする**．
派 damaging（害を与える）
関 damn（けなす）〔←だめと判定する〕

The drought has severely *damaged* [=affected] the crops in the fields.　日照り続きで畑の作物はひどくやられた．

Avoid too much sun, which can ⌈cause *damage to* [=*damage*] your skin.　皮膚に悪いので日光に当たり過ぎないようにしなさい．

Walking is less *damaging to* the knees than jogging.　ウォーキングはジョギングよりもひざへの負担が少ない．

dangerous /déɪndʒərəs/

語源は〈danger(危険) ous(多い)〉である.**危険な,危害を加えそうな**.
派 danger「危険」.

It is *dangerous* to leave a young child at home alone. 幼い子を家の中でひとりにしておくのは危険だ.

Don't forget that there is *danger* in exposing your skin to extreme UV rays. 強い紫外線に皮膚をさらすと危険だということを忘れないように.

dark /dáːrk/

原義は〈暗い〉である.**光が乏しくて暗い,色が黒っぽい,雰囲気が暗い**.d- は〈光から離れる〉イメージ.
派 darken(暗くなる);darkness(暗闇)
関 dim(薄暗い)

It was *dark* inside the cave and we couldn't see very well. 洞窟の中は暗くてよく見えなかった.

Small children are afraid of *the dark*. 幼い子どもは暗がりを怖がるものだ.

The sky *darkened* [=clouded over] suddenly and then the rain poured down in torrents. 空が急に暗くなり雨が激しく降り始めた.

The news of the terrible tragedy *darkened* [=threw cold water on] the mood of celebration. 恐ろしい惨事のニュースで祝賀の雰囲気に水が差された.

data /déitə/

原義は〈与えられたもの〉である．**(提供された) データ・資料**．例えば，ある場所の今の気温は18度というのは，情報として捉えると a piece of data (データの一つ) となる．一つひとつのデータを集積すると，平均気温や温暖化の傾向を考察するための data (データ) となる．
関 database (データベース)〔←検索用データの集積〕

He helped me to find and retrieve the *data* I had lost.　彼は，僕がなくしてしまったデータを見つけて修復してくれた．

The personal *data* [=information] you provided will be kept confidential.　頂いた個人情報を外部に漏らすことはありません．

date /déit/

原義は〈与えられた日にち情報〉である．**(記録に与えられた日) 日付→ (割り振る日) →デート；年代を定める，日付を書く，デートする**．
派 update (更新する)　関 data (データ)；dot (点を打つ)；up-to-date (最新の)〔←本日までの〕

What *date* is today? =What *date* is it today? =What's *the date* today? =What's today's *date*?　今日は何日ですか．　▶What day is today?「今日は何曜日ですか」

What *date* was it when Hiroshima was bombed?　広島が原爆を落とされたのはいつでしたか．

We'd like to decide the *date for* our next session.　次の集会の日取りを決めたいと思います．

This site is *updated* daily.　このサイトは毎日更新される．

dawn /dɔ́ːn/

語源は〈daw=day(太陽が) n=ing(出かかっている)〉である. **夜明け, 新しい時代の始まり**.
関 day (日)

The travelers set off before *dawn* [=daybreak] to beat the heat of the day.　旅人たちは日中の暑さを避けるために夜明け前に出発した.

Human beings have created so many things since the *dawn* [=beginning] of civilization.　人類は文明の黎明(れいめい)期以来, 多くのものを生み出してきた.

day /déɪ/

原義は〈太陽が照っている時〉である. **(夜に対する) 昼間, (人が活動する) 一日, (時間単位としての) 一日**.
派 daily (毎日の)　関 dawn (夜明け)

We are enjoying warm weather here with temperatures around 30 degrees by *day* and 20 degrees at night.　こちらでは, 日中は30度ぐらい, 夜は20度ぐらいで暖かな気候に恵まれています.

How was your day?　今日はどうだった?　▶具体的に何かを想定していう時は, How did it go today?「今日はうまくできた?」

His *days* are numbered, suffering from terminal cancer.　彼は末期癌を患っており, 余命わずかだ〔←日数が数えられるほど〕.

Your email always makes ⌈my *day* [=me happy].　あなたからのメールをもらうといつもうれしくなるよ.

dazzle /dǽzl/

語源は〈daze(ぎらぎら)le(繰り返し)〉である.**ぎらぎらしていて目をくらませる**.
関 daze(茫然とさせる)

I try not to drive at night; I hate being *dazzled* [=blinded] by the headlights of oncoming vehicles.　夜間の運転はしないようにしているよ．対向車のヘッドライトに目がくらむのが苦手だ．

The talented dancer *dazzled* [=amazed] the audience with his turns and jumps.　ダンサーは見事なターンとジャンプで観衆を魅了した．

dead /déd/

原義は〈死んでいる〉である.**(すでに)死んでいる・枯れている・動かない**.　d- は〈離れる・落ちる〉イメージ．
派 deadly(命にかかわる)
関 deep(深い)〔←表面からずっと離れている〕; die(死ぬ)〔←命から離れる〕; deaf(聞こえない)

The man was ⌈shot *dead* [=to death] on the street by an unidentified person.　その男は誰かに通りで銃殺された．

Be sure to pick off the *dead* flowers so that new flowers will grow in their place.　次の花が咲くように，枯れた花は摘み取るようにしなさい．

The clock is beginning to lose time. The battery is going *dead* [=dying].　時計が遅れ始めた．電池が切れかかっているんだ．

deadline /dédlàin/

語源は〈dead (無効になる) line (線)〉である. **無効になる境界線→締め切り**.

I worked very hard on the report, and managed to *make the deadline*.
レポートを懸命に頑張って締め切りに間に合わせた. ▶make [=meet/beat] the deadline「締め切りに間に合わせる」

If you don't get a paper in by the *deadline*, you could lose points or fail. 論文は締め切りまでに出さないと点が悪くなるか不合格になる.

deaf /déf/

原義は〈音から離れている〉である. **耳が遠い→耳が聞こえない**. d- は〈離れる〉イメージ.
関 dead (死んでいる)

My mother is a little bit *deaf* [=hard of hearing]. 母は少し耳が遠い.
The girl was born *deaf* but she can communicate using sign language.
あの子は生まれつき耳が聞こえないが, 手話で意思の疎通ができる.

deal /díːl/

原義は〈分け与える〉である。**分ける→物事をさばく・扱う→取引する；(分け与える)量・分量**。d- は〈(手元から)放す・離す〉イメージ。
派 dealer（業者）　関 dole（施し物）

Make sure you *deal* the cards face down so that no one can see them.
誰にも見えないようにトランプを伏せて配ってね。

We *deal* in second hand and old books on a wide range of subjects.
当店ではさまざまな分野の古本や古書を扱っています。

Many shoppers are looking for the best *deals* possible online.　できるだけ安くていい買い物をしたいとネットで検索する人が多い。

How do you *deal with* difficult people in your workplace?　職場の気難しい人にはどう対応していますか。

decay /dɪkéɪ/

語源は〈de（外へ）cay（落ちる）〉である。**崩れ落ちる→腐敗する**。d- は〈離れる〉イメージ。
関 cascade（小さな滝）〔←水が落ちる〕; deteriorate（悪化する）

There is a brown spot on my front tooth. I wonder if it is *decaying*.
前歯に茶色の斑点があるの。虫歯になりかけているんじゃないかしら。

You'd better get your *decayed teeth* treated before they start to ache.
虫歯は痛み始めるまえに治療しなさいよ。

Ants will often build their nests in *decayed* [=rotten] wood.　アリはよく朽ちた木に巣をこしらえる。

deceased /dɪsíːst/

語源は〈de (離れて) ceased (行った)〉である. **向こうへ行った→あの世へ行った→最近亡くなった**. the deceased で「故人, 故人たち」の意.
関 cease (止む)

The funeral service was held for only the immediate family of *the deceased*.　葬儀は故人の近親者のみで行われた.

We put flowers on the grave of *deceased* relatives.　先祖の墓に花を供えた.

deceive /dɪsíːv/

語源は〈de (外す) ceive (取る)〉である. **奪う→欺く**.
派 deceit (詐欺)　関 receive (受け取る)

Don't be *deceived* [＝fooled] by appearances.　外見にだまされないようにしなさい.

We often *deceive* ourselves *into* thinking that what we believe is always the best and true.　私たちは自分の信じることはいつも最善で真実であると思い込みがちである.

decide /dɪsáɪd/

語源は〈de(離す) cide(切る)〉である. **思い"切る"→決"断"する**.
派 decision(決定)
関 concise(簡潔な)〔←すっ"切り"している〕

The mayor *decided* not to run again, because he is losing his mental and physical strength.　市長は, 気力や体力が衰えてきたので再出馬しないことに決めた.

It's not something you should *decide* by yourself; have a talk with your parents.　これはあなたが自分だけで決めるようなことではないから, 両親と相談しなさい.

Have you *decided* where you are going to college?　どこの大学へ行くのか決めたの.

declare /dɪkléər/

語源は〈de(強く) clare(はっきり言う)〉である. **力強く宣言する, 申告する**.
派 declaration(宣言)　関 clear(はっきりさせる)

The new government of Japan has *declared* that it attaches great importance to Asian diplomacy.　日本の新政権はアジア外交を重要視するとの宣言をした.

A state of emergency has been *declared* in the area, due to a toxic gas leakage at the chemical plant.　化学工場の有毒ガスが漏れたために, 一帯に非常事態が宣言された.

What do I need to *declare* at customs?　税関では何を申告する必要がありますか.

decline /dɪkláɪn/

語源は〈de(下方へ)cline(傾ける)〉である.**傾く,衰える,断る**.cline- は〈傾く〉イメージ.
関 recline(もたれる)〔←後ろに+傾ける〕

The birthrate has been *declining* steadily [=There has been a steady *decline* in the birthrate] in Japan.　日本では出生率が徐々に下がっている.

The quality of students' handwriting has *declined* because of their over-reliance on technology.　テクノロジーに頼り過ぎて学生の手書き文字が下手になっている.

The manager *declined* [=turned down] our request for an interview.　監督は私たちのインタビューの申し込みを断った.

decrease /動 dìːkríːs, 名 díːkriːs/

語源は〈de(下へ)crease(増える)〉である.**(マイナス成長する)→減少する;減少**.
関 increase(増える)

There has been a steady *decrease* [=decline] in the number of people who feel their situation has gotten better.　生活状況がよくなったと思う人の数がだんだんと少なくなっている.

Violent crime in New York City has been *decreasing* [=dropping] for the last three decades.　ニューヨーク市の暴力犯罪はここ 30 年間減少している.

decide, declare, decline, decrease

dedicate /dédəkèit/

語源は〈de(強く)dicate(言う)〉である．**神に宣言して努力を誓う→達成に向けて専心努力する，捧げる．**
派 dedication（献身）
関 devote（捧げる）〔←強く＋誓う〕

Nelson Mandela *dedicated* [＝devoted] his life to bettering the lives of the oppressed people in South Africa.　ネルソン・マンデラは，迫害された南アフリカの人々の生活向上のために命を捧げた．

The staff of our school is quite *dedicated* [＝devoted] and is always there to help and offer advice.　僕たちの学校の教職員はとても献身的で，いつでも力になって助言してくれる．

deep /díːp/

原義は〈深い〉である．**(表面から下に向かって)深い，(手前から奥に向かって)深い，奥行きがある．** d- は〈(表面から)離れる〉イメージ．
派 deepen（深刻になる）；deeply（深く）；depth（深さ）
関 dead（死んでいる）；dip（浸す）

The snow is several inches *deep* on the ground.　雪は地面に数インチ積っている．

Make sure the water is *deep* enough before jumping in.　飛び込む時はまず十分深さがあることを確かめなさい．

In softball *how deep* is the center field fence?　ソフトボールではセンターのフェンスまで奥行きはどれくらいあるの？

The bookcase is 200cm wide, 45cm *deep*, and 190cm high.　この本棚は幅200センチ，奥行き45センチ，高さ190センチです．

defeat /dɪfíːt/

語源は〈de(反)feat(作る・成す)〉である. **成功を阻止する→打ち負かす;(成功ならず)敗北**.
関 feat(偉業)

He admitted *defeat* before the final results of the election were announced.　彼は選挙の最終結果が発表されるのを待たず,敗北を認めた.

The defending champion *defeated* [=beat] the challenger by 6th round KO.　チャンピオンが挑戦者を6回ノックアウトで退けた.

defend /dɪfénd/

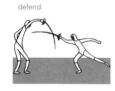

defend

語源は〈de(外す)fend(打ち込む)〉である. **相手の攻撃をかわす→防御する;(世論に抗して)擁護する**.
派 defendant(被告)〔←原告(plaintiff)の責めをかわす立場の人〕; defensive(防衛的な)
関 fence(柵)〔← defense(防御)〕; offend(傷つける)〔←へ+打ち込む〕

Immunity is our body's ability to *defend* [=protect] itself against infections.　免疫とは感染症に対して防御する人体の能力のことだ.　▶defend oneself against 〜「〜から身を守る」

It is regrettable that nobody *defended* [=spoke for] him against the false accusations.　誤った非難に対して誰も彼を擁護しなかったことは遺憾である.　▶defend+人+against 〜「〜に対して人を弁護する」

define /dɪfáɪn/

語源は〈de (ちゃんと) fine (区切る)〉である．**意味の範囲を区切って意味を明確にする，定義する**．
派 definition (定義); definitive (明確な); definitely (確かに)
関 finish (終える)〔←区切りをつける〕

How do you *define* [=explain] the concept of "culture"? 文化の概念をどう定義しますか．

The federal government didn't have any *definitive* [=clear-cut] evidence that Iraq possessed chemical weapons. 連邦政府は，イラクが化学兵器を持っているという確たる証拠は何も握っていなかった．

defy /dɪfáɪ/

語源は〈de (否定) fy (従う)〉である．**権威・権力に従わない，反抗する，無視する**．
関 fidelity (忠実)

Many parents openly *defied* [=challenged] the school authorities by withholding their children from school. 多くの親は子どもの登校を拒否して，公然と学校当局へ反抗した．

He *defied* [=disobeyed] the order to appear in court. 彼は出廷命令に従わなかった．

degree /dɪgríː/

語源は〈de(下へ)grade(歩む)〉である.**(段階を踏む)→段階,度合い,程度,地位,学位.**
関 grade(等級)

It was around 20 *degrees* Celsius this morning.　今朝は摂氏 20 度ぐらいでした.

David took a *degree* in geology at Oxford University.　デビッドはオックスフォード大学で地質学の学位を取った.

To what *degree* [=extent] do you agree with this policy?　この政策にどの程度賛成なの?

delay /dɪléɪ/

delay

語源は〈de(離して)lay=leave(置いておく)〉である.**そのままにしておく→着手・行動を遅らせる;遅れ.**

We decided to *delay* [=postpone] our departure until the weather improves.　天候が回復するまで出発を延ばすことにした.

The group arrived ⌈safely after a two-hour *delay* [=two hours later than the scheduled time]⌉.　一行は 2 時間遅れで無事到着した.

I think you need to see a doctor without *delay* [=before it's too late].　手遅れにならないうちに医者に診てもらわないといけないと思うよ.

deliver /dilívər/

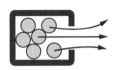

語源は〈de (外へ) liver (解放する)〉である. **(窮屈なところから) 広々とした所へ出す**.
派 delivery (配達, 出産)　関 liberate (解放する)

The medical team *delivered* the baby by Cesarean section.　医師たちは赤ちゃんを帝王切開で出産させた.《窮屈なところ＝子宮》

Barak Obama *delivered* [＝gave] *a speech* on a nuclear-free world in Prague.　バラク・オバマは核兵器のない世界についてプラハで演説した.《窮屈なところ＝口腔》

We will *deliver* [＝ship] the goods as soon as your order and payment are confirmed.　注文と支払いが確認されしだい, 品物を発送致します.《窮屈なところ＝倉庫》

demand /dimǽnd/

語源は〈de (強く) mand (任せる)〉である. **(任せきる)→責任を負わせる→要求する；要求**.「任せるよ！」は裏を返せば〈命令〉である.
派 demanding (骨の折れる)
関 command (命令する)〔←強く＋任す〕

The hijackers *demanded* the release of their imprisoned comrades.　ハイジャック犯たちは捕虜の解放を要求してきた.

Some parents give in to their children's *demands* thoughtlessly.　子どもの要求に軽率に応じてしまう親がいる.

The job is physically *demanding* [＝tough] and you have to stay and work outdoors all day.　この仕事は肉体的にきつく, 終日戸外で働かなくてはいけない.

demonstrate /démənstrèɪt/

語源は〈de(強く) monstrate(示す)〉である．**内在する能力や力を表に出してきちんと示す**．
派 demonstration(デモ)〔←胸中の意志・要求を行動で表に示すこと〕
関 monster(怪物)〔←凶兆の現れ〕; monument(記念碑)〔←過去の業績を示すもの〕

Honda *demonstrated* the latest development of its humanoid robot ASIMO.　ホンダは人型ロボット，アシモの最新の開発状況を実演して見せた．

The instructor *demonstrated* how to use the computer to access the information we need.　指導員はパソコンで必要とする情報にアクセスする方法をやって見せてくれた．

People *demonstrated* [=staged a *demonstration*] against Hamas' incessant rocket attacks against Israel's civilians.　人々はハマスのイスラエル市民に対する絶えざるロケット攻撃に抗議してデモを行った．

depend /dɪpénd/

語源は〈de(下へ) pend(垂れる)〉である．**ぶら下がる→寄りかかる，依存する→条件に左右される**．on は〈ぶらさがり・寄りかかり〉の対象を示す．
派 dependence(依存); dependent(頼っている); independence(独立)〔←否+依存〕
関 pendant(ペンダント)〔←首にぶら下げるもの〕

Kuwait's economy ⌈heavily *depends* [=is heavily *dependent*] *on* oil production.　クウェートの経済は石油の生産に大きく依存している．

"Would you do me a favor?" "That *depends*."　「頼みがあるんだけどといい？」「内容によるわ」　▶ That *depends* (*on* what it is). が言外に意味される．

People who are *dependent on* drugs or alcohol are not in control of their own lives.　薬やアルコールに依存している人は生活の自制ができない．

depress /dɪprés/

depress

語源は〈de（下へ）press（押す）〉である．**(気持ちや景気を) 落ち込ませる**．
派 depression（鬱，不況）　関 press（押す）

Fans will feel *depressed* [=let down] when their team loses.　ひいきのチームが負けるとファンは落ち込むものだ．

The thought of having to retake the exam ⌈*depressed* him [=made him feel *depressed*]．　再試験を受けなきゃいけないかと思うと彼は憂鬱になった．

The Lehman Shock brought about a worldwide economic *depression*.　リーマン・ショックは世界的経済不況を引き起こした．　▶リーマン・ショック：2008年9月に米国の名門投資銀行であるリーマン・ブラザーズの破綻による衝撃．

descend /dɪsénd/

語源は〈de（下方へ）scend（登る）〉である．**降りる，下る；由来する**．
派 descendant（子孫）；descent（降下）
関 ascend（登る）

The aircraft started *descending* [=its *descent*] for landing.　飛行機は着陸のために降下を始めた．

It is dangerous for a bicyclist to *descend* [=go down] steep slopes fast.　自転車で急坂をスピードを出して下るのは危険だ．

describe /dɪskráɪb/

語源は〈de(下へ)scribe(書きつける)〉である. **見たことをことばにして書きつける→描写する(対象の姿形や様子・内容をことばによってスケッチする)**.
派 description(描写;記述) 関 script(脚本)

Will you *describe* the man who threatened you? あなたを脅した男はどんな風貌でしたか.

There are no words to *describe* the beauty of the Earth seen from space. =The beauty of the earth seen from space is *beyond description*. 宇宙から見た地球の美しさはことばにならないほどだ.

What word best *describes* this novel? この小説のことを一言でいうとどうなりますか.

deserve /dɪzə́ːrv/

語源は〈de(十分)serve(役立つ・資する)〉である. **人の行為・業績が評価・賞罰を受けるにふさわしい**.
関 serve(仕える)

"I am thinking of having a week off." "Well, you've been working day and night. You *deserve* it." 「1週間休みを取ろうと思っているんだ」「君は日夜懸命に働いているのだから当然だよ〔←休暇をとる資格がある〕」

I hate to say this, but you don't *deserve* the salary you receive. 言いたくはないけど君は給料分の働きをしていないよ.

I certainly said some harsh things to John, but he *deserved* it. 確かにジョンにはひどいことを言ったが,当然のことを言っただけだよ.

design /dɪzáɪn/

語源は〈de (下に) sign (印をつける)〉である. **下絵を描く→設計する；設計, 図柄→〜することを意図する**.
派 designer (デザイナー)　関 sign (署名する)

I love the new *design* that the company chose for its logo.　その会社がロゴ用に選定した図柄が気に入っている.

This book is *designed* [=intended] to teach students how to write good sentences.　この本は学生によい文章の書き方を教えることを意図して書かれています.

How would you *design* [=plan] your retirement, if I may ask?　よろしければ, 退職後はどんな生活を考えておられるか教えてください.

desire /dɪzáɪər/

語源は〈de (強く) sire (星) を望む〉である. **よい星の巡りを求める→切に求める；欲望**.
派 desired (望みどおりの)；desirable (望ましい)
関 consider (考える)〔←しっかり星を観察する〕

There are many boys who desire [=have a *desire*] to be a professional athlete.　プロの運動選手になりたがっている少年が多い.

My new job ⌈*leaves nothing to be desired* [=is perfectly satisfactory]; I have a high salary, an office with a good view, and nice colleagues.　今度の仕事は申し分なしだ. 高給でオフィスからの眺めもよければ, いい同僚もいる.

Your efforts don't always ⌈bring the *desired* results [=pay].　努力がいつも望みどおりの結果をもたらすとは限らない.

destination /dèstənéɪʃən/

語源は〈destin=destine（予定された）ation（ところ）〉である。**(定めて行く) 目的地**。
派 destine（運命づける）；destiny（運命）

Paris is one of the most popular tourist *destinations* in the world.　パリは世界で最も人気のある観光地の一つである。

His new business, which lacks proper plans, is *destined* [=doomed] to fail anyway.　計画性のない彼の商売はいずれ破綻(はた)する運命にある。

You can control your own *destiny* at least to a certain degree.　運命は少なくともある程度は自分で左右できるものだ。

destroy /dɪstrɔ́ɪ/

語源は〈de（壊す）stroy（築く）〉である。**築かれたものを壊す→破壊する，滅ぼす**。
派 destruction（破壊）；destructive（破壊的な）
関 structure（建物）

Drinking too much alcohol can *destroy* [=damage] the normal function of the liver.　酒の飲みすぎは肝臓の正常な働きを壊しかねない。

Most of the town was completely *destroyed* by the lava flows.　町の大部分が溶岩流によって全壊した。

detail /díːteɪl/

語源は〈de (離す) tail (切る)〉である. **(細かく切り分けた) 細部・詳細**.
関 tailor (テーラー)〔←裁断する人〕; retail (小売する)〔←切り売りする〕

The company's *details* are not given in this brochure. Full *details* are available at our web site.　会社の詳細はこのパンフレットには記していません. 詳しくはホームページに出ています.

Please explain *in detail* your new sales strategy.　あなたの新しい販売戦略を詳しく述べてください.

detect /dɪtékt/

語源は〈de (外す) tect (覆い)〉である. **覆いを取り外す→覆いを取って潜んでいるものを見つけ出す**.
派 detective (刑事, 探偵)〔←隠れている事実を探り出す〕　関 protect (保護する); protector (防具)〔←身体を覆う〕

I stopped my car as I *detected* a strong smell of gasoline.　ガソリンの臭いがひどくしたので車を止めた.

Mercury was *detected* in the drinking water.　水銀が飲料水から検出された.

The *detectives* have as yet found no clues leading to the arrest of the girl's murderer.　刑事たちはまだ, 少女の殺人犯の逮捕に結びつく手がかりを見つけていない.

determine /dɪtə́ːrmən/

語源は〈de (はっきり) termine (限界を定める)〉である. **漠然とした内容・範囲・量をはっきり定める→決める, 定める.**
派 determined (断固としている); determination (決意)　関 terminate (終わらせる); term (学期)〔←限られた期間〕

Genes *determine* many of our personal characteristics, such as gender and skin color.　遺伝子は性や肌の色など個人の多くの特徴を決める.

Longevity is to some extent *determined* by one's lifestyle.　寿命はある程度, 人の生活習慣によって決まる.

If you're *determined*, you can do anything.　やる気さえあれば, 何でもできるよ.

develop /dɪvéləp/

語源は〈de (解く) velop (包み)〉である. **成長の種・疾病の因子が殻を破って伸びていく→進展する, 発症する.**
派 developing (発展途上の, 高まりつつある); development (発達, 開発)　関 envelope (封筒)

I'm relieved to know that my baby is *developing* normally.　赤ちゃんが順調に成長していると (医者から) 聞いてほっとした.

Most children start to *develop* a sense of right and wrong by the age of four.　4歳ごろになると, ほとんどの子どもは善悪の判断がつくようになる.

My son *developed* asthma when he was two.　息子は2歳の時, ぜんそくを発症した.

Tension *developed* between Japan and China over the Senkaku islands.　尖閣諸島をめぐって日中間で緊張が高まった.

diagnose /dàɪəgnóʊs/

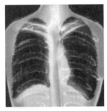

語源は〈dia(直に・横切って) gnose(診る・知る)〉である. **体に直(じか)に探りを入れて病名を知る→診断する**.
派 diagnosis (診断)
関 know (知る); ignore (無視する) 〔←否+知る〕

My father was *diagnosed* ⌈as having [=with] stomach cancer.　父は胃癌と診断された.

We are waiting for the doctor's *diagnosis*.　医者の診断が出るのを待っている.

diameter /daɪǽmətər/

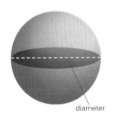
diameter

語源は〈dia(横切って) meter(測る)〉である. **(中心を横切って測った) 直径**.
関 radius (半径)

The Japanese one-yen coin is 2 centimeters ⌈in *diameter* [=across].　1円硬貨は直径が2センチだ.

How long is the earth in *diameter*? =How long is the *diameter* of the earth?　地球の直径はどれくらいですか.

All the residents living within a 10 kilometer *radius* of the chemical plant were evacuated.　化学工場の半径10キロ以内の住民はすべて避難させられた.

die /dáɪ/

原義は〈生命が消える〉である.**(動物・人が) 死ぬ, (植物が) 枯れる**. d- は〈離れる・落ちる〉イメージ.
派 dead (死んでいる); death (死)

His father *died* [=passed away] last month after a long battle against illness.　彼の父は長い闘病生活の後，先月亡くなった．

A seven-year-old boy *died* [=was killed] in a car accident.　7歳の子が車の事故で死んだ．

The crops in this region are *dying* [=withering] in the long drought.　この地域の農作物は長い日照りで枯れかかっている．

diet /dáɪət/

原義は〈生き方・食べ方〉である.**(日常的に摂取する) 食事, (治療などのために内容を規定した) 食事; 食事療法をする**.
派 dietary (食事の)

She eats a *diet* rich in fiber.　彼女は繊維の多い食事をする．

I have been advised to change my *diet* to control my weight.　体重を制限するために食事内容を変えるように言われている．

What is the best *diet* for diabetes?　糖尿病に一番よいのはどんな食事ですか．

I'm *dieting* [=on a *diet*] but not losing any weight.　ダイエットして (食事療法をして) いるんだけど，体重がちっとも減らないの．

different /dífərnt/

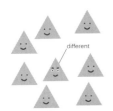

語源は〈differ(異なる)ent(状態である)〉である. ①**一方がもう一方とは異なっている**, ②**互いに異なっているものがいろいろある**.
派 differ(異なる); difference(相違)

I just don't understand what you are saying. Can you explain it in a *different* [=another] way? どうもおっしゃることがわかりません. 別の言い方で説明してもらえますか.

During the time when dinosaurs lived, the earth was much *different from* the way it looks today. 恐竜が生きていた時代の地球は現代の様相とはひどく異なっていた.

There are *different* [=various] ways to look at things. 物事にはいろいろな見方があるものだ.

difficult /dífikəlt/

語源は〈dif(でない)ficult(容易な)〉である. **容易でない→(行為の成就が)難しい・(人の気質が)難しい**.
派 difficulty(困難) 関 facile(容易な)

Grammatical exceptions make it *difficult* to learn a new language. 文法上の例外は新しい言語の習得を難しくしてしまう.

My son has become rebellious and *difficult* to deal with recently. 息子がこのごろ反抗的で扱いが難しくなった.

dig /díg/

原義は〈土を掘る〉である．**掘り出す→潜んでいるものを掘り起こす**．
関 ditch（溝）

The farmers *dug* a ditch to drain water from the pond for irrigation.
農夫たちは池から灌水用の水を引くために溝を掘った．

The reporter tried hard to ⌈*dig up* [=uncover] the truth behind the incident.　記者は事件の真相を見つけ出そうと懸命だった．

dip /díp/

原義は〈水につける〉である．**物を液体に浸す**．
派 dipper（ひしゃく）; the Great Dipper（北斗七星）〔←ひしゃくの形〕
関 deep（深い）

Dip [=Soak] the carrot seeds in water overnight before planting.
ニンジンの種は植える前に一晩水に漬けておきなさい．

We use a *dipper* to scoop out water from the bathtub and rinse ourselves before getting into the tub.　私たちは湯船に入る前に風呂の湯をひしゃくですくって体を洗います．

direct /dərékt/

語源は〈di (離れる) rect (まっすぐ)〉である. **目的に向けてまっすぐに引く (指導する)；まっすぐに (当てる・向ける)；まっすぐの**.
派 director (監督)；direction (指導, 指示, 方向)；directly (直接に)
関 correct (訂正する)

The board of education *directs* [=controls] and manages most of the school affairs.　教育委員会は学校関係のほとんどの事柄を取り仕切る.

When you *direct* [=aim] the camera at your subject, the camera selects the appropriate settings for you.　このカメラは, 被写体に向けると適切な設定を選んでくれる.

I took a *direct* [=non-stop] flight from Narita to Sydney. =I flew to Sydney *direct*(*ly*) from Narita.　成田からシドニーへ直行便で行った.

Hibiya Park is 500 meters away in this *direction*.　日比谷公園はこちらの方向に500メートル行ったところです.

dirty /də́ːrti/

語源は〈dirt (汚れ) y (の)〉である. **汚れた→不潔な→わいせつな**.
派 dirt (土, 汚れ)

I don't like boys with *dirty* fingernails.　爪を汚くしている男の子は嫌いよ.

John was thrown out of the game because he repeated a *dirty* [=foul] play.　ジョンは反則を繰り返したので退場になった.

The movie is rated X because it has some *dirty* [=obscene] scenes.　この映画はわいせつな場面があるので成人向けに指定されている.

We drove through the bumpy *dirt* road to the lake.　でこぼこした土の道を運転して湖に着いた.

disappear /dìsəpíər/

語源は〈dis(否)appear(現れる)〉である. **姿が見えなくなる→視界から消える**.
派 disappearance(消滅)

The man *disappeared* into the crowd shortly after being questioned by police. 男は職務質問を受けた直後に人ごみに姿をくらました.

The morning mist *disappeared* [=cleared away] as the sun came up. 太陽が昇ると朝霧は消えて行った.

The aircraft *disappeared* [=vanished] from the radar screen. 機影はレーダーから消えた.

Most bruising will *disappear* [=go away] in a week or so. たいていの打撲傷は1週間かそこらで消えるものだ.

disappoint /dìsəpɔ́ɪnt/

語源は〈dis(外す)appoint(指名する)〉である. **予定の指名をはずす→肩透かしを食らわす・がっかりさせる**.
派 disappointing(期待はずれの);disappointment(落胆, 期待はずれ)

I was *disappointed* [=sad] not to find my name on the list of successful candidates. 合格者名簿に自分の名前がなかったのでがっかりした.

He had been expected to win but finished in a *disappointing* seventh place. 彼は優勝候補だったが, 期待はずれの7位に終わった.

To our disappointment, the game was rained out. 残念ながら, 試合は雨天中止となった.

disaster /dɪzǽstər/

語源は〈dis (それる) aster (星)〉である. **星の巡りからそれること→運が悪いこと→災難, 災害, 大失敗**.
派 disastrous (災害を引き起こす)
関 ill-starred (星まわりの悪い, 不運な)

He argued that the collapse of the dam was a human-made *disaster*, rather than a natural *disaster*. 彼は, ダムの崩壊は天災ではなく人災だと主張した.

David's second challenge was a complete *disaster* [=failure]; he had to stop the race halfway due to a sudden knee pain. デビッドの二度目の挑戦は散々だった. 急にひざが痛み出してレースを途中棄権する羽目になったのだ.

discharge /dɪstʃɑ́:rdʒ/

語源は〈dis (出す) charge (詰め込む)〉である. **溜まっているものを吐き出す→負担・拘束から解放する**.
関 charge (詰め込む)

The minister was *discharged* [=released] from the hospital today after being treated for a mild heart attack. 大臣は軽い心臓発作の治療を受けていたが, 今日退院した.

The factory was charged for *discharging* its wastewater into local waterways. 工場は汚水を近くの河川に垂れ流していたことで告発された.

discipline /dísəplən/

語源は〈dis (分ける) cipline (聞く)〉である. **聞き分けさせる→しつける→叱る;しつけ, 自制**.
関 disciple (弟子) 〔←しつける〕

Parents should not neglect to *discipline* [=neglect *disciplining*] their children.　親は子どものしつけを怠ってはならない.

Why can't cats be *disciplined* [=trained] like dogs?　猫はなぜ犬のようにしつけることができないの.

You have been keeping up your exercise routine. I admire your *discipline*!　君は日課の運動をちゃんとやっているね. 君の自制力には感心するよ!　▶exercise routine とは, 毎日決めて行う walking, jogging など, 健康のための運動のこと.

discourage /dɪskə́ːrɪdʒ/

語源は〈dis (外す) courage (やる気)〉である. **やる気をそぐ→思いとどまらせる, 落胆させる**.
派 discouragement (落胆)
関 encourage (励ます)

Although Mary worked hard on learning Spanish, she was *discouraged* by her slow progress.　メアリーはスペイン語を懸命に勉強したが, なかなか向上しないのでがっかりした.

Parents should *discourage* their children from eating foods with too much　sugar.　親は子どもに砂糖を多く含む食品を食べさせないようにするべきだ.　▶discourage+人+from ~「(人) に~することを思いとどまらせる」

Cold and icy weather *discourages* us from leaving our homes.　凍えるような天気だと人は家から出たくなくなるものだ.

discover /dɪskʌ́vər/

語源は〈dis (外す) cover (覆う)〉である．**覆いを取る→中が見える→発見する・見つけ出す**．
派 discovery (発見, 発覚)　関 cover (覆う)

The mother *discovered* her son's talent for music when he was four years old.　母親は，息子が4歳の時に音楽の才能があることを見抜いた．

It was a relief to *discover* that our son wasn't involved in the bullying.　息子がいじめに関わっていないことが分かってほっとした．

Copernicus *discovered* that the earth is not in the center of the universe but it circles the sun.　コペルニクスは，地球が宇宙の中心ではなく太陽の周りを回っていることを発見した．

discuss /dɪskʌ́s/

語源は〈dis (分ける) cuss (たたく)〉である．**問題の塊を砕いて考える**．日本語でも議論のための原案を「たたき台」という．
派 discussion (議論)
関 percussion (打楽器)；concussion (脳しんとう)〔←頭部を強く打つ〕

We want to *discuss* [=have a discussion about] environmental problems.　環境問題について話し合いをしましょう．

The staff *discussed* [=had a *discussion* about] how to raise the fund for the project.　職員はプロジェクトのための資金をいかに調達するか話し合った．

disease /dizí:z/

語源は〈dis(否)ease(楽)〉である **体調が楽でない→病気**. illness や sickness が〈病気の状態〉を指すのに対して,disease は〈個々の病気〉を指す.
関 malaise(不快)〔←悪い+楽〕

High blood pressure is not a *disease* but a symptom of some other underlying *disease*. 高血圧は病気ではなく,潜んでいる何か他の病気の症状である.

I hear that he is bedridden [=confined to bed] with an incurable *disease*. 彼は不治の病で寝たきりだそうだ.

Most *diseases* are caused by your unhealthy lifestyle—poor diet, lack of exercise, and inadequate sleep. たいていの病気は不健康な生活習慣,例えば,適切でない食事,運動不足,睡眠不足が原因で起こる.

---

disguise /dɪsɡáɪz/

語源は〈dis(外す)guise(装い)〉である. **普段の装いを変える→本人・実態とは違う姿・様子にする;変装**.
関 guise(外観)

The director of the kindergarten *disguised* himself as a Santa Claus to entertain the children. 園長さんはサンタクロースに変装して園児たちを喜ばせた.

Tom didn't try to *disguise* [=hide] the fact that he was gay. トムは自分がゲイであることを隠そうとはしなかった.

This defeat could be *a blessing in disguise* for my son. I think he was becoming a bit over confident. 今回の敗北は,息子にとってかえってよかったかもしれないよ.少し自信過剰気味になっていたようだから. ▶a blessing in disguise「不運に見える幸運」

dish /díʃ/

原義は〈円盤〉である．**大皿・皿→（皿に盛った）料理**．
同様の日本語に〈鍋＝鍋料理〉がある．
関 disk（円盤）

I always help Mom *do the dishes* [＝with the *dishes*].　僕はいつも母の皿洗いを手伝う．▶do the dishes「食器を洗う」

Sushi is my favorite Japanese *dish* [＝food].　日本料理でいちばん好きなのは寿司だ．

dismiss /dɪsmís/

語源は〈dis（外へ）miss（送る）〉である．**（考え・提案を）追い払う→無視する，却下する；（人を）追い払う→解雇する**．
派 dismissal（解雇，却下）
関 mission（派遣）〔←送り出す〕

The board *dismissed* [＝rejected] his suggestion as impossible.　委員会は彼の提案を実行不可として却下した．

Temporary workers are usually the first to be *dismissed* [＝fired] when a company must downsize.　会社がリストラを実施する時に，最初に解雇の対象になるのは，たいてい非正規雇用者だ．

display /dɪspléɪ/

語源は〈dis (外へ) play=ply (折り込む)〉である．**折り込みを外へ開く→開いて内容を見せる；展示**．パソコンの画面を display というのは，ディスクの中に折り込んである情報を画面上に開示するから．

She *displayed* [=showed] exceptional singing talent in the musical.
彼女はそのミュージカルで非凡な歌唱力を見せた．

Click this icon to *display* [=show] weather information. 天気情報を画面に出すにはこのアイコンをクリックしてください．

African watercolor art are ⌈on *display* [=displayed] at the museum.
アフリカの水彩画がこの美術館に展示されている．

dispute /dɪspjúːt/

語源は〈dis (反対に) pute (考える・思う)〉である．**反対に考えて訴える→異論を言う，言い争う；論争**．
関 compute (計算する)；reputation (評判)〔←返り＋思い〕

They have good reason to *dispute* [=oppose] the government's proposal. 彼らが政府案には賛成できないのは当然だ．

There often arises a territorial *dispute* [=disagreement] between neighboring countries. 隣国間では領土問題がよく起こる．

dish, dismiss, display, dispute

distance /dístəns/

語源は〈dis(離れて) stance(立っている)〉である. **(離れている双方間の) 距離；相手との距離を置く**.
派 distant (遠くにいる)
関 stand (立つ)；stance (立場)

Be sure to keep enough *distance from* the car ahead of you. 前の車との車間距離を十分とるようにしなさい.

I live「within commuting *distance* of [=close enough to commute to] Tokyo. 東京の通勤圏に住んでいる.

Distance yourself [=Keep yourself away] *from* tainted money. 汚れた金には関わらないようにしなさい.

The Moon is about 380,000 kilometers *distant* [=away] *from* the Earth. 月は地球から約38万キロ離れている.

district /dístrɪkt/

語源は〈di(分けた) strict(引かれた)〉である. **(行政的に区分された) 区域, (特徴的に区分される) 地域**.
関 strict (厳しい)〔←緊張を強いた〕

In Japanese Diet elections, a candidate does not have to run in the electoral *district* where he or she resides. 日本の国会議員選挙では, 候補者は自分の住む選挙区から立候補する必要はない.

Niigata is a leading rice producing *district* [=area] in Japan. 新潟は日本の米どころの一つだ.

The bank is located in the financial *district* of Kabutocho. その銀行は兜(かぶと)町の金融街にある.

disturb /dɪstə́ːrb/

disturb

語源は〈dis (外へ) turb (かき乱す)〉である. **平静・平安をかき乱す**.
派 disturbance (騒動, 妨害)
関 turbine (タービン, 原動機) 〔←気体をかき混ぜる〕; turbulent (荒れ狂う)

Don't *disturb* [=interrupt] me. I am busy working.　じゃましないで. 仕事で忙しいのだから.

His wife was *disturbed* [=bothered] by unfounded rumors about her past.　彼の妻は自分の過去についての根も葉もないうわさに心を乱された.

divide /dɪváɪd/

語源は〈di (離して) vide (分ける)〉である. **分ける→分割する**.
派 dividend (配当金) 〔←分け前〕; divisible (割り切れる); division (区分, 割り算)
関 individual (個別の) 〔←不可+分割できる〕

Even numbers are numbers that ⌈can be *divided* [=are *divisible*] by two.　偶数とは 2 で割り切れる数のことである.

Tokyo is *divided into* 23 wards.　東京は 23 区に分かれている.

The teacher *divided* [=separated] the students *into* four groups, each with a different assignment.　教師は学生を 4 グループに分けて, それぞれに課題を与えた.

The town is *divided* in two over the issue of projected nuclear power plant.　町は原発計画の問題で二分されている.

divorce /divɔ́:rs/

語源は〈di（離れる）vorce（向ける）〉である．**(相手を向こうへ追いやる) →相手を離婚させる；離婚**．
関 divert（そらす）

When did they *get divorced*? ＝How long have they been *divorced*?
彼らはいつ離婚したの．

They *got ⌈a divorce ⌊＝divorced⌉* two years ago. ＝They have been *divorced* for two years.　彼らは2年前に離婚した．

We *got a divorce* by mutual consent.　私たちは協議離婚した．

Julie is a *divorced* mother with two children.　ジュリーは離婚していて，二人の子どもがいる．

do /dú:/

原義は〈置く→用意する〉である．**(～を) ちゃんとする・しっかりする→役立つ**．
関 deed（行為）

My father *did* what he liked and seldom worried about tomorrow.
父は好きなことをやって，将来のことを思い煩うことがなかった．

How are you *doing* with your business nowadays?　最近，商売はどうですか．

"I got divorced." "You *did*? Why?"　「私，離婚したのよ」「離婚したって？なんで？」

His advice didn't *do* me any good. ＝His advice wasn't helpful to me at all.　彼のアドバイスはちっとも役立たなかったよ．

doctor /dá:ktər/

語源は〈doct (教える) or (人)〉である．**医者，博士→(うまく治す)→あちこち直す→あちこち改ざんする**．
関 doctrine (教義)；document (公文書，記録書類)〔←教示する文書〕

You'd better go and see a *doctor*.　医者に診てもらいに行きなさいよ．

He is a *doctor* of engineering.　彼は工学博士だ．

An accountant was accused of *doctoring* [=cooking] the books.　会計係が帳簿の改ざんで訴えられた．　▶books=accounting books「会計簿」

dog /dɔ́:g/

原義は〈犬〉である．**犬→(惨めな) 犬；(犬のようにうろうろ) まとわりつく**．
派 doggie (ワンちゃん)〔小児語：doggyともつづる〕

Take your *dog* for a walk [=Walk your *dog*] every day.　犬は毎日散歩させなさい．

His administration was *dogged* [=haunted] by scandals and suspicions of corruption.　彼の政権はスキャンダルや汚職疑惑につきまとわれた．

He has been leading *a dog's* [=wretched] *life* since he lost his job.　彼は失業してから惨めな生活をしている．

An ex-convict complained that he was treated like a *dog* while in prison.　元囚人が在獄中にひどい扱いを受けたと訴えた．

domestic /dəméstɪk/

語源は〈domest(家庭)ic(の)〉である. **家庭内の→国内の；家で(飼う・使う・起こる)**.
関 dome (ドーム, 丸天井)

Domestic violence is increasing, due partly to increasing urbanization. 家庭内暴力が増えているのは，都会化が進んでいることも影響している．

They sell a wide range of *domestic* [=household] appliances from kettles to washing machines at the store. この店では，やかんから洗濯機まで広範囲の家庭用品を売っている．

I prefer *domestic* vehicles. 僕は国産車のほうが好きだ．

While most horses are *domestic*, others remain wild. たいていの馬は家畜〔←家で飼われている〕であるが，野生のままの馬もいる．

---

door /dɔ́ːr/

原義は〈戸〉である. **戸→玄関→一戸，一軒；(開けると〜へ通じる) 門，道**.

When there is a knock at the *door*, it is important not to rush to answer it without checking who is there. 玄関でノックの音がしたら，誰なのか確かめないであわてて出ることのないようにしなさい．

My parents live just a few *doors* [=houses] away from us. 両親は私たちの家からほんの数軒離れたところに住んでいる．

Email has opened the *door* to quick and inexpensive interpersonal communication. 電子メールは敏速で廉価な個人間の交信の道を開いた．

double /dʌ́bl/

語源は〈dou (二) ble (重ねる)〉である．**二重にする；二重の→二倍になる；二人用の**．
関 duplicate (複製の)〔←重複〕

Never allow your children to ride *double* (on a bike).　子どもに (自転車の) 二人乗りを決してさせないようにしなさい．

He tried to *double* his income by doing some side jobs.　彼はいくつかのアルバイトをして収入を倍増させようとした．

Ichiro hit a *double* deep into center field.　イチローはセンターの深いところへ二塁打を放った．　▶a single「単打」, a triple「三塁打」

doubt /dáut/

語源は〈doubt (二重になる)〉である．**前提の意見 (一番目の意見) に対して疑問あるいは否定の意見 (二番目の意見) を加える→前提の意見を疑う・否定的に考える；疑い**．
派 dubious (疑わしい)；doubtful (どうも疑わしい〔疑問〕，ありそうにない〔否定的〕)

They say that he's single, but I *doubt* that's true.　人は彼を独身だと言うが，私はそうでないと思う．《否定的意見の表明》

They say that he's single, but I *doubt if* that's true.　人は彼を独身だと言うが，本当かどうかは疑わしい．《疑問の表明》

There is simply no room to *doubt* what she had said in the letter.
彼女が手紙の中で言ったことは全く疑う余地がない．

down /dáun/

原義は〈高い所から低い所へ〉である．**下方へ→落ち込んで→倒れて**．

It got bitterly cold when the sun went *down* [=the sun set]. 日が沈むとひどく寒くなった．

The stock markets have been trending *down* since the start of this year. 今年になってから株市場は下降気味だ．

Just the thought of exams makes me feel *down* [=blue]. 試験のことを思うだけで気分が落ち込む．

I had been *down* with a cold last week. 先週は風邪で伏せっていた．

draft /drǽft/

原義は〈引く〉である．**(引き込まれるように吹く) すきま風，(ペンで引く) 草案，(引き抜く) 徴兵，(引き出す) 為替手形**．

There was a *draft* coming from somewhere and I was freezing. どこからかすきま風が入ってきて凍えるように寒かった．

I have just finished writing a rough *draft* for my graduation thesis. 卒業論文の草稿〔←おおまかな下書き〕を書き終えたばかりだ．

He tried to dodge the *draft* by pretending to be insane. 彼は精神異常を装って徴兵を免れようとした．

I sent my application fee by bank *draft*. 申し込み料金を銀行為替手形で送った．

drag /drǽg/

原義は〈引きずる〉である．**引きずる→事がだらだら続く**．draw（す〜っと引く）に比べて drag には〈接地面との摩擦〉が感じられる．

Don't *drag* the table, you'll scratch the floor! テーブルを引きずらないで，床に疵(きず)がつくでしょう！

Alligators *drag* [=pull] animals like dogs and pigs under water to drown them. ワニは犬や豚のような動物を水中に引きずり込んで溺死させる．

The territorial dispute over the Kuril Islands has *dragged on* for more than five decades. 千島列島をめぐる領土問題は 50 年以上にわたって長引いている． ▶drag on「（会議などが）だらだら続く」

drain /dréɪn/

原義は〈（水を引いて）流し出す〉である．**水を抜く，排水する，水気を切る**．
派 drainage（排水）　関 drought（干上がり）

This soil *drains* well. = This soil has good *drainage*. この土地は水はけがよい．

Try to *drain* [=get] water out of your ears after swimming. 泳いだ後は耳から水気を抜くようにしなさい．

I'm afraid all the investments ⌈*went down the drain* [=came to nothing] in the end. 残念ながら投資はすべて水泡に帰したのではないかと思う．

draw /drɔ́ː/

原義は〈引く〉である．**ぐ〜と引く，引き寄せる，引き込む**．筆記具で線を引く：*draw* a line（線を引く），*draw* a map（地図を描く），*draw* a cartoon（マンガを描く），*draw* a circle（円を描く），*draw* a sketch（スケッチを描く）　派 drawer（引き出し）；drawing（絵，製図）　関 drink（飲む）

He *drew* [=took] a deep breath and dived into the water.　彼は大きく息を吸って水中に潜った．

You have to *draw* the line between private and public affairs.　公私のけじめをつけなくてはいけないよ．　▶draw the line「線引きをする」

Casinos *draw* [=attract] gamblers as honey *draws* [=attracts] bees.　蜜がミツバチを呼ぶようにカジノはギャンブラーを引きつける．

Most children love *drawing*.　子どもはたいていお絵描きが好きだ．

dream /dríːm/

原義は〈夢〉である．**（眠っている時に見る）夢，（将来実現したい）夢**．
派 dreamy（夢見心地の）

I had a terrible *dream* last night.　昨晩，嫌な夢を見た．

He won the finals and felt as if he were in a *dream*.　彼は優勝して夢のような気がした．

"Is there a heaven?" "Oh, yeah. It's the place where *dreams* come true."　「天国ってあるの？」「うん，あるよ．天国はね，夢がかなう所なんだ」

I felt it was only a *dream* that would never be realized.　それは決して実現することのない夢に過ぎないように思えた．　▶realize a dream=make a dream come true「夢を実現する」

dress /drés/

原義は〈まっすぐに引く〉である. **(引いてまっすぐにする)→きちんとする→仕上げる→装う**. dr- は〈引っ張る〉イメージ.
派 dressing (ドレッシング)〔←サラダを覆う〕
関 address (演説する)

Do you have to *dress* a certain way at work? ＝Do you have a *dress* code at your workplace?　あなたの職場では服装の規定がありますか.

"What should I wear to the party?" "It's casual, so you don't have to *dress up* much."　「パーティには何を着ていったらいい?」「気軽な集まりだから,あまりおめかししなくていいよ」

Can you *dress* yourself in a kimono? ＝Can you put on a kimono by yourself?　着物をひとりで着られますか.

How〔＝With what〕do you *dress* your salad?　サラダのドレッシングは何にしますか.〔←サラダに何をかけますか〕

drill /dríl/

原義は〈穴をこじ開ける〉である. **(ぐい〜っと) こじ開ける；(ぐい〜と引き込むように) 訓練する**.

The company started *drilling*〔＝boring〕for oil and gas beneath the seabed off the coast of the Falkland Islands.　その会社は, フォークランド諸島沿岸沖の海底に石油とガスを求めて掘削を始めた.

Parents must repeatedly *drill*〔＝instill〕basic manners into their children.　親は子どもに基本的な行儀を繰り返し教え込まないといけない.

drink /dríŋk/

原義は〈飲む〉である. **飲み物を飲む**, **酒を飲む**. dr- は〈(水を喉に) 引き込む〉意味合い. 固形物 (錠剤, 粉薬, 胃カメラ) を飲み込む時は swallow という.
派 drinkable (飲用できる); drinker (酒飲み)
関 dry (乾かす)〔←水分を吸い取る〕; draw (引き込む)

Do you want something to *drink*? 何かお飲み物はいかがですか.

Let's *drink* to one another's health and happiness! お互いの健康と幸福を祈って乾杯しましょう! ▶「乾杯!」は Cheers! / Toast! / Bottoms up! などという.

I'll go out for a *drink* with my coworkers on Friday night. 金曜日の夜は同僚と飲みに出かけるよ.

Dick was arrested for「*drunk* driving [=driving under the influence (of alcohol)]. ディックは飲酒運転で逮捕された.

---

drive /dráiv/

原義は〈牛の群れを駆り立てる〉である. **(御するのがやっかいな対象・重量感のある対象を) 動かす**; **運転**, **(難事に向かう) やる気**, **政治的運動**.
派 driver (運転手); driving (激しい)〔←駆り立てるような〕
関 address (演説する); drove (家畜の群れ)

Do you「*drive* to work [=go to work by car]? 車で通勤するの? ▶work「勤め・職場」

Cowboys would *drive* cattle to market before the invention of trucks and trains. トラックや列車の発明以前は, カウボーイが牛を追って市場へ運んでいた.

Tom is talented enough, but he lacks *drive* and determination. トムは才能があるのに, 気力や根性がない.

We had a *driving* rain last night. 昨夜はひどい土砂降りだった.

drop /drɑ́:p/

原義は〈落ちる〉である. **(重力に引かれて) 大地に落ちる**, **(程度・割合が) 落ちる**, **(ある状態に) 落ち込む**, **(ある状況から) 消える・脱落する**.　dr- は〈引く〉イメージ.
関 drip (したたる)；droop (垂れ下がる)

A monkey *dropped* from the tree.　サルが木から落ちた.

Birth rates in Britain have *dropped* rapidly.　英国の出生率は急激に低下した.

The boy was exhausted and *dropped* off to sleep as soon as he hit the pillow.　少年は疲れ切っていたので床に着くやすぐに寝入った.

She *dropped out* of college. ＝She is a college *drop-out*.　彼女は大学を中退した.

---

drown /drάun/

原義は〈溺れる〉である. **溺れ死ぬ**, **溺れ死なせる**.
派 drowning (溺れかかっている)

A baby can *drown* in only a few inches of water.　赤ん坊はわずか数インチの水位でも溺れることがある.

The man was charged with animal cruelty after he *drowned* his cats in a pond.　男は飼猫を池で溺死させたので動物虐待で訴えられた.

The lifeguard helped a *drowning* boy in the sea.　救助員が海で溺れかかっている少年を助けた.

drug /drÁg/

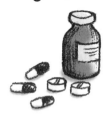

原義は〈植物を乾燥させて (dried) 作った薬〉である. **(健康回復のための) 薬, (非合法的な) 薬.**
関 dry (乾かす)

This is the most common over-the-counter *drug* [=medicine] for hay fever.　これがもっともよく使われている花粉症の市販薬です.　▶ over-the-counter「医師の処方の要らない」

He admitted using *drugs*.　彼は麻薬を使っていることを認めた.

He is ⌈*on drugs* [=a *drug* addict].　彼は麻薬中毒だ.　▶ be on drugs「麻薬を常用している」

dry /dráɪ/

原義は〈水が引き切っている〉である. **乾いている, 干上がっている;乾く;乾かす, 水気を拭き取る.**
関 drink (飲む); drought (日照り); drug (薬)

The weather has been very *dry* for the past three weeks.　この3週間少しも雨が降っていない.

The laundry ⌈is not *dry* [=hasn't *dried*] yet.　洗濯物がまだ乾いていない.

This blanket is machine-washable and easy to *dry*.　この毛布は洗濯機で洗えて乾きも早い.

How do you *dry* your laundry when it is rainy?　雨の日は洗濯物をどうやって乾かすの.

She *dried* herself on a bath towel after getting out of the bath.　彼女は風呂から出るとバスタオルで身体をふいた.　▶ dry oneself「体を拭く」

due /d(j)úː/

due

原義は〈負債を負っている〉である. **(借金がある)** →支払うべきである→しかるべきである→そうであるのが当然である.
派 duly (予定どおりに, しかるべく) 関 debt (借金)

The train is *due* to arrive at ten. 列車は 10 時到着の予定です.

The payment for the rent is *due* on the first day of each month. 家賃の支払いは毎月一日になっている.

He will get back into shape *in due time*. 彼はそのうち〔←しかるべき時間が過ぎたら〕元気になるでしょう.

"I am pregnant." "Really! Congratulations. When is「the baby *due*〔=your *due* date〕?" 「私, 妊娠してるの」「ほんとう！おめでとう. で, 予定日はいつ？」

---

dull /dÁl/

原義は〈頭が鈍い〉である. **鈍い→切れが悪い→退屈である→不活発である**. 音的に「だるい」と似ている.
関 dolt (うすのろ)

I sometimes feel a *dull* pain in my stomach after eating. 食後, ときどき胃に鈍痛がする.

You can't cook well with *dull* [=blunt] knives. 包丁の切れが悪いと料理はうまくできないよ.

Business has been remarkably *dull* [=slow] in the provinces. 地方では景気が極端に悪い.

during /dˈəːrɪŋ/

during

語源は〈dure (持ちこたえる) ing (間に)〉である. **〜の間ずっと (全期間)**, **〜の間に (一部期間)**. during+〈特定の期間〉. for+〈不特定の時間〉.

The wind blows mostly from the sea *during the day*.　風は, 日中はたいてい海から吹いてくる.

I met many of my old friends *during* my stay at my parents' home.　実家に帰っている間, 多くの旧友に会った.

Her husband served in the army for two years, *during* which [=*during* which time] she lived alone.　夫が2年間兵役に服していたので, その間彼女はひとりで暮らした.

---

dust /dˈʌst/

原義は〈細かなほこり〉である. **ほこり, 粉;ほこりを払う, 粉末を振りかける**.

A thick layer of *dust* covered everything [=Everything is thickly covered with dust] and cobwebs hung in the corners of the room.　いろいろなものに厚くほこりが積もって, 部屋の隅々にはクモの巣がかかっていた.

Would you please wipe the *dust off* the screen with a soft cloth?　画面のほこりをやわらかい布で拭き取ってくれませんか.

Mom always *dusts* the crepes *with* powdered sugar before serving them.　母はいつもクレープに粉砂糖をまぶして出してくれる.

duty /d(j)úːti/

語源は〈du（負っている）ty（こと）〉である．**（負っている・果たすべき）義務・職務；（払うべき）関税**．
関 debt（借金）

Employees must carry out their *duties* faithfully for the sake of the company.　従業員は会社のために忠実に職務を果たすべきである．

He is *off duty* today.　彼は，今日は非番です．　▶ be on duty「勤務中」

An *off-duty* policeman was arrested on suspicion of drunk driving.
非番の警官が飲酒運転の容疑で捕まった．

They sell *duty-free* goods at this shop.　この店では免税品を売っている．

dye /dáɪ/

原義は〈染める〉である．**布や髪を染める**．

Mom, may I *dye* my hair blonde?　お母さん，髪をブロンドに染めていい？
What color should I *dye* my gray hair?　白髪をどんな色に染めたらいいですか．

each /íːtʃ/

原義は〈個々の〉である.**(ある全体・全部の中の) それぞれ, めいめい, おのおの.** each は個体の全部に意識を置きながら各個体に注目する.

Each person is entitled to live freely.　(AさんもBさんもCさんも) 誰でも自由に生きる権利がある.

You should live *each* moment of your life to its fullest.　人生の刻一刻を目いっぱい生きなさい.

The team steadily improved with *each* game they played at Koshien.　このチームは甲子園での試合ごとに着実に成長した.

I'd go to see my grandparents *each* summer.　昔は祖父母のところへ毎夏遊びに行っていた.

---

eager /íːgər/

原義は〈しきりに望む〉である.**しきりに〜したいと思う, 熱心である.**
派 eagerly (しきりに)
関 overeager (熱心すぎる)

He is an *eager* reader of modern American literature.　彼は現代アメリカ文学の熱心な読者だ.

I think the critic *is* overly *eager to* find fault with new writers' works.　この批評家は新人作家の作品にどうも難癖をつけ過ぎると思う.

The review made me *eager to* read the book.　書評を読んでその本をとても読みたくなった.

early /ə́ːrli/

語源は〈ear (早く) ly (に)〉である. **一続きの事柄が経過する中で初めのほうの時期・時間に.**

early

Gamba Osaka scored two goals ⌈in the *early* stages of the game [= *early on* in the game]. ガンバ大阪は試合の早い段階で 2 ゴール入れた.

He ran for governor in his *early* thirties. 彼は 30 代前半で知事選に立候補した.

I always come *early* to work. The *early* bird catches the worm! 僕は出勤が早いんだ. 早起きは三文の徳 (早起きの鳥は虫にありつける) だからね.

earn /ə́ːrn/

原義は〈収穫を得る〉である. **働いて報酬を得る, 努力して評価を得る.**
派 earnings (賃金, 報酬)

My brother *earns* [=makes] his living by trading stocks. 兄は株を売買して生計を立てている.

Teachers have to *earn* [=gain] their students' respect. 教師は生徒たちの尊敬を得ることが大事だ.

Average monthly *earnings* rose by 2% this year. 今年は平均月収が 2% ほど増えた.

earth /ə́:rθ/

原義は〈地面〉である. **地面**, **大地**, **地球**.
派 earthen (陶製の) 関 earthquake (地震)

I felt the *earth* [=ground] shake beneath my feet.　足下の地面が揺れるのを感じた.

In one second, light travels seven and a half times around the *Earth*.　光は1秒間に地球を7周半回る.

Why *on earth* do you want to move to such a remote countryside?　いったいどうしてあんな片田舎に引っ越したいの？　▶ on earth =among all the possibilities「こともあろうに」

easy /í:zi/

原義は〈近くにある〉である. **(近くにある)** →すぐ目的に届く→楽に手にできる→**楽な**, **ゆったりした**.
派 ease (容易さ, 和らげる); easily (容易に); easygoing (物事に対して気楽に構える)

It's not *easy* to forgive those who hurt you.　あなたを傷つけた相手を許すのはなかなかできることではない.

Computers make it *easy* to collect and store data. =Computers help us collect and store data *easily*.　コンピュータによってデータの収集と保存が楽にできる.

You're just a bit too serious about everything; you should take things *easy* and relax more.　君はなんでも少し真剣になり過ぎるよ. 物事を気楽に捉えてもっと楽になさいよ.

eat /íːt/

原義は〈食べる〉である．**人や動物が食べる，虫が食う，酸などが物を腐食する**．

My boy is in a growing stage and *eats* a lot.　息子は育ち盛りでよく食べる．

The lettuce in the garden has been *eaten* by worms.　菜園のレタスが虫に食われているよ．

How often do you ⌜*eat out* [=go out to *eat*]?　どれくらいの頻度で外食しますか．

Rust had *eaten into* the metal parts of the fence.　柵の金属部がさびで腐食していた．

---

echo /ékou/

原義は〈こだま〉である．**こだまする；こだま→音や声が響く→繰り返す**．

My footsteps alone *echoed* [=Only the *echoes* of my footsteps could be heard] on an empty and quiet street.　私の足音だけが人通りのない静かな通りに響いた．

Many of Basho's haiku poems have ⌜*echoed* down [=come down to us] through the ages.　多くの芭蕉の俳句が世代を超えて語り継がれてきている．

ecology /ɪkάːlədʒi/

語源は〈eco(住みか)logy(研究)〉である.**(住環境の研究)→生態学,生態,自然環境**.
派 ecological(生態系の)
関 economy(経済);ecosystem(生態系)

He is interested in the *ecology* [=the *ecological* behavior] of honeybees.　彼はミツバチの生態に興味を持っている.

We need to save energy to protect the natural *ecology* [=environment].　私たちは自然環境を守るためにエネルギーを節約する必要がある.

economy /ɪkάːnəmi/

語源は〈eco(住みか)nomy(やりくり)〉である.**(世帯のやりくり)生計・節約→(社会のやりくり)経済**.
派 economic(経済上の);economics(経済学);economize(節約する);economist(経済専門家)
関 ecology(生態学)

The government is planning a huge tax cut in order to stimulate the *economy*.　政府は景気を刺激するために大型の減税を計画している.

For *economic* [=financial] reasons, he had to give up on going to college.　彼は経済的理由で大学進学を諦めねばならなかった.

Living in the country is more *economical* [=cheaper] than living in the city.　田舎暮らしのほうが都会暮らしよりも安くつく.

edge /édʒ/

原義は〈鋭くとがった所〉である．**刃先→端・縁（edge があると相手に切り込める）→威力・優位が保てる；優勢**．

Don't sit on the *edge* of your chair.　いすの縁に座らないようにしなさい．

Let's walk down to the water's *edge*.　波打ち際まで行ってみよう．

Careful with that knife — it's got a very sharp *edge*!　そのナイフは刃先が鋭いから注意して！

Because of my experience I had the *edge* [=the advantage] over the other applicants.　経験があるので，他の志願者よりも有利だった．

educate /édʒəkèɪt/

語源は〈e（外へ）duc（引き）ate（出す）〉である．**人の能力を引き出す**．
派 educated（教養のある）；education（教育）；educational（教育的な）

Mozart was *educated* by his father when the Mozart family toured around Europe.　モーツァルトは，家族がヨーロッパを巡業中は父から教育を受けた．

His brother is an *educated* and interesting man.　彼の兄さんは教養があっておもしろい人ですよ．

Where did Murasaki Shikibu get her *education*?　紫式部はどこで教育を受けたのですか．

I find this program is very *educational*.　この番組はとても教育的だと思う．

effect /əfékt/

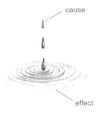

語源は〈ef(外へ) fect(作る)〉である. **活動の外側に作り出されるもの→影響, 結果, 効果**.
派 effective(効きめがある)
関 affect(影響を与える); efficient(効率的な)

Chemotherapy may cause side *effects*.　化学療法は副作用が起きることが多い.

The *cause and effect* of this phenomenon is yet to be apparent.　この現象の因果関係はまだはっきりしていない.

The new bill, if passed, will come into *effect* [=force] in approximately one year.　新しい法案は通過すれば, ほぼ1年で実施されるだろう.

Excessive exercise may have an adverse *effect* on your health.　過度の運動は健康に逆効果をもたらしがちだ.

---

effort /éfərt/

語源は〈ef(外へ) fort(力)〉である. **力を出す→頑張って取り組む; 頑張り, 努力**.
派 effortlessly(容易に)　関 force(力)

It was quite an *effort* to finish the assignment within 30 days.　この課題を30日で仕上げるのはとても骨が折れた.

You need to make more *effort* to attain the goal you set.　立てた目標を達成するにはもっと頑張らないとだめだよ.

The magazine is advertising extensively *in an effort to* increase its readership.　その雑誌は読者拡大のために大々的に宣伝をしている.

The mechanic repaired my very old car「without *effort* [= effortlessly].　整備士は僕の年代物の車を難なく修理してくれた.

either /íːðər/

語源は〈ei(常に)ther(どちらか)〉である. **二つのうちどちらでも**.

A good footballer can kick the ball hard with *either* foot.　うまいサッカー選手はどちらの足でも強く蹴れる.

Most newspapers predicted that the election *could go either way*.　ほとんどの新聞が，今度の選挙はどちらに転ぶか分からない（勝利がどちらにも行き得る）と予測している.

In democracy people can take part in government *either* directly *or* indirectly.　民主主義では，人はみな直接的あるいは間接的に政治に参加できる.

If you don't go, I wo*n't either*.　君が行かないのなら僕も行かないよ.

elaborate /ɪlǽbərət/

語源は〈e(尽くす)laborate(力を込める)〉である. **念入りに仕上げる；手の込んだ→ことばを尽くして言う→もっと詳しく述べる**.
派 elaboration(詳細)　関 labor(労働)

The interior decoration of the hall is too *elaborate* [=complicated] for my taste.　このホールの室内装飾は凝り過ぎていて僕の趣味ではない.

The company is *elaborating* [=working out] a sales strategy for the Middle East market.　会社は中東市場への販売戦略を練っている.

Would you please ⌈*elaborate* a bit more [=add a bit more detail]⌉ on your suggestion?　君の提案をもう少し詳しく述べてくれませんか.

elderly /éldərli/

語源は〈elder (年長の) ly (状態)〉である．**年を重ねた；年輩者**．an old person を遠回しに an elderly person, a senior citizen ということがある．
派 elder (年上の)

He has an *elderly* mother in a nursing home.　彼は老人ホームに年老いた母親がいる．

I feel「*elderly people* [=the *elderly*] used to be more respected in our culture than they are today.　この社会では，年輩者は今日よりもっと尊敬されていたように思う．

I have two *elder sisters*.　私には姉が二人います．

elect /ilékt/

語源は〈e (出す) lect (選ぶ)〉である．**議員や委員を選び出す→選挙する**．
派 election (選挙)　関 select (選ぶ)〔←抜く＋選ぶ〕

Barack Obama was *elected* president on Nov. 4, 2008.　バラク・オバマ氏は 2008 年 11 月 4 日に大統領に選ばれた．

An *election* promise is a promise made to the public by a politician who is trying to win an *election*.　選挙公約とは，政治家が選挙に勝とうとして一般の人々にする約束である．

Which party will win the next general *election*?　次の総選挙で勝つのはどの政党だろう？

electricity /ɪlèktrísəti/

語源は〈electric（電気の）ity（状態）〉である．**電気，電流．** ラテン語 electrum は「琥珀」の意であるが，これを摩擦することによって静電気ができたことに由来する．
派 electric（電気の，電動の）; electrical（電気に関する）; electrify（電化する）

How much money do you spend on *electricity* per month? 月にどれくらい電気代がかかりますか．

A hybrid car is powered by both gasoline and *electricity*. ハイブリッドカーはガソリンと電気で動く．

Don't touch *electric* appliances with wet hands or you may get an *electric* shock. 電気製品には濡れ手で触らないようになさい，でないと感電するかもしれないから．

---

element /éləmənt/

原義は〈自然界の基本要素〉である．**あるものを構成する基本的要素・元素・要素．**
派 elementary（基礎の，初歩の）

An atom is the smallest particle of an *element* that cannot be divided or broken up. 原子は元素の中の最小の粒子で，これを分割することはできない．

Trust is the most important *element*［＝asset］for success in business. 商売で成功するために最も大切な要素は信用である．

The temple is remarkably well kept for 250 years of exposure to the *elements*［＝the weather］． この寺は250年も風雪にさらされている割には驚くほど見事に保存されている．　▶the elements から〈風，雨，雪，日光など〉が連想される．

---

elderly, elect, electricity, element 247

eliminate /ɪlímənèɪt/

語源は〈e (出す) liminate (敷居)〉である．(**敷居から追い出す**)→**領域から追い出す→不必要なものを取り払う，敗者を除外する**．
派 elimination (排除, 消去)
関 limit (限度)；subliminal (意識下の)〔←下＋意識の域〕

I think trade barriers should be completely *eliminated* [=removed]. 貿易障壁は全部取り払うべきだと思う．

His team was *eliminated* [=defeated] in the first round of the tournament. 彼のチームはトーナメントの1回戦で敗退した．

Use the process of *elimination* to reach the right answer. 消去法を使って正解を求めなさい．

else /éls/

語源は〈el (他) se (の)〉である．**その他の，その他に**．
関 elsewhere (どこか他の所で)

Who else did you see? 他に誰に会ったの．

Would you like anything *else*? 他に何か欲しいですか．

I am sorry. I mistook you for somebody *else*. すみません．人違い〔←あなたを他のある人と間違えた〕でした．

Let me see, I had something *else* to say. え～と, 他に言うことあったんだけど……．

When you are in love, nothing *else* in the world matters. 恋に落ちると世間の他のことは目に入らなくなる．

embarrass /ɪmbérəs/

embarrass

原義は〈em (中に) barrass (棒を投げ入れる)〉である. **ボウ害する→人の気持ちをまごつかせる, 人にばつの悪い思いをさせる**.

派 embarrassing (まごつかせるような); embarrassment (当惑)　関 bar (棒)

Take care not to *embarrass* a person in public.　人前で人に恥をかかせないように気をつけなさい.

It is really *embarrassing* when you call a person by a wrong name.　相手の名前を間違って呼んだ時は実にばつが悪いものだ.

I don't mind *embarrassing* [=humiliating] myself by asking for help in time of need.　困った時に助けを求めるのは (恥ずかしくても) 気にしません.

emerge /ɪmə́ːrdʒ/

語源は〈e (外へ) merge (水中)〉である. **(水中から姿を現す)→不意に姿を現す**.

派 emergence (出現); emergency (緊急事態): シャーク (shirk) や海坊主が突然頭を出したら emergency (緊急事態) だ!
関 merge (混じる); immersion (没頭)

When it gets warm enough many insects begin to *emerge* [=come out] from their nests.　暖かくなるとたくさんの虫が巣から出てくるようになる.

We store canned foods and drinks for an *emergency*.　非常時に備えて缶詰食品や飲料を貯蔵している.

The *emergency* number for police is 110.　警察への非常電話番号は110番だ.

eliminate, else, embarrass, emerge

emotion /ɪmóʊʃən/

語源は〈e (外に) motion (気持ちの動き)〉である. **外に表れる気持ちの動き→感情 (fear, anger, joy, sorrow など)**.
派 emotional (感情的な, 感動的な)
関 move (感動させる)

He always tries to discuss things without being controlled by his *emotions*.　彼は感情的になって〔←感情に支配されて〕議論をすることがないようにいつも心がけている.

Showing *emotion* in public is considered indecent in many cultures.　人前で感情をあらわにするのははしたないと多くの社会で思われている.

Try not to be so *emotional*, try to behave more rationally!　そんなに感情的にならないで, もっと理性的に振る舞ってちょうだい!

He gave a very *emotional* [=moving] farewell speech to his colleagues.　彼の同僚たちへの送別の辞はとても感動的であった.

emphasize /émfəsàɪz/

語源は〈em (強く) phasize (見せる)〉である. **中に込めて見せる→気持ちを込めてことばにする→強調する**.
派 emphasis (強調)

It has been *emphasized* that saving energy is the key to combating climate change.　省エネこそが気候変動に対処する鍵になると強調されている.

The doctor lectured on lifestyle and health with special *emphasis* on the role of diet.　医者は生活の仕方と健康について講演をし, 特に食事の役割を強調した.

employ /implɔ́i/

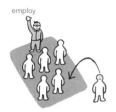

語源は〈em (中に) ploy (重ねる)〉である. **(職場に人を重ねる)→雇う;(問題に方法を重ねる)→用いる**.
派 employer (雇用者); employees (被雇用者, 従業員); employment (雇うこと, 雇われること); unemployed (失業している)

Employers will be prosecuted for *employing* children and young people illegally.　雇用者は子どもや若者を不法に雇用すると起訴される.

The arrested man was *unemployed* of no fixed address.　逮捕された男は住所不定で無職だった.

I'm a freelance photographer, meaning I am *self-employed*.　私はフリーランスの写真家, つまり自営ってことです.

You can *employ* [=use] a web site to advertise your products and services.　商品や事業を宣伝するためにホームページが利用できる.

---

empty /émpti/

原義は〈ふさがっていない〉である. **空いている→(容器が)空である;空にする→(他の容器に)注ぎ込む**.〈空にする〉と〈注ぐ〉は表裏一体の動作である.

The room was bare and *empty* except for two plastic chairs in the center.　部屋はがらんとして, 中央にプラスチック製のいすが二つある他は何もなかった.

The medicine is taken on an *empty* stomach with a glass of water in the morning.　この薬は朝の空腹時にグラス (コップ) 一杯の水で飲みます.

Try to「*empty* your bladder [=urinate] before you go to bed.　寝る前に小用をすませるようにしなさい.　▶bladder「膀胱」

The Yodo River *empties* [=flows] into Osaka Bay.　淀川は大阪湾へ注いでいる.

enable /inéɪbl/

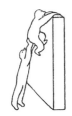

語源は〈en (する) able (できる)〉である. **あることが力となって〜を可能にする**.
関 able (〜ができる)

The scholarship *enabled* [=allowed] me to study agriculture further in Australia.　この奨学金のお陰で, オーストラリアでさらに農業の研究を続けることが可能になった.

I think traveling abroad *enables* [=helps] us to widen our views of the world and ourselves.　海外旅行は私たちの世界観や人生観を広げるのに役立つと思う.

encounter /ɪnkáʊntər/

語源は〈en (〜に) counter (逆らう)〉である. **相手に出会う, 事態に出くわす**.
関 counter (逆らう); counterblow (〔ボクシングで〕カウンターパンチ)

This economic depression is by far the worst one we have ever *encountered* [=experienced].　この不況はこれまで経験した中で最悪の不況だ.

What should I do if I *encounter* [=run across] a bear in the wilderness?　原野でクマに出くわしたら, どうすればいいですか.

encourage /ɪnkə́ːrɪdʒ/

語源は〈en (入れる) courage (勇気)〉である. **勇気づける, 励ます**.
派 encouraging (励ましになる); encouragement (激励)
関 discourage (落胆させる)

The runner was *encouraged* to pick up speed by the cheers of his family and friends.　ランナーは家族や友達の声援に励まされてスピードを上げた.

The patient's constant efforts to regain his lost skills is very *encouraging* to everybody.　この患者の失った機能を回復するための絶えざる努力は, 皆を元気づけるものだ.

Thanks for your *encouragement*. I will keep on working hard !　激励ありがとう. 努力を続けるよ!

---

end /énd/

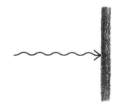

原義は〈細長いものの端〉である. **端→終点→目的; 終わる; 終わらせる**.
派 endless (限りない)

The pencil is with an eraser at an *end* for easy correction.　この鉛筆はすぐ訂正できるように端に消しゴムがついている.

The post office is at the *end* of this street on the right-hand side.　郵便局はこの通りを突き当たって右手にあります.

The *end* doesn't always justify the means.　目的が正しければ手段を選ばなくてもよいとは限らない.

Here's where the story *ends*.　お話はここでおしまい.

The death of Emperor Hirohito *ended* [=brought to an *end* of] an era.　裕仁天皇の死は一つの時代の終わりをもたらした.

---

enable, encounter, encourage, end

endure /ɪnd(j)úər/

語源は〈en (する) dure (堅固)〉である. **堅固にする→困難に持ちこたえる→がまんする**.
派 endurance (忍耐)　関 durable (長持ちする)

The man who was wrongly convicted had to *endure* [=put up with] being in prison for many years.　その人は無実の罪で何年も獄中生活に耐えねばならなかった.

Having *endured* [=gone through] many difficulties, George finally realized his dream of becoming a doctor.　多くの苦労に耐えてジョージはついに医者になる夢を実現させた.

enemy /énəmi/

語源は〈en (非ず) emy (友達)〉である. **友に非ず→敵**.
関 amiable (好感の持てる); amity (友好)

The man has a lot of *enemies* because he often criticizes others harshly.　あの男は他人をひどくけなすことがよくあるので敵が多い.

Racism is the *enemy* of freedom and equality.　人種差別は自由と平等の敵である.

Snakes have many *natural enemies* such as raccoons, skunks, owls, hawks, and other animals.　ヘビは, タヌキ, スカンク, フクロウ, タカなど多くの天敵がいる.

engage /ɪngéɪdʒ/

語源は〈en (する) gage (担保・契約)〉である.**(担保にする)→約束・契約をする→深くかかわる**.
派 engagement (婚約, 取り決め)
関 mortgage (担保); wage (賃金)〔←労使間の契約〕

He seems to be *engaged* [=involved] in illegal drug transactions. 彼は不法な麻薬の取引に手を染めているらしい.

I don't like to ⌈*engage* in a long conversation [=talk for a long time] over the phone. 電話で長話をするのは嫌いだ.

I had to refuse because of a *prior engagement*. 先約があるので断わらなければならなかった.

enhance /ɪnhǽns/

語源は〈en (する) hance=high (高い)〉である.**価値や質を高める**.
派 enhancement (高揚, 向上)

Those students' motivation for learning has been *enhanced* [=increased] dramatically after applying a new teaching method. 新しい教授法を導入すると, 学生たちの学習意欲は劇的に向上した.

The government aims to *enhance* [=improve] social welfare systems. 政府は社会福祉制度の向上をもくろんでいる.

enjoy /ɪndʒɔ́ɪ/

語源は〈en (中へ) joy (喜び)〉である. **(〜の喜びの中へ入る) →楽しむ**.
派 enjoyable (楽しい); enjoyment (楽しみ)
関 joy (喜び)

Now you can *enjoy* movies and music on your smart phone.　今ではスマホで映画や音楽が楽しめる.

I really ⌜*enjoyed* myself at [=*enjoyed*] the concert.　コンサートはとても楽しかったよ.

enormous /ɪnɔ́ːrməs/

語源は〈e (はずれる) norm (基準) ous (様子)〉である. **並はずれている, 桁はずれである**.
関 norm (基準, ノルマ); normal (通常の)

Most dinosaurs were *enormous* [=massive] in size.　たいていの恐竜は巨大であった.

Enormous [=Gigantic] waves generated by the earthquake that hit the northern coast of the island.　地震による巨大な波が島の北岸を襲った.

enough /ınʌ́f/

語源は〈e (ちゃんと) nough (手に入れる)〉である. **どうやら十分である→どうやら (必要に) 間に合う→程よい**.

We have ⌈*enough* time [=time *enough*]⌉ to finish the project.　プロジェクトを完成させるには十分時間がある.

He is*n't* smart *enough* to go to college.　彼は大学へ行くほど頭がよくない.

You can overcome these problems, if you are determined *enough*.　やる気さえあれば, これらの問題は克服できるよ.

You should drive *fast* enough on the expressway.　高速道路では適切な速度で運転しないとだめだよ.

---

ensure /ınʃúər/

語源は〈en (する) sure (確か)〉である. **物事の起きることを確実にする, (達成や質などを) 保証する**.
関 sure (確かで); surely (確かに)

This carefully controlled low-fat, low-calorie diet will *ensure* [=make sure] you lose weight.　この入念に調整された低脂肪・低カロリーの食事療法で確実に減量できる.

This mark *ensures* [=guarantees] the quality of the product.　このマーク (印) は製品の質を保証するものだ.

enter /éntər/

原義は〈～の中へ〉である．**(場所に) 入る**, **(活動に) 入る**.
派 entry (加入)；entrance (入口)

When I *entered* the woods, a monkey appeared out of nowhere.　森に入るとサルが 1 匹ひょっこり (どこからともなく) 現れた．

When did you *enter* college?　いつ大学に入ったの．　▶特定の大学なら enter the college とする．

Why did Japan *enter* the war against the allied forces?　なぜ日本は連合軍と戦争を始めたの．

entertain /èntərtéin/

語源は〈enter (間に) tain (保つ)〉である．**互いの間の関係を取りもつ→相手をもてなす**.
派 entertainer (芸人)；entertainment ([自分をもてなす] 娯楽, [他人をもてなす] 接待)
関 maintain (維持する)

I'll be home late this evening. I have to *entertain* customers after work.　今夜は遅くなるよ．仕事が終わってからお客さんの接待があるのでね．

How do you *entertain* yourself when you're home alone?　家で一人の時はどう (過ご) しているの．　▶entertain oneself「一人で楽しく過ごす」

He is one of the most popular *entertainers* in Japan.　彼は日本で最も人気のある芸人の一人だ．

Watching sports on TV is my favorite form of *entertainment*.　テレビでスポーツ観戦するのは私の大好きな娯楽 (の形態) だ．

entire /intáiər/

語源は〈en（否）tire（触れる，欠ける）〉である．**あれもこれも欠けることなく全ての・全部の**．
派 entirely（完全に）

My father spent his *entire* [=whole] life in his hometown, working on a farm.　父は農業をしながら生まれ故郷で生涯過ごした．

I am in *entire* [=complete] agreement with his view.　彼の意見に大賛成だ．

Sorry for the failure, which was *entirely* [=completely] my fault.　うまく行かなくてごめんなさい．すべて私が悪かったのです．

environment /inváiərnmənt/

語源は〈environ（周りを囲む）ment（状態）〉である．**人の生活に影響を及ぼす周りのありさま，環境**．
派 environmental（環境の）

To create a better working *environment*, smoking has been banned in our office.　快適な労働環境にするために，私たちの職場は禁煙になっている．

I want to raise my children in「a rich natural *environment* [=rich natural surroundings].　子どもは自然の豊かな環境で育てたいと思う．

equal /íːkwəl/

1+1+1=3

語源は〈equ（平ら）al（である）〉である．**等しい→釣り合う→向き合う仕事をこなす能力がある**．
派 equality（平等）；equally（等しく）；equation（方程式）
関 equinox（春分，秋分）〔←等しい＋夜〕

The length of the day and night is almost *equal* on the spring and fall *equinox*.　春分と秋分の日は昼と夜の長さがほぼ等しい．

Will you cut the pizza into eight *equal* pieces?　ピザを8等分してくれますか．

Five times five *equals*［＝is *equal* to］25.　5×5は25です．

Robert is an expert negotiator; there is no one else who is *equal* to the task.　ロバートは交渉のベテランだ．この仕事をこなせるのは彼をおいて他にはいないよ．　▶be equal to ～「～に対応できる」

equip /ɪkwíp/

原義は〈装備する〉である．**器具や設備を備える**．
派 equipment（設備，用具）

The kitchen is *equipped* with a refrigerator, dishwasher, microwave oven, and all the standard cooking utensils.　この台所は冷蔵庫，皿洗い機，電子レンジ他一般調理用具がすべて備わっている．

The victims were poorly *equipped* for camping in the snowy mountain.　遭難者たちは雪山でキャンプするには装備が不十分だった．

What kind of *equipment*［＝gear］do you need for a long-distance bicycle trip?　自転車旅行にはどんな装備が要りますか．

equivalent /ɪkwívələnt/

語源は〈equi(等しく) valent(価値がある)〉である。**一方の数量・価値がもう一方の数量・価値と同じである**。
関 value(価値)

There was a time when one US dollar was *equivalent* [=equal] to 360 Japanese yen.　1米ドルが360円(と同じ価値)の時代があった。

Applicants for the position must have a bachelor's degree or *equivalent* qualification.　この職の志願者は学士号かそれに同等する資格を有することが必要である。

Japan's Diet is the *equivalent* [=counterpart] of America's Congress.　日本の国会は米国の議会に相当する。

escape /ɪskéɪp/

語源は〈es(外へ) cape(外套(がいとう))〉である。**(外套を脱ぎ捨てる)→拘束の場から脱出する、難を逃れる**。
関 capture(捕らえる); cape(外套)

Did anyone ever *escape from* this prison?　この刑務所から脱獄した人が今までにいますか。

People often drink to *escape from* stress and pain in our lives.　人は生活のストレスや苦痛から逃れるためによく酒を飲む。

I narrowly *escaped* a car accident when a front tire of my car blew out.　前輪のタイヤがパンクした時、危うく事故を起こしそうになった。

All the passengers just got out of the bus before it caught fire. It was *a narrow escape*.　乗客全員はバスが火を吹く直前に脱出した。危機一髪であった。　▶a narrow escape「かろうじて難を逃れること」

essence /ésns/

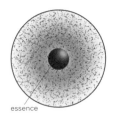

原義は〈実在すること〉である．**実在の中心にあるもの→本質，核．**
派 essential（不可欠な，中核をなす）; essentials（不可欠なもの）; essentially（本質的に）
関 presence（存在）

The *essence* of education is to provide students with knowledge and skills necessary for happy and fulfilled lives.　教育の本質は，生徒に幸福で充実した生活をするための知識と技能を与えることだ．

Flexibility is *essential* [=crucial] to any athlete.　柔軟性はすべての運動選手に不可欠だ．

Computer skills are one of the basic *essentials* [=necessities] for students' success.　コンピュータの技能は，学生が好成績を修めるための基本的必須事項の一つだ．

establish /istǽbliʃ/

原義は〈e（ちゃんと）stablish（確立する）〉である．**しっかり打ち立てる→確立する，創設する．**
派 establishment（確立，施設）　関 stable（安定した）

When and by whom was the university *established* [=founded]?　この大学はいつ，誰によって創立されたのですか．

His guilt was *established* [=confirmed] through DNA testing.　彼の有罪は DNA 鑑定によって確定した．

The hotel is located very close to business *establishments* such as restaurants, supermarkets, and banks.　このホテルは，レストラン，スーパーマーケット，銀行などの商業施設にとても近いところにある．

estimate /動 éstəmèɪt, 名 éstəmət/

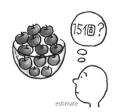

原義は〈(数量の) 狙いをつける〉である．**数量や価値を見積もる，推し量る；見積り**
派 estimation (評価，見積り)
関 aim (狙う)；esteem (尊重する)〔←価値を置く〕

I *estimate* that we've spent about ¥1,500,000 on the project up to now.　このプロジェクトに今まで約 150 万円かかった計算になる．

"What is the *estimated* age of the Earth?" "The Earth is *estimated* to be 4.6 billion years old."　「地球の推定年齢はどれくらいですか」「地球はほぼ 46 億年と推定されています」　▶4.6 billion＝four point six billion

What is your *estimate* of the total cost of living as a student in the UK?　英国では学生の生活費の総額は概算でいくらになりますか．

eternal /ɪtə́ːrnl/

語源は〈etern (永遠) al (の)〉である．**果てしなく長く続く．**
派 eternity (永遠)；eternally (永遠に)

Eternal

"Is our soul *eternal* [＝immortal] after death?" "It is an *eternal* puzzle of life, I think."　「死後も魂は生き続けるの？」「それは生命の永遠の問題だと思う」

Is there anything that continues to exist *eternally* [＝through *eternity*]?　永遠に存在し続けるものって何かありますか．

ethnic /éθnɪk/

原義は〈民族の〉である. **ある民族の, ある民族特有の**.
派 ethnicity（民族意識）

This restaurant serves a variety of *ethnic* dishes, from Mexican, Middle Eastern to Asian.　このレストランではメキシコ, 中東, アジアまでのさまざまな民族料理を出す.

Ethnic identity used to play an important role in getting a job in the US.　米国では, どの民族に属するかが就職の場合に重要な要件であった.

The number of employees from *ethnic* minority groups has increased in our company.　わが社では少数民族出身の従業員が増えた.

evaporate /ɪvǽpərèɪt/

語源は〈e（外へ）vapor（蒸気）ate（する）〉である.
蒸発する；蒸発させる.
派 evaporation（蒸発）　関 vapor（蒸気）

Water is continuously *evaporating* from the ground and the sea through solar energy.　水は大地や海から太陽エネルギーによって絶えず蒸発している.

Your body loses moisture through *evaporation* from pores in the skin.　人体は皮膚の毛穴からの蒸発によって水分を失う.

even /íːvn/

原義は〈平ら〉である.**(双方が) 同等である；(〜であってもやはり同じである)→それでもなお，それでもやはり.**
派 evenly (均等に)

The score is still *even* [=tied] *after* the 8th inning. 得点は8回を終わってまだ同点だ．

An *even number* can be divided by two with no remainder. 偶数は2ですっきり〔←余りなしで〕割り切れる． ▶an odd number「奇数」

The boys performed very well, *even though* they lost the finals. 決勝戦では敗れたけれど少年たちはとてもよくやった．

My father goes out for a walk, *even when* it rains hard. 父は雨のひどい時でも散歩に出かける．

evening /íːvnɪŋ/

原義は〈遅い時間〉である.**(日没時) 夕刻，夕方，(日没後就寝時までの時間) 晩，夜．**一日を日照時間で分けると day (昼) と night (夜)，生活時間帯で分けると morning (朝)，afternoon (午後)，evening (晩) になる．

We usually spend the *evening* watching television. 夜はたいていテレビを見て過ごす．

Venus is the first star that can be seen in the western sky in the *evening*. 金星は夕方，西の空に見られる一番星だ．

event /ivént/

語源は〈e (出る) vent (来る)〉である. **(起きてくる) 出来事・事件**. 日本語の「出"来"事」と発想が同じ.
派 eventual (最終的な); eventually (結果的に)

The police are looking for people who witnessed the *event* [= incident]. 警察は事件の目撃者を探している.

His encounter with the teacher was an *event* that changed his life completely. その先生との出会いは彼の人生を一変させた〔←一変させる出来事だった〕.

He *eventually* [=finally] rose to the position of vice president. 彼はついに副大統領の地位にまで昇りつめた.

ever /évər/

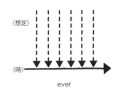

原義は〈常に, いつでも〉である. **どんな時でも, すべての時を含めて**.
関 evergreen (常緑樹, 常緑の)

Do you *ever* go to the movies? 君は映画に行くことはあるの?

I think Pele is the best soccer player *ever* [=of all time]. ペレは歴代最高のサッカー選手だと思う.

And they lived happily *ever* after. そして二人はいつまでも幸せに暮らしました. ▶昔話の終わりの常套句.

Did you *ever* see a catfish? =Have you *ever* seen a catfish? (今までに) ナマズを見たことある?

every /évri/

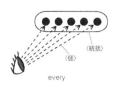
every

語源は〈ever(全て)y(において)〉である. **全ての, あらゆる**. 各個体に注目しながら, それら個体の全部を総括的に捉える.

Every cell in your body needs oxygen to live. 身体の全ての細胞は生きるために酸素を必要とする.

The rescue team made *every* effort [=all possible efforts] to save the victims. レスキュー隊は被災者を救うために最善を尽くした.

The bus leaves the airport *every* 30 minutes. 空港から30分ごとにバスが出ている.

evidence /évədəns/

evidence

語源は〈e(外へ)vid(見える)ence(状態)〉である. **内に潜む存在をはっきり外に出して見せるもの(証拠・根拠)**.
派 evident(明白な);self-evident(自明の)
関 video(ビデオ)

There is enough *evidence* that smoking is responsible for lung cancer. 喫煙が肺癌の原因になるということには十分な証拠がある.

Is there any *evidence* to support your assertion? 君の主張を裏付ける証拠がありますか.

It is *evident* [=obvious] that the existing pension system won't be sustainable for future generations. 現行の年金制度が将来の世代にわたって維持できないことは明白である.

It is *evident* [=clear] to everyone that he is involved in the incident. 彼がその事件に関与していることは誰の目にも明らかだ.

evolve /ɪváːlv/

語源は〈e (外へ) volve (転がす)〉である.**(巻物を開く)→展開する→進化する**.
派 evolution (進化);evolutionary (進化の)
関 involve (巻き込む);volume (本,巻物)

Darwin argued that humans and apes *evolved from* a common ancestor.　ダーウィンは,人間とサルとは共通の祖先から進化したと主張した.

These fossils reveal how fish *evolved into* four-legged land animals.　これらの化石を見ると,どのように魚が四足の陸上動物に進化したかが分かる.

Darwin's *theory of evolution* isn't compatible with what the Bible says.　ダーウィンの進化論は聖書の内容と矛盾する.

exact /ɪgzǽkt/

語源は〈ex (尽くす) act (行う)〉である.**突き詰めた→厳密な**.
派 exactly (厳密に)

Do you remember the *exact* date when the symptoms began?　この症状が初めて出たのは正確には何日だったか覚えていますか.

The police have been unable to identify the *exact* cause of the accident as of now.　警察はこれまでのところ,事故の原因をはっきりと特定できていない.

I'm not *exactly* sure, but maybe the hard disk went wrong.　はっきりは分からないけど,たぶん,ハードディスクの故障だよ.

I remember *exactly* where I was and what I was doing on September 11, 2001.　同時多発テロの日,自分がどこで何をしていたかはっきり覚えているよ.

examine /ɪɡzǽmən/

語源は〈ex（しっかり）amine（計る）〉である．**じっくり調べる→検査する→試験する**．
派 examination（試験，調査）

I have my teeth *examined* [=checked] by a dentist periodically.
定期的に歯医者に歯を診てもらっている．

The security guard *examined* [=checked] my identification card and allowed me to enter the premises. 守衛は僕の身分証明書を調べて構内へ通してくれた．

We have a final *examination* [=test] at the end of the course. この講座の終わりに最終試験がある．

You are supposed to take an annual medical *examination* [=checkup].
毎年，健康診断を受けることになっている．

excel /ɪksél/

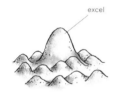

語源は〈ex（外へ）cel（上がる）〉である．**抜きん出る，傑出する**．
派 excellent（優れている）；excellence（優秀さ）

My son ⌈*excelled* in [=was good at] math and became a science student. 息子は数学がよく出来たので理系に進んだ．

The MC did ⌈an *excellent* [=a very good] job at keeping everything moving smoothly. 司会者がすばらしく全てが順調に進んだ． ▶MC=Master of Ceremonies「宴会・儀式の司会者」

The company is known for its technical *excellence*, quality innovation, and the service. この会社は技術の優秀さ，品質の改善およびサービスのよさで知られている．

except /ɪksépt/

語源は〈ex（外へ）cept（取る）〉である．**外へ取り出す→取り除く；〜を除いて**．except は目的語に名詞の他，前置詞句，that 節，wh 節をとる．
派 exception（例外）；exceptional（例外的な）

Everyone was excused *except* John who picked the fight. けんかを仕掛けたジョン以外は皆許してもらえた．《except+名詞》

It will be sunny across the whole country *except* in the area of Kanto. 関東地方を除いて全国的に晴れるでしょう．《except+前置詞句》

I walk every day *except* when it rains heavily. 雨がひどい時以外は毎日，ウォーキングします．《except+wh- 節》

The food was pretty good *except* that it was a bit too spicy for the kids. 料理は子どもたちには少し辛すぎたけどとてもおいしかった．《except+that 節》

exchange /ɪkstʃéɪndʒ/

語源は〈ex（外へ）change（変える）〉である．**やりとりする，交換する；交換**．
関 change（変える）

We *exchange* business cards to introduce ourselves to each other. 互いの紹介のために名刺を交換する．

The residents had a meeting to *exchange* opinions and ideas about the security of the community. 住民は集会を開いて，地域の安全について意見や考えを出し合った．

Where can I *exchange* yen *for* US dollars? 円の米ドルへの両替はどこでできますか．

excite /ıksáıt/

語源は〈ex (外へ) cite (呼ぶ)〉である．**興奮を呼び起こす→わくわくさせる**．
派 excited (興奮した)；exciting (興奮させる)；excitement (興奮)

The legendary hero has *excited* the imagination of writers and artists for a long time.　この伝説的英雄は昔からずっと作家や画家の想像力を刺激してきた．

He is very *excited about* becoming a father soon.　彼はもうすぐ父親になるのでわくわくしている．

It's very *exciting* to see a friend again after many years of absence.　長年会っていない友との再会はとてもわくわくする．

excuse /ıkskjú:z/

語源は〈ex (外へ) cuse (責める)〉である．**責めをそらせる→許してやる**．
関 accuse (責める)

The women employees with young children have been *excused* from working overtime.　幼い子どものいる女性従業員は残業を免除されている．

Mom eventually *excused* me as I promised not to tell lies again.　もううそはつかないと約束したので母さんはやっと許してくれた．

Excuse me for not having answered your email sooner.　メールの返事が遅れたことをお許しください．

To be *excused* [＝To take a leave of absence] from work on medical grounds, you need a doctor's certificate.　健康上の理由で会社を休むには医者の証明が要る．

execute /éksəkjùːt/

語源は〈ex (外へ) secute (追求する)〉である。**とことんやり通す→計画を遂行する;(刑をやりぬく) 極刑にする**.
派 execution (遂行; 処刑); executive (重役, 高官)〔←業務の遂行者〕

The company is going to *execute* [=carry out] a CO_2-reduction plan suggested by the government. この会社は政府の勧める二酸化炭素削減計画を実行する予定である.

He was tried and *executed* [=put to death] as a spy from the enemy country. 彼は裁判にかけられ, 敵国のスパイだとして処刑された.

exercise /éksərsàɪz/

語源は〈ex (外へ) ercise (囲い)〉である。**拘束を解いて行動する, 潜在する力を行使する, 運動する; 運動**.

Police powers must be *exercised* [=used] with respect to people's human rights. 警察権力は人々の人権を尊重して行使されねばならない.

How much ⌈do I need to *exercise* [=*exercise* do I need] to lose weight? 減量するにはどれくらい運動すればいいのですか.

Walking is said to be one of the best *exercises* for keeping fit. ウォーキングは健康維持にいちばんよい運動の一つと言われている.

exhaust /ɪgzɔ́ːst/

語源は〈ex(外へ)haust(吐き出す)〉である. **エネルギー・資源を出し尽くす；排気ガス→疲れ果てさせる**.
派 exhausting(ひどく疲れる)

Conventional energy resources, such as fossil fuels, will be *exhausted* [=used up] in the not-too-distant future.　化石燃料のような従来のエネルギー資源は，遠くない未来に使い果たされるだろう.

Car *exhaust* affects our environment.　車の排気ガスは環境に悪影響を与える.

I'm *exhausted* [=tired out] after a hard day's work.　今日は忙しかったのでくたくただ.

Today was the most *exhausting* [=tiring] day; we had three tests one after another.　今日はとても疲れる日だったよ. つぎつぎと3つも試験があったんだ.

exhibit /ɪgzíbɪt/

語源は〈ex(外へ)hibit(持つ)〉である. **(内にあるものを外へ持ち出す)→見せる→展示する；展示会**.
派 exhibition(展示会)

The award-winning photos are now *exhibited* [=on *exhibit*] at a local gallery.　入賞写真は地元の画廊で展示中だ.

Mozart *exhibited* [=showed] his amazing talent for composition in his childhood.　モーツァルトは子ども時代にすばらしい作曲の才能を発揮していた.

exist /ɪgzíst/

語源は〈ex(外へ)(s)ist(立つ)〉である.**(外に立つ)→ちゃんと存在する**. be(いる・ある)を強調した語.
派 existing(現在ある);existence(存在)
関 resist(逆らう)〔←反対に+立つ〕

Fossils are the remains of a plant or animal that *existed* sometime in the distant past. 化石とは遠い昔のある時期に存在した動植物の遺骸である.
▶ remains「残存物」((常に複数形で))

Many believe that newspapers would「cease to *exist* [=disappear] in the near future. 新聞は近い将来なくなるだろうと思う人がたくさんいる.

Most are unhappy with the *existing* [=ongoing] pension system. ほとんどの人が現行の年金制度に不満をもっている. ▶ unhappy=dissatisfied「不満である」

expand /ɪkspǽnd/

語源は〈ex(外へ)pand(張る)〉である.**(バーンと広がる)→四方八方へ広がる**. pan- は〈破裂して四方八方へ広がる〉イメージ. 類義語 extend は,ある一定方向への広がりについていう.
派 expansion(拡張)
関 panacea(万能薬)〔←全部+治療〕

Normally, things *expand* [=become larger] when heated and contract when cooled. 通常,物は熱せられると膨張し,冷やすと収縮する.

I'm introverted, have no friends outside of the work place; how should I *expand* [=widen] my social circle. 私は内向的で,職場以外には友達がいません. どうしたら社交の輪を広げられるでしょうか.

expect /ikspékt/

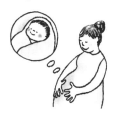

語源は〈ex(外へ)pect(目をやる)〉である. **かなたを見やる→前もって推測する, 予期する, 期待する.**
派 expectation(予測, 期待); expectancy(予測値); expected(予想される)

A natural disaster comes when ⌈least *expected* [=you least *expect* it]. 天災は思わぬときにやってくるものだ.

The response from our customers has been much better than (we) *expected*. 顧客の反応は予想よりうんとよい.

When you do good to others, do you *expect* something in return? 他人に親切にした時に見返りを期待しますか.

She is *expecting* [=going to have a baby]. 彼女は赤ちゃんが生まれる.

expend /ikspénd/

語源は〈ex(出す)pend(重さを計る)〉である. **(価値を計って代価を出す)→(金・時間・労力)を費やす.**
派 expense(出費); expensive(値段が高い); expenditure(支出) 関 spend(費やす)

Even when you are asleep, your body *expends* [=uses] energy. 寝ている時でも身体はエネルギーを使っている.

If you have a health insurance, you will pay 30 percent of your medical *expenses* [=costs]. 健康保険があれば医療費の3割を払うことになります.

I normally avoid *expensive* restaurants or hotels. 高価なレストランやホテルはたいてい避ける.

We tried to survive by limiting *expenditures*. 支出を抑えて生き残りを図った.

experience /ɪkspíəriəns/

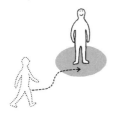

語源は〈ex (ちゃんと) peri (試みる) ence (こと)〉である. **やってみること→経験, 体験；体験する, 感じる.**
派 experienced (経験豊かな)
関 peril (危機)〔←大変な体験〕; experiment (実験); expert (経験豊かな専門家)

Do you have any *experience* of [=Have you ever *experienced*] living abroad?　海外生活の経験がありますか.

Check with your physician if you *experience* [=feel] any pain or discomfort that concerns you.　気になる痛みや不快感があったら医者に診てもらいなさい.

He is a very *experienced* surgeon, having performed more than 500 heart transplants.　彼は500件以上もの心臓移植を行っているベテラン外科医だ.

expire /ɪkspáɪər/

語源は〈ex (外へ) pire (息をする)〉である. **(息を吐き尽くす)→息絶える→期限が切れる.**
派 expiry (期限切れ); expiration (期限終了); expiry [expiration] date (賞味期限)
関 inspire (発奮させる)〔←入れる+息〕

The wounded man *expired* [=breathed his last breath] before the ambulance arrived.　負傷者は救急車の到着前に息絶えた.

The term of the incumbent governor will *expire* [=come to an end] next spring.　現知事の任期は来春で切れる.

Don't let your driving license *expire* by mistake. =Don't forget to renew your driving license.　運転免許証の更新を忘れたらだめだよ.

explain /ikspléin/

語源は〈ex（外へ）plain（平ら）〉である. **(平らにして出す)→難しいことを平たく言う**.

派 explanation（説明）　関 plain（平易な；平原）

The president *explained* [=made clear] the company's management policy to the new employees.　社長は新入社員に会社の経営方針を説明した.

Let me *explain* to you [=give you an *explanation* of] why we should embark on the new enterprise.　なぜこの新規事業に乗り出すべきかを説明します.

explode /iksplóud/

語源は〈ex（外へ）plode（パ〜ンとたたく）〉である. **パ〜ンと破裂する・爆発する**.

派 explosion（爆発）；explosive（爆発性の, 爆発物）

I looked outside and saw fireworks *exploding* beautifully in the night sky.　外を見ると，花火が夜の空に美しく大きな音を立てて打ち上がっていた.

The world's first atomic bomb *exploded* over Hiroshima on August 6, 1945.　世界で最初の原子爆弾が1945年8月6日広島上空で炸裂(さくれつ)した.

There was a gas *explosion* in the coal mine and many miners were killed or injured.　炭鉱でガス爆発があり，多くの坑夫に死傷者が出た.

exploit /ɪksplɔ́ɪt/

語源は〈ex(外へ)ploit(折り込んだ)〉である. **(埋もれているものを外へ出す)→活用する→うまく利用する→つけこむ**.
派 exploitation (活用, 搾取)
関 explicit (明白な)〔←外へ+折り込んだ〕

Lots of corporations in advanced countries are *exploiting* [=taking advantage of] low-wage labor in developing countries.　先進国の多くの企業が発展途上国の安い労働力をうまく利用している.

The corporation was attempting to *exploit* [=take advantage of] a tax loophole.　その会社は税法の抜け穴につけ込もうとしていた.

explore /ɪksplɔ́ːr/

語源は〈ex(外へ)plore(あふれる)〉である. **気持ちが外に向かう→未知の領域をあちこち探る・巡り歩く**.
派 explorer (探検家)

The government intends to *explore* [=look for and find] every possibility of settling the dispute amicably by direct negotiation with South Korea.　政府は韓国と直接交渉を行って, 論点を友好的に解決できるあらゆる可能性を模索する意向である.

The hotel is located near Yokohama Port and China Town and offers a convenient location from which to *explore* Yokohama.　このホテルは横浜港や中華街に近いので, 横浜の散策には絶好の起点になります.

export /動 ɪkspɔ́ːrt, 名 ékspɔːrt/

語源は〈ex（外へ）port（運ぶ）〉である．**外へ運ぶ→輸出する；輸出，データを移す**．
派 exporter（輸出国，輸出業者）
関 import（輸入する）

Japan *exports* vehicles to many countries; its *exports* of cars, trucks, and buses rose 2.3% in April from a year earlier.　日本は車を多くの国に輸出している．同国の乗用車，トラック，バスの輸出高は，前年の 4 月に比して 2.3% 伸びた．　▶exports「輸出高」《複数形》

I would like to know how to *export* [=send] Excel data to a Word document.　エクセルのデータをワードの文書に移す方法を教えてください．

India is the world's largest producer and *exporter* of tea.　インドは世界最大の紅茶の生産国であり輸出国である．

expose /ɪkspóʊz/

語源は〈ex（外へ）pose（置く）〉である．**覆いをはいで中身をさらす→身をさらす→さらけ出す**．
派 exposed（露出した）；exposure（さらすこと）
関 pose（ポーズをとる）

Sara was wearing a short shirt that *exposed* [=showed] her belly button.　サラはへそが見える短いシャツを着ていた．　▶belly button=navel「へそ」

Rub sunscreen on the *exposed* parts of your body if you have to spend a long time in the sun.　日なたに長くいるときは，露出しているところに日焼け止めを塗りなさい．

Continuous *exposure* to loud noise may damage hearing.　ひどい騒音に絶えずさらされていると，聴力に障害が起きることがある．

express /iksprés/

語源は〈ex(外へ)press(押す)〉である.**(感情や考えを外へ押し出す)→表現する**.
派 expression(表情,表現,数式)
関 impress(印象づける);press(押す)

Try to *express* yourself clearly in your own words.　自分の考えを自分のことばではっきり表現するように努めなさい.

Words cannot *express* [=I cannot find words to tell you] how much I miss you.　どれほどあなたを恋しく思っているかことばでは表現できません.

She looked at me with a confused *expression* [=look] on her face.　彼女は困惑した表情でぼくを見た.

In the *expression* x+y=7, x would be 2 if y is 5.　数式 x+y=7 において,yが5ならxは2になる.

extend /iksténd/

語源は〈ex(外へ)tend(伸ばす)〉である.**ある方へ向けて伸ばす→延長する**.extend は〈線的拡がり〉,expand は〈面的・汎方向的拡がり〉のイメージ.
派 extension(拡張,延長);extensive(広範囲にわたる);extent(範囲,程度)　関 attend(出席する)

Please *extend* [=also send] my regards to the rest of your family.
ご家族のみなさんによろしくお伝えください.

Cutting the stem underwater will *extend* [=lengthen] the life of cut flowers.　水切り(水中で茎を切る)をすると切り花の寿命を延ばせる.

To report breaking news on a train accident, NHK's evening news was *extended* by 30 minutes.　列車事故の特報のために,NHK の夕方のニュースは30分延長された.

extinct /ɪkstíŋkt/

語源は〈ex(外へ)tinct(突く)〉である.**(突いて外へ出された)→存在が消された**.
派 extinction(絶滅) 関 extinguish(火を消す)

"When did dinosaurs become *extinct*?" "They ⌈went *extinct* [=died out]⌋ about 65 million years ago." 「恐竜はいつごろ絶滅したの?」「恐竜は6500万年前頃に絶滅した」

Frogs around the world are ⌈on the brink of *extinction* [=in danger of dying out]⌋. 世界中のカエルが絶滅の危機に瀕している.

extinguish /ɪkstíŋgwɪʃ/

語源は〈ex(外へ)tinguish(突く)〉である.**(火の存在を押しのける)→火を消す**. 同義の put out(火を消す)はこの語源をなぞっている.
派 extinguisher(消火器)(fire extinguisher ともいう)
関 extinct(絶滅した);sting(刺す)

To *extinguish* [=put out] a fire most effectively, aim the *extinguisher* nozzle at the base or center of the fire. もっとも効果的に消火するためには,消火器のノズルを火の元か中心に向けなさい.

If the fire is bigger than you are, it's too big to put out with an *extinguisher*. もし火が人より大きくなっていたら,消火器で消すことはできない.

extreme /ɪkstríːm/

語源は〈extre (外) me (最も)〉である. **(一番外の→普通から一番離れている)→極端な**.
派 extremely (極度に)
関 extra (余分の); exterior (外の)

My mother has an *extreme* [=radical] view on abortion and calls an abortionist a murderer.　母は中絶について極端な考えを持っていて、中絶をする医者のことを「殺人者」って言うのよ.

If you pee outside in an *extremely* cold region, your pee will freeze before hitting the ground.　極寒の地の戸外でおしっこをすると、おしっこが地面に着くまでに凍ってしまう.

eye /áɪ/

原義は〈目〉である. **目, 見抜く力;(好奇・疑心の)目で見る, 視線を投げる**.

I'm just going out for a moment. Will you keep an *eye* on the kids?　ちょっと出かけてくるので、子どもたちを見ていてくれない？

I couldn't believe my *eyes* when I saw my name on the list of winners.　当選者リストに自分の名前を見た時は目を疑ったよ.

John saw a man who was *eyeing* [=looking at] him suspiciously.　ジョンは自分を怪しげに見つめている男の姿が目に入った.

fabric /fǽbrɪk/

原義は〈巧妙につくったもの〉である. **(巧妙に編み上げた) 布地, (巧妙に組み上げた) 組織**. fa- は〈つくる〉の意味合い.
派 fabrication (でっち上げ); fabricate (でっち上げる)〔←ことばを巧妙に紡いでうそ話をつくる〕
関 factory (工場)

The *fabric* [=cloth] is soft to the touch and feels good on the skin. この生地は触れるとやわらかで肌触りがよい.

Can the Internet change and enrich the *fabric* [=structure] of our society? インターネットが我々の社会の構造を変えて豊かにできるだろうか.

The woman *fabricated* [=invented] a story about being assaulted in the street. その女性は通りで襲われたと, うそ話をでっち上げた.

face /féɪs/

原義は〈(造作された) 顔〉である. **顔, 面; 面する, 直面する**. fa- は〈つくる〉の意味合い. 顔は造作の極み.
派 facial (顔の)　関 surface (表面)

It was so windy and blowing right in my *face*. 風がとても強くて顔にまともに吹きつけた.

The owner *faced* [=confronted] a serious problem that was beyond his control. オーナーは自分ではどうしようもない難問に直面した.

This living room ⌈*faces south* [=looks to the south]⌉ so you can enjoy sunshine. この居間は南向きなので日当たりがよい.

facilitate /fəsíləteìt/

語源は〈facility（容易）ate（する）〉である．**物事の成就をはかどるようにする**．
派 facilities（施設）〔←活動を助けるための設備〕; facilitation（取りまとめ）; facilitator（進行役）
関 facile（安易な）; faculty（学部）

There are many language aids available that will *facilitate* your language learning [=make your language learning more efficient]. 言語学習を効率的にする言語教材がたくさんある．

You can enjoy various hot spring *facilities*, such as an open-air bath, a sauna, and a fitness room. 露天風呂，サウナ，フィットネス・ルームなどいろいろな温泉施設が楽しめます．

fact /fækt/

語源は〈（成された）こと〉である．**実際に起こったこと，事実，現実**．fact- は〈つくる，成す〉の意．
派 factual（事実上の）
関 factory（工場）; fiction（作り話）

It is a *fact that* countless wars have been caused by religious differences. 宗教の違いが原因で幾多の戦争が起こっているのは事実である．

The government could no longer ignore the *fact that* unemployment was still rising. 政府は失業率が依然高くなっていることをもはや無視するわけにいかなかった．

How old were your children when you taught them *the facts of life*? 赤ちゃんがどうやって生まれるのかを教えたのは，お子さんが何歳の時でしたか．
▶ the facts of life「（子どもに教える）生殖の事実」

factor /fǽktər/

語源は〈fact (つくる) or (人・物)〉である. **(物事を成り立たせる・生み出す) 要因**.
関 faction (〔つくる〕派閥, 党); fashion (〔形づくる〕様式)

Finding a job that matches your interest is an important *factor* in your happiness.　興味と一致する仕事を見つけることが幸せの大切な要因だ.

One's physical appearance should never be a *factor* when hiring an employee.　容姿が雇用の際の条件になってはならない.

factory /fǽktəri/

語源は〈fact (物をつくり出す) ory (場)〉である. **工場, 製造所**.
関 fabric (織物); fact (事実); manufacture (製造する)

He owns a furniture *factory* in the suburbs.　彼は郊外に家具製造所を持っている.

The firm is outsourcing their clothing manufacturing to *factories* in China.　この会社は衣服の製造を中国の工場に委託している.　▶outsource「(業務を外部の組織に) 委託する」

faculty /fǽkəlti/

原義は〈facul(容易につくる)ty(こと)〉である.**(物事をこなす)才能→(才能を有する集団)→教授陣,教員団,学部**.
関 facility(器用さ)

This robot has the *faculty* of speech. このロボットは話す能力がある.

He worked for a private research institute before becoming a *faculty* member at Waseda University. 彼は早稲田大学の教員になる前は民間の研究所に勤めていた.

The *faculty* [=teaching staff] meet(s) every second Tuesday of the month at 3:00pm. 教師たちは毎月第2火曜日の午後3時から会議をする.
▶ faculty は集合名詞で,〈ひとまとまり〉と感覚すると単数扱い,〈複数の構成員〉と感覚すると複数扱い.

---

fade /féɪd/

原義は〈衰弱する〉である.**色や活力がだんだんと衰える**.

Red paint *fades* [=discolors] faster than other colors. 赤色の塗装は他の色よりもはやくあせる.

As time passed, my memories of the summer I spent with him slowly *faded away* [=grew dim]. 時がたつにつれて,彼と過ごした夏の思い出はだんだんと薄れていった.

fail /féɪl/

原義は〈不足する〉である.**(期待に届かない)→うまくできない,ちゃんとやらない;失敗する.**
派 failure（失敗, 不履行）
関 false（偽りの）; fault（過失）

Students who *failed* math have to repeat it.　数学（の単位）を落とした学生は再履修を受けないといけない.

When forced to prove that he was drug free, the athlete *failed* to show up for a dope test.　薬物使用をしていないことを証明すべきだと言い渡されているのに, その選手はドーピング検査に現れなかった.

failure /féɪljər/

原義は〈fail（できない）ure（こと）〉である.**(期待通りにならない)失敗, 機能不全, 怠慢.**
派 fail（失敗する）

After several business *failures*, Steve Jobs rose to become the head of a global enterprise.　スティーブ・ジョブズ氏はいくつかの事業で倒産を経験したが, 世界的企業のトップに上りつめた.

A power *failure* brought the train to a stop in the tunnel for an hour.　停電で電車はトンネル内で1時間立ち往生した.

If not taken as instructed, this medicine may result in liver *failure*.　指示どおりに服用しないと, この薬は肝臓疾患を起こすことがある.

faint /féɪnt/

原義は〈見せかけの〉である．**かすかに感じる，わずかにある**．
派 faintly（かすかに）　関 feign（ふりをする）

There is still a *faint* [=slight] hope that she may be cured.　彼女が治る希望はまだわずかにある．

The room retained a *faint* [=slight] smell of her perfume.　部屋には彼女の香水のかすかな匂いが残っていた．

I don't have the *faintest* [=slightest] idea of what the stock market is like.　株式市場がどんなものかちっともわからないわ．

There are billions of stars that are too *faint* [=dim] to be seen by your eyes.　肉眼では見えないかすかな光の星が何十億とある．

fair¹ /féər/

原義は〈美しい〉である．**(わだかまりがなくすっきりして) 公平・正当な，天気がよい，相当な→まずまずの**．
派 fairly（相当，かなり）

Do women get *fair* treatment at your work place?　あなたの職場では女性は公平な扱いを受けていますか．

The *fair* [=fine] weather has been predicted to hold until this evening.　この好天は今夕までもつと予報されている．

I found that the house for sale was in *fairly* [=rather] good condition.　売りに出ている家はかなりよい状態だったよ．

fair² /féər/

原義は〈祭日〉である. **農業祭→品評会→見本市, 展示会, 博覧会**.
関 festival (祭り)

Each year agricultural *fairs* [=shows] are held in many places across the country during the harvest season. 毎年,収穫期に全国各地で農業祭が催される.

The Tokyo International Anime *Fair* attracts the attention of people throughout the world every year. 東京国際アニメフェアは毎年, 世界中の人々の関心を呼んでいる.

faith /féɪθ/

語源は〈fai (信頼する) th (こと)〉である. **(自分・他者・ことば・神への) 信頼**.
派 faithful ((心が) 正直である, 〔記述が〕本当である)

After such series of scandals, it's very hard to restore people's *faith* in politics. こんなスキャンダルの連続では, 人々の政治への信頼を回復することは難しい.

The guide dog is very *faithful to* its master and it always tries to protect him from any dangers. その盲導犬は主人にとても忠実で, どんな危険からも主人を守ろうとします.

She gave a *faithful* [=true] account of what had happened to her. 彼女は身の上に起こったことを正直に話した.

fake /féɪk/

原義は〈(本物に)似せる〉である. **似せる；偽物；偽りの**.

The man's signature in the hotel register was ⌜a *fake* [=*faked*]. 男のホテルの宿泊名簿の署名は偽りであった.

Does the actor have *fake* [=artificial] hair of some kind or is it his own? この俳優は髪に何か細工してるの,〔←かつらあるいは添え髪〕それとも地毛なの?

Don't you think her boobs look *fake*? 彼女の胸はうそっぽくないか?
▶ boobs=breasts「胸」

fall /fɔ́ːl/

原義は〈(支えを失って)落ちる〉である. **落ちる, 倒れる, (ある状態に)落ち入る**.

They say that Isaac Newton discovered the law of gravitation by seeing an apple *fall* from a tree. アイザック・ニュートンは, リンゴが木から落ちるのを見て万有引力の法則を見つけたそうだ.

Several roadside trees *fell* in the storm last night. 昨夜の嵐で街路樹が数本倒れた.

My son works very hard late into the night but constantly *falls behind*. 息子は夜遅くまでよく勉強するのに, いつも周囲から後れをとっている.

I had a hard time *falling* asleep after seeing the movie. その映画を見た後, なかなか寝つけなかった.

false /fɔ́ːls/

false

原義は〈真実を裏切る〉である．**本当でない，偽っている**．

派 falsely（誤って），falsify（ごまかす）；fallacy（〔真実を裏切る〕誤った考え）

関 fail（失敗する）〔←期待を裏切る〕

The prime minister gave a *false* [=unfounded] hope to people by pledging what he was not sure if he could do.　首相は，できるかどうか確信のないことを公約して，人々に虚しい期待を与えてしまった．

I only wear *false* [=fake] eyelashes when I go out.　つけまつげをするのは外出の時だけです．

He had been imprisoned for many years on *false* [=wrong] *charges*.　彼は冤罪(えんざい)（無実の罪）で長年投獄されていた．　▶on ～=due to ～

It is a *fallacy* [=false notion] that the function of the brain declines as we grow older.　年を取ると脳の働きが衰えてくるというのは誤った考えである．

fame /féɪm/

原義は〈人びとがよく話題にする〉である．**評判，名声**．

派 famous（有名な）；famed（有名な）

関 fate（運命）〔←神が告げる〕；fable（物語）；infant（小児）〔←否+話す〕

David Beckham won international *fame* [=renown] as a peerless soccer player in Great Britain.　デビッド・ベッカムは英国の抜群のサッカー選手として国際的に有名になった．

Honolulu is *famous* [=known] *for* Waikiki beach and Diamond Head.　ホノルルはワイキキビーチとダイアモンドヘッドで有名だ．

familiar /fəmíljər/

아 이 우 에 오
unfamiliar

語源は〈family（家族）ar（的な）〉である．**（家族のように）よく知っている，親しみのある，打ち解けた．**
派 familiarity（十分な知識）；familiarize（慣れさせる）；family（家族）

あ い う え お
familiar

I majored in engineering, and so I'm *familiar* [=at home] *with* using computers.　工学を専攻したのでコンピュータの使い方には通じている．

It was so good to have seen so many old *familiar* faces at the class reunion.　同窓会で多くの昔馴染みの顔に会えたのはとても楽しかった．

family /fǽmli/

原義は〈住人〉である．**家族→（同種の）族・群．**
派 familiar（親しい）

"How big is [=How many members are there in] your *family*?" "We are a *family* of four with two kids aged 6 and 8."　「家族は何人ですか」「4人家族で，6歳と8歳の子どもがいます」

"Do you know that a tiger is a member of the cat *family*?" "Yes, it looks like a big cat with black stripes."　「トラはネコ科だということを知ってる？」「知ってるよ，トラは黒の縞のある大きな猫みたいだ」

I hope my son will take over the *family business* after graduation.　卒業後は息子に家業を継いでもらいたいと思っている．

famine /fǽmɪn/

語源は〈fam(飢え)ine(状態)〉である．**不作による食糧不足，飢饉(きん)**．
関 famish(飢えさせる)

Millions of Africans are suffering from starvation and disease brought on by *famine*.　何百万人ものアフリカ人が飢饉のもたらす飢えや病気で苦しんでいる．

Unless the current warming trend is stopped, many areas of the world will be threatened by periodic droughts and *famines*.　現在の温暖化傾向が止められないと，世界の各地は周期的に干ばつと飢饉に脅かされることになるだろう．

fan /fǽn/

原義は〈熱狂的な人〉である．**(有名人・スポーツチームなどの)ファン**．fan は fanatic(熱狂者)の短縮形．
派 fanatic(狂信的な)

I'm *a* big *fan of* Murakami Haruki; I get and read his new book as soon as it is published.　私は村上春樹の大ファンで，発売されるとすぐに買い求めて読みます．

I am a baseball *fan* [＝lover], particularly, a Hanshin Tigers *fan*.
僕は野球が大好きで，とくに阪神タイガースのファンです．　▶lover「愛好者」

fancy /fǽnsi/

原義は〈想い描く〉である．**(ちょっとした) 思いつき，空想；〜したいような気がする；(空想的な) おしゃれですてきな，高級な．**
関 fantasy (夢想)

Mike's interest in becoming a singer is not just a passing *fancy* [=whim]; he has applied to a music college.　マイクの歌手になるという気持ちは気まぐれじゃないよ．音楽大学に志願してるんだから．

Fancying [=Imagining] himself the Sakamoto Ryoma of politics, he left the party for his principle.　彼は政界の坂本龍馬たらんとして，信念を貫くため離党した．

We had dinner at a very *fancy* [=elegant] restaurant in Ginza.　銀座のとてもすてきなレストランで食事をした．

---

fantasy /fǽntəsi/

原義は〈思い描く〉である．**(非現実的なことを思い描く)→夢想・幻想．**
派 fantastic (素晴らしい) 〔←夢見るような〕
関 fancy (空想)

In the story a girl named Alice falls down a rabbit hole into a *fantasy* [=magical] world populated by strange creatures.　物語の中では，アリスという名の少女がウサギの穴に落ちて，奇妙な動物たちの住む不思議の国へ行く．

Most girls *have a fantasy* of being loved by a strong and handsome guy.　女の子ならたいてい強くてハンサムな人に愛されることを夢見るものだ．

The trip was *fantastic* [=wonderful] in every way, and each day passed as if in a dream.　この旅はすべてが素晴らしく，毎日が夢のようだった．

far /fάːr/

原義は〈越えて〉である．**遠くに，遠くから，はるかに；反対側の．**

How *far* down [=How deep] can you dive?　君はどれくらいの深さまで潜れる？

How *far* apart should I plant tulip bulbs?　チューリップの球根はどれくらいの間隔で植えたらいいの？

The beam of the lighthouse can be seen from as *far* as 20 kilometers away.　この灯台の光は20キロも離れた所から見える．

From Earth, we cannot see the *far* [=other] side of the moon.　地球から月の裏側を見ることはできない．　▶the near [=front] side of the moon「月の表側」

fare /féər/

原義は〈行く〉である．**事を進めていく，やっていく；(旅をするための) 料金・運賃，(食卓に出す) 料理．**

I wonder how the children are *faring* [=doing] after their parents divorced.　両親が離婚してから子どもたちはどうしているのかしら．

What's the *fare* from Hakata to Tokyo by *Shinkansen*? [=What is the *Shinkansen* fare from Hakata to Tokyo?]　博多から東京までの新幹線の料金はいくらですか．

Vegetarian dishes are now standard *fare* [=menus] in many restaurants in America.　野菜料理は，多くのアメリカのレストランで標準メニューになっている．

farm /fάːrm/

原義は〈農作物〉である.**(作物を耕作したり家畜を飼育したりする)農場；飼育する,(魚などを飼育する)養殖場；養殖する.** 元来は地代として「定期的にちゃんと納める農作物」の意で，firm（ちゃんと固定した）と関連がある．
派 farmer（農場経営者）；farming（農業）
関 firm（しっかりした）

Nearly all the food that we eat comes from crops and livestock raised on *farms*. 私たちの食べる食料のほとんどは，農場で育てられる農作物と家畜によっている．

Oyster *farming* [＝aquaculture] is very popular in Japan. 日本ではカキの養殖がとても盛んだ．

In general, people prefer the taste of wild fish to that of *farmed* [＝farm-grown] fish. 一般に，人は養殖魚よりも天然魚の味を好む．

fashion /fǽʃən/

語源は〈fash（つくる）ion（こと）〉である.**特定の形(形式・流儀),今の形(流行);形づくる.**
派 fashionable（流行の）　関 factor（要因）

My son wears underwear as outerwear, as is the *fashion* right now. 息子は下着を上着として着ているが，これは今はやりのファッションです．

Brush your hair *in this fashion* [＝way] for at least 5 minutes every day. 毎日，少なくとも5分間はこのようなやり方で髪をブラッシングしなさい．

I can swim *after a fashion* [＝to some degree], but I'm certainly not as good as you. どうにか泳げるけれど，君のようにうまくは泳げないよ．

The exterior of the aquarium was *fashioned* [＝modeled] after the shape of a dolphin. この水族館の外観はイルカの形を模して造られている．

fast /fǽst/

原義は〈力を込めて〉である．**力を込めて速く・しっかり，じっくり**．
派 fasten（ぐいと締める）; fastener（ファスナー）

The pitcher can throw a ball *as fast as* 160 kilometers per hour. この投手は 160 キロもの速球が投げられる．

I keep my watch five minutes *fast*. 私は時計をいつも 5 分進めている．

We tied the boat *fast* to the pier. ボートを桟橋にしっかりつないだ．

I was *fast* [=sound] asleep and didn't feel the earthquake. ぐっすり眠っていたので地震には気づかなかった．

Fasten your seatbelts as we are taking off shortly. 間もなく離陸しますのでシートベルトを締めてください．

fat /fǽt/

原義は〈脂肪のかたまり〉である．**でっぷり太った**．
派 fatty（脂肪分の多い）

My dad is slim build but he is beginning to put on *fat* [=weight] around the belly. 父さんは細身だけど，おなかの周りに脂肪がつき始めている．

Fat [=Overweight] people are likely to develop high blood pressure, or cardiovascular diseases. 肥満だと高血圧や心臓血管の病気になりやすくなる．

People who are under stress tend to reach for *fatty* and sugary foods. 人はストレスがあると脂っこいものや甘いものを欲しがるようになる．

fatal /féɪtl/

語源は〈fate (運命) al (の)〉である．**死ぬことになる，やがて死ぬ→一大事である**．運命の行きつくところは死である．
派 fatally (致命的に)；fatalities (死亡者)

If left untreated, most cancers ⌈are *fatal* [=lead to death]． 治療しないでいると，ほとんどのがんは命取りになる．

There appears to be a *fatal* flaw in his marketing strategy． 彼の市場戦略には致命的欠陥があるように思う．

The mayor's reputation was *fatally* damaged by losing the case. 敗訴によって市長の評判は致命的打撃を受けた．

The number of traffic *fatalities* [=deaths] in Japan has been on the decline in recent years． 日本の交通事故死者数は近年減少傾向にある．

fate /féɪt/

原義は〈神により告げられしこと〉である．**(神のお告げ) 天命，運命，(究極の運命) 死，滅亡．**
派 fatal (死に至る)
関 fable (おとぎ話)；fame (名声)

She has never complained about her illness, just accepts it as her *fate* [=as being inevitable]． 彼女は自分の病気について不平をもらしたことがなく，自分の宿命としてしっかり受け入れている．

The governor's ⌈*fate* was sealed [=luck ran out] with the discovery of bribery from a construction company． 建設会社からの収賄が発覚して知事の命運は尽きた．　▶seal [=decide] one's fate「人の運命を決定づける」

fatigue /fətíːg/

原義は〈使い尽くす〉である. **心身の疲労**.

Recently, I began to feel ⌈unusual *fatigue* [=unusually tired] after a day's work.　最近，一日の仕事の後，ひどい疲れを覚えるようになった．

He fell down in bed, worn out with *fatigue* both physically and mentally.　彼は心身ともに疲れ切ってベッドに倒れ込んだ．

My grandfather can do more than 20 push-ups without *fatigue* [= without getting tired].　おじいちゃんは平気で〔←疲れることなく〕20回以上も腕立て伏せができるよ．

fault /fɔ́ːlt/

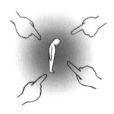

原義は〈期待を裏切る〉である.**(不注意による) 過失，誤り，(出来が完全でない) 欠陥**．
関 fail (失敗する)

The mother said, "It's my *fault* that my son got autism."　母親は「息子が自閉症になったのは自分のせいだ」と言った．

My husband is always *finding fault with* the way I do things. Even the smallest things seem to be major issues to him.　夫はいつも私のやり方に文句ばかり言う．ささいなことでも彼には大ごとみたいなの．　▶find fault with ～「～のあら探しをする」

fatal, fate, fatigue, fault

favor /féɪvər/

favor

原義は〈好きな気持ちが湧く〉である．**好意，賛成**．
派 favorite（大好きな）；favorable（好都合な）；favorably（好都合に）；favoritism（えこひいき）
関 fever（熱）

Would you mind doing me a *favor*?　お願いがあるのですが．▶他に，Could you do me a *favor*? / Could I ask a *favor* of you? / Could I ask you a *favor*? などという．

Are you *in favor of* capital punishment or opposed to it? ＝Are you for or against the death penalty?　死刑に賛成ですか，それとも反対ですか．

The wind is blowing in a *favorable* direction [＝*favorably*] for the ski jumpers.　風向きはスキージャンプの選手たちに有利になっている．

favorite /féɪvərət/

原義は〈favor（気に入り）ite（の人）〉である．**お気に入りの人・物，一番人気**．
派 favor（好意）；favoritism（えこひいき）

Who is your *favorite* writer [＝the writer you like most]?　一番好きな作家は誰ですか．

Parents should treat their children fairly without any *favoritism* [＝partiality].　親は子どもたちをえこひいきせずに公平に扱わねばならない．▶partiality「不公平，えこひいき」

In most cases, I think betting on the *favorites* is the best and the safest.　たいていの場合，本命に賭けるのが最善で一番安全だと思う．▶bet on the favorite「(競馬などで) 一番人気に賭ける」

fear /fíər/

原義は〈体験することに対する恐れ〉である. **恐れ, 不安;
体験することを不安に思う, 怖がる.**
派 fearful（恐れている）

As the interview came nearer, I ⌈was overcome by *fear* [=began to feel fear]. 面接試験が近づくと, 不安にかられた.

Just as I *feared* [=was afraid], my husband was sued for the possession of drugs. 恐れていたとおり, 夫が麻薬の所持で訴えられた.

My daughter has always been scared of water; how can I help her overcome her *fear* of water? 娘はいつも水にびくびくするの. どうしたら水の恐怖を克服させてやれるかしら.

Do you have a *fear* [=Are you *fearful*] of death? 死ぬのは怖いですか.

feature /fíːtʃər/

原義は〈身体・顔の造り〉である. **造り, 目鼻立ち→特徴→特別記事; 特徴とする, 特集する.**
関 feat（偉業）; feasible（実現可能な）

His *features* are sharp and well-defined, giving us an impression of a philosopher. 彼の顔は端正で彫が深く, 哲学者のような印象を与える.
▶ well-defined「輪郭がはっきりしている」

What are the *features* [=characteristics] of the new electric car?
新しく出る電気自動車の特徴はどういった点ですか.

What *features* or articles in this issue interested you most? この号で一番面白かった特集, あるいは記事は何ですか.

The magazine *features* the interviews with the new cabinet members.
この雑誌は新閣僚とのインタビュー記事を特集している.

fee /fíː/

fee

原義は〈奉仕に対して払う代金〉である.**(受益に対して払うべき)料金,謝礼**.領主が,土地の使用料を奉仕で払うことを条件に農民に与えた耕作地を feud と言ったことに由来する.
関 feudal(封建制の)

The medical school lasts six years and the tuition *fees* alone cost as much as 2,000,000 yen a year.　医科大は6年過程で,授業料だけでも年間200万円になる.

Shipping and handling *fees* are not included in the prices.　送料および手数料は定価に含まれていません.

feed /fíːd/

原義は〈食物を与える〉である.**動物にえさをやる,子どもや病人に食べ物を与える**.
関 breastfeed(赤ん坊を母乳で育てる);fed up(うんざりした);food(食べ物)

We *feed* our dogs [=Our dogs *get fed*] twice a day.　うちの犬には一日に2度えさをやる.

How long should I *breastfeed* my baby?　母乳を与える期間はどれくらいですか.

I'm ⌈*fed up* [=sick and tired] with TV commentators constantly criticizing others.　絶えず他人の批判ばかりしているテレビの評論家にはうんざりだ.

feel /fíːl/

原義は〈触れる〉である．**触れる→体に感じる→心に感じる→〜と思う**．
派 feelers（触角）; feeling（感覚, 雰囲気, 気持ち）

Your hands and feet *feel* cold when your blood circulation gets worse.　血液循環が悪くなると手足が冷く感じる．

The continents are moving all the time, although we cannot *feel* it.　知覚できないが大陸は常に移動している．

It always *feels* good *to* get into a cozy bed after a hard day's work.　一日の忙しい仕事の後，心地よいベッドに潜り込むのはいつも快感だ．

I *feel that* his essay is very good but can still be improved in some ways.　彼の論文はとてもいいけれど，まだ改善の余地があると思う．

I don't *feel like* doing anything today.　今日は何もする気がしない．

female /fíːmeɪl/

female　　male

原義は〈femina（乳を含ませる人）〉である．**(性別を意識して) 女性，雌；女性の，雌の**．元の femina が現在の female になったのは 14 世紀ごろで，male（男性）と対照させるためである．
派 feminine（女らしい）; feminism（男女同権主義, フェミニズム）; feminist（男女同権主義者）

The majority of the cases who develop osteoporosis are *females* [=women].　骨粗鬆(そしょう)症になる患者の大半は女性だ．　▶osteoporosis /àːstioupəróusəs/＝porous bone

Mrs. Chiaki Mukai was the first *female* [=woman] Japanese astronaut.　向井千秋さんは日本人最初の女性宇宙飛行士だった．

Can you distinguish male chicks from *female* chicks?　ひよこの雄雌の区別ができますか．

fertile /fə́ːrtl/

語源は〈fer（運ぶ）tile（性質をもっている）〉である．**(運ぶ→生み出す）→豊かに生み出す素地がある．** fer-〈運ぶ→生み出す〉は bear（運ぶ→生む），carry（運ぶ→生む）の意味の展開と同じ．
派 fertility（肥沃）；fertilize（土地を肥沃にする）；fertilizer（肥料）　関 ferry（フェリーで運ぶ）

The soil in this neighborhood is very *fertile* [=rich], producing large amounts of rice and wheat.　このあたりの土地はとても肥沃で，米や小麦がよくできる．

His new anthology is the product of the poet's *fertile* [=rich] imagination.　彼の新しい詩集は詩人の豊かな想像力のたまものだ．

When you apply *fertilizer* for [=*fertilize*] your plants, be sure not to overdose.　植物に肥料をやる時は，やり過ぎないように気をつけなさい．

fever /fíːvər/

原義は〈熱〉である．**(身体の不調による）熱→（気持ちの高揚による）熱狂．**
派 feverish（熱っぽい）
関 favor（〔気持ちを熱くして〕好む）

I would advise you to keep the baby in the hospital till the *fever* [=temperature] settles down.　赤ちゃんは熱が下がるまで入院させておくほうがいいと思いますよ．

If you go to London in June you can enjoy and feel the *fever* [=excitement] of Wimbledon Tennis Championships.　6月にロンドンに行けば，ウインブルドン・テニス選手権の熱気が感じられますよ．

few /fjúː/

原義は〈数がほんの少しだけ〉である．**少ない数を否定的に捉えると few，肯定的に捉えると a few** という．例えば，人数が約 20 人で，場所を夏の浜辺とするなら，「おや，今日は少ない」と思って，There are *few* people on the beach today. と発想するだろうが，もし同じ人数を厳寒の浜辺に見つけたら，There are *a few* people on the beach today. と描写するはずである．

This medicine causes *few* side effects. この薬は副作用がほとんどない．

This medicine causes *only a few* side effects. この薬は副作用がごくわずかにある．

This medicine causes a *few* side effects. この薬は副作用が少々ある．

This medicine causes *quite a few* side effects. この薬は副作用がかなりある．

fiction /fíkʃən/

語源は〈fic (つくる) tion (こと)〉である．**(頭で作る) 創作，(頭ででっち上げる) うそ，作り話**
派 fictional (架空の)；fictitious (でっち上げの)
関 fact (事実)

The movie is based on *fiction* [=fictional], but I think it's possible to happen in real life. この映画はフィクションだけど，現実の生活でも起こりうることだと思う．

The defendant's alibi turned out to be a complete *fiction* [=fabrication]. 被告のアリバイはまったくのでっち上げだった．

Sherlock Holmes isn't a real person; he is a *fictional* [=an imaginary] character created by Arthur Conan Doyle. シャーロック・ホームズは実在の人物ではなく，アーサーコナン・ドイルによる架空の人物だ．

field /fíːld/

原義は〈野原〉である．**野原，現地→（活動の）分野，競技場→球をさばく→質問をさばく．**

A spring breeze is gently blowing over a *field* of wildflowers.　春のそよ風が花の咲く野原をゆったりと吹いている．

He is an expert in the *field* of dentistry, specializing in implant treatment.　彼は歯科のベテランで，特にインプラント治療を専門にしている．

She took her class on *a field trip* to a fish market.　彼女はクラスの生徒を校外学習で魚市場へ連れて行った．　▶a field trip「実地見学旅行」

The presenter was poised and deftly *fielded* [=handled] questions from the floor.　発表者は落ち着きがあり，会場からの質問を上手にさばいた．

fight /fáit/

原義は〈けんかする〉である．**（敵と）戦う，（困難・障害と）闘う．**
派 fighter（戦士，戦闘機）　関 firefighter（消防士）

The couple stopped *fighting* [=arguing] over money after they separated their finances.　その夫婦は会計を別々にしてからはお金のことでけんかをしなくなった．

When the town announced that a nuclear power plant would be constructed, many residents decided to *fight* against the decision in court.　町が原発の誘致を発表すると，多くの住民はその決定に対して裁判で争うことを決めた．

figure /fígjər/

語源は〈fig (つくった) ure (もの)〉である．**(物事の実体・量を形に描き出した) 数字・表；(形を描く) 姿・人物；(実体・内容を描き出して) 理解する・表す**．

Business is certainly recovering in *figures* [=numbers], but we don't really feel it.　数字の上では景気は確かに回復してきているが，実感はない．

She woke up sensing something strange, and noticed a dark *figure* standing still outside the window.　彼女は異様な気配を感じて目を覚ますと，黒い人影が窓の外にじっと立っているのに気付いた．

I can't *figure out* [=understand] what the author is saying in the article.　この論文で著者が何を言わんとしているのか分からない〔←意味が描き出せない〕．

---

file /fáil/

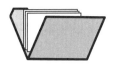

原義は〈ひも〉である．**書類をひもで綴じる→ファイルにする；ファイル→書類にして提出する**．ファイルの綴じ込み用具は〈ひも→バインダー→コンピュータ〉と変遷している．
関 filament (フィラメント)〔←ひもの形状をしている〕

You should save the *file* frequently as you do your work on the computer.　パソコンで仕事をする時は頻繁にファイルを保存する必要がある．

Many people *file* [=apply] for divorce on grounds of incompatibility.　性格の不一致を理由に離婚申請を出す人が多い．

Being dissatisfied with the judgment, the suspect *filed* [=brought] a lawsuit demanding a retrial.　容疑者は判決を不服として再審を求める申請を出した．

fill /fíl/

原義は〈いっぱいに満たす〉である．**容器・場所の空間を液体や物で満たす**．
派 filling（〔歯の〕詰めもの，〔パイなどの〕中身）
関 full（あふれるほどの）；fulfill（果たす，満たす）

We usually *fill* the bathtub halfway to save water.　水の節約のために，たいてい浴槽の半分までしか水を入れません．

I had a small cavity and got it *filled*.　小さな虫歯があったので詰めてもらった．

Don't forget to *fill out* the registration form.　登録用紙は記入漏れのないようにしてください．

final /fáɪnl/

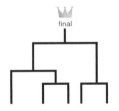

語源は〈fin（終わり）al（の）〉である．**最後に起きる，最後の→ことの成否を決定づける；決勝戦**．
派 finalize（試行錯誤を経て決定する）；finally（ようやく，最後には）
関 finish（終える）

They are making a *final* attempt to save the company from bankruptcy.　彼らは会社を破産から救うために最後の試みをしている．

Tiger Woods easily made the cut to advance to the *final* round.　タイガー・ウッズは予選を軽く通過し決勝ラウンドへ進んだ．　▶make the cut「〔ゴルフ〕予選を通過する」

Please let us know as soon as your itinerary ⌈is *finalized* ［＝takes shape］．　旅行の日程がはっきり決まったら知らせてください．

finance /fáɪnæns/

語源は〈fin(終わり)ance(にすること)〉である.**(終わりにする)→(購入・受益を代金の支払いによって完成させる)→資金の調達をする**.
派 financial(財政上の); financially(財政的に)
関 finish(完成させる)

That sounds like a good idea, but how will you *finance* [=get money for] the project? その企画はよさそうだけど,資金の調達はどうするのですか.

The young man traveled the world, *financing* [=supporting] himself by doing jobs along the way. 青年は先々で仕事をやって稼ぎながら,世界中を旅した.

Many department stores in Japan have been experiencing *financial* problems. 日本では経営不振の問題を抱えている百貨店が多い.

find /fáɪnd/

原義は〈出会う〉である.**(たまたま)見つける,(探して)見つける**.
派 finding(見つけること,見つけたこと,結果)

I thought you would be interested in this article that I *found* in the magazine. 雑誌で見つけたのだけど,この記事は面白いと思うよ.

Whales are *found* [=seen] in many oceans and seas around the world. クジラは世界中の多くの海洋や海域で見られる.

Don't you *find* that girl attractive? あの娘,いけてると思わない?

He is scheduled to present his *findings* from his six-month field study in Africa. 彼は6か月のアフリカでの現地調査で分かったことを発表することになっている.

fine /fáin/

原義は〈終わり〉である．**(完了している→仕上がっている)→罰金を課す；罰金→細かい→申し分ない→立派である**．原義の〈終わり〉はイタリア映画の FINE (= END) でお馴染み．
関 finish（完成させる）

When we arrived at Tokyo station, a *fine* [=misty] rain was falling outside.　東京駅に着いた時，外は霧雨が降っていた．

My boy was ill yesterday, but he's feeling *fine* [=better] today!　息子は，きのうは体調がすぐれなかったけど，今日はいいわ！

"We need about five days to fix it." "*That's fine*" [="OK"]!　「修理は5日くらいかかります」「かまいませんよ」

I was *fined* [=got a ticket ordering to pay] 5,000 yen for illegal parking.　違法駐車で5,000円の罰金を食らった．▶この fine は〈罰金を科す〉の意．罪を終わりにする (=始末する) ために罰金を科すことに由来．

finger /fíŋgər/

原義は〈(物をつかむ)指〉である．**指；指で触る**．足指は toe．
関 fist（握りこぶし）

On which *finger* do you wear a wedding ring?　結婚指輪はどの指にはめますか．

The little girl timidly *fingered* [=ran her *fingers* along] the carved tiger figurine.　少女は彫り物のトラの像に恐る恐る指をはわせた．

finish /fíniʃ/

語源は〈fin (終わり) ish (する)〉である. **終わりにする→完了する, 仕上げる；終わり.**
関 final (最終の); finance (財政); fine (罰金); define (明確にする)

There were a few elderly runners who *finished* [=completed] the race ahead of me.　僕より先にゴールしたお年寄りが何人かいたよ.

I don't like being forced to *finish* [=eat up] all the food I am served.　出された食事を全部残さず食べるように言われるのは嫌だよ.

If the truth becomes known, he is *finished* [=done for].　事実が知れると, 彼はおしまいだ.

As the race neared the *finish* [=end], it became a match race between two horses.　レースがゴール近くになると, 2頭のマッチレースとなった.

fire /fáɪər/

原義は〈火〉である. **火→火を放つ→弾を放つ→首にする.**
関 firearms (銃器); fireworks (花火); fuel (燃料); flame (炎)

The protesters ⌈*set fire to* many vehicles [=set many vehicles *on fire*] and hurled rocks at government troops.　抗議の人たちは多くの車輌に火を放ち政府軍に投石をした.

Cook the peas over a *low fire* for about 20 minutes.　エンドウ豆は弱火で20分ほど煮なさい.　▶ over a *high fire*「強火で」

A policeman can only *fire* [=*open fire*] in self-defense.　警官は正当防衛を条件とした時だけ発砲できる.

The manager was *fired* [=dismissed] because of the continuous poor performance of his team.　監督はチームの不振が続くので解雇された.

firm /fə́:rm/

原義は〈頑丈な〉である．**外からの力に抗してぐらつかない**．名詞では「会社，商社」の意であるが，原義の〈売買契約をしっかり行うところ〉に由来する．
派 firmly（確固として）
関 confirm（確認する）; farm（農場）

Make sure that your mattress is *firm* [=hard] enough to support your body.　マットレスは，体を支えるのに十分な堅さがあるものにしなさい．

We should stand *firm* against terrorism.　テロリズムには頑として屈しないことが大切だ．

He used to work for a trading *firm* [=company] in Kobe.　彼は以前，神戸の貿易商社で働いていた．

first /fə́:rst/

原義は〈fore（前の）st（最上級を示す）〉である．**一番目の，最初に現れる**．
関 fore（前の，前方の）; former（前の，元の）

Turn left at the *first* light and you'll see a parking lot ahead on your left.　最初の信号を左へ曲がると，左手前方に駐車場がありますよ．

What is the *first* thing you would do if you won a lot of money?　大金が手に入ったとして，まずやることは何ですか．

Former heavyweight champion Muhammad Ali appeared in public *for the first time* in decades.　元ヘビー級チャンピオンのモハメド・アリが数十年ぶりに〔←数十年で初めて〕大衆の前に姿を現した．

fish /fíʃ/

原義は〈魚〉である．**魚，魚類，魚肉；釣りをする→漁(する)る**．魚類は集合的に捉えて単複を問わないのが普通．fishes という時は種類が意識される．
派 fishery（漁場，漁業）；fishing（魚釣り）
関 fisherman（漁師）

I'm beginning to like *fish* better than meat as I get older.　年を取ってくると肉よりも魚が好きになってきた．

"How was the *fishing*?" "I caught about 30 trout."　「釣りはどうだった」「マスが 30 匹ほど釣れたよ」

He *fishes* for a living. ＝He is a professional *fisherman*.　彼は漁業で生計を立てている．

Everyone is always *fishing for* compliments and confirmation.　誰でもいつも人からほめられ，認められたがっているものだ．

fit /fít/

原義は〈ぴったり当てはまる〉である．**サイズ・形がぴったり合う→適する，ぴったりの**．

I often have trouble finding ⌈shoes that *fit* well [＝*well-fitting* shoes]⌉ because my feet are so wide.　僕は足幅が広いのでぴったり合う靴を見つけるのによく苦労する．

If you choose a career that doesn't *fit* [＝suit] your personality, you may become confused or unhappy.　性格に合わない職業に就くと困ったり落ち込んだりすることが多い．

Animals live in a world where only the *fittest* survive.　動物は最も環境に適するものだけが生き延びる世界に住んでいる．　▶the law of the survival of the fittest「適者生存の法則」

fix /fíks/

原義は〈くっつける〉である．**ちゃんと固定させる→(故障を)ちゃんと直す,(問題を)ちゃんと解決する．**
派 fixed（〔時間等が〕決められた）
関 prefix（接頭辞）〔←前+くっつける〕; suffix（接尾辞）〔←後+くっつける〕

I need someone to help me *fix* [=install] an air-conditioner onto the wall. 壁にエアコンを取り付けるのに誰か手伝ってくれる人が要る．

Would you check and *fix* [=repair] my PC that keeps freezing? パソコンがたびたびフリーズするのだけど，診て直してもらえない？

It's time for you to face the problem directly and take steps to *fix* [=resolve] it before it's too late. 手遅れにならないうちにその問題にちゃんと向き合って解決の手段をとる時期だ．

flag /flǽg/

原義は〈旗〉である．**旗; 垂れ下がる, 活力がなくなる．**
派 unflagging（衰えない）　関 flabby（たるんだ）

The enemy raised a white *flag* to signal their surrender after two days of bloody clashes. 敵は2日間の激戦の後，白旗を上げて降伏をした．

The runner who was leading the race was beginning to *flag*. 先頭を走っていた走者が疲れを見せ始めた．

flat /flǽt/

原義は〈平らな〉である．**平らな→ぺしゃんこ→(勢いがなくて) 気の抜けた**．
派 flatten (ぺしゃんこにする，台無しにする)
関 floor (床)

Most of the Netherlands is *flat*, though it has some hilly lands.　オランダはいくつかの丘陵地帯はあるが，ほとんどが平坦だ．

The car battery will go *flat* [=dead] if the lights are left on.　車のバッテリーはライトを点けたままにしていると上がってしまう．

I have *flat feet* [=am flat-footed] but can move just as well as anyone else.　僕は偏平足だけど，他の誰とも同じように運動できるよ．

I got a *flat tire* (while) cycling to work this morning.　今朝，通勤の途上で自転車がパンクした．

flavor /fléɪvər/

原義は〈(漂う) 香り〉である．**風味；風味を添える**．
派 flavoring (味付け，香料)

Keep the coffee beans in an airtight container to retain [=keep] their freshness and *flavor*.　コーヒー豆は，密封容器に入れて新鮮さと香りが逃げないようにしなさい．

Strawberry *flavoring* [=taste] in toothpaste make me gag.　練り歯磨きのイチゴの香りは吐きそうになるよ．

I like *mint-flavored* ice cream best.　ミント味のアイスクリームがいちばん好きだ．

flesh /fléʃ/

原義は〈(やわらかい) 肉〉である. **動物の肉, 魚の肉, 果物の果肉**.
派 fleshy (肉付きのよい); fleshly (肉感的な)

Animal *flesh* [=meat] is high in essential nutrients such as fat, protein, and minerals.　動物の肉は脂肪, 蛋白質, ミネラルといった必須栄養素を多く含んでいる.

The *flesh* [=meat] of the tuna is highly prized for use in sashimi.　マグロ (の身) は刺身の具としてとても珍重されている.

The *flesh* [=body] of the cherry is juicy and sweet, but the pit is inedible.　サクランボの果肉は甘くてジューシーだが種は食べられない.

Most *flesh-eating* [=carnivorous] animals prey on grass-eating animals.　たいていの肉食動物は草食動物を捕食する.

---

flex /fléks/

原義は〈曲げる〉である. **手足を曲げる**.
派 reflex (反射)〔←再び+曲がる〕; flexible (融通が利く); flexibility (融通性)

The wrestler *flexed* [=bent] his arms to show off his muscles.　レスラーは両腕を曲げて力こぶを見せびらかした.

Be stubborn with your vision, but *flexible* [=adaptable] with your plans.　理想にはこだわり, その (実現のための) 計画には融通性をもってあたりなさい.

The professor ⌈is *flexible* [=has *flexibility*]⌉ in his thinking, (being) ready to take young people's ideas into account.　あの教授は考え方に柔軟性があって, 若者の考え方を考慮する余裕がある.

float /flóut/

原義は〈浮かぶ〉である. **水面や大気の中でゆらゆら漂う**.

関 fleet（艦隊）〔←悠然と大洋に浮かんでいる〕; flow（流れる）

I like *floating* [=lying] on my back in the water, looking up at the blue sky and the white clouds. 海に仰向けに浮かんで, 青い空や白い雲を見るのが好きだ.

Oil is often seen *floating* on the water in and around the port. 港の中や周りで, 油が浮いているのをよく見かける.

Clouds of volcanic ash *floating* [=drifting] over Europe are causing many flight delays and cancellations. ヨーロッパ上空を漂っている火山灰の雲は, 多くの飛行便の遅れや欠航を引き起こしている.

flock /flá:k/

原義は〈羊の群れ〉である. **ふわふわした群れ; 群がる**.
牛馬の群れは a herd, オオカミ・猟犬などの群れは a pack という.

We saw *a flock of* goat grazing on the grassland. ヤギの群れが野原で草を食んでいた.

Many people *flocked* [=gathered] in front of the store and waited for the start of the sale of a revolutionary gadget named iPad. 多くの人が,「アイパッド」と名付けられた画期的な装置の発売開始を待って店頭に群がった.

Bats commonly fly *in flocks* [=in groups]. コウモリはふつう, 群れて飛ぶ.

flood /flád/

原義は〈あふれる〉である. **水があふれ出る;洪水**.
関 flow (流れる)

The company was *flooded* [=inundated] with orders from across the country after their product was featured on TV. テレビで製品が特集されると, 会社に全国から注文が殺到した.

Lots of people lost their homes and lands in the *flood*(s). 洪水で多くの人が家や土地を失った.

floor /fló:r/

原義は〈(平たい) 床(ゆか)〉である. **フロア, 階→底;床を張る**. カタカナ語のフローリングは通例〈木製の床材〉を指すが, flooring (床張り材) には, 木製 (wood) の他にコンクリート (concrete), タイル (tile), 石 (stone) などがある.
関 flat (平たい)

The exhibit of paintings and sculptures is on the library's third *floor* and is open to the public without charge. 絵画と彫像の展示は図書館の3階で催されており, 無料で一般公開している.

We have replaced the carpet in the living room with a hardwood *floor*. 居間のカーペットを板張りの床に変えた.

What kind of *flooring* is best for a kitchen? 台所に一番よいのはどんなフローリング (床張り) ですか.

flour /fláuər/

原義は〈flower=flour(小麦の花部分)をひいてつくった小麦粉〉である. **小麦粉, (穀物の) 粉**.
関 flower (花); flourish (栄える)〔←花+になる〕; soybean flour (黄粉(きな))

Dredge the chicken with *flour* [=*Flour* the chicken] before frying.
油で揚げる前に鶏肉を小麦粉でまぶしなさい.

Kanazawa *flourished* [=prospered] as a castle town in the Edo period.　金沢は江戸時代に城下町として栄えた.

flow /flóu/

原義は〈水が流れる〉である. **水がゆらゆら流れる, 髪がさらりと垂れている, 水があふれる, 潮が満ちる**. flo- は〈たゆたう水〉のイメージ.
関 flood (洪水); float (漂う)

The Ishikari River *flows* [=runs] through Asahikawa and Sapporo before reaching the sea.　石狩川は, 旭川, 札幌を抜けて海に流れ込んでいる.

My sister has long *flowing* hair that reaches her waist.　姉は, 腰まで届くほど髪を長く垂らしている.

In general, fish bite well when the tide is *flowing* [=coming] in.
一般的に, 潮が満ちてくる時に魚の食いがいい.

flower /fláuər/

原義は〈花がふっくら咲く〉である. **花・草花, 開花；開花する**. flo- は〈膨(ふく)らみ〉のイメージ.
派 flowery（花模様の）

The *flowers* are beginning to blossom and the trees are budding.
草花は咲き始め，木々は芽吹いている.

Cut *flowers* stay fresh for several days if they are taken care of properly.　切り花は適切な管理をすれば，数日間新鮮さが保てる.

"In which season do daffodils bloom?" "Daffodils *flower* in spring."
「ラッパスイセンはどの季節に咲きますか」「ラッパスイセンは春に咲きます」

The dogwood is *in flower* [＝bloom] just outside of our living room window.　居間の窓の外にハナミズキが花を咲かせている.

fluctuate /flʌ́ktʃuèɪt/

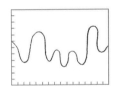

原義は〈ゆらゆら揺れる〉である. **（水準や価格が）上がったり下がったり揺れ動く**. flu- は〈波がゆらゆら〉のイメージ.
派 fluctuation（変動）
関 fluent（流れるような）；fluid（流動的な）

Currency exchange rates *fluctuate* [＝vary] continuously, being updated every 15 minutes.　通貨交換レートは絶えず変動しているので，15分ごとに更新されている.

Blood pressure *fluctuates* [＝goes up and down] during the course of a day.　血圧は一日の中で変動する.

fly /fláɪ/

原義は〈空中を飛ぶ〉である.**鳥や飛行機が空を飛ぶ,飛行機で飛ぶ;飛行機を飛ばす;時間が飛ぶように過ぎる**.
派 flight (飛行); flyer (ちらし, 飛行士)

He *flies* [=pilots] his own airplane.　彼は自家用機を操縦する.

You can 「*fly direct* [=take a direct *flight*] from Sapporo to Naha.
札幌から那覇へ直行便があります.

Time *flies* [=goes by fast] when you're having fun.　楽しい時は時間が過ぎるのが早いものだ.

What is the arrival time of the *flight* from Tokyo?　東京からの便は何時に到着しますか.

Most birds have hollow bones that are designed for *flight* [=flying].
ほとんどの鳥は飛翔 (ひしょう) のために骨が中空になっている.

focus /fóʊkəs/

原義は〈炉〉である.**(燃焼する所)→焦点・関心の中心;焦点を合わせる, 関心を集中させる**.
派 focal (焦点の)　関 fuel (燃料)

My *focus* right now is on losing weight as quickly as possible for the upcoming summer season.　今, 心がけていることは, 夏までにできるだけ早く減量することです.

"Do I have to *focus* the camera manually?" "No, this is auto-focus. All you have to do is point and press the button."　「このカメラは手動で焦点を合わせないといけないの?」「いや, 自動焦点だから, カメラを向けてボタンを押すだけでいいよ」

It takes a few seconds for our eyes to *focus* in the dark.　暗がりで目の焦点が合うには数秒かかる.

fog /fɑ́:g/

原義は〈立ち込めた霧〉である. **霧；霧が立ち込める**.
fog は〈濃い霧〉, mist は〈薄い霧〉の意味合い.
派 foggy（霧がかかっている, 〔思考などが〕もやもやしている）

I awoke to find that the area was covered in *fog* [＝the area *fogged* in]. 目を覚ますと辺りは霧に覆われていた.

At the start of our hike, it was still dark, and *foggy*. ハイキングに出かける時は, まだ暗くて霧がかかっていた.

Now, correct me if I'm wrong, because my memory's a bit *foggy* [＝unclear]. 私の記憶は少しあいまいだから, 間違っていたら直してくださいね.

The future of the new party is quite *foggy* [＝uncertain]; only time will tell. 新党がどうなるかは極めて不透明で, 時が経ってみないと分からない.

fold /fóuld/

原義は〈折る〉である. **折り重ねる, 包み込む**.
派 folder（紙ばさみ, フォルダー）〔←データをまとめて入れる容器〕 関 twofold（二重の, 二倍の）

Fold the napkin in half to form a triangle. ナプキンを半分に折って三角形を作りなさい.

Mom *folds* the laundry and puts it in piles for each person. 母さんは洗濯物をたたんで, 各人ごとに分けて積み重ねておく.

The use of electricity increased more than *twofold* last year. 昨年は電力使用量が 2 倍以上増えた.

follow /fá:lou/

原義は〈~の後をたどる〉である．**~の後を追従する，~の次に来る**．
派 follower（支持者，信者）

There are signboards along the road, so you can *follow* [=be guided by] them to the museum. 道路沿いに標識があるので，それに従って行けば博物館に着きます．

I don't watch soccer games on TV, but it's still fun to *follow* [=check] how the teams are doing on the internet. サッカーの試合はテレビでは見ないが，ネットでチームの様子を確かめるのはやはり楽しいものだ．

The instructor spoke quickly and unclearly, I couldn't *follow* what he was saying. 講師が早口で不明瞭な発音でしゃべったので，何と言っているのか分からなかった．

fond /fá:nd/

原義は〈ばかな〉である．**(ばかみたいに) 好きである**．
派 fondly（優しく）; fondle（いとおしむようになで回す）

Mom *is fond of* (singing) karaoke, and every weekend she invites several friends to sing with. 母さんはカラオケが大好きで，週末になると友だちを数人呼んで一緒に歌っている．

Those classmates who met for the first time in many years talked *fondly* [=nostalgically] about their good old days. 久しぶりに再会した旧友たちは，古きよき昔のことを懐かしむように話していた．

food /fú:d/

原義は〈食べ物〉である．**食べ物**，**食料**，**料理**，**糧**(かて)，**植物の栄養**．種類を強調する場合は複数形 foods を使う．
関 feed（食べ物を与える）

Rice is the staple *food* [=ingredient] in Japanese cuisine. 米は日本食の中心的食材である．

At most karaoke bars, they serve drinks and light *food*. たいていのカラオケ店では，飲み物と軽い食事が出る．

Plants make *food* [=nutrients] by photosynthesis. 植物は光合成によって栄養を作る．

This book provides plenty of *food for thought* for those who are going into the world. この本には，社会人になる人達に糧になることがたくさん載っている．

fool /fú:l/

原義は〈ふいご〉である．**(中身が空(から)っぽ)→内容がない人→ばか；ばかにする，ふざける**．
派 foolish（ばかな）

You can't *fool* me! ばかにしないでよ！

Bill has been *fooling* [=hanging] *around*, not trying to get a job. ビルは仕事を探そうともせず，ぶらぶらしている．

He felt like a *fool* for having trusted such a moneymaking scheme. 彼はあんなもうけ話を信用してばかなことをしたと思った．

It was *foolish* [=silly] of you to call an ambulance as you just felt a chill. 寒気がしたぐらいで救急車を呼ぶなんてばかげているよ．

foot /fút/

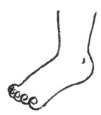

原義は〈足〉である. **足 (くるぶしから下の部分) →足元, 下部.**
関 footstep (足音, 足跡); footnote (脚注); barefoot (素足で, 素足の)

The boxer barely *got to his feet* [=stood up] before he was counted out.　ボクサーはノックアウトになる前にからくも立ち上がった.　▶レフリーは 10 カウントで KO の宣告をする.

My son has turned twenty; I think he should *stand on his own feet* [=take care of himself] now.　息子は 20 歳になりました. もう自立してもらわなければと思っています.

If you come across a question, use the Help button at the *foot* of the screen.　分からないことがあったら, 画面下のヘルプボタンを使いなさい.

---

for /fər/

原義は〈前へ向かう〉である. **(対象に気持ちが向かう) →〜のために, 〜へ向かって, 〜に対して, 〜の範囲で.**
関 fore (前の)

This train is (bound) *for* Tokyo and stops at the main cities along the way.　この列車は東京行きで, 途中, 主要都市に止まります.

What are you here *for*? =Why are you here?　何しにここに来たの?

What is this tool *for*?　この道具は何に使うの?

I'd like to sleep *for* a little while.　少し (の間) 眠りたい.

Mike felt sorry *for* what he had done to his brother.　マイクは弟にしたことを後悔した.

What is the weather forecast *for* today?　今日の天気予報はどうですか?

force /fɔ́ːrs/

原義は〈強い〉である．**(強い) 勢い，武力→力を出す→力で動かす→強制する**．類義語 power は「内に溜まっている力」，force は「外に噴出する力」といえる．
派 forceful（力あふれる）
関 effort（努力）〔←力を込める〕

The *force* of the wind knocked down many trees during the hurricane.　ハリケーンによる強風で多くの木々が倒れた．

Nobody *forced* [＝compelled] me to quit; it was my own decision.　私に辞めるよう誰が強いたわけでもありません．自分で決めたことです．

She was a little frightened and *forced* herself to relax [＝made an effort to relax].　彼女は少し怖かったので努めて平静になろうとした．

The late prime minister, Kakuei Tanaka, captivated the nation with his *forceful* [＝convincing] personality.　故田中角栄首相は力強い個性で国民を魅了した．

forecast /fɔ́ːrkæst/

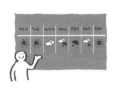

語源は〈fore（前もって）cast（投げる）〉である．**前もって予測・予想を投げかける；予測**．
派 forecaster＝weatherperson（天気予報士）
関 broadcast（放送する）

What is the weather *forecast* [＝report] for Fukuoka tomorrow?　明日の福岡の天気予報はどうですか．

Heavy rain is *forecast* [＝predicted] for the weekend.　週末は大雨の予報が出ている．

Japan's economic growth rate for the coming year is *forecast* [＝estimated] to be around two percent.　来年の日本の経済成長率はおよそ2％と予測されている．

foreign /fɔ́:rən/

原義は〈戸外に〉である。**(領域外の)→外国の→(自分とは)異質の→自分には縁がない**。
派 foreigner（外国人）
関 forest（森）〔←戸外にある場所〕

Try not to use *foreign* [=borrowed] words unless there are no Japanese alternatives.　日本語で表現できる場合は外来語を使わないようにしなさい。

Doing deskwork in an office all day is *foreign* [=alien] to Mike's nature, who is very active and energetic.　事務所で終日事務の仕事をするのは，とても活動的なマイクの性(しょう)に合わない。

The concept of same-sex partners is quite *foreign* [=unthinkable] to the older generation.　同性結婚という考えは年輩の世代にはとてもありえないことだ。

---

forest /fɔ́:rəst/

語源は〈for（越えて）est（ある）〉である。**(越えて向こうにあるもの)→森**。その昔，住居の向こうにあるものは森であった。
派 forestry（林業）　関 foreign（外国の）

The hunter went into the *forest* [=woods] in search of game.　猟師は獲物を求めて森に入った。

Many *forests* [=woodlands] in the world are facing serious threat of extinction due to human industrial activities.　多くの世界中の森林が人間の産業活動のために絶滅の危機に瀕している。

Some people cannot see the *forest* [=woods] for the trees. =Some people focus only on small details and fail to grasp the whole picture.　細かなところにとらわれて全体像が掴(つか)めない人がいる。〔木を見て森を見ず〕

forget /fərgét/

R
FOGET

語源は〈for（怠る）get（得る）〉である．**(持っていた物を失う)→記憶を失う→忘れる，うっかり物を置き忘れる．**
派 forgetful（忘れっぽい）
関 forsake（見捨てる）；forswear（誓って放棄する）

I'll never *forget* [=fail to remember] all the good and bad times we went through together.　苦楽を共に歩んだあの日々のことを決して忘れはしません．

You should learn to forgive and *forget* for the sake of your peace of mind.　心の平静のために，許して忘れることを覚えるべきだと思う．

Please ⌈don't *forget* [=remember] all your belongings when you get out of the bus.　バスから降りる時は忘れ物がないように気をつけなさい．

Being *forgetful* seems to be a normal part of aging.　忘れっぽくなるのは自然な老化現象ように思える．

---

forgive /fərgív/

forgive

語源は〈for（強く）give（与える）〉である．**(すっかり与える)→相手に譲る→過ちを許す．**
派 forgiveness（寛容）；forgiving（寛大な）
関 forbear（我慢する）；forbid（禁ずる）

Please *forgive* me for not answering you sooner.　返事が遅れてごめんなさい．

If you repent I will *forgive* you, but people in general are not that *forgiving*.　すまないと思うのなら許すけど，人はそんなに甘くはないよ．

I don't expect *forgiveness* [=to *be forgiven*] but please understand that I did not do it out of spite.　許しを乞うわけではありませんが，決して悪気（やるぎ）でやったのではないことは分かってください．

form /fɔ́ːrm/

原義は〈(固定した)形〉である．**形→体型→体調；形になる**．

派 formative (形成の)

Cold medicines are commonly taken *in the form of* [=as] tablets or capsules.　風邪薬はふつう，錠剤やカプセルの形で飲まれる．

We learned how a typhoon *forms* [=develops] and behaves in science class.　理科の授業で，台風がどうしてできるのか，どのような動きをするのかを学んだ．

What children hear and see around them during their *formative years* may have a lot of influence on their personal character.　子どもが成長期に自分の周囲で見聞きすることは，人格形成に大きな影響を及ぼすだろう．

---

formal /fɔ́ːrml/

formal　　casual

語源は〈form (形) al (に沿った)〉である．**形式的な，格式ばった，正規の**．

派 formality (儀礼的行為)《通例複数形》; formally (正式に)

"Yours faithfully" is too *formal* [=stiff] for usual email communication.　"Yours faithfully" は普通のメール交信には堅すぎる．

My father was not *formally* educated [=got no *formal* education] beyond grade school, but he made a great success in the construction business.　父は小学校を終えてから正式な教育を受けていないけれど，建設業で大成功した．

Being brought up in an open and casual culture, I hate *formalities* and ceremonies.　僕は開放的で気さくな環境で育ったので，儀礼的なことや儀式が嫌いだ．

former /fɔ́:rmər/

former

語源は〈form (前の) er (〜より《比較級》)〉である。**今より前の→以前の**.
派 formerly (以前は)　関 fore (前の)

I got the horrible news that a *former* colleague [=an ex-colleague] of mine was killed in a car accident.　職場の元同僚が交通事故で亡くなったというむごい知らせが入った.

Of the two plans, I personally prefer *the former* (to the latter).　2つの計画についていうと, 個人的には前者のほうが (後者より) いいと思う.

They hired a new hitting coach who had *formerly* [=previously] been playing for the Giants.　あのチームは, 昔ジャイアンツでプレーしていた打撃コーチを雇った.

forth /fɔ́:rθ/

語源は〈前方へ〉である. **前へ, 先へ**.
関 forthcoming (まもなくやって来る); fore (前の)

The plan for transforming the Japanese Archipelago was ⌈*put forth* [=announced] by the then prime minister, Kakuei Tanaka in 1972.　日本列島改造論は, 1972年に当時の首相だった田中角栄によって提案された.

An eyewitness finally ⌈*came forth* [=appeared] and said that the missing boy was killed.　ようやく目撃者が現れて, 行方不明になっている少年は殺されたと証言した.

Little kids love rocking ⌈*back and forth* [=to and fro] on a swing.　幼い子はブランコでゆらゆらこぐのがとても好きだ.

fortune /fɔ́ːrtʃən/

原義は〈運ぶこと・生むこと〉である.**(運ぶ)→運命→幸運→富・財産**. for- は fer-〈運ぶ・生む〉と同根：conifer（針葉樹）〔←松かさ＋生む〕, ferry（フェリー）
派 fortunate（恵まれている）；fortunately（運よく）

It's my *fortune* [=I'm fortunate] to have become friends with you. あなたと友だちになれて幸いです.

He lost much of his *fortune* [=money] on the stock market. 彼は株で多額の損失をした.

It was *fortunate* [=lucky] for him that the cancer was detected early enough. がんが早期発見できたのは彼にとって幸いだった.

forward /fɔ́ːrwərd/

語源は〈for（前）word（方向）〉である.**前方へ；転送する, 先へ進める；前衛**.

When a person becomes sleepy in a sitting position, the head falls *forward*. 人は, 座った状態で眠くなると頭は前へ垂れる.

Please *forward* this mail to anyone who might be interested in our events. このメールを私たちの催しに興味をもってもらえそうな人たちに転送してください.

We are ⌈*looking forward to*⌉ [=eagerly waiting for] the start of the baseball season. 野球のシーズンが始まるのを心待ちにしています.

He plays *forward* [=as a *forward*] for Kashima Antlers. 彼は鹿島アントラーズのフォワードだ.

fossil /fá:sl/

原義は〈fosse (掘った) ile (もの)〉である. **(掘り出された) 化石**.
派 fossilize (化石化する)

The coelacanth is a living *fossil* previously believed to have gone extinct at the time of the dinosaurs.　シーラカンスは，以前には恐竜の時代に絶滅したと考えられていた生きた化石である.

We must limit using *fossil* fuels by increasing solar energy use.　太陽エネルギーの活用を増やして，化石燃料の使用を抑えないといけない.

found /fáund/

原義は〈底〉である. **元・基礎を築く**.
派 founder (創業者)；foundation (創立, 財団)
関 fund (基金)；profound (底が深い)

Waseda University was *founded* [=established] by Okuma Shigenobu in 1882.　早稲田大学は 1882 年，大隈重信によって創立された.

Matsushita Konosuke was the *founder* of Panasonic Corporation, formerly known as Matsushita Electric Industrial Co.　松下幸之助は，以前は松下電器として知られていたパナソニックの創業者だ.

Foundations are organizations that aid research, cultural progress, and social welfare.　財団とは研究や文化の進展や社会福祉を援助する組織のことである.

fraction /frǽkʃən/

原義は〈壊れたもの〉である. **断片→ほんの少量；分数**.
関 fracture (破損)；fragile (壊れやすい)

A car accident can happen in ⌈*a fraction of* a second⌉ [=a matter of seconds] due to momentary carelessness.　車の事故はちょっとの油断で一瞬にして起こる.

Only *a fraction of* [=Only a small number of] seedlings survived the unusual cold weather in March.　3月の異常な寒さに耐え抜いた苗木はほんの一握りにすぎない.

Do you know how to convert a *fraction* into a percentage?　分数をパーセンテージ (百分率) に換えることができますか.

fragile /frǽdʒəl/

原義は〈frag (壊れ) ile (やすい)〉である. **衝撃を与えるとすぐに壊れる**.
関 frail (ひ弱な)；fraction (断片)

If you don't get enough calcium from your diet, your bones are likely to become *fragile* [=brittle].　食事から十分なカルシウムを取らないと骨がもろくなりやすい.

These glasses are very *fragile* [=breakable] and need to be packed properly to avoid breakage.　これらのグラスは壊れやすいので，破損しないように適切に梱包する必要があります.

frame /fréɪm/

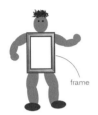

原義は〈枠〉である. **がっちりした枠, 額縁** (<ruby>額縁<rt>がくぶち</rt></ruby>), **フレーム；枠に入れる**.
関 framework（枠組み）

If we get trapped in a negative *frame* [=state] *of mind*, we only tend to see the dark side of things.　人は否定的な気分に陥ると, 物事の暗い面ばかり見る傾向になる.

He is a very tall man, with a muscular *frame* [=body].　彼はとても長身で筋肉質の体格をしている.

Why don't you ⌈*frame* the picture [=put the picture in a *frame*]?　この絵は額に入れたらどう?

frank /fræŋk/

原義は〈自由な〉である. **こだわりなく言える**.
派 frankly（率直に）; frankness（率直さ）

Could you give us your *frank* [=honest] opinion on this?　この点について忌憚 (<ruby>忌憚<rt>きた</rt></ruby>) のないご意見をいただけますか.

I think the author's description of the murder scene is too *frank* [=graphic] for young readers.　この著者の殺人現場の描写は, 若い読者にはあからさまに過ぎると思う.

Frankly [=To be honest], I don't understand people who don't give up smoking.　正直に言って, たばこを止めない人の気持ちが分からないわ.

fraud /frɔ́:d/

原義は〈ごまかすこと〉である. **詐欺 (さぎ), いんちき.**
派 fraudulent (詐欺の)　関 frustrate (いらいらさせる)

The doctor was arrested on suspicion of tax *fraud* [=evasion].　その医者は脱税容疑で逮捕された.

I think most of the weight-loss supplements are *fraudulent* [=phony].　たいていの減量に効くというサプリメントはいんちきだと思う.

free /frí:/

原義は〈解放されている〉である. **束縛 (権威・義務・弱点など) から解き放たれている.**
派 freely (自由に); freedom (自由)

What do you do in your *free* [=spare] *time*?　余暇には何をしますか.

I got this *free* [=for nothing].　これをただでもらった.

A large gas tank provides longer continuous operation, *free from* [=without] frequent refueling.　ガソリンタンクが大きいと, 頻繁に給油しなくても長く運転できる.

Please *feel free to* ask any questions.　質問があれば何でも遠慮なくお聞きください.

freeze /fríːz/

原義は〈凍りつく〉である. **(水・水道管・気持ち・パソコンが) 凍りつく**.
派 freezer (冷凍室); freezing (凍(い)てつくような)
関 frost (霜)

Does Niagara Falls *freeze* in winter?　ナイアガラの滝は冬には凍りますか.

I awoke this morning to find our water pipes completely *frozen*.　起きてみると, 水道管がすっかり凍っていた.

His blood *froze* [=ran cold] at the sight of roaring flames.　燃え盛る炎を見て彼は血の凍る思いがした.

Reboot your computer when it *freezes*.　パソコンがフリーズしたら再起動しなさい.

frequent /fríːkwənt/

原義は〈定期的に繰り返す〉である. **しばしば起こる, しばしば訪れる**.
派 frequently (頻繁に); frequency (多発, 頻度)

There are *frequent* [=many] flights between Naha and other large cities in Japan.　那覇と他の日本の大都市を結ぶ飛行便は多くある.

Typhoons are *frequent* in Japan [=often hit Japan] during summer and autumn.　日本では夏から秋にかけて台風がよく来る.

This lake is *frequented* [=visited] by many kinds of migratory birds.　この湖はいろいろな渡り鳥がよく来る.

fresh /fréʃ/

fresh

原義は〈生まれ出た〉である.**出来立ての,生き生きしている,新鮮な→生のまま→混じり気(塩分)がない**.
派 freshness(新鮮味)

I woke up *fresh* [=well-rested] after a good night's sleep.　よく眠ったのでさわやかな目覚めだったよ.

Vendors were selling various sea foods *fresh* from the ocean.　行商人が捕れ立ての魚介類を売っていた.

Grapes are eaten either *fresh* or dried.　ブドウはそのままでも干しても食べられる.

Some fish can live in either salt water or *fresh water*.　魚の中には海水でも淡水でも生きられるものがいる.

friend /frénd/

原義は〈好きな人〉である.**友人,友だち**.
派 friendly(好意的に)　関 friendship(友好関係)

We became *friends* when she was in my class last year.　私たちは去年,彼女が私のクラスにいた時に友だちになった.

Japan has long been America's best *friend* [=ally] in Asia.　日本は長い間,アジアではアメリカの一番の友好国だ.

My dog is *friendly* to people, but not to dogs.　うちの犬は人にはなつくが犬にはそうではない.

Email exchanges help us keep and cultivate our *friendship*, even though we live far apart.　私たちは互いに遠く離れているが,Eメールのおかげで友情を保ち,育むことができる.

from /frəm/

原義は〈〜へ向かって進む〉である．**(物事の起点を表して)〜から**．

I knew of it *from* a friend of mine.　そのことは友人から聞いて知っている．

Every year, thousands of people die of complications *from* [=caused by] common cold.　毎年，風邪をこじらせて〔←風邪が原因の合併症で〕何千人もの人が死亡する．

When walking my dog, how should I keep it *from* urinating everywhere?　犬を散歩させている時，所かまわずおしっこするのをやめさせるにはどうしたらいいのでしょう．

These shirts are made *from* [=out of] recycled plastic bottles.　これらのシャツはリサイクルのプラスチックボトルから作られています．

front /fránt/

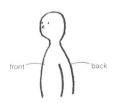

原義は〈額(ひたい)〉である．**(額)→前面，正面，最前列；前線，最先端**．
派 frontier（辺境，前線，最先端）

She takes a seat close to *the front of* the class.　彼女は教室の前の方の席に座る．

A dog was standing *in front of* the bus, preventing it from starting.　犬が1匹，バスの前にいたので，バスは発車できなかった．

I sat at the *front* [=first] row of the bus for a better view.　景色がよく見えるように，バスの一番前の席を取った．

For safety, let your baby sleep on her back, not on her *front* [=tummy].　安全のために，赤ちゃんはうつ伏せではなく仰向けに寝かせなさい．

fruit /frúːt/

原義は〈実り〉である. **(実った) 果実, (実った) 成果.**
派 fruitful (実りの多い); fruity (果物のような味わい [香り]の)

Fruit is both healthy and delicious, so it makes an ideal dessert.
果物は健康によくておいしいので, 理想的なデザートになる.

An apple tree will usually begin to bear *fruit* in the fourth or fifth year.　リンゴの木はふつう, 4年目, 5年目あたりから実をつけ始める.

The government's investment on higher education is beginning to bear *fruit*.　政府の高等教育への投資は成果が出始めている.

The party's election strategy proved *fruitful* [=successful], winning the majority of the votes.　党の選挙戦略は過半数を獲得し成功した.

---

frustrate /frʌ́streɪt/

原義は〈欺く〉である. **成就を妨げる→いらいらを生じさせる.**
派 frustrating (いらいらさせる); frustration (不満; 挫折)　関 fraud (詐欺)

The city authorities *frustrated* the residents' attempt to hold a protest meeting.　市当局は住民の抗議集会の計画を妨害した.

Most new mothers get 「*frustrated with* [=upset by] their babies' continuous crying.　新米の母親はたいてい, 赤ん坊が泣きつづけるといらいらしてしまう.

It is very *frustrating* [=annoying] getting caught in a traffic jam especially when we're in a hurry.　急いでいる時に渋滞に引っかかると, とてもいらいらするものだ.

fry /fráɪ/

原義は〈こんがり焼く〉である．**油で揚げる・炒(いた)める**．
関 frying pan（フライパン）

Shall I *fry* the potatoes or boil them?　ジャガイモは揚げましょうか，それとも煮ましょうか．

Fry the onions on a low heat until they become light brown.　タマネギを弱火で淡いきつね色になるまでいためなさい．

I have *fried* eggs, bacon, toast, and coffee for breakfast.　朝食は，目玉焼き，ベーコン，トースト，それにコーヒーです．

fuel /fjúːəl/

原義は〈炉〉である．**石炭・石油などの燃料；燃料を供給する，気持ちを燃え立たせる**．
関 fire（火）；focus（中心，焦点）

The gauge showed my car was running out of *fuel* [=gas].　燃料計がそろそろガス欠になることを示していた．

Uranium is used to *fuel* [=supply fuel to] nuclear plants.　原発の燃料供給にウラニウムが使用される．

How do you *fuel* [=inspire] your spirit when you feel down?　気持ちが落ち込んだ時は，どうやって気力を奮い立たせますか．

fulfill /fulfíl/

語源は〈ful (いっぱいに) fill (満たす)〉である．**求めるもの・求められるものを完全に満たす**．
派 fulfillment (成就，満足感)

The applicant must *fulfill* [=meet] the following requirements for admission to the college. 志願者は，この大学への入学に際して次のような条件を満たさないといけない．

He has *fulfilled* [=realized] his long cherished dream of becoming a professional singer. 彼はプロの歌手になるという長年の夢を実現した．

full /fúl/

原義は〈(水が) いっぱいである〉である．**容器にいっぱいである→全部を満たしている**．
派 fully (十分に)　関 fill (満たす)

She stood motionless with her eyes *full* of [=brimming with] tears. 彼女は目に涙をいっぱいためて立ち尽くしていた．

The parking lots in the downtown area are all *full*. 繁華街の駐車場は全部満車だ．

A glass of wine can be described as half *full* or half empty, depending on how you see it. グラスに入っているワインは，見方によって半分入っている，あるいは半分なくなっていると表現できる．

"Would you like some more bread?" "No thank you. I'm really *full*." 「もう少しパンはどうですか」「いいえ，もうおなかいっぱいです」

fun /fʌ́n/

原義は〈ふざける〉である. **やると面白く愉快になること**. fun は主観的に〈体験して面白い・わくわくして面白い〉ことについて, 類義語 interesting (面白い) は客観的に〈関心を引いて面白い〉ことについていう.
派 funny (こっけいな)

We had so much *fun* in Hawaii.　ハワイはすごく楽しかったよ.

I am really having *fun* watching the World Cup Soccer games on TV.　テレビでサッカーのワールドカップを大いに楽しんでいる.

No matter how busy you are, try to find the time to do something *fun*.　どんなに忙しくても, 何か楽しいことをする時間を見つけるようにしなさい.

I don't find it much *fun* to drive.　僕は車の運転がそんなに楽しいことと思わない.

function /fʌ́ŋkʃən/

語源は〈func (行う) tion (こと)〉である. **(行う) 機能・役割 ; 作動する, 機能する, (行う) 儀式・パーティー**.
派 functional (機能的な)

"What is the *function* [=role] of the stomach?" "It *functions* [=works] as the main part of the digestive system."　「胃の役割は何ですか」「胃は消化組織の一番主要な器官として働きます」

My computer has ceased to *function* [=operate] beyond turning on.　コンピュータが電源を入れても〔←電源は入るがそれ以上は〕作動しなくなった.

Let's plan a *function* [=party] when the project is finished.　この企画が完成したら, 打ち上げ (パーティー) をしましょう.

fund /fʌ́nd/

原義は〈底〉である. **基→(事業の基となる) 基金・資金；資金を提供する**.
派 fundamental (根本をなす)；fundamentally (根本的に)
関 found (基を築く)

This concert is planned to raise *funds* [=money] for children orphaned by traffic accidents.　このコンサートは交通遺児のための資金を募るために計画されました.　▶funds「基金」((通例複数形で))

What percentage of my salary should go to the company's retirement *fund*?　収入の何割を会社の退職年金のために払うことになりますか.

This research is *funded* [=supported] by a grant from the government.　この調査は政府の交付金を受けている.　▶grant「補助金」

---

funeral /fjúːnərəl/

原義は〈葬式〉である. **葬式，葬儀**.
関 funeral director (葬儀屋)；funeral home (葬儀会館)

Are you going to attend his *funeral*?　彼の葬儀に出席しますか.

I think a *funeral* is not only for the dead but for the survivors; they need to share their sorrows with others.　葬儀は死者のためだけでなく遺族のためでもあると思う. 遺族の人たちは悲しみを他の人たちと分かち合う必要があるからだ.

furniture /fə́:rnɪtʃər/

原義は〈furnit（備える）ure（もの）〉である．**備えられたもの→備品，調度品，家具**．いすやソファーやベッドなどの集合体を furniture という．意味の抽象性が高いので複数形をとらない．
関 furnish（備える，供給する）；furnishings（備え付け家具）

Furniture should be arranged so that people can move about smoothly in a room. 　家具は，人が部屋の中をスムーズに動けるように配置しないといけない．

We *furnished* [＝provided] the room with chairs, a table, a sofa, a refrigerator, and other necessities. 　部屋にいすやテーブル，ソファー，冷蔵庫，その他の必需品を備え付けた．

further /fə́:rðər/

further

語源は〈furth＝forth（前へ）er（～より《比較級》）〉である．**もっと進める，さらにもっと**．

For *further* [＝more] information, please contact us directly. 　詳細については私どもに直接お問い合わせください．

This chapter is *further* [＝again] divided into three sections. 　この章はさらに3つの項に分かれている．

We do not see any point in going *further* into the problem than this. 　これ以上この問題に深入りしても意味がないと思う．

fuss /fÁs/

原義は〈騒ぎ立てる〉である.**ささいなことに大騒ぎする**.fuss に〈騒音〉が感じられる.
派 fussy(気難しい)

The crew got the job done quickly without any *fuss* [=without any argument]. 作業チームは不満を言い合うことなく迅速に仕事を成し遂げた.

If you ask me, you are ⌈making a *fuss* [=fussing] about your children's education. 私に言わせれば,君は子どもの教育にあれこれと騒ぎすぎだよ.

Susie is very *fussy* [=particular] about how she dresses. 彼女は服装にとてもこだわる.

futile /fjú:tl/

語源は〈fut(流れ) ile(やすい)〉である.**(流れやすい)→努力が流れてしまう(骨折り損)**.
派 futility(無益) 関 fuse(溶ける)

Any effort you make studying a foreign language is *futile* [= pointless] if your knowledge of your own language isn't good enough. 自分の母語がしっかりしていないと,外国語をいかに懸命に学ぼうとも成果は生まれない.

Any war is *futile* [=fruitless] whatever reason it is fought for. 戦争は,どういう理由で戦われようとも,結局は無意味なものだ.

future /fjúːtʃər/

原義は〈やがて来る〉である. **(やがて来る時)→将来・未来**.

I wonder what kind of *future* our offspring(s) can expect.　我々の子孫にはどんな未来が待っているのだろうか.

No decision on this issue is likely in the near *future*.　この件に関しての決定は近々には出ないだろう.

I reject the notion that newspapers have no *future* in the Internet age.　インターネットの時代に新聞の将来性はないという見方は違うと思う.

gain /géɪn/

原義は〈求めて得る〉である. **獲得する, 増す, 新たに得る**.
派 gainful (利益の上がる)

Recently, compact cars have been *gaining* (in) popularity.　最近, 小型車の人気が出ている.

The parents gradually *gained* confidence in handling their baby.　両親は, だんだんと赤ちゃんの扱いに自信がついてきた.

I *gained* [=put on] five kilos in the first five months after moving here.　ここに越してから5か月で5キロ増えた.

"Nothing ventured, nothing *gained*" suggests that if you never take a risk you will never succeed.　「虎穴に入らずんば虎子を得ず」とは, 危険を冒さないことには何も得られないということを言っている.

game /géɪm/

原義は〈娯楽〉である．**(楽しむ) ゲーム**，**試合**；**(狩って楽しむ) 獲物**．
関 gamble (賭け事)

Did you attend the *game* or watch it on TV?　その試合を見に行ったの，それともテレビで見たの？

Japan won the *game*, coming from behind to win 2-1.　日本は逆転し，2対1で試合に勝った．

Have you ever shot any *game* with a rifle?　ライフル銃で獲物を撃った経験がありますか．

gap /gǽp/

原義は〈裂け目〉である．**割れ目**，**穴**，**すき間**，**空白**；**格差**．
派 gape (大きく口を開ける)；gaping (ぽっかり穴のあいた)

A cat was looking directly at me through a *gap* in a wooden fence.　木の柵のすき間から猫がじっと私をにらんでいた．

How should we fill the *gap* created by his quitting?　彼が辞めたことで生じた穴をどうやって埋めたらいいだろうか．

There still remains a *gap* [=difference] between male and female salaries.　依然として男女間の賃金格差がある．

Her husband's death had left a *gaping* hole in her heart.　夫を亡くして彼女の心にぽっかりと穴があいた．

garbage /gáːrbɪdʒ/

原義は〈食べ残し〉である。**生ごみ；ごみ同然のがらくた**．

Garbage [＝Kitchen waste] should be bagged and placed in the container on the designated collection day.　生ごみは，指定の収集日に袋に入れてコンテナの中に入れておかないといけません．

There's nothing but *garbage* [＝trash] on TV tonight.　今夜のテレビはがらくたばかりだ．

garden /gáːrdn/

原義は〈（囲まれた）庭〉である．**庭，庭園，菜園；庭いじりする，庭仕事をする**．
派 gardener（庭師）；gardening（庭仕事）

How often should we water the *garden* in summer?　夏は庭の水やりはどのくらいの頻度でしますか．

My father really likes *gardening* and is always planting seeds and tilling the soil.　父は庭いじりが大好きで，いつも種をまいたり土を耕したりしている．

Yesterday it never got warm enough for us to *garden* [＝do gardening].　昨日はちっとも暖かくならなかったので，庭仕事をしなかった．

gas /gǽs/

原義は〈混沌 (chaos) とした気体〉である. **気体, ガス, ガソリン (gasoline)**. ガソリンは短縮して gas というが, liquid（液体）であり, 気体 (gas) ではない.
派 gasoline（ガソリン）; gaseous（ガス状の）

How much are the average monthly water, *gas*, and electricity bills for a family of four?　4人家族の場合, 水道, ガス, 電気の1か月の料金は平均いくらですか.

Unlike the earth, Jupiter isn't a terrestrial planet but a *gaseous* one.　木星は, 土で固まった地球とは違ってガス状の惑星である.

What should I do if I smell *gas* indoors?　家の中がガス臭かったらどうすればいいですか.

She had mistakenly stepped on the ˈ*gas pedal* [=accelerator] rather than the brake.　彼女は誤って, ブレーキではなくアクセルを踏み込んだ.

gather /gǽðər/

原義は〈集める〉である. **物や人を一か所に寄せ集める; 断片情報を寄せ集めて推測する**. -g- には〈群れる〉意味合いがある：amon*g*, *g*roup, min*g*le（混ぜる）, *g*regarious（群生の）
関 together（一緒に）

Thousands of fans *gathered* to watch the game on a big screen.　何千人ものファンが大型スクリーンで試合を見るために集まった.

Gather data without being influenced by your own preferences or biases.　自分の好みや偏見に左右されないように情報を収集しなさい.

It took me a whole week to *gather* my thoughts and write this essay.　この論文の構想をまとめて書くためにまる一週間かかった.

I *gather* from what he said that the mayor has decided to resign.　発言から推測すると, 市長は辞職を決めたように思う.

gene /dʒíːn/

原義は〈種(しゅ)を生み出すもの〉である. **(種を生み出す) 遺伝子**.
派 genetic (遺伝子の)
関 gender (〔社会的役割としての〕性, ジェンダー)

Show business seems to be in her *gene* [=blood]; her mother was a singer and her father was a dancer.　芸能界で働くことは彼女の血筋のようだ. 母親は歌手で, 父親はダンサーだった.

I think my nearsightedness is totally *genetic* [=hereditary]; I've worn glasses ever since I can remember.　僕が近視なのはどうみても遺伝だと思う. 物心ついたときからめがねをかけているんだから.

Changing *gender* roles have dramatically altered our lives at work and at home.　性的役割が変化したために, 職場や家庭で生活が劇的に変わってきた.

---

general /dʒénərəl/

語源は〈gener (種) al (～にわたる)〉である. **ある種の全体にわたる傾向〈全般的, 一般的〉;〈全体を指揮する〉大将, 将軍**.
派 generally (一般的には); generic (一般的な)

This book is written with the *general* [=lay] reader in mind.　この本は一般読者を対象として書かれている.

It is ⌈*generally* true [=true *in general*]⌉ that women live longer than men.　一般的に女性のほうが長生きというのは事実である.

The Rhine flows *generally* [=more or less] north.　ライン川はほぼ〔←均(なら)すと〕北へ向かって流れている.

Generic medicines are less expensive than the original ones.　一般薬 (ジェネリック薬品) は開発薬よりも安価である.

generate /dʒénərèɪt/

語源は〈gener (生まれ) ate (させる)〉である. **発生させる, 生じさせる**.
派 generation ((生み出された) 世代)

Static electricity is *generated* [=caused] by friction.　静電気は摩擦によって起こる.

The serial bomb blasts *generated* [=created] chaos in the whole city and a curfew was imposed.　連続爆破事件は全市に混乱を巻き起こし, 厳戒令 (外出禁止令) が敷かれた.

We have to convey the tragic nature of the atomic bombing to future *generations*.　原爆の悲惨さを後の世代に伝えなくてはいけない.

generous /dʒénərəs/

語源は〈gener (よい生まれ) ous (～のあふれた)〉である. **(生まれのよい) →心が広い→惜しみなく与える**.
派 generosity (心が広いこと, 気前のいいこと)
関 gentle (温厚な)

Mike knows everything about computers and is very ⌈*generous* in sharing [=willing to share] his knowledge.　マイクはコンピュータのことは何でも知っていて, いろいろなことを快く教えてくれる.

The student came to Japan for the first time and was very much impressed by the *generosity* [=kindness] of his host family.　その学生は日本に初めて来たが, ホストファミリーの親切にとても感動した.

gene, general, generate, generous 351

gentle /dʒéntl/

原義は〈よい生まれの〉である.**性格・人柄がいい→性格が穏やかである,天候や様子が穏やかである**.
派 gently（穏やかに）
関 generous（寛大な）〔←生まれのよい〕

He looks *gentle* [=kind], but he is very insistent on what he believes. 彼は温厚に見えるが,芯は強い〔←信念は曲げない〕.

When you are relaxed, your breathing tends to be slow and *gentle* [=light]. リラックスすると,呼吸はゆっくり穏やかになるものだ.

gesture /dʒéstʃər/

語源は〈gest（運ぶ）ure（こと）〉である.**(身の運び)→身のこなし,しぐさ,意思表示**.carry oneself（振るまう）と同じ発想.カタカナ語の「ジェスチャー」が含む〈思わせぶりな態度〉の意はない.
関 digest（消化する）〔←砕いて+運ぶ〕

France gifted the Statue of Liberty to USA as a *gesture* [=sign] of friendship. フランスは友好のしるしとしてアメリカに自由の女神像を贈った.

I thought his apology was ⌈an empty [=a token] *gesture*. 彼が誤ったのは口先だけだと思った.

get /gét/

原義は〈手に入れる〉である. **〜を手に入れる, 〜の状態になる.**
関 beget (生じさせる) 〔← be (強め) get (得る)〕

Get [=Buy] a detergent, please, if you go shopping. 買い物に行くのなら洗剤を買ってきてちょうだい.

What do you *get* [=What is the total] if you multiply three by six? 3に6を掛けるといくつになりますか.

Do you *get* [=understand] what I mean? 僕の言いたいことが分かった？

Dad put me on his shoulders to *get* a better view of the parade. 父さんはパレードがよく見えるように僕を肩車してくれた.

When I fell off from the bike, I *got* scratches on my leg and elbow. 自転車で転んで脚と肘に擦り傷を負った.

---

gift /gíft/

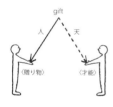

語源は〈give (与え) t (られたもの)〉である. **人が人に与える贈り物；天が人に与える才能；贈り物をする, 才能を与える.**
派 give (与える)

They say it is bad when it rains, but rain is a *gift* [=blessing] from Nature. 人は雨が降ると天気が悪いというが, 雨は天からの恵みである.

My daughter *gifted* ⌐me *with* a shirt [=a shirt *to* me] for Father's day. 父の日に娘がシャツを贈ってくれた.

She is a *gifted* [=talented] singer, blessed with a unique voice and beauty. 彼女は類(たぐい)まれな声と美貌にめぐまれた才能ある歌手だ.

give /gív/

原義は〈与える〉である．**与える，譲歩する**．
派 gift（贈り物）

What should I *give* my friend for her birthday?　友だちの誕生日祝いに何を贈ろうかな．

I'll *give* you five more minutes to prepare your answer.　答えを出すまであと5分与えましょう．

She *gave* a piano recital for the victims of the earthquake.　彼女は震災による被災者たちのために，ピアノ演奏会を開いた．

To reach an agreement on this issue, I feel both sides need to *give* in on some points.　この問題で合意を得るには，双方がいくつかの点で譲り合う必要があると思う．

---

glad /glǽd/

原義は〈気持ちが輝く〉である．**うれしく思う**．
派 gladly（喜んで）

I'm very *glad* [=happy] to hear you are feeling better.　体調がよくなっていると聞いてうれしいよ．

"Will you help me with my homework?" "I'll be *glad* [=happy] to."　「宿題手伝ってくれない？」「いいよ〔←喜んでするよ〕」

She *gladly* [=willingly] accepted his invitation to dinner.　彼女は，彼が食事に誘ってくれたので喜んで受けた．

glass /glǽs/

原義は〈ぎらぎら輝くガラス〉である．**ガラス**（不可算名詞），**ガラス製のコップ**，**グラス**（可算名詞），**めがね**《複数形で》．gl- は〈輝き〉のイメージ．日本語の〈ぎらぎら〉に音が似ている．
派 glassy（ガラスのような，生気のない）；glassful（コップ一杯の）　関 glassware（ガラス製品）

Glass is a transparent, shiny substance that breaks rather easily.　ガラスは透明できらきら輝き，壊れやすい素材である．

You look better with *glasses* [＝eyeglasses]（on）．　君はめがねが似合うよ．

His eyes are always *glassy* [＝dull] and bloodshot, due to his addictive drinking.　彼の目はアルコール中毒のために，いつもとろんとして，充血している．

When brushing your teeth, use a *glassful* of water instead of running the tap.　歯磨きは水道を流しっぱなしにしないで，コップ一杯の水でしなさい．

global /glóubl/

語源は〈globe（地球）al（に関わる）〉である．**全世界に関わる**．
派 globe（球体，地球，世界，地球儀）；globalize（国際化する）

Many businesses today operate and compete on a *global* [＝worldwide] scale.　現代の企業の多くは世界規模で展開し競争している．

We can read the local news from every corner of the *globe* [＝world] on the Internet.　インターネットで世界の隅々からのニュースを読むことができる．

Can you locate the island of Kauai on the *globe*?　この地球儀でカウアイ島はどこにあるか指せますか．

give, glad, glass, global

gloomy /glúːmi/

語源は〈gloom（薄暗がり）y（の）〉である．**薄暗い→陰鬱な．**
派 gloom（憂鬱）

We have been having *gloomy* weather for almost ten days.　当地は，とてもうっとうしい天気がもう10日近く続いています．

The Bank of Japan gave a *gloomy* [＝pessimistic] picture on productivity growth.　日銀は生産力の伸びに関して悲観的見解を示した．

glow /glóu/

原義は〈赤み，輝き〉である．**灼熱（しゃくねつ）の光，夕焼け，紅潮；真っ赤に燃える，輝く．**
関 glory（栄光）；gloss（光沢）

High above us, the full moon was *glowing*.　頭上高く満月が輝いていた．

The *glowing* colors of the sunset that we saw in Tahiti were breathtaking.　タヒチで見た入り日の燃えるような色彩は，息を飲むほどだった．

When his Daddy returned, the little boy's face *glowed* with happiness.　お父さんが帰ってくると，幼い男の子の顔は喜びに輝いた．

go /góu/

原義は〈行く〉である. **行く《進行・展開》→〜になる《結果》→消えて行く《消失・不在》**.

Please let us know what is *going* on [=happening] in your new life in Tokyo? 東京での新生活の様子を知らせてください.

I have been out of work for a few months and my savings ˈare almost *gone* [=have nearly run out]. ここ数か月, 職がなくて貯えもほとんど無くなってきた.

I ask my neighborhood friends to water the garden when we're *gone* [=away from home] for a long time. 長く留守にする時は近所の友だちに庭の水やりを頼みます.

goal /góul/

原義は〈レースのゴールライン〉である. **(苦労の後, 達する) ゴール, (苦労して目指す) 目標**.

Japan's two *goals* came from free kicks in the first half of the game and Shinji Okazaki scored an insurance *goal* in the latter part of the game. 日本は, 前半にフリーキックから2ゴールを得て, 岡崎慎司が後半に試合を決めるゴールを入れた. ▶insurance＝decisive「決定的な」

When you set *goals* [=targets], draw up a lesson plan, chart your progress, and reward yourself. 目標を立てるときは練習計画を作り, 進歩の過程を図表にして自分に褒美を与えるようにしなさい.

god /gάːd/

原義は〈神〉である．**(万能の) 神．(崇(あが) める) 神**．
派 goddess（女神） 関 godsend（恩恵, もっけの幸い）

Tenjin shrines are dedicated to a Heian period scholar, Sugawara Michizane, who was deified as a *god* of learning.　天神様は平安時代の学者で，学問の神として崇拝されている菅原道真を祭った神社だ．

No one complains against earthquakes because they believe they are 「*acts of God* [＝beyond their control].　地震は自然現象〔←不可抗力〕と考えているので，誰も文句を言うものはいない．

Only God knows [＝No one knows] what will happen in the future.　将来どうなるかは神のみぞ知ることである．

---

gold /góuld/

原義は〈黄色〉である．**(黄色に輝く) 金**．
派 golden（金色の, 貴重な）

Gold is soft enough to work with.　金は軟らかいので細工がしやすい．

The forthcoming election is a *golden* [＝great] opportunity for us to put an end to the bureaucrat-controlled government.　今度の選挙は，官僚支配の政治に終止符を打つ絶好の機会だ．

Nagashima and Oh contributed to building up the *golden age* of professional baseball in Japan.　長嶋と王は日本プロ野球の黄金期を築くのに貢献した．

good /gúd/

原義は〈適している〉である. **適している, 有効である, 得意である.**
派 goods（品物）〔←複数形で,「所有すべきよいもの」が元来の意〕

It's a *good* thing that we don't have noisy, nagging, fastidious neighbors.　騒がしくて気難しく口うるさい近所がいなくて幸いだ.

The ticket is *good* [=valid] only on the day of purchase.　この切符は購入当日に限り有効だ.

How long ⌈is a PC *good for* [=does a PC last] if we use it normally?　パソコンは通常の使い方でどのくらい持ちますか.

Bob is pretty *good* at fixing things.　ボブは物を修理するのがとても上手だ.

He owns a furniture store specializing in imported *goods*.　彼は輸入品専門の家具店を持っている.

---

govern /gʌ́vərn/

原義は〈舵（かじ）を取る〉である.**（国・地域・組織を）治める.**
派 government（政府）; governor（知事）; gubernatorial（知事の）; governance（制御）

In the fall of 2009, the Democratic Party of Japan took power from the Liberal Democratic Party that had long *governed* [=ruled] the country.　2009年の秋, 民主党はこの国を長く治めてきた自民党から政権を奪った.

Our social behavior is unconsciously *governed* [=controlled] by traditions and customs of our own culture.　私たちの社会的行動は, 気づかぬうちに社会のしきたりや習慣に左右されている.

Who will run ⌈for *governor* [=in the *gubernatorial* election]?　知事選に誰が出るの？

grade /gréɪd/

原義は〈階段〉である.**(階段)→階級・等級;等級を付ける**.
派 gradual (徐々の); gradation (グラデーション) 〔←色調・濃淡の段階的変化〕
関 degree (度合い)

My *grades* in the last term were terrible.　前学期の僕の成績は散々だった.

We should be through with *grading* and submitting the *grades* by Friday.　金曜日までに採点を終えて成績を提出しなければいけません.

How is the vocational aptitude test *graded*?　職業適性検査はどんなふうに採点されるのですか.

gradual /grǽdʒuəl/

語源は〈gradu (階段) al (の)〉である.**段々の, 徐々の**.
派 gradually (徐々に)

In time, a *gradual* increase in global temperature may become beyond our control.　地球の温度が徐々に上がっていくと, やがては制御できない状態になるかもしれない.

Grandpa *gradually* learned how to use the word processing software on his PC.　おじいちゃんはパソコンのワープロ (言語処理) ソフトの使い方を徐々に身に付けた.

graduate /動 grǽdʒuèit, 名 grǽdʒuət/

語源は〈gradu (階段) ate (する)〉である.**段階を経て卒業する；卒業生**.
派 graduation (卒業)

She *graduated* from a local university and obtained a teacher's license.　彼女は地元の大学を卒業して，教員免許を取得した．

He is a college *graduate*. ＝He has a college degree.　彼は大学を卒業している．

What are your plans after *graduation*?　卒業後は何をするつもりですか．

grain /gréin/

原義は〈穀物の粒〉である.**(麦・米・トウモロコシなどの) 穀物**.
関 granary (穀物倉)

Most of the local farmers are growing *grain* [=cereals] and vegetables.　当地のほとんどの農家は穀物と野菜を作っている．

There is not *a grain* [=particle] *of* truth in what the suspect says.　容疑者の言っていることには真実のかけらもない．

grant /grǽnt/

grant

原義は〈信じる〉である.**(信じて)要求を聞き届ける→与える,認める；(要求を受け入れて与える)助成金**.
派 grantee (受給者)

The family fled to the United States from Cuba and the government *granted* them asylum.　家族はキューバから米国へ脱出し,政府は家族の亡命を受け入れた.　▶asylum /əsáıləm/

My father became ill and lost his job; he is thinking of applying for ⌜a *grant* of welfare benefits [＝a welfare *grant*]⌝.　父は病気になり,職を失ったので生活保護(受給)の申請を考えている.

Because of a stroke, he can't do many of the things that he used to *take for granted*.　彼は脳卒中のために,以前はできるのが当たり前と思っていた多くのことができなくなっている.　▶take ～ for granted「～を当然と考える」

grasp /grǽsp/

原義は〈しっかり握る〉である.**しっかり握る,しっかり把握する；把握**.
派 grasping (貪欲な)〔←日本語の「握り屋」と同じ発想〕 関 grapple (取っ組み合う); grip (強く握る)

Mom gently *grasped* my shoulders and said, "Don't worry; eventually time will solve the problem."　母は優しく私の両肩をつかんで「心配しないで.時間がいずれ問題を解決してくれるのだから」と言った.

My boy, who is five years old, already has a good *grasp* [＝understanding] of the concept of percentage.　息子は5歳だけど,もう百分率の意味がちゃんとつかめている.

grass /grǽs/

原義は〈(緑の伸びる)草〉である. **草, 牧草, 芝生**.
関 grasshopper (キリギリス) 〔←草+ぴょんぴょん〕; grow (成長する); green (緑)

Grass is one of the most varied families in the plant kingdom.　草は植物界でもっとも種類の多い種族の一つだ.　▶grass は, 芝生から竹 (bamboo) までの多種類の草をいう.

Don't walk on *the grass*. ＝Keep off *the grass*.　芝生に入らないで.

People tend to think that the *grass* is always greener on the other side of the fence.　人はいつも, 隣の家の芝生の方が青い (自分の持っている物より他人の物のほうがよい) と思いがちである.

grave /gréiv/

原義は〈墓穴〉である. **深刻で重々しい; 墓**. gr- は〈重さ・重厚さ〉のイメージ.
派 gravity (重力)　関 gravel (砂利 (じゃり))

We have *grave* [＝serious] concerns about the nuclear development in North Korea.　我々は北朝鮮の核開発のことを非常に心配している.

What a child learns at home lasts until the *grave*.　《諺》三つ子の魂百まで〔←子どもが家庭で身につけることは墓場までもつ〕.

Your center of *gravity* moves forward when you are pregnant.　妊娠すると身体の重心は前に移動する.

To keep the weeds from spreading, we spread *gravel* over the yard.　雑草がはびこるのを防ぐため庭に砂利を敷きつめた.

great /gréɪt/

原義は〈大きい〉である. **大きい, たくさん, すばらしい**.
gr- は〈大きさ・重さ〉のイメージ.
派 greatly（非常に）

A *great* [=Very] many books and articles have been written about Jesus, his life, and his teaching.　イエスの人柄，人生，教えについて，非常に多くの本や論文が書かれている．

There was a *great* [=large] turnout at the fair this year; it was a *great* [=huge] success.　今年の見本市にはたいそうな人出があって大成功だった．

When you are in love, life feels so *great* [=nice].　恋をしていると，人生がすばらしく感じられる．

green /gríːn/

greens

原義は〈草の色〉である. **緑→野菜, 緑の草木；未熟な**.
派 greenery（緑の草木）
関 greenhouse（温室）; green belt（緑地帯）; grass（草）

The three primary colors of light are red, blue, and *green*.　光の三原色は赤と青と緑だ．

When I was young, I was often reminded to eat *greens* [=vegetables].　小さいころ，野菜を食べるようにとよく注意された．

Green [=Unripe] tomatoes are edible, and can be used to make all sorts of tasty treats.　トマトは熟れていなくても食べられるので，いろいろな御馳走をつくるのに使われる．

greet /gríːt/

原義は〈あいさつする〉である．**あいさつする→出迎える**．
派 greeting（あいさつ）

We *greet* each other [=exchange *greetings*] by saying, "konnichiwa" with a slight bow.　私たちは軽く会釈しながら，「こんにちは」と言ってあいさつを交わす．

The Olympic champion was *greeted* [=welcomed] as a hero by thousands of excited fans.　金メダリストは何千もの熱狂的ファンにヒーローとして迎えられた．

We exchange New Year *greetings* by sending cards. ＝We exchange new year's *greeting* cards.　私たちは年賀状を送って新年のあいさつを交わす．

---

grip /gríp/

原義は〈ぐいっと握る〉である．**握る，つかむ→気持ちをつかむ**．
関 greedy（欲張りな）〔←握って放さない〕; grasp（しっかり握る）

He *gripped* [=took hold of] the reins and kicked the horse to make him start moving forward.　彼は手綱を握って馬に蹴りを入れて走り始めた．

Worn down tires don't *grip* the road well, so they are unsafe.　すり減ったタイヤは路面をよくとらえないので危険だ．

The doctor's announcement of a new treatment for diabetes *gripped* [=attracted] the attention of many medical workers.　医師の発表した糖尿病の新しい治療法は多くの医療従事者の関心を引いた．

ground /gráund/

原義は〈底・大地〉である．**大地→（依って立つところ）立場，根拠，理由；根拠を～に置く，飛行機を地上に留め置く．**
派 grounder（〔野球で〕ゴロ）；groundless（根拠のない） 関 grow（育つ）

You need to put manure into the *ground* [=soil] before planting. 植え付け前に土に肥しをすき込まないといけない．

His argument always rests on firm *grounds* [=reasons]. 彼の意見はいつもしっかりした根拠に基づいている．

All the planes had to be *grounded* until the typhoon passed. 台風が通過するまで全機が地上待機を強いられた．

The accusations against those dismissed proved to be *groundless* [=false]. 解雇された人たちへの告発は不当であることが判明した．

group /grúːp/

原義は〈かたまり〉である．**"ぐるっ"としたかたまり→集団，グループ；グループ分けする．**
関 crop（収穫物）〔←かたまり〕；grove（〔こんもりとまとまっている小さな〕森）

Human blood is categorized into four main *groups* that are referred to as blood types. 人の血液は大きく4つ（の類）に分類され，それは血液型と呼ばれる．

Children may play in *groups* who share the same personality. 子どもは自分と同じような性格の子とグループを作って遊ぶ傾向がある．

In most Japanese high schools, students are *grouped* [=classified] into two types; science-oriented students and language-oriented ones. 日本の高校では，生徒は理系と文系の2つの型に分けられることがほとんどである．

grow /gróu/

原義は〈大地に育つ〉である. **育つ→だんだんと~になる；育てる，生やす**.
派 growth（成長，増大）
関 grass（草）；ground（大地）

They say couples *grow* to look like each other over time. 夫婦はだんだんと互いに似てくるものだとよくいわれる.

New hybrid vehicles are coming to the market to meet the *growing* [=increasing] demand for fuel efficiency. 燃費のいい車の需要の高まりに応えるために，新しいハイブリッド車が市場に出てきている.

We are *growing* vegetables like carrots and cucumbers in containers. ニンジンやキュウリなどの野菜をコンテナ容器に植えて栽培している.

guarantee /gèrəntí:/

原義は〈大丈夫であると請け合う〉である. **質や結果を保証する；保証**.
派 guarantor（保証人）

Give us a try, and we will *guarantee* satisfaction. =We are sure that you will be satisfied with our service. 私どもにお任せくださいれば，ご満足いただけることを保証します.

Publication from a leading publishing company 「doesn't always *guarantee* [=isn't necessarily a *guarantee* of] good results. 大手出版社の出版物だからといってよく売れる〔←売れることを保証する〕とは限らない.

guard /gáːrd/

原義は〈見張る〉である. **見張る, 警戒する, 用心する**.
派 guardian（保護者，後見人）
関 guard [=watch] dog（番犬）; regard（〜と見なす）

Our next-door neighbor keeps a dog to *guard* their house.　隣の人は番犬を飼っている.

The White House has been *guarded* by Secret Service agents.　ホワイトハウスは機密諜報（ちょうほう）員たちによって警備されている.

guess /gés/

原義は〈推測する〉である. **推測する, 言い当てる；推測**.
関 guesswork（当て推量）

"Who will win Wimbledon this year?" "Your *guess* is as good as mine.[=I'm not certain about it, either.]"　「今年のウインブルドンは誰が優勝するだろうか」「僕にも分からないよ」

My *guess* is [=I *guess*] that the current government won't last long.　現政権はあまり長持ちしないと思うよ.

guest /gést/

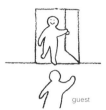

原義は〈よその人〉である. **(もてなしを受ける) 客・来賓**.
関 host (〔客をもてなす〕主催者)

We are having *guests* [=company] tomorrow. 明日はわが家に来客があります.

The last Prime Minister was the *guest* [=invited] speaker at the conference. 前総理が総会のゲストスピーカーだった.

guide /gáɪd/

原義は〈世話する〉である. **案内する；案内係, ガイド, 指導する, 誘導する**.
派 guidance (案内)

He *guided* [=showed] us around Kanazawa. 彼は金沢を案内してくれた.

This article will *guide* [=advise] you as to how to deal with difficult people at work. この記事は, 職場で気難しい人にどう対応したらよいかについて助言している.

A *tour guide* will travel and accompany the guests throughout the tour. この旅行は全行程にガイドが添乗します.

Missiles are *guided* [=directed] to their targets by various *guidance* systems. ミサイルは種々の誘導方式によって目標地点に誘導される.

guilty /gílti/

原義は〈負い目のある〉である. **(法的に) 罪を犯した；(感情的に) 後ろめたさをもつ**.
派 guilt (犯罪；罪悪感)

An ex-actress was found *guilty* of shoplifting jewelry from a department store.　元女優がデパートで宝石を万引きして有罪となった.

I always feel *guilty* [＝uneasy] when I leave the office earlier than my colleagues.　同僚より早く退社する時はいつも気が引ける.

I feel *guilty* [＝a sense of *guilt*] whenever I do not finish a meal.　出された食事を残すといつもすまない気がする.

habit /hǽbət/

原義は〈持つ (have) ようになったもの〉である. **(持つようになったもの) →身についたもの→癖, 習慣**.
派 habitual (習慣的な)
関 habitat (生息地)；inhabit (生息する)；inhabitant (居住者)《通例複数形》

Old *habits* die hard. ＝Long-standing habits aren't easy to change or stop.　昔からの癖はなかなか変えられない.

Bob has a *habit* of running his fingers through his hair when he is deep in thought.　ボブは考え込むと髪の毛を指でかき上げる癖がある.

Form [＝Get into] the *habit* of clearing your desk after each day's work is done.　仕事が終わったら毎日, 机の上を片付ける習慣をつけなさい.

You may cease to be trusted if tardiness becomes *habitual* [＝chronic].　遅刻を繰り返していたら信用を失ってしまうことになる.

hair /héər/

原義は〈頭髪〉である. **(頭に生える毛) 髪**（集合名詞），**毛**（可算名詞）；**(人や動物の) 体毛**.
派 haircut（散髪，ヘアカット）；hairy（毛深い）

John tends to worry if his *hair* gets a bit long.　ジョンは髪が少しでも伸びると気にしがちだ.

When playing tennis, he wears a *hair band* to keep his *hair* out of his eyes.　彼はテニスをするとき，髪の毛が目にかからないようにヘアバンドをする.

If you find a *hair* in your food, you may lose your appetite.　料理に髪の毛が入っていたら食欲を失いがちになる.

How often do you get your「*hair* cut [=*haircut*]?　散髪はどれくらいの頻度でしてもらいますか.

half /hǽf/

原義は〈切り分ける〉である. **半分，半端**.
派 halve（半分にする）　関 halfway（中途で，中間で）

He moved to Hiroshima about「*half* a year [=a *half* year] ago.　彼は半年前に広島へ引っ越した.

If you cut an apple *in half*, you'll get two *halves* of an apple.　リンゴを半分に切ったら半個のリンゴが二つになる.

John is rather lazy and disorganized; he always does things *halfway*.　ジョンはひどく怠惰でいい加減で，いつも物事を中途半端にやってしまう.

I「left *halfway through* [=excused myself from] the party because I had to make the last train home.　僕は，帰宅の最終電車に間に合うよう，パーティーを中座した.

hand /hænd/

原義は〈つかむ手〉である. **(物をつかむ) 手；手助け；手渡す**. h- は〈つかむ〉のイメージ：hunt (猟をする), hold (保つ), hug (抱きしめる), hoist (つり上げる)
派 handful (一握りの)；handy (便利な)

You'd better not walk with your *hands* in your pockets.　ポケットに手を入れて歩かないようにしなさい.

Could you ⌈give me a *hand* [=help me] with the dishes?　皿洗いを手伝ってもらえる？

A representative of the audience *handed* [=gave] a bouquet of flowers to the speaker.　聴衆の代表が講演者に花束を渡した.

There are only ⌈a *handful* [=a small number] of tickets left for the final match.　決勝戦のチケットは残りわずかです.

handle /hǽndl/

handle

語源は〈hand (手) le (道具)〉である. **取っ手；手でさばく, 取り扱う**. h- は〈つかむ〉のイメージ.
派 handling (取り扱い, 対応)

How should I *handle* [=deal with] my rebellious children?　反抗的な子どもたちをどう扱ったらいいでしょうか.

The problem was so complex that we decided to let a lawyer *handle* [=deal with] it.　問題がひどく複雑なので弁護士に任せることにした.

Rembrandt's masterful *handling* [=rendering] of light has been recognized by many people.　レンブラントの見事な光の扱い方は多くの人に認められている.

hang /hǽŋ/

原義は〈(物を) つるす〉である．**物をつるす；(物が中空に) 漂う，(人がうつろに) ぶらつく．**
関 hangover (二日酔い)

My mom *hangs* the washing on the line on sunny days.　母さんは晴れた日には洗濯物をロープに (つるして) 干します．

A slim TV can be *hung* on the wall as a picture frame.　薄型テレビは，額のように壁に掛けることができる．

The prisoner *hanged* himself in his cell.　囚人は独房で首つり自殺した．
▶「首をつる」の意では hang-hanged-hanged と規則変化する．

The morning mist is *hanging* [＝drifting] over the lake.　朝霧が湖面上に漂っている．

happen /hǽpən/

語源は〈hap (偶然) en (〜なる)〉である．**事がたまたま起こる，人がたまたま〜する．**
派 happening (出来事)　関 happy (幸せな)

This is the total picture of what *happened*. ＝Here's how it all *happened*.　これが事の全容です．

Don't concentrate on falling asleep because it will not *happen* if you force it.　無理に眠ろうとすると眠気が起こりませんよ．

I *happened* to see my former teacher at the bus stop.　バス停で昔の先生に偶然出会った．

happy /hǽpi/

語源は〈hap (偶然) y (〜の)〉である. **(巡り合わせ・遭遇が) 幸いである, うれしく思う, 満足に思う.**
派 happiness (幸福)　関 happen (起こる)

She looks *happy* [=cheerful] and excited today.　今日の彼女はとても上機嫌のようだ.

Will you marry me? I will do anything to make you *happy*.　結婚してくれる？幸せにするために何だってするよ.

I'm *happy* [=glad] to know that you became the father of a daughter.　娘さんが生まれて父親になられたと聞いて喜んでいます.

I'm not *happy* [=satisfied] with this apartment; the ceiling isn't high enough.　このアパートは, 天井が低いので気に入らないの.

hard /hɑ́ːrd/

原義は〈力強い〉である. **しっかりとして硬い→(相手にすると) 攻略しにくい.**
派 harden (硬くする)；hardship (苦難)
関 hardware (ハードウェア, 金属製品)

My old dog can't eat *hard* [=tough] food anymore.　うちの老犬は硬い餌はもう食べられない.

We learn most of the important things in life ⌈the *hard* way [=through trial and error].　人は人生で大切なことのほとんどは苦労して学び取るものだ.

Some people have *a hard* [=difficult] *time* controlling their appetite, resulting in getting too fat.　食欲の抑制が苦手で, 肥満になってしまう人がいる.

hardly /háːrdli/

語源は〈hard（厳しい）ly（様態）〉である．**難しい状態にある→ほとんど～が起こらない**．

The man was so drunk he could *hardly* [=barely] remember what happened to him.　男はひどく酔っていて，自分に何が起こったのかほとんど思い出せなかった．

It's「*hardly* surprising [=not a big surprise] that Bob won the first prize; I know how good he is and how much he prepared for the competition.　ボブが1等賞を得たのはさほど驚くことではない．彼がどれほど優秀で，またコンクールのためにどれほど多くの準備をしてきたかをちゃんと知っていますから．

harm /háːrm/

原義は〈（精神的・肉体的）苦痛〉である．**（物事・精神・身体に）害・傷を与えること**．
派 harmful（有害な）; harmless（無害である）

Too much exercise can「*do* more *harm* than good [=be *harmful*].　運動のやり過ぎは身体に有害無益だ．

Smoking during pregnancy can「*harm* [=cause damage to] the health of both the mother and her unborn baby.　妊娠中の喫煙は母子の健康を害する．

harvest /háːrvəst/

原義は〈刈り取る〉である．**刈り取る；収穫する；収穫**．h- は〈つかむ〉のイメージ．

A good rice *harvest* [=crop] is in prospect this year. 今年の稲は豊作が見込まれている．

I *harvested* [=picked] a few cucumbers from the vegetable garden this morning. 今朝，菜園でキュウリを数本収穫したよ．

haste /héɪst/

原義は〈急ぐこと，大急ぎ〉である．**大急ぎで行動すること**．

派 hastily（大急ぎで）；hasty（慌ただしい）；hasten（急がせる）

Don't act or respond ⌈*in haste* [=in a hurry]⌉ when you think more thought is needed. もっと考えなければいけないと思う時は，性急に行動や返答をしないようにしなさい．

Haste makes waste. =When we act too quickly, we are likely to end up with poor results. 《諺》せいては事を仕損じる．

You shouldn't make a *hasty* conclusion, based on just a few facts. ほんのいくつかの事例だけで，性急な結論を下してはいけない．

hate /héɪt/

原義は〈悲しむ〉である. **(悲しむ)→嫌だと思う, ひどく嫌う**.
派 hatred (憎しみ) 〔← hate+red (様態)〕

I *hate* cockroaches; just looking at them makes me sick.　私はゴキブリが大嫌いで, 見るだけで気分が悪くなるの.

Hitler *hated* [＝had *hatred* towards] Jews.　ヒトラーはユダヤ人を忌み嫌った.

I used to *hate* going back to school after the long summer vacation.　長い夏休みの後, 登校するのはとても嫌だった.

I *hate* to hear people talking bad things about others behind their backs.　人が他人の悪口を陰でしゃべっているのを聞くのは嫌だ.

have /hév/

原義は〈つかむ〉である. **所有する, 人や動物を身近に持つ, 病気・能力などを持つ, 経験する, 状況をもたらす**.
関 heave (持ち上げる); hold (つかむ)

I *have* a cell phone with me at all times.　私はいつでも携帯電話を持ち歩いている.

Have you ever *had* any serious illnesses?　重病にかかったことがありますか.

Although my grandpa is 90, he *has* an excellent memory.　祖父は90歳だがとても記憶力がよい.

My son *had* me worried when he said he was quitting the job.　息子が仕事を辞めると聞いて心配になった.

head /héd/

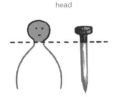

原義は〈頭〉である．頭，物の上部；(組織の)長；(頭を向ける)→向かう；(頭(かしら)になる)→率いる．
派 heading (標題)
関 headache (頭痛)；headline (見出し)；headlong (真っ逆さまに)

Stroke the dog on the *head*. 犬の頭をなでてやりなさい．

Kids who are good at abacus can do very fast calculations「*in their head* [=mentally]. そろばんが得意な子は暗算がすばやくできる．

A powerful typhoon is *heading* toward Japan's main island. 強い台風が本州へ向かっている．

The Vice-chairperson temporarily *heads* [=chairs] the committee until the chairperson resumes office. 座長が復職するまで副座長が委員会を仕切る．

heal /híːl/

原義は〈完全にする〉である．(全(まった)うな状態にする)→傷を治す・癒やす．
派 healer (癒やすもの)；health (健康)；healthy (健康な，健康によい)；healthful (健康によい)
関 healthcare (健康管理)；whole (完全な)

My eyes are bloodshot; should I see a doctor, or just let it *heal* itself? 目が充血しているが，医者に行くか，それとも自然治癒に任せたほうがいいですか．

His knee injury will take a few months before it's all *healed* [=cured]. 彼の膝の負傷は全治には数か月かかる．

Don't worry, time「is a *healer* [=will *heal* your pain]. 心配はいらない，時が薬だよ．

Egg is「a *healthy* [=*healthful*] and nutritious food. 卵は健康によい栄養の豊かな食品だ．

hear /híər/

原義は〈耳にする〉である。**聞く，耳にする，聴く．**
派 hearing（聴力，傾聴，聴聞会）

I *heard* someone call my name in the crowd.　人だかりの中で，誰かが私の名前を呼ぶのが聞こえた．

I don't know if that's true, but that is what I *heard*.　本当かどうか分からないけど，そのように聞いたんだ．

How often do you *hear from* your mother?　お母さんからの連絡はよくあるの？

You should *hear* [=listen to] what both sides have to say.　両者の言い分に耳を傾けるようにしなさい．

heart /hά:rt/

原義は〈心臓〉である．**（臓器としての）心臓，（感情の宿る）心・気持ち，物事の中心．**
関 heartfelt（心からの）；heartwarming（心温まる）

Athlete's *hearts* may beat slower than those of non-athletes.　スポーツ選手の心臓は，普通の人より心拍数が少ないことが多い．

My boyfriend is ten years older than me, but age doesn't matter as long as he has a good *heart* [=nature].　私の彼氏は10歳年上だけど，よい性格であれば年齢は関係ないわ．

The concept of freedom lies at the *heart* [=center] of human rights.　人権の根底には自由という概念がある．

heat /híːt/

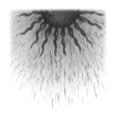

原義は〈熱(hotness)〉である. **熱, 暑さ；熱する, 暖める**.
派 heater（ヒーター, 暖房器具）; heating（暖房）
関 hot（暑い）

Animals and plants seem to be recovering after the *heat* of summer.
夏の暑さが去って，動物も植物も元気を取り戻しているようだ．

This region is cold in winter and hot in summer; I advise you to install air conditioners that can both *heat* [=warm] and cool your rooms.　この地方は，冬は寒くて夏は暑いので，冷暖房のできるエアコンを取り付けるのがいいですよ．

Things got *heated* [=confrontational] at the hearing when a woman challenged the Mayor.　一人の女性が市長に異議を唱えたので公聴会は熱くなった．

heaven /hévn/

原義は〈(地上を覆う)天空〉. **天空→天国**. h- は〈覆う〉のイメージ．
派 heavenly（天の，天国の）

The evening star is always seen in the *heavens* [=sky] just after the sunsets.　宵の明星は日没後(の空)にいつも見える．　▶heaven は「空」の意では通例，複数形．

Both *heaven* and hell are imaginary places.　天国も地獄も想像上の場所である．

A baby is a gift from *Heaven* [=God].　子どもは天[神]からの授かりものだ．

I felt as if I were in *Heaven* [=Paradise], soaking in the hot spring.
温泉につかっていると極楽にいる思いだった．

heavy /hévi/

原義は〈heav（重なって）y（状態）〉である．**多量である→重い→重苦しい**．重いものを引き上げる（heave）と，反作用で腕に重い感じ（heavy）が生じる．
派 heavily（重く，濃密に）　関 heave（持ち上げる）

Heavy [=high] taxes are often imposed upon imports to protect domestic industries.　国内産業を保護するために，しばしば輸入品に重税がかけられる．

My legs feel *heavy* [=sluggish] because I had to keep standing all day.　一日中立ちっぱなしだったので，脚が重たい．

Avoid eating *heavy* and fatty foods at night.　夜，こってりした油っこいものは食べないようにしなさい．

Tokyo is one of the most *heavily* [=densely] populated cities in the world.　東京は世界で最も人口密度の高い都市の一つだ．

hectic /héktɪk/

原義は〈消耗させるような〉である．**(人を消耗させるほど) すべきことが多い，慌ただしい**．雰囲気・状況の「慌ただしさ」をいうので人を形容できない．

It was *hectic* [=busy] today. = I had a *hectic* day today.　今日は目が回るほど忙しかった．

Our daughter is leading a *hectic* [=busy] life as an office worker and mother.　娘は会社勤めして母親でもあるので，多忙な生活を送っている．

help /hélp/

原義は〈助ける〉である．**他者の物事の進展を助ける；手助け，援助．**
派 helpful（役立つ）；helpless（身動きのとれない）

Will you *help* [=assist] me with setting up my own website?　自分のホームページを作るのを手伝ってくれませんか．

GPS will *help* you locate where you are in an instant.　GPSを使えば現在地がすぐに分かる．▶GPS =global positioning system「衛星利用測位システム」

You'll have to learn to ⌈*help yourself*⌉ [=be independent] after finishing school.　卒業したら自活するようにしないといけないよ．

We need *help* [=assistance] with the pets while we are away.　留守中にペットの世話をしてくれる人が要る．

here /híər/

原義は〈ここに〉である．**ここに，ここで，ここへ．**話者からの位置関係を示す時，英語ではhere（ここ），there（あそこ）と二様にいう．

Fall ⌈is *here*⌉ [=has come upon us] at last.　やっと秋になった〔←秋がここに来た〕．

Here we are! =We have arrived.　（ここに）着いたよ！

I wish you were *here* with me!　あなたがここにいてくれたらいいのに！

"May I please see your ID?" "Yes, of course. *Here it is*."　「本人証明書を見せてもらえますか」「はい，もちろん．これです」

hesitate /hézətèɪt/

原義は〈粘りつく〉である.**(粘りついて)決断が遅い→躊躇(ちゅうちょ)する→どうしようかとためらう**.
派 hesitant (ためらいがちな); hesitation (ためらい)
関 adhere (くっつく); adhesive (粘着性の); cohere (密着する)

Don't *hesitate* to let me know if I'm wrong.　間違っていたら遠慮なく言ってください.

Some students *hesitate* [=are shy] to say what they think unless they are asked to.　生徒の中には, 問われないと自分の意見を言うのをためらう者がいる.

She was *hesitant* [=unsure] about taking the medicine, worrying about its side effects.　彼女は副作用を心配してその薬を飲むことをためらった.

hide /háɪd/

原義は〈覆い隠す〉である.**物や身柄を見られないように覆い隠す**. h- は〈覆う〉のイメージ.
派 hidden (隠された)　関 hide-and-seek (かくれんぼ)

She did not *hide* [=conceal] the fact that she was (a) lesbian.　彼女は自分がレスビアンであることを隠さなかった.

I followed the pickpocket, but he skillfully ⌈*hid himself*⌋ [=went into hiding] in the crowd.　スリを追ったが, 彼は巧みに群衆の中に姿をくらました.

The mountains became *hidden* from view by those newly-built buildings.　山並みは新しく建ったビル群のために見えなくなった.

high /háɪ/

high

原義は〈高い〉である. **(高さ・位置・程度が) 高い**. highという時, 視線の先は対象物の頂点に注がれている. 類義の tall は丈のあることをいうので, 視線は対象物の足元から頂点までの長さに注がれている.
派 height (高さ, 高所, 絶頂); heighten (高くする); highly (非常に)　関 highlight (最大の山場, 強調する)

The flood water rose waist *high* [=deep]. 洪水は腰 (の高さ) まで達した.

Mount K2 is the *second-highest* mountain in the world, after Mount Everest. K2 峰はエベレストに次ぐ世界第二の高峰である.

The moon was *high* in the sky, shedding a silver light all over. 月は空高く, 銀色の光を一面に注いでいた.

A diet *high* [=rich] in fiber helps regulate your bowel movements. 繊維質の多い食事は便通を整えるのに役立つ.

hinder /híndər/

語源は〈hind (後ろに) er (置く)〉である. **物事の進行を遅らせる, 邪魔する**.
派 hind (後部の); hindrance (妨害)
関 behind (〜の後ろに)

The delivery of newspapers was *hindered* [=slowed] by the storm. 嵐のために新聞の配達が遅れた.

His poor education *hindered* [=prevented] him from becoming a government officer. 彼は学歴不足のために役人になれなかった.

The college wanted to install the latest computer system, but the cost was a *hindrance* [=barrier]. 大学は最新のコンピュータ装置を導入しようと思ったが, 費用が障害となった.

hint /hínt/

原義は〈ヒントを与える〉である．**さっとほのめかす，さりげなくにおわせる；暗示，気配，ヒント**．

The mayor resigned suddenly ⌈without *hinting* [=with no *hint*] that he was thinking of doing so.　市長は辞める気配を見せることなく突然辞職した．

If you have no idea, I'll give you a *hint*.　分からないならヒントを出しましょう．

The article includes helpful *hints* [=tips] for parents with overly shy kids.　この記事には，ひどい人見知りをする子どもをもった親に参考になるひけつがある．

---

history /hístəri/

原義は〈出来事についての話（story）〉である．**歴史，経歴，事歴；自然界についての記述**．
派 historic（歴史に残る）；historical（歴史に関する）
関 story（話）

We know war begets nothing but destruction, but *history* is repeating itself, again and again.　我々は，戦争が破壊しかもたらさないことを知っているのに，歴史は絶えず繰り返している．

Submit a resume detailing your education and work *history* [=experience] before the interview.　面接までに学歴と職歴の詳細を記した履歴書をお送りください．

Does anyone in your family have a *history* of cancer?　家族でどなたかがんの病歴のある人がいますか．

hit /hít/

原義は〈当てる〉である. **たたく, ぶつかる；ふと気づく；襲う**.

To loosen a stubborn jar lid, try to *hit* [=tap] the side of the lid with a spoon several times.　きつく締まった瓶のふたを緩めるには, ふたの縁をスプーンで数回たたいてみなさい.

The foul ball *hit* the umpire in his most sensitive spot.　ファウルボールは審判の急所に当たった.

It suddenly *hit* me that I was missing a dental appointment.　歯医者の予約をしていたことを忘れていたことにはっと気づいた.

A strong quake *hit* [=struck] Kobe area on January 17, 1995.　大地震が1995年1月17日神戸地方を襲った.

---

hold /hóuld/

原義は〈握る〉である. **物を手の中にとどめる→物・事をある状態に保つ**. h- は〈つかむ〉イメージ.
派 holder (所有者, ホルダー)；holding (持ち株)
関 have (持つ)

Always *hold* the railing when climbing up and down the stairs.　階段を昇り降りする時はいつも手すりをつかむようにしなさい.

The abdomen *holds* [=contains] digestive organs.　腹部には消化器官が納まっている.

I hope the weather will *hold* [=continue to be good] through the weekend.　天気がこのまま週末までもてばいいと思っている.

How long can you ⌈*hold* your breath [=stop your breathing]?　どれくらい息を止めることができますか.

hole /hóul/

hole

原義は〈うつろな所 (hollow place)〉である. **穴, くぼみ；理論などの欠陥**.
関 hollow (うつろな)

I have [=There is] a *hole* in my sock. Will you mend it, Mom?　靴下に穴が開いているよ. 母さん, 直してくれる?

Tennis balls are *hollow*, with nothing in the middle.　テニスボールは中に何も入っておらず中空だ.

The miners' eyes and cheeks are *hollow* [=sunken] from working under very harsh conditions.　過酷な状況下で労働しているので, 坑夫たちの目や頰はくぼんでいた.

holiday /hɑ́:lədèɪ/

原義〈holy (神聖な) day (日)〉である. **(祭典のために労働をしない日)→祝日, 休日**.
関 holy (神聖な, 尊い) 〔← whole (完全な, 欠陥・汚れのない) y (状態)〕

No mail is delivered on Sunday(s) and national *holidays* except for express mail.　日曜と祝日には, 速達を除いて郵便の配達はない.

We took a 10-day *holiday* [=vacation] in Okinawa.　沖縄で10日間の休暇を取った.

Jerusalem is a *holy* [=sacred] place to Christians, Muslims, and Jews.　エルサレムはキリスト教徒, イスラム教徒, ユダヤ教徒にとって聖地である.

home /hóum/

原義〈住んでいる所〉である．**家**，**家庭**，**生息地**；**家へ**，**本拠地の**；**しっかり中へ**．類義語 house は〈人が住む建物〉，home は〈人が暮らす場〉である．
派 homeless（家のない）

She left *home* after graduating from high school.　彼女は高校を卒業すると実家を出た．

Come any time; I'm going to ⌈be *home* [=stay at *home*] all weekend.　週末は家にいるので，いつでもいらっしゃい．

Most teams do better ⌈at *home* [=in their *home* games] than on the road.　たいていのチームはアウェーよりホームゲームのほうが成績がいい．
▶ than (they play) on the road＝than they play away「遠征して試合するよりも」

honest /á:nəst/

原義は〈尊敬・信用 (honor) のある〉である．**言行に包み隠しがない**．
派 honestly（正直に）；honesty（正直）
関 honor（誉れ）

Give me your *honest* [=true] feeling about your new boss.　新しい上司のことを率直に言ってどう思ってるの．

That can't be true! Why can't you be *honest* [=truthful] with me?　そんなことあるわけないでしょ！どうして正直になれないの．

If you would like to know my *honest* [=candid] opinion, I think you shouldn't quit the job now.　正直に（意見を）言わせてもらえば，仕事をいま辞めるのはよくないと思うよ．

I think it was *an honest* [=innocent] *mistake*. Don't blame him that way.　わざとやったミスじゃないと思うよ．彼をそんなに責めないで．

honor /ɑ́:nər/

原義は〈名声〉である．**名誉，光栄；栄誉をたたえる**．
派 honorary（名誉の）; honorable（名誉となる）
関 honest（正直な）

Sally got the first prize in the piano contest, so we decided to have dinner「in her *honor* [=to *honor* her]．　サリーがピアノコンテストで1位になったので，お祝いに食事会をすることにした．

National teams fight for the *honor* [=glory] of their countries．　国代表のチームは国家の名誉のために戦う．

It's「an *honor* [=a privilege] for me to attend the conference representing the community．　地域を代表してこの会議に参加するのは光栄です．

---

hope /hóup/

原義は〈期待に胸をはずませる〉である．**～になりたいと望む，期待する；希望，期待**．
派 hopeful（期待している，有望な）; hopefully（できれば）

Hope this email finds you well．　お元気でいらっしゃることでしょう〔このメールが元気なあなたを見つけることを望んでいます〕．　▶メールの冒頭で用いる常とう句．

Don't give up *hope*; this is not the end．　（望みを）あきらめちゃだめよ．これでおしまいじゃないのだから．

I am *hopeful* [=full of hope] for my son's future．　僕は息子の将来に期待している．

Hopefully, [=I hope] business will get better soon．　景気が早くよくなるといいのですが．

horizon /həráɪzn/

原義は〈境界線〉である．**水平線，地平線→（見渡しのきく）範囲，視野**．
派 horizontal（水平の）；horizontally（水平に）
関 aphorism（格言）〔←世事に輪郭を引き簡潔にまとめ上げた文句〕

I watched the sun set into the *horizon*.　太陽が地平線[水平線]に沈むのを見た．　▶前置詞は，into の他，over, on, in, below などが可能．

Reading enriches our knowledge and broadens our *horizons* [= views of the world].　読書は知識を豊かにし，視野を広げてくれる．

This ivy grows *horizontally* [=sideways] as well as vertically [= upward].　このツタは縦にも横にも伸びる．

hospital /hɑ́ːspɪtl/

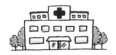

原義は〈巡礼・旅人を受け入れる所〉である．**(病人を受け入れる)病院**．
派 hospitalize（入院させる）；hospice（緩和医療施設）
関 host（受け入れる）；hotel（ホテル）

Five people including the bus driver were taken to (the) *hospital* after the accident.　その事故で運転手を含め5人が病院に搬送された．

Following the operation my sister was *in the hospital* for three more days just in case.　姉は手術後，大事を取ってもう3日間入院していた．

Many people who ate at the restaurant were *hospitalized* for food poisoning.　そのレストランで食事をした多くの人が食中毒で入院した．

His father's condition was terminal and he was moved to the *hospice* ward.　彼の父親は末期症状なので緩和病棟へ移された．

host /hóust/

原義は〈他人・客〉である. **(客を) 接待する人**；**(行事・大会を) 主催する**.
派 hostess（女主人）
関 hospital（病院）; hotel（ホテル）; hostile（敵の）〔←他者〕

The couple *hosted* [=had] a dinner party for their friends and colleagues.　夫妻は友人や同僚のために食事会を開いた.

Which country is going to *host* the next Summer Olympics.　次の夏期オリンピック開催国はどこ?

Denmark will be the *host* country for the climate change conference next year.　デンマークは来年, 気象変動に関する会議を主催する.

He has been the *host* of the quiz show since its inception.　彼は番組が始まってからずっとこのクイズ・ショーの司会をやっている.

---

hostage /há:stɪdʒ/

hostage

語源は〈host（とらわれた）age（状態）〉である. **人質状態**, **人質**. 語源的に host とは無関係. h- は〈つかむ〉のイメージ.

A Japanese journalist who was held *hostage* [=as a hostage] in Afghanistan has been freed.　アフガニスタンで人質となっていた日本人ジャーナリストが解放された.　▶hostage は「人質状態」, a hostage は「人質」となる.

human /hjúːmən/

原義は〈(天上の神に対して) 地上の〉である.**(全能ではない) 人間,(生物としての) 人間;(感情に揺れ動く) 人間的な,(生態的に) 人間の.**
派 humanity (人間らしさ);humanism (人間主義)
関 human being (人間);human beings (人類)

The champion is only *human* [=a human being]; he has his share of weakness like everyone else.　チャンピオンだって人間だから, 皆と同じように弱点もある.

The accident investigation committee indicated that the crash was 「due to *human* error [=the fault of a person not the failure of a machine].　事故調査委員会は, 墜落は人為的ミスによることを示唆した.

This virus infects both *humans* and animals, sometimes resulting in a fatal fever.　このウイルスは人間にも動物にも感染し, 時に高熱で死に至ることもある.

humble /hʌ́mbl/

原義は〈地面に着くほどに〉である.**(地面に着くほどに) 頭の低い, 位・質の低い;(地面に着くほどに) おとしめる, 負かす.** hum- は〈土〉を連想させる:human (〔地上の〕人間), humid (〔土のように〕湿っぽい)

I felt *humbled* [=awkward] when I found myself among the best players in the country.　全国レベルの精鋭選手の中に入ると引け目を感じた.

The Nobel Prize winner comes from a *humble* [=poor] background; his mother was a single parent who worked to send him to college.　このノーベル賞受賞者は貧しい生い立ちで, 片親の母親は働いて彼を大学に行かせた.

He is very *humble* and modest about his past achievements.　彼は謙虚で慎み深く, 過去の自分の業績のことを得意気にしゃべることがない.

hundred /hʌ́drəd/

原義は〈hund (100) red (数) → 100〉である. **100**. 101 は a hundred one, または a [one] hundred and one と読む. 201 は two hundred one, または two hundred and one と読む.

Several *hundred* people have been killed in the riot.　数百人がその暴動で死亡した.

Hundreds of townspeople attended the funeral for the landslide victims.　地滑りの犠牲者の葬儀に何百人もの町民が参列した.

I have heard the song *hundreds* of times and it still moves me every time.　その歌を幾度となく聴いているが, 聴くたびに感動する.

He won the 100-meter freestyle by a *hundredth* of a second.　彼は100メートル自由形を100分の1秒差で制した.　▶ by two hundredths of a second「100分の2秒で」

---

hungry /hʌ́ŋgri/

原義は〈おなかの空いた〉である. **空腹である, 飢えている；物事を強く求めている**.
派 hunger (飢え, 渇き)；hungrily (飢えたように)

I couldn't get to sleep sooner, as I went to bed *hungry* [=with empty stomach] last night.　昨夜は, 空腹のままで床についたので寝つきが悪かった.

You need to get *hungry* enough to appreciate the food well. *Hunger* is the best sauce!　食事をちゃんと味わうには適度に空腹でないといけない. 空きっ腹にまずいものなしだよ！　▶ sauce「(味を良くする) ソース」

Many children whose parents are too busy working may be *hungry* for parental affection.　仕事で忙しい親を持っている子どもは, 親の愛情に飢えていることが多い.

hunt /hʌ́nt/

原義は〈狩をする〉である **狩猟する；捜し求める，追跡する**．h- は〈つかむ・覆う〉を連想させる．
派 hunter（狩りをする人，〔他の動物をねらう〕どうもうな動物）；hunting（狩り）

People used to just *hunt* and fish before the dawn of civilization.　文明の始まる前は，人間はただ狩猟と漁で暮らしていた．

The police are *hunting* [=*on the hunt*] for clues (linking) to the robbery.　警察は強盗事件の手がかりを捜索している．

Most of the students start *hunting* [=looking] *for jobs* at least one year before graduation.　ほとんどの学生は，卒業の少なくとも1年ほど前から就職活動を始める．

hurry /hə́ːri/

原義は〈(はっとして) 急ぐ〉である．**急ぐ；急がせる**．
派 unhurried（ゆったりした）
関 scurry（小走りする）；rush（急ぐ）

Take your time. There's no need to *hurry* [=rush].　ゆっくりやってね．急ぐ必要はないから．

She *hurries* home after work to look after her children.　彼女は仕事を終えると，子どもたちの世話をするために急いで帰宅する．

Whatever it may be, I hate being *hurried through*.　何であれ，せかされるのは嫌いだ．

I'm *in a hurry* to get things done. May I call you back later?　今，急ぎの用事をしているの．後からかけ直していい？

hurt /hə́ːrt/

原義は〈打ちつける〉である. **身体・感情を傷つける, 事態を害する.**
派 hurtful (有害な, 感情を害する)

Sorry if you felt offended. I didn't mean to *hurt* [=offend] you.　もし気分を悪くされたのならごめんなさい. そんな〔←悪くさせる〕つもりじゃなかったの.

"What happened to your leg?" "I *hurt* it playing soccer."　「脚どうしたの？」「サッカーやっていて痛めたんだ」

The minister's inappropriate remark about minorities has badly *hurt* [=damaged] his image.　大臣の少数民族に対する軽率な発言は, 彼の印象をひどく悪くした.

He was bullied by *hurtful* information posted on the Internet.　彼は傷つくような情報をネットに流されていじめられた.

---

ice /áɪs/

原義は〈氷〉である. **氷；氷で冷やす.**
派 iced (氷で冷やした)
関 ice cube (〔冷蔵庫でつくる〕角氷)；icicle (つらら)

In a few more days, the *ice* on this pond will be thick enough to skate on.　もう数日で, この池の氷は十分にスケートできる厚さになるよ.

I've grown fond of the *iced* coffee they serve at this café.　このカフェのアイスコーヒーがとても好きになった.

A good speaker often starts a speech ⌈by telling a joke to *break the ice* [=using a joke as an icebreaker] with the audience.　演説のうまい人は, 聴衆との雰囲気を和らげるためにジョークでスピーチを始めることが多い.

▶ break the ice「座の緊張を解く」

idea /aɪdíːə/

原義は〈頭に思いつく形〉である. **(頭に形成される) 考え, 意見, 思想, 意図.**
関 ideal (理想の)

I'm not sure what to do with the problem? Do you have any *ideas*?　この問題はどうしたらいいのかわからないよ. 何かいい考えはない？

How do you ⌈get your *ideas* [＝come up with *ideas*]⌉ for your novels?　小説の構想はどうやって得るのですか.

Our son is coming home on Friday. I think ⌈the *idea* is [＝he means]⌉ to spend the three consecutive holidays leisurely with us.　息子は金曜日に帰省します. 3連休をわが家でゆっくり過ごすつもりだと思います.

ideal /aɪdíːəl/

語源は〈idea (考え) al (の)〉である. **(考え通りの) 理想の, 申し分ない.**
関 idea (考え)

The location of the hotel is *ideal* for seeing all the attractions of the city.　そのホテルは, 街の名所を全部見てまわるのに理想的な場所にあります.

What would your *ideal* partner be like?　あなたの描く理想的な結婚相手はどんな人ですか.

As a solution to the problem it was far from *ideal*.　この問題の解決法として, このやり方は理想とは程遠かった.

identity /aɪdéntəti/

語源は〈identi（同一）ty（状態）〉である．**ある人に関する付帯情報が本人そのものと一致すること**．

派 identify（〔同一である・そのものである〕と突きとめる）; identical（双方がまったく同じである）

The fugitive murderer may have undergone plastic surgery to hide his *identity*.　逃亡中の殺人犯は，姿を見破られないように顔の整形手術をしている可能性がある．

Doctors can now *identify* [=determine] the causes of symptoms by using samples such as urine, saliva, and blood.　現代では，医者は尿や唾液，血液などの検体を使って症状の原因を突きとめることができる．

In many countries, the fiscal year and calendar year are not *identical* [=the same].　多くの国では，会計年度と暦年とは同じでない．

idle /áɪdl/

原義は〈空の〉である．**人や機械が本来果たすべき活動をしていない様子→（人が）時を無為に過ごす；（機械が）動いていない，空回りしている**．

Because he is preparing for college exams, our son has no time to be *idle*.　息子は大学入試の準備のため，のんびりしている時間はない．

My bike ⌈has been lying *idle* [=hasn't been used] for many months since I injured my leg.　脚をけがしたので，僕の自転車は何か月も使われていない．

Don't leave the engine *idling* needlessly.　必要もないのにエンジンをかけっぱなしにしておいてはだめだよ！

if /ɪf/

原義は〈もし～ならば〉である. **(ある状況を設定して) そうであるならば；(ある状況を設定して) そうであるかどうか.**

"What happens *if* it rains?" "We'll still go unless it rains heavily."　「雨の場合はどうなるの」「大雨でなければ行きます」

If you weren't a scientist, what would you be?　もし科学者になっていなければ，何になっていましたか.

He is definitely one of the best writers, *if not* the greatest.　彼は一番ではないにしても，間違いなく最も優れた作家の一人だ.

I have to ask my mom *if* I can come to the party.　パーティーへ行ってもいいかどうか，母さんに聞かないといけないわ.

I wonder *if* she remembers me.　彼女は私のことを覚えているかな.

---

ignore /ɪɡnɔ́ːr/

ignore

語源は〈i（否）+gnore＝know（知る）〉である. **知ろうとしない→注意を払わない，無視する.**
派 ignorance（無知）；ignorant（無知である）
関 diagnose（診断する）；know（知る）

How come my boyfriend *ignores* [＝doesn't care about] me when he is around his friends?　私の彼は，彼の友達が一緒の時はどうして私のことをかまってくれないのかしら.

The boys went fishing, *ignoring* [＝disregarding] the warning that the typhoon was coming.　少年たちは台風が近づいているという警告を無視して釣りに行った.

He *ignores* [＝doesn't respond to] all my emails, and won't pick up my calls.　彼は私のEメールに全然返事をくれないし，電話をかけても取ってくれない.

ill /íl/

原義は〈害を及ぼす〉である．**体調・状況がよくない，質(%)の悪い**．
派 illness (体調不良，病気)

I always feel *ill* [=sick] after drinking alcohol.　僕は酒を飲んだら決まって気分が悪くなる．

Her 15-month-old son has been very *ill* [=sick] with the flu for more than five days.　彼女の15か月になる男の子は，インフルエンザで5日以上も伏せっている．

Comets were once believed to be omens that brought *ill* [=evil] fortune to the world.　彗星(慈)はかつて，社会に不吉をもたらす前兆だと信じられていた．

illustrate /íləstrèit/

語源は〈il (に) luster (光) ate (する)〉である．**(〜に光を当てる)→(光を当てて)明瞭に描き出す→図解・イラストを入れる，例を挙げて明瞭にする**．
派 illustrious (輝かしい)；illustration (イラスト)
関 luster (光沢)

Now I'll give a few examples to *illustrate* [=clarify] my point.　話の論点を明瞭にするために，いくつかの例を挙げましょう．

The book is *illustrated* with drawings and photographs, all of which are in color.　この本にはカラーの挿絵や写真が入っている．

Every war *illustrates* the difficulties of understanding different cultures and religions.　どの戦争も，異なった文化や宗教を理解することの難しさを物語っている．

imagine /imædʒin/

原義は〈像 (image) を心に描く〉である. **想像する**.
派 image (心に描かれる像, 鏡に映る像, 写真に映る像); imagination (想像); imaginary (想像上の)

Can you *imagine* how the final game would go tomorrow? 明日の決勝戦はどんな試合になるか予想できますか.

Can a dog recognize his reflection in the mirror as his own *image*? 犬は鏡に映った自分の姿を自分であると認識できますか.

Haiku readers have to use their *imagination* to fill in the unsaid. 俳句は想像力を働かせ行間を補って読まなければならない.

Godzilla isn't a real dinosaur but an *imaginary* [=invented] creature for science fiction movies. ゴジラは実在した恐竜ではなく, SF映画に出る想像上の動物だ.

---

imitate /íməteìt/

原義は〈写す〉である. **しゃべり方や動作をまねる→他の物に似せる**.
派 imitation (模造品)

That comedian is very good at *imitating* [=mimicking] famous singers. あの喜劇役者は有名歌手の物まねがとてもうまい.

Younger children often *imitate* [=copy] the way their older siblings do. 下の子は, 兄や姉のすることをよくまねるものだ.

The suspect robbed the convenience store by threatening the cashier with an *imitation* [=a fake] gun. 容疑者は, 模造銃でレジ係を脅してコンビニで強盗を働いた.

immediate /ɪmíːdiət/

語源は〈im (否) mediate (中間)〉である. **(中間に何もない)→間髪を置かない様子**.
派 immediately (すぐに)

The government response to the disaster was not *immediate* [=soon] enough, leaving the victims in a terrible condition for a long time.　政府の災害対策が遅れたので, 被災者を長期間悲惨な状況のまま置くことになった.

He had been seriously affected with hypertension, but the *immediate* [=direct] cause of his death was a lung failure.　彼は高血圧がひどかったが, 直接の死因は肺疾患だった.

The flowers were drooping, but they began to recover *immediately* [=instantly] after watering.　花はしおれていたが, 水をやるとたちまち元気を取り戻してきた.

important /ɪmpɔ́ːrtnt/

語源は〈im (に) port (運ぶ) ant (ほどの)〉である. **(中に運び込むほどに) 重要な, 大切な**.
派 importance (重要性); importantly (重要なことには)
関 import (輸入する)

Train noise is an *important* [=serious] problem to those who live near the railway lines.　鉄道の沿線に住んでいる人には列車の騒音は深刻な問題だ.

I cannot overemphasize the *importance* of a good family background for children.　子どもにとってよい家庭環境が大切であることは, いくら言っても言い過ぎにはならない.

Diet and exercise are good for weight loss and, more *importantly*, for your health.　食事制限と運動は減量に効果があるが, もっと重要なことは健康にいいことだ.

impress /imprés/

語源は〈im (に) press (押しつける)〉である. **よい印象を与える**.
派 impression (印象); impressive (よい印象を与える)
関 press (押しつける); express (表現する)

The new car *impressed* the users with its super-high gas efficiency. ＝The new car's super-high gas efficiency was very *impressive* to the users.　その新車は非常に優れた燃費で消費者の心を捉えた.

My *impression* about people in Okinawa is that they are cheerful and easy-going. ＝I have the *impression* that people in Okinawa are cheerful and easy-going.　私は, 沖縄の人たちは明るくて楽天的だという印象をもっている.

Neat and clean streets make a good *impression* on visitors.　きれいで清潔な通りは訪れた人たちによい印象を与える.

improve /imprúːv/

語源は〈im (に) prove (価値)〉である. **〜に価値をもたらす→価値を高める→改善する**.
派 improvement (改善)

The rain will probably continue until tonight, but it will *improve* [＝clear up] tomorrow.　雨は今夜まで残ると思われますが, 明日は好天になるでしょう.

The company has *improved* [＝increased] sales by introducing a new model.　会社は新しい機種を市場に出して売り上げを伸ばした.

in /ɪn/

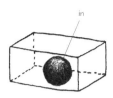

原義は〈一定の空間・時間・状況の中に〉である. **〜の空間・時・状況 (の中) に[で]**.

He was *in* and out of (the) hospital for several years before his death.　彼は,死ぬまでの数年間は入退院を繰り返していた.

His new novel is coming out *in* two months.　彼の新しい小説はあと2か月すると刊行される.　▶in+時間「〜の時間が経過した時点で」

I was *in* college *in* the late 1970's. Back *in* those days, we had no computers or cell phones.　私は1970年代の後半に大学生だったが,当時はコンピュータも携帯電話もなかった.

The soldier was wounded *in* the arm and leg *in* action.　兵士は交戦中に腕と脚を負傷した.

incident /ínsədənt/

語源は〈in (に) cident (降りかかる)〉である. **降りかかってくる不都合な出来事,不意に起こる事件**.
派 incidence (発生率); incidental (付随的な); incidentally (偶然に, ついでながら)
関 accident (事故)

The school authorities covered up the *incident* so as not to affect the pride and morale of the students.　学校当局は,事件が学生たちの誇りと士気に影響を与えないようにその事件を隠ぺいした.

The demonstration went off without *incident* [＝a hitch].　デモは事無く行われた.

Quite *incidentally*, I found some useful information for my thesis in the book.　全く偶然に,論文に有益な情報をその本で見つけた.

include /inklú:d/

include

語源は〈in (中に) clude (閉じ込める)〉である．**総体の中に～を含む**．
派 including (～を含めて); inclusive (～を含んだ)
関 conclude (締めくくる)

The price of gasoline *includes* a tax of about 50 percent.　ガソリン価格には約50パーセントの税金が含まれている．

My interests *include* [＝are] reading, gardening, music, and star watching.　僕の興味は読書，庭いじり，音楽，それに天体観測です．

More than 300 delegates *including* Nobel laureates attended the conference.　ノーベル賞受賞者を始め，300人を上回る代表者たちが会議に参加した．

The price, *inclusive of* [＝including] accommodation and breakfast, is 30 dollars.　料金は宿泊と朝食を含めて30ドルです．

increase /動 inkrí:s, 名 ínkri:s/

語源は〈in (中に) crease (伸びる)〉である．**だんだんと増える；増加**．
派 increasing (ますます増える)
関 crescent (上弦の月) 〔←満月へと成長する〕; create (生み出す); decrease (減少する)

Begin with a short run and *increase* the distance gradually.　短い距離から走り始めて徐々に距離を伸ばしなさい．

Skill *increases* with practice. ＝*Increase* in skill comes from practice.　実践することで技術は伸びてくる．

There has been *increasing* [＝growing] criticism regarding the sloppy management of the pension system.　年金制度のいい加減な管理に対して批判が高まっている．

independent /ìndɪpéndənt/

independent

語源は〈in (否) dependent (ぶら下がって)〉である. **(ぶら下がっていない)→頼っていない→自立している**.
派 independence (独立); independently (自力で)

My sister is so *independent* that she rarely asks others to help her in anything. 姉はとても自立心が強いので, 何であれ他人に助けを求めることはほとんどない.

Jawaharlal Nehru became India's first prime minister when the country won its *independence* in 1947. ジャワハラル・ネールは, インドが1947年に独立したときに最初の首相になった.

I've taken some guided tours, but now want to travel *independently* [=alone]. いくつかのツアーに参加したが, これからは個人で旅行をしたいと思っている.

individual /ìndəvídʒuəl/

語源は〈in (否) dividual (分割できる)〉である. **(これ以上分割できないひとかたまり)→個**.
派 individualism (個人主義); individuality (個性); individually (個々には) 関 divide (分割する)

Class size is a major factor in giving as much *individual* attention to students as possible. クラスの人数は, できるだけ個々の生徒に気を配るための重要な要件だ.

Sometimes we need to sacrifice the right(s) of the *individual* for our group or society. 集団や社会のために個人の権利を犠牲にしなければならないこともある.

industry /índəstri/

語源は〈indu (中に) stry (築く)〉である. **(努力して築く)→勤勉→生産→産業**.
派 industrial (産業の); industrious (勤勉な); industrialize (産業化する)　関 structure (構造)

Tourism is now one of the largest *industries* [=businesses] in many countries.　観光業は多くの国で今や主要産業の一つとなっている.

Ninomiya Kinjiroh was admired as the symbol of *industry* and integrity.　二宮金次郎は勤勉と誠実さの象徴としてあがめられた.

Industrial robots have been widely used in many manufacturing *industries*.　産業ロボットは多くの製造産業で広く使われている.

He is *industrious* [=hard-working] and frugal.　彼の生活態度は勤勉で質素だ.

inevitable /ɪnévətəbl/

語源は〈in (否) evitable (避けられる)〉である. **避けようのない→運命づけられた**.
関 evade (逃れる)

She accepted her husband's early death as *inevitable* [=her fate].　彼女は, 夫に早く死なれたのは運命だと諦めた.

Some side effects are *inevitable* [=sure to happen] with most drugs.　たいていの薬はなんらかの副作用は避けられない.

influence /ínfluəns/

語源は〈in (中に) fluence (流れ込む)〉である. **流れ込んで影響を与える**. flu- は〈流れ〉のイメージ.
関 flu (インフルエンザ, 流行性感冒); fluid (流体)

Television has a great *influence* on children's personality development. =Television greatly *influences* the way children's personality develops.　テレビは子どもの人格形成に大きな影響を与える.

He was arrested for「driving under the *influence* of alcohol [=drunk driving].　彼は飲酒運転で捕まった.

inform /infɔ́:rm/

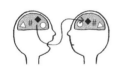

語源は〈in (中に) form (形)〉である. **頭の中に情報を形成する**. figure out〈形が形成される→理解する〉と発想が似ている.
派 information (情報)

Please keep me *informed* [=posted] about how you are doing.　近況をお知らせ〔←私に情報がもたらされた状態にして〕ください.

The police are asking for *information* from anyone who witnessed the incident.　警察は事件を目撃した人からの情報を求めている.

I have attached an article「for your *information* [=hoping it will interest you].　ご参考までに記事を添付しました.

ingredient /ɪŋgríːdiənt/

語源は〈in (中に) gredi (入る) ent (要素)〉である. **中に入っている構成要素 (食材・原料), 物事を成立させる大切な要件**.

What are the *ingredients* [=is the recipe] for this soup?　このスープの材料は何ですか.

Humor is an effective *ingredient* [=factor] of a speech.　スピーチを魅力的にする上でユーモアは大切な要素だ.

injure /índʒər/

語源は〈in (否) jure=just (正しい)〉である.**(不当な状態にする)→傷つける→身体・感情・名誉を傷つける**. injure は「事故などによる負傷」, hurt は「軽いけが」に用いる.
関 injury (負傷, 損傷)

I was *injured* in a car accident.　車の事故で負傷した.

The crushing defeat *injured* [=wounded] the champion's pride.　ひどい負け方をしたので, チャンピオンのプライドが傷ついた.

He survived the accident without serious *injuries* [=being seriously injured].　彼は事故で重傷を負わなくて済んだ.

The actress sued the magazine for *injury* [=damage] to her dignity and reputation.　女優は自分の尊厳と名前を汚すとしてその雑誌を訴えた.

input /ínput/

語源は〈in (中に) put (入れる)〉である. **入力；(入力された) データ, (知っている) 情報；入力する**.
関 output (出力, 生産高)

I need your *input* [=information] on how I should prepare for the exam. 受験準備にあなたのアドバイスが欲しい.

At the end of the day, the manager ⌈*inputs* the sales figures [=puts the sales figures into the computer]. 一日の終わりに, 支配人は売上高をパソコンに打ち込む.

instruct /instrʌ́kt/

語源は〈in (中に) struct (築く)〉である. **相手の頭の中に必要情報を築く**.
派 instruction (教育, 指示)；instructor (指導者)

The doctor *instructed* [=advised] young people on the dangers of smoking and drinking. 医師は若い人たちに喫煙と飲酒の危険性について説いた.

You must read manufacturer's *instructions* [=directions] carefully before using the pesticide. 殺虫剤を使う前に使用説明をちゃんと読まないといけない.

The government introduced English language *instruction* [=teaching] in elementary schools. 政府は小学校に英語教育を導入した.

ingredient, injure, input, instruct

insult /ɪnsʌ́lt/

語源は〈in(上に)sult(跳びかかる)〉である. **傷つくことばを浴びせかける**. 元来は「襲う」の意であったが,現代では〈ことばで襲う〉の意でのみ使われる.
関 assault(襲う);result(結果として生じる)

I was deeply *insulted* [=offended] when my teacher said, "Didn't you copy someone else's writing?" 先生に「誰か他の人の作文を写したんじゃないの?」と言われてとても傷ついた.

The fans shouted *insults* [=abusive words] at the players who were miserably defeated. ファンたちは, 惨敗した選手たちに野次(やじ)を飛ばした.

insure /ɪnʃúər/

語源は〈in=en(する)sure(確実)〉である. **確実にする→保証する→保険をかける**.
派 insurance(保険)

Did you ⌈get your house *insured* [=*insure* your house] against fire? 自宅に火災保険を掛けましたか.

What does your car *insurance* cover? あなたの自動車保険はどういった保障内容ですか.

intend /inténd/

語源は〈in (に) tend (伸ばす)〉である. **〜に気持ちを向ける→〜しようという気持ちになる**.
派 intention (意図)

He *intends* ⌜that his son should [=to let his son] inherit his business. 彼は息子に自分の店を継がせるつもりである.

For what purpose do you *intend* to use your computer? (お客様は)どんな目的でパソコンを使うつもりですか.

What age group is this book *intended* [=meant] for? この本はどの年代向けですか.

I have no *intention* [=thoughts] of quitting my present job. 今の仕事を辞めるつもりはありません.

---

interest /ínt(ə)rəst/

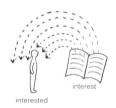

interested

語源は〈inter (中に) est (いる)〉である. **対象の中に入っている→関わる→興味を持たせる；興味**.
派 interesting (興味深い)

It *interested* me [=I found it *interesting*] to learn that the president of our company is from the same hometown as mine. 会社の社長が同郷の出身と知って興味をもった.

The media has been following the incident with great *interest*. メディアはその事件を非常な関心をもって追っている.

After his wife's death, he seems to have lost his *interest* in everything. 妻の死以後, 彼は何事にも興味を失ったようだ.

interfere /ìntərfíər/

語源は〈inter(相互) fere(打つ)〉である. **相互に打ち合う→相手の妨げをする→干渉する**.
派 interference (干渉, 介入)

We shouldn't *interfere* [=meddle] in the affairs of other families. 他家のことに干渉しないほうがいい.

Don't *interfere*. Leave me alone!　邪魔しないで, ほっといてよ！

The player got a five-minute penalty for *interference*.　その選手は, 妨害行為で5分間プレー停止のペナルティーを受けた.

international /ìntərnǽʃənl/

語源は〈inter(間=際) national(国の)〉である. **国家間の→国を超えての**.
派 internationally (国際的に)　関 nation (国家)

He is a pianist with an *international* fame. =He is an *internationally* famous pianist.　彼は国際的に有名なピアニストだ.

Haneda Airport handles both domestic and *international* flights.　羽田空港は国内便も国際便も扱っている.

interrupt /ìntərʌ́pt/

語源は〈inter(間) rupt(割る)〉である。**間に割り込む→他者の行動の邪魔をする**。

派 interruption(中断, 妨害)　関 rupture(破裂)

Don't *interrupt* me while I'm talking.　私が話しているのだから(横から口出しして)邪魔しないでよ。

My sleep is *interrupted* [=disturbed] by frequent urination during the night.　私は夜間しばしばトイレに行きたくなるので, 睡眠が妨げられます。

I hate commercial *interruptions* in the middle of programs. =I hate that commercials *interrupt* the natural flow of programs.　番組の途中で割り込むCMが嫌いだ。

into /íntə/

語源は〈in(中) to(へ)〉である。**(あるところへ)進入する→(ある状態に)変化する**。

As the day turned *into* night, the festive mood rose and prevailed over the town.　日が落ちて夜になると, お祭りムードは高まって町中が沸いた。

He decided to get *into* local politics as a city councilor.　彼は市会議員として地元の政界に入る決心をした。

The rioting in the capital continued late *into* the night.　首都での暴動は深夜まで続いた。

My daughter is *into* [=crazy about] the actor.　娘はあの俳優に夢中になっている。

introduce /ìntrəd(j)úːs/

語源は ⟨intro (中へ) duce (引く)⟩ である．**中へ引き入れる→未知の情報を導き入れる→新規のことを導入する．**
派 introduction (紹介，導入，最初の経験)
関 reduce (減少させる)

The substitute teacher *introduced* herself to the class.　代理の先生はクラスの生徒たちに自己紹介をした．

Older generations are reluctant to *introduce* new technology in the workplace.　年輩の人たちは，職場に新しい技術を導入するのをためらう．

You need *a letter of introduction* to apply for the position.　この職に応募するには紹介状が必要です．

My first ⌈*introduction* to [=encounter with] personal computers was in my early thirties, about thirty years ago.　私が初めてパソコンに接したのは 30 代初めのころで，かれこれ 30 年ほど前になる．

---

invent /ìnvént/

語源は ⟨in (上に) vent (来る)⟩ である．**(〜に来る→〜に現れる) →なかったものを作り上げる (発明，捏造(ねつぞう))．**
派 invention (発明，捏造) ; inventor (発明家)

Thomas Edison was a great *inventor*; he *invented* hundreds of things we use today.　トーマス・エジソンは偉大な発明家で，私たちが現代使っている何百もの製品を発明した．

He *invented* an excuse for not going to work.　彼は欠勤の口実を作った．

Parts of the drama are true, but much of it is *invention*.　このドラマは部分的には史実通りだが，多くは作り話だ．

invite /inváit/

語源は〈in (中へ) vite (求める)〉である．**人を招く (意図的)，不本意な事を招く (無作為)．**
派 invitation (招待); inviting (人目を引く)

The boss *invited* us to dinner after work.　仕事が終わると，上司は食事に誘ってくれた．

Susie is complaining about her parents who constantly *invite* themselves over to her place for the weekend.　スージーは，両親が週末にいつも彼女の家に押しかけてくることに不平を言っている．

Don't *invite* trouble by intruding into other people's private lives.　他人の私生活に入りこんでトラブルを引き起こしてはだめだよ．

The weather in Tahiti is warm and *inviting* [=enticing].　タヒチの天候は暖かくてさわやかである．

involve /inváːlv/

語源は〈in (中に) volve (転がる)〉である．**巻き込む→入り組む→〜ということになる．**
派 involvement (巻き添え; 介入)
関 evolve (発展する); revolve (回転する); volume (容量)

A truck and three cars were *involved* in the accident.　トラック1台と車3台が事故に巻き込まれた．

Parents should not get too much *involved* in their grown-up children's lives.　親は成人した子どもたちの生活にあまり入り込まないほうがよい．

Studying a foreign language *involves* [=means] learning about new ways of thinking as well as those of communication.　外国語を勉強すると未知のコミュニケーション法と発想法を学ぶことになる．

iron /áɪərn/

原義は〈鉄〉である. **鉄, 鉄分→鉄製品→アイロン→アイロンをかける；鉄のように強固な**.
派 ironed (アイロンのかかった)；ironing (アイロンかけ)

Iron deficiency can cause weakness, anemia, and fatigue.　鉄分が不足すると，虚弱，貧血，疲労などを引き起こすことがある.

Would you please *iron* these dresses, mom?　母さん，ドレスにアイロンかけてちょうだいね.

The president ⌈has a will of *iron* [＝is iron-willed]; he is determined to realize what he had promised.　大統領は鋼鉄のように強固な意志を持っており，公約したことは断固実現させる気概をもっている.

issue /íʃuː/

語源は〈is (外へ) sue (出る)〉である. **(出てくる) 印刷物；(表沙汰になる) 問題；発刊する，発令する**.

Protection of one's privacy has become a major *issue* in this technologically advanced society.　今日のようなテクノロジーの発達した社会では，個人のプライバシーを守ることが大きな問題となっている.

School bullying is featured in this month's *issue* of "Classroom Management."　学校におけるいじめが「学級経営」の今月号に特集されている.

A tsunami warning has been *issued* for the coasts of the Pacific.　津波警報が太平洋沿岸に発令された.

it /ɪt/

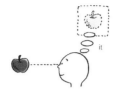

原義は〈それ〉である. **(例の) それ, (話題にしている) それ, (環境として存在している) それ.**

"Where is today's paper?" "*It* is over there." 「今日の新聞はどこ?」「あそこだよ」

Many working mothers have a hard time caring for a child after *it* is born. 働く母親は子どもの誕生後, 養育に大変な苦労をする人が多い.

Julie scarcely gets angry, or if she is, she won't show *it*. ジュリーはあまり怒らないし, もし怒っても (怒りを) 顔に出さない.

I don't like *it* when people sit directly across from me at an empty restaurant. 誰もいないレストランで, 自分のすぐ向かいの席に座られるのは嫌だ.

item /áɪtəm/

原義は〈(項目を数える時に言う) 同じく〉である. **品物, 品目;項目, 記事.**
派 itemize (箇条書きにする)

There are a lot of *items* [=topics] to discuss at today's meeting. 今日の会議で議論することがたくさんある.

When we eat out, my husband always orders the same *item* as mine on the menu. 外食すると, 夫はいつも私と同じものを注文するのよ.

I saw an *item* [=article] in today's local paper about a man who was arrested for hit and run. 今日の地方紙に, ひき逃げで捕まった男の記事が出ていたよ.

jealous /dʒéləs/

語源は〈jeal=zeal(熱中)ous(いっぱい)〉である. **嫉妬して, うらやましい**.
派 jealousy(嫉妬, ねたみ)

A married man may sometimes feel *jealous* of his unattached friends.　結婚している男は, 時に独身の友だちをうらやましく思うものだ.

We feel *jealous*, more or less, of our successful friends.　人は, 成功した友だちのことを多少はうらやましく思うものだ.

I can't help but be very *jealous* whenever my boyfriend talks to other girls.　私って, ボーイフレンドが他の女の子に話しかけているといつも嫉妬してしまうの.

job /dʒá:b/

原義は〈仕事の一つ〉である. **ある仕事; 仕事内容**.
派 jobless(失業中の)

What is your *job*? ＝What do you do?　お仕事は何ですか.

He was offered and took a consulting *job* at a bank after retiring from politics.　彼は政界を辞めた後, 銀行の顧問の仕事に誘われ着任した.

The pitcher did a good *job*; he allowed only one run with nine strikeouts.　この投手はみごとな働きをした. わずか1失点で9三振を奪ったのだ.

The *jobless* [＝unemployment] rate remains stalled at more than ten percent.　失業率は依然10パーセントを越え, 低調なままだ.

join /dʒɔ́ɪn/

原義は〈くっつける〉である．**別々のものを合わせる，別々のものが一緒になる．**
派 joint（関節）

The island is *joined* [=connected] to the mainland by a bridge.　この島は橋で本土とつながっている．

Would you like to *join* [=come with] us for lunch at a Chinese restaurant?　中華料理店で僕たちと一緒に食事しませんか？

The two banks ⌈*joined* together [=merged] to form the ABC Bank.　両銀行は合併して ABC 銀行になった．

joke /dʒóʊk/

原義は〈冗談，ふざけ〉である．**相手を面白がらせるための冗談，取るに足らない冗談．**
関 jest（冗談）

At first I took it as a *joke*, but then it really seemed like he was telling the truth.　最初は冗談だと思ったが，彼はどうも本当のことを言っているように思えた．

I meant it as a *joke*, but he took it seriously.　冗談のつもりで言ったのだけど，彼は真剣に受け取った．

Don't take it seriously; he was only *joking*.　深刻に考えるなよ．彼は冗談で言ったんだよ．

It's *no joke* to smoke as many as forty or more cigarettes a day.　1日にタバコを 40 本以上も吸うなんて，冗談じゃないよ．

jealous, job, join, joke

journal /dʒə́ːrnl/

語源は〈jour(日)al(の)〉である.**日々の記録→(個人的)日記,日誌→(社会的)雑誌,専門誌**.
派 journalist(新聞・雑誌・放送記者);journalism(マスコミ業界)

I've been keeping a *journal* [=diary] since I got married.　結婚してからずっと日記をつけている.

Sometimes I forget to write in my *journal* [=diary].　ときどき日記をつけるのを忘れてしまう.

The doctor regularly writes columns for medical *journals*.　その医師は医学雑誌に定期的にコラムを書いている.

He has been working as a reporter in broadcast *journalism*.　彼は記者として放送業界で仕事をしている.

journey /dʒə́ːrni/

原義は〈一日の旅〉である.**旅,旅行**.「日帰り旅行」はa day tripというのが普通.

We made a *journey* to Paris to see the sights.　パリへ観光旅行した.

Our *journey* to Paris to see the sights was wonderful.　パリへの観光旅行はすばらしかった.

joy /dʒɔ́ɪ/

原義は〈喜び〉である．**喜び，喜びをもたらすもの．**
派 joyful（喜ばしい）；joyous（喜びあふれる）
関 enjoy（楽しむ）

Reading books is one of my greatest *joys*.　読書は私の最大の楽しみの一つだ．

Sara jumped for *joy* at the news she had been long waiting for.　サラは待ち焦がれていた知らせに小躍りして喜んだ．

One cannot be educated without experiencing the *joys* and sorrows of life.　人生の喜びと悲しみを経験することなくして人は成長できない．

I love the *joyful* [=joyous] atmosphere towards the end of the year.　僕は年の瀬の高揚した雰囲気が好きだ．

judge /dʒʌ́dʒ/

語源は〈ju（法）dge（言う）〉である．**法に照らして裁く→評価を決める；判事，審査員．**
関 just（公平な）；jury（裁判員団）；juror（裁判員）；judicature（司法）

People should be *judged* [=assessed] by their deeds, not their words.　人はことばではなくて行動で評価されるべきだ．

Judging from her looks in the photo, she seems to be very well.　写真で見ると彼女は元気そうだね．

Have you ever *judged* [=participated in] a case as a juror?　裁判員として事件の審理に参加したことがありますか．

She served as a *judge* in the piano competition.　彼女はこのピアノコンクールの審査員を務めた．

juice /dʒúːs/

原義は〈絞り汁〉である.**(果物・野菜・肉の)汁,(果物・野菜の)ジュース;分泌液**. ju- は〈絞りの圧迫〉が感じられる.
派 juicer(ジューサー,果汁搾り器);juicy((ステーキなどが)ジューシーな;〔うわさなどが〕関心をそそる,きわどい)

I use a *juicer* to make apple *juice*.　私はジューサーを使って,りんごジュースを作ります.

When making gravy from meat *juices*, skim off as much fat as possible.　肉汁からグレービーソースを作るときは,できるだけ脂肪分を取り除くようにしなさい.

The stomach secretes digestive *juices* [=liquids].　胃は消化液を分泌する.

jump /dʒʌmp/

原義は〈ぴょんと跳ぶ〉である.**跳び上がる,衝動的に飛びつく**. ju- に〈押しつけ〉が感じられる. jump とは足を使って大地を押しつけて跳ねること.

How can I stop my cat from *jumping* up onto the dining table?　うちの猫は食卓に飛び乗ってしまうのだけど,どうやったらやめさせられるだろうか.

A few children are enjoying *jumping* rope on the playground.　子どもたちが遊び場で縄跳びをして遊んでいる.

Frogs can *jump* but they can't fly.　カエルは跳ねることはできるが,飛ぶことはできない.

Don't *jump* to conclusions before you have the facts.　事実を確かめないで結論を急ぐのはだめだよ.

junior /dʒúːnjər/

語源は〈juni (若い) or (〜より《比較級》)〉である. **年下の, 後輩の**.
関 juvenile (年少の)

My brother is three years ⌈my *junior* [*junior* to me]. = My brother is *junior* to me by three years. 弟は3歳年下だ.
Robert is a *junior* partner in the office. ロバートは職場の後輩だ.

just /dʒʌ́st/

原義は〈ちょうど合っ〉である. **ちょうど;(ちょうど→余分がない) やっと;(ちょうど→ちゃんと) 法に合う**.
派 justice (正義); justify (正当化する)

My teacher looked *just* as embarrassed as I was when I saw him in the nude theater. ストリップ劇場で先生に会ったら, 僕と同じくらい気まずそうな様子だった.

The bridge is *just* [=only] wide enough for two cars to pass each other. その橋は2台の車がやっと行き交える幅しかない.

"Didn't you see Ted?" "He was here *just now*." 「テッド見なかった?」「さっきまでここにいたよ」

I don't believe there is a ⌈*just cause* [=good reason] for starting any war. いかなる戦争も, 始めるのに大義などないはずだ.

keep /kíːp/

原義は〈じっとする〉である.**(変化が起こらないように)そのままの状態を保ち続ける**.
関 keepsake（形見）

Keep your hands [=Make sure your hands are] clean when preparing meals. 食事の準備をする時は，手を清潔にしておきなさい．

Just be yourself and *keep* [=stay] cool and composed throughout the interview. 面接を受ける時は，自然体で冷静に落ちついているように心掛けなさい．

You need to learn how to *keep* moisture from damaging your clothes and other stuff in the closet. クローゼットの中の衣類などが湿気で傷まないようにする方法を知っておく必要があるよ．

key /kíː/

原義は〈かぎ〉である．**鍵**(かぎ)，**(成否の)鍵；重要な；ピアノなどの鍵**(けん) → **(鍵の出す)音の調子**．
関 keyboard（パソコンのキーボード，楽器の鍵盤）

Making a proper plan and following it through is the *key* [=secret] to meeting a deadline. 適切な計画を立てて，それをちゃんとこなしていくことが締め切りに間に合わせるひけつだ．

Albert Einstein was one of the *key* [=central] figures in the development of modern physics. アルバート・アインシュタインは，現代物理学の発展における中心人物の一人だった．

That boy sings loud(ly) and ⌈off *key* [=out of tune] whenever we do a chorus. コーラスをすると，あの子は決まって大きな声で調子はずれの歌い方をする． ▶off key「キーをはずして」

kick /kík/

原義は〈蹴る,蹴とばす〉である．**脚で強く蹴る；蹴り，キック**．
関 kickoff（キックオフ）

Poor swimmers tend to *kick* their legs too much, splashing lots of water up and around. 泳ぎの下手な人は脚をひどくバタつかせ，水しぶきをまき散らして泳ぎがちだ．

He ⌈gave the ball a powerful *kick* [=kicked the ball powerfully]⌉ to score the winning goal. 彼は力強くボールを蹴って決勝のゴールを決めた．

The baseball season has ⌈*kicked off* [=started]⌉, announcing that the spring has just arrived across the archipelago. 野球のシーズンが始まって，列島にあまねく春の到来を告げた．

---

kill /kíl/

原義は〈突き刺す〉である．**危害を加えて殺す；植物を枯らす；効果を損なう；薬が痛みを軽減する；時間・機会をつぶす**．
派 killer（死に至らせる病気；殺人者）

On December 8th, 1980, John Lennon was shot ⌈and *killed* [=to death]⌉ outside his apartment in New York City. 1980年12月8日に，ジョン・レノンはニューヨークのアパートの前で撃たれて死んだ．

Don't use too much pepper so as not to *kill* [=spoil] the natural taste of the food. 食べ物の自然な味が損なわれるので，コショウを使いすぎるとだめですよ．

Many workers *kill* [=spend] time on their way home in cafés and shops to avoid the traffic. 帰宅時に交通の混雑を避けるために，カフェや店で時間をつぶす通勤者がけっこういる．

kind /káɪnd/

原義は〈生まれたままの〉である. **無垢(く)な→性格のよい→親切な；(同じ生まれの)→同種の→種類**.
派 kindness（親切な行為）； kindly（親切にも）

It is very *kind* of you to let me know about that website. It will be of great use to me.　あのサイトを教えてくれてありがとう. とても役立つと思います.

They say my girl friend is「*kind of*［＝a bit］fat but I still like the way she looks.　人は, 僕のガールフレンドはちょっと太り気味だと言うんだけど, 僕はやはり彼女の容姿が好きなんだ.

She knows all *kinds* of things surrounding the show business— singers, actors, dancers, and their backgrounds.　彼女は芸能界のあらゆることに通じている. 歌手や俳優, ダンサー, それに彼らの境遇も.

---

kitchen /kítʃən/

原義は〈料理する (cook) 所〉である. **(家庭の) 台所, (レストランなどの) 調理場**.

It was commonly accepted in our society that men were to stay out of the *kitchen*. ＝That the *kitchen* is not the place for men used to be common sense in our culture.　私たちの社会では, 男子厨房に入らずということが世間の常識だった.

We grow leafy vegetables in the *kitchen garden*.　菜園で葉物野菜を作っている.

knee /níː/

原義は〈曲がる〉である。**(脚の曲がる部分である) ひざ**.
kne- には〈曲げる〉の意味合いがある：knuckle (こぶし)
〔←指を曲げた時に出る指関節〕
派 kneel (ひざまずく)

She *knelt down* [=dropped down on her *knees*] beside her dying mother and prayed.　彼女は死の迫った母親のそばにひざまずいて祈りを捧げた．

The dog growled at me when I approached him *on hands and knees*.　四つんばいになって近づくと，犬はうなり声を上げた．

knock /náːk/

原義は〈(こぶしを丸めて) ノックする〉である．**ドアや窓をノックする，こぶしや固いもので打ちつける，打撃を与える**．

I *knocked* on the door but got no answer.　戸をノックしたが，返事がなかった．

The teacher *knocked* on the desk to attract the attention of some absent-minded students.　教師は，ぼんやりしている生徒に注目させるために教卓をたたいた．

I fear the strong wind will *knock* [=blow] *off* the cherry blossoms that are just beginning to bloom.　強風で咲き始めたばかりの桜が吹き飛ばされないかと心配だ．

know /nóu/

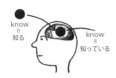

原義は〈わかる〉である. **～を知っている, ～を知る.**
派 knowingly（故意に）
関 diagnose（診断する）; ignore（無視する）

He *knows* all the Beatles' lyrics *by heart*.　彼はビートルズの曲の歌詞を全部暗記している.

Rodin is best *known* [＝recognized] for his sculpture, *The Thinker*.　ロダンは彼の彫刻「考える人」で一番よく知られている.

We've *known* each other by chance while traveling.　私たちは旅行している時にたまたま知り合いになった.

Someone in my office has *knowingly* [＝deliberately] deleted my mail in the inbox.　職場の誰かが故意に僕の受信メールを削除していた.

knowledge /ná:lɪdʒ/

語源は〈know（知る）ledge（行動）〉である.**（知ること）→知識, 認識, 情報.**
派 knowledgeable（知識の豊富な）

It's「common *knowledge* [＝widely believed] that the Universe started as a result of a big bang 13.8 billion years ago.　宇宙は138億年も前にビッグバンによって始まったということは常識だ.

The photos I took had been used in the magazine without my *knowledge*.　この雑誌に私の撮った写真が知らないうちに使われていた.

My mom「has good *knowledge* of [＝is familiar with] traditional herbal medicine.　母は漢方薬に詳しい.

To my knowledge [＝As far as I am aware], my brother has been to Taiwan twice.　僕の知っている限りでは, 兄は台湾に二度ほど行っている.

labor /léɪbər/

原義は〈物事がうまく運べない〉である．**物・事の運びに力を労する；重労働**．
派 laborer（労働者）；laborious（骨の折れる）
関 elaborate（手の込んだ）

The president has *labored* [=struggled] to convince the opposition party to accept their proposal.　大統領は，野党に自分たちの案が受け入れられるように手を尽くして説得にあたった．

Many job seekers will not take a job that requires manual *labor*.　肉体労働を嫌う求職者が多い．

How long does *labor* usually last during a first-time birth?　初産の時，陣痛はどれくらい続くものですか．

Mining is *laborious* [=backbreaking], and the risk of injury is high.　鉱山で働くのは重労働で，けがの危険性も高い．

---

lack /lǽk/

原義は〈欠けていること〉である．**不足，欠乏；必要なものを欠く**．
派 lacking（〜が不足している）

He is constantly complaining about *lack* of time, while using up time doing trivial things.　彼はつまらないことに時間を使って，いつも時間がないとこぼしている．

Don't worry, no one ever died just from *lack* of sleep.　心配するなよ，眠れなくて死んだやつはいないんだから．

His theory *lacks* [=is *lacking* in] convincing evidence.　彼の論は説得力のある根拠に欠けている．

land /lǽnd/

原義は〈(海から見た) 陸〉である. **土地, 国土, 所有地**; **上陸する, 着陸する, 着地する**.
派 landing ((飛行機などの) 着陸)
関 landlord (家主, 地主)

The *land* that the farmer sold is going to be developed into a residential property. 農夫の売った土地は宅地用に造成される.

The Pilgrims *landed* at Plymouth in the year 1620. 清教徒たちはプリマスに1620年に上陸した.

The typhoon is expected to *land* [=make landfall] somewhere near Kagoshima. 台風は鹿児島付近に上陸するものと思われます.

A cat can *land* on its feet, even when dropped upside down. 猫は逆さまに落としても足からうまく着地できる.

landscape /lǽndskèɪp/

語源は〈land (土地) scape (状態・様子)〉である. **目に映る景色・様相**; 目に映る風景をよくする→**造園する, 景観をよくする**.
関 landscape gardener (庭師)

When making a *landscape* photo, you should first learn how to frame it properly. 風景写真を撮るには, まず適切な構図のとり方を身につける必要がある.

With the advent of electronic books, the publication *landscape* [= situation] is changing at a rapid pace. 電子書籍の出現によって出版界の様相が急激に変化し始めている.

Good *landscaping* around your home will add value to your property. 家の周りの景観をよくすると地所の価値が上がる.

language /lǽŋgwɪdʒ/

原義は〈舌〉である. **伝達のための言語；言い方, ことば遣い.**
関 linguistics（言語学）

<ことば>

"Silent Night" has been translated into more than three hundred *languages*, and is sung all over the world. 「聖夜」は, 300以上もの言語に訳されて世界中で歌われている.

Children acquire *language* unconsciously, so the kinds of speech they hear have a great impact on their *language* development later in life. 子どもは無意識に言語を身につけるので, 彼らが耳にすることばは以後の言語の発達に大きな影響を及ぼす.

You need to「watch your *language*［=be careful about the words you use］. ことば遣いに気をつけないといけません.

lap /lǽp/

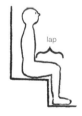

原義は〈スカートのすそ〉である.**（スカートのすそが覆う）ひざの部分, ひざ；（スカートのすそがぐるり）一周；（スカートのすそに覆われているように）庇護(ひご)に囲まれた状況.**
関 laptop（ラップトップ［ノート型パソコン］）

I managed to overtake the leader in the final *lap* of the race. 最後の一周で先頭を追い抜いた.

Some pets truly live in the *lap* of luxury; special imported food, a weekly visit to a professional haircut and massages are just a part of their lives. ペットの中にはとてもぜいたくな環境で生活をしているものがいる. 特製の輸入食を食べ, 毎週のように理容やマッサージを受けに行く, などは彼らの生活のほんの一端である.

large /lá:rdʒ/

原義は〈潤沢である様子〉である．**通常よりも量や数が多い**．
派 largely（主として）

How *large* was the audience?　聴衆はどれぐらいの人数でしたか．

Japan is a small country with a *large* population.　日本の国土は小さいが人口は多い．

The Australian economy is *largely*〔＝mainly〕based on natural resources.　オーストラリアの経済は主として天然資源に頼っている．

Two men were arrested but one man is still *at large* ten days after the robbery.　二人は捕まったが，強盗事件後 10 日経っても一人はまだ逃走中だ．

▶ be at large「（監禁されず）自由状態である，未逮捕である」

---

last¹ /læst/

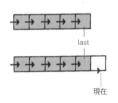

原義は〈一番遅い（last＝latest）〉である．**最後の→一番最近の→直前の**．

It was about six months ago that we *last* met.　この前会ってからほぼ半年になるね．

The *last* thing we need are politicians who are only interested in getting people's votes.　得票のことばかり考えてる政治家はまったく必要としない〔←優先順位の最後にくる〕．

Last but not least, everything we sell has a ten-year warranty.　最後に，これは重要なことですが，私ども商品はすべて 10 年間の保証がございます．

last² /lǽst/

原義は〈ずーっとそのままの状態で続く〉である. **(一定期間) 続く, 長持ちする.**
派 lasting (長持ちする)

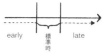

How long did the earthquake *last*? どれくらい揺れが続いたの.

How long does a music copyright *last* [=remain valid]? 音楽著作権の有効期間はどれくらいですか.

Fossil fuels won't *last* forever. 化石燃料はいつか枯渇する〔←永遠に続くわけではない〕.

Alkaline batteries are *long-lasting*. アルカリ電池は寿命が長い.

late /léɪt/

原義は〈定刻に遅れている〉である. **物事が時間的に基準より遅れて起こる様子.**
派 later (後で)

I had to work *late* (into the night) to meet the deadline. 締め切りに間に合わせるために, 遅くまで仕事をしなくてはいけなかった.

The mother noticed her son is a bit ⌈*late* in starting to talk [=delayed in his speech]. 母親は息子のことばが少し遅れていることに気づいた.

We usually let our kids ⌈sleep *late* [=sleep in] on weekends. 週末はたいてい, 子どもたちに朝寝させているわ.

The Beatles had profound influence on the *later* development of pop music. ビートルズは, その後のポップミュージックの発展に大きな影響を与えた.

lately /léɪtli/

語源は〈late (最近) ly (ころに)〉である.**このごろ,近ごろ**.通例,現在完了形と共に使う.

She hasn't been looking very well *lately*. 彼女は近ごろ,顔色があまりよくないように見える.

She has been one of the busiest actresses in Hollywood *lately*. 彼女は最近ハリウッドで最も忙しい女優の一人だ.

I've not seen Bob *lately*. Have you? 最近,ボブを見かけないのだけど,あなたは (見かけた)?

launch /lɔ́ːntʃ/

原義は〈弾丸をドーンと打ち放つ〉である.**(華々しく) 打ち上げる, (企画などを) 打ち出す**.

NASA will *launch* another high-tech weather satellite next year. NASA (米国航空宇宙局) は来年,もう一つハイテク気象衛星を打ち上げる予定だ.　▶NASA =National Aeronautics and Space Administration

The company *launched* a glasses-free 3-D TV late last year. この会社は昨年末,めがねのいらない 3D テレビを発売した.　▶3-D =Three Dimensional

laundry /lɔ́:ndri/

語源は〈laund（洗う）ry（場・物）〉である．**洗濯場，クリーニング店；洗濯物，洗濯すること．**
派 launder（洗濯する）　関 lavatory（手洗い，トイレ）

Before the coming of automatic washing machines, we used to ˈwash *laundry*［＝do (the) *laundry*］by hand.　自動洗濯機の出現までは洗濯物を手洗いしていたのですよ．

My husband *does the laundry* for our family.　夫が家族の洗濯物を洗ってくれます．

Three bank officers were arrested on suspicion of *money laundering*.　銀行役員が3人，マネーロンダリング（資金洗浄）の容疑で逮捕された．
▶ launder は〈不法所得の汚れたお金を洗ってきれいな金に見せかける〉の意．

law /lɔ́:/

原義は〈置く〉である．**（定め置く規則）→遵守すべき法律，スポーツのルール，科学的法則．**
派 lawful（合法である）; unlawful（不法である）; lawyer（弁護士）　関 lawsuit（訴訟沙汰）; lay（置く）

It is ˈagainst the *law*［＝*unlawful*］to carry guns and swords in public.　公共の場で銃や刃物を携帯することは違法になる．

They say that Isaac Newton discovered the *law* of gravity when he saw an apple fall from a tree.　アイザック・ニュートンは木から落ちるりんごを見て重力の法則を発見したと言われている．

The *lawyer* helped the company avoid a *lawsuit* from the employees.　弁護士の助言で，会社は従業員から出された訴訟問題を回避できた．

lay /léɪ/

原義は〈横たえるように置く〉である．**人を横たえる，物を敷く，テーブルなどを敷設する**．類義の stand は〈立てるように置く〉の意味合い．

The rescuers gently *laid* the injured person on the stretcher. 救助隊員はけが人を担架にゆっくり寝かせた．

We *laid* sheets of newspaper on the floor to catch paint splatters. ペンキの跳ねを防ぐために床に新聞紙を敷いた．

Dad *laid* [=put] aside the newspaper he had been reading and turned on the television. 父は読んでいた新聞を横に置いてテレビをつけた．

Due to the depression, many workers have been *laid off* for an indefinite period of time. 不景気のために，多くの労働者が無期限で解雇されている．

---

lazy /léɪzi/

原義は〈のんびりしている〉である．**さぼり気味の，意欲のない，動きの鈍い**．
派 lazily（のんびりと，ゆっくりと）；laziness（怠惰）

I have a very *lazy* person on my staff who endlessly gossips at work. さぼってばかりで，いつも無駄話をしているやつが職場にいる．

I know I should work harder, but I'm feeling *lazy*. もっと頑張らないといけないと分かってるんだけど，どうもやる気にならないんだよ．

The cat stretched out from his nap and walked *lazily* towards the food. 猫が眠りから覚めて伸びをして，のそりのそりと餌に向かった．

The mother blamed her son's bad grades on *laziness*. 母親は，成績が悪かったのは怠けているからだと息子を叱った．

lead /líːd/

原義は〈道を案内する〉である．**先頭に立って進む，率いる；〜へ導く・至らせる；〜な生活を送る**．
派 leading（先頭に立つ，主要な）；leader（指導者）
関 leadership（リーダーシップ，指導力）

Untreated hypertension can *lead to* serious diseases, including stroke, heart disease and kidney failure. 高血圧をそのままにしておくと，卒中，心臓疾患，腎臓病など重篤な病気になる可能性がある．

Where does this road *lead* (to)? この道はどこへ続いているの？

My son *leads* his team as captain. 息子はキャプテンとしてチームを率いている．

Hawaii's *leading* [=number one] source of income is tourism. ハワイの一番の収入源は観光業だ．

He has been *leading* a quiet *life* after retirement. 彼は退職後，ゆったりとした生活を送っている．

leak /líːk/

原義は〈したたる〉である．**容器から液体や気体が漏れる；秘密・情報が洩(も)れる**．
派 leakage（漏洩(ろうえい)）；leaky（漏れやすい）

The explosion was caused by a gas *leak*. 爆発はガス漏れによるものだった．

A secret government video footage *leaked out* on to the Internet. 政府の秘密ビデオ映像がインターネット上に漏出した．

There is a site that *leaks* secret information anonymously. 匿名で秘密情報を漏出させるサイトがある．

lean /líːn/

原義は〈坂になる〉である．**傾く，傾ける；寄りかかる，頼る．**
関 cline（傾く）

He is a libertarian, *leaning* a bit to the left.　彼は自由主義者だが，やや左がかっている．　▶ one's political leanings「(人)の政治的指向」

The old man rose to his feet *leaning* heavily *on* his cane.　老人はよたよたとつえにもたれながら立ち上がった．

Everyone should be determined to live their old age without *leaning* [=depending] *on* others.　誰でも，老年期を他の人に頼ることなく生きるという気概をもつべきだ．

learn /lə́ːrn/

原義は〈道をたどって経験する〉である．**(経験を通して)知識を身につける，事柄を知る．**
派 learner（学習者）

I have just *learned* [=been informed] that I am pregnant with twins.　私は双子を妊娠していることが分かった．

I failed to *learn* to ride a bicycle [=learn how to ride a bicycle], because I was weak during my childhood.　子どもの時に病弱だったので，自転車に乗ることを覚えそこねた．

I don't like beer and wine. Can we *learn* to enjoy the taste of alcohol?　ビールやワインがだめなの．お酒の味が分かるようになれるかしら．

I had to go over it many times before I *learned* my speech *by heart*.　スピーチを暗記するまでに何度も繰り返し練習した．

least /líːst/

little　less　least

原義は〈最も小さい〉である．**数量や程度が最も少ない**．little の最上級．

He didn't have the *least* idea of what his wife had in mind.　彼は，妻がどんなことを計画しているのか皆目見当がつかなかった．

What the author states in the article is unfair to the defendant *to say the least*.　著者が論文の中で述べていることは，控えめに言っても被告に不公平だ．

However busy I am, I have *at least* one hour a day to spend with my kids.　どんなに忙しくても，最低 1 時間は子どもと過ごすようにしている．

Children are born innocent; *at least* I think they are.　子どもは純真無垢（む く）なものとして生まれてくる；少なくとも私はそうだと思う．

leave¹ /líːv/

原義は〈場所を離れる〉である．**ある所から離れる→ある所の物・状態を残して去る→そのままの状態にしておく**．

Please *leave* a message after the beep.　ピーという音の後に伝言を残してください．

"What will happen, if I *leave* my acne untreated?" "It may *leave* permanent scarring on the skin."　「このにきびを放っておくとどうなりますか」「肌に跡が残って消えなくなってしまうかも知れません」

I'll *leave* the matter up to you. ＝I'll let you take care of the matter.　この件は君に任せるよ．

leave² /líːv/

原義は〈許可〉である．**縛りからの解放→許可；休暇**．

How much do you get paid while on maternity *leave*?　産休の期間はいくら給料が出るの．

I took a paid *leave* from work to take care of my kid who caught a cold.　子どもがかぜを引いたので有給休暇を取った．

You look tired. Why don't you take a *leave* of absence for a few days?　君は疲れているよ．少し休暇を取ったら？

left /léft/

left

原義は〈左手〉である．**左側；左派，左翼**．
派 lefty（左利きの人）
関 left-handed（左手の，左利きの）

Turn *left* [＝Make a *left* turn] at the next light.　信号を左に曲がりなさい．

As you walk down the street towards the east, my house will be *on your left*.　通りを東に向かって進むと，私の家は左手にあります．

When going up to Tokyo on the Shinkansen, you will see Mt. Fuji *to your left*.　新幹線で東京へ向かっていると左手に富士山が見えてきますよ．　▶ to one's left「(離れて) 左手に」

The President writes 「with his *left* hand [＝*left-handed*].　大統領は左手で書く．

leg /lég/

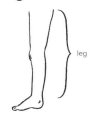

原義は〈脚〉である．**人や動物の脚→（テーブルなどの）脚→（旅の）一行程**．

How long can you stand on one *leg*? 片足でどれくらい立てますか．

I feel more comfortable sitting with my *legs* crossed than with my legs outstretched. 僕は脚を投げ出すより，組んで座るほうが楽だ．

I stubbed my toe against the *leg* of the table. テーブルの脚に指をぶつけてしまった．

legal /líːgl/

語源は〈leg=law（法律）al（の）〉である．**法律に関係する，法律にかなう**．
派 illegal（違法の）; legally（法律上）

The victims took *legal* action against the government over drug-induced sufferings. 被害者たちは政府を相手取って薬害の法的行動を起こした．

The fishermen were arrested for catching more fish than the *legal* limit. 漁師たちは乱獲の罪で（「法外に」魚を取ったので）逮捕された．

In Japan, a person *legally* becomes an adult at age twenty. 日本では法的には20歳になると大人とみなされる．

lend /lénd/

(borrow)

原義は〈貸す〉である．**(金・物を) 一時的に貸し与える**．
関 loan (貸し付ける)

I have a friend who often *lends* me DVDs of movies that he thinks I'd like.　私の好みと思われる映画のDVDをよく貸してくれる友だちがいる．

Dad *lent* me his car as my car was in the garage being repaired.　僕の車は修理工場に出しているので，父さんが車を貸してくれた．

Celebrities should know better than to 「*lend* their names to such shady enterprises [=allow their names to be used for such shady enterprises].　有名人は，そのような怪しげな会社に名前を貸すことにもう少し慎重になるべきだよ．

less /lés/

原義は〈量・程度がより少ない〉である．**基準よりも少ない様子**．
派 lessen (減らす)；lesser=less (より少ない)

In the United States, tea is *less* popular than coffee.　アメリカでは紅茶はコーヒーほど飲まれない．

If you serve or order *less* food, you will inevitably eat *less*. ＝A sure way to eat *less* is to serve or order *less* food.　腹八分目のひけつは食事の量や注文を少なめにすることだ．

It's becoming *less and less* common for people to use conventional home phones.　従来の固定電話を使う人がどんどん少なくなっている．

lesson /lésn/

原義は〈講読〉である. **(知識・技術を学ぶ) 授業・レッスン, (体験して学ぶ) 教訓・知恵.**
関 lecture (講義)

What *lessons* can we learn from the incident? この度の事件から, 私たちは何を教訓にすればいいでしょうか.

She gives private piano *lessons* at home. 彼女は家でピアノの個人教授をしている.

I'm never going to drink and drive again. I've *learned my lesson*. もう二度と飲酒運転はしません. もうこりごりです.

let /lét/

原義は〈縛りを解く〉である. **好きにさせる, 気ままにさせる；起こるに任せる.**

You need to show your ID at the campus gate to be *let* in. 構内に入るには門のところで ID の提示が必要だ.

Let me think about it a little bit because I've never expected such a question. そのような質問は予想していなかったので, 少し考えさせてください.

My boyfriend is very generous, but I can't always *let* him pay for me. 私の彼はとても気前がいいのだけど, いつも彼に払わせるわけにはいかないわ.

Let it happen naturally because sleep won't come if you force it. 無理に寝ようと思っても眠りはやってこないので自然に任せなさい.

letter /létər/

語源は〈let=put(置く→書く)er(もの)〉である. **(書き置く)文字;(文字で書いた)手紙・文書→文学**.

Write your name and address in *block letters*. =Print your name and address.　名前と住所は楷書でお願いします.

My doctor wrote *a letter of introduction* for me to get treated by a specialist.　かかりつけの医師は,専門医の治療を受けるために紹介状を書いてくれた.

Many news sources are biased; don't believe everything reported *to the letter*.　ニュースの出所は偏向していることがよくあるから,記事を鵜(う)のみにするとだめだよ.　▶to the letter「文字通りに, 正確に」

level /lévl/

原義は〈天秤(てんびん)〉である. **水平→水準→高さ;水平にする→(立っているものを)なぎ倒す**.

Add one *level* teaspoon of salt and two *level* teaspoons of sugar.　茶さじすり切り一杯の塩と同じく二杯の砂糖を加えてください.

Whenever possible, teachers should speak to children at their eye *level*.　教師はできるかぎり,生徒の目線で話しかけるのがいい.

The plane *leveled off* at 8,000 meters.　飛行機は高度8000メートルで水平飛行に入った.

We need to *level* [=prepare] the soil for sowing.　種をまくのに畑をならす必要がある.

liberal /líbərəl/

語源は〈leber (解放) al (状態である)〉である.**(縛り・拘束から解放されて) 自由である→偏見がない；惜しみなく与える**.「一般教養科目」を liberal arts というのは〈専門・専攻の縛りがない科目〉の意味合いから.
派 liberalization (自由化)；liberalism (自由主義)
関 liberty (自由；勝手, せんえつ)

He has a *liberal* attitude [=is unbiased] towards uneducated persons. 彼は学歴の無い人に対して分け隔てがない.

There are some colleges that are too *liberal* [=easy] in granting degrees. 学位をいとも簡単に出してしまう大学がある.

I'd like to *take the liberty to* say that some criticisms you made about my article are not right. 私の論考に対しての貴殿の批判は当を得ていないとあえて (遠慮をほどいて) 言わせてもらいます.

lie¹ /láɪ/

原義は〈横たわる〉である.**(物・事が) 存在する**.
関 lay (横たえる)

The woman found a girl *lying* unconscious, with blood on her face. 女性は, 顔を血だらけにして意識を失って倒れている女の子を見つけた.

We never know what *lies* ahead [=will happen in the future]. 一寸先は闇だ〔←前方に何が横たわっているか分からない〕.

The town *lies* [=is nestled] in a broad and peaceful valley. その町は広々としたのどかな山里にある.

Japan *lies* to the east of mainland China. 日本は中国本土の東側に位置している.

lie² /lái/

原義は〈うそ〉である．**うそをつく，ごまかす．**
派 liar（うそつき）

Why did you ⌈*lie* to me [=tell me a *lie*]?　どうしてうそをついたの．

She *lied* about her age.　彼女は年齢を偽った．

Photos can serve as the strongest evidence as they never *lie*.　写真は裏切らないので最強の証拠となる．

life /láif/

原義は〈生きる〉である．**生命，生活，人生，生物．**
派 live（生きる）; alive（生きている）
関 lifespan（寿命）; lifestyle（生き方）

Do you believe in *life* after death?　あの世を信じますか．

Life isn't always what we expect it to be.　人生はままならないものだ．

How long is the *life* of a laptop computer battery?　ノートパソコンの電池はどれくらいもちますか．

Is there *life* on other planets?　他の惑星にも生物はいますか．

The Iraq War claimed the *lives* of thousands of U.S. soldiers and hundreds of thousands of Iraqis.　イラク戦争は，何千人もの米兵の命と何十万ものイラク人の命を奪ってしまった．

lift /líft/

原義は〈上部へ持ち上げる〉である. **引き上げる→取り除く**.
関 lift-off (打ち上げ)

The father *lifted* [=raised] his child over his shoulders so she could have a better view of the parade.　父親はパレードがよく見えるように子どもを肩車した.

The fog gradually *lifted* [=cleared] as the sun came up.　太陽が昇ると霧は徐々に晴れてきた.

The government is making every possible effort to *lift* [=end] the ban on commercial whaling.　政府は商業捕鯨の禁止令を解くためにあらゆる努力をしている.

light¹ /láɪt/

原義は〈光〉である. **明かり→(物事に思考の光を当てる) 考慮；明るい**.
派 lighten (明るくする)；lightning (稲妻)

Turn out [=Turn off] the *lights* when you leave the room.　部屋を出る時は明かりを消してください.

We walked along ⌜the sandy beach and tide pools *lit* by the moon [= the *moonlit* sandy beach and tide pools].　月明かりの砂浜と潮だまりを散歩した.

The government has to review the policy *in (the) light of* the feedback it got from the people.　政府は国民の反応を見て政策を見直す必要がある.　▶ in (the) light of ～「～を考慮して」

light² /láɪt/

原義は〈軽い〉である. **(重さが) 軽い, (数量・程度が) 軽い.**
派 lighten (軽減する); lightly (軽く, そっと)

Hot air is *lighter* than cold air.　熱い空気は冷たい空気より軽い.

I always try to travel *light* [=with less baggage].　いつも身軽な旅を心がけている.

We had a *light* [=thin] rain this morning.　今朝, 小雨が降りました.

I take a *light* [=small] meal before my workout.　僕は運動する前に軽い食事をする.

like¹ /láɪk/

原義は〈似ている〉である. **似ている→似つかわしい; 同種のもの→好ましい→好む.**
派 likable (人に好かれる); liking (好み)
関 dislike (～を嫌う)

What is it that you don't *like* about me?　私のどこが気に入らないの?

I *like* him, but he doesn't *like* me back.　彼に片想いなの〔私は好きだけど, 彼には好かれていない〕.

I have someone I would *like* you to meet. I think you'll *like* her.　あなたに会って欲しい人がいるの. きっとその人を気に入ると思うわ.

Like attracts *like*. =Birds of a feather flock together.　類は友を呼ぶ.

like² /láik/

原義は〈似ている〉である.**(外見や性質が)似ている, 〜と同じような.**
派 likely (ありそうな)

Our teacher told us what it was *like* to live in the Edo period.　先生は江戸時代の生活がどんなだったか話してくれた.

"What's her husband *like*?" "He's very friendly."　「彼女の夫はどんな人なの」「気さくな人だよ」

Ted is a careful driver; it's not *like* him to get a ticket for speeding.　テッドの運転は慎重なのに,スピード違反の切符を食らうとは彼らしくないね.

Most immigrants are attracted to large cities *like* Toronto and Vancouver.　たいていの移住者はトロントやバンクーバーのような大都市にあこがれて来る.

likely /láɪkli/

語源は〈like(似ている)ly(様態)〉である.**どうも〜らしい,どうも〜になりそうである.**
関 likelihood (見込み,可能性)

"Will they expand their business?" "That's「not *likely*［=unlikely］to happen in this economy."　「彼らは商売を拡張するのだろうか」「この経済状況ではあり得ないよ」

How *likely* is it that he'll be reelected?　彼が再選される可能性はどうだろう？

Researchers say overweight people are three times more *likely* to suffer a heart attack.　研究者によれば,肥満の人は心臓発作に襲われる恐れが3倍になるそうだ.

limit /límət/

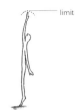

原義は〈境界〉である．**越えられない限度，許される範囲**．
派 limited（限られた，乏しい）; limitation（限度）; limitless（無限の）
関 eliminate（排除する）

I understand that you would like to do everything possible to keep the house clean, but there are *limits*.　家をきれいにするために何でもしたいというのは分かるけれど，程度ものだよ．

Freedom does have *limits* [＝lines] that should not be crossed.　自由には超えてはならない一線がある．

If you knew you had a very *limited* amount of time to live, what would you most want to do?　もし生きられる時間がごく少ないと分かったら，あなたは何を一番したいですか．

---

line /láɪn/

原義は〈ひも〉である．**(ひも状の) 線，ロープ**;**(人の並び) 列**;**(単語の並び) 行，ことば**;**(種類の並び) 分野，職業，品物**．
関 linear（直線上の）

There were lots of people waiting *in line* to get into the stadium.
球場に入るために多くの人が列を作っていた．

There needs to be a definite *line* drawn between punishment and abuse.　懲罰と虐待行為ははっきり区別しないといけない．

Most Japanese can sing at least a few *lines* of the song "Sakura."
日本人ならたいてい，歌曲「さくら」の少なくとも数節は歌える．

Lots of souvenir shops *line* the main street. ＝The main street *is lined* with lots of souvenir shops.　たくさんのみやげ店が本通りに軒を連ねている．

link /líŋk/

原義は〈つながる輪〉である.**(〜への) つながり, (相互の) つながり.**
派 linkage (連鎖, つながり)

The airport *is linked* to the city center by trains and buses in less than thirty minutes.　空港から都心へは30分足らずで電車かバスで行ける.

There is conclusive data showing the *link* [=relationship] between smoking and lung cancer.　喫煙と肺がんの関連を示す明白なデータがある.

list /líst/

原義は〈目録・名簿〉である.**一覧表；一覧表にする.**
派 listing (記載事項, 一覧表)

The magazine published a *list* of [=*listed* and published] the top ten Christmas movies the whole family can enjoy.　この雑誌は家族で楽しめるクリスマス映画のベストテン (の一覧) を載せている.

List [=*Make a list* of] at least five things you like about yourself.
自分の好きなところを少なくとも5つ挙げてごらんなさい.

listen /lísn/

原義は〈耳を傾ける〉である. **耳を傾けて聞く**.
派 listener (ラジオの聴取者)

He *listened*, but couldn't hear her well because of the noise from the vacuum cleaner.　彼は耳を傾けたが, 掃除機の音がやかましくて彼女の言うことがよく聞こえなかった.

Did you ⌜*listen to* [=hear] the local news this morning?　今朝のローカルニュース, 聞いた?

None of this would have happened if you'd *listened* to me.　私の言うことを聞いていたら こんなことにはならなかったのに.

I stopped reading to *listen for* the strange sounds from upstairs.　階上から妙な音がするので, 本から目を離して耳を澄ませた.

little /lítl/

原義は〈小さな〉である. **ちっちゃな, ほんのちょっぴりの**.

This washing machine is designed to use as *little* water as possible.　この洗濯機はできるだけ少量の水で済むように作られている.

There is *little* time left to turn the game for us.　(試合で) 逆転するにはもう時間がほとんどない.

She often drops in on us for a *little* chat.　彼女はうわさ話をしによく来る.

He is big, but speaks in a *little* voice.　彼は, 体はでかいけど声は小さい.

I loved going to the zoo with Dad when I was *little*.　幼いころ, 父さんと動物園に行くのが大好きだった.

live¹ /lív/

原義は〈とどまる〉である. **(とどまって) 住む→ (逝くことなく) 生きる**.
派 living (生計)

Where do you *live*? どこに住んでいるの.

How long does a turtle *live* [=stay alive]? カメはどのくらい生きるの.

These days with you will remain in my memory for as long as I *live*. 一緒に過ごした日々は生涯忘れないでしょう.

Do you have any favorite quotes or words to *live by*? 何か座右の銘 (生きる指針となることば) がありますか.

After losing their only son, the parents seem to have nothing to *live for*. ひとり息子を失って, 両親は生き甲斐 (生きる目的) をなくしたように見える.

What does the earthworm *live on*? ミミズは何を食べて生きているの.

live² /láɪv/

原義は〈場を離れない〉である. **生きている；その場で, 実況で, 生で.** alive (生きている) の a- が消失したもの.
派 lively (活発な)

live

Don't touch the wire ! It's *live*. その線さわっちゃだめ！ 電気が来ているよ.

I hate cutting the head off of a *live* [=living] fish. 生きた魚の頭を切り落とすのは嫌だわ.

The title match will *air live* [=will be broadcast in real time] on NHK. タイトルマッチは NHK で生放送される.

load /lóud/

原義は〈運搬〉である．**(運搬する) 荷物；荷物を積む→負担→仕事量**．
派 unload (積み荷を降ろす)
関 download (ダウンロードする)；workload (仕事量)

He put half a *load* of laundry in the machine. 彼は1回分の洗濯物の半分を洗濯機に入れた．

These shoes will reduce the *load* on your back and knees. この靴は腰やひざにかかる負担を軽くします．

Farmers were *loading* [=filling] the truck with heavy sacks of grain on their shoulders. 農夫たちは重い穀物袋を肩に載せてトラックに積み込んでいた．

We need to spread the *workload* [=amount of work] fairly among the employees. 社員の仕事量を平等に割り振らないといけない．

loan /lóun/

原義は〈貸す〉である．**貸し付ける；貸し付け，ローン (借金)**．
関 lend (貸し出す)

I forgot my wallet. Would you *loan* [=lend] me five thousand yen? 財布を忘れちゃった．5千円貸してもらえる？

How should we prepare to take out a home *loan*? 住宅ローンを受けるにはどんな用意が必要ですか． ▶ home loan＝housing loan

Some of the exhibited items are *loans* [=*loaned / on loan*] from other museums. 展示品の中には，他の博物館から借りているものがある．

local /lóukl/

語源は〈loc(場所)al(の)〉である. **(全域から見て)ある特定地域の, 地元の, 局部の.**
派 locate(位置する); locally(地元で, 現地で)
関 local time(現地時間)

We often climb *local* hills for exercise and pleasure.　運動と楽しみのために近辺の山によく登る.

Dentists often use *local* anesthesia during dental work.　歯科医は治療の際, 局部麻酔をよく使う.　▶anesthesia /ænəsθíːʒə/

locate /lóukeɪt/

語源は〈loc(場所)ate(にする)〉である. **物の存在する場所をつきとめる;物をある場所に存在させる.**
派 location(所在場所, ロケ地); local(地元の)

A sky-map helps us *locate* and identify stars and constellations.　星座表を使うと星や星座の位置と名前が分かる.

The international space station is *located* about 220 miles above the Earth's surface.　国際宇宙ステーションは地上約220マイルの位置にある.

lock /lá:k/

原義は〈錠を下ろす〉である．**(鍵を使って) ロックする**．
派 unlock (錠を開ける)；locker (ロッカー)

Make sure you *lock* the car before you leave.　車を離れるときは，ちゃんとロックするようになさい．

The thief seems to have used a wire to pick the *lock*.　泥棒はワイヤーを使って錠をこじ開けたようだ．

She had been ⌈*locked up* in her house [=under house arrest] for many years by the government.　彼女は政府によって何年も自宅軟禁されていた．

long /lɔ́:ŋ/

原義は〈沿ってなが〜い〉である．**(距離が) なが〜い，(時間が) なが〜い；(短い待ち時間も長く思われるほどに) 慕う，あこがれる**．

Last night, I came home late after ⌈a *long day* [=spending many hours] at work.　昨夜は職場で仕事が忙しかったので，遅くに帰宅した．

It was the *longest* [=hardest] day for the students who had to take five exams on the same day.　一日に5科目の試験があったので，学生には大変な日だった．

Elderly people often ⌈*long for* [=miss] the good old days when life was simpler and slower.　お年寄りは，生活がもっと単純でゆっくりしていた古きよき昔を懐かしむことが多い．

look /lúk/

原義は〈見つめる〉である．**(対象に) 目を向ける；(対象が) 〜のように目に映る**．

関 lookout（見張り台）

What's wrong? You *look* sick.　どうしたの？ 顔色が悪いよ．

I'm not happy with the way you *look* with dark glasses on.　あなたがサングラスかけている姿は好きじゃないわ．

The government has to *look for* ways to cut spending as much as it can.　政府は歳出をできる限り削る方策を探らないといけない．

When crossing streets, *look* [＝watch] *out* for speeding cars and trucks.　通りを横断する時は，スピードを出している車やトラックに用心しなさい．

Babies need to be *looked after* [＝taken care of] in every way.　赤ん坊はいろいろと手がかかるものだ．

loose /lú:s/

原義は〈(結びが) ほどけている〉である．**緩んでいる，(縛りから) 放たれている**．

派 loosen（緩める）；loosely（緩く）　関 lose（失う）

The screw on the door is getting *loose*; you need to tighten it.　ドアのねじが緩くなっているよ．締めておかないと．

Don't let a dog *loose* [＝free] in the car. I recommend a pet carrier.　車の中では犬を放しておいてはだめだよ．ペットキャリアーを使うといいよ．

The government *loosened* [＝eased] the restriction imposed on livestock products from foreign countries.　政府は輸入畜産物に関する規制を緩和した．

lose /lúːz/

原義は〈消滅する〉である. **(持っているものを) 失う, 負ける**.
派 loser (敗者); loss (喪失, 失敗); lost (失った, 道に迷った)

Tens of thousands of people *lost* their homes and loved ones in the tsunami.　何万もの人が家や愛する人たちを津波で失った.

Can you stand and put your socks on without *losing* your balance?　立ったままバランスを崩さずに靴下がはけますか.

I believe you have nothing to *lose*; it is worth taking a chance.　失うものは何もないのだから, やってみる価値があると思うよ.

---

lot /láːt/

原義は〈くじ〉である. **くじ→ (くじによる) 割り当て→ (くじが割り当てる) 運命→ (割り当ての) ひと山, 土地**.
派 lottery (宝くじ)
関 allot (割り当てる); parking lot (駐車場)

Let us ⌈draw *lots* to decide [=decide by *lot*]⌋ who will pay the bill.　勘定を誰が払うか, くじ引きで決めよう.

It's like a ghost town with *lots* [=plenty] *of* abandoned homes, vacant *lots* [=spaces], and empty streets.　空き家や空き地, 誰もいない通りが多くて, まるでゴーストタウンのようだ.

My mother looks ⌈*a lot* [=much]⌋ younger than her age.　母は年齢よりずっと若く見える.

loud /láud/

原義は〈聞こえる〉である．**声・音が大きい，よく聞き取れる；(服装が) 派手な．**
派 loudly (大声で)

The television isn't *loud* enough; would you turn up the volume, please? テレビの音がよく聞こえないよ．ボリューム上げてくれない？

I don't like ⌈TV commercials that are too *loud* [=the *loudness* of the TV commercials]． やかましいテレビコマーシャルは嫌いだ．

The opposition party *loudly* criticized the proposed bill. 野党は提出された法案を声高に非難した．

You should avoid wearing ⌈too *loud* clothes [=clothes with very loud colors] at work. 職場ではあまり派手な服装はよしたほうがいいよ．

---

love /lʌ́v/

原義は〈欲する〉である．**(気持ちを全部預けて) 好きである．**
派 lovely (愛くるしい，すてきな)；lovable (愛すべき)；loving (愛情の込もった)

I *love* you. 好きだよ． ▶定訳「愛しているよ」は，love に含まれる内からの気持ちの発露を伝え切らない．

List the things you *love* most and hate most about cell phone communication. 携帯電話について，とても気に入っている点と嫌いな点を挙げなさい．

"Would you like to go to the beach tomorrow?" "I'd *love* [=very much like] to." 「明日，海辺に行かない？」「喜んで」

We *fell in love* the instant we saw each other. 私たちは互いに一目ぼれした．

low /lóu/

原義は〈低い位置にある〉である. **低い**, **気持ちが落ち込んでいる**.
派 lower（降ろす，低くする）

We saw the crescent moon hanging *low* in the sky over the lake.
三日月が湖上の空低くかかっていた.

Dizziness often occurs when your blood pressure is *lower* than normal.　血圧が低すぎるとめまいが起こりやすい.

My son is feeling so *low* after breaking up with his girlfriend.　息子は失恋してひどく落ち込んでいる.

You need to *lower* [=reduce] the oven temperature to 160 degrees.
オーブンの温度を160度に下げなさい.

luck /lʌ́k/

原義は〈巡り合わせ〉である. **たまたまの運**, **幸運**.
派 lucky（運のよい）；luckily（運よく）

Good *luck*!　うまく行きますように!

Unfortunately, *luck* was not on our side.　残念ながら我々に運がなかった.

Don't blame *luck* for a failure. Try to figure out where it went wrong.
失敗を運のせいにしてはだめだよ. どこがいけなかったのか考えなさい.

I feel very *lucky* [=fortunate] to be involved in this fieldwork.　この実地研修に参加できてとても幸いだと思う.

Luckily, when we were in Japan the cherry blossoms were at their best.　日本へ行った時は運よく桜が満開だった.

mad /mǽd/

原義は〈変わる〉である.（平常心が変わる）→**怒っている**, **夢中である**, **狂っている**.
派 madly（狂ったように）; madness（狂気）

My girlfriend got *mad* [=angry] when I told her my image of an ideal partner. She took what I said the wrong way. 伴侶となる人の理想像を話したら，誤解して彼女は怒ってしまった．

What are you so *mad* about? Calm down and tell me what happened. 何をそんなに怒っているの．落ち着いて，どうしたのか話してごらん．

That incessant factory noise is ⌈driving me *mad* [=annoying me very much]. ひっきりなしの工場の騒音には気が狂いそうだよ．

---

mail /méɪl/

原義は〈郵袋〉である.**（集合的に）郵便物**, **（制度としての）郵便**, **メール**；**郵送する**, **メールする**.
関 email=electronic mail（電子メール）; mail order（通信販売）

We will accept the copy of your manuscript either by *email* or postal mail. 文書の原稿は電子メールでも郵送でも受け付けます．

I check my computer ⌈for *email* [=to see if I've gotten any *email*] every day after dinner. 毎日夕食後，メールチェックします．

Would you *mail* [=post] this letter for me, please? この手紙を投函してくださいね．

I usually get tickets and books by *mail* order. チケットや本はたいてい通販で購入します．

low, luck, mad, mail

main /méɪn/

原義は〈力がある〉の意. **全体の中でもっとも重要である**. ma- は〈力〉のイメージ.
派 mainly (主として)
関 might (力); may (可能性がある)

Our *main* [=head] office is located close to Tokyo Railway Station. 本社は東京駅の近くにあります.

The *main* [=major] advantage of cycling to work is being able to avoid traffic jams. 自転車通勤で一番いいのは渋滞を避けられることだ.

So far, the reviews of the film have been *mainly* [=mostly] positive. これまでのところ, この映画の評判はほとんどが好意的だ.

major /méɪdʒər/

語源は〈maj (大きい) or (もっと)〉である. **あるグループの中で他よりも大きく重要である**.
派 majority (大多数, 〔得票・議席の〕過半数)

White blood cells play a *major* [=significant] role in the human immune system. 白血球は人間の免疫システムの上で重要な役を果たしている.

As for the election system, no *major* changes are expected in the near future. 選挙制度に関しては, 近々に大きな変更があるとは思われない.

My brother ⌈is a law *major* [=majors/specializes in law] at Kyoto University. 兄は京都大学で法学を専攻している.

The *majority* [=More than half] of the students who come to this school are from out of town. この学校の生徒の過半数は町外から来ている.

make /méɪk/

原義は〈力をこめてつくる〉である．**物をつくり出す，状態をつくり出す；状態が生じる**．ma- は〈力〉の意味合いをもつ．make の背景に〈人の努力・自然の力・組み合わせの妙〉が感じられる．

派 maker（製造者，製造業者）; making（製造）
関 makeup（化粧）

"What *makes* a good parent?" "Hard to say in a few words; parenting is a skill that is learned over a period of time." 「どうしたらいい親になれる？」「簡単には言えないわ．長くかかって身に付けるものだから」

What *makes* humans different [=distinguishes humans] from other animals? 人間が他の動物とは異なるゆえんはなんですか．

The sumo wrestler isn't big enough, but he *makes up for* it with great agility. この力士は小柄だが，巧みな動きで軽量を補っている．

Can you *make* [=build] a fire without using matches or a lighter? マッチやライターを使わずに火を起こすことができる？

---

manage /mǽnɪdʒ/

manage

語源は〈man（手）age（行為）〉である．**いろいろ手を尽くして事を成す**．

派 manager（監督）〔←いろいろと手を尽くす人〕; manageable（扱いやすい）; management（経営，管理）

Many young mothers find it very hard to *manage* both work and children. 仕事と子育てを両立させるのは難しいと感じている若い母親が多い．

The firm had a difficult time making ends meet, but they *managed* somehow. 会社は帳尻合わせに苦しんだが，どうにか乗り切った．

We have to *manage* [=make do] with 20,000 yen for the rest of the month. 月末まで2万円でやりくりして生活しないといけない．

manner /mǽnər/

原義は〈物事を扱う方法〉である．**方法，態度；行儀・マナー**．英語で manners というのは manner（態度）の抽象的意味が複数形になると具体性を帯びるから．

The chairperson's forceful *manner* [=way] of speaking offended all the members of the board. 議長が威圧的な物言いをしたので，委員たちはみな気分を害した．

Where are your *manners* [=Have you no *manners* =Mind your *manners*], Tom? Thank your uncle for his help. トム，お行儀はどうしたの？ 叔父さんにちゃんとお礼を言いなさい．

We want to raise a *well-mannered* [=well-behaved] child. 行儀のよい子どもに育てたいと思う．

manufacture /mænjəfǽktʃər/

語源は〈manu（手）facture（つくる）→〈手で物をつくる〉〉である．**機械で物を作る→製造する；口実をうまく作る**．
派 manufacturer（メーカー）；manufacturing（製造，製造業） 関 manual（手動の，手引き）

The company *manufactures* [=produces] automotive parts for Toyota. この会社はトヨタの自動車部品を作っている．

It's illegal to *manufacture* [=make] or sell alcohol without a license. 許可なしに酒を造ったり売ったりするのは違法だ．

He *manufactured* [=invented] a story to escape being fined. 彼は罰金を逃れようとして話をでっち上げた．

many /méni/

原義は〈人や物の数がかなり多い〉である. **漠然とした数の多さをいう.**

Are there *many* female students in your department? あなたの学部に女子学生は多いですか.

"Suzuki" is ⌈one of the *many* family names [=a common family name] in Japan. 「鈴木」は日本にとても多い姓の一つです.

The vocal group released five albums ⌈in as *many* years [=in five years]. このボーカルグループは5年間に5枚のアルバムを発売した. ▶in as many years [days/weeks]「(前述の数と) 同数の年[日/週]で」

How *many* times [=How often] do I have to tell you to clean up the room? 部屋を掃除しなさいって何回言わせるの.

---

march /má:rtʃ/

原義は〈歩行する〉である. **行進する→時間などが確実に進む.**

Hundreds of people ⌈*marched* on the streets to protest [=made a protest *march*] against the company's unfair dismissal. 会社の不当解雇に抗議して, 何百人もの人が街頭デモを行った.

People and things come and go as time and tide *march* on. 人も世事も, 歳月の進むにつれて生まれては消えていく.

mark /máːrk/

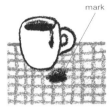

mark

原義は〈縁(ふち)〉である．**印，記号→印をつける→評価する**．
派 marked（著しい，目立つ）; markedly（著しく）; marker（目印，マーカーペン）

Don't leave coffee *marks* on the tablecloth, please. ＝Be careful not to *mark* the tablecloth with your coffee. テーブルクロスにコーヒーのしみを残さないように気をつけて．

Those signposts on a roadside *mark* [＝indicate] the distance from a given point. 道路脇の標識は一定の地点からの距離を示している．

Mark [＝Check] the items which apply to your mental and physical conditions. あなたの心身の状態に該当する項目に印を付けなさい．

My son got a good *mark* in math this semester. 息子は今学期，数学の成績がよかった．

market /máːrkət/

原義は〈売買の場〉である．**市場→取引き**．
派 marketable（よく売れる）; marketing（販売促進，マーケティング）

There is a huge and growing *market* for electronic publications. 電子書籍には巨大な発展市場がある．

You need to do *market* research before venturing into any business. どんなビジネスでも始める際は市場調査をする必要がある．

Do you grow crops for the *market* or for private consumption? 作物は市場用に，それとも自家用に作っているのですか．

The *market* [＝business] has been slow recently. 最近は景気が振るわない．

marry /mǽri/

原義は〈結婚する〉である．**結婚する**．
派 marriage（結婚）; married（結婚している, 既婚の）; unmarried（未婚の）

"Is your daughter *married*?" "Yes, she has been *married* for three years and has a child." 「娘さんは結婚しているの？」「ええ、結婚して3年になり、子どもが一人います」

Today many Japanese tend to get *married* later in life than they used to. 日本人は昔よりも晩婚の傾向がある．

Most *unmarried* people would like to be *married*, but some remain *unmarried* by choice. 未婚の人の多くはできれば結婚したいと思っているが、中には、あえて独身を通す人もいる．

mass /mǽs/

原義は〈こねたかたまり〉である．**ひとかたまり；大量の**．
物理学では mass は「質量」．
派 massive（大規模の）

We have an apple tree in the backyard which produces *masses* of apples in autumn. 秋になるとたわわに実をつけるりんごの木が裏庭にある．

You can see only a portion of an iceberg; the greater part of the *mass* is beneath the water. 氷山で見えるのはほんの一部だけだ．かたまりの大部分は水面下にある．

The *mass* production of items is usually done by using an assembly line. 物品の大量生産は普通、流れ作業によって行われる．

The patient died of *massive* bleeding during the operation. 患者は手術中に大量出血によって死んだ．

master /mǽstər/

原義は〈(雇い人に対する)主人〉である．**物事を自由に駆使できる→難事を克服する→名人**．
派 mastery (熟達, 支配)
関 mastermind (立案者, 黒幕); masterpiece (傑作)

Would you give me some tips on how to *master* [=learn] a foreign language?　外国語を習得するこつを教えていただけませんか．

My brother, who owns a store, doesn't like being part of any organization because he wants to be his own *master*.　兄は自営の店を持っているが，何事にも拘束されたくないのでどんな組織に属するのも嫌う．

Osama bin Laden *masterminded* [=pulled the strings behind] the Sept 11, 2001 attacks.　オサマ・ビンラディンは9・11テロの首謀者であった．

"*Twelfth Night*" is one of Shakespeare's comedic *masterpieces*.　『十二夜』はシェークスピアの傑作喜劇の一つだ．

match /mǽtʃ/

原義は〈対のものとつり合うこと〉である．**つり合わせる→調和する；試合させる；試合**．

Your coat doesn't *match* [=go well] with your pants.　上着とズボン(の色やデザイン)がつり合っていないよ．

The young rookie was no *match* for the veteran pitcher.　新人はベテランピッチャーの相手にならなかった．

The baseball *match* scheduled for today was rained out.　今日の予定の試合は雨で中止になった．

material /mətíəriəl/

原義は〈物が作られる素〉である. **原料, 材料→素材→資料.**
関 matter (物質)

Which building *materials* are most commonly used in this region, concrete, stone, steel, or wood?　この地域ではどんな建築資材が一番よく使われますか. コンクリート, 石材, 鋼材, あるいは木材ですか.

Teachers need to prepare teaching *materials* while they are not in the classroom.　教師は教室にいない時は教材を準備しないといけない.

---

matter /mǽtər/

原義は〈もの〉である. **(具体的な) 物, 物質, (抽象的な) もの→物事, 事態；問題となる→重要である.**
関 material (材料)

Radioactive *matters* [=substances] were detected in the water off the nuclear power plant.　原発沖の海水から放射性物質が検出された.

What's the *matter* [=What's wrong] with you?　どうしたの？

Tom drives with reckless speed; *it is only a matter of time* before he causes a traffic accident.　トムは滅茶なスピードで運転する. 事故を起こすのは時間の問題だよ.

Height doesn't *matter* much to me but I'd prefer to marry someone close to my height.　背丈はたいして気にならないけど, できるならあまり身長差のない人と結婚したい.

may /méɪ/, might /maɪt/

原義は〈可能性がある〉である. **〜かもしれない**《可能性の推量》→（起こり得る）→**〜してもよい**《可能性の実現》.
関 main（主要な）; might（力）

Dad *may* forgive me, or he *may* not.　父さんは許してくれるかどうか分からない.

I don't think so, but I *may* [=could] be wrong.　僕はそうは思わないけど, 間違っているかも.

This *may* not be true. =It is possible (that) this is not true.　これは本当ではないかもしれない.

The sky looks threatening; it *might* rain for a while.　雲行きが怪しい. ひと雨来るかもしれない.

May [=Can] I leave the rest up to you?　あとはお任せしていいですか.

maybe /méɪbi/

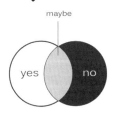

語源は〈may（知れない）be（〜である）〉である. **ひょっとすると**. 文頭で用いるのが普通. 類義語 perhaps よりも気さくな感じ.

"Will you go to the party?" "*Maybe, maybe* not."　「パーティーに行くの?」「はっきり分からない」

I never really thought about twitting. *Maybe* it would be fun.　ツイッターについては考えたことはなかったよ. ひょっとして面白いかもね.

Maybe you should read the manual again.　もう一度説明書を読み直したほうがいいんじゃない. ▶Maybe を文頭に加えると, 軟らかい調子になる.

There are still many *maybes* [=uncertainties] involved in predicting an earthquake.　地震予知にはまだまだはっきり分からないことが多い.

mean /míːn/

原義は〈〜と考える〉である.**(潜んでいる) 本意・意思を言い表す→意味する；〜するつもりである**.
派 meaning（意味）；meaningful（意味のある）；meaningless（意味のない）

C *means* [＝signifies] "average" on a school report card.　通知表のCは「可」を表す.

It's Monday tomorrow, which *means* the start of a new workweek.　明日は月曜日，つまり，また1週間の仕事が始まるってことだ.

The writer's dairy was not *meant* to be read by the public.　その作家の日記は，公開するつもりで書かれたものではなかった.

There are occasions when you should not say what you *mean* [＝actually have in mind].　本音を言わないほうがいい場合もある.

---

measure /méʒər/

原義は〈測定する〉である.**計る→〜ほどの重さ・長さがある；計測 (計る)，対策 (図る)**.
派 measurement（寸法，サイズ）

The nurse *measured* [＝took] my blood pressure.　看護師は血圧を測ってくれた.

The pool *measures* 25 meters *long*, 10 meters *wide* and 1.5 meters *deep*.　このプールは長さ25メートル，幅10メートル，深さ1.5メートルである.

You need to take legal *measures* to address those personal property issues.　そのような私有不動産の問題に対処するには法的手段をとることが必要だ.

media /míːdiə/

原義は〈介在する媒体〉である．**情報の媒体であるテレビ・ラジオ・新聞・雑誌などの総体**．med- は〈中間→媒介〉の意味合い．
派 mediate（調停する）
関 mass media（マスメディア）; news media（報道機関）

President Obama's speech in Prague on a "nuclear-free world" attracted a lot of ⌈attention from the *media* [=media attention].「核兵器のない世界」に関するオバマ大統領のプラハでの演説は，メディアの大きな注目を集めた．

A third party was brought in to *mediate* between labor and management.　労使間の調停に第三者が入れられた．

---

medicine /médəsn/

原義は〈癒し〉である．**(治療のための) 医療**; **(治療のための) 医薬**．
派 medical（医療の）; medication（薬による治療）

If you have loose bowels, take the *medicine* within 30 minutes after each meal.　下痢の時は，毎食後 30 分以内にこの薬を飲んでください．

My grandma believes in traditional *herbal medicine*, and she doesn't like to take pills and *medicines* very much.　祖母は漢方を信じているので，錠剤や薬を飲むのをあまり好まない．

Science-based modern *medicine* [=*medical* progress] has worked to extend human life.　科学的現代医療は寿命の伸びをもたらしている．

Are you ⌈on any *medication* [=taking any *medicine*]?　今，何か薬を飲んでいますか．

meet /míːt/

原義は〈出会う〉である.**(計画して) 会う→ (たまたま) 出会う→ (必要条件に) 合う・かなう**.類義語 see は〈会う〉,meet は〈出会う〉の意味合い.
派 meeting (会合)

I'd like you to *meet* my colleague Bill.　同僚のビルを紹介するよ.

The moment my eyes *met* hers, we fell in love.　僕たちは目が会ったとたんに恋に落ちた.

He *met* his wife [=They *met* each other] at work.　彼らは職場結婚だ〔職場で出会った〕.

The club *meets* every day after school hours.　クラブ活動は毎日放課後です.

The website is designed to *meet* the growing demand for health information.　このサイトは健康情報の需要拡大に応えるために設けられている.

melt /mélt/

原義は〈溶ける〉である.**固体が溶ける,感情が和らぐ**.

It's been a long and terrible winter, but the snow is finally *melting* [=thawing].　冬は長く厳しかったけど,雪がようやく解け始めている.　▶thaw /θɔ́ː/

The reactor had *melted down* because they failed to cool it down early enough.　冷却が遅れたために原子炉がメルトダウン (溶解) した.

My anger「*melted away* [=died down] when I realized how she had struggled in vain.　彼女は大変な努力をしたが,うまくいかなかったことを知って私の怒りは消えた.

memory /méməri/

原義は〈頭 (mind) に納めること〉である．**記憶していること；記憶する能力**．
派 memo (連絡メモ)；memorable (記憶に残る)；memorial (記念の，記念碑)；memorize (記憶する)

The Fukushima nuclear accident *brought back memories* of Chernobyl in Ukraine in 1986.　福島原発事故は，1986年のウクライナでのチェルノブイリ原発事故を思い出させた．

I have no *memory* of the Tokyo Olympics as I wasn't old enough.　幼かったので東京オリンピックの記憶はない．

He drew a map from *memory* for us, but we failed getting to the destination. Our *memories* are often unreliable.　彼は記憶を頼りに地図を描いてくれたが，目的地にうまく行けなかった．記憶は往々にしてあやふやなものだ．

mention /ménʃən/

原義は〈相手の頭 (mind) に入れる〉である．**手短に述べる，軽く (話題に) 触れる；言及すること**．
関 comment (意見を述べる)

He briefly *mentioned* [=talked about] his family.　彼は家族のことを少し話した．

My husband hadn't *mentioned* anything to me about his illness before he was hospitalized.　夫は入院するまで自分の病気のことは何も言わなかった．

There was no ⌈*mention* of [=reference to] the issue at the meeting.　その件は会議では話題に上らなかった．

message /mésɪdʒ/

message

語源は〈mess(送られた)age(もの)〉である. **伝言, 趣旨, 通達, メール**.

He is out right now. May I take a *message*? 彼は今, 出かけています. 何か伝言を承りましょうか.

Thank you for your *message* [=email]. メールをありがとう.

What *message* do you want to get across to the new employees? 新入社員に伝えたいことは何ですか.

As there was no answer, I left a *message* on her answering machine. 彼女に電話したけど出なかったので, 伝言を留守電に入れておいた.

---

method /méθəd/

method

語源は〈met=meta(求めて)hod(歩む道)〉である. **(求める道筋)→方法**.

派 methodical(秩序ある);methodology(方法論)

What is the most widely used *method* for classifying books in the library? 最も広く普及している図書の分類法は何ですか.

We need to develop more efficient *methods* for mastering a foreign language. 外国語習得のもっと効率的な方法を開発する必要がある.

He reads and studies randomly and lacks *method*. 彼はやみくもに学ぶが, 一貫性がない.

middle /mídl/

語源は〈mid(真ん中)le(辺り)〉である. **中間の, 中程度の**.

Greece was *in the middle of* an economic crisis.　ギリシアは経済危機の真っただ中にあった.

Personal computers came on the market *in the middle of* 1970s.　パソコンは1970年代の中ごろに市場に出てきた.

I grew up as the *middle* child [＝I am the middle one] of three sisters.　私は3人姉妹の真ん中です.

mild /máild/

原義は〈やわらかい〉である. **気候・気質・性質などが穏やかである**.
派 mildly (穏やかに)

mild

We've been having a very *mild* winter.　とても穏やかな冬日が続いています.

My husband is「*mild* in nature [＝mild-mannered] and rarely becomes angry or irritated.　夫は温厚なので怒ったり, イライラしたりすることがほとんどない.

This is a *mild* medicine with little or no adverse side effects.　これは副作用のほとんどない軽い薬です.

Mastering a foreign language is, *to put it mildly*, a demanding job.　外国語の修得は控えめに言っても, なかなか厄介なことだ.

mind /máind/

mind 〈思考の座〉

原義は〈頭に入れる (記憶・思考)〉である. **気を配る, 気にする；(思考する) 頭**. mind は〈思考の座〉, heart は〈感情の座〉の意味合い.
派 mindful (気を配った); mindless (心ない)

Do you *mind* if I ask about your family? ご家族のことを尋ねてもいいですか〔かまわないですか〕.

What're important things to *keep in mind* in buying stocks? 株を買う際に心得ておくべき大切なことは何ですか.

"How much money do you earn?" "*Mind* your own business!" 「いくら稼いでいるの」「余計なおせっかいよ〔自分自身の仕事を気にかけなさい〕」

Now, he is ⌈of two *minds* [=wavering] about going to college. 彼は大学へ行くべきかどうか迷っている.

---

minute /名 mínət, 形 main(j)úːt/

原義は〈細かな〉である. **(1 時間を細かく分けた) 分 (ぷん)；細かな**.
関 mini (小型(の))

The office is only ⌈ten *minutes'* walk [=a ten-*minute* walk] from my home. 事務所は家から歩いてほんの 10 分です.

You're too quick to decide; why don't you wait for a *minute* [=while/moment]? 速断はだめだよ. もう少し待ったらどうなの.

I expect the bus to come ⌈at any *minute* [=very soon]. バスはもうじき来ると思います.

He remembers everything well and told about our days in school in *minute* detail. 彼は何でもよく覚えていて, 学生時代のことをこまごまと語った.
▶ in minute detail「こと細かに」

miss /mís/

原義は〈的を外す〉である. **(目的物) を取り逃がす；(会えなくて) 寂しく思う；(事故をからくも) 逃れる.**
派 missing (見当たらない)

You feel the cell phone's vibration, so you won't *miss* incoming calls in a noisy place.　携帯電話の振動を感じるから, 騒がしいところで連絡が入っても逃すことはない.

I have *missed* you so much!　会えなくて寂しかったわ！

I *miss* the days when we had nothing to worry about and played outside till it got dark.　無邪気に暗くなるまで外で遊んでいたあのころが懐かしい.

Fortunately, the typhoon that was heading for this area *missed* us.　幸い, こちらに向かっていた台風はそれた.

mission /míʃən/

語源は〈miss (送る) sion (こと)〉である. **(役目を与えて送り出す) 使節団→伝道, 布教→使命, 任務.**
派 missionary (宣教師)
関 admit (認める)；dismiss (退ける)

Many self-defense officials have been sent on a *mission* to get rid of debris and rubble in the disaster-stricken area.　多くの自衛隊員が被災地のがれきの撤去をするために派遣された.

The Red Cross has a *mission* of providing help and hope to people in need.　赤十字は貧しい人々に援助と希望を与える使命をもっている.

mistake /məstéɪk/

語源は〈mis（誤って）take（取る）〉である．**判断を誤る，思い違いをする**．

mis✗take

If you live actively, you'll make *mistakes*. But if you learn from them, you'll be a better person.　積極的に生きていると誤りを犯しがちだが，誤りから学べば向上できる．

Don't worry about it. Anyone can make the same *mistake*.　心配しないで．誰でも同様の誤りはするかもしれないよ．

I missed the first half of the concert, as I *mistook* the starting time.　開始時間を勘違いして，コンサートの前半を聞き逃した．

mix /míks/

原義は〈混ぜ合わせる〉である．**あるものが別のものと混ざる；人が他の人や環境と打ち解ける**．
派 mixture（混合）；mixed（混ざった，複雑な）

Mix [=blend] sugar, flour and milk to make a paste.　砂糖，小麦粉，牛乳を混ぜて生地を作りなさい．

Oil will not *mix* with water. =Oil and water don't *mix*.　油は水とは混ざり合わない．

She is from Italy but *mixes* [=gets along] well in our community.　彼女はイタリア出身だが，私たちの社会にうまく解け込んでいる．

Fathers often have *mixed* feelings about their daughter's marriage.　父親は娘の結婚には複雑な思いをすることが多い．

moderate /mάːdərət/

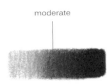
moderate

語源は〈moder(方式)ate(のある)〉である. **形を逸脱していない→節度のある→ほどよい**.
派 moderation(節度);moderately(そこそこに, 適度に)
関 moderato(《音楽》ほどよい速度で)

Most symptoms of human diseases can be classified into mild, *moderate*, or severe.　人間の病気の症状はたいてい, 軽症, 普通, 重症に分けられる.

The economic recovery is continuing ⌜at a *moderate* pace [= gradually].　経済は徐々に回復しつつある.

Drinking ⌜a *moderate* amount of alcohol [=alcohol in moderation] may be good for your health.　ほどほどの酒は体によい場合が多い.

modern /mάːdərn/

語源は〈mode(ぴったりはまる)rn(状態)→現代の〉である. **新しく現代的な**.
派 modernization(現代化);modernize(現代化する)

modern

Thanks to *modern* [=present-day] medicine, some deadly diseases have become things of the past.　現代医学のお陰で, 致命的な病気のいくつかが過去のものになっている.

China has been trying to *modernize* [=update] its industries for the past two decades.　中国はこの20年, 国の産業の近代化に努めている.

moment /móumənt/

原義は〈(動く)瞬間〉である. **短い時間→瞬間, 少しの時間→ある機会・場合**.
派 momentary (一瞬の); momentarily (一瞬, ちょっとの間)

You should not rush. Wait for the right *moment* before you quit your job. 慌てないで. 仕事を辞めるのなら潮時 (適切な時) を待ちなさい.

There was total silence for a *moment* in the hall before the winner was announced. 優勝者の発表前, ホールは一瞬静まりかえった.

"Excuse me, Sara, do you have a *moment* [=minute]?" "I'm afraid I'm busy right now." 「サラさん, ちょっと時間ある?」「ごめん, 今, 取り込んでいるの」

There were several *moments* in my life when I thought I might die. 死ぬのではないかと思った時が何度かある.

money /mʌ́ni/

原義は〈貨幣〉である. **金**.
派 monetary (通貨の, 金銭の)

Things are still tough with our business; more *money* is going out than coming in. 我々の商売は依然として厳しい状況で, 支出が収入を上回っている.

Does a lawyer make good *money*? 弁護士ってもうかるの?

The company was short of *money*, so it could not expand into potential foreign markets. その会社は資金不足のため, せっかくの海外市場へ乗り出すことができなかった.

The government has tightened its *monetary* policy in order to avoid inflation. 政府はインフレ抑止のために国の金融政策を引き締めた.

mood /múːd/

原義は〈気分〉である．**ある場における心持ち・気分・雰囲気**．
派 moody（気分が変わりやすい，不機嫌な）

What's your *mood* [=frame of mind] right now before the final?
決勝戦を前にした今の気持ちはどうですか．

I am not in the *mood* to talk to anybody now. =I don't feel like talking to anybody.　今は誰とも話す気になれない．

Watch out for the new boss; she is very *moody* [=temperamental].
新しい課長は気をつけたほうがいい，大変な気分屋だよ．

more /mɔ́ːr/

原義は〈もっと大きい〉である．**数量・程度が他と比べてより多い・大きい**．much, many の比較級として用いられる．

Asthma affects *more* than one million children each year. It is *more* common among boys *than* girls.　ぜんそくは毎年 100 万人を超える子どもがかかる．女児よりも男児に多い．　▶asthma /ǽzmə/

What is described here is the fact. *No more and no less.*　ここに述べられていることが現実です．これ以上でも以下でもありません．

I've already broken up five times. *No more* men for me.　もう 5 回も別れているの．男はもうたくさんだわ．

It will take him a few *more* days to fully recover.　彼が完治するにはあと数日かかる．

most /móʊst/

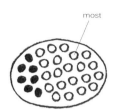

原義は〈もっと大きい〉である．**数量・程度が最も多い・大きい．**
派 mostly（ほとんどは）

I love playing sports, baseball *most* of all.　スポーツをするのが好きで，特に野球が大好きです．　▶ most of all「何よりも一番」

I had to work *most* of the weekend to make up for lost time.　遅れを取り戻すために，週末のほとんどは仕事をしなくてはいけなかった．

The plan went very well for the *most* part.　企画はほとんどがとてもうまくいった．

The weather for today will be *mostly* cloudy.　今日の天気はおおむね曇りでしょう．　▶ partly cloudy「ときどき曇り」

---

motivate /móʊṭəvèɪt/

語源は〈motive（動機）ate（づける）〉である．**何かをする動機を与える，やる気にさせる．**
派 motivation（動機づけ）; motive（動機）
関 move（動かす）

The teacher is very good at *motivating* her students.　この先生は生徒のやる気を促すのが上手だ．

I have lost *motivation* to keep studying. I wonder how I can stay *motivated* in schoolwork.　勉強する意欲がなくなってしまった．どうしたらやる気を持ち続けられるだろうか．

When you don't sleep well, you may feel low and *unmotivated* [= depressed].　睡眠が十分でないと，気分がすぐれず，やる気がなくなりがちだ．

mountain /máuntn/

原義は〈積み上げたもの,隆起〉である. 山.
派 mountaineer (登山家); mountaineering (登山); mountainous (山の多い)　関 mound (盛り土)

On Saturday, I usually have a *mountain* of laundry to do, besides other neglected household duties.　土曜日にはたいてい,放っておいた家事の他に山のような洗濯物がある.

Japan is, in fact, a *mountainous* country; there are very few Japanese who cannot see a *mountain* or a hill from their residential quarters.　日本は,実のところ山国です.住んでいる地域から山や丘陵が見渡せない人はほとんどいません.

mouth /máuθ/

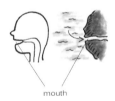

mouth

原義は〈口〉である. 口→ **(口から発する) ことば**. m-の音は両唇を合わせるので口・声・音を意識することになる: moo (もーと鳴く), moan (うめく), mute (無言である), murmur (つぶやく), mutter (ぶつぶつ言う)
派 mouthful (一口分)

Don't talk with your *mouth* full.　口に食べ物を頬張ったまま話すのはよしなさい.

The *mouth* of the river [＝The river's *mouth*] was so wide that we barely saw the other shore of the river.　河口はとても広くて対岸はほとんど見えないほどだった.

The restaurant's popularity spread by word of *mouth*.　そのレストランの人気は口コミで広まった.

Watch your *mouth* [＝language].　ことば遣いに気をつけて!

move /múːv/

原義は〈押して(物を)動かす〉である. **(物を)動かす, 人が引っ越す；(心を)動かす**.
派 moving (感動的な)；movement (動き, 運動)
関 emotion (感情)；motivate (やる気にさせる)

I want to *move* the table. Would you help me?　テーブルを動かしたいんだけど, 手伝ってくれる？

If you're *moving* overseas, I recommend you buy a car locally.　海外へ引っ越すのなら, 車は現地で調達するのがいいと思う.

She「was *moved* to tears by [=became very emotional and was in tears reading] her mother's heartfelt letter.　彼女は母の心のこもった手紙を読み, 感動して涙を流した.

"How was the movie?" "It was very good and very *moving* at the last scene."「映画, どうだった」「とてもよかった. ラストシーンは感動的だったよ」

much /mʌ́tʃ/

many

much

原義は〈多量〉である. **漠然とした量の多さ, 程度の高さ**をいう.

He doesn't have *much* money.　彼はお金をあまり持っていない.

How *much* does it hurt「to pierce your nose [=getting your nose pierced]?　鼻にピアスするのは(どれほど)痛いですか.

I try to have as *much* time as possible to spend with my family.　家族と過ごす時間をできるだけ多く持つようにしている.

"Your son is *much* taller than you." "Yes, he certainly is."「息子さんはあなたよりうんと長身だね」「ええ, そうなんです」

Much to my surprise [=To my great surprise], I was awarded the first prize.　とても驚いたことに, 私, 1等賞を取ったのよ.

multiply /mʌ́ltəplài/

語源は〈multi（たくさん）ply（重ねる）〉である。**(どんどん重ねる)→どんどん増える→掛け算する**.
派 multiple（多数の）; multiplication（掛け算, 増殖）

Mosquitoes *multiply* [=breed] in stagnant water like in a ditch or a pool.　蚊は溝や水たまりなど, よどんだ水の中で繁殖する.

The flu virus enters through the nose or mouth and *multiplies* mainly in the lungs.　インフルエンザ・ウイルスは鼻や口から侵入し主に肺で増殖する.

Multiplying any number by zero makes zero.　どんな数でもゼロを掛けるとゼロになる.

murder /mə́ːrdər/

原義は〈死〉である. **故意に人を殺す；殺人**.
派 murderer（人殺し）　関 mortal（死に至る）

A woman was *murdered* [=killed] in her downtown apartment.　女性が繁華街のアパートで殺害された.

He was charged with attempted *murder*.　彼は殺人未遂で告訴された.

The *murder* suspect is still at large.　殺人容疑者はまだ捕まっていない.

A middle-aged man was responsible for the mass *murder* [=killing] of young people attending a summer camp.　サマー・キャンプに参加していた若者たちを大量殺人した犯人は中年の男だった.

muscle /mÁsl/

語源は〈mus (ハツカネズミ) cle (丸い)〉である. **(ハツカネズミのように丸まった) 筋肉**.
派 muscular (筋肉の)

He has strained the *muscle* at the back of the thigh.　彼は大腿(だい)の後ろ側の筋肉の筋を痛めた.

Every strong swimmer「is very *muscular*［＝has a *muscular* body］.　強い水泳選手はみな筋肉質だ.

---

must /mÁst/

原義は〈〜すべき〉である.**(動作に威圧・義務を加えて)〜しなければならない；(判断に威圧・確信を加えて)〜に違いない**.

You *must* get the car registered before you drive a new car.　新車を買ったら運転する前に車を登録しなければいけない.

You *must* not go to the theater alone; children under ten should be accompanied by an adult.　一人で映画館に行ってはいけないよ. 10歳以下の子は大人の付き添いが必要なのだから.

My baby began to cry again; he *must* have a wet diaper.　あら, 赤ちゃんがまた泣き出したわ. きっとオムツがぬれてるのよ.

"Why did I say that to my boss?" "You *must* have been very upset."
「なんであんなこと課長に言ったのだろう」「動転していたに違いないよ」

name /néɪm/

原義は〈物の名前〉である．**名前→名前を付ける→指名する，名前を挙げる**．
派 namely（すなわち）

His replacement is yet to be *named* [=appointed]. 彼の後任はまだ任命されていません．

Name what you think is the most important event in the 20th century. 20世紀で一番重要だと思う事件を挙げなさい．

Tasmania is *named after* Abel Tasman, who was the first explorer to sight the land. タスマニアは，最初に島を見つけた探検家であるアーベル・タスマンにちなんでいる．

narrow /nǽloʊ/

原義は〈幅が狭い〉である．**幅が狭い→心が狭い→ぎりぎりのところ**．
派 narrowly（かろうじて）

Japan looks long and *narrow* on the map. 日本は地図で見ると細長く見える．

The road will *narrow* [=become *narrow*] after you pass the town. 町を過ぎると道路は狭くなります．

The gymnast won the gold medal by a *narrow* margin. =The gymnast *narrowly* won the gold medal. その体操選手は僅差で金メダルを獲得した．

It was fortunate that we *narrowly* missed an accident. 事故をすんでのところで免れたのは幸いだった．

nation /néɪʃən/

原義は〈生まれ〉である．**(ある地に生まれた)国民→(国民で構成する)国家**．
派 national(国の);nationalism(民族主義);nationalist(民族主義者);nationality(国籍);nationally(全国的に)
関 nationwide(全国的な)

Economic problems of a country often require「cooperation among *nations*［＝international cooperation］． 一国の経済問題が国家間の協力を必要とすることが多い．

"What is his *nationality*?" "He is a Vietnamese."「彼の国籍はどこですか」「ベトナムです」

Kimigayo (The Emperor's Reign), was adopted as *the national anthem* of Japan in 1888.「君が代」は1888年に日本の国歌として採択された．

native /néɪtɪv/

語源は〈nat(生まれ)ive(ながらの)〉である．**ある土地に生まれついた→土着の→生来の**．

He is a *native* speaker of English from London. 彼はロンドン出身で英語が母語です．

Shinto is the *native*［＝indigenous］Japanese religion. 神道は日本の土着の宗教です．

The term *Indians* is still used, but *Native Americans* has caught on, especially in the media. インディアンという用語は今でも使われているが，ネイティブ・アメリカンと呼ぶのが普通になり，ことにメディアではそうなっている．

nature /néɪtʃər/

語源は〈nat (生まれる) ure (こと)〉である. **(生まれたままの) 自然→ (生まれもった) 性質**.
派 natural (自然のままの);naturally (当然, 生まれつき)

I usually go to a lakeside to enjoy the beauty of *nature* in the summer.　夏はたいてい, 自然の美しさを楽しむために湖畔へ出かけます.

My son is introverted *by nature*; he prefers to be in his room alone.　息子は内向的〔←生まれつき内気〕で, 部屋に一人こもるのを好む.

A wig should look as *natural* [=genuine] as possible.　かつらはできるだけ自然に見えるのがいい.

Let your hair dry *naturally* if you have time.　時間があれば, 髪は自然に乾かしなさい.

near /níər/

原義は〈近い〉である. **(距離・時間・程度・関係が) 近い状態である;近づく**.
派 nearby (最寄りの)

Summer vacation is drawing *near* [=getting closer].　夏休みが近づいてきた.

Excuse me. Is there a bicycle shop *near* here?　すみませんが, この近くに自転車屋さんはありますか.

Summer vacation is ⌈*nearing* the end [=coming to an end].　夏休みが終わりに近づいてきた.

More details will be announced as the date *nears*.　もっと詳しいことは当日が近づいてからお知らせします.

necessary /nésəsèri/

語源は〈ne=not（否）cess（譲る）ary（の）〉である．**（譲ることの出来ない→無くなると困る）→必要な**．
派 necessarily（必然的に）；necessity（必要性，必需品）

Is it really *necessary* for elementary school children to carry mobile phones?　携帯電話を小学生が持つことが本当に必要ですか．

Some people have to work long hours out of *necessity*.　仕方なく長時間働かなくてはいけない人もいる．

Development of technology does not *necessarily* lead to human happiness and well-being.　技術の進歩が人間の幸福や福利に結びつくとは限らない．

They struggled to obtain the *necessities* of life during the war.　人々は戦時中，生活必需品を手に入れることに苦労した．

---

need /níːd/

原義は〈困窮〉である．**欠けている要素・条件を取り込む必要がある；必要**．
派 needy（非常に貧しい）

Always take enough rest when you *need* it.　休養は，必要な時にいつもちゃんと取るようにしなさい．

There's something I *need* to tell you.　あなたに言わなければならないことがある．

There's no *need* to suffer silently; you should openly ask him to carry out what he promised.　黙って我慢することはないよ．彼に約束はちゃんと果たすように言わなきゃ．

We raised money and necessities for ⌈*needy* people [=those *in need*]⌉．貧しい人たちのために金と生活用品を募った．

nature, near, necessary, need

negotiate /nəgóuʃièɪt/

原義は〈障害を乗り越える〉である．**他者との問題を協議する，取り決めのために話し合う**．
派 negotiation（交渉）

When purchasing in bulk, you can *negotiate* a reduced price.　まとめ買いするときは値引き交渉ができますよ．

The *negotiation* failed to come to an agreement.　交渉は物別れに終わった．

neighbor /néɪbər/

語源は〈neigh=near（近くの）bor（住人）〉である．**近くに住んでいる人**．
派 neighboring（近隣の）；neighborhood（近所，付近）

Avoid loud arguments with your housemates that will get your *neighbors*' attention.　大きな声で家の人と口論すると，隣人たちの関心を買ってしまいますよ．

What are the *neighboring* [=surrounding] cities of Fukuoka?　福岡市に隣接しているのは何市ですか．

You may find the *neighborhood* boring with no shops and places to enjoy yourselves.　この辺りはお店も遊ぶ所もなくて退屈に思うでしょう．

Harlem used to be considered a high-crime *neighborhood* [=area].　ハーレムは，昔は犯罪の多い所と思われていた．

new /n(j)úː/

原義は〈新しい〉である. **(出来たばかりの)新しい→(これまで存在しなかった)新たな**.

old   new

派 newly（新しく, 最近）; newcomer（新人, 初心者）; news（ニュース）〔← new＋(thing)s〕

New to the fair this year is a local drama club which will present a traditional comedy.　今年の祭りの新たな出し物は, 地元の演劇クラブが上演する伝統喜劇です.

This is a *newly* formed nonprofit organization, whose mission is to raise money and support the earthquake orphans.　これは新規のNPO組織で, 震災孤児のための基金と支援を目的にしている.

It is *news* [＝a surprise] to us that your brother will run for election. 君の兄さんがこの選挙に出馬するとはびっくりしたよ.

---

next /nékst/

語源は〈ne（＝near 近く）xt（＝est 最上級）〉である. **(一番近い)→(順序がすぐ)次の, (位置がすぐ)隣の**.

NEXT→

Who is the lady standing *next to* the President?　大統領の横に立っている女性は誰ですか.

The store will be closed for renovation for the *next* three weeks. この店は, 改修のためにこれから3週間ほど休みになります.

He finished *next* to last in the final of a 100-meter sprint.　彼は100メートル走決勝でビリから2番目だった.

When can we see each other *next*?　今度, いつ会える?

The conference will be held in Rio *the year after next*.　大会はリオデジャネイロで再来年開催される.

nice /náɪs/

原義は〈きれいな〉である. **すてきな→心地よい→親切な**.
派 nicely（上手に）

I love travelling, but it's also *nice* to be back home.　旅が好きだけど, 家に帰るのもまたいいものだ.

I think you will look *nice* with shorter hair.　髪を短くしたらよく似合うと思うよ.

Here, it's *nice* and warm most of the fall season.　当地は, 秋はたいていさわやかで暖かです. ▶nice and cool/quiet/breezy/sunny などのように表現して〈心地よさ・快適さ〉を強調する.

It's *nice* of you to say so.　そう言ってくださってうれしく思います.

night /náɪt/

原義は〈(光のない)夜〉である. **夜, 夜間, 晩**.
派 nightly（夜の）
関 overnight（一夜で, 一晩中）; nightmare（悪夢）

It is a beautiful moonlit *night*, with a pleasant breeze on the beach.　きれいな月明かりの夜で, 浜辺には心地よい風が吹いている.

It seems to have rained last *night*; the asphalt is still wet.　昨夜は雨が降ったようで, アスファルトがまだぬれている.

The mother spent many sleepless *nights* tending her critically injured child.　母親は重傷の子どもに付き添って, 何日も眠れない夜を過ごした.

When「*night* falls [=it gets dark], those crickets in the bush start singing in chorus.　夜になると茂みのコオロギが一斉に鳴き始める.

no /nóu/

原義は〈けっして〜でない〉である．**存在しない**，**(否定の答えとして) いいえ**．

"Do you need a ride?" "*No*, thank you. My son is picking me up."
「便乗されますか」「いいえ，結構です．息子が迎えに来てくれますので」

I have *no* idea what happened to him.　彼に何が起ったのか知りません．

It is *no* joke that my husband has been misdiagnosed for the past five years.　夫が5年間も誤診を受けていたなんて冗談じゃない．

"I don't think it's right." "*No*, it isn't."　「それ，間違っていると思うよ」「確かに間違っているね」

No breakfast is complete *without* a fragrant coffee.　朝食に香り高いコーヒーはなくてはならない．

---

note /nóut/

原義は〈印〉である．印→**書き付け**，**覚え書き**；**(音階が印してある) 音符**；**(心に印すべき) 注目**，**特徴**．
派 notable（目立つ，卓越した）
関 noteworthy（注目すべき）

May I ask you to take *notes* of the meeting?　会議の記録をお願いできますか．

I resent seeing scribbled *notes* in the margin of books I borrow from the library.　図書館で借りた本の余白に書き込みがあるのを見ると不快になる．

Can you read ⌈musical *notes* [＝music]?　音符が読めますか．

They had a long meeting over the problem, but nothing of *note* [＝importance] came out of the discussion.　その問題で長時間会議をしたけれど，注目すべき結論は何も出なかった．

nice, night, no, note　495

nothing /nʌ́θɪŋ/

語源は〈no (零) thing (物・事)〉である. **何もないこと, 内容が何もないこと**.

This method works like *nothing* else.　この方法は他にないくらいの効果がある.

I did *nothing but* hang around all day.　一日中ぶらぶらしていた〔ぶらぶらする以外は何もしなかった〕.

Don't hesitate. Just go for it. You have *nothing* to lose.　躊躇(ちゅうちょ)しないで, 思い切ってやってみろよ. だめ元だよ〔失うものは何もないよ〕.

Without software, a computer is *nothing* more than a plastic box.　ソフトがなければ, コンピュータはプラスチックの箱に過ぎない.

notice /nóʊtəs/

語源は〈not=know (知る) ice (こと)〉である. **通知, 気づき；〜に気づく**.
派 noticeable (目立つ)；notion (観念, 考え)；notify (知らせる)

A renewal *notice* will be sent to you about four weeks before your license expires.　免許の更新通知は, 免許の切れる4週間前にお手元に送られます.

The parents *noticed* [=became aware of] their daughter's strange behavior.　両親は娘の異常な行動に気づいた.

"What is the first thing you *notice* when you meet a new person?" "Their eyes. They really are the windows to the soul."　「初対面の時に最初に注目するのはどこですか？」「目です. 目は心の窓ですから」

now /náu/

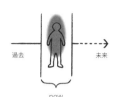

過去　　now　　未来

原義は〈いま〉である．**今は，このごろは，現代は；今すぐ．**

His condition seems stable, at least for *now* [=the mean time]. 彼の容態は今のところ安定している．

I didn't know until *now* that you are from the same hometown as mine. あなたが同郷だったとは今まで知りませんでした．

Have you been thinking of studying abroad? If so, *now* is the time to take action. 留学を考えているのなら，今こそ行動に移す時だ．

Good-bye for *now*. （しばらくの間）さようなら．

My daughter is late; she should have been home *by now*. 娘の帰りが遅いわ．もう帰っている時間なのに．

---

number /nʌ́mbər/

原義は〈数〉である．**(数えて得られる) 数，(数を表す) 数字・番号；数が～に達する．**
派 numerous（多数の）
関 Arabic numerals（アラビア数字）

We still often see Roman *numbers* [=numerals] on a clock face. 今でも時計の文字盤にローマ数字をよく見かける．

There are ⌈*a number of* [=several] options to choose from based on your individual needs. 個人の要望に応じていくつかの選択肢があります．

Traffic fatalities across the country *number* [=The *number* of traffic fatalities across the country amounts to] nearly five thousand annually. 全国の交通事故死者数は年間 5,000 人近くに達する．

object /名 á:bdʒɪkt, 動 əbdʒékt/

語源は〈ob（向こうへ）ject（投げる）〉である．**(関心を向けて投げる) 目的・対象物；(向かって投げる) 反対する**．
派 objection（反対，異議）　関 eject（追放する）

I have become farsighted; I can see distant *objects* clearly, but cannot near ones.　遠視になってしまった．遠くの物ははっきり見えるけど，近くの物は見えないの．

There were few who *objected* to my proposal.　私の提案に反対する人はほとんどいなかった．

objective /əbdʒéktɪv/

語源は〈object（物）ive（的な）〉である．**(遠くに置いて見る) 客観的な；(遠くに置いた) 目標**．
派 objectively（客観的に）；objectivity（客観性）
関 subjective（主観的な）

It's hard to ⌈be *objective* [＝think *objectively*] about one's own faith.　自分自身の信仰について客観的に見るのは難しい．

You need more *objective* [＝concrete] evidence to support the theory.　その理論を裏づける客観的証拠がもっと必要だ．

It is very important to set specific *objectives* in the beginning of planning.　計画を立てる時は，最初に具体的目標を設定することが大切だ．

observe /əbzə́:rv/

語源は〈ob (〜を) serve (保つ)〉である. **(じっと目をやる→注意を注ぐ)→観察する, 規則を守る**.
派 observation (観察); observatory (観測所); observer (評論家, 観察者)

Parents are invited to *observe* their child's class once a month.　月に一度, 親が子どもの授業を参観する日がある.

Since the beginning of time, people have *observed* how the Moon waxes and wanes.　原始以来, 人は月の満ち欠けを観察してきた.

Bike riders must also *observe* [=obey] traffic rules.　自転車に乗る人も交通規則をちゃんと守らないといけない.

obvious /á:bviəs/

語源は〈ob (上に) vious (道の)〉である. **(行く手にある)→明白である**.
派 obviously (明らかに)
関 previous (以前の)〔←前＋行程〕

It's *obvious* [=clear] why they have broken up.　あの人たちが別れた理由は明白よ.

It may be stating the *obvious*, but you can't proceed with the project without money.　当たり前のことを言うようですが, 金がないことには企画は進められないよ.　▶ state the obvious「当たり前のことを言う」: 相手の明白すぎる発言に対して Don't state the obvious. / It's obvious. / I know. などと応じる.

Obviously, this is not genuine.　明らかにこれは本物じゃないよ.

occasion /əkéɪʒən/

語源は〈oc(へ)casion(落ちる)〉である. **(事が降りかかる)時・場合；出来事**.
派 occasional(ときどきの)；occasionally(ときどき)
関 case(場合, 事件)

"We're planning to have a party." "What's the *occasion* [=What is the party for]?"　「パーティーを計画しているんです」「何のパーティーですか」

You need to take an *occasional* break from work.　仕事から離れてときどき休みを取ることが必要だよ.

My son calls me *occasionally* to let me know how things are going.　息子はときどき電話で近況を知らせてくれる.

occur /əkə́ːr/

語源は〈oc(へ)cur(走る)〉である. **(〜のほうへやって来る→現れる)→ふと起こる→ふと思い浮かぶ**.
派 occurrence(出来事)　関 current(現行の)

Heartburn often *occurs* [=happens] after eating a heavy meal.　胸やけは, こってりした食事をした時に起こりやすい.

It never *occurred* to me to contact [=I never thought of contacting] my birth mother who left us when we were young.　幼いころ私たちを見放した生みの母に, 連絡を取ろうと思ったことはない.

Getting stuck in the traffic is *an everyday occurrence* in big cities.　渋滞に巻き込まれるのは都会では日常茶飯事だ.

odd /ɑ́:d/

原義は〈余り〉である．**余り→はみ出し→(偏り，傾き)→勝ち目，確率**．

We often find one *odd* sock left in the laundry. 洗濯物に靴下が片方だけ残っていることがよくある．

It took twenty *odd* years to build the sea wall. 防潮堤の建設に二十数年かかった．

Here, the ⌈*odd* numbered houses [=houses with *odd* numbers] are on the left side of the street. ここでは，奇数番地の家が通りの左側にある．
▶an odd number「奇数」

The *odds* [=chances] are extremely slim that you will win the lottery. 宝くじに当たる確率はきわめて低い．

of /ʌ́v/

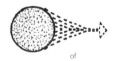

原義は〈〜から離れて〉である．**分離・発生の元 (根源，部分，所属，原因，理由) を示唆する**．

They had three children, *of* whom only the youngest survived to adulthood. 彼らには子どもが3人いたが，そのうち末っ子だけが成人した．

You may think it strange, but there are many who have a fear *of* dogs. 変に思うかも知れませんが，犬恐怖症の人も多くいます．

When Tom came, the four *of* us went out to the party. トムが来たので，私たち4人でパーティーに出かけた．

He quit school *of* his own will to become a fisherman. 彼は漁師になるために自分の意志で学校を辞めた．

off /ɔ́ːf/

原義は〈〜から離れて〉である．①**(活動を離れる)→休んで，止めて．**②**(静止を離れる)→始動して．**①離れる場に視点を置くと〈消失・不在・不接触〉，②離れる動きに視点を置くと〈始動・勢い〉と捉えられる．

He is *off* today. 彼は今日，休みです．

I decided to take a week *off* work [=from work]. 仕事を1週間休むことにした．

Keep your hands *off* the exhibits. 陳列品に触れないでください．

The ship was wrecked *off* the coast of Miura. 船は三浦海岸沖で難破した．

She hustles her children *off* to school every morning. 彼女は毎朝，子どもたちを学校へせかせて送り出す．

The plane *took off* as scheduled. 飛行機は定刻に離陸した．

offer /ɔ́ːfər/

語源は〈of (へ) fer (運ぶ)〉である．**援助・提案などを相手に差し向ける．**

I was *offered* a job at a shoe store, but I turned it down. 靴屋で働かないかと言われたけれど，断った．

I'd like to *offer* a couple of comments on the subject in question. 問題の件について少し意見を述べたく思います．

We don't need any help for the time being, but thank you very much for *offering*. 今のところ援助は要りませんが，お申し出に感謝します．

office /ɑ́ːfəs/

原義は〈仕事をする〉である.**(職務を果たす地位) 職,官職**;**(仕事する場) 事務所, 役所**.
派 official (職務上の, 高官); officially (正式に); officer (警官, 役員)

His *office* is on the fourth floor near the elevator. 彼の事務所は4階エレベーターの近くにあります.

Do you go to the *office* every week day? 平日は毎日, 会社ですか.

There are eight presidents who died ⌜in *office* [=before his term ended]. 任期中に亡くなった大統領が8人いる.

The President of the United States is elected to *office* by the citizens. アメリカの大統領は国民によって選出される. ▶ office = the White House

often /ɑ́ːfn/

原義は〈しばしば〉である. **たびたび, 何度も**.

How *often* do you use your cell phone? 携帯電話をよく使いますか.

There was snow on the roofs and grass, which doesn't happen very *often* in this area. 屋根や芝生に雪が積もっていたけど, 当地では珍しいことです.

Adults do not drink soft drinks as *often* as young people. 大人は若者ほど頻繁にソフトドリンクを飲まない.

oil /ɔ́ɪl/

原義は〈オリーブ〉である．**食用油・石油；潤滑のために油を差す．**
派 oily（〔髪・肌などが〕脂っぽい，〔食べ物が〕油っこい）

Do you paint in *oils* or watercolors?　油絵の具で描くの？それとも水彩絵の具で？

You should clean and *oil* [=lubricate] the chain when it begins to make a noise.　チェーンから雑音が出るようになったら，きれいにしてオイルを差しなさい．

The last time I went to the restaurant, I found the food too *oily* [=greasy].　この前そのレストランに行ったときは，料理がとても油っこかった．

---

old /óʊld/

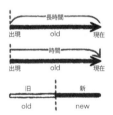

原義は〈時間が経った〉である．**（存在している総時間が長い）古い，（存在時間が〜ほどである）〜ほど時間がたっている；（現存前の存在）旧の，前の．**
関 old-fashioned（旧式の）; age-old（長年の）

This carpet is getting pretty *old* now.　このじゅうたんはもう随分古くなっている．

The baby is just a week *old*.　この赤ちゃんは生後1週間です．

"This PC is only a month *old*." "What did you do with your *old* computer?"　「このパソコンは買ってからほんの1か月です」「前のパソコンはどうしたの」

How old do you have to be to drive a car legally?　法的に車が運転できるのは何歳からですか．

on /ɑːn/

原義は〈乗っかっている〉である. **乗っかっている→～上にある《上面への接触》→接触している《付着》→かかわっている《関係》→頼っている《依存》**.

〈接触〉　〈活動〉

It is illegal to work *on* a tourist visa. 観光ビザで働くのは違法だ.

The actor was *on* TV yesterday. あの俳優は昨日テレビに出ていた.

Don't leave the oven *on*. オーブンに火をつけたまま離れてはだめよ.

Women usually spend more time *on* housework than men do. 概して女性は男性より家事に時間を費やす.

Fire crews are always *on standby* in case of emergency. 消防隊員は非常時に備えて常に待機している.

This car runs *on* electricity. この車は電気で動く.

---

once /wʌ́ns/

語源は〈on=one (一) ce (度)〉である. **一度；ひとたび～すると**.
関 twice (二度)

I walk for about thirty minutes *once* a day, after work. 仕事の後, 一日一回 30 分ほど散歩する.

The store doesn't seem to be as thriving as it ⌈*once* was⌉. [=used to be]. この店は以前のようには繁盛していないようだ.

Young people may don't know it, but he was *once* a national hero. 若い人たちは知らないかも知れないが, 彼はかつて国民的英雄だった.

Once a nuclear war broke out, there would probably be no way to control it. ひとたび核戦争が起きると制御不能になるだろう.

one /wʌ́n/

原義は〈一つ〉である．**(最初に思い浮かぶ) 奴 (やつ) →例の奴**．ことばが乱暴になるが，one は〈奴 (やつ)〉という感じでとらえると体得しやすい．

"Which *one* will you take?" "I'll take this *one*." 「どれ〔←どのやつ〕を取りますか」「これ〔←このやつ〕にします」

It always seems that as we settle *one* problem, a new *one* arises. いつも，一難去ってまた一難，って様相だ．

Four large islands and many smaller *ones* make up Japan. 4つの大きい島と多くの小さい島で日本はできている．

To ban smoking is *one* thing, but to ban smokers is quite *another*. 喫煙を禁じるのと，喫煙者を締め出すのとはまったく別のことだ．

only /óunli/

語源は〈on=one (一つ) ly (だけ)〉である．**ただ一つの；ほんの，単に**．

Ken is an *only* child. ケンは一人っ子だ．

Wars *only* bring destruction and nothing else. 戦争は破壊をもたらすばかりだ．

There were *only* a certain number of jobs available for those with no degrees. 学歴がない人にはほんの限られた仕事しかなかった．

Don't worry. It is *only* natural to get nervous before an important exam. 心配しないで．大切な試験の前に緊張するのはごく自然だ．

open /óupən/

open　open

原義は〈蓋が開いている〉である. **(覆い・扉を) 開く** → **(気持ち・情報・空間を) 解放する**; **開いている, 解放されている**.
派 opening (開始, 始め, 穴, 空き); openly (公然と)

The new airport will ⌈be *open* [=*open*]⌉ in March next year.　新空港は来年3月にオープンする.

The board held an *open* discussion about future plans for the community.　理事会は地域の将来計画について公開討論会を開いた.

You should do fireworks only in an *open* space.　花火は空き地でしなくてはいけません.

We don't have any *openings* [=available posts] right now.　当社は今, 職に空きはない.

---

opinion /əpínjən/

語源は〈opini (考える) ion (こと)〉である. **(考えた) 意見・見解, 世論**.
派 opinionated (自己の意見に固執する, 頑固な)
関 option (選択) 〔←考えて選ぶ〕; opinion poll (世論調査)

What is your *opinion* about his suggestion?　彼の提案を君はどう思う?

This is only ⌈one person's [=my personal]⌉ *opinion*.　これは私の個人的意見にすぎません.

It has always been my *opinion* that women are more stable and stronger than men both mentally and physically.　女性のほうが心身ともに男性より安定して強い, というのが私の変わらぬ持論です.

I'd like a second *opinion* before I make a decision.　決める前に別の人の意見を聞いてみたいと思います.

opportunity /ɑ́ːpərt(j)úːnəti/

語源は〈op(へ向けて) portuni(港) ty(状態)〉である.**(風が港方向へ向いている)→(寄港に)条件が好都合である→事を成すよい機会, チャンス**. 日本語でも「追い風が吹いている(好条件である)」という.

I think we need to be patient and wait for the right *opportunity*.　我慢してチャンスを待ったほうがいいと思う.

Bob failed, but he saw it as an *opportunity* to improve his skills.　ボブは失敗したが, 能力を向上させるいい機会だったと考えた.

You have to be ready to take an *opportunity* [=a chance] when it comes your way.　自分に運が向いてきた時に運をつかむ準備をしておきなさい.

opposite /ɑ́ːpəzɪt/

語源は〈op(対して) posite(置いた)〉である. **反対側に位置する；まったく逆の；逆のもの**.
派 oppose(反対する); opposition(反対)

Many may think so, but the *opposite* is true.　そう考える人が多いが, 事実は逆だ.

"What is the *opposite* of 'rural'?" "It's 'urban.'"　「『田舎の』の反対語は?」「『都会の』です」

I found a woman sitting *opposite* [=across from] me on the train was sobbing.　列車の反対側に坐っている女性がすすり泣いているのに気づいた.

Do you favor or *oppose* [=Are you for or against] restarting nuclear reactors?　原子炉の再稼働に賛成ですか, 反対ですか.

option /άːpʃən/

語源は〈opt (選ぶ) tion (こと)〉である. **いくつかの候補から選ぶこと, 選択するもの, いくつかの候補から選べること (選択権・選択肢があること)**.
派 opt (選ぶ); optional (選択できる)〔←必須でない〕
関 opinion (意見)

Computer skills have become more a necessity than an *option* [= have become essential] to everyone. コンピュータが使えることはもはや, 誰にとっても必須〔←選ぶものではなく不可欠〕になった.

When the city's residents need a place for recreation, there are many *options* open to them. 市民がレクリエーションの場がほしい時は, いろいろな選択肢があります.

Attending after-school programs is *optional* [=is up to each person]. 課外授業への参加は各自の選択に任せられている.

or /ɔ́ːr/

原義は〈他の〉である. **それとも, (別の言い方をすると) つまり; ～がなされないと…になってしまう**. other → o'r → or と変遷している.

Can I get you a cup of coffee *or* something? コーヒーか何かどうですか.

There is no air *or* water to erode the surface of the moon. 月面を侵食する空気や水はない.

The temperature in a car parked in the sun may rise to 50 degrees centigrade *or* more. 日なたに駐車している車の車内温度は, 50℃あるいはそれより高くなることがある.

Take a break once in a while, *or* you'll get sick. ときどき休憩しないと, 体を壊してしまうよ.

order /ɔ́ːrdər/

order

原義は〈整然と並ばせる〉である.**(きちんと並ばせる)順序→(きちんと並ばせる)命令・注文(する)→(きちんと並ばせる)秩序**.
派 orderly (整然とした)
関 ordinary (普通の); money order (為替) 〔←現金に替え為(し)める. いわば「換金命令書」のこと〕

The authors' names are listed in alphabetical *order*.　著者名はアルファベット順に出ています.

When you are ready to *order*, please press the button.　注文が決まりましたら, ボタンを押してお知らせください.

People don't like to be ⌈*ordered* around [=told what to do in a bossy way].　人はあれこれ指図されたくないものだ.

It will take several years for them to restore *order* to the country.　その国の治安の回復には数年かかるだろう.

ordinary /ɔ́ːrdənèri/

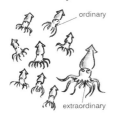
ordinary
extraordinary

語源は〈ordin (通常) ary (の)〉である. **普通の, 並みの**.
派 extraordinary (並外れた)　関 order (秩序)

There are some who can't do *ordinary* things or lead a normal life, because of their mental illness.　精神疾患のために普通のことができない, または通常の生活が送れない人がいる.

People often say Tom is strange, but he seems quite *ordinary* [= normal] to me.　トムは変だと人はよく言うが, 僕にはごく普通に思える.

I often find that those high-priced brand goods are *ordinary* [= average] in quality.　高価なブランド品が並みの品質であることがよくある.

organize /ɔ́ːrgənàɪz/

語源は〈organ(器官・組織)ize(〜をにする)〉である.
組織を構成する→個々を整理して全体をうまく展開させる.
派 organization(組織);organized(入念に計画された)
関 organ(器官)

The World Cup is *organized* by FIFA, the International Football Association.　ワールド・カップはFIFA(国際サッカー連盟)によって運営されている.

Due to lack of proper *organization* at home or office, we often feel frustrated and irritated.　家や職場がきちんと整頓されていないために,しばしば嫌になったりいらいらしたりするものだ.

Workplace safety should be the first priority for any *organization* [= corporation].　職場の安全がどんな組織にとっても第一優先であるべきだ.

original /ərídʒənl/

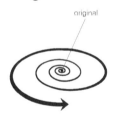

original

語源は〈origin(起源)al(の)〉である.**最初の(もの),独創的な(もの),元の(もの)**.
派 originally(もともとは);originate(生じる);origin(〔物事の〕始まり);originality(独創性)

The *original* plan had to be changed, because of a rise in material prices.　資材の価格が上がったために,当初の計画を変更しなければならなかった.

The singer had *originally* [=initially] wanted to be a drummer.　あの歌手はもともとドラマー志望だった.

Buddhism *originated* in India around the fifth century B.C.　仏教は紀元前5世紀ごろにインドで生まれた.

The *origin* of Kabuki is very old, going back to the early Edo period.　歌舞伎の起源は古く江戸時代初期にさかのぼる.

other /ʌ́ðər/

原義は〈もう一方の〉である. **もう一方の (もの), 別の (もの), その他の (もの)**.

I know Sydney and Melbourne. What *other* famous cities are there in Australia?　シドニーとメルボルンは知ってるけど, オーストラリアで他にはどんな都市が有名ですか.

The dates of the event were announced, but no *other* details are yet known.　イベントの開催日は発表になったが, その他の詳細はまだ知らされていない.

Don't try to force your opinion on *others* [=*other* people].　自分の考えを他人に押しつけないようにしなさい.

otherwise /ʌ́ðərwàɪz/

語源は〈other (別の) wise (方法で)〉である. **その他の方法で, そうでなければ, それとは違ったふうに**.

We happened to sit next to each other on that flight; I could never have met him *otherwise*.　私たちはたまたま, あの飛行機で隣り合わせに座ったの. それがなかったら彼と知り合うことはなかったわ.

You should apply for it; *otherwise* you will miss the opportunity.　それに応募しなさいよ, でないとチャンスを逃してしまうよ.

The defendant denies his involvement in the smuggling, but it's hard to imagine *otherwise*.　被告は密輸にはかかわっていないというが, そうとしか思えない〔←違ったふうに考えるのは難しい〕.

ought /ɔ́ːt/

原義は〈借りがある〉である. **〜しなければならない, 〜であるのが当然である.**
関 owe (借りがある)

People wishing to increase the strength of the heart and lungs ⌈*ought* to [=have to] exercise at least three to four times per week.　心肺能力を高めたい人は, 少なくとも週3, 4回運動すべきである.

Mr. Tanaka ⌈*ought* to get [=deserves] a raise; he is hardworking and energetic.　田中さんは昇給されて当然だ. とても勤勉で精力的だから.

out /áut/

原義は〈中から外へ〉である. **(外から見ると) 姿が現れる；(中から見ると) 姿が消える.**

He stuck his tongue *out* at the camera just for fun.　彼はふざけてカメラに向かって舌を出した.

The moon came *out* over the mountains.　月が山の端に現れた.

Speak *out* if you have something on your mind.　気がかりなことがあるのなら思い切って言いなさい.

I washed the shirt twice, but I couldn't get the stain *out*.　シャツを二度も洗ったけど, しみは取れなかった.

I dropped in on him but he was *out*.　彼の家に立ち寄ったが留守だった.

outcome /áutkʌ̀m/

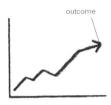

語源は〈out (外へ) come (出る)〉である.**(出てくる) 結果・成果**.

How do you predict the *outcome* [=results] of the presidential election?　大統領選挙の結果はどうなると思いますか.

Pitching mostly determines the *outcome* [=win or loss] of baseball games.　野球ではほとんどの場合，投手力が勝敗を左右する.

outside /àutsaɪd/

語源は〈out (外) side (側)〉である.**外側, 外部；外の；外へ, 外で**.
派 outsider (部外者)

It's snowing *outside*, thick and soft.　外はしんしんと雪が降っています.

The series of the incidents needs to have an *outside* investigation [=investigation from *outside*].　一連の事件は外部による調査が必要だ.

Things are often deceiving when seen from *outside*.　物事は外見では事実とは違うように見えることが多い.

over /óuvər/

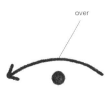

語源は〈ov=up(上)er(もっと)〉である. **〜の上を覆って《関連》, 〜の上に位置して《支配》, 〜の上をずっとたどって《完了》.**
派 overly (過度に)

What is their disagreement *over* [=about]?　何について彼らは意見が合わないのですか.

You need to have more control *over* your emotions.　感情をもっと抑えられるようになりなさい.

When will this horrible recession be *over*?　このひどい不景気はいつ終わるのだろうか.

The game was *over* in an instant.　決着はすぐについた.

owe /óu/

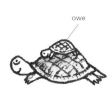

原義は〈物品を入手する〉である. **手に入れる (所有する)→支払いの義務がある→〜すべきである→(成果などが) 〜に負っている.**
派 owing (未払いの, 帰すべき)
関 own (所有する); ought (〜すべきである)

I *owe* you a drink. You bought me a beer last time.　僕がおごるよ. この前は君がビール代を払ってくれたから.

"Why did you give up the plan?" "I think I'm *owed* some kind of explanation."　「どうして計画をやめてしまったの」「その訳をお話しなくてはと思っています」

I *owe* what I am today *to* my parents.　今日の僕があるのは両親のお陰だ.

Owing to strong winds, flights are being temporarily suspended.　強風のため, 現在, 運航を見合わせています.

own /óʊn/

原義は〈所有する〉である．**所有する；自分独自の．**
派 owner（所有者）
関 ownership（所有権）；owe（借りがある）

After working as an apprentice chef for five years, my brother realized his dream—to *own* his *own* business.　兄はシェフの見習いとして5年働いた後，自分の店を持つ夢を実現させた．

Until suffering from a heart attack, my grandma lived *on her own* [= without anyone's help].　心筋梗塞を患うまで，祖母は自活していた．

pain /péɪn/

原義は〈刑罰〉である．**(肉体的)痛み，(精神的)苦痛；痛む；苦痛を与える．**
派 painful（痛みを起こす，苦痛になる）
関 punish（罰する）；painkiller（鎮痛剤）

I have a *pain* in the lower part of my abdomen from time to time.　ときどき下腹部が痛みます．

I am having a difficult time with *pain* from arthritis.　関節炎の痛みで苦しんでいます．

It *pains* us [=It is a *pain* for us =It is *painful* for us] to have to change the plan halfway.　計画を半ばで変更しなければならないのはつらいことだ．

paint /péint/

原義は〈装飾する〉である. **ペンキ, 塗料；ペンキを塗る**.
派 painter（画家）; painting（絵画）

We're going to *paint* the house green, because the color probably matches best with the surroundings.　おそらく緑が最も周囲と融け合うので, 家を緑色に塗るつもりだ.

To prevent wood rot you need to apply *paint* on the deck every couple of years.　木材の腐食を防ぐために, 2, 3年ごとにデッキをペンキで塗ることが必要です.

pair /péər/

原義は〈等しい〉である. **（双方が等しい）一揃(ぞろ)い, 一組, 一対；一対にする, ペアになる**.
関 compare（比較する）

If you have two *pairs* of walking shoes, wear them alternately.　ウオーキングシューズを2足持っているなら, 交互に履くようにしなさい.

They say that a cat and a mouse don't ⌜make a good *pair* [=get along well with each other]．　ネコとネズミは相性が悪いと言われている.

Most wines ⌜*pair* well [=make a good *pair*] with oysters.　たいていのワインはカキとよく合う.

The students are *paired* for practicing the dance.　ダンスの練習をするために, 生徒たちはペアを組む.

paper /péɪpər/

原義は〈紙〉である.**紙→書類,論文,新聞**.紙がイグサの一種である papyrus (パピルス) を材料としていたことに由来している.
派 paperless (ペーパーレスの)
関 paperwork (事務作業)

Take a piece of *paper* and a pencil and draw your own portrait.　紙と鉛筆を用意して,自分の似顔絵を描いてください.

Well, it sounds good *on paper*, but we always have to prepare for something unexpected.　確かに理論上はそれでいいけど,常に想定外のことを覚悟しておかないといけないよ.

The *paper* you presented was well-researched and very useful.　あなたが提出した論文は,調査がよくできていてとても価値がある.

I read about it in the local *paper*.　そのことについては地元紙で読んだわ.

parent /péərənt/

語源は〈par (生む) ent (人)〉である.**親;親になる,子育てをする**.
派 parental (親としての)

Parents can have a huge impact on the growth and development of their children.　親は子どもの心身の成長に大きな影響を与える.

Single parents [=One-parent families] are growing in number, especially in western countries.　片親の家庭が,ことに西欧の国で増えている.

Parent birds hunt for food for their young until they are old enough to feed themselves.　親鳥はひな鳥が自活できるまで,エサを捕ってきて与える.

Some young people don't know how to *parent* [=bring up] their children properly.　若い親の中には適切に子育てができない者がいる.

park /páːrk/

原義は〈囲われた場所〉である. **庭園, 公園, 遊園地, 競技場；駐車場→駐車する**.
派 parking（駐車）；parking lot（駐車場）

We usually walk at a nearby *park*.　たいてい近くの公園で散歩する.

I saw the slugger hit a thrilling home run out of the *park*.　あの強打者が豪快な場外ホームランを打ったのを見たよ. ▶ball park「野球場」

Don't *park* near the construction site.　建設現場の近くに駐車しないでください.

part /páːrt/

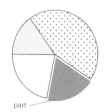

原義は〈一部〉である. **部分；分ける, 別れる**.
派 partial（部分的な）；partly（部分的に）
関 partner（相手, 連れ合い）

What do you think is the best *part* of living in a big city?　都会に住むことの一番の利点〔よい部分〕は何だと思う？

We don't have「the *part* that needs to be replaced〔＝the replacement *part*〕and have to order it from the manufacturer.　交換部品がないので, メーカーに注文することになります.

The mother couldn't bear the thought of「*parting* with〔＝separating from〕her only son who will join the military.　母親は入隊する一人息子との別れを思うと耐えがたかった.

particular /pərtíkjələr/

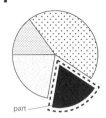

語源は〈particle (細かな部分) ar (の)〉である. 細かな部分に関わる〉である. **特別の, 細かなところまでこだわる**.

派 particularly (とりわけ)　関 particle (微粒子)

They are very *particular* about running their Shinkansen trains on time.　(JRは) 新幹線を定刻通りに走らせることにとても留意している.

My father is very *particular* [=fussy] about coffee.　父はコーヒーの味にこだわりがある.

Is there a *particular* [=specific] reason to drink vegetable juice before a meal.　食事の前に野菜ジュースを飲むのは何か特別な理由があるのですか.

I cook for myself, but I don't like it *particularly* [=in particular].　自炊しているけど, 特に料理が好きってことではない.

party /pá:rti/

語源は〈part (部分) y (集合状態)〉である. **(社会全体から見て部分を構成する人の集合体) →パーティー (集まり), 一団, 一行, 政党**.

Who are you going to invite to the *party*?　パーティーには誰を招くの?

Parties of players from each country are arriving at the Olympic village.　各国の選手団がオリンピック村へつぎつぎと到着している.

The ruling *party* barely managed to attain a majority in both Houses.　与党が両院でからくも過半数を維持した.

We need to hear *third-party* opinions from people outside the company.　社外から第三者の意見を聞く必要がある.

pass /pǽs/

原義は〈歩む〉である．**通過する→通過させる→過ごす→渡す；通過許可・利用許可の証明券；山道**．
派 passable (まずまずの)〔←まずまず通過できる〕
関 passage (通路, 〔文章などの〕一節); passenger (乗客); passport (旅券)

There is a truck behind that is trying to *pass* us. 僕たちを追い越そうとしているトラックが後ろにいる．

The issue pending for a long time has finally *passed*. 長い間の懸案がやっと通過した．

I just let his criticism *pass* without comment. = I didn't make a fuss about his criticism. 彼からの非難には反論せずやり過ごした．

Some characteristics are *passed on* by heredity. 性格には遺伝するものがある． ▶pass on 〜「(疾患・才能などを) 〜に受け継ぐ」

---

past /pǽst/

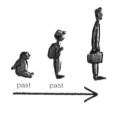

原義は〈通過した〉である．**過ぎ去った；過去，過去の出来事**．

He has been living in Kanazawa on business for the *past* several years. 彼はここ数年，仕事で金沢に住んでいる．

TB is not a disease of the *past* even in advanced countries. 結核は，先進国でも過去の疾病ではない．

I'd like to live and enjoy the present; the *past* is something I'm not really interested in. 私は現在を生き，楽しみたい．過去のことにはあまり関心がないわ．

particular, party, pass, past 521

patient /péɪʃənt/

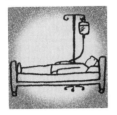

語源は〈pati (苦しむ) ent (人)〉である. **(治療を受けている) 病人；辛抱強い，我慢強い**.
派 patience (我慢, 根気)；patiently (辛抱強く)；impatient (いらいらした)

The number of diabetic *patients* has been on the increase. 糖尿病の患者が増加している. ▶diabetic /dàɪəbétɪk/

Be *patient* with others who are slower or less capable than you. 相手があなたより仕事が遅かったりうまく出来なかったりしても、いらいらしないようにしなさい.

It is easy to lose your *patience* [=temper] when you are depressed, or tired. 落ち込んでいたり疲れていたりすると感情的になりやすい.

pay /péɪ/

原義は〈平衡を保つ〉である. **受益に対して償う・払う；出費・努力に対して成果を得る；給料**.
派 payable (支払うべき)；payment (支払い)

Can I ask how much you *pay* for water every month? 毎月いくらほど水道代を払いますか.

You are supposed to *pay* the bills if you ask her out on a date. 君が彼女を誘うのなら、勘定は君が払うのが常識だよ.

Human beings will *pay* for their indiscriminate destruction of the environment. 人類は止めどない環境破壊のしっぺ返しを食らうだろう.

It doesn't *pay* to be too humble in a job interview. 就職の面接では、あまりへりくだるといい結果につながらない.

people /píːpl/

原義は〈人々〉である. **人々, 世間一般の人；住民, 国民**.
関 popular（人気のある）

There are more than 500 *people* [=persons] in the audience.　聴衆は500人を上回っている.

Don't care about what *people* think about you; follow what your heart says.　人の評判を気にすることなく，心の赴くところに従いなさい.

The government should work for the *people*, definitely not the other way around.　政府は国民のために働くべきで，断じてその逆ではない.

The North Korean *people* [=citizens] have not been told the truth about what is happening in the world.　北朝鮮国民は世界で起こっている事実を知らされていない.

percent /pərsént/

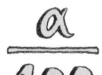

語源は〈per（〜につき）cent（100）〉である. **(100分のいくつになるかを示す) パーセント**.
派 percentage（割合）

Polls show only thirty *percent* of the voters are for revision of the constitution.　世論調査では憲法改正に賛成する有権者は30％に過ぎない.

"Do you agree?" "I agree with you 100 *percent*.=I couldn't agree with you more."　「君は賛成する？」「大賛成だよ」

What is the *percentage* of people in your country who are overweight?　あなたの国では肥満者の比率はどれくらいですか.

perfect /pə́ːrfikt/

語源は〈per(完全に)fect(作る)〉である. **完全で申し分ない状態である.**
派 perfection(完璧); perfectionism(完全主義); perfectly(申し分なく)

My life isn't *perfect*, but I'm pretty happy with it.　私の暮らしは満点ではないけれど,とても満足している.

The authorities tried to minimize the problems by saying no system is *perfect*.　当局は,完璧なシステムなどないと言って問題を矮小(わいしょう)化しようとした.

Don't try to make anything *perfect*; *perfectionism* [=striving for *perfection*] often leads to frustration.　何でも完璧にしようとするとだめよ.完璧主義はしばしば挫折につながるのだから.

perform /pərfɔ́ːrm/

語源は〈per(完全に)form(行う)〉である. **役割を果たす,機能を発揮する,演じる.**
派 performance(演技,出来映え); performer(演じる人)
関 outperform(〜より優れている)

Generally boys ⌈*perform* better than [=*outperform*]⌋ girls on a math test.　一般的に,男子のほうが女子より数学のテストの出来がいい.

You can ⌈make your computer *perform* better [=improve your computer's *performance*]⌋ by adding additional memory.　メモリーの容量を増やせば,コンピュータの性能が上がる.

In the final tournament, winning is more important than *performance*.　決勝トーナメントでは内容よりも結果が重要だ.

perhaps /pərhǽps/

語源は〈per(通して)hap(偶然)s(に)〉である. **(偶然によって)→ひょっとすると**.

Perhaps George will come to the concert; we may possibly run into him there. ひょっとして,ジョージはコンサートに来るかもしれない.もしかしたら出会うかもしれないよ.

The parents are hoping that she'll *perhaps* change her mind. 両親は,ひょっとすると娘が考えを変えてくれるのではないかと思っている.

I'm too busy today. *Perhaps* it would be better if you came back another day. 今日はとても忙しくしています.後日改めて来られるといいのですが.
▶ perhaps によって,陳述に〈断定しない→押しつけない→丁寧さ〉が生まれている.

---

period /píəriəd/

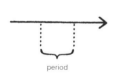

period

語源は〈peri(巡る)od(道筋)〉である. **(事象の始めから終わりまでを巡る時間)→(物事の出現・活動している)期間,時期,時代**.
派 periodical(定期刊行物)
関 periscope(潜望鏡)〔←周り+観測〕

Most teenagers go through a *period* of rebelling. 十代の多くは反抗期を経験する.

So much seems to have changed in a short *period* of time since the turn of the century. 今世紀に入ってからわずかの間に非常に多くのことが変わったように見える.

Do less exercise during your *period*. 月経のときは,運動量を落としなさい.
▶ period は menstruation(月経〔←月ごとに巡りくるもの〕)の婉曲語.

We have math in the next *period*. 次の時間は数学だ.

person /pə́ːrsn/

原義は〈登場人物〉である. **(一人ひとりの) 人間**.
派 personal (個人的な); personally (個人的に); personality (人柄, 性格; 有名人)

The admission fee is 500 yen *per person*.　入場料は一人 500 円です.
A certain *person* told me about it.　ある人がそのことを私に話してくれた.
What is your teacher like as a *person*?　先生は個人的にはどんな人ですか.
I met this guy online and I think he is nice, but I haven't met him「*in person* [＝*personally*].　この人は出会い系サイトで知り合った人で, いい人だと思うけど, 直接会ったことはないのよ.　▶in person「本人が直接に, 自分で」

pick /pík/

原義は〈つつく〉である. **(つつく)→摘み取る→選ぶ; (つつく)→つつき回す, ほじくる**.
関 peck (つつく); pickpocket (すり)

I'll *pick* you *up* at the station.　駅まで車で迎えに行きます.
The members of the singing group were *picked* from more than 500 applicants.　このグループの歌手たちは 500 人もの応募者の中から選ばれた.
I accidently left the key inside the car. Will you help me *pick* the lock?　うっかり車の中に鍵を忘れちゃった. なんとかして開けてもらえない?
▶pick a lock「鍵以外のものを使って (ピッキングで) 解錠する」
I tell my husband not to *pick* his nose in public.　夫に人前で鼻をほじくるのはやめてって言ってるのよ.

picture /píktʃər/

原義は〈描く〉である．**絵に描く，写真にする；絵，写真；心に描く，理解する；物事の概要・概観．**
派 picturesque（絵のように美しい）　関 depict（描く）

Let's draw a *picture* of your mother for Mother's Day.　母の日のためにお母さんの絵を描きましょう．

Can you *picture* what life was like in the Edo period?　江戸時代の生活がどんな様子だったか想像できますか．

The police are getting the whole *picture* of the crime.　警察は事件の全容をつかみつつある．

piece /píːs/

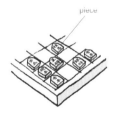

原義は〈切れ端〉である．**（切れ端）→断片→（総体の中の）一個．**

What *piece* of music is this?　これ，なんていう曲？

How many *pieces* of baggage can we travel with free of charge?　手荷物は何個まで無料で携行できますか．

The sculptor is working on a large *piece* which is to be exhibited in the entrance of a hotel.　その彫刻家はホテルの玄関に飾られる大作（作品）に挑んでいる．

To understand the mechanism, we took apart the computer *piece by piece* and put it back together again.　コンピュータの仕組みを理解するために，部品を一個一個分解し，さらに組み立てた．

person, pick, picture, piece 527

place /pléɪs/

原義は〈(平たい)場所〉である. **場所；場所を定める, 場所に置く**. put が〈置く〉なら, place は〈丁寧に置く〉の意味合い.
関 replace (〜に取って代わる)

I stayed at my parents' *place* [=house] for the night.　その夜は両親の家に泊まった.

My dentures don't ⌈stay *in place* [=fit well] and cause discomfort to the gums.　入れ歯がしっくりしないので, 歯茎が気持ち悪い.　▶in place「しかるべき所に」

I saw the floor was stained ⌈in *places* [=here and there].　床があちこち汚れていた.

Where is the best place to *place* [=install] the smoke detector?　この煙探知機はどこに取り付けるのが一番いいですか.

plain /pléɪn/

plain

原義は〈平らな〉である. **(煩雑でない・飾りのない)→分かりやすい, 質素である, ありのままの**. 素うどんの素(す)とイメージするのも一興.
派 plainly (率直に)　関 explain (説明する)

Government officials may use jargon and clichés rather than *plain* language.　役人は平易な言い方をせず, 難解な表現や決まり文句を使うことが多い.

He wears *plain* ties.　彼は無地のネクタイをする.

I wonder how to dress up my *plain* white T-shirt?　白無地のTシャツはどう着こなしたらいいかしら.

The *plain* fact is that there's no scientific way to predict an earthquake accurately.　早い話〔←率直な事実は〕, 地震を正確に予測する科学的方法はないってことだ.

plan /plǽn/

原義は〈(平たい)図面〉である.**図面,計画表,計画；計画する**.
関 plane (飛行機)〔←平たい〕; plate (皿)〔←平たい〕

Do you have any *plans* for the weekend?　今週末は何か予定ある？

How do you *plan* the trip?　旅行はどんな予定にするの？

My *plan* [=What I *planned*] didn't work out as well as I thought.　私の計画は思ったように進まなかった.

A young architect was commissioned to draw a *plan* for the new city hall.　若い建築家が新市役所の設計図作製を委託された.

plant /plǽnt/

原義は〈苗木を植え込む〉である.**(苗などを)植える,(思想を)植え付ける,(爆弾を)仕掛ける；植物；(大地に設置する)設備,工場**.
関 plantation (大規模農園)

I *planted* several daffodil and tulip bulbs in our back yard.　裏庭にスイセンとチューリップの球根を植えた.

The professor tried to *plant* the seeds of doubt about common beliefs in the minds of his students.　教授は,世間の常識に疑いを持つような精神を学生に植え付けるように努めた.

The oxygen in the air we breathe comes from *plants*.　私たちが吸う大気中の酸素は植物から発生している.

The new *plant* will start operation in June.　新工場は6月から操業を開始する.

plastic /plǽstɪk/

語源は〈plast (しっくい) ic (的な)〉である. **(固形の硬い) プラスチック, (軟らかい) プラスチック, ビニール.**
関 plaster (しっくい)〔←自由な形にできる〕

Kitchen workers wear *plastic* gloves to keep the food they serve safe and clean.　調理人は, 提供する料理を安全で清潔に保つためにビニール手袋をしている.

She recently had *plastic* [=cosmetic] surgery to lift the breasts.
彼女は最近, 胸を豊かに見せる整形手術をした.

play /pléɪ/

原義は〈展開する〉である. **(競技・演目・遊びなどを) 展開する.** 審判の試合始めの合図 play ball! は〈ボールゲームを展開せよ〉が本意.
派 player (選手, 演奏者, ゲームをする人)

Japan *played* against the United States for the Women's World Cup championship.　日本は女子ワールドカップサッカーの決勝でアメリカと戦った.

For a practice game, how they *play* the game is more important than winning.　練習試合では, 勝敗よりも試合内容〔←どのように試合を運ぶか〕が大切だ.

Robert is to *play* [=act the part of] Macbeth.　ロバートがマクベスを演ずることになっている.

He was a former stage *player*.　彼は昔, 舞台俳優をしていた.

Deal five cards to each *player*.　トランプを各人に 5 枚配ってください.

please /plíːz/

原義は〈気持ちを和ませる〉である. **楽しませる；(楽しんでくださいの気持ちを込めて) どうぞ**.
派 pleased (満足した)；pleasant (気持ちのいい)；pleasure (喜び)

"Coffee or tea?" "Coffee, *please*." 「コーヒーか紅茶はいかがですか」「コーヒーをください」

I sometimes visit my hometown to *please* my parents. 両親を喜ばせるためにときどき田舎に帰る.

Hawaiian music is *pleasant* to the ear. ハワイアンは耳に心地よい.

Camping in the woods is one of my greatest *pleasures*. 森でキャンプするのは大きな楽しみの一つだ.

plus /plʌ́s/

原義は〈足す〉である. **〜に加えて**. pl- は〈重ねる→加える〉のイメージ.
関 plural (複数)

"How much is six hundred *plus* three hundred?" "Nine hundred."
「600 に 300 を加えるといくつ?」「900」

You must pay back every dollar borrowed, *plus* [＝and] interest.
借りた全額と利子を返さないといけません.

The anchorwoman has unsurpassed beauty *plus* [＝and] intelligence.
あのキャスターは比類ない美人で，かつ知性がある.

pocket /pá:kət/

語源は〈pock（袋）et（小さな）〉である．**ポケット；ポケットに物や手を入れる，ポケットにこっそり手を入れて盗む．**
関 pickpocket（すり）

He reached into his *pocket* for his wallet.　彼は財布を出そうとしてポケットに手を入れた．

He was at the desk with one hand in his *pocket*, resting his cheek on the other.　彼はポケットに片手を入れ，頬づえをついて〔←もう一方の手に頬をのせて〕机に向かっていた．

The accountant had *pocketed* [=embezzled] part of the money deposited by their clients.　会計係は顧客の預金の一部を着服していた．

poem /póʊəm/

原義は〈想像の歌〉である．**一編の詩．**
派 poetry（〔文学としての〕詩）；poet（詩人）；poetic（詩的な）

The Japanese have the world's shortest *poetry* form—haiku. A haiku *poem* has only 17 syllables.　日本人は世界最短の詩の形式である俳句を持っている．俳句はわずか 17 音節だけである．

The work of children's *poet* Kaneko Misuzu has recently become quite popular.　童謡詩人である金子みすずの作品は近年，とても有名になってきた．

He has long been interested in *poetry* and literature in general.　彼は長年，詩と文学一般に興味を持っている．

point /pɔ́ɪnt/

原義は〈とがった先端〉である.**点→要点, 大切な点; 指摘; 指さす, 〜を…に向ける; 段階**.
派 pointed (とがった); pointless (無駄な)

"My brother finally got a job." "That's not the *point*. I'm afraid he isn't suited to be a salesperson."　「兄はやっと就職できたよ」「そういう話ではないのだよ〔←それはどうでもいいことだ〕.彼は営業マンに向いていないと思うんだ」

Don't throw a firework or *point* it at someone.　花火を投げたり,他人に向けたりしてはいけません.

His anxiety rose to a *point* [＝level] at which it was no longer bearable.　彼の不安はもう耐えられないほどにひどくなった.

police /pəlíːs/

原義は〈国家〉である.**警察**.「警察」は署員のことを指すのが通例なので,集合的名詞として扱い,複数形で呼応する.個人の警官は a police officer や policeman, または policewoman という.

He was arrested by *the police* for dangerous driving.　彼は危険運転で警察に捕まった.

I'm going to report what I had witnessed to *the police*.　目撃情報を警察に通報するよ.

policy /pá:ləsi/

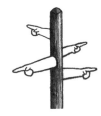

原義は〈統治〉である. **政策, 方針**.
派 politics (政治); political (政治の); politically (政治的に)

I agree with the German's energy *policy* to shut down all the nuclear power plants.　ドイツの全原発閉鎖のエネルギー政策に賛成だ.

What is your *policy* [=approach] regarding corporal punishment at home?　家庭での体罰についてあなたの方針はどうなんですか.

poll /póul/

原義は〈頭→頭数〉である. **(賛否の頭数を調べる) 世論調査; 投票, 投票数; 世論調査をする**.
関 polling station (投票所)

Today's national policy seems to be too much influenced by the public opinion *polls*.　今の国政は世論調査の動向に左右され過ぎているように思える.

Recent *polls* show that the support rate for the new cabinet is down from seven to nine points from last month.　最新の世論調査によると, 新内閣の支持率は先月より7〜9ポイント落ちている.

NHK *polled* 2,000 randomly selected adults nationwide and 1,581 people responded.　NHKは無作為に全国の有権者2000人にアンケートをとり, 1581人から回答を得た.

pollute /pəlúːt/

原義は〈pol(すっかり)+lute(汚す)〉である. **汚染する**.

派 pollutant(汚染物質);pollution(公害)

Seas and rivers have been *polluted* [=contaminated] by industrial and domestic waste.　海や川は産業や家庭廃棄物によって汚染されている.

Workers are making desperate efforts to stop radioactive *pollution* [=contamination] from the exploded nuclear power plants.　作業員は,爆発した原発からの放射能汚染を止めるために必死の努力を続けている.

poor /púər/

原義は〈少ない〉である. **(金・才能・質・量が) 乏しい**.
派 poorly(乏しく,不十分に);poverty(貧乏)

There are some who are too *poor* to go (and) see a doctor.　貧しくて医者にかかれない人もいる.

The *poor* little girl was abused by her stepmother.　かわいそうに,幼い少女はまま母から虐待を受けた.　▶憐れみ・同情を感じる対象に冠する形容詞. 日本語では,「かわいそうに」などと副詞的に表現するのが普通.

Unskilled workers are usually *poorly* paid.　技量のない従業員はたいてい給料が低い.

popular /pá:pjələr/

語源は〈popul（人びと）ar（の）〉である． **人びとに広まった，人びとに好まれる．**
派 popularity（人気）　関 people（人びと）

Hula has recently 「become *popular* [=grown in popularity] in Japan.　フラダンスが最近，日本ではやっている．

It is a *popular* [=common] belief that we shouldn't take a bath when we are having a cold.　風邪を引いたときは入浴しないほうがいいということは一般常識だ．

population /pá:pjəléɪʃən/

語源は〈populate（人びとの住む）tion（状態）〉である． **住民数，全住民；（生物の）個体数，個体群．**
派 populate（（人を）住まわせる）

What [=How large] is the *population* of Tokyo?　東京の人口はどれくらいですか．

India has a *population* of more than one billion.　インドの人口は10億以上だ．

The fish *population* in coastal waters has decreased due to overharvesting.　乱獲によって近海の魚の数が減っている．

position /pəzíʃən/

語源は 〈posit (置く) ion (こと)〉 である. **(置かれた) 位置, 立場, 地位, 職;(構える) 態度, 姿勢.**
関 positive (肯定的な, 前向きな)

How can I find the *positions* [=locations] of the planets and constellations in the night sky? どうしたら, 夜空の惑星や星座の位置が分かりますか.

We need to clarify our *position* [=attitude] on the issue before the coming meeting. 次の会議までに, この件についての我々の立場をはっきりさせておかないといけない.

I saw a few people in the audience who were asleep in a sitting *position*. 座ったまま居眠りしている聴衆が何人かいたよ.

---

positive /pá:zətɪv/

語源は 〈posit (置く) tive (性質の)〉 である. **(立場・意見がちゃんとしている)→確信がある, 肯定的な.**
派 positively (肯定的に) 関 position (位置)

No *positive* [=good] change is happening in our lives since the new government started last year. 昨年の新政権の誕生以後, 私たちの生活になんら好転の兆しはない.

She was tested *positive* for HIV. 彼女は HIV 検査で陽性反応が出た.

Think *positively*; you need to forget the past and start living afresh. 前向きに考えなさい. 過去のことは忘れて心機一転, 再出発すべきだよ.

possibility /pɑ́:səbíləti/

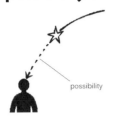

原義は〈possible (可能である) ity (状態)〉である. **起こり得る見込み, 可能性**.

A nuclear war seemed a real *possibility* in 1962 when US and USSR were caught up in political conflict over Cuba. 1962年, 米ソがキューバをめぐって政争に巻き込まれた時, 核戦争が現実に起こる可能性があった.

My wife seems to be suffering from morning sickness; there is a strong *possibility* [=likelihood] that she is pregnant. 妻はつわりのような症状があるようなので, 妊娠の可能性がきわめて高い.

possible /pɑ́:səbl/

原義は〈poss (可能) ible (である)〉である. **(努力すると) 起こりうる, (ひょっとすると) 起こりうる**.
派 possibly (たぶん); impossible (不可能である, 容易でない, 我慢できない)

Try to avoid driving through residential areas as shortcuts if *possible* [=you can]. 近道のために住宅街を車で通り抜けることは, できるだけ避けなさい.

We will do everything *possible* [=we can] to meet your expectations. 当社は, お客様のご希望に添えるようにできるだけの努力をします.

The Prime Minister is now in an *impossible* [=a helpless] situation; he has lost the confidence of his own party. 首相は自分の党の信頼をも失って今や窮地に陥っている.

post /póust/

原義は〈置く〉である. **(情報を置く)→知らせる, 公表する, 郵送する.**
派 postage (郵送料)

Keep us *posted* [=updated] on how things are going in your new town. 新天地での様子を知らせてね.

You can *post* [=send] your comments on line or write them to us. ご意見をメールや郵便で投稿できます.

A dog's unique performance has been *posted* on YouTube. 珍しい犬の演技がユーチューブに動画投稿されている.

What is the *postage* for this package? この小包の郵送料はいくらですか.

---

pound /páund/

原義は〈どんどんとたたきつける〉である. **たたき続ける.**

The president *pounded* [=beat] the desk to make his point clear. 大統領は机をたたいて, 自分の主張をはっきりさせようとした.

When my turn finally came, my heart began *pounding* [=beating]. 自分の番が来ると心臓の鼓動が高鳴り始めた.

power /páuər/

原義は〈力があること〉である。**(潜在的)力・能力→動力・電力；権力をもっている人，強国**．
派 powerful（力強い）; powerless（無力な）; powered（動力源となっている）

He suffered a stroke and lost the *power* [=faculty] of speech. 彼は脳梗塞を患って話す能力を失った．

We had *power failure* [=The *power* was out] yesterday for about 2 hours. 昨日，2時間ばかり停電があった．

Kim Jong-un came to *power* after his father died in 2011. キム・ジョンウンは父親が2011年になくなってから，権力の座についた．

This PC is battery *powered* [=operated], so it needs to be charged regularly. このパソコンは充電式なので，定期的に充電が必要だ．

practical /præktıkl/

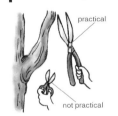

原義は〈practic（実践の）cal（的な）〉である．**実用に向いている**．
派 practically（事実上）; practice（練習する）

It is not *practical* [=It's *impractical*] to use a washing machine when you only have a few towels to wash. ほんの数枚のタオルを洗うのに洗濯機を使うのは合理的でない．

Right now, there is no complete and *practical* [=efficient] way to prevent hackers from causing damage to network systems. 現在のところ，ハッカーのネットワークシステムへの妨害を防ぐ完璧かつ有効な方法はない．

practice /prǽktɪs/

原義は〈実行する〉である．**実践**《目的を持って実行すること》，**習慣**《常に実践すること》，**(向上を目指す)練習**，**開業**《法や医における実践》；**実践する**，**練習する**，**開業する**．
派 practical（実用的な）；practitioner（〔医師・弁護士などの〕開業者）

Please try to attend at least four *practices* [=rehearsals] before the performance.　発表会までに少なくとも4回の練習に参加するようにしてください．

His suggestion sounds good, but the problem is how to「put it into *practice*[=make it happen].　彼の提案はよさそうだけど，問題はいかに実践するかだよ．

He *practices* what he preaches.　彼は他人に説くところを自分でも実践する．

She *practices* law in the areas of civil and criminal procedures.　彼女は民事と刑事訴訟の弁護士として開業している．

praise /préɪz/

原義は〈値踏みする〉である．**評価する→ほめる**；**称賛**．
派 praiseworthy（賞賛に値する）
関 price（価格）；prize（賞）

Her new piece was highly *praised* [=admired] by many critics.　彼女の新作は批評家に高く評価された．

The nation was full of *praise* for their national team's performance in the World Cup.　国代表のワールドカップでの活躍に国民は絶賛を送った．

pray /préɪ/

原義は〈(求めて) 祈る〉である. **神に祈る, 物事の成就を祈る**.
派 prayer (祈り)

May I ask what you *prayed* to God for the new year?　新年にどんなことを祈ったの.

I *pray* your recovery is quick and smooth. ＝I pray for your quick and smooth recovery.　回復が早く順調であるようにお祈りします.

My late mother used to begin the day with a *prayer*.　亡くなった母は, 一日を祈りで始めていた.

predict /prɪdíkt/

語源は〈pre (前) dict (言う)〉である. **未然のことを前もって予言・予測する**.
派 prediction (予言);predictable (予想どおりの)

Who could have *predicted* [＝foreseen] the collapse of such a long-established bank?　誰があのような老舗銀行の崩壊を予測できただろうか.

Today is *predicted* [＝forecast (ed)] to be mostly cloudy.　今日は, おおむね曇りであると予報されている.

prefer /prɪfə́ːr/

語源は〈pre(前に)fer(運ぶ)〉である．**好きなほうを前に運び出す→〜のほうを好む**．
派 preferable (より好ましい)；preferably (なるべくなら)；preference ([優先的] 好み)

I *prefer* snowy days to rainy days. =I like snowy days better than rainy days.　雨の日よりも雪の日のほうが好きだ．

I'm not sure which of these computers is *preferable*.　これらのパソコンのうち，どれがいいのか分からない．

Their price and performance are almost the same; which you choose depends on your personal *preference*.　値段も性能もほとんど同じだから，どちらにするかは個人の好みによる．

pregnant /prégnənt/

語源は〈pre(前)gnant(生まれる)〉である．**妊娠している**．
派 pregnancy (妊娠)

My wife's seven months *pregnant* now.　妻は妊娠7か月です．

How soon can you know if you're *pregnant*?　妊娠したかどうかはいつごろ分かるの．

How much weight should I gain during my *pregnancy*?　妊娠中の体重は普通，どれくらい増えるの？

prepare /prɪpéər/

語源は〈pre (前) pare (そろえる)〉である. **前もって物を用意する；心の準備をする**.
派 preparation (準備)

My mother always gets up early to *prepare* lunchboxes for us.　母さんはいつも早起きして私たちのお弁当を作ってくれる.

The school authorities weren't *prepared for* the drastic cut of the budget.　学校 (当局) は大幅な予算削減に備えていなかった.

The doctor told me to *prepare* for surgery if the medication fails.　医師に, 薬の効果がない場合は手術を覚悟するように言われた.

Have you *prepared* well for the final exams?　期末試験の準備はちゃんとできているの？

present /形 préznt, 動 prɪzént/

語源は〈pre (前に) sent (いる)〉である. **目の前にいる, 目の前にある；目の前に〜を出す**.
派 presentation (贈呈, 発表)；presently (現在は)
関 absent (欠席して)

These pieces of earthenware were discovered near the *present* day town Yayoi [=what is now the town of Yayoi].　これらの土器は現在の弥生町近辺で発見された.

The court rendered judgment without the「defendant being *present* [=*presence* of the defendant].　被告が不在のまま裁判所は判決を言い渡した.

The committee *presented* its final report on education reform to the president.　委員会は教育改革に関する最終報告を学長に提示した.

preserve /prizə́ːrv/

語源は〈pre（前もって）serve（保つ）〉である．**先手を打って（腐らないように）保存する**．
派 preservation（保存）；preservative（防腐剤）

We paint the deck in order to *preserve* [=protect] the wood longer. 木材が長持ちするようにデッキに塗装する．

"How can I *preserve* radishes?" "I pickle them in vinegar." 「大根の保存はどうしたらいい？」「私は酢漬けにするよ」

Robert is very conservative; he only wants to *preserve* [=maintain] the status quo. ロバートはとても保守的な人で，現状維持を欲するばかりだ．

No *preservative* is used in any of our food products. 我が社の食品には防腐剤はいっさい使用していません．

---

press /prés/

原義は〈押しつける〉である．**〜に対して押しつける**．
派 pressure（重圧）
関 depress（落ち込ませる）；impress（印象づける）；express（表現する）

The little girl *pressed* her lips against the windowpane, trying to make a funny face. 少女は窓ガラスに唇を押しつけて，ひょうきんな顔をしようとしていた．

I wish I could come to the concert, but I am「very *pressed* for time [=too busy and have no time] right now. コンサートに行きたいけど，今，時間に追われているのよ．

The mother is under a lot of *pressure* [=stress] with her newborn baby crying all the time. 生まれたばかりの赤ん坊が泣いてばかりなので，母親はとてもいらいらしている．

pretend /prɪténd/

語源は〈pre(前に) tend(張る)〉である．**繕いの表情を張る→見栄を"張る"→見せかける**．
派 pretentious (見栄を張った)；pretense (見せかけ)

It's no use *pretending* to be a different person.　自分を装っても無駄だ．

Jane ⌈*pretended* not to be [=tried not to look] nervous but she could not help it.　ジェーンは緊張感を悟られないようにしたが，出てしまった．

She *pretended* not to know anything, because she didn't want to be involved in the trouble.　トラブルに巻き込まれたくないので，彼女は何も知らぬふりをしていた．

pretty /príti/

原義は〈かなりかわいい〉である．**かわいい→けっこういける，相当である**．

Toddlers are very charming and *pretty*.　よちよち歩きの子は愛らしくてかわいい．

It is *pretty* [=rather] cold today.　今日はけっこう寒い．

Synonyms are words that have ⌈*pretty* much [=quite] the same meaning.　類義語とは，かなり似かよった意味を持つ語のことだ．

prevent /privént/

語源は〈pre (前に) vent (来る)〉である. **前に出て通せんぼうする→立ちはだかる**.
派 prevention (予防)；preventive (予防のための)

The government might not *prevent* [=stop] the economic crisis easily because it is a global problem. 全世界的な問題だから, 政府は容易にこの経済危機を避けられないだろう.

Those errors could have been *prevented* [=avoided] if they had been a bit more careful. もう少し注意していたら, これらの間違いは防げただろう.

Prevention's better than cure. 予防は治療に勝る.

---

previous /príːviəs/

語源は〈pre (前の) vious (道に)〉である. **事柄の発生が先行している→(時間的・順序的に)より以前に起こっている**.
派 previously (以前は)
関 obvious (明白な)；via (〜経由で)

I wish I could be there, but I have a *previous* [=prior] engagement on that day. 参加したいのですが, 当日は先約があるのです.

May I ask who was the *previous* [=former] owner of the house. この家の前の持ち主はどなたでしたか.

We don't have any kids together, but she has two children from a *previous* [=former] marriage. 私たちの間に子どもはありませんが, 妻には前の結婚で 2 人の子どもがいます.

price /práɪs/

原義は〈ほうび〉である.**(得るものに対する) 代価；値段を決める, (失うものに対する) 代償**.
関 praise (ほめる)；prize (ほうび)

"What is the *price* of gasoline now?" "It's about 150 yen per liter."
「ガソリンは今, いくらですか」「リッターあたり 150 円くらいです」

This smart phone is *priced* [=selling] at 60,000 yen.　このスマートフォンは 6 万円で売っている.

The player had to accept a pay cut as the *price* [=result] of his poor performance last season.　その選手は昨シーズンの成績が振るわなかったので, 減給を受け入れざるを得なかった.

principle /prínsəpl/

〈行動の指針〉

語源は〈princi (最初) ple (の)〉である.**(行動・考え方の根本を成す) 原理・原則・主義**.
関 prince (王子)

Muslims don't eat pork「on *principle* [=as a rule].　イスラム教徒は主義として肉を食べない.

Both had reached agreement「in *principle* [=basically] but the details are yet to be worked out.　双方は基本的に合意に達したが, まだ詳細は検討の余地がある.

print /prínt/

原義は〈押し付けて印を付ける〉である．**印刷，焼付け，活字体；印刷する，焼き付ける，活字体で書く．**
派 printer（印刷機）；printing（出版の〜刷）

What was the first book ever *printed* [=published] in the world?　世界で最初に印刷された本は何ですか．

The book is「no longer in *print* [=now out of *print*]．この本は絶版になっている．

Please *print* your name and address. =Please write your name and address in *print*.　住所氏名は活字体で書いてください．▶ in cursive「筆記体で」

Shall I *print out* the recipe on the site for you?　このサイトのレシピを印刷しましょうか．

priority /praɪɔ́:rəti/

priority

語源は〈prior（より前に）ity（状態）〉である．**他よりも先んじてすべきこと，優先すること．**
派 prior（より前の，事前の）

Do things in the order of *priority* [=importance].　優先順に仕事をしなさい．

They should make safety a *priority* [=Top *priority* should be given to safety] under any environment.　どんな場合でも安全第一でなければならない．

price, principle, print, priority 549

prison /prízn/

語源は〈pris (捕らわれた) on (状態)〉である. **拘束, 拘置；拘置所, 刑務所.**
派 prisoner (囚人, 捕虜)；imprisonment (禁固)

The soldier was taken *prisoner* in Hanoi and died in *prison*.　兵士はハノイで捕虜になり, 獄死した.

The clerk was sentenced to three months' *imprisonment* for forgery.　その事務員は文書偽造で禁固3か月の実刑を受けた.

private /práɪvət/

語源は〈pri (前へ) vate (離す)〉である. **(他と引き離す) →他者との関わりを許さない状態；(公的でない) 私的な, 民間の.**
派 privacy (プライバシー)；privately (個人的に)；privatize (民営化する)

May I speak with you「in *private* [＝privately]?　個人的にお話ししたいのですが?

You all have the right to do what you want in *private* [＝secret] unless it causes harm to others.　誰でも他人に迷惑をかけないかぎり, 私的に好きなことをする権利がある.

Lawyers should take due care to protect the *privacy* [＝secrecy] of their clients.　弁護士は依頼人のプライバシー (秘密) を守るように十分注意を払うべきだ.

prize /práɪz/

原義は〈ほうび〉である.**(価値ある実績に対する)賞；価値を認める→重要と考える**.
関 praise (ほめる)

My daughter won the gold *prize* in the piano competition.　娘はピアノ・コンクールで金賞を取った.

Oysters are highly *prized* [=thought of] as food containing rich minerals and vitamins.　カキはミネラルとビタミンが豊富な食べ物として珍重されている.

probably /prá:bəbli/

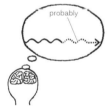

語源は〈prob (証明) able (できる)〉である.**(証明できそうな)→どうやらそうなりそうな→おそらく, きっと**.
類義語 maybe の確信の度合いは 50 % 程度だが, probably は 80 〜 90%ほどである.
派 probable (ありそうな)；probability (見込み)

It will *probably* snow tomorrow.　明日はおそらく雪だよ.　▶Maybe it will snow tomorrow.「明日は雪になるかも」

It is highly *probable* [=There is a high *probability*] that the baby is infected with influenza virus.　この赤ちゃんはウイルスに感染している可能性が高い.

problem /prá:bləm/

語源は〈(前に) blem (投げ出されたもの)〉である. **(行く手を遮る) 問題, 難題, 試験問題.**
派 problematic (問題のある)

My grandpa is having a *problem* going to sleep.　おじいちゃんは寝つきが悪い.

Using too much fertilizer on your plants can cause *problems*.　植物に肥料をやり過ぎると害になりかねない.

Install anti-virus software on your computer before ⌜it has *problems* [=*problems* happen].　問題が起きる前に, ウイルス対策ソフトをインストールしておきなさい.

proceed /prəsí:d/

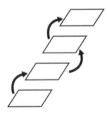

語源は〈pro (前へ) ceed (進む) →次へ進む〉である.
継続する, 次へ進む.
派 procedure (手順); process (過程, 加工する)

How is your preparation for the exam *proceeding* [=going]?　試験準備は進んでいますか.

Can we *proceed* [=go on] to the next item on the agenda?　次の議題に移っていいですか.

When it comes to effective use of a computer, you should first learn the cut-and-paste *procedure* [=method].　パソコンを効率的に使うには, まずカットアンドペーストの仕方を覚えるといいよ.

process /prá:ses/

語源は〈pro（前へ）cess（行く）〉である．**(物事が進行する) 過程，方法；加工する，処理する．**
派 proceed（前進する）; procession（行列）; processor（〔コンピューターの〕プロセッサー）

We often arrive at the right answer by the *process* of elimination.
消去法によって正しい答えにたどり着けることがよくある．

Do you believe that some food can slow the aging *process*?　食べ物によって老化を遅らせることができるということは本当だと思いますか．

Try to eat natural foods, rather than *processed* ones as often as possible.　できるだけ加工食品よりも自然食品を食べるようにしなさい．

---

produce /prəd(j)ú:s/

語源は〈pro（前に）duce（引く）〉である．**(前に引き出す) →つくり出す，制作する．**
派 producer（生産者，製作者）

Rubbing your hands together *produces* [=creates] heat on your palms.　手をこすり合わせると手の平に熱が生じる．

He has *produced* [=made] unique and innovative animated films for children.　彼は子ども向けの独特で斬新なアニメを制作した．

There's nothing like the taste of your homegrown *produce* [=vegetables and fruit].　自分で育てた作物の味にかなうものはない．

product /prá:dəkt/

語源は〈pro(前に)duct(引き出されたもの)〉である．**(原料を加工して作り出される)製品**．
派 production(生産, 生産物); productive(生産的な)

In general, Japanese *products* have a reputation for high quality.
一般的に日本製品は品質がよいという評価を受けている．

The *production* of eco-friendly, compact cars has been increasing recently.　最近，環境に優しい小型車の生産が増えている．

Building *productive* [=constructive] relationships with other people is not as simple as it seems.　他人とよい(実りある)関係を築くのは意外に難しいものだ．

professional /prəféʃənl/

語源は〈profession(専門職)al(の)〉である．**職業としている，プロの→プロ級の；専門家**．
派 professor(教授); professionally(仕事上)

Her son has not had voice lessons, but sings like a *professional* [= *professional* singer].　彼女の息子は歌のレッスンを受けたことがないが，プロ歌手のように見事に歌う．

The problem is very complicated; I think you need *professional* help from an experienced lawyer.　問題がとても複雑なので，ベテランの弁護士による専門的な助けが必要だと思う．

Teaching is one of the leading *professions* for women in our country.
先生という職は，この国では女性がもっとも活躍している職業の一つだ．

profit /prá:fət/

語源は〈pro(前へ)fit(作る)〉である. **(生み出す) もうけ**, **利益**.
派 profitable (利益になる); nonprofit (非営利的な)

The way they do business ended up putting *profits* ahead of consumers' safety. 彼らの商売の仕方は, 消費者の安全よりも利益を優先するようになってしまった.

I believe honesty ˈfinally proves *profitable* [=pays in the long run] for any business. どんな商売でも, 正直にやることが結局は利益につながると信じている.

This is a *non-profit* website that aims to improve your communication skills. これは, 皆さんのコミュニケーション能力の向上を目的とした非営利のサイトです.

program /próugræm/

語源は〈pro(前もって)gram(書いたもの)〉である. **(内容を前もって書き記した) プログラム**, **番組**; **コンピュータに (前もって) 作動指示を書き込む**, **プログラムを書き込む**.
派 programmer (プログラマー); programming (プログラミング)

Could you recommend any good TV *program* for children? 子ども向けのよいテレビ番組はありませんか.

How a baby develops is *programmed* [=written] in the genes. 赤子がどのように成長していくかは遺伝子に書き込まれている.

I'm learning how to *program* a computer. コンピュータのプログラミングを学んでいます.

product, professional, profit, program

progress /prɑ́:gres/

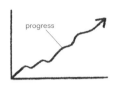

語源は〈pro（前へ）gress（進む）〉である．**進歩する，進展する；進歩，進展．**
派 progression（前進）；progressive（進歩的な）；progressively（しだいに）

Trade liberalization among countries has made much *progress* in the past several years.　諸国間の貿易自由化はここ数年で大きな進展をしている．

Cancer treatment has been making steady *progress*.　がん治療は着実に進歩している．

Your morning sickness will ease up as your pregnancy *progresses*.　つわりは妊娠の経過につれて和らいでいきますよ．

As the war *progressed*, it became evident that they couldn't win and end it as was planned.　戦局が進むにつれ，計画通りに勝利し，終結させることができないことが明らかになった．

project /名 prɑ́:dʒekt, 動 prədʒékt/

語源は〈pro（前に）ject（投げる）〉である．**(前もって打ち出す) 企画；企画する，前に投影する．**
派 projector（映写機，プロジェクター）；projection（見通し，映写）
関 subject（話題，テーマ）

I'm working on a *project* for young mothers who are interested in continuing their career.　私は，仕事を継続していきたいと考える若い母親のためのプロジェクト（企画）に取り組んでいる．

A planetarium is a theater with a rounded ceiling onto which images of the stars and planets are *projected*.　プラネタリウムとは，丸天井に星の映像を投影するようになっている劇場のことだ．

promise /prá:məs/

語源は〈pro (前に) mise (送る)〉である. **(人の前に言質を差し出す) →約束する→見込む**.
派 promising (前途有望な)
関 compromise (妥協する)

College degrees can't necessarily *promise* a good job.　大学卒であればよい職に就けるとは限らない.

The people are very much disappointed by the new leader who is breaking his numerous campaign *promises*.　国民は，新しい指導者が多くの公約を破っているのでひどく落胆している.

"*Promise* you won't do it again." "I *promise*."　「そんなこと二度としないって約束しなさい」「約束するよ」

promote /prəmóut/

語源は〈pro (前へ) mote (動かす)〉である. **事柄を前へ推し進める→促進させる**.
派 promoter (主催者); promotion (促進, 昇進)

He has been *promoted* to the head of the department.　彼は課長に昇進した.

The novelist attended several autograph sessions across the country to *promote* [=advertise] her new book.　その小説家は，新刊書を宣伝するために全国各地のサイン会に出た.

proof /prúːf/

原義は〈試す〉である．**試験して適切であると証明する →証拠，証明．**
派 prove (証明する)
関 proofread (校正する)；probe (探り針，調べる)
〔←検査読み〕

What *proof* do you have [＝How do you *prove*] that one's blood type links to one's personality?　血液型が性格に関連性があることにどんな証拠がありますか．

Scientifically, there's no *proof* of any connection between them.
科学的には相互の関連性に何の証拠もありません．

I always have my English essays *proofread* [＝checked] by a native speaker.　私はいつも英語の論文をネイティブスピーカーにチェックしてもらっている．

proper /prɑ́ːpər/

proper　not proper

原義は〈固有の〉である．**(個に特有の) →本来の→適切な，ふさわしい．**
派 properly (適切に)；property (財産)

Vitamins are critical to the *proper* [＝normal] function of your body.
ビタミンは私たちの体の適切な働きのために必須の栄養素です．

John changed his job again; he doesn't seem to have ever had a *proper* job.　ジョンはまた仕事を変えたけど，彼はこれまでちゃんとした仕事に就いたことがないようだ．

"How long will the tomatoes last?" "They last one or two weeks if they are *properly* stored."　「トマトはどれくらいもつの？」「適切に保管すれば1，2週間はもつよ」

property /prá:pərti/

語源は〈proper (自己の) ty (ものである)〉である. **(自己のものとして所有する) 財産・家屋・宅地**.
派 proper (固有の)

My neighbor's cat always comes into our *property* and urinates in the backyard. 隣の猫がいつも，うちの敷地に入ってきて裏庭でおしっこをする.

We grow a vegetable garden, using a small corner of our *property*. 宅地の片隅を使って菜園で野菜を育てています.

proposal /prəpóuzl/

語源は〈pro (前へ) pose (置く) al (こと)〉である. **(他者の前に出す) 提案, (相手に出す) 結婚の申し込み**.
派 propose (提案する)

We had to withdraw the *proposal* due to a sudden change of the plan. 方針が急に変わったので提案を引っ込めるはめになった.

The government is planning to *propose* a reform of the tax system before long. 政府は近々に税制改革案を提出する予定だ.

Jim *proposed* to her and she ⌈said "yes" [=accepted his *proposal*]. ジムは彼女に結婚を申し込み，受け入れられた.

prospect /prá:spekt/

語源は〈pro (前もって) spect (見る)〉である。**(遠くを見渡す)→展望, 期待, 期待の候補**.
派 prospective (予想される)
関 spectacular (目を見張るような)

The boys are excited by the *prospect* [=thought] of playing games at the big stadium.　少年たちは大きな球場で試合できるという期待でわくわくしている.

He's shown great potential and will certainly be a top *prospect* among the rookies this year.　彼は大きな将来性を見せており, 今年のルーキーの中では間違いなく最も期待できる選手だ.

protect /prətékt/

語源は〈pro (前を) tect (覆う)〉である. **前を覆って中身を護る**.
派 protective (保護のための); protection (保護); protector (防具)
関 detect (発見する)

Builders and firefighters wear helmets and goggles「to *protect* [=for the protection of] their eyes.　建設業者や消防士は, 目を保護するためにヘルメットやゴーグルをつける.

The intellectual property such as patents and copyrights is *protected* by law.　特許や著作権のような知的財産は法によって保護されている.

protest /próutest/

語源は〈pro（前で）test（証言する）〉である。**(不条理・矛盾に対して) 公然と反対を訴える, (正当性を) 主張する；抗議, 異議.**
派 protesters（抗議者）
関 Protestant（新教徒, プロテスタント）

The victim's widow *protested* at the leniency of the sentence.　被害者の妻は判決が甘いと抗議した.

The director resigned *in protest* at the decision.　理事は決定に抗議して辞任した.

The residents began a sit-in *protest* against the construction of the treatment plant.　住民はゴミ処理場の建設に反対して座り込みを始めた.

proud /práud/

語源は〈pro（前にいる）ud（状態）〉である。**(上位にいる) →誇りをもっている→威張っている.**
派 pride（誇り）；proudly（得意げに）

Your achievements are something to be *proud* of.　君の業績は誇るべきものだ.

There are some who are *proud* and arrogant in the presence of junior workers.　部下に威張ったり横柄な態度を取ったりする人がいる.

It's time to give up your *pride* and ask for their help.　メンツを捨てて援助を求める時だよ.

prove /prúːv/

語源は〈pro（前へ）ve（置く）〉である．**本当であると示す・判明する**．
派 proof（証拠）

How are you going to *prove* it is your wallet?　それがあなたの財布だとどうやって証明しますか．

All his efforts *proved* [=turned out to be] nothing.　彼の努力は成果が得られなかった．

It has been scientifically *proven* [=shown] that one's mental state of mind affects one's ability to heal from an illness.　人の精神状態は，その人の病気の回復力に影響することが科学的に立証されている．

---

provide /prəváɪd/

語源は〈pro（前を）vide（見る）〉である．**（見通して必要に備える）→必要な物を供給する・用意する，必要条件を与える**．
派 provided（～という条件で）
関 improvise（即席に作る）〔←否+用意する〕

This book *provides* [=gives you] detailed information about how to troubleshoot a computer.　この本はパソコンのトラブル解決法を詳しく教えてくれる．

There are many unemployed grownups who can't afford to *provide* for themselves.　自活できない多くの失業者がいる．

If you deny our suggested plan, you need to *provide* [=show] us with an alternative for further discussion.　我々の提案に反対するのであれば，議論を進めるために対案を出すべきだ．

public /pʌ́blɪk/

語源は〈publ(人びと) ic(の)〉である．**人びと一般の・大衆に開かれた，公共の；皆に知られた．**
派 publicly (公の場で)；publish (公にする)；publicity (衆目, 評判)；publication (出版)

Some mothers don't feel comfortable breastfeeding ⌈*in public* [=in front of other people]．　母親の中には，人前で自分の乳を赤ん坊に飲ませるのを嫌う人もいる．

The true cause of her death hasn't been made *public* [=known to us]．　彼女の本当の死因は公表されていない．

The incident attracted great *publicity* [=public attention]．　その事件は世間の耳目を集めた．

publish /pʌ́blɪʃ/

語源は〈publi(公) ish(にする)〉である．**公にする→発表する，出版する．**
派 publisher (出版社)

This magazine is *published* [=issued] every second week．　この雑誌は隔週で発行されている．

If you have your own healthy recipe, why don't you ⌈get it *published* [=make it public] online?　あなた独特の健康レシピがあるのなら，ネット上に掲載しなさいよ．

pull /púl/

原義は〈引き抜く〉である. **引く, 引っ張る**.

You only need to *pull* the tab up to open the cans of beverages. 飲み物の缶はタブを引き上げるだけで開けられる.

My train was slowly *pulling out of* the station, when I rushed to the platform. ホームに駆けつけたら, 電車はゆっくり駅を出て行くところだった.

He ⌈*pulled off* [=pulled his car over to the side of] the road as the tire started clunking. 彼は, タイヤがゴトゴトと異音を立て始めたので道路脇に車を寄せた.

purchase /pə́ːrtʃəs/

語源は〈pur (～に向けて) chase (追う)〉である. **買い求める, 購入する；買い入れ, 購入**. purchase が「購入する」なら buy は「買う」のイメージ.
関 chase (追跡する)

I usually *purchase* [=buy] souvenirs at duty-free shops when abroad. 海外ではたいてい免税店でみやげ物を買う.

You can *purchase* [=buy] any music you love directly from the website. ネット上のサイトから直接, 好きな音楽を自由に購入できる.

For many people, a home may be a once-in-a-lifetime *purchase* [=buy], so you should take time before making a decision. 多くの人にとって, 家は生涯一度の買い物だから, じっくり時間をかけて決めるべきだ.

purpose /pə́ːrpəs/

語源は〈pur (前へ) pose (置く)〉である. **(自分の前に置く) 目的・目標**.

派 purposely＝on purpose (故意に)

What's the main *purpose* [＝aim] of your entering this college?　この大学へ入学した主な目的は何ですか.

There seems to be some evil *purpose* [＝intention] behind it.　裏に何かたくらみがありそうだ.

You may use these photos solely for personal, noncommercial *purposes*.　これらの写真は，個人的，非営利目的に限って利用してよろしい.

This is a multi-*purpose* hall that can be used for events such as weddings, banquets, conferences, and seminars.　これは多目的ホールで，結婚式，宴会，会議，研修会などに利用できます.

pursue /pərs(j)úː/

語源は〈pur (を) suit (追う)〉である. **獲得を目指して追いかける**.

派 pursuit (追求,〔求める〕楽しみ, 趣味)

My brother moved to Tokyo to *pursue* [＝seek after] a career in music as soon as he graduated from a local high school.　兄は音楽で身を立てようとして，地元の高校を出るとすぐに東京へ引っ越した.

Princess Aiko has been constantly *pursued* by the press since she was born.　愛子さまは，生まれた時から常にマスコミに追いかけられている.

Cycling is a popular outdoor *pursuit* [＝activity] being enjoyed by young and old.　サイクリングは，若者にも年輩者にも楽しまれている人気のある野外活動だ.

push /púʃ/

原義は〈押しやる〉である. **密着して圧力を加える, 前へ押し進める；押すこと.**

The car was stuck in the snow and would not move no matter how hard we *pushed*.　車が雪にタイヤをとられて, いくら押しても動かなかった.

The boy seems (to be) tired; he has always been *pushed* by his parents to get good grades.　その子は疲れているように見える. いつも両親によい成績を取るようにせきたてられているのだ.

It's good to be energetic, but you shouldn't *push yourself* too much.　精力的であるのはいいのだけど, あまり頑張り過ぎてはだめだよ.

She tried to *push* her anxiety out of her mind. ＝She tried not to think about her anxiety.　彼女は不安を払拭 (ふっしょく) しようとした.

---

put /pút/

原義は〈ある場所に物を置く〉である. **ある場所に置く, ある状態に置く；（考えを頭から出して）口にする, 文字にする.**

I *put* [＝placed] the indoor plants near the window for sunlight.　日光に当てるために観葉植物を窓際に置いた.

He *put* [＝wrote] his signature on the document as a witness.　彼は目撃者として調書に署名した.

I can't *put* the excitement I have into words.　この感動はことばになりません.

To put it mildly, the new mayor is a reformer. He is trying to change all the old rules and systems of the city.　新市長は, 控えめに言っても改革者だ. あらゆる旧来の規則や制度を変えようとしている.

qualify /kwáːləfàɪ/

語源は〈quali (質・中身) fy (存在させる)〉である. **(中身がある)→ある資格がある, 資格を与える**.
派 qualification (能力, 資格); quality (質)

The top three teams in this division ⌈*qualify* for playing [=are qualified to play] in J-league.　このグループの上位 3 チームが J リーグでプレーする資格を得る.

Our son is very good at numbers, wishing to ⌈*qualify* [=be *qualified*] as a school math teacher.　息子は数学が得意で, 学校の数学教師の資格を取ることを希望している.

quality /kwáːləti/

語源は〈quali (ある質) ity (状態)〉である. **物の質, 品質;質がよい, 品質がよい**.
派 qualify (資格を与える)

It is *quality*, not quantity, that counts.　大切なのは量ではなくて, 質だよ.

The wine they produce is of top *quality*. =They produce top *quality* wine.　この会社のワインは最高級だ.

quarter /kwɔ́:rtər/

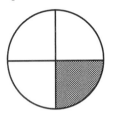

原義は〈4番目〉である．**4分の1 →一区画，界隈**．
派 quarterly（季刊の，季刊誌）；quartet（四重奏）

In most areas of the earth the seasons are divided into *quarters*.　地球上のたいていの地域で季節は4つに分かれる．

Nearly three-*quarters* of people over 65 have some symptoms of the disease caused by high blood pressure.　65歳以上の4分の3近くが高血圧による何らかの病状をもっている．

Because the Shibuya *quarter* [=area] has the latest and most colorful fashions, the youth are attracted to it.　渋谷界隈は，最新のカラフルなファッションがあるので若者が集まる．

question /kwéstʃən/

原義は〈求める・追及する〉である．**(不明の答え・不審の原因を追及すべく) 質問する；質問**．
派 quest（探求）；questionnaire（アンケート用紙）
関 request（要求する）

Only one quarter of the people *questioned* said that they support the projected construction of the dam.　計画しているダムの建設について問われ，賛成と答えた人は，25％に過ぎなかった．

I often *question* whether more advancement in science and technology is really necessary.　僕は，科学や技術がこれ以上進歩することが本当に必要なのだろうか，と疑問に思うことがよくある．

"How do they know modern humans originated in Africa?" "It's a good *question*."　「どうして現代人はアフリカ起源だと分かるのですか」「いい質問だね」

quick /kwík/

原義は〈生き生きしている〉である．**(動きや理解が) すばやい**．
派 quicken (早める)；quickly (早く)

My brother is *quick* to point out the cause of the malfunction of a computer.　兄はパソコンの不具合の原因究明がすばやくできる．

The girl is ⌈*quick* to learn [=a *quick* learner].　あの少女は物覚えが早い．

Don't be too *quick* [=hasty] to conclude that you are not gifted; great talents are slow to mature.　自分は才能に恵まれていないと速断してはだめだよ．大器は晩成するのだから．

December slips by *quickly* with the endless list of things to do.　12月は，することがいっぱいあってあっという間に過ぎてしまう．

quiet /kwáɪət/

原義は〈(活動がやんで) 静かな〉である．**人や機械が物静かである，場が静かである**．
派 quietly (静かに，そっと)
関 quit (やめる)

Children should learn to keep *quiet* [=silent] while they are in the movie theater.　子どもは，映画館では静かにしていることを身に付けなければいけない．

My husband is a fairly *quiet* person, sort of an easy person to get along with.　私の夫はとても物静かで，つき合うのが楽な人なのよ．

This electric car is *quiet*, fast, and emission free.　この電気自動車は，音が静かで速く走れて排気ガスが出ません．

quit /kwít/

原義は〈〜から身を引く〉である．**身を引く→活動をやめる**．活動の場から**身を引く**（quit）とその場は**静か**（quiet）になり，場の雰囲気が**すっきり**（quite）する．
関 quiet（静かな）; quite（かなり）

Quitting [=Giving up] smoking is not easy; many people need professional help to make it successfully. たばこをやめるのは容易ではない．医者の助けがないとうまくできない人が多い．

The taxi driver *quit* [=gave up] his job as his eyesight began to fail. タクシー運転手は視力が落ちてきたので仕事を辞めた．

quite /kwáit/

原義は〈(解放されて)すっきり〉である．**かなり→すっかり→本当に**．
関 quit（〔会社などを〕辞める）

It has already gotten *quite* dark outside. 外はもうすっかり暗くなっている．

We cycled all the way from Amsterdam to Paris. It was *quite* an experience. アムステルダムからパリまで自転車旅行した．それはすばらしい体験だった．

She has made *quite a* success in the field of chemistry. 彼女は化学の分野で大きな成功を収めた． ▶ quite a 〜「かなりの〜」

quote /kwóut/

原義は〈一部を言う〉である．**ある文言を引き合いに出す，文言を引用する**；**引用文**．
派 quotation（引用）

Shakespeare is the most often *quoted* author in the world. シェークスピアは世界で一番多く引用される作家だ．

People often *quote* [=extract] a passage or phrase from Shakespeare's works in their speaking and writing. 人は，話したり書いたりする際，シェークスピアの作品中の一節や成句を引用することが多い．

race¹ /réis/

原義は〈流れ〉である．走る→**競争する，先を急ぐ**．
派 racing（競走，競馬）

The police *raced* [=hurried] to the scene and caught the men in the act. 警察は現場へ急行し，男たちを現行犯逮捕した．

Researchers around the world are *racing* [=striving] to find better treatments for cancers. 世界中の研究者たちはがんのよりよい治療法を見つけようと競っている．

How many will「enter the *race* [=run] for mayor of the city? 市長選に何人立候補するのだろうか．

In Japan, horse *racing* is very popular as a betting sport. 日本では，賭け対象のスポーツとして競馬に人気がある．

race² /réɪs/

原義は〈同種〉である. **同一の種族・民族・人種**.
派 racial（人種の）；racism（人種差別）；racist（人種差別主義者, 人種差別的な）

People are apt to believe that one's own *race* is superior to other races.　人は, 自分の属する種族が他の種族よりも優れていると思い込みがちだ.

Racial discrimination is still being practiced in not a few countries in the world.　人種差別は, 今でもけっこう多くの国で起こっている.

rain /réɪn/

原義は〈雨〉である. **雨；雨が降る**.
派 rainy（雨の, 雨降りの）
関 rainbow（虹）；rainfall（降水量）；rainstorm（風雨）

It *rained* the whole day.　一日中, 雨だった.

The *rain* is pouring outside.　外は雨がひどく降っている.　▶the rain は〈体験している雨〉.

I got drenched in the *rain* on the way home from school.　下校の途中, 雨にあってびしょぬれになった.　▶the rain は〈体験した雨〉.

It's better not to paint today because a *rain* is expected tonight.　今夜は雨になりそうだから, 今日はペンキ塗りはよしたほうがいいよ.　▶a rain は〈頭に描いた雨〉.

It is *rainy* [=wet] here in Nagasaki.　ここ長崎は雨です.

raise /réɪz/

原義は〈上げる〉である．**高い位置・段階へ引き上げる→子どもを育てる**．raise は〈引き上げる〉，rise は〈上がる〉．

The government is planning to *raise* [=hike] the price of cigarettes, up to about 700 yen a pack. 政府は，たばこの値段を1箱700円程度に値上げしようとしている．

Being overweight may *raise* [=increase] the risk of developing many health problems. 肥満になるとさまざまな健康障害を引き起こす危険性が増えかねない．

Most mothers say *raising* boys is harder than *raising* girls. ほとんどの母親が，男の子を育てるほうが女の子よりやっかいだと言う．

range /réɪndʒ/

原義は〈並べる〉である．**ひとつながり→幅，広がり；〜から…までの幅がある**．
関 arrange（並べる，整える）

What is the price *range* for compact electric cars? 小型電気自動車の値段の幅（最安値〜最高値）はどれくらいですか．

The prices of these houses *range* [=span] from about $70,000 to $100,000. これらの家の値段は7万ドルから10万ドル（までの範囲）です．

He is able to run 100 meters in the 10-second *range*. 彼は100メートルを10秒台で走れる．

rapid /rǽpɪd/

原義は〈強奪する〉である．**すばやい→急速な；急流**．
派 rapidly（速く，急速に）；rapidity（速さ，急速）

Old people may find it very difficult to catch up with the *rapid* progress of communication technology.　年輩の人は通信技術の急速な進歩について行けないことが多い．

The current is very *rapid* [=swift] at the strait.　この海峡では潮の流れが速い．

rare /réər/

原義は〈まばら〉である．**たまにしか起こらない，珍しい**．
派 rarely（まれに）；rarity（希少さ）

Snow is *rare* [=It *rarely* snows] in Hawaii except on its high mountains.　ハワイでは，高い山以外では雪はめったに降らない．

The shark is *rarely* [=scarcely] seen in shallow waters.　浅い海域ではサメはめったに現れない．

Rare metal is very expensive because *rarity* [=scarcity] begets value.　レアメタルが高価なのは希少価値ゆえだ．

rate /réɪt/

原義は〈見積もる〉である. **割合・比率, 心拍数；価値・能力をランク付けする.**
派 rating（評価, 支持率）; ratio（比率）
関 overrate（過大評価する）

What's [=How much is] the exchange *rate* of US dollar to Japanese yen? 日本円に対する米ドルの為替レートはいくらですか.

The unemployment *rate* increased two points in August. 失業率は8月に2ポイント上昇した.

Athletes at rest commonly have a heart *rate* less than 60 beats a minute. 運動選手は通常, 静止時の心拍数が60を下回っている.

The university is highly *rated* for its research. この大学は研究実績が高く評価されている.

rather /rǽðər/

原義は〈気がはやる〉である.**（気がはやる）→～のほうへ気が傾く→むしろ→かなり.**
関 rash（早まった）

People should be judged by their character *rather than* their skin color. 人は, その人の肌の色ではなく性格で判断されるべきだ.

She said, "I'*d rather* be dead than be forced to marry someone." 彼女は「誰かとの結婚を強要されるのなら死んだほうがましだ」と言った.

I'*d rather* stay home than go out in this weather. この天気では外出したくない〔外出するより家にいたい〕.

I'*d rather* not be seen with you. =We should not be seen together. I don't know what people would say about us. 私たち, いっしょにいるところ見られるとまずいわ. どんなことを言われるか分からないよ.

reach /ríːtʃ/

原義は〈目的地にたどり着く〉である. **目的地・目標に到達する；たどり着ける範囲・距離**.

Our ability to remember what we learn *reaches* its peak in our early teens.　習ったことを記憶する能力は十代の初めごろ最高になる.

Japan was the only Asian team to have *reached* the quarterfinals.　準々決勝に進出したのはアジアの中では日本だけだった.

Would you please get that book for me? I can't *reach* the shelf.　その本を取っていただけますか. 棚に届きませんので.

After listening carefully to the opponents, we were able to *reach* a mutually agreeable conclusion.　相手側の言い分をしっかり聞いたので，双方が納得のいく結論に至ることができた.

---

read /ríːd/

原義は〈勘ぐる〉である. **文字・本・表示・事態を読む，読み解く**.
派 reader（読者）；reading（読書）

His novels, having been translated into Japanese, are widely *read* in Japan.　彼の小説は日本語に訳され，広く読まれている.

My mom used to *read* stories to me at bedtime.　母さんは寝る前によく物語を読んでくれていた.

As of now, my daughter is unable to *read* music, but she plays the piano by ear.　娘はまだ楽譜が読めないが，聞き覚えでピアノを弾いている.

"How good are you at *reading* maps?" "I'm hopeless with maps."　「地図はうまく読める？」「全然だめなのよ」

ready /rédi/

原義は〈準備が整った〉である. **準備できている→すぐに行動が起こせる→今にも事が起こる**.
派 readily (〔人が〕快く；簡単にできる)；readiness (快くすること, 意欲)

"Dinner is *ready*!" "Thanks, I'm coming." 「食事の用意できたよ！」「ありがとう．すぐ行きます」

I'm busy getting *ready* for the exam. 試験準備で忙しくしています．

How long do you ⌈take to get yourself *ready* [=spend grooming yourself] before going out? 出かける前の身支度にどれくらい時間をかけますか．

Our new teacher said, "I'm always *ready* to help you when you're in trouble." 新任の先生は「君たちが困った時はいつでも快く助けるよ」と言ってくれた．

real /ríːəl/

語源は〈re (本物) al (の)〉である. **(想像ではなくて)実際の, (うそではなくて)本当の**.
派 reality (現実)；realistic (現実的な)；realize (現実にする)；really (本当に)

What's the singer's *real* [=true] name? あの歌手の本名はなんていうの？

Movies for a while help us to escape from *reality*. 映画はしばし現実を忘れさせてくれる．

He's making his dream ⌈a *reality* [=come true]. 彼は自分の夢を実現させつつある．

The laws of the universe may seem complicated but in *reality* it is quite the opposite. 宇宙の法則は複雑そうに見えるけど，実際は真反対です．

realize /ríːəlàɪz/

語源は〈real (現実) lize (にする)〉である. **不確かであった事物を目のあたりにする・現実にする, 現実を悟る, 〜であると気づく.**

派 real (現実の); realization (認識)

After working a few months, he *realized* [=found] that he wasn't suited for the job. 数か月働いてみると, 彼は自分はその仕事に向いていないことに気づいた.

When you *realize* [=notice] you've made a mistake, take immediate steps to correct it. 間違いをしたと気づいたら, すぐに訂正の手段を取りなさい.

After years of serving as an apprentice he ⌜*realized* his dream [= made his dream *real*]⌝ by opening his own shop. 彼は何年も見習いとして修業し, 自分の店を開く夢を実現させた.

really /ríːli/

語源は〈real (本当) ly (に)〉である. **本当に, 本当は;(驚いて) 本当!**

派 real (現実の)

"I climbed Mt. Fuji this summer." "Oh, *really*." 「今年の夏, 富士山に登ったのよ」「まあ, 本当!」

The village is *really* [=truly] beautiful; its natural surroundings are breathtaking. その村は実に美しく, 自然は息をのむほどだ.

My daughter *really* [=very much] likes drawing; she is always with a painting pad. 娘は本当に絵が好きで, いつもお絵かき帳を持ち歩いている.

I heard Jim was sick in bed. Is he *really* [=surely] coming? ジムは病気で伏せっていると聞いたけど, 本当に来るって?

reason /ríːzn/

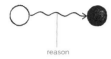

原義は〈じっくり考える〉である. **論理的に考える；理由**.
派 reasonable (道理にかなった)；reasonably (まあまあ)

Everything happens for a good *reason*.　何事もしかるべく理由があって起こるものだ.

There is no *reason* not to use these convenient communication tools.　こんな便利な通信ツールを使わない手 (理由) はないよ.

You did your best. You don't have the slightest *reason* to feel ashamed.　君は最善を尽くしたのだから，ちっとも恥じ入ること (理由) はないよ.

After retirement, he seems to have lost ⌈his *reason* for living [=what makes his life worth living]⌉.　退職後，彼は生き甲斐 (生きる理由) をなくしたようだ.

rebel /rébl/

語源は〈re (反抗して) bel (戦う)〉である. **権威に反逆・反抗する**.
派 rebellion (反乱)；rebellious (反抗的な)
関 bellicose (好戦的な)

Some members of the ruling party *rebelled* against the government and voted against the bill.　与党議員の何人かが政府に逆らって法案に反対票を投じた.

Teenagers may be *rebellious* [=disobedient] towards their parents.　十代のころは親に反抗しがちである.

The riot police were mobilized to put down the student *rebellion*.　機動隊が学生の暴動を鎮圧するために出動した.

recall /rɪkɔ́ːl/

語源は〈re (元へ) call (呼ぶ)〉である.**人を呼び戻す→記憶を呼び戻す (思い出す)→製品を呼び戻す (リコールする)**.

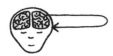

Steve Jobs had been *recalled* [=called back] to his former post.　スティーブ・ジョブズは元の職に呼び戻された.

He gets emotional whenever he *recalls* [=remembers] the years he spent with his beloved siblings.　彼は愛しい兄弟たちと過ごした年月のことを思い出すといつも感傷的になる.

The company started *recalling* more than 12,000 automobiles that were produced between 2009 and 2010.　会社は,2009から2010年までに製造した12,000台もの車のリコールを始めた.

---

receive /rɪsíːv/

語源は〈re (元に) ceive (受ける)〉である.**物を受け取る,傷などを受ける,人を迎える**.
派 receipt (領収書, レシート); reception (歓迎, 受信状態); recipient (受領者); receiver ([電話の] 受話器)
関 deceive (奪う)

Every day he *receives* [=gets] a lot of messages from his blog readers.　彼は毎日,ブログの読者から多くのメールを受け取っている.

The student *received* [=sustained] injuries in her head and spinal cord in a road accident.　その学生は交通事故で頭と脊髄に負傷した.

Many communities willingly *received* [=welcomed] those radioactive refugees from Fukushima.　多くの地域で,福島の放射能から逃れてきた人達を快く受け入れた.

I'm sorry sir, but we cannot give you a refund without a *receipt*.　申し訳ありませんが,レシート (領収書) がないと払い戻しはできません.

recent /ríːsnt/

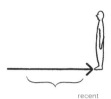

語源は〈re (とても) cent (新しい)〉である. **ほんの最近に (起こった)**.
派 recently (ついこの間, 最近)

His findings were featured in a *recent* issue of *Science*. 彼の発見したことが「サイエンス」誌の最近号に特集された.

We have experienced record-breaking hot summers in *recent* years. 近年, 記録的猛暑の夏を経験している.

Until very *recently* this housing area was used for farming. この宅地はごく最近まで農業用地だった.

recognize /rékəgnàɪz/

語源は〈re (再び, はっきり) cognize (知る)〉である. **改めて～だと気づく, ～の存在を認める**.
派 recognition (認識)

Many celebrities wear disguises so as not to be *recognized* [= known] in public. 人前で気づかれないように変装する有名人が多くいる.

We often don't *recognize* [=know] what we've got until we lose it. 人は, 恵まれているものを失って初めてその価値を知ることが多い.

The police discovered some bodies charred beyond *recognition* [= identification] in the ruins of the fire. 警察は, 焼け跡から判別できないほどに焼け焦げた数人の遺体を発見した.

recommend /rèkəménd/

語源は〈re（繰り返し）commend（ほめる）〉である．**(〜を強くほめる) →推薦する**．
派 recommendation（推薦）　関 commend（ほめる）

We *recommend* [=advise] that you use the water left in the tub to do the laundry.　お風呂の残り湯を洗濯に使うことをお勧めします．

Rice porridge is *recommended* [=I recommend rice porridge] as a diet for those who feel feverish with a cold.　風邪で熱っぽい時はかゆがお勧めです．

Would you please write a letter of *recommendation* for me?　推薦状を書いていただけませんか．

record /rékərd/

語源は〈re（再び）cord（心）〉である．**(しっかり心に留める) →記録する**．
関 cordial（心を込めた）

An experienced staff member *records* [=makes a *record* of the] proceedings.　ベテランの職員が議事録をとる．

All the music was *recorded* live at Carnegie Hall.　全曲ともカーネギーホールでライブ録音されたものだ．

The defendant has a previous criminal *record*.　被告には前科がある．

We experienced a *record* high temperature of 40 degrees Celsius last week.　先週，40°Cという記録的な高温を経験した．

recover /rɪkʌ́vər/

recover

語源は〈re (再び) cover (覆う)〉である．**再び傷・欠損を覆う→元通りにする→回復する，取り戻す．**
派 recovery (回復，取り戻し)

Kobe *recovered* quickly [=made a quick *recovery*] from the earthquake disaster that hit the area in 1995. 神戸は 1995 年，同地域を襲った震災から急速な復興を遂げた．

Many businesses find it very difficult to *recover* [=bounce back] from such a huge disaster. 多くの企業にとってそのような大災害から立ち直るのは容易ではない．

The police *recovered* my car that was stolen and abandoned at a vacant lot. 警察は空き地に乗り捨てられていた盗難車を取り戻してくれた．

reduce /rɪd(j)úːs/

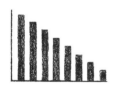

語源は〈re (後ろへ) duce (引く)〉である．**(引き戻す)→減少・縮小させる．**
派 reduction (減少，削減) 関 introduce (紹介する)

You had better *reduce* [=limit] the intake of animal fats. 動物性脂肪の摂取を控えめにしてください．

Top leaders should try their best to *reduce* the number of nuclear warheads around the world. 首脳は世界の核弾頭の数を減らす努力を尽くすべきだ．

You can magnify or *reduce* [=shrink] images by clicking this icon. このアイコンをクリックすると，画像を拡大あるいは縮小できます．

Poor diet may lead to a *reduction* in immunity. 粗末な食事をしていると免疫力が落ちかねない．

refer /rifə́:r/

語源は〈re(元へ) fer(運ぶ)〉である. **しかるべきところへ差し向ける**.
派 reference (参考, 参照)〔←疑問を差し向けること〕

Please *refer* me to someone who can read and translate Italian? イタリア語を読んで翻訳できる人を紹介してくれませんか.

Please *refer* me to any papers or books on the subject. このテーマに関する論文や書籍を何か教えてください.

What does "it" at the head of the sentence *refer* to? 文頭の it は何を指していますか.

I usually use a Post-it note while reading for later *reference*. 本を読む時は, あとから参照できるように付箋をよく使います.

reform /rifɔ́:rm/

語源は〈re(元へ) form(形づくる)〉である. **つくり直す→改善する→矯正する**.
関 reformation (改善)

The Government needs to *reform* [=amend] its pension system before it runs out of money. 政府は, 資金が枯渇する前に年金制度を改革する必要がある.

After being released from prison, he *reformed* [=mended his ways] and worked as a cook. 彼は出所後, 更生して料理人になって働いた.

refuse /rɪfjúːz/

原義は〈re（元へ）fuse（注ぐ）〉である．**(注ぎ返す) → 受け付けない→拒絶する**．
派 refusal（拒絶）　関 confuse（混乱させる）

He flatly *refused* our request for an interview.　彼はインタビューの申し出をきっぱり断った．

The girl gave birth to a baby boy, but she *refused* to reveal who the father was.　少女は男の子を産んだが，誰が父親なのか明かすことを拒んだ．

I gave them a polite *refusal* to the job offer.　彼らの仕事の誘いを丁寧に断った．

regard /rɪgáːrd/

語源は〈re（再び）gard（見る）〉である．**〜にしっかり目を向ける→〜であると見る→目を向ける；敬意，配慮**．
派 regarding（〜に関して）；regardless（〜のいかんにかかわらず）　関 guard（見張る）

The neighbors *regarded* [=looked upon] him as something of a crank.　近所の人たちは彼を一風変わった人だと思っていた．

May we have more information *regarding* [=concerning] food allergies for young children.　幼い子どもの食物アレルギーに関する情報をもう少し教えてもらえますか．

Everyone must be treated equally, *regardless* of [=without *regard to*] race, religion, or sex.　人種，宗教，性別にかかわりなく，すべての人は平等に遇されるべきだ．

regret /rɪgrét/

語源は〈re (再び) gret (嘆く)〉である. **したこと・起こったことを悔む, 後悔する；後悔**.
派 regrettable (遺憾な)　関 grief (悲嘆)

We may *regret* not the things we tried to do, but the things we didn't try.　私たちは試みたことよりも, 試みなかったことを後悔することがよくある.

I don't make much money, but I have ⌈no *regrets* [=never felt sorry] about my choice of career.　お金はもうからないけど, この職業を選んだことは少しも悔いていない.

It is *regrettable* [=to be *regretted*] that young people have been spending less and less time reading books.　若い人が本を読む時間が減ってきているのは残念だ.

regular /régjələr/

語源は〈regul (規定) ar (のような)〉である. **規則的な, 通常の, 普通の**.
派 regularly (規則正しく)；regulate (規定する)；regulation (規定)

The student council meets ⌈on a *regular* basis [=*regularly*].　生徒会は定期的に会合を開いている.

They say people who take *regular* exercise are less likely to be depressed.　定期的に運動する人は気分が滅入ることが少ないそうだ.

Check your mirrors *regularly* to know where other vehicles are around you.　他の車両が周囲のどこにいるか確認するために, ときどきバックミラーに目をやりなさい.

reject /rɪdʒékt/

原義は〈re(元へ) ject(投げる)〉である. **逆に投げ返す→受け取らずにつき返す→不良品を廃棄する**.
派 rejection(却下)
関 jet(ジェット機);inject(注入する)

My application for visa extension was *rejected* [=turned down].
ビザの延長申請は認められなかった.

Many of the expired foods they sell at the convenience stores are *rejected* [=thrown away]. コンビニの賞味期限を過ぎた食品の多くは廃棄される.

You should expect many *rejections* before you make a contract.
契約するまでに何度も断られることは覚悟しといたほうがいいよ.

---

relate /rɪléɪt/

語源は〈re(元へ) late(運ぶ)〉である.**(あることを別のあることにつなぐ)→関連づける,(あることをことばでつなぐ)→〜のことを語る**.
派 related(関連のある);relation(関係, 関連);relationship(結びつき, 人間関係);relative(身内, 親戚);relatively(比較的)

High cholesterol and hypertension are closely ⌈*related* to⌉ [=connected with] each other. 高コレステロールと高血圧は互いに密接な関連がある.

The old man *related* [=told] a dreadful story of his experience in Nazi concentration camps. 老人はナチの強制収容所の恐ろしい体験について話をした.

Japan normalized its diplomatic *relations* with China in 1972. 日本は1972年に中国と国交正常化を果たした.

release /rɪlíːs/

語源は〈re（元へ）lease（放つ）〉である．**縛り・拘束をほどいて解き放つ→解放する，公表する，発売する．**
関 press release（プレスリリース〔報道機関への発表〕）

The reporter interviewed hundreds of people, and *released* his findings in today's paper.　記者は，数百人にインタビューして判明したことを今日の新聞で発表した．

The band will *release* a new album soon.　このバンドは新しいアルバムをもうすぐ発売する．

The list of successful candidates will be *released* [=published] on the college's website.　合格者名簿は大学のホームページで発表される．

My package was *released* from [=went through] customs without any trouble.　私の荷物は難なく税関を通った．

remain /rɪméɪn/

語源は〈re（後ろに）main（残る）〉である．**趨勢(すうせい)・傾向に染まらないでそのままの状態にとどまる．**
派 remainder（残り）；remaining（残りの）；remains（遺跡，残り物）

A fingerprint will *remain* unchanged during a person's lifetime.　指紋の形は生涯変わらないままである．

The disease *remains* [=lies] dormant for several days before its symptoms appear.　この病気は発症するまでに数日間潜伏する．

There are only three minutes *remaining* [=left] until the exam hours expire.　試験終了まで 3 分しか残っていない．

The boy was told to *remain* behind after school as a punishment.
その子は罰で放課後居残るように命じられた．

remember /rɪmémbər/

語源は〈re (再び) member (考える)〉である. **思い浮かべる→覚えている→きちんと認識する**.
派 remembrance (記憶, 回想)

Please *remember* to feed the dog.　犬に餌をやるのを忘れないで.

It's important to *remember* people's names for better communication.　人の名前を覚えておくことはよりよいコミュニケーションのために大切だ.

Sometimes my grandma can't *remember* [=think of] the names of my family members.　おばあちゃんはときどき, 家族の名前を思い出せないことがある.

Remember not to use compliments too often or they will start to sound insincere.　ほめ過ぎないようにしなさい, ほめてばかりだとわざとらしくなってしまうよ.

---

remind /rɪmáɪnd/

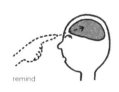

語源は〈re (再び) mind (頭に入れる)〉である. **忘れていること・注意すべきことを思い出させる**.
派 reminder (思い出させるもの, 督促状)

This photo *reminds* me of [=takes me back to] my childhood days.　この写真を見ると子どものころを思い出す.

Let me *remind* you that I'm always ready to talk with you.　(念のために言いますが) 私はいつでも相談に乗る用意がありますよ.

The audience was *reminded* to turn their cell phones off.　聴衆は携帯電話の電源を切っておくように言われた.

remove /rɪmúːv/

語源は〈re(後ろへ) move(動かす)〉である.**(ある場から後退させる)→取り除く**.
派 removal(除去)

What's a good way to *remove* stains from the carpet?　カーペットのしみを取るにはどうしたらいいですか.

Remove [＝Delete] my name from the phone book.　電話帳から私の名前を削除してください.

She decided to have her breast *removed* [＝cut out] after quitting chemotherapy.　彼女は化学療法をやめて乳房を切除してもらう決心をした.

repeat /rɪpíːt/

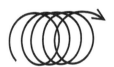

語源は〈re(再び) peat(求める)〉である.**(何度も求める)→繰り返す,繰り返し言う**.
派 repeatedly(繰り返して); repeater(再履修生,常客); repetition(繰り返し)

He vowed to himself never to *repeat* those mistakes.　彼は,こんな失敗は繰り返さないぞと心に誓った.

I'm afraid I don't follow you. Could you ⌈*repeat* it [＝say it again], please?　ちょっと分からないのですが,もう一度言ってくださいませんか.

I had to *repeat* a year in high school.　高校時代に1年間留年しなければならなかった.

His father has been in and out of the hospital *repeatedly*.　彼の父親は入退院を繰り返している.

replace /rɪpléɪs/

語源は〈re（再び）place（置く）〉である．**（代わりのものを元来のところへ置く）→新しいものが古いものに取って代わる→取り替える．**
派 replacement（代わりの人[物]） 関 place（置く）

Replace your brush when the bristles begin to wear. 毛が傷んできたら歯ブラシを替えなさい．

You can *replace* fear with confidence by preparing for it as much as you can. 準備を尽くせば，不安を自信に替えられるよ．

The ace pitcher is going to join another team; we need someone to *replace* him. エースピッチャーが他チームに移籍するので，彼に代わる投手が必要だ．

reply /rɪpláɪ/

語源は〈re（元へ）ply（折る，重ねる）〉である．**（折り返す）→返答する．**
関 apply（応用する）

Thank you for your quick *reply* [＝answer]. 早速のご返事，ありがとう．

I asked, "Are you sure you will make it?" "Yes," she *replied* with confidence. 「ちゃんとできるの？」と聞いたら，彼女は「できる」って自信を持って答えた．

I'm writing to ⌈*reply to* [＝answer] your questions. 質問への返信を書いています．

report /rɪpɔ́ːrt/

語源は〈re (元へ) port (運ぶ)〉である。**(依頼者の元へ入手情報を運ぶ) →報告する；報告**.
派 reportedly (伝えられるところによれば)；reporter (報道記者)

The crash happened a few minutes after the pilot *reported* engine trouble.　操縦士がエンジン・トラブルを報告して数分後に墜落した.

Our teacher asked us to *report* on the excursion to the zoo.　先生は動物園への遠足について感想を書くように言った.

He immediately *reported* the incident to the police.　彼は事件をすぐに警察に連絡した.

request /rɪkwést/

語源は〈re (再び) quest (求める)〉である。**強く求める，要求する；要求**.
関 question (質問する)〔←答えを求める〕

The family *requested* that the police arrest a man who was stalking their nineteen-year-old daughter.　家族は，19才の娘にストーカー行為をしている男を逮捕してもらうように警察に依頼した.

The union made several *requests* about improving their working environment.　組合は労働環境の改善に関していくつかの要求をした.

research /rí:sə̀:rtʃ/

語源は〈re (再び) search (調べる)〉である. **じっくり調査する；調査**.
派 researcher (研究者)
関 search (探す)

Recent *researches* [=studies] show laughter has a beneficial effect on the human system. 最近の研究によると，笑うことは人体によい効果があるそうだ．

The doctor is *researching* [=investigating] the relationship between stress and blood pressure. 医師はストレスと血圧の関係を調査している．

reserve /rɪzə́:rv/

語源は〈re (奥に) serve (保つ)〉である. **他者が触れないように保っておく→使わないで取っておく→保管する**.
派 reservation (予約)

I *reserved* [=booked] a table for five of us at the Chinese restaurant. 例の中華料理店に私たち5人の席を予約した．

Let's *reserve* this wine for our wedding anniversary. このワインは結婚記念日用に取っておきましょう．

The school *reserves* [=retains] the right to expel students who break the school's regulations. 学校には校則を守らない学生を退学させる権利がある．

resource /ríːsɔ̀ːrs/

語源は〈re(再び) source(湧き出る)〉である. **(湧き出る) 資源, (能力の湧き出る) 人材**.
派 resourceful (やり繰りの上手な)〔←難事に際して知恵が湧く〕

There is an urgent need to increase human *resources* in nursing old people.　高齢者介護サービス関係の人材を早急に増やすことが必要である.

Japan lacks natural *resources* and has to depend on import to a great extent.　日本は天然資源が少ないので, 輸入に大きく頼らないといけない.

respect /rɪspékt/

respect

語源は〈re(再び) spect(見る)〉である. **(繰り返し見る) →重視する→尊重する; 尊敬, (注目する) 点**.
派 respectable (尊敬すべき)

The students *respect* the teacher a lot for his knowledge. ＝The students have a lot of *respect* for their teacher's knowledge.　生徒たちは先生の学識をとてもすごいと思っている.

My exam preparation is perfect in「all *respects*［＝every way］.　試験準備はすべて (の点で) 完璧だ.

respond /rɪspɑ́:nd/

語源は〈re (元へ) spond (応じる)〉である. **〜に反応する, 返答する**.
派 response (反応, 返事); responsive (反応のよい)

How did the audience *respond*? =What was the *response* of the audience? 聴衆の反応はどうでしたか.

Students are likely to become *less responsive* in class to their teachers as their grades advance. 生徒は学年が進むにつれ, 授業中の先生に対する反応が悪くなる傾向がある.

responsibility /rɪspɑ̀:nsəbíləti/

語源は〈responsible (責任がある) ity (状態)〉である. **責任**.
派 responsible (責任のある)

All the parents have a *responsibility* [=duty] to raise their children until they are old enough to support themselves. 親はみな, 子どもが自立できるまで養育する責任がある.

If you want to do it anyway, take full *responsibility* for the results. どうしてもやるというのであれば, どうなろうと責任を負いなさい.

If you return the purchase, the cost of the shipping is 「your *responsibility* [=on you]. 返品の場合, 送料はあなたの負担になります.

No one has claimed *responsibility* for the explosion. 爆破の犯行声明はどこからも出されていない. ▶claim responsibility for 〜「〜の犯行声明を出す」

rest /rést/

語源は〈re（後ろに）st（立つ）〉である．**（後ろに残る）残余；（後ろに残る→表に出ない）休息；休息する**．
派 restful（やすらぎを与える）；restless（落ち着かない）
関 stand（〜の状態である）

Today is the first day for the *rest* [＝remaining days] of your life.
今日は残りの人生の最初の日だ．

Just sign your name and I will write the *rest*.　署名だけしてちょうだい．あとは私が記入するから．

About three-fourths of the students are natives; the *rest* are mainly from other Asian countries.　4分の3が本国人学生で，あとは主に他のアジア諸国からの学生です．

You seem to be tired. Get a good night's *rest*.＝*Rest* well for the night.　疲れているようだね．今夜はぐっすり休みなさい．

---

result /rɪzʌ́lt/

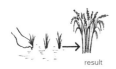

語源は〈re（元へ）sult（跳ねる）〉である．**（跳ね返って結果を生む）→結果をもたらす；結果**．
関 insult（侮辱する）〔←〜に飛びかかる〕

The company's poor planning *resulted* [＝ended up] in huge deficits.
会社のずさんな計画が莫大(ばくだい)な赤字をもたらしてしまった．

The *results* [＝outcomes] of treatment for cancer have been improving yearly.　がん治療の成績は年々よくなっている．

Butterflies often lay eggs on green vegetables; the *resulting* caterpillars feed on and destroy those vegetables very quickly.　チョウは緑色野菜によく卵を生みつける．孵化(ふか)した〔←その結果生まれた〕青虫は野菜をたちまち食べ尽くしてしまう．

return /rɪtə́ːrn/

語源は〈re (元へ) turn (返る)〉である．**元の所・状態へ戻る**．
派 returnee (帰国子女)；returnable (返却できる)

We *returned* yesterday from a seven-day trip to Hokkaido. 昨日，7日間の北海道の旅から帰ってきました．

You must *return* the books within fourteen days. 本は14日以内にお返しください．

He wants to *return* [=come back] to the old post after medical treatment. 彼は療養後復職したいと思っている．

You should *return* to original intentions, if you're in doubt about what you're doing. やっていることに迷いが生じたら，初志に立ち返りなさい．

---

review /rɪvjúː/

語源は〈re (再び) view (見る)〉である．**見直す→点検する，復習する；復習→批評する；批評**．
関 view (考察する)

I entered the appointment in my calendar but I forgot to *review* [=check] it in time. カレンダーに予約を書き入れていたのに，それを見直すのを忘れてしまい，間に合わなかった．

I *reviewed* [=went over] important things we learned in preparation for the exam. 重要な学習事項をおさらいして試験に備えた．

Mr. Smith has been ⌈*reviewing* books [=writing book *reviews*]⌋ for newspapers for a long time. スミスさんは長年，新聞に書評を書いている．

rich /rítʃ/

原義は〈力のある〉である. **金がある, 豊かである, 豊富である**.
派 richly (豪華に); richness (豊かさ)

I think *rich* [=wealthy] people should pay more taxes.　金持ちはもっと税金を払うべきだと思う.

We had a *rich* [=good] harvest of corn this year.　今年はトウモロコシが豊作だった.

Liver is *rich* [=high] in vitamin D.　レバーはビタミンDが豊富だ.

The book is 「*rich* in [=packed with]」 ideas about developing imagination and creativity.　この本には想像力や独創性を養うアイディアがたくさん載っている.

ride /ráɪd/

原義は〈馬に乗る〉である. **自転車・バイクに乗る；乗り物に乗って行く**.
派 rider (乗る人, 騎手)

Did you ever *ride* a camel?　ラクダに乗ったことがありますか.

He *rides* his bicycle to work every day.　彼は毎日, 自転車で通勤する.

I'll *give you a ride* if you want; the museum is a good way from here.　博物館はここからけっこう遠いですよ. よければ, 車にお乗りください.

right /ráɪt/

原義は〈正しい,まっすぐな〉である.**適切な,ちょうどいい,ぴったりの**.

派 righteous (正しい);rightful (正当な);rightly (当然のことながら)

Keep the *right* distance with everyone if you want to have a good and long relationship with each other.　よい関係を長く続けたければ,誰であれ適切な距離を保つようにしなさい.

What may be *right* for you may not be *right* for others.　あなたにとって都合のいいことが,他の人にはそうでないかも知れません.

You mean you need one more week to finish the job, *right* [= correct]?　仕事を仕上げるにはもう1週間必要ってことだね.

---

rise /ráɪz/

原義は〈上がる〉である.**上がる《上昇》,沸き起こる《発生》**.
関 raise (上げる)

The water level *rises* every spring due to snow melt.　春になると雪解けのために水位が上がる.

Every civilization *rises* and falls.　どんな文明も盛衰がある.

The *rise* and fall of water is caused by gravitational forces of the moon and the sun.　潮の満ち引きは月と太陽の引力によって起こる.

Prices have been 「on the *rise* [=going up].　物価が高騰してきた.

The Nile *rises* [=starts] near the equator and flows into the Mediterranean Sea.　ナイル河は赤道近くで源を発し,地中海へ流れ込んでいる.

risk /rísk/

原義は〈危険に飛び込む〉である.**何かを求め,新境地に至るために出くわす危険；危険を冒す**.
派 risky（危険な）

Being overweight ⌈puts you at *risk* for [=may increase your risk of developing] diabetes.　肥満になると糖尿病になる恐れが生じる.

Where there is no *risk*, there is no achievement.　危険を冒さなければ,何事も成就しない.

You have to *risk* loss if you want to make money on the stock market.　株でもうけようとするなら損失を覚悟する必要がある.

He *risked* all his savings on his new business.　彼は蓄えの全てを新しい仕事に賭けた.

role /róul/

原義は〈役者の役割の配当を書いた巻物〉である.**割り振られた役,役割**.
関 roll（名簿,目録）；role model（手本とされる人）

Japan must *play* a leading *role* in the effort to eliminate nuclear weapons from the world.　日本は核兵器廃絶へ向けて主導的役割を果たさなければならない.

The actor started his career, playing a minor *role* in the movie.　俳優はその映画で端役を演じることで役者業を始めた.

Steve Jobs is a *role* model for many of those who want to challenge old authorities and traditions.　スティーブ・ジョブズは,旧来の権威や伝統主義に挑もうとする多くの人たちの模範となっている.

room /rúːm/

原義は〈空間〉である. **空間; (空間に仕切りを入れた)部屋**.
派 roomy (広びろとしている)

Is there *room* for one more person in your car?　もう一人乗れますか.

There is no *room* for compromise on this matter.　この問題には妥協の余地はありません.

The bus we chartered was nice as we had *room* to spread out.　貸切りバスは散らばって座れる余裕があったので快適だった.

route /rúːt/

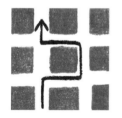

原義は〈(切り開いた)道〉である. **(出発点から目的地までの)道・経路**.
派 routine (お決まりのこと, いつもの手順)

I'd rather take a scenic *route* [=road] than a superhighway.　高速道より景色のいい道路を走りたいわ.

"Do you jog after work?" "Yes, that's my daily *routine* [=practice]."
「仕事が終わったら, ジョグするの?」「うん, 毎日のことなんだ」

rule /rúːl/

原義は〈定規〉である．**規定する→定める→統率する；規則**．
派 ruler（支配者，定規）

For thousands of years, African lions have *ruled* [＝dominated] the savannah.　何千年もアフリカライオンはサバンナを支配してきた．

It is against the *rules* [＝It's illegal] to ride a bicycle on a sidewalk.　歩道を自転車で走るのは規則違反だ．

run /rʌ́n/

原義は〈走る〉である．**走る，（機械が）動く，（店などを）経営する，（水や時などが）流れる，（性質などが）遺伝する**．
派 runner（走者）；running（長年の，維持する）：running costs（維持費）

This car *runs* almost 25 kilometers on a liter of gas.　この車はリッター当たり 25 キロ近く走る．

We let the dog *run* free in the yard.　うちの犬は庭に放し飼いしている〔←自由に走り回らせている〕．

His father *runs* a bakery in Tokyo.　彼の父は東京でパン屋を経営している．

Don't leave the tap *running* while you brush your teeth.　歯磨きの時，蛇口から出る水を流しっぱなしにしてはだめですよ．

Nearsightedness tends to *run* [＝be inherited] in the family.　近視は子どもに遺伝しやすい．

sad /sǽd/

原義は〈うんざり〉である.**(うんざり→むなしい)→悲しい**.
派 sadden (悲しませる); sadness (悲しみ)
関 satisfy (満足させる)

I ⌈felt *sad* at leaving [=was saddened by having to leave] so many friends behind.　多くの友人と別れるのは悲しかった.

My *sadness* was deepened at the sight of victims who lost their beloved ones.　愛する人たちを失った被災者たちの姿に悲しみが深まった.

safe /séɪf/

safe

原義は〈無傷〉である.**(傷を受けそうな状態から自由である)→安全である**.
派 safely (安全に); safety (安全)　関 save (助ける)

Flying is one of the *safest* forms of travel.　飛行機は最も安全な交通手段の一つだ.

I think you should get a flu shot. It's better to be *safe* than sorry.　インフルエンザの予防接種をしたほうがいいと思うよ. 用心するに越したことはない〔←悔やむより大事をとるほうが賢明だ〕.

Whenever I go out to drive, my dad says, "Drive *safely*!"　私が車で出かける時, 父はいつも,「安全運転でね」と言ってくれる.

Safety comes first when you're behind the wheel.　運転時は安全第一である.

same /séɪm/

same

原義は〈一つ (single)〉である。**同じである，同様である**。
関 simple (単純な)

I am the *same* age as that singer.　ぼくはあの歌手と同い年だよ．

We are from the *same* high school and played on the *same* baseball team.　僕たちは同じ高校の出身で同じ野球部でプレーしていました．

I am of the *same* opinion as you.　あなたと同様の意見です．

"Have a nice day!" "The *same* to you."　「いい日にしてね！」「あなたもね」〔←同じことばをあなたにも〕

save /séɪv/

原義は〈傷を受けないようにする〉である。**窮地に陥らないようにする〈守る・助ける〉→将来に備えて取っておく〈蓄える・控える〉**。save は〈窮地への陥落を防ぐ（予防）〉，help は〈窮地からの引き上げ（救助・治療）〉の意味合い．
派 saving (節約，貯金)
関 safe (安全な)

We used a rope to *save* ourselves from falling.　落下しないようにロープを使った．

The couple is *saving* money [＝putting money aside] for their children's education.　夫妻は子どもの教育に備えて貯金をしている．

Everyone is being encouraged to *save* energy.　皆がエネルギーを節約するように奨励されている．

say /séɪ/

原義は〈～であると言う〉である. **～と言う, ～であると言う**.
派 saying (ことわざ)

Sara *said*, "I am sick." =Sara *said* that she was sick.　サラは気分が悪いと言った.

Let's eat out this evening. What do you *say*?　今晩は, 外食しましょうよ. どう?

Fifty passengers are *said* to have been seriously or slightly injured.　50人の乗客が重軽傷を負ったそうだ.

We want to know「what you have to *say* [＝your opinion] about the issue.　この件についてあなたの意見を知りたいと思います.

search /sə́ːrtʃ/

原義は〈あちこち探し回る〉である. **物・人・情報の所在を求めてあちこち探し回る；捜索**.
関 seek (求める)；research (研究する)

Paul *searched* for information on the college he wants to attend on the Internet.　ポールは志望大学の情報をインターネットで検索した.

I often have to *search* the whole house for my misplaced car keys just before leaving.　僕は出掛ける直前になって車のキーが見つからず, 家中を探し回ることがよくある.

The man stopped by the police was questioned and *searched*.　警察に呼び止められた男は尋問とボディーチェックを受けた.

second /sékənd/

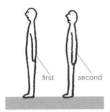

原義は〈次に来る〉である．**二番目の；(分($\frac{ふん}{ふん}$)の次に来る時間単位) 秒**．
派 secondary (二次的な)；secondhand (中古の，間接的な)　関 sequence (続いて起こること)

This is the *second* time it's happened.　こうなったのはこれで 2 度目だ．

John is "*second to none* [=better than anyone else] in rope skipping.
縄跳びでジョンにかなうものは誰もいない．

I'm having *second* thought(s) about changing my job.　転職するのはよそうと思っている．　▶have second thoughts about 〜「〜について考え直す」

I've enjoyed every *second* [=moment] I have been with you.　あなたといっしょにいる時間〔←刻々のすべて〕はとっても楽しかったわ．

There are a lot of children suffering from *secondhand* [=passive] smoking.　受動喫煙の被害を被っている子どもが多い．

---

secret /síːkrət/

語源は〈se (離して) cret (分けた)〉である．**(他者の目から引き離す)→他者に知られないようにする《内密》・奥の手《ひけつ》**．
派 secretly (密かに)；secretary (秘書官)；secrecy (秘密)

Why do you keep it a *secret* from your friends that you got engaged?
なぜ婚約したことを友だちに隠すの．

The doctor decided to keep it *secret* from the patient that his cancer is terminal.　医師はがんが末期であることを患者に言わないことにした．

My *secret* for good skin is using makeup sparingly.　私の美肌のひけつは化粧を控えめにすることです．

secure /sɪkjúər/

語源は〈se（離して）cure（心配）〉である．**(心配をなくす)→きちんとした状態にする→安全にする；安定した．** 派 security（保護，安心） 関 care（注意）

Make sure the ladder is leaning against something *secure* [=stable]. はしごは安定したものに立てかけるようにしなさい．

The government has taken no effective action to *secure* [=bring about] the release of many abductees in North Korea. 政府は，北朝鮮にいる多くの拉致被害者の解放を確実にする効果的な行動を取っていない．

Cozy beds may give your cats a sense of *security*. 気持ちよい寝床は猫に安心感を与える．

see /síː/

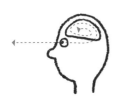

原義は〈(目に) 見える〉である．**見える→出会う→体験する，(脳で) 見る→分かる，(心で) 見る→注意を払う．**

They are *seeing* [=going out with] each other. 二人は交際している．

In my whole life, I haven't *seen* this much snow in this area. この地方でこんな大雪は経験がない．

"Did Santa come?" "Yes, mom. I *saw* my wish came true." 「サンタさん来た？」「うん，ママ，ぼくの願いがかなったよ」〔←願いの実現を体験した〕

I couldn't *see* [=understand] what he meant to say. 彼が何を言いたかったのか分からなかった．

seed /síːd/

原義は〈まく〉である. **種をまく→種→種ができる→種を除く**.
関 sow (〔種を〕まく); semen (精液); seminar (ゼミ)〔←知識の伝播〕

Even giant trees grow from a tiny little *seed*.　巨木も小さな種から育つ.

Seasoned roasted pumpkin *seeds* make a healthy snack.　味付けして焼いたかぼちゃの種は, 体によい軽食になる.

Most summer flowers *seed* [=produce *seeds*] in the fall.　夏の花はたいてい秋に種を付ける.

You first need to peel and *seed* [=remove *seeds* from] tomatoes to make ketchup.　ケチャップを作るには, まずトマトの皮をむいて種を取り除きなさい.

The top four teams will be *seeded* for the first round.　上位4チームは, 1回戦はシードされる.

---

seek /síːk/

原義は〈求める〉である. **(糧・場・手段を) 求める**.
関 search (捜し求める)

Bullied students are often unwilling to ⌈*seek* help from others [=turn to others for help].　いじめを受けている生徒は, 他の人に助けを求めることをためらうことが多い.

The president is *seeking* [=running for] a second term in the next election.　大統領は次の選挙で2期目を目指している.

He moved to Tokyo to *seek* [=pursue] a career as a writer.　彼は作家になることを目指して東京に移り住んだ.

seem /síːm/

原義は〈～にふさわしい〉である. **～のように見える・思える**.
派 seemingly (外見上は)

Challenge it with all your heart; walls are never as solid as they *seem* [=appear]. 全力で挑戦しなさい. 壁は思うほど高くはないものだよ.

The guy *seems* [=appears] curt, but kind at heart. あの人はぶっきらぼうに見えるが, 根は優しいのよ.

I can't *seem* to be friends with him again. 彼とは仲直りできそうもないわ.

sell /sél/

原義は〈放す〉である. **金と引き替えに物を売る, 販売する**.
派 seller (売り手, 販売会社)

His Naoki prize work has been *selling* well. 彼の直木賞作品はよく売れている.

What is the biggest *selling* point of this car? この車のセールスポイントは何ですか.

Tickets for today's game are *sold out*. 今日の試合のチケットは売り切れです.

In job interviews, getting yourself noticed is the key. Don't *sell* yourself *short*. =Don't downplay your abilities. 就職の面接では注目してもらうことが大切だ. 売り込みを遠慮してはだめだよ.

send /sénd/

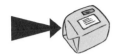

原義は〈行かせる〉である. **物を発送する, 人を行かせる**. se- は〈離す・放す〉の意味合い.
派 sender（差出人）

The fishery company *sends* [=ships] fish and seafood by air.　この水産会社は魚介類を空輸している.

Fill out the form and *send* it back to us.　用紙に記入の上, 返送してください.

Please *send* [=extend] my best regards to your family.　ご家族に皆さんによろしくお伝えください.

The Government *sent* some experienced officials to North Korea to negotiate on the abduction issue.　政府は拉致問題の交渉のために, ベテランの高官を数人北朝鮮へ派遣した.

sense /séns/

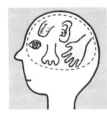

原義は〈感じる〉である. **感じる《感覚》, 分かる《分別・意味》**.
派 sensible（分別のある）; sensitive（敏感な）; oversensitive（意識過剰な）

A solitary person may lack the *sense* [=appreciation] of humor.　孤独な人はユーモアのセンス（感覚）に欠けることが多い.

Toward the end of summer we 「often feel a *sense* of [=may have a feeling of] fatigue or weariness.　夏の終わりごろになると, 疲れやだるさを感じることが多い.

Dogs have an excellent *sense* of smell.　犬は鋭い嗅覚を持っている.

The boy 「*sensed* [=was aware] that he was not liked by his classmates.　少年は, 自分はクラスの仲間に好かれていないと感づいていた.

sentence /séntns/

原義は〈sent (感じる, 思う) ence (行為)→考え方〉である. **(考え方→意見)→文→判決文→判決を言い渡す**.
関 sentiment (感想, 感傷); sentimental (感傷的な)

In English, the first letter of a *sentence* is capitalized.　英語では, 文頭の文字は大文字で書かれる.

The defendant was「given a life *sentence*［=*sentenced* life in prison］.　被告は終身刑を言い渡された.

---

separate /sépərèit/

語源は〈se (離して) parate 配置する〉である. **本来はつながっているものを引き離す→分ける; 分かれている**.
派 separately (個別に); separation (分離)

You often take your work home with you; I think you should *separate* your work from your personal life.　君はよく仕事を家に持ち帰るけど, 仕事と私生活は分けたほうがいいと思う.

Belgium is *separated* from England by the English Channel.　ベルギーはイギリス海峡で英国と隔てられている.

We are now living「*separate* lives［=*separately*］, because my husband is working as a resident employee in Vietnam.　夫がベトナムで駐在員として働いているので, 私たちは別居中です.

serious /síːəriəs/

原義は〈真剣な〉である．**(事態が) 重大である→(人が) 真剣になる**．
派 seriously (真剣に)；seriousness (まじめ，深刻)

Nursing care for older people has become a *serious* problem in Japan.　日本では高齢者の介護が深刻な問題になっている．

"I'm engaged to a man who is twenty years my senior." "Are you *serious* [=for real]?"　「20歳年上の人と婚約したの」「本当?」〔←マジで?〕

If you are *serious* about becoming an actor, you need to go to an acting school in Tokyo.　俳優になることを真剣に考えているのなら，東京の俳優養成所に行かないとだめだよ．

Don't take it so *seriously*. I just said about a possible but rare case.　そんなに真剣に受け取らないで．万一のことを言っただけだよ．

serve /sə́ːrv/

原義は〈人に仕える〉である．**人のために仕える→職務を務める→食事を出す**．
派 server (〔コンピューターネットワークの〕サーバー)；service (奉仕，事業，業務；点検する)
関 deserve (～に値する)

In Korea, all men are required to *serve* in the military for about two years.　韓国では男性は皆，ほぼ2年間兵役に就くことになっている．

Carter *served* [=had been in office] as president of the US from 1977 to 1981.　カーターは1977年から1981年まで米国大統領を務めた．

Pickles were *served* as an appetizer.　ピクルスが前菜として出された．

The heater isn't working properly. We need to call a repair *service*.　ヒーターがうまく作動していないよ．修理サービスに電話しなくちゃ．

set /sét/

原義は〈座らせる〉である．**ある位置に置く，ある状態に置く**．

派 setting（背景，場面）　関 sit（座る）

A protester *set* himself on fire.　抗議者が自分の身体に火を放った．

Do you *set* your alarm clock even on your day off?　休みの日でも目覚ましをかけるの？

Don't rush. *Set* your own pace [＝Pace yourself]!　あせらないで．マイペースで！

I have my hair cut and *set* every month.　毎月，髪をカットしてセットしてもらう．

---

settle /sétl/

原義は〈座らせる〉である．**試行錯誤したりさまよった挙げ句に落ち着く**．

派 settler（移住者）; settlement（集落）〔←移住者たちが住み着いた所〕

I will write as soon as I am *settled*.　（新天地に）落ち着きましたら，お便りします．

The problem has been *settled* [＝solved].　問題は解決した．

The price of gasoline will *settle* at around 150 yen per liter.　ガソリンはリッター150円あたりに落ち着くでしょう．

The craftsman is very thorough and will not ⌈*settle* for [＝be satisfied with]⌋ a less than perfect job.　あの職人はとても几帳面で，完璧に仕上げないと満足しない．

sex /séks/

原義は〈(生物を雄雌に分ける)性〉である．**性別，性，性行為**．se- は〈分ける〉の意味合い．
派 sexism (性差別主義); sexual (性の); sexuality (性行動); sexy (性的魅力のある)

How soon can you tell the *sex* [=gender] of a baby? 赤ちゃんの性別は妊娠後どれくらいで分かりますか．

Premarital *sex* used to be considered sinful. かつて婚前交渉は不道徳だと思われていた．

Even just a generation ago, many careers were limited to ⌈one *sex* [=either men or women]. ほんの一世代前までは，多くの職業は男と女どちらかのものと決まっていた．

shadow /ʃǽdou/

原義は〈影(かげ)〉である．**物が光をさえぎってできる(輪郭をもった)影**．類義語 shade は物が光をさえぎってできる(薄暗い部分をなす)陰(かげ)．
派 shade (影); shady (陰になった，明瞭でない)

I saw my *shadow* much longer than I am in the evening light. 夕日のつくる僕の影は，実際の背丈よりもずっと長かった．

A cyclist was taking a rest in the *shade* of an elm tree. サイクリストが一人，ニレの木陰で休んでいた．

shake /ʃéɪk/

原義は〈小刻みに震える〉である. **震える，上下に揺さぶる**. sh- は〈震えが空気を切る音〉のイメージ.
派 shaky（震える，ぐらつく）　関 shock（衝撃を与える）

We *shook* with fear when we noticed huge waves coming from over the sea.　海の向こうから押し寄せる巨大な波に気づいて恐怖で震えた.

My hands *shake* [=are *shaky*] whenever I hold something in the air.　僕の手は何か物を持ち上げるといつも震える.

Shake the bottle before you use it.　使用前にびんをよく振ること.

shall /ʃæl/, should /ʃúd/

原義は〈義務がある→相手の意見に従う，意見を聞く〉である.（疑問文で）**〜しましょうか，〜すべきでしょうか**.

Shall I make coffee?　コーヒーをお入れしましょうか.

Shall I open the window?　窓を開けましょうか.

How early *should* I get to the airport?　空港にはどれくらい早めに行けばいいですか.　▶should は発言に「〜したほうがいい」の意味合いを生む.

You *shouldn't* drink and drive.　飲酒して運転してはいけない.

A present for me? You *shouldn't have*!　僕にプレゼント?そんなにしなくていいのに!　▶You shouldn't have.「わざわざすみません」（お礼のことば）

shape /ʃéɪp/

原義は〈形〉である．**形→形を整える→好調である**．
派 shapeless（不格好な）

I've learned how to draw *shapes* on the screen.　パソコン画面に形を描くことができるようになった．

The dancer looks out of *shape* with a bloated belly.　あのダンサーは腹が出ていて引き締まった身体に見えない．

This car isn't *in good shape*.　この車は調子が悪い．

Hardships may help *shape* a strong and independent character.　困難に出くわすと，強くて自立的な性格を形成するようになるだろう．

share /ʃéər/

原義は〈切り分ける〉である．**一つのものを複数人で分け合う《分配，共有》**．sh- は〈分ける時の切る音〉のイメージ．
関 shareholder（株主）

May I *share the table*?　相席させてもらえますか．

Nobel Peace Prizes were *shared* by three women.　ノーベル平和賞は3人の女性が受賞した〔←賞を分けた〕．

I *share* your feelings completely. ＝I feel quite the same way.　あなたのお考えにまったく同感です．

Thank you for *sharing* [＝letting me know] the information.　情報をいただいてありがとう．

Sharing your troubles with others will help unload your worries.　悩みを他の人に打ち明けると気持ちが楽になる．

sharp /ʃɑ́ːrp/

原義は〈鋭い〉である．**鋭い，とがった，辛らつな**．
派 sharpen（鋭くする）; sharply（鋭く）

Don't let children play with *sharp* pointed objects.　子どもたちに先端のとがった物で遊ばせないようにしなさい．

The old man is hard of hearing, but he still has a *sharp* mind.　あの老人は耳は遠いけど，頭はピカピカだよ．

Will you please *sharpen* this kitchen knife?　この包丁をといでくれませんか．

I turned *sharply* to avoid a dog that ran onto the road.　道路に飛び出してきた犬をよけようと急ハンドルを切った．

ship /ʃíp/

原義は〈舟〉である．**船；船で運ぶ→輸送する**．舟による物資の運びが運搬の原型．
派 shipment（輸送）

I prefer travelling slowly by *ship*.　ゆっくりした船旅が好きだ．

We will *ship* [=send] your orders as soon as we receive your payment.　代金を受け取り次第，注文品をお送りします．

Hundreds of cars to be exported were waiting for *shipment* at the port.　何百台もの輸出車が港で積み込みを待っていた．

shock /ʃá:k/

原義は〈打撃〉である.**(感情や身体への)ショック・衝撃;ショックを与える**.
派 shocking (ぎょっとさせる)　関 shake (揺さぶる)

Don't touch the wire; you'll get a *shock*.　電線に触ったら,感電するよ.

Their mother's sudden death「was a great *shock* to the family [= shocked the family greatly].　母親の急死は家族に大きなショックだった.

I wear thick-soled shoes that absorb the *shock* [=impact] on the legs.　脚への衝撃を吸収する厚底の靴を履きます.

shoot /ʃú:t/

原義は〈打ち出す〉である.**発射する,撃つ,シュートを放つ;(ぐいぐい伸び出る)新芽**.
派 shooting (銃撃)
関 shot (発砲);troubleshoot (機械を修理する,調停する)〔←トラブル+射落とす〕

The man *shot* randomly at people on the street.　男は通りがかりの人たちに見さかいなく発砲した.

The policeman *shot* the gun into the air to threaten the man on the rampage.　警官は銃を空へ向けて発射し,暴れる男を威嚇した.

If you saw *a shooting star* right now, what would you wish for?
流れ星を今見たら,何を願う?

I noticed that a few new *shoots* are coming out on the vines of roses.
バラのつるに新芽がいくつか出ていた.

shop /ʃá:p/

原義は〈仕切り部屋〉である.**(仕切られた) 仕事場，店**
→**買い物をする**.

派 shopping (買い物)　関 workshop (工房, 研修会)

Some *shops* sell goods and others sell services.　店には, 物を売る店とサービスを売る店がある.

They are planning to start and run「a flower *shop*[=a florist].　彼らは花屋を開店する計画をしている.

We「go *shopping*[=*shop*] at the supermarket on Friday.　金曜日にスーパーへ買い出しに行く.

I often「do *shopping*[=shop] online.　私はよくネット通販を利用する.

short /ʃɔ́:rt/

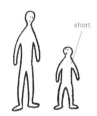

short

原義は〈切り落とす〉である.**(切り落とした)→短い→足りない**.

派 shortage (不足); shorten (短くする); shortly (まもなく)

Life is too *short* to waste any time worrying about little things.　人生は小さなことにくよくよして時間を浪費するには短すぎる.

I began to feel *short* of breath while climbing stairs.　階段を昇るときに息切れがするようになった.

Which is the *shorter* route to take?　どちらを行けば近道になりますか.

He was just a few points *short of* passing the exam.　彼はほんの数点足りなくて試験に落ちた.

shot /ʃάːt/

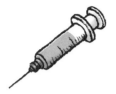

原義は〈撃つ〉である．**発砲，撮影，注射，(狙ってみる) 試み，賭け．**
関 shoot (発射する)

A few *shots* were heard, breaking the silence of the night.　夜の静寂を破って数発の発射音が聞こえた．

I got some good *shots* of my kids playing.　子どもたちが遊んでいるよい写真が撮れた．

Did you get ⌈a flu *shot* [=a *shot* for the flu] this year?　今年，インフルエンザの予防注射をしましたか．

We have nothing to lose. Let's give it a *shot* [=try].　失うものは何もないのだから，やってみようよ．

show /ʃóu/

原義は〈示す〉である．**そのままでは見えないものを見せる；(感性・態度・性質などを) 示すこと．**
派 showy (派手な，目立つ)

He *showed* me the surgical scar on the chest.　彼は胸にある手術の傷跡を見せてくれた．

The decision was voted by a *show* of hands.　決定は挙手で決められた．

Shall I *show* you around the neighborhood?　近所をご案内しましょうか．

I was very nervous but tried not to *show* it.　ドキドキしたが表情に出ないようにした．

The game is being *shown* [=broadcast] live on NHK.　その試合はNHKで生中継している．

sick /sík/

原義は〈病気である〉である. **病気である；うんざりする, 気分が悪くなる.**
派 sickness（体調不良）

He has been *sick* [=ill] with stomach cancer for nearly two years.
彼はもう2年近く胃がんを患っている.

We are getting *sick* of snow this winter. 今年の雪にはもううんざりだ.

I can't handle the smell of fish that makes me *sick* to my stomach.
僕は魚の臭いをかぐと気分が悪くなってどうにもならない.

Most pregnant women get *morning sickness*. 妊婦はたいていつわりを経験する.

side /sáid/

原義は〈横腹〉である. **側面, 側；ある側につく.**
派 sideward（横に） 関 sidewalk（歩道）

My obesity may be inherited from my mother's *side* of the family.
僕の肥満は母方の家系からの遺伝のようだ.

Which *side* of the road do you drive on in Korea? 韓国では道路のどちら側を運転するの？

The most common *side effect* of cold medicine is sleepiness. かぜ薬にいちばんよくある副作用は眠気だ.

They were arguing, but I didn't want to take *sides*, so I kept silent.
彼らは言い合っていたけど, どちらの側にもつきたくなかったので黙っていた.

What party do you *side* with? どの党を支持していますか.

sight /sáɪt/

語源は〈sigh (見る) t (こと)〉である. **視覚, 視力;眺め, 見方;目にする.**
関 eyesight (視力);sightseeing (観光)

I can't stand even the *sight* of an octopus.　タコは見るのも耐えられないの.
Carrying a cell phone has become a common *sight* in contemporary society.　携帯電話を持ち歩くのは現代社会では普通の光景になった.
There is only one house *in sight*, out on the horizon.　地平線の向こうに家が一軒だけ見えた.
Captain Cook was the first European to *sight* the eastern coast of Australia in 1770.　クック船長は, オーストラリアの東岸を1770年に最初に目にしたヨーロッパ人だった.

---

sign /sáɪn/

原義は〈しるし〉である. **(背後にある意味・現象を伝えるしるし) 兆し, (本人であるしるし) サイン;署名する.**
派 signal (合図);signature (署名)
関 design (設計する)

There was no *sign* of life in the house.　その家は人が住んでいる気配がなかった.
Will you *sign* [=write your *signature*] here?　ここに署名してください.
How do you say, "I love you." in *sign language*?　手話で "I love you." ってどう表現するのですか.

silence /sáiləns/

語源は〈sil(静かな)ence(状態)〉である. **静けさ, 沈黙**.
派 silent (静かな); silently (黙って)

We need to hear the *silence* of those who are socially disadvantaged. 社会的弱者の声なき声を聞かないといけない.

Bullied students often suffer in *silence*. いじめを受けている生徒は黙って我慢することが多い.

He is a *silent* [=quiet] person and never gets a word in. 彼は物静かな人だから口出しなどしない.

The "k" is *silent* [=isn't pronounced] in "knee." "knee" の "k" は発音されない.

The accused used the right to remain *silent*. 被告は黙秘権を使った.

similar /símələr/

語源は〈simil(一つ)ar(の)ような〉である. **同一のような→同じような**.
派 similarity (類似点); similarly (同様に)
関 simulate (模擬で行う, よく似た状態をつくり出す); simple (単純な)

He is *similar* in character to his father. 彼は親父さんに性格が似ている.

What is *similar* [=the *similarity*] between the two works? その二つの作品の類似点は何ですか.

There is some *similarity* in the way they sing. 彼らの歌い方はどこか似たところがある.

We can't *simulate* [=create] weightlessness on earth. 無重力状態は地上では作り出せない.

simple /símpl/

complex

simple

語源は〈sim (同じ) ple (重なり)〉である. **(ひと重なりの) →単純な**.
派 simply (単に, とても)
関 same (同じ)；similar (似ている)

I prefer「a *simple* lifestyle [=living simply]. 簡素な生活のほうが好きだ.

I always try to write in *simple* [=plain] language. いつも簡潔な言い回しで書くようにしている.

You signature is too *simple*; it can be easily forged. あなたの署名は単純すぎて, 簡単にまねされちゃうよ.

since /síns/

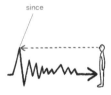
since

原義は〈その後 (after that)〉である. **〜して以来；〜だから**. 文脈により「その後〜である《以後》」, あるいは「その後どうなる《因果》」の意味合いをもつ. 端的に,「以来」→「由来」→「理由」となる.

I haven't seen him *since* last week. 先週から彼に会っていない.

She's been skating *since* childhood [=she was a child]. 彼女は子どもの時からスケートをしている.

Since [=As] you've finished all your homework, you may go out and play. 宿題は全部やったから遊びに行っていいよ.

You may take the magazine *since* [=as] I've read it. その雑誌はもう読んだので持って行っていいよ.

sit /sít/

原義は〈座る〉である．**座る，座っている，座ったままで動かない．**
関 sit-ups（腹筋運動）; set（置く）

I had to *sit up* late for several nights in order to get it finished.　それを完成させるために数日夜遅くまで起きていなければならなかった．

Every day when the school is off, my boy *sits* [=stays] at home playing computer games.　学校が休みの日はいつも，うちの子は家にこもってゲームばかりしている．

The economic depression is too severe to「*sit back and wait* [=let it goes as it may].　この不況はもはやゆっくり構えてはいられないほど深刻だ．　▶ sit back and watch「傍観する」

---

site /sáit/

原義は〈占める場所〉である．**（事柄・事象が存在する）場；場所を設定する．** place（場所）に特定性が加わると site になる．

We hate living near the *site* [=location] of the waste treatment facility.　廃棄物処理場の近く（の場所）に住むのは嫌だ．

This *site* [=website] provides information about fantastic places to visit.　このサイトは観光地情報を提供しています．

The *siting* of nuclear waste facilities [=Where to locate nuclear waste facilities] can be controversial.　核廃棄物保管所をどこにする建設するかは，大きな議論を呼ぶだろう．

situation /sìtuéɪʃən/

語源は〈situ (置く) ation (こと)〉である. **(置かれた) 状況・場所**.
派 situate (位置づける)

How is the city's financial *situation*?　市の財政状況はどうなっていますか.

I'm worried about the current political *situation* in Islamic countries.　イスラム諸国の現今の政治状況が心配である.

The town is *situated* [=located] on a plateau high up in the Andes mountain range.　その町はアンデスの山並みに囲まれた高原にある〔←位置している〕.

sleep /slíːp/

原義は〈(す〜と) 眠る〉である. **眠る, 睡眠を取る；眠り**.
派 asleep (眠って)；sleepy (眠い)；sleepiness (眠気)
関 slumber (まどろむ)

I can't *sleep* for the heat.　暑くて眠れない.

I sometimes find myself *sleeping* in class.　授業中にときどき居眠りすることがある.

Did you have a good *sleep*? = Did you *sleep* well?　よく眠れましたか.

He felt pleasantly *sleepy* [=drowsy] in the warm sunshine shining through the window.　彼は窓から差し込む温かい日差しに心地よい眠気を感じた.

I almost ⌈*fell asleep* [=dozed off]⌉ while driving.　うっかり居眠り運転をしかけた.

slow /slóu/

原義は〈(力が抜けて)のろい〉である。**遅い、のろい；緩める**。
派 slowly (ゆっくりと)

Business has been *slow* [=sluggish] since the turn of the year.　今年になってから景気が悪い。

You've got to ˈ*slow* down [=reduce your speed] when you approach a school zone.　スクールゾーンに近づく時は徐行しなければならない。　▶speed down とはいわない。

Alcohol *slows* [=dulls] brain activity.　酒は脳の働きを鈍らせる。

The automobiles cause pollution and that can surely harm us *slowly*.　車は環境を汚すので、じわじわと私たちに害を与えている。

---

small /smɔ́ːl/

原義は〈小さい〉である。**(大きさが)小さい、(数が)少ない、(物事の程度が)ささいな**。
派 smallness (微小)

The copier is *small* enough to sit on the desk.　このコピー機はこの机にちょうどいい大きさだ。

The world grows *smaller* as technology accelerates communication and transportation.　技術が交信と交通を加速するにつれて、世界はだんだん小さくなっている。

Wow, you and I are from the same hometown! It sure is a *small* world [=It's a *small* world after all].　えっ、君と僕とは同郷なんだ！ ほんとに世間は狭いね。

smoke /smóuk/

原義は〈煙〉である. **煙；煙る，喫煙する.**
派 smoked（燻製(くんせい)の）；smoker（喫煙者）；smoky（煙っている）

My father neither *smokes* nor drinks.　父は酒もタバコもやらない.

Where there's *smoke*, there's fire. ＝There is no *smoke* without fire.
《諺》火のないところには煙は立たない〔←うわさはむげに否定できない〕.

I was caught *smoking* a cigarette at school and was suspended for a week.　学校で喫煙しているところを見つかって，1週間の停学になった.

society /səsáɪəti/

語源は〈socie（人びとが交わる）ty（こと）〉である. **(人びとの行き交う) 社会，世間；(同志の集まり) 協会.**
派 sociable（社交的な）；sociability（社交性）；socialize（つき合う）
関 associate（～と…を関連づける）

Every *society* has its own culture and way of life.　どんな社会でも独特の文化や生活習慣があるものだ.

Society has become more dependent on technology than ever before.
社会はこれまでにないほどテクノロジーに依存するようになった.

They established the American Cancer *Society* that provides money for scientists who are studying cancer.　がんを研究している科学者に資金を提供する「米国癌協会」を設立した.

solve /sá:lv/

語源は〈so(離す)lve(解く)〉である.**(もつれを解き放つ)問題を解決する**.
派 solution(解決)

War has not *solved* any problems. It created more all the time.　戦争は何ら問題を解決した試しがない.いつも問題を増幅してきただけだ.

Don't worry about such little things; time will *solve* everything.　そんなささいなことを心配することないよ.時間が何でも解決してくれるよ.

I'll see if I can come up with a *solution* for the problem.　その問題の解決策を思いつくか考えてみましょう.

some /sʌ́m/

原義は〈いくらかの〉である.**いくらかの;(ある程度の)→相当の**.物事の存在・数量を漠然と捉える.

Would you like *some* milk in your coffee?　コーヒーにミルクを入れましょうか.

There are *some* people who get a thrill out of teasing others.　他人をいじめてスリルを味わう人がいる.

Some people never seem to get fat *while others* are always on a diet.　食べてもちっとも太らない人もあれば,いつも食事制限している人もいる.

That was *some* party!　結構なパーティーだったよ.　▶時に皮肉に響くこともある.

soon /súːn/

原義は〈やがて，まもなく〉である．**(ある時を基準に) 物事の発生までの時間が短い．**

How *soon* do I have to make a reply?　いつまでにご返答すればよろしいですか．

How *soon* can I eat after the surgery?　手術後いつから食べられますか．

If you miss a dose, take it *as soon as* you remember.　もし服用を忘れていたら，気づいた時にすぐに飲みなさい．

No sooner had I started speaking on the cell phone *than* it ran out of battery.　携帯電話で話し始めた途端に電池切れになった．

---

sorry /sάːri/

語源は〈sore（痛んで）y（いる）〉である．**〜のことで心が痛む，すまなく思う．**
関 sore（痛む）

I'm sorry I've kept you waiting.　待たせてごめんなさい．

"I feel we should have prepared better." "It's too late to be *sorry*."
「もっとしっかり準備しておくべきだったと思うよ」「悔やんでもあとの祭りだよ」

Stop feeling *sorry* for yourself, and make a positive change in your life.　自分のしたことを悔むのはもうやめて，生き方の転換を図りなさい．

sort /sɔ́ːrt/

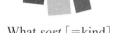

原義は〈振り分ける〉である. **種類別に分ける**；**種類**.
派 sorter（選別機）

What *sort* [=kind] *of* careers are there in sociology? 社会学を修めるとどんな就職口がありますか.

My hometown is *the sort* [=kind] *of* place where everyone knows everyone else. 私の田舎は誰でも互いを知っているような所だよ.

Trash must be separated and *sorted* into plastics, glass, and paper. ごみは分けて，プラスチック，ガラス，紙に分類しないといけない.

sound /sáund/

原義は〈(うねる)音〉である. **音；響く，～のように響く・思われる**.
派 soundly（ぐっすりと）
関 sonar（音波探知機）；surround（取り囲む）

Aren't you getting a cold? Your voice *sounds* hoarse. かぜ，引きかけてない？ 声がかすれているよ〔←かすれて聞こえる〕.

His logic doesn't *sound* sensible to me. 彼の論理はどうも理解しがたい.

You shouldn't have said that in that way; what you suggested doesn't *sound like* you. あんなふうに言うべきじゃなかったよ. あの意見は君らしくないね.

source /sɔ́ːrs/

原義は〈(湧き出る)源〉である. **発生源；調達する**.
関 surge (せり上がる)；outsource (外部委託する, 調達する)

Carrots are a good *source* of fiber and vitamin A.　ニンジンは食物繊維とビタミン A が多く摂取できる.

What is the main *source* of income for the city?　この市の主な収入源は何ですか.

The reporter refused to reveal the news *source*.　記者はニュースの発信源を明かそうとしなかった.

We *source* all the vegetables sold in our stores from local farms.　我々の店で売っている野菜はすべて, 地元の農家から買い付けたものです.

space /spéɪs/

原義は〈空間, 間隔〉である. **スペース (空間), 間隔**.
派 spacious (広びろとした)

The room has been furnished to give a feeling of *space*.　この部屋は家具の配置がいいので広びろとした感じがする.

Always keep enough *space* [=distance] between your car and the one ahead.　常に前車との車間を十分に取りなさい.

spare /spéər/

原義は〈控える〉である．**全体の中の一部のみを使う→倹約する，惜しむ，残す；余分の，予備の；予備品．**
派 sparing (少ない)；sparingly (控えめに)
関 spare key (合い鍵)；spareribs (豚の骨付きあばら骨)《複数扱い》

Thank you so much for *sparing* the time out of your busy schedule.　お忙しいのに，時間を割いていただいて本当にありがとう．

We have no time to *spare*. Could you hurry up a little please?　時間的余裕がありません．もう少し急いでいただけませんか．

During the World War II, Kyoto was *spared* from much of the destruction.　第二次世界大戦中，京都は壊滅的被害をほとんど免れた．　▶ be spared「(被害などから) 免れる」

He ⌈is *sparing* with his praise [=praises people very little]⌉.　彼は人をあまりほめない．

---

speak /spíːk/

原義は〈ことばを発する〉である．**話す，しゃべる．**
派 speaker (演説者，スピーカー)；speech (しゃべり，スピーチ)；speechless (口がきけない)

She *speaks* with a Kyoto accent.　彼女は京都弁で話す．

His mother lost her *speech* [=voice] after the surgery on the throat.　彼の母親は咽喉(?)の手術後，しゃべることが出来なくなった．

The child ⌈is slow in *speech* [=*speaks* very little for his age]⌉.　その子はことば (の発達) が遅い．

source, space, spare, speak

speed /spíːd/

原義は〈急ぐ〉である. **速力；急ぐ，急がせる**.
派 speedy（迅速な）; speedily（迅速に）

You need *speed* and endurance for the 1500-meter race.　1500メートル走では速さと持久力が要求される.

I *sped* [=hurried] along the highway, feeling the spring breeze through the window.　車窓からの春風を感じながら高速道路を飛ばした.

He was caught *speeding* [=breaking the speed limit].　彼はスピード違反で捕まった.

The Bank of Japan took steps to「*speed up* the [=ensure speedy] recovery from deflation.　日本銀行はデフレからの回復を早めるための策を打った.

spend /spénd/

原義は〈費やす〉である. **金・時間・労力を費やす**.
派 spending（支出）　関 expend（費やす）

We *spend* about one-third of our lives asleep.　我々は人生の三分の一を寝て過ごす.

I *spent* more money than I made last month.　先月は赤字だった〔稼ぎより出費が多かった〕.

Many women *spend* a lot of time and energy to be beautiful.　多くの女性は，きれいになるためにたくさんの時間と努力を費やす.

spot /spá:t/

原義は〈小さな点〉である. **地点, 斑点；しみを付ける；見つける**.
派 spotless (汚れのない)

My dog has several black *spots* on his nose.　うちの犬は鼻に黒い斑点が数個ある.

He was thrown out of the car from the backseat, and died *on the spot*.　彼は後部座席から投げ出されて即死した〔←その場で死んだ〕.

The comet was first *spotted* [=discovered] by a Japanese amateur astronomer.　この彗星(すい)は日本のアマチュア天文家によって最初に発見された.

spread /spréd/

原義は〈広げる〉である. **かたまりを全面に広げる, 手や脚を伸ばす**.
関 widespread (普及している)

You can *spread* [=divide] the payments over a certain number of months.　支払いは数か月に分けて分割できます.

In Japan, it is illegal to *spread* [=scatter] cremated ashes freely in the sea.　日本では, 遺灰を勝手に海にまくのは違法だ.

HIV is still *spreading* [=increasing] worldwide.　HIV 感染症は依然, 世界的に広がっている.

stable /stéibl/

stable　　　unstable

語源は〈st（立って）able（いる）〉である. **(動かない) → 安定している**.
派 stability（安定性）; stabilize（安定させる）
関 stand（立っている）; establish（設立する）

My father has to remain in the hospital for another month, but his condition is *stable*.　父はもう1か月入院しないといけないが, 容態は安定している.

The price of crude oil has been *unstable*. ＝There's no *stability* in the price of crude oil.　原油価格が不安定だ.

staff /stǽf/

原義は〈支えるもの〉である. **組織を支える（員＋員＋員＋員）→部員, 職員, スタッフ**. 組織内の〈複数の構成員〉が総体的にイメージされる.

These victim support organizations are *staffed* by volunteers.　これらの被災者支援団体のスタッフはボランティアである.

How big is the sales *staff* of this company?　この会社の営業部員は何人ぐらいいますか.

She has been「*on the staff*［＝a member of the *staff*］of NHK for over twenty years.　彼女は20余年 NHK の職員を務めている.

stage /stéɪdʒ/

原義は〈立つ所〉である. **舞台;(進展過程の一つの)段階**.
関 stand (立つ)

Palliative care is provided for those patients who are in the last *stage* of cancer.　がんの末期患者のために緩和ケアが施される.

He has become a very important figure on the political *stage* [= arena].　彼は政治の舞台で大物になった.

stand /stǽnd/

原義は〈立つ〉である. **立つ→立ち続ける→我慢する**.
関 distance (立つ); constant (絶え間ない); contrast (対照); stable (安定している); stage (舞台); standard (標準の); stay (とどまる)

He *stands* 164 centimeters and weighs 60 kilos.　彼は身長164センチ, 体重60キロだ.

Grand champion, Futabayama, won 69 bouts in a row in 1939; the record ⌈still *stands* today [=is yet to be broken]⌉.　横綱双葉山は1939年に69連勝したが, その記録はいまだ破られていない.

I can't *stand* [=put up with] the way he treats me.　彼の私に対する振る舞いは我慢できない.

The draft for the speech is OK as it *stands* [=is].　スピーチの草稿はそのままでいいです〔←修正の必要はない〕.

standard /stǽndərd/

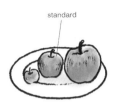

原義は〈兵の集結地点を示す旗〉である．**基準，標準；標準の，標準となる．**
派 standardize（規格化する）　関 stand（立つ）

Always set high *standards* for your work.　仕事をする時はいつも，高い基準を設けるようにしなさい．

His performance is below [=not up to] *standard* for pro leagues.
彼の技量はプロでやれる水準ではない．

The first performer is the *standard* by which all others are judged.
最初の演技者は，以降の演技者の判定の基準になる．

start /stá:rt/

原義は〈跳ねる〉である．**さっと動き始める→始める，始まる；開始．**
派 startle（びっくりさせる）

List the words that *start* [=begin] with the letter "z."　"z"で始まる単語を挙げなさい．

The meeting *starts* [=begins] at 10 a.m.　会議は10時に始まります．

Let's get *started* with the third lesson on page fifty-one.　51ページの3課から始めましょう．

The exhibition lasts for a month *starting* [=beginning] tomorrow.
展示会は明日から1か月間，開催される．

state /stéɪt/

原義は〈(確たる) 有り様〉である. **状態；(しっかりと)述べる**.
派 statement (声明)

How do you find the present *state* of things in the economic reform?
経済改革の現状をどう思いますか.

Proper breathing may control your *state* of mind as well as your body.　正しい呼吸法は, 身体だけでなく精神状態も整えることができる.

"We will overcome this difficult situation," the president *stated* [= spoke] simply.　「我々はこの難局を乗り越える」と, 大統領はきっぱり宣言した.

stay /stéɪ/

原義は〈立っている〉である. **場所にとどまる；変更・変化なくとどまる**.
派 statue (彫像)　関 stand (立っている)

Some supermarkets *stay* open on New Year's day.　元日に開いているスーパーもある.

Getting old is inevitable, but try to *stay* young in mind and heart.
歳を取るのは仕方ないけど, 気持ちは若いままでいるように努めなさい.

I hope the weather will *stay* nice into this weekend.　週末まで好天がもちますように.

Stay away from people who speak ill of others behind their backs.
他人の悪口を陰で言うような人とは関わらないようにしなさい.

step /stép/

原義は〈足で踏む〉である. **一歩一歩歩く；歩み, 段階**.
関 stamp（踏みつける）

She went up onto the stage with a quick and light *step*.　彼女は軽い足取りで舞台へ上がっていった.

The company has just taken the first *step* towards its reconstruction after the disaster.　会社は被災後, 再建に向けてようやく最初の一歩を踏み出した.

His ideas always seem to be one *step* ahead of the times.　彼の考えはいつも時代に一歩先行しているようだ.

The steps are wet and slippery. *Watch your step*!　階段はぬれて滑りやすいよ. 足元（足の運び）に気をつけて！

---

still /stíl/

原義は〈じっとして動かない〉である. **じっとした, 静かな；依然そのままである**.
派 stillness（静けさ）　関 stall（立ち止まる）

When the explosion happened, it felt as if time was standing *still*.　爆発の瞬間は, まるで時が止まっているようだった.

Some students can't sit *still* in class.　授業中にじっと座っていることができない子どもがいる.

My father is 70 and is *still* working part time.　父は70歳だが, まだパートで働いている.

stop /stá:p/

stop

原義は〈穴をふさぐ〉である．**(流れをふさいで止める)→動きを止める**．
関 stuff（詰め込む）

They have to *stop* [＝put a *stop* to] Iran's nuclear development before it is too late.　イランの核開発を今のうちにやめさせなければならない．

Stop being so negative; we should start with things we can do.　そんなに落ち込まないで；できることから始めればいいのよ．

My boy is completely addicted to video games. He just can't *stop* playing them.　うちの子ったらゲームに夢中なの．どうしてもやめられないのよ．

I think the rain will *stop* [＝let up] before long.　もうすぐ雨は上がると思う．

Stop and think before you act.　行動する前にじっくり〔←立ち止まって〕考えなさい．

---

store /stɔ́:r/

原義は〈蓄え〉である．**物を蓄える；(情報・知識の)蓄え；(品物を蓄えて売る)店**．
関 restaurant（レストラン）〔←再びエネルギーを蓄えるところ〕; restore（回復する）

Instructions for controlling the mechanisms of life are *stored* [＝programmed] in DNA.　生命体の仕組みを制御する指示は，DNAの中にプログラムされ〔組み込まれ〕ている．

The camel *stores* fat in its hump.　ラクダはこぶの中に脂肪を蓄えている．

Store the bulbs in a dry, airy place.　球根は湿気の少ない風通しのよい場所に保管しなさい．

story /stɔ́ːri/

原義は〈事実についての話〉である．**事実に基づく話→想像力によって生み出す話，物語．**
関 history (歴史)

The smile on his face told the *story*.　彼の笑顔から事の次第がどうであったか分かった．

A clown doesn't have to say very much because his action tells the *story*.　道化師は，身振りで物語を伝えるのであまりしゃべらなくてよい．

You shouldn't judge people or things by hearing only one side of the *story*.　一方の意見だけで人や事態を判断してはならない．

It is best to compare the same *stories* told by different reporters.　同じ事件の経緯をいろいろなレポーターの記事で比べてみるのが一番いい．

---

stress /strés/

原義は〈圧迫する〉である．**重圧をかける，強調する；重圧，強調．**
派 stressful (ストレスの多い)
関 distress (苦悩); strain (引っ張る，締め付ける)

I feel a lot of *stress* [＝pressure] with this job.　この仕事はプレッシャー(重圧)がかかる．

Good music helps me ease the *stresses* [＝pressures] of daily life.　よい音楽は毎日の生活のストレス(緊張感)を和らげてくれる．

He *stressed* [＝emphasized] the importance of early childhood education.　彼は幼児教育の大切さを強く訴えた．

Just thinking about being interviewed ⌈is *stressful* [＝makes me feel *stressed*]．　面接を受けることを思うだけで緊張する．

struggle /strʌ́gl/

原義は〈もがく〉である. **困難を打ち破ろうと懸命に努力する；苦闘**.

Boxers have to *struggle* [=make an all out effort] to lose weight before a fight. ボクサーは試合をする前に減量に苦労しなければならない.

Some Euro countries are *struggling* [=suffering] economically. ユーロ加盟国の中には経済的に苦しんでいる国がある.

All living things are destined to *struggle* [=fight] for existence. すべての生物は生存のために戦うことが宿命だ.

study /stʌ́di/

原義は〈専念する〉である. **じっくり学ぶ，研究する；じっくり観察する**.
派 student (学生)；studious (熱心な)

He is *studying* [=majoring in] mathematics at Kyoto University. 彼は京都大学で数学を専攻している.

She *studied* [=examined] my face secretly to make sure I was not offended. 彼女は，僕が気分を害していないか確かめようとこっそり僕の顔を観察した.

People in ancient times used to tell fortunes by *studying* [=observing] the stars. 昔の人は星の動きを調べて予言していた.

stuff /stʌ́f/

原義は〈すき間に詰める〉である. **詰め込む；(詰まった) 物質, 要素, 素質.**
関 stop (止める)

He *stuffed* [=packed] food and spare clothes in his rucksack. 彼はリュックに食料と着替えを詰め込んだ.

"Would you like some more?" "No, thank you. I'm *stuffed* [=I've had enough]." 「もう少しいかがですか」「いいえ結構です. 満腹です」

The investigator examined all the *stuff* [=things] in his bag. 捜査員は彼のバッグの中身を全部調べた.

Do you have ⌈all your *stuff* [=everything with you]? 忘れ物はありませんか〔←持ち物は皆ありますか〕.

---

subject /名形 sʌ́bdʒekt, 動 səbdʒékt/

語源は〈sub (下に) ject (投げる)〉である. **(投げ出す) 話題, 主題, 主語；(投げ出されて～の前で) お手上げ状態である, ～に対して支配・統制を受ける.**
派 subjective (主観的な)
関 project (企画)〔←前に＋投げる〕

Anti-aging is a *subject* [=topic] of great interest to health freaks. 老化防止は健康オタクの人たちの格好の話題だ.

All things including customs and morals are *subject to change* over time. 習慣や道徳を始め, すべてのことは時とともに変化するものだ.

This document is ⌈not *subject to* [=available without infringing] copyright. この文書は自由に用いてよろしい〔←版権に抵触することなく利用できる〕. ▶be subject to ...「…が課せられる」

succeed /səksíːd/

語源は〈suc（次に）ceed（来る）〉である．**次につながる（継続する）→途切れずに首尾よくつながる（成功する）**．

派 success（成功）; successful（うまくいく）; successfully（何とか）; succeeding（次の）; successive（連続する）

Who did Donald Trump *succeed* as president?＝Who was the president before Donald Trump?　ドナルド・トランプは誰のあとを引き継いで大統領になりましたか．

I have no doubt that he will *succeed* [＝be *successful*] in his new business.　彼は今度の商売で間違いなく成功すると思う．

suffer /sʌ́fər/

語源は〈suf（下に）fer（運ぶ）〉である．**（重圧・苦労を背負う）→〜で苦しむ;（損害・痛みを受ける）→〜に襲われる**．
派 sufferer（患者）; suffering（苦痛）
関 ferry（フェリー）〔←運ぶもの〕

He *suffered* a heart attack while playing basketball.　彼はバスケットボールをしているときに心臓発作に襲われた．

He *suffers from* heart disease.　彼は心臓病を患っている．

What else can cause more *suffering* than war?　戦争以上に人を苦しめるものが他にあるだろうか．

Buddha mentioned four human *sufferings*, living, aging, illness, and death.　ブッダは四つの人間の苦しみ，生・老・病・死があると言った．

suggest /səgdʒést/

語源は〈sug（下から）gest（運ぶ）〉である．**(下から差し出す) →控えめに意見を出す，さりげなく表す**．
派 suggestive（思わせぶりな）; suggestion（提案）

"This doesn't work well." "I *suggest* [=have a *suggestion* that] you call the consumer complaint department." 「これ，うまく作動しないよ」「消費者苦情係に電話しなさいよ」

Some lyrics are too *suggestive* [=sexy] for prime time TV shows. テレビのゴールデンタイムの番組にしてはあまりに思わせぶりな歌詞のものがある．

suit /súːt/

原義は〈従う，追う〉である．**(従う→合わせる) →うまくかみ合う；(上下そろいの) スーツ；(追う) →追及→告訴**．
派 suitable（適している）; suitably（適切に）

I finally found a job that ⌈*suits* me best [=is ideal for me]. やっと理想の仕事が見つかった．

A cold climate doesn't *suit* [=agree with] me. 寒冷な気候は私の体に合わない．

Do you have to wear a dark *suit* in your workplace? 職場では黒っぽいスーツを着用しないといけないの？

He ⌈*filed a suit* [=started legal proceedings] against the employer. 彼は雇用主を相手取って訴訟を起こした．

sum /sˊʌm/

原義は〈加えた合計→頂上〉である. **一番上→（全体をまとめ上げた）合計**.

派 summary（概要）；summarize（要約する）；summit（頂上）

You need a large *sum* [=amount] of money to repair the house. 家の改修は多額の金がかかる.

What is the *sum* [=total] of the angles in a triangle? 三角形の内角の総和はいくらですか.

Sum up [=*Summarize*] your main points at the end of your presentation. プレゼンの終わりに要点をまとめて言いなさい.

sun /sˊʌn/

原義は〈太陽〉である. **太陽, 日光, 日なた**.
派 sunny（晴れている）
関 sunlight（日光）；sunset（日の入り）；sunrise（日の出）；sunscreen（日焼け止め）；sunshine（日差し）

The rain has stopped and *the sun* is ⌈coming out [=beginning to shine]⌉. 雨がやんで日が差してきた.

The sun was in my eyes and I failed to see the traffic light. 太陽が目に入って信号が見えなかった.

Cats love basking [=bathing] in *the sun*. 猫は日なたぼっこが好きだ.

It becomes dark quickly after *the sun* sets in late autumn. 晩秋には日が落ちるとすぐに暗くなる.

supply /səpláɪ/

語源は〈sup(次に)ply(重ねる)〉である. **必要に応じて〜を供給する;供給, 支給, 支給品.**
派 supplier(供給者)

This company *supplies* [=provides] parts and components to leading automobile manufacturers.　この会社は大手自動車メーカーに部品を調達している.

Our bodies need a constant *supply* of oxygen in order to stay alive.　私たちの体は, 生きていくために酸素の供給を絶えず必要としている.

It is reported that North Korea needs food *supplies* from other countries.　北朝鮮は他国からの食糧支援が必要だと報道されている.

support /səpɔ́ːrt/

support

語源は〈sup(下から)port(支える)〉である. **倒れないように支える→活動を支える, 支持する;支持.**
派 supporter(支持者); supportive(支えとなる)

While going to college, he *supported* [=maintained] himself by working part-time.　彼はアルバイトで自活しながら大学へ通った.

Do you *support* [=Are you for] the current government?　現政権を支持しますか.

The investigators found no evidence to *support* [=prove] any charges of criminal activity.　捜査官は刑事告発につながる証拠を何も見つけられなかった.

suppose /səpóuz/

語源は〈sup(下から)pose(置く)〉である. **そっと考えを述べる→どうも～であると思う**.
派 supposed(〔事実であると〕言われている); supposedly(一般的に言われているところでは)
関 propose(提案する); oppose(反対する)

Which team do you *suppose* [=think] will win? どのチームが優勝すると思いますか.

How many hours a week are you *supposed* to work? 週当たり何時間働くことになっていますか.

You *are supposed to* take any lost and found items to the police. 落し物を見つけたら警察に届けないといけない〔←届けることになっている〕.

---

sure /ʃúər/

原義は〈しっかりした〉である. **確実な, きっと(～である)《主観性の強い確信判断》**. 類義語 certain は客観性の強い〈確信判断〉の意味合い.
派 surely(確かに)　関 ensure(確実にする)

"That's Sarah's father." "Are you *sure*?" 「あれはサラの父親だよ」「確かなの?」

Both teams are of the same strength; *it's sure to* [=*I'm sure that* it will] be a close game. 両チームの力は互角だから, きっと接戦になるよ.

Make sure that the front door is locked. 玄関の戸は必ず鍵を掛けてね.

surround /səráund/

語源は〈sur（越えて）ound（うねる）→（うねりあふれるように）取り囲む〉である. **取り囲む**.
派 surroundings（環境）　関 sound（音）〔←うねる〕

An island is *surrounded* by water on all sides, while a peninsula is *surrounded* by water on only three sides.　島は四方を海に囲まれているが，半島は三面だけ囲まれている.

Surround yourself with positive people who believe in you and inspire you.　あなたを信用し，元気をもらえるような前向きな人と交際しなさい.
▶ surround oneself with ...「自分の周りに…を置く」

It took me a while to get used to my new *surroundings* [= environment].　新しい環境に慣れるのにしばらくかかった.

survey /sə́ːrveɪ/

語源は〈sur（上から）vey（見る）〉である. **(物事を)見渡す→調査する**.
派 surveillance（監視）
関 supervise（監督する）〔←上から＋見る〕

A recent *survey* found that 70 percent of all adults over 50 wear glasses for driving.　最近のある調査によると，50歳以上の運転者の70％がめがねを使用するそうだ.

NHK *surveyed* randomly selected 1,000 people and asked which party they support.　NHKは無作為に選んだ1,000人にアンケートを取り，どの政党を支持するか調べた.

survive /sərváɪv/

survive

語源は〈sur(越えて) vive(生きる)〉である. **困難・苦境を越えて生き続ける**.
派 survival(生存); survivor(生存者)

It's a miracle: the entire population of 360 people in this community *survived* the tsunami.　この地区の360人全員が津波に命を奪われなかったのは奇跡だ.

I don't make enough money. I am wondering how I will *survive* on my low wages.　十分な稼ぎはない. この低収入でどうやって生活していくか考えているんだ.

He ⌈is *survived* by [=died, leaving behind] his wife and three children.　彼は妻と3人の子どもを残して他界した.

---

suspect /動 səspékt, 名形 sʌ́spekt/

語源は〈sus(下から) spect(見る)〉である. **(密かに見る→控えめに判断する)→〜ではないかと思う; 容疑者**.
派 suspicion(容疑, 疑い); suspicious(疑わしい)

He reads an astronomical magazine regularly. I *suspect* he loves watching the stars.　彼は定期的に天文雑誌を読んでいる. 彼は星空観測が好きなんだろうと思う.

As I *suspected* the bus was so crowded that I could barely move.　案の定, バスは満員で身動きできないほどだった.

Chemicals used in agriculture are *suspected* of causing cancer.　農薬はがんの原因になるかもしれないと考えられている.

system /sístəm/

語源は〈sy(共に)stem(配すること)〉である.**各部分を配して組み上げたもの→システム(仕組み)**.人体は究極の system である.
派 systematic(組織的な)

Some foods can boost your immune *system*, preventing you from getting a cold and other diseases. 食べ物の中には,免疫機能を高め,かぜや諸々の病気の予防に効くものがある.

The subway *system* in Tokyo is the most highly used, convenient transit *system* in the world. 東京の地下鉄網は世界でもっとも利用者の多い便利な交通システムである.

Heavy drinking is not good for your *system*. 深酒は体に悪い.

take /téɪk/

原義は〈手でつかむ〉である.**(つかむ→取る)持って行く,連れて行く;態度を取る,考えを取る;時間を取る**.
関 touch(触れる)

Take your umbrella with you just in case. 念のために傘を持って行きなさい.

Take it easy! 気楽にね〔←気楽に受け止めて〕! ▶take(受け止める)+it(事・状況を)+easy(楽に)

The government urged corporations to *take* cyber attacks seriously and be prepared. 政府は企業に,サイバー攻撃を真剣に受け止め対策を講じるように促した.

How long does it usually *take* to get a driver's license? 運転免許の取得にはふつう,どれくらいの日数がかかりますか.

talent /tǽlənt/

原義は〈価値〉である. **価値ある才能**.
派 talented (才能豊かな)

She has a real *talent* for [=is really *talented* at] playing the piano.
彼女はピアノの本当の才能がある.

People often lament, "I just don't have any *talents* to achieve anything," but I think everyone has the potential to be good at something. 人はよく「私って何の才能もないの」って嘆くけど, 誰でも何かに上達する可能性は持っていると思う.

talk /tɔ́ːk/

原義は〈しゃべる〉である. **しゃべる**. talk は〈しゃべる〉, tell は〈語る〉, speak は〈話す〉の意味合い.
派 talkative (話し好きな)

I can't stand being alone. I always need someone to *talk* with. 私ってひとりぼっちが耐えられないの. いつも誰かと話してないとだめなの.

Don't *talk* to me now. I'm busy. 今話しかけないで. 忙しいから.

My students won't stop *talking* [=whispering] in class. 私の受け持ちの生徒たちは, 授業中の私語をどうしてもやめないのよ.

tall /tɔ́ːl/

原義は〈背丈が高い〉である．**背が高い；〜ほどの背丈・高さがある**．tall は〈全長に着目して高い〉，high は〈頂点に着目して高い〉の意味合い．

Being *tall* is advantageous for most of the sports.　背が高いことはたいていのスポーツで有利に働く．

The Tokyo Sky Tree stands at 634 meters *tall*.　東京スカイツリーは高さ634メートルだ．

Don't slouch and try to stand *tall* all the time.　猫背にならないように，いつも背筋を伸ばしているように努めなさい．

target /tá:rgət/

語源は〈targ (盾) et (小さな)〉である．**射撃の的→目標；目標に定める，標的にする**．

We failed to meet the month's sales *target* [=goal] by five percent.　月間売り上げ目標に5パーセント及ばなかった．

This magazine *targets* [=The *target* audience of this magazine is] teenage gamers.　この雑誌は十代のゲーマーを読者対象にしている．

The newly launched computer models are *targeting* [=*targeted* at] elderly users.　新型コンピュータは高齢のユーザーを狙っている．

task /tǽsk/

原義は〈課せられた仕事〉である. **義務としてすべき仕事, 任務；仕事を課す**.
関 tax (税)

Don't think too far ahead; focus on the *task* at hand. あまり先案じせず, 今, すべきことに集中しなさい.

It is ⌈quite a *task* [=not an easy *task*]⌉ for me to write a paper in English. 英語で論文を書くのは僕にはとてもやっかいなんだ.

She is ⌈*tasked* with [=assigned the job of]⌉ checking the execution of the budget. 彼女は予算執行の監査を任されている.

taste /téɪst/

原義は〈舌の感触〉である. **舌の感触→①味；味がする. ②味→好み→嗜好(しこう)**.
派 tasty (味がよい)

Food *tastes* better outdoors. 戸外で食べると, うんとおいしく感じる.

I *tasted* the soup to see if it was salty enough. スープの塩味がちゃんとついているか味見した.

She is too skinny for my *taste*. 彼女は僕の好みからするとやせすぎだ.

He is very business-minded and has little *taste* for literature. 彼は商売一辺倒で, 文学の趣味などはほとんどない.

Oh, your house looks great. You have good *taste* in furniture. まあ, すばらしいお宅ですね. 家具の趣味がとてもいいわ.

teach /tíːtʃ/

原義は〈指し示す〉である. **教える**.
派 teacher（教師）; teaching（教職, 教育）
関 self-taught（独学の）

Dad *taught* me how to ride a bike when I was five or six. 父さんは, 私が5, 6歳のころ, 自転車の乗り方を教えてくれた.

My husband ⌈is a math *teacher* [=*teaches* math] at a local high school. 夫は地元の高校で数学を教えている.

I've been *teaching* myself German because I'm going to travel in Germany next year. 来年, ドイツを旅するので, ドイツ語を独学している.

tear¹ /téər/

原義は〈引き裂く〉である. **布や紙を引き裂く, 皮膚・じん帯などを裂傷する**.

He *tore* the manuscript to pieces and threw them into the trash can. 彼は原稿をびりびり破ってゴミ箱へ投げ入れた.

He *tore* [=ripped] his pants on a barbed wire fence. 彼は有刺鉄線の柵にズボンをひっかけて破ってしまった.

I partially *tore* a ligament in my ankle during soccer practice. サッカーの練習中にくるぶしのじん帯を部分断裂した.

tear² /tíər/

原義は〈涙〉である．**涙**．

I just couldn't hold back my *tears* when I heard the news. その知らせを聞いた時，涙を抑えることができなかった．

She couldn't tell the story without *tears* [=*tears* in her eyes]. 彼女は涙なしにそのことを話すことはできなかった．

The child *burst into tears* upon entering into the darkness of the theater. その子は映画館の暗闇に入るとわっと泣き出した．

tell /tél/

原義は〈語る〉である．**出来事について語る，きちんと言う，言いつける；分かる，判別する**．tell は〈語る〔←話の内容を意識している〕〉，類義語 talk は〈しゃべる〔←話す行為を意識している〕〉の意味合い．
派 tale (物語)；teller (〔銀行等の〕窓口係)

Why didn't you bring your umbrella? I *told* you it would rain! どうして傘を持ってこなかったの．雨になるって言ったでしょ．

Don't ask why; here, you are supposed to do as you're *told*. つべこべ言わずに，ここでは言われた通りにしなさい．

How do you *tell* an edible mushroom from an inedible one? 食べられるキノコと毒キノコはどうやって区別するの．

tend /ténd/

原義は〈張り出す〉である. **(〜へ向かう) 傾向がある.**
派 tendency (傾向)

Shy children *tend* to be nervous around people they don't know well.
恥ずかしがりやの子は知らない人と一緒にいると緊張しがちだ.

Some people ⌈*tend* to [=are likely to] gain weight easily.⌉　太りやすい傾向の人がいる.

People have a *tendency* to talk too fast when they're nervous.　人は緊張すると早口になる傾向がある.

term /tə́ːrm/

原義は〈区切り〉である. **(時間の長さを限る) 期間, 期限；(状況を限る) 条件, 関係；(意味範囲を限る) 用語, 専門語.**
派 terminate (終わらせる)；terminal (末期の；〔空港・鉄道などの〕ターミナル)　関 determine (決める)

The mayor's *term* of office expires next January.　市長の在任期間は1月で切れる.

On what *terms* are you employed?　どういう条件で雇用されているのですか.

The teacher teaches science ⌈using simple *terms* [=without using technical language]⌉.　先生は易しいことばを使って理科を教えてくれる.

Eggs are superb *in terms of* overall nutritional value.　卵は総合的に栄養価がある点でとても優れている.

text /tékst/

原義は〈編む〉である．**文を編む→メールする**；**文言**，**本文**，**メール**，**テキスト**．
派 textual（文章の）
関 context（文脈）；textbook（教科書）；text message（メール〔の文言〕）；texture（感触，手触り）

We aren't allowed to *text* [=send] a personal message while on the job. 仕事中に私信をメールすることは許されていない．

I just got a *text* [=message] from a colleague. 同僚からメールが来た．

I love the *text* [=words] and tune of the song. この歌の詩もメロディーも好きだ．

thank /θǽŋk/

原義は〈心から思う〉である．**心から思う→感謝する**．thank と think（思う）は同系語．
派 thankful（ありがたく思っている）；thankfully（ありがたいことに）；thanks（感謝）

I'm a bit late. *Thank* you for waiting. 少し遅れてしまいました．待っていただいてありがとう．

Please extend my *thanks* [=gratitude] to everyone in the family. ご家族の皆さんへもありがとうと（感謝の気持ちを）お伝えください．

I bought him a meal ⌈as a *thank-you* [=to show *thanks*] for his help. 彼に手伝ってもらったお礼に食事をおごった．　▶thank-you「礼，感謝のしるし」

then /ðén/

原義は〈その時〉である．**その時，それから，それなら．**

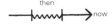

I would like to have it finished by *then* [=that time]. その時までに仕上げておきたいと思います．

His first album came out in 2010, and *then* six months later it ranked number 1 in sales. 彼の初めてのアルバムは2010年に出たが，(それから) 6か月後には売り上げランキング1位になった．

The Great Buddha Statue of Nara was built in 752. Nara was *then* [=at that time] the capital of Japan. 奈良の大仏は752年に建立された．奈良は当時，日本の首都であった．

thing /θíŋ/

原義は〈事件〉である．**(抽象的な) 物事，事柄 → (具体的な) 物．**

What do you think is the most important *thing* in your life? あなたの人生でもっとも大切なことは何だと思いますか．

We're going to take *things* easy this Christmas and just rest. 今年のクリスマスはのんびり過ごし [物事を楽にとらえて]，専ら休むつもりです．

This book tells you about how *things* [=the world] will be in 2050. この本は，2050年には世界がどうなっているかについて語っている．

Lots of nice ⌈*things* for the kitchen [=kitchen utensils] are on sale in this store. この店でたくさんの台所用品が特売されている．

think /θíŋk/

原義は〈考える〉である。**～であると考える；～について考える，思いつく．**
派 thinking（考え方；思慮深い）; thought（考え）; thoughtful（思いやりのある）

I *think* very much so.　本当にそうだと思う．

The teacher makes the students *think* before she gives answers.　その先生は解答をする前に生徒に考えさせる．

Thinking about it again [=On second thought], I *think* your choice was right.　考え直してみると，あなたの選択は間違ってなかったと思う．

Think again [=*Think* over again]: it could cost you.　よく考えてごらん．大変なことになるかも知れませんよ．　▶ think again は〈再考の促し〉の常とう句．

Her *thinking* [=*thinking* ability] remained clear into her nineties.　彼女の思考力は 90 代になっても明晰（めいせき）であった．

---

threat /θrét/

原義は〈押しつける〉である．**威圧，脅迫．**
派 threaten（脅す）; threatening（脅迫的な）

We are not going to yield to any *threat* of violence.　我々はいかなる暴力の脅しにも屈しない．

We eventually chased out a pushy salesman by *threatening* to call the police.　警察に電話すると脅して，やっとのことでしつこい押し売りを退散させた．

The mayor received a *threatening letter* saying, "Do not run for the next election, or it will cost you your life."　市長は，「今度の選挙に立候補すると命がありませんよ」という脅迫状を受け取った．

through /θrúː/

原義は〈～を貫いて〉である．**～を通じて，通り抜けて，終わって．**
関 throughout (至る所に); thorough (徹底的な)

We don't want younger generations to have to *go through* miserable war experiences.　若い世代の人たちに悲惨な戦争を経験させたくない．

We fly to Seattle *through* [=by way of] Honolulu.　ホノルル経由でシアトルへ行きます．

Oops, I just drove *through* a red light.　おっと，赤信号を突っ切っちゃった．

I usually get information I need *through* computers.　必要な情報をたいていパソコンで得ている．

Sensibilities nurtured when young continue *through* life.　幼い時に育まれた感性は生涯（を通して）続く．

throw /θróu/

原義は〈回す→腕を回して投げる〉である．**さっと投げる，投げかける．**

Let's play catch. *Throw* me the ball [=the ball to me] first and I'll *throw* it back.　キャッチボールしようよ．ボールを投げて，投げ返すから．

The starting pitcher didn't *throw* as well as he was expected to.　先発投手は期待されたほどの投球ができなかった．

The rider hit the guardrail and he was *thrown* from the motorcycle.　ライダーはガードレールに衝突し，バイクから投げ出された．

He *threw* himself onto the bed and fell asleep instantly.　彼はベッドに身を投げ出すや，たちまち寝入った．

tight /táit/

原義は〈密な〉である．**ぎゅーっと詰まった→余裕のない**．
派 tighten（しっかり締める）; tightly（きつく）; tightness（窮屈，ひっ迫）

The old dress was just a little *tight* around the waist, but otherwise it fit perfectly.　昔のドレスは腰回りがちょっときつかったけど，他はぴったりだった．

Because my income decreased by about ten percent, I have to live on a very *tight* budget.　収入が1割ほど減ったので，予算を切り詰めて生活しないといけない．

I have a very *tight* [=busy] schedule for the next few weeks.　来週から2, 3週間はスケジュールが立て込んでいる．

time /táim/

原義は〈時間〉である．**時間，時；時刻を合わせる，かかる時間を計る**．
派 timing（タイミング，間のとり方）; timely（ちょうどよい時の，タイムリーな）

What is the *time* now? = What time is it?　今，何時ですか．

He plays video games whenever he has *time*.　彼は暇さえあればテレビゲームをしている．

Don't worry; I'll propose to her when the *time* comes.　心配しないで．(しかるべき)時期がきたらプロポーズするよ．

The poems Yosano Akiko produced were very liberal and sensual *for the time*.　与謝野晶子の歌は当時としてはとても自由で官能的だった．

There are *times* [=occasions] when smiling is not appropriate.　ほほ笑みを見せてはいけない場面もある．

tire /táiər/

原義は〈疲れさせる〉である. **体を疲れさせる, 体が疲れる；気持ちをうんざりさせる.**
派 tired (疲れた)；tiring (骨の折れる)

The workout has really *tired* me *out*. =I was *tired out* by the workout.　トレーニングで疲れ切った.

I am *tired* [=sick] *of* being told to exercise and lose weight.　運動して減量しなさいといつも言われてうんざりしている.

You may *tire* [=get *tired*] easily for the first few days after the surgery.　手術後の数日間は疲れが出やすいかも知れません.

It was very *tiring* [=exhausting] but really fun.　(それをするのは) 疲れたけど, とてもおもしろかった.

---

to /tú/

原義は「～へ」である. **活動の到達先 (場所, 状態, 時期, 結果など) を指す.**

The tide pool was not deep, but my legs got wet *to* the knees.　潮溜まりは深くはなかったが, ひざまでぬれた.

Children were singing *to* their teacher's piano. 生徒たちは先生のピアノに合わせて歌っていた.

We have only five weeks *to* [=till] the entrance exams.　入試まで5週間しかない.

Mom used to sing me *to* sleep.　母さんはいつも, 歌を歌って私を寝かしつけてくれた〔←眠るまで歌を歌ってくれた〕.

tongue /tˊʌŋ/

原義は〈舌〉である．**舌；(舌から発する) ことば・言語**．
関 tongue twister (早口ことば)

Watch your *tongue* [=Be careful what you say], boy!　君，ことばには気をつけなさい！

Be careful not to burn your *tongue*; these potatoes can be pretty hot.　舌をやけどしないように．ジャガイモはとっても熱いはずだから．

I know her name! It's just *on the tip of my tongue*.　彼女の名前知ってるよ．え〜と，のどまで出かかっているのだけど．

Portuguese is her *mother tongue*. =She grew up speaking Portuguese.　彼女の母語はポルトガル語です．

top /tάːp/

原義は〈頂上の部分〉である．**一番高い所，上部，表面**．
関 tip (先端)

What are the *top* ten songs that you recommend?　お薦めのベストテン (上位 10 曲) の歌は何ですか．

Hard work has brought him to the *top* [=best] of the class.　よく勉強したので，彼は成績がクラスで 1 番になった．

Among the most popular forms of exercise, walking usually *tops* [=ranks the first of] the list.　人気のあるスポーツではたいてい，ウォーキングが 1 位にランクされる．

We missed the bus, and *on top of* that it started raining.　バスに乗り遅れた上に雨が降り始めた．　▶ on top of 〜「〜に加えて」

tire, to, tongue, top 665

total /tóutl/

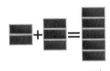

語源は〈tot (全部) al (の)〉である. **全部の；合計；合計すると〜になる**.
派 totally (完全に)

total

It will cost 2,500 yen ⌈*in total* [=all together]. =The *total* will be 2,500 yen.⌋　合計で 2500 円になる.

What is the *total* of twelve plus eight?　12+8 (の合計は) いくつですか.

Donations for the victims *totaled* [=amounted to] twenty-five million yen.　被災者への義捐金は 2500 万円に達した.

He was born with congenital glaucoma and became *totally* [=completely] blind by the age of seven.　彼は先天性の緑内障で 7 歳の時に全盲になった.　▶congenital glaucoma /kəndʒénətl glɔːkóumə/

touch /tʌ́tʃ/

原義は〈触れる〉である. **接触する→心に触れる→問題に触れる→傷つける (触る=障る)**.
派 touchy (神経質な)

Tilt your head to the right and left until your ear almost *touches* your shoulder.　首を左右へ肩に着くほど傾けなさい.

The audience was deeply *touched* [=moved] by the musical.　観衆はそのミュージカルにとても感動した.

I have *a touch of* a cold. =I have a slight cold.　少しかぜ気味です.
▶a touch of 〜「少しの〜」

Don't ask about her academic background as she is very *touchy* [=sensitive] about it.　彼女の学歴については聞かないほうがいいよ, とても気にしているから.

tough /tʌ́f/

原義は〈粘っこい〉である．**圧力になかなか屈しない，攻略しがたい，厳しい．**
派 toughness（頑健さ，たくましさ）

Would you teach me how to ⌈make *tough* meat tender [＝soften meat]? 硬い肉を軟らかくするのはどうしたらよいですか．

It's *tough* [＝challenging] to have to leave one's familiar place, after one gets very old. 高齢になって住み慣れた場所を去るのはつらいことだ．

Many argue that a law that punishes employees by dismissing them for drunk driving is too *tough* [＝severe]. 酒気帯び運転で免職にするのは厳しすぎるという人が多くいる．

---

tour /túər/

原義は〈周回する〉である．**ツアー，旅行；各地を巡る．**
派 tourist（観光客）
関 turn（回る）; detour（迂回（うかい））〔←それて＋回る〕

tour→

We ⌈made a *tour* of [＝toured] various temples and shrines in Kyoto. 京都各地の寺社巡りをした．

The exhibition is ⌈now *on tour* [＝currently touring] across the country. この展示会は現在，全国各地を巡回している．

We *detour* [＝make a detour] around the heaviest traffic during morning rush hours. 朝のラッシュアワーには渋滞を避けて迂回する．

towards /tɔ́ːrdz/

語源は〈to (〜へ) wards (向けて)〉である. **〜のほうへ, 〜のころ.**

Go *towards* the railway station and take the first turn on your right.　駅のほうへ向かって行き, 最初の曲がり角を右へ進みなさい.

The movie is going to be released *towards* the end of this year.　その映画は年末ごろに公開になる.

town /táun/

語源は〈囲まれた土地〉である. **(行政上の) 町, (生活の場としての) 町.**
関 townspeople (町民)

I live in a *town* in Hokkaido near the Ishikari River.　石狩川近くの町に住んでいます.

We're going to be *out of town* this Friday through next Monday.　この金曜日から来週の月曜日まで家を留守にします.

The President is back in *town* and back at work after taking a family vacation.　大統領は家族との休暇を終えて, (ワシントンに) 帰り, 執務を再開している.

track /trǽk/

原義は〈引く〉である．**引いた痕→足跡→行路；跡を追う→追跡する．**

関 trace（形跡）；trade（取引する）；trek（徒歩で行く）

He was so absorbed in reading a book that he lost *track* of time. 彼は本に夢中になって時の経つのも忘れていた．

To「keep their business *on track* [=revive its ailing business], the company decided to reduce its workforce by ten percent. 経営再建〔←軌道に乗せる〕のために，会社は 10% の人員削減を決定した．

Detectives *track* [=monitor] every place you visit and every person you meet. 探偵は訪ねる場所や会う人をくまなく突きとめる．

trade /tréɪd/

原義は〈道〉である．**道を行き来する→交易する→商売する；商売，仕事．**

派 trader（商人，トレーダー）；trading（証券取引）
関 track（通路）；tread（踏みつける）

Barbers learn their *trade* [=jobs] through on-the-job training. 理髪師は見習いで仕事を覚える．

Early explorers *traded* directly with the Native Americans. 初期の探検者たちは，ネイティブ・アメリカンと直接会って物品の交換をした．

You may need to *trade* time for money in order to survive. 生活のために，時間をお金と引き換えにしなければならないことはよくある．

train /tréɪn/

train

原義は〈引く〉である. **引っ張る→導く→(〜へ向けて) 訓練する;(引っ張る)列, 流れ;電車.**
派 training(トレーニング, 訓練); trained(訓練を積んだ); trainer(〔動物の〕調教師,〔スポーツの〕コーチ)

He is now *training* to be a care manager at a medical center. 彼は医療センターで介護士になる訓練をしている.

I've *trained* [=taught] my dog to sit. うちの犬におすわりができるようにしつけた.

Because he used good graphics, we were able to follow his *train of thought* more easily. 彼は分かりやすい図表を使ったので,彼の説明〔←考えの過程〕にたやすくついて行けた.

A company of traders with *a train of* camels was journeying across the desert. ラクダの隊列を連れた商人の一団が砂漠を旅していた.

---

travel /trǽvl/

原義は〈苦労して移動する〉である. **(人が)動く, 旅する;(物・事が)伝わる.**
派 traveler(旅行者)

I always *travel* independently, not as part of a package tour. 団体旅行ではなく,いつも個人旅行をする.

Even when it is overcast, UV rays can *travel* [=pass] through clouds. 曇っていても紫外線は雲を通過する.

Bad news *travels* [=spreads] fast while good news *travels* slowly. 人に関する悪いうわさはすぐに広がり,よい話は伝わりにくいものだ.

treat /tríːt/

原義は〈引く〉である. **(相手を引き入れる)→もてなす→治療する**.

派 treatment（対応, 治療）; untreated（未治療の）

Don't be so upset about the task. After you finish it, I'll ⌈*treat* you to lunch［＝buy you lunch］. 仕事のことでそんなに気落ちするなよ. ちゃんとできたら食事おごるよ.

If left *untreated*［＝unattended］, gum disease can cause heart problems. 歯周病はそのままにしておくと心臓病を起こしかねない.

We should *treat* everyone with respect, regardless of who they are. 相手がどんな人であろうとも, 敬意をもって接しなければいけない.

trip /tríp/

原義は〈ひょいと動く〉である. **ひょいひょい歩む→ちょっとした旅；(ひょいと引っかかる)→つまずく**.
関 trap（わな）

Have a nice *trip*! いい旅をしてください!

Our class took a *field trip* to the fish market. 私のクラスは魚市場へ校外学習に行った.

We took a *trip* to the shopping mall this morning. 今朝, ショッピングモールへ行ってきた.

Toddlers often *trip* on the rug. よちよち歩きの幼児は敷物によくつまずく.

trouble /trʌ́bl/

原義は〈(平安・安定を) かき乱す〉である. **悩ます, 苦しめる；もめ事, 心配事**.
派 troublesome (面倒な)；troubleshoot (故障を解決する)　関 turbulent (混乱した)

You look disappointed; what is *troubling* [=bothering] you?　沈んでいるようだけど, 何を悩んでいるの.

The *trouble* [=The *trouble* I have] with my hair is that it is very stiff and coarse.　僕の髪のやっかいなところはひどい剛毛なんだよ.

Asthma sufferers may have *trouble* breathing during physical exercise.　ぜんそく持ちの人は, 運動中に呼吸困難になることがある.

If you are *in trouble*, read the section on troubleshooting before you call the *trouble* hotline.　問題があれば, 苦情処理係に電話する前に「故障かな, と思ったら」の箇所をお読みください.

true /trúː/

原義は〈がっちりしている〉である. **発言が事実と合致している**.
派 truly (本当に, とても)；truth (真相)

How can such things be *true* [=real]?　そんなことが本当にあるの？

Men in general live less long than women; this is especially *true* of those who are survived by their spouses.　一般に男性は女性に比べて短命であるが, ことに, 連れ合いが先に亡くなった場合にこの傾向が強い.

I'm not sure ⌈of the *truth* of this story [=that this story is *true*].　その話が事実かどうかは自信がありません.

The *truth* is that researchers know very little about when and where earthquakes will occur.　実は専門家も, いつどこで地震が起こるかほとんど分かっていない.

trust /tríst/

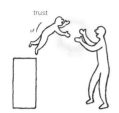

原義は〈信頼する〉である. **信用する；確信する**.
派 trustee（理事）〔←信頼されて任される人〕；
trustworthy（信頼できる）

How can you *trust* a person who you came to know only through online communication?　交信だけで知った相手をどうして信頼できるの？

If you put your *trust* in me, I will not let you down.　信用してくれるなら，裏切りはしません．

A wildlife *trust* [=conservation society] saves land from development so that animals can live there without threat.　野生動物保護協会は土地開発を規制して，動物が脅威を感じることなく住めるように努めている．

try /trái/

原義は〈ふるいにかける〉である. **試してみる，やってみる；裁判にかける**.
派 trial（裁判，試用〔期間〕）；trying（つらい）

She *tries* not to take things negatively.　彼女は物事を否定的に考えないようにしている．

Would you like to *try* a new blend of coffee?　コーヒーのブレンドを変えたんだけど飲んでみる？

Your patience is *tried* [=tested], when you are involved in an endless traffic jam.　我慢強さは果てのない交通渋滞に巻き込まれた時に試される．

The suspect is going to「be *tried* [=put on *trial*] for theft.　容疑者は窃盗罪で裁判にかけられる．

turn /tə́ːrn/

原義は〈曲がる〉である. **回る,転回する,(性質や様子などが)変わる;順番**.
関 tour (旅行); turbine (タービン, 原動機)

At most places the tide *turns* twice a day.　たいていの場所で潮の流れは一日に2度変わる.

My mom will *turn* 50 next month.　母は来月で50才になる.

Why did he suddenly *turn* cold towards me?　どうして彼は急に私に冷たくなったのかしら？

Things *took a turn* for the worse. ＝Things went from bad to worse.　状況は悪化した.

We took *turns* driving to Sendai.　仙台まで交替しながら運転した.

under /ʌ́ndər/

原義は〈〜の下に〉である. **〜より下の位置に, 〜の状況下に**.

If you are caught in a thunderstorm, do not take shelter *under* trees.　戸外で雷雨にあったら，木の下で雨宿りしないように.

Some social activists have been *under* house arrest in China.　中国で何人かの社会活動家が軟禁状態になっている.

In Japan, marriage isn't legal for those *under* sixteen「years of age [＝or below].　日本では，16歳未満の結婚は法的に認められない.

understand /ˌʌndərstǽnd/

語源は〈under（下に）stand（置く）〉である．**(ある状況下に置く)→様子・内容を理解する．**
派 understandable（理解できる）；understandably（当然）；understanding（理解）

I *understand* that you had no intention of hurting me with what you said.　あなたが悪口のつもりで言ったのではないことは分かっているよ．

The goal of sociology is to help students *understand* how the world works.　社会学の目標は，学生に世界がどのように動いているかを理解させることにある．

I could hardly make myself *understood*, because I couldn't speak English well.　英語がうまく話せなかったので，私の考えを理解してもらえなかった．

---

union /júːnjən/

語源は〈uni（一つ）ion（状態）〉である．**(一つにまとまった) 組織，連合国家，労働組合．**
派 unit（単位）；unite（結合する）；unity（統一性）

You need to form a *union* to bargain with the employer.　雇用主と交渉するために労働組合を結成する必要がある．

Your voice will be stronger in *union* with those of coworkers than alone.　意見は仲間と一緒に発したほうが一人で言うより効力がある．

unique /juː(ː)níːk/

unique

語源は〈uni(一つ)que(の)〉である.**唯一の→類のない**.

派 uniqueness(独自性) 関 unicycle(一輪車)

Your fingerprint is *unique to* you.　あなたの指紋はあなた独自のものだ.

This is a *unique* [=great] opportunity that allows you to widen your experience.　これは見聞を広げるまたとない機会だ.

He speaks with a *unique* [=an unusual] accent.　彼は独特ななまりで話す.

universe /júːnəvə̀ːrs/

語源は〈uni(一つ)verse(回る)〉である.**(ぐるりと巻き込むごとく全体を含む)→全世界, 宇宙**.

派 universal(普遍的な)

Describe the image you have of the *universe*.　あなたが宇宙についてもっているイメージはどんなものか言ってごらん.

My hometown was the whole *universe* [=world] to me when I was a child.　幼いころは生まれた町が世界のすべてだった.

It's a *universal* [=common] fact that nobody likes going to the dentist.　歯医者に行きたくないのは誰だって同じことだ.

unless /ənlés/

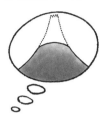

語源は〈on less (than) より少ない条件で〉である. **(〜でない条件で) →〜でない限り**.

I won't go *unless* you go. =If you do not go, I won't go either. 君が行かないのなら僕も行かないよ.

You can't apply for the job ⌈*unless* you've got [=if you don't have] the experience. この仕事は経験がないと応募できない.

He should be in the office ⌈*unless* he is [=if he isn't] out for lunch. 彼は食事に出かけていない限り, 会社にいるはずだ.

You need to water the garden, ⌈*unless* it rains [=if it doesn't rain]. 雨が降らないなら, 水やりしないとだめだ.

until /əntíl/

語源は〈un=up to (〜へ) till (〜まで)〉である. **〜まで**.
関 till (〜まで)

She remained unmarried *until* [=up to when] her fiancé finished college. 彼女は婚約者が大学を卒業するまで結婚しなかった.

Sorry for not being able to reply *until* now. 今までご返事できなくてごめんなさい.

I have to work in office *until* late this evening. 今夜は遅くまで会社で仕事しないといけない.

You don't realize what you have *until* it's gone. 持っているものの価値は失って初めて分かる.

up /ʌ́p/

原義は〈上方へ〉である．**上へ→立って→起きて→現れて→（上がって）いっぱいまで→（上がって）尽きて**．
派 upper（上側の，上位の）

Look *up* at the moon; it's full.　月を見てごらん，満月よ．

I had to stay *up* late to finish my homework.　宿題を終えるために遅くまで起きていなければならなかった．

The garbage truck came around to pick *up* the trash.　ごみ収集車がごみを回収しにやってきた．

Don't stop until time is *up*.　（制限）時間いっぱいまで頑張りなさい．

update /動 ʌ̀pdéɪt, 名 ʌ́pdèɪt/

語源は〈up＝up to（～へ）date（今日）〉である．**（今日にする）→最新にする，情報を更新する；新しい知らせ**．
up-to-date（最新の）の変形．

Keep me *updated* [＝posted] if any news comes up.　何か変ったことがあったら知らせてください．

Please *update* your address book, since I have moved.　引っ越したからアドレス帳を更新してね．

With an online textbook, this kind of information would be constantly *updated* [＝added].　電子書籍ならば，この種の情報は随時更新される．

Thank you for the *update*.　近況を知らせてくれてありがとう．

upon /əpɑ́:n/

語源は〈up (上に) on (の上に)〉である. **〜の上に**, **〜の際に**.

Upon the death of his father [＝As soon as his father died], the son took over the business.　父親がなくなるとすぐ, 息子が商売を継いだ.

The snow season is ⌈*upon* us [＝already here].　雪の季節がすでにやって来ています.

Now is a good time to reflect *upon* [＝on] our family's history.　家の歴史を振り返ってみる好機だ.

Success depends *upon* [＝on] your previous preparation.　うまくいくかどうかは君の準備次第だ.

upper /ʌ́pər/

語源は〈up (上へ) er (もっと)〉である. **片方より上側の**, **上位の**. up の比較級.

"Where is the cat?" "Did you check the *upper* rooms?"　「猫はどこ?」「2階を見た?」

My daughter licks her *upper* lip when she sees something delicious.　おいしそうなものを見ると, 娘は上唇をなめる癖がある.

The boy is in the *upper* half of the class.　その少年は成績がクラスで上位半分に入っている.

use /動 júːz, 名 júːs/

原義は〈道具を使う〉である．**道具・金・エネルギー・能力・人などを使う；使用**．
派 usable (使える)；used (中古の)；useful (役立つ)；useless (無益な)　関 usual (いつもの)〔←いつも使うような〕；utensil (台所用具)；utilize (利用する)；utility (実用性，利用者)

There is no *use* dwelling upon what has happened with regret.　済んだことをあれこれ悔やんでも無駄だ．

Try to make the best *use* of your time.　時間を最大限に活用せよ．

It won't be so expensive if you buy a *used* one.　中古品を買えばそんなに高価ではないよ．

What you learn in class isn't always *useful* [=helpful] in the real world.　学校で学んだことが実社会で必ずしも役立つとは限らない．

Theory is *useless* [=worthless], unless it's applied.　理論も活用されなければ無用である．

usual /júːʒuəl/

unusual

usual

語源は〈use=use (使う) al (性質の)〉である．**(よく使う) →いつもの，普段の**．
派 usually (たいていは)；unusual (まれな)
関 use (使う)

The hotel charges more than the *usual* fees on weekends.　このホテルは，週末は通常料金より高い．

Yesterday we went to the movies, which is what we *usually* do on Friday.　きのう，映画を見に行きましたが，金曜日にはたいてい行くことにしています．

We're having *unusual* [=abnormal] weather lately.　最近，天気が異常です．

value /vǽljuː/

原義は〈力がある〉である. **価値, 価格；評価する.**
派 valuable (価値のある)；valuables (貴重品)
関 equivalent (同等の, 同等のもの)

The *value* of the company's stock continues to rise gradually. この会社の株価は徐々に上がっている.

Don't *take* manufacturer's advertisements *at face value*. 企業広告をいつも額面通りに受け取ってはだめだ.

Please leave your *valuables* in the safe. お出かけの際は, 貴重品は金庫へ保管ください.

Our house and land were *valued* [=assessed] at fifty million yen. 家と土地が5千万円と査定された.

---

vary /véəri/

原義は〈変化する〉である. **同一のものについて様態が変化していく《変容》, 同種のものについて内容が種々である《多様》.**
派 variable (変わりやすい)；varied (いろいろな)；variety (多種)

The flora *varies* [=changes gradually] as you climb higher. 登るにつれて植生が変わっていく.

Roses *vary* in [=Roses come in a variety of] shapes and sizes. バラは形や大きさがさまざまである.

The wind is *variable* [=changeable] in direction in and around the stadium. この球場の周辺では風向きが変わりやすい.

---

use, usual, value, vary

victim /víktɪm/

原義は〈(神に捧げる)生贄(いけにえ)〉である. **犠牲者, 被害者**.
派 victimize (犠牲にする)

Most of the flood *victims* [=sufferers] have been moved to temporary shelters.　洪水の被災者のほとんどが仮設住宅へ移った.

My elderly neighbor has become a *victim* of an "It's me, Grandma!" scam.　隣の老人が「オレオレ」詐欺の被害者になった.

Cabbages in my garden have「fallen *victim* to [=been eaten by]」hungry worms.　菜園のキャベツが食欲旺盛な害虫にやられてしまった.

view /vjúː/

原義は〈眺め〉である. **事物が目に映る《光景》; 事物が心に映る《見解》**.
派 viewer ((テレビなどの)視聴者)
関 vision (視力, 洞察力); viewpoint (視点, 観点); review (再検討する)

The *view* [=sight] from the mountaintop is breathtaking.　山頂からの眺めは圧巻だ.

Many stars too faint to be seen in urban areas come into *view* [=sight] in the country.　都市部では見えない多くの星が田舎では見える.

His *view* [=theory] of life is terribly conservative and old-fashioned.
彼の人生観はひどく保守的で古くさい.

We may *view* [=regard] slow children as lazy ones. ＝Slow children may be *viewed* as lazy ones.　成績が悪い子をとかく怠け者と見る傾向がある.

violence /váɪələns/

語源は〈viol（暴力）ence（状態）〉である．**人を傷つける暴力**．
派 violent（乱暴な，激しい）; violate（違反する，侵害する）

Don't give in to *violence* and threats.　暴力や脅迫に屈してはいけない．

Aggressive person may resort to *violence* as a means to express anger and frustration.　高圧的な人は怒りや不満を暴力に訴えることが多い．

My husband gets *violent* [=out of control] when he is drunk.　夫は酔っぱらうと暴力的になる．

A *violent* [=strong] explosion occurred at the factory due to a gas leak.　ガス漏れのために工場で大きな爆発が起こった．

virtual /vɜ́ːrtʃuəl/

原義は〈力のある〉である．**ほとんど実際に近い，実質上の**．
派 virtually（事実上）

A major power failure brought the metropolis to a *virtual* [=practical] standstill.　大停電が首都をほとんどまひ状態にした．

Computer graphics can produce a *virtual* [=practical] reality.　コンピュータ・グラフィックスは仮想現実を作り出せる．

He was a *virtually* [=an almost] unknown writer before he won the prize.　彼はその賞を取るまではほとんど無名の作家だった．

visible /vízəbl/

語源は〈vis (見る) ible (できる)〉である. **目に見える；明らかな**.
派 visibility (視界)；vision (映像)；visual (視覚の)

Venus is usually the first star to 「become *visible* [=be seen] in the west as the dusk begins to fall.　金星は, 暗くなると西の空に見えてくる最初の星だ.

He made *visible* [=obvious] progress in drawing.　彼は目に見えて絵がうまくなった.

visit /vízət/

語源は〈vis (見に) it (行く)〉である. **会いに行く→訪問する→見舞う；訪問**.
派 visitation (視察)；visitor (訪問者)
関 advice (助言)

My wife and I take turns *visiting* my father in the hospital.　妻と私が交互に, 入院している父を見舞っている.

It is always good *visiting* [=accessing] his web site.　彼のサイトにアクセスするのは楽しい.

Is this your first *visit* [=trip] to Japan?　今回が最初の日本訪問ですか.

voice /vɔ́ɪs/

原義は〈声〉である. **人の声**, **意見**；**意見を言う**.
関 vocal (声の, 声高の)；vote (投票する)；vowel (母音)

The singer has a rich *voice* that carries well.　この歌手はよく通る声だ.

Excessive drinking and smoking may damage your *voice*.　酒やたばこの飲み過ぎは声を痛めることがある.

People began to *voice* [=express] their opinions by way of blogging and tweeting.　人々はブログやツイッターで自分の意見を言い始めた.

volume /vάːljəm/

原義は〈巻物〉である. **(分厚い) 本**→**容量**, **大きさ**.
関 evolve (進化する)；involve (巻き込む)

Would you ⌈turn the *volume* up [=turn up the volume]?　音量を上げていただけませんか.

We usually measure liquids by *volume*, not by weight.　液体はたいてい, 重量ではなく容量で計る.

Traffic *volume* [=The amount of traffic] on this road went down visibly after the bypass opened.　バイパスが開通後, この道路の交通量は目に見えて減った.

The encyclopedia is published in three *volumes*.　この百科事典は3巻仕立てだ.

vote /vóut/

原義は〈願う〉である。**(自己の声を) 票に託す→投票する→決める**。vote による賛否の表明は，投票・挙手・発声・拍手などがある。
派 voter (投票者)　関 vow (誓う); voice (声)

I think people who don't pay taxes shouldn't have the right to *vote*.　税金を払わない人は選挙権をもつべきではないと思う。

Who will you *vote for* in the upcoming mayoral election?　今度の市長選挙では誰に投票しますか。

There are 52 *votes* in favor, 12 against and 3 blank ballots.　賛成 52 票，反対 12 票，白票 3 です。

wait /wéɪt/

原義は〈見張って待つ〉である。**出現や発生をじっと待つ；待機**。
派 waiter / waitress (接客係)

I had to *wait* in line for an hour to get the tickets.　チケットを手に入れるために 1 時間並んで待った。

I can hardly *wait* to see him again.　彼との再会が待ちきれないわ。

We'll just have to *wait and see*—there's nothing we can do at the moment.　様子を見るしかないよ。今のところどうしようもないから。

She doesn't know how to ⌈*wait on* [＝serve] customers.　彼女はお客への対応がなってないね。

Finally, my turn came, but it was ⌈worth the *wait* [＝worth *waiting*].　やっと私の番が来たけど，待った甲斐があった。

walk /wɔ́ːk/

原義は〈ぐるぐる回る〉である．**あちこち歩く→歩く，歩かせる；散歩→歩行→人生の歩み**．
派 walking (歩くこと，ウォーキング)；walker (歩行器)

My boy *walks* to and from school every day.　うちの息子は毎日，徒歩通学する．

The sand on the beach was too hot to *walk on* in bare feet.　浜辺の砂は熱すぎて裸足で歩けなかった．

I *walk* the dog [=*take* the dog *for a walk*] every evening.　夕方はいつも犬を散歩させる．

People from all *walks of life* [=types of work] joined the protest meeting.　さまざまな職種の人たちが抗議集会に参加した．

wall /wɔ́ːl/

原義は〈周りを囲む〉である．**壁，内壁，障壁；壁で囲う**．wa- は〈ぐるり〉の意味合い：walk 〔←ぐるぐる歩く〕，watch 〔←あちこち見張る〕，wander 〔←あちこち歩く〕

She hangs quilts on the *walls* of the living room.　彼女は居間の壁にキルトを飾っている．

Becoming suspicious of other people, he built a *wall* around himself.　彼は他人に懐疑的になって，自分の周りに壁をこしらえてしまった．

Walls of water flooded over the land.　まるで水の壁が陸地を襲ってきた．

He is *walled in* by a mountain of papers.　彼は書類の山に囲まれている．

want /wʌ́nt/

原義は〈欠落している〉である．**欠けている→欠落を埋めたがる→必要なものを欲する**．
派 wanted（指名手配された）；unwanted（望まれない）

I'll help you. How do you *want* it done?　手伝うよ．どうして欲しいの？

There are many parents who *want* their children to learn to speak English.　子どもには英語を話せるようになって欲しいと思う親が多くいる．

Our former neighbor is *wanted* for an attempted murder by the police.　かつて隣に住んでいた人が，殺人未遂の容疑で警察に指名手配されている．

warm /wɔ́ːrm/

原義は〈暖かい〉である．**(気温・衣服・心が) 暖かい**．
派 warmth（暖かさ）

It's cold outside; be sure to keep *warm* when you go out.　外は寒いから，外出の時は温かくして出かけなさい．

The nurse had a *warm* and caring nature; she always sided with the weak.　その看護師は温かく思いやりのある性格で，いつも弱者の味方した．

You need to *warm up* before exercising, or you might have a muscle cramp.　運動の前にウオームアップし〔←体を温め〕ないと筋肉がつることがある．

warn /wɔ́ːrn/

原義は〈目を見開くよう警告する〉である. **危険を警告する, 〜しないよう注意する.**
派 warning（警告）　関 watch（見張る）

He *warned* [=advised] his young daughter to come home before it got dark.　彼は幼い娘に，暗くなる前に帰宅するよう注意した.

Getting short of breath is a *warning* sign that something may be wrong in your heart or lungs.　息切れがするのは，心臓か肺のどこかが悪いかもしれないという兆候である.

A *warning* sign reads: "Poisonous snakes inhabit the area."　警告板に「毒蛇生息区域」と書いてある.

waste /wéist/

原義は〈虚しさ〉である. **(金・時間・労力を) 無駄にする；無駄遣い, 不用物.**
派 wasteful（無駄の多い）　関 devastate（荒廃させる）

All my efforts ⌈were *wasted* [=came to nothing]; the data I stored had gone instantly.　保存していたデータを一瞬に失って，これまでの努力が水の泡になった.

Don't *waste* money *on* clothes you don't need.　必要のない服にお金を無駄遣いしたらだめよ.

The movie was a *waste* of time.　この映画は時間の無駄だったよ.

Disposal of industrial *wastes* leads to problems of water, soil, and air pollution.　産業廃棄物の処理は，水，土壌，大気汚染の問題につながる.

watch /wɑ́:tʃ/

原義は〈見張る〉である．**目を見開いてじっくり見る**．
派 watchful（用心深い）　関 wake（目覚める）；warn（警告する）

I usually stay at home and *watch* a football game on TV on Sunday evenings.　日曜日の夜はたいてい家にいて，サッカーをテレビで観戦する．

We need someone to *watch* [=look after] our children while we're at work.　勤めに出ている間，子どもたちを見ていてくれる人が要る．

The doctor *watched* the patient for signs of serious illness.　医師は，患者に何か重大な病気の兆候があるのではないかと注意して診察した．

I ˈhave to *watch* the time [=should make sure what the time is]; I'm going to meet my relatives at three-thirty at the station.　時間に気を付けていないと．3時半に親戚の人たちを駅に迎えに行くことになっているの．

water /wɑ́:tər/

原義は〈水〉である．**水，水域；水をやる**．
派 watery（水っぽい）
関 waterfall（滝）；wet（湿った，雨の）

If you use the air-conditioning, you may find *water* dripping from under your car.　空調を使うと，車の下から水が滴っているのに気づくことがよくある．

Some foreign vessels were operating in Japanese *waters*.　何隻かの外国漁船が日本の海域で操業していた．

We *water* the garden every morning and evening in summer.　夏は，朝と夕方に庭に水をやる．

wave /wéɪv/

原義は〈波〉である．**揺れる，波立つ；手を振る．**
派 waver（揺れ動く）；wavy（揺れ動くような）；wavelength（波長，考え方）

I *waved* goodbye to her and drove away. 彼女に手を振って別れを告げ，走り出した．

The willow leaves are *waving* [＝rippling] in the breeze. ヤナギが風にそよいでいる．

She has long *wavy* hair. 彼女は長いウェーブのかかった髪をしている．

---

way /wéɪ/

原義は〈道〉である．**目的に至る道→道のり，方向，進路；方法．**
関 way of life（生活様式）

Everything is going well, but there is still a long *way* to go before it is fully accomplished. 万事順調だが，成就までにはまだまだ長い道のりがある．

On my way home from work, I often drop in at a bookstore. 仕事の帰りに，よく本屋に立ち寄る．

Homosexuals shouldn't be persecuted; they are born that *way*. 同性愛は責められるべきではない．そういうふうに生まれついているのだから．

That's no *way* to speak to your parents. 親にそんな口をきいてはだめだよ．

That's the *way* things are. ＝Life's like that. ＝That's life. 世の中って所詮，こんなものさ．

weak /wíːk/

原義は〈軟弱な〉である．**丈夫でない，十分な抵抗力がない**．
派 weaken（弱くする，弱くなる）; weakness（弱さ）

My arms are too *weak* to do pushups.　腕の筋肉が弱いので腕立て伏せはできない．

I'*m weak in* [=am not good at] math.　私は数学に弱い．

Stressful conditions may *weaken* [=reduce the function of] your immune system.　ストレスがあると免疫力が落ちることがある．

I have a *weakness* for alcoholic drinks. ＝I give in easily to the temptation of alcoholic drinks.　私は酒に目がない．

wear /wéər/

原義は〈着る〉である．**着る→身につける→（やがてすり切れてくる）→すり減る**．
派 weary（疲れ果てた）

Do I have to *wear* a tie for the party?　パーティーにはネクタイをして行かなくてはいけないの？

She *wears* [=puts on] more makeup than she used to.　彼女は昔より化粧が濃い．

Front tires *wear (out)* faster than rear tires.　前輪のタイヤのほうが後輪のタイヤよりも早くすり減る．

weather /wéðər/

原義は〈吹きすさぶ風〉である．**天気→荒天，風雨；風雨にさらす，風雨をしのぐ．**
関 wither（しぼむ）

The *weather* looks great for today. 今日は天気がよさそうだ．

"Are you going to the beach tomorrow?" "It depends on the *weather*." 「明日，海に行く？」「天気次第だね」

Older mountains are less jagged due to the effects of *weathering*. 古い山は風化作用のために山容が険しくない．

Our company managed to *weather* [＝get through] the global financial crisis. 我が社は，なんとか世界的経済危機を乗り切れた．

week /wíːk/

S,M,Tu,W,Th,F,S

原義は〈7日の経過で変わる月の形〉である．**7日間→週**
派 weekly（週一度の）
関 week day（平日）；weekend（週末：土曜日と日曜日）
weekend は〈週末→休日〉の意を内包しているので〈Saturday＋Sunday〉を指す．

What day of the *week* do you like best? 何曜日が一番好きですか．

We live in town during the *week* and go to the country for the weekend. 平日は町で暮らし，週末は田舎で過ごします．

In the mid 1960's, Japan gradually introduced the five-day *workweek*. 1960年代半ばから，日本は徐々に週五日制を導入し始めた． ▶workweek「週労働時間」

I often spend time with my parents *on weekends*. 週末はよく両親と一緒に過ごします．

weigh /wéɪ/

原義は〈重さがかかる〉である.**重さを量る,重さがある**.
派 weight（重さ）

How much do you *weigh*? ＝What is your *weight*?　体重はどれくらいですか.

My baby *weighed* about three and a half kilograms at birth.　私の赤ちゃんは生まれた時，約3.5キロだった.

Women tend to gain *weight* after getting married.　女性は結婚すると体重が増えがちだ.

welcome /wélkəm/

語源は〈well（喜んで）＋come＝comer（来訪者）〉である.**歓迎；歓迎する；歓迎される**.

You are *welcome* to join our club. ＝We are happy to have you in our club.　クラブへの加入を歓迎します.

You're *welcome* [＝Feel free] to eat anything in the refrigerator.
冷蔵庫の中のものは何でもご自由にどうぞ.

We had a *welcome* [＝*welcoming*] party for the new employees.
新入社員の歓迎会を開いた.

Don't *overstay your welcome*; everything has its own right time.
長居しないようにしなさい．なんでも頃合いというものがあるのだから．　▶overstay one's welcome「長居する」

wet /wét/

原義は〈ぬれた〉である. **ぬれた, 雨の**.
関 water（水）

The ground became so *wet* that they gave up continuing the game.
グラウンドが水浸しになったので試合を途中でやめた.

We got *wet* [=drenched] to the skin by the sudden heavy rain. 急な土砂降りでびしょぬれになった.

When you are nervous, your hands and armpits may get *wet* with sweat. 緊張すると, 手や脇の下が汗で湿ることがある.

It has been unseasonably cold and *wet* since the turn of the month.
今月になって, 季節外れの寒さと雨が続いている.

what /wάt/

原義は〈何〉である. **何？《疑問》, 何と！《驚き》；(〜する) もの**.

What's [=How much's] the sales tax in your country? あなたの国では消費税はいくらですか.

What I don't like about the telephone is that it can abruptly interrupt *what* the other one is doing. 電話の嫌いな点は, いきなり相手のやっていることを邪魔してしまうことになりかねないことだ.

What's done is done. It cannot be changed. 過去のことは過去のこと. 変更は不可能だ.

What a sight! なんて (すばらしい[ひどい]) 光景でしょう！

when /wén/

原義は〈いつ〉である. **いつ，〜する時・場合，〜である時に**.

When is the press conference?　記者会見は何時からですか.

When something is wide, it takes up a lot of space from side to side.　幅が広いということは，端から端までの空間を広く取ることである.

Please tell me how you enjoyed the trip *when* you return.　帰ったら旅のみやげ話をしてね.

My father is very particular *when it comes to* coffee.　コーヒーのことになると，父はとてもうるさい.

where /wéər/

原義は〈どこ〉である. **どこへ，どこで；〜である場所**.

Do you know *where* you are?　(移動中に) ここがどこか分かりますか.

Where have you been all day?　一日中どこへ行ってたの？

This is *where* many go wrong; they believe everything that they read in books and papers.　多くの人が誤ってしまうことだけど，活字になっているとなんでも信じ込んでしまう.

He has worked hard to get *where* he is today.　彼は努力して，今の〔←今いる〕自分を築いた.

whether /wéðər/

原義は〈どちらか〉である. **〜かどうか；〜のこと**.

She is yet uncertain *whether* to take a job or to go to college.　彼女はまだ，就職か大学進学か迷っている.

It doesn't matter *whether* [=if] you win by an inch or a mile; winning's winning.　辛勝か大勝かは問題ではない．勝ちは勝ちなんだから．

Cell phones have become part of your daily life *whether* you like it or not.　携帯電話は，好むと好まざるにかかわらず，今や生活の一部となっている．

which /wítʃ/

原義は〈どっち〉である. **どちら；〜のこと**.

Which color do you like for your room's wallpaper?　部屋の壁紙にはどの色が好き？

They're all so pretty. I don't know *which* one to choose.　みんなきれいで，どれを選んでいいか分からないわ．

You may be constipated, in *which* case you need to eat more high fiber foods.　便秘になるかもしれないが，その時は繊維を多く含むものを食べる必要がある．

while /wáɪl/

原義は〈〜の間〉である．**〜の間，〜の時；(ちょっとした)時間；〜なのに，〜だけど．**

Wear a wide-brimmed hat *while* watching sporting events in the sun.
日なたでスポーツ観戦する時は，広縁の帽子をかぶりなさい．

The boss said, "Give me a *while* to think over your suggestion."
課長は「君の提案について少し考える時間をください」と言った．

It's been a *while* since I used this machine, so I don't remember exactly how to do it.　この機械を使うのは久しぶりなので，扱いを正確に覚えていない．

While epilepsy cannot be cured, it can be successfully controlled.
癲癇(てんかん)は治ることはないが，うまく抑えることはできる．

who /húː/

原義は〈誰〉である．**誰が，誰を；〜する人．**

First, let's decide *who* does what.　最初に，役割分担〔←誰が何をするか〕を決めよう．

The company is looking to hire those *who* know programming.　会社はプログラミングのできる人を求めている．

Bill is not *who* you think he is. He is such a lovely person.　ビルは君が思っているような人じゃないよ．彼はとてもすてきな人だよ．

What may seem ordinary to the people *who* live there can be surprising to those who do not.　そこに住んでいる人にとっては平凡に見えることが，そうでない人には思いがけないと感じられることがある．

whole /hóul/

原義は〈完全な〉である．**丸ごとの；全部**．
関 wholesale（卸売り）

Not wanting to be suspended again, I decided to change my *whole* lifestyle.　停学になるのはもうまっぴらなので，生活態度をすっかり変えようと決心した．

Be sure to choose *whole* [=unrefined] grains. You should, for example, eat brown rice rather than white.　精白していない穀物を選ぶようにしなさい．例えば，白米よりも玄米を食べるように．

Watermelons are sold *whole*, in halves, or quarters.　スイカは，丸ごとか，半分，あるいは4分の1に切って売られている．

why /wáɪ/

原義は〈なぜ〉である．**なぜ；理由**．

"Can I see you tomorrow?" "*Why not*?"　「明日，会える？」「いいとも」

Why is it that if you tickle yourself it doesn't tickle?　自分の身体をくすぐっても，くすぐったくないのはなぜですか．

I need to look after my elderly parents, which is *why* I moved to my hometown.　高齢の両親の世話のために故郷に帰った．

wide /wáɪd/

原義は〈幅広い〉である．**幅広い，〜ほどの幅をもつ**．
派 widen（広くする）; width（幅）; widely（広く）
関 widespread（広範囲にわたる）

The film has appealed to a *wide* audience.　この映画は多くの観客の心をとらえた．

He is leading the election by a *wide* margin.　彼は他候補を大きくリードしている．

Mastery of foreign languages provides a *wide* range of career choices.　外国語を習得しておくと職業の選択肢が広がる〔←広い範囲の選択肢をもたらす〕．

The bridge is 250 meters long and 6.5 meters *wide* [= in *width*].　この橋は，長さ250メートル，幅6.5メートルだ．

---

wild /wáɪld/

原義は〈野生の〉である．**野生の→自然のままの；感情のおもむくまま**．
派 wildly（荒々しく）; wildness（荒野）
関 wildlife（野生生物）

Can a pet dog survive in the *wild*?　飼い犬は野外に放っても生き抜けますか．

They say *wild* fish tastes better than farmed fish.　天然魚は養殖魚より味がいいと言われている．

The crowd *went wild* when the singer appeared on the stage.　観衆は歌手が舞台に登場するとわっと沸いた．

will /wíl/, would /wúd/

原義は〈～しようと思う〉である．**～するつもりである，～であろう；意志．**

I *will* be there in fifteen minutes.　15分ほどでそちらに着きます．

What do you think *will* happen to the heroine in the end?　最後にはヒロインはどうなると思う？

Where there's a *will*, there's a way.　《諺》意志があれば，道は開ける．

Would you be able to post this parcel for me?　この小包を出しに行ってもらえますか．　▶wouldは発言に「慎み・控え目」な意味合いを生む．

Would Friday at 6 pm suit you?　金曜日の夕方6時はいかがでしょうか．

I *would* prefer to eat ice cream.　アイスクリームをいただきたいのですが．

---

win /wín/

原義は〈勝ち取る〉である．**試合・競争・選挙に勝つ；賞・名声・欲しいものを得る．**
派 winner（勝者，受賞者）；winning（勝利を得た）

How did you *win* her heart?　どうやって彼女のハートをつかんだの？

He *won* [＝earned] fame with his debut novel.　彼はデビュー作の小説で有名になった．

Don't play the lottery. Your odds of *winning* are awful!　宝くじはやめておきなさい．当たる確率は最低だよ．

wish /wíʃ/

原義は〈(心を込めて)願う〉である. **〜したいと切望する；切望，願望.**
派 wishful（切望している）

"Why were you demoted?" "I *wish* I knew [＝I myself want to know why]." 「なんで降格されたの？」「私こそ知りたいわ」

I *wish* I studied harder when I was at school.　学校時代にもっと勉強しておけばよかったと思っている.

It is *wishful* thinking on her part that she could succeed without a degree.　彼女が大学を出なくてもうまくやれると考えるのは，希望的観測に過ぎないよ.

with /wíθ/

原義は〈〜に相対して〉である. **〜を用いて《手段》, 〜と一緒に《同行・同伴・保持》, 〜に対して《対立》.**

Cut off the dead branch *with* the shears.　枯れ枝を剪定鋏(せんていばさみ)で切り落としなさい.

It is very unsafe to give fish *with* bones to a cat.　骨の付いた魚を猫に与えるのは危険だ.

What should I wear *with* these pants?　このズボンに合わせて何を着たらいい？

You shouldn't take work home *with* you.　仕事は家に持ち帰らないように.

I am down *with* the flu.　かぜでダウンしています.

wonder /wʌ́ndər/

原義は〈～に驚く〉である．**すばらしさに驚く→不思議に思う→どうしてだろう→～かしら**．
派 wonderful（すばらしい）
関 wow（うわ～〔間投詞〕）

Have you ever *wondered* how computer programs work?　コンピュータのプログラムがどんな仕組みになっているのか，考えたことがありますか．

I was *wondering* if you could help me with this issue.　この件であなたにお手伝いしてもらえないかと思っています．

It is no *wonder* that a married couple without children keeps lots of pets.　子どものいない夫婦がペットをたくさん飼っているのは別に不思議じゃないよ．

Crying can work *wonders* on healing your pains and sorrows.　泣くことは心痛や悲しみを癒すのにすばらしい効果を発揮する．

wood /wúd/

原義は〈薪（たきぎ）〉である．**薪→木材→森**．
派 wooded（木々の茂った）; wooden（木製の）

What is the best *wood* for decks or porches?　デッキやベランダに最適の木材は何ですか．

I often go for a hike in the *woods* in summer.　夏はよく森へハイキングに行きます．

The camping ground was beautifully *wooded* with birch, aspen, maple, and cedar.　キャンプ地はカバ，ポプラ，カエデ，スギなどの樹木で美しく囲まれていた．

I prefer *wooden* [=*wood*] cutting boards to plastic ones.　木製のまな板のほうがプラスティックのものより好きです．

word /wə́:rd/

原義は〈話す〉である. **単語, ことば；発言, 約束**.
派 wordy（言い回しがくどい）

Choose your *words* carefully when describing a handicapped person.
障害者について語る時はことばを慎重に選びなさい.

I like the *words* of the song.　この歌の歌詞が好きだ.

I've never heard a *word* of gossip about the actor.　あの俳優の浮いた話を聞いたことがない.

I was surprised when the fortuneteller's *words* came true.　占い師の言ったことが本当に起こったので驚いた.

work /wə́:rk/

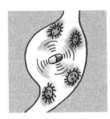

原義は〈働く〉である. **働く, 効果が出る；仕事, 作品**.
派 worker（労働者）；working（労働の, 作業用の）
関 workout（訓練, トレーニング）；workshop（作業場, 講習会）

Both my parents *work*.　両親とも働いています.

If over-the-counter medicine does not *work*, then you need to see a medical professional.　市販の薬が効かないときは，専門医に診てもらう必要がある.

I go straight home after *work* [=the day's *work* is done].　私は仕事が終わったら家へ直行します.

John Keats is a national poet of England and his *works* are enjoyed worldwide.　ジョン・キーツは英国の国民的詩人で，彼の作品は世界中で読まれている.

world /wə́ːrld/

原義は〈人の世〉である. **世界, 社会, 世間.**
関 worldwide (世界規模の)

He worked for a news agency, which took him around the *world*.
彼は通信社に勤務し, 世界中を飛び回っていた.

I felt that the *world* was against me. 世間はみな, 自分に反対しているように感じた.

You've got a lot to learn about the *world*. 君はまだ社会について学ぶことが多くある.

worry /wə́ːri/

原義は〈絞める, ひねる〉である. **気持ちを鬱屈させる→心を悩ます；心配, 心配事.**
派 worried (心配した)；worrying (気がかりな)

I understand you don't want to「get your parents *worried* [=to *worry* your parents], but it's not good to keep your *worries* inside. 両親を心配させたくないというのは分かるけど, 悩みを内にため込むのはよくないよ.

I cannot sleep—my daughter's health is *worrying* me. 娘の健康のことが心配で眠れません.

Most *worrying* [=What *worries* us most] is that young people have been failing to have a dream for their future. 最も気がかりなのは, 若者が将来に夢を抱けないでいることだ.

worth /wə́:rθ/

原義は〈~ほどの価値がある〉である. **(時間・金・労力を費やす) 価値がある**.
派 worthy (価値のある); worthwhile (〔時間をかける〕価値がある)

It's not going to be easy, but it's *worth* it. それは簡単じゃないけど, やる価値があるよ.

His live performance was *worth* the money. 彼のライブ公演は料金を払うかいがあった.

We have two suggestions both of which are, I think, ⌈*worthy* of consideration [=*worth* considering]. 2つの提案をいただいているが, 双方とも検討に値すると思います.

This book is *worthwhile*; it covers the topic thoroughly. この本は読む価値がある. テーマがくまなく記述されているからだ.

---

write /ráit/

原義は〈文字を刻む〉である. **文字・手紙・メール・物語・詩・曲などを書く**.
派 writer (作家); writ (令状); writing (書かれた文字); written (書面による)

It is taking me a long time to *write* this computer program. このプログラムを書くのに随分時間がかかっています.

Could I borrow something to *write* with? 何か書くもの (筆記具) をお借りできますか.

She is ⌈a singer who *writes* and composes her own songs [=a singer song writer]. 彼女は自分の歌を作詞作曲する.

I went to that new restaurant last night. The food was *nothing to write home about*. 昨晩, 新しいレストランに行ってみたけど, 料理はたいしたことなかったよ. ▶nothing to write home about「特筆すべきことでない」

wrong /rɔ́ːŋ/

原義は〈ねじれた〉である. **真っ当でない→間違っている；悪いこと，不正.**
派 wrongly（間違って）

The waiter served us ⌈the *wrong* food [=different food from what we ordered]. ウエイターは注文とは違う料理を運んできた.

I don't mean to complain but what's *wrong* [=the problem] *with* my playing video games? 不平を言うわけじゃないけど, テレビゲームやってどこが悪いの.

When do children start to know right from *wrong*? 子どもはいつごろから善悪の区別がつくようになるの？

These figures don't add up to the right total! Where did I *go wrong*? 計算が合わないよ. どこで間違えたのかな.

---

year /jíər/

原義は〈年〉である. **年，年間.**
派 yearly（毎年の）

Her mind is still sharp, and she looks *years* younger than she is. 彼女の頭はまださえていて，年よりもうんと若く見える.

I spent most of my teenage *years* in Seoul. 十代の大半をソウルで過ごした.

My son is in his first *year* at high school. 息子は高校の1年生です.

In Japan, the school *year* starts in April. 日本では新学年度は4月に始まる.

yet /jét/

原義は〈まだ〉である. **いまだ**.

Haven't you received the results of your health check *yet*? まだ検診結果は受け取っていないの?

Women's baseball ⌈isn't a major sport *yet* [=is *yet* to be a major sport]. 女子野球はまだ主流の競技ではない.

I haven't spoken to my parents yet [=I still haven't spoken to my parents], so don't know if I can go to the party. まだ親に相談していないので, パーティーに行けるかどうか分からない.

yield /jíːld/

〈屈する〉
〈生じる〉

原義は〈与える〉である. **生み出す**, **屈する**. 「相手側に与える→生み出す. 相手側に与える→譲る→屈する」と考える.

The ocean floor could *yield* many as yet undiscovered natural resources. 海底から未発見の天然資源が多量に産出する可能性がある.

Term deposits *yield* better returns than ordinary deposits. 定期預金のほうが普通預金よりも多くの利子が付く.

Many young people start smoking by *yielding* to peer pressure. 仲間の圧力に負けてタバコを吸い始める若者が多い.

Here, you must *yield* to traffic coming from another direction by waiting and allowing it to go first. ここでは, 別の方向から接近してくる車を優先するために, 停車して先に通さないといけない.

young /jʌ́ŋ/

young

原義は〈幼い〉である. **発生後時間が長く経っていない；動物・鳥の赤ちゃんたち**.

派 youth（若いころ，若者）; youthful（若者持有の）

We are twins. I'm *younger* by fifteen minutes.　私たちは双子です．私のほうが15分遅く生まれたの．

The night is still *young*. Let's go for more drinks at another bar.　まだ宵の口だよ．もう一杯やろうよ．

She married *young*, and now has three children.　彼女は若くして結婚したので，もう3人の子持ちだ．

A female polar bear usually gives birth to one or two *young* [= babies] in winter.　ホッキョクグマの雌は冬季に1, 2頭の子どもを産む．

---

zero

原義は〈空 (から)〉である. **(皆無)** →ゼロ，零，数字の0

Our chances of success are virtually *zero* [=nonexistent].　成功する可能性はほとんどない〔←事実上ゼロだ〕．

It's supposed to fall five degrees below *zero* tonight.　今夜は氷点下5度になるそうだ．

The thick fog has reduced visibility almost to *zero* [=its lowest point].　濃霧で視界はほとんど見えなくなった．

The number one million is written as one followed by six *zeros*. = One million is a one with six *zeros* after it.　百万は1の後ろに0が六つ付く．

索　引

*見出し語，派生語・関連語，および解説中の関連語句とその掲載ページ（太字は見出し語）を示しています．

A

a	**2**
ability	2
able	**2**, 252
about	**3**
above	**3**
abroad	**4**
absence	4
absent	**4**, 544
absentee	4
absolute	**5**
absolutely	5
abuse	**5**
accept	**6**
acceptable	6
acceptance	6
access	**6**
accessible	6
accident	**7**, 403
accidental	7
accord	**7**
accordingly	7
account	**8**, 174
accountable	8
accountancy	8
accountant	8
accuse	**8**, 271
achieve	**9**, 129
achievement	9
across	**9**
act	**10**
action	**10**
active	10
activist	10
activity	10
actor	10
actual	**11**
actually	11
acute	188
add	**11**
addition	11
additional	11
additive	11
address	**12**, 231, 232
adhere	383
adhesive	383
admission	12
admit	**12**, 478
advance	**13**
advanced	13
advancement	13
advantage	**13**
advantageous	13
advice	**14**, 684
advise	14
affair	**14**
affect	**15**, 244
affirm	156
afflict	156
afford	**15**
affordable	15
afraid	**16**
after	**16**
afternoon	265
again	**17**
against	**17**
age	**18**
agency	18
agent	**18**
age-old	504
ago	**19**
agree	**19**
agreement	19
agriculture	184
ahead	**20**
aid	**20**
aim	**21**, 263
aimlessly	21
air	**21**
airy	21
alive	446, 453
all	**22**
allot	458
allow	**22**
allowance	22
almost	**23**
alone	**23**
along	**24**, 65
already	**24**
alternate	25
alternative	**25**
alternatively	25
amiable	254
amity	254
among	**25**, 349
amount	**26**
analogue	**26**
analogy	26
analysis	**27**
analyst	27
analyze	27
ancestor	**27**
ancestry	27
anniversary	**28**, 29
announce	**28**
announcement	28
annual	28, **29**
annually	29
another	**29**
answer	**30**
anticlimax	137
anxiety	30
anxious	**30**
anxiously	30
any	**31**
apart	**31**
apartheid	31
apartment	**31**
aphorism	390
apologize	**32**
apology	**32**
appeal	**32**
appear	**33**
appearance	33
appetite	148
apply	**33**, 591
appoint	**34**

appointment 34	attempted 46	bare **56**	biased 70
appreciate **34**	attend **46**, 280	barefoot 325	bicycle **71**
appreciation 34	attendance 46	barren 56	bid **71**
approach **35**	attention 46	barrier **56**	bidder 71
approval 35	attentive 46	base **57**	bidding 71
approve **35**	attitude **47**	basement 57	big **72**
Arabic numerals 497	attract **47**	basin 57	bike 71
area **36**	attraction 47	bat **58**, 60	bilingual **72**
arena 36	attractive **47**	battle 58	bill **73**
argue **36**	audience **48**	bay 58	bind 73, 82
argument 36	audio equipment 48	bear **59**, 100	binding 73
arm **37**	author 48	beard **59**	bit **74**
around **37**	authority **48**	bearing 60	bite **74**
arrange **38**, 573	authorize 48	beat 58, **60**	bitter **75**
arrangement 38	automatic **49**	become **61**	bitterly 75
arrest **38**	automatically 49	before **61**	bitterness 75
arrival 39	available **49**	beget 353	blame **75**
arrive **39**	average **50**	begin **62**	blank **76**
art **39**	avoid **50**	beginning 62	blaspheme 75
article **40**	avoidable 50	behalf **62**	bleed **77**
ascend 204	award **51**	behave **63**	blind **76**
ask **40**	aware **51**	behavior 63	block **77**
asleep 626	awareness 51	behind 63, 384	blood **77**, 78
aspect **41**	away **52**	being **64**	bloody 77
assault 410		belief **64**	bloom 77, **78**
assemble **41**		believe **64**	blossom **78**
assembly 41	B	bellicose 579	blow **79**
assess **42**		belong 24, **65**	board **79**
assessment 42	back **52**	belongings 65	boast **80**
asset **42**	background 52	below **65**	body **80**
assist **43**	baggage **53**	belt **66**	boil **81**, 169
assistance 43	bake 169	bench 54	boiler 81
assistant 43	balance **53**	bend **66**	bomb **81**, 83
associate **43**, 628	balanced 53	beneath **67**	bombard 81
association 43	ban **54**	beneficial 67	bombardment 81
assume **44**	band 82	benefit **67**	bond 73, **82**
assumption **44**	banish 54	beside **68**	book **82**
at **44**	bank **54**, 55	besides **68**	booking 82
atmosphere **45**	banker 54	betray **69**	boom 81, **83**
atmospheric 45	banking 54	betrayal 69	boost **83**
attack **45**	bankrupt 54, **55**	between **69**	booster 83
attempt **46**	bankruptcy 55	beyond **70**	border **84**
	bar **55**, 249	bias 70	borderline 84

712

Word	Page
bore	**84**
boredom	84
boring	84
born	**85**
borrow	**85**
boss	**86**
bossy	86
both	**86**
bother	**87**
bottom	**87**
bottom line	87
bottomless	87
bow	**88**
bowel	**88**
brace	**89**
bracelet	89
brain	**89**
branch	**90**
brand	**90**
bread	90
break	**91**
breakfast	91
breastfeed	302
breath	**91**
breathe	91
breed	**92**
breeder	92
breeze	**92**
breezy	92
bribe	**93**
bribery	93
bridge	**93**
bright	**94**
brim	**94**
bring	**95**
brink	**95**
brisk	**96**
briskly	96
brittle	**96**
broad	**97**
broadcast	**97**, 115, 326
broadcaster	97
broaden	97
broadly	97
browse	**98**
browser	98
bubble	**98**
bud	**99**
budget	**99**
build	**100**
builder	100
building	100
burden	59, **100**
burial	102
burn	**101**
burst	**101**
bury	**102**
business	**102**, 103
busy	102, **103**
buy	**103**
buyer	103
by	**104**

C

Word	Page
calculate	**104**
calculation	104
calf	**105**
call	**105**
calm	**106**
camouflage	**106**
camp	**107**
can	**107**
canal	124
cancel	**108**
cancellation	108
cancer	**108**
Cancer	108
candid	**109**
candidate	**109**
candle	109
canny	107
cap	**109**, 110
capability	110
capable	109, **110**, 111
capacity	**110**
cape	109, 261
capital	**111**
capitalism	111
capitalist	111
capitalize	111
captain	109
capture	110, **111**, 261
care	112, 185, 607
career	**112**
carefree	113
careful	112, **113**
carefully	113
careless	113
carrier	113
carry	**113**
cascade	194
case	**114**, 115, 123, 500
cash	**114**
cast	97, 114, **115**
casual	114, **115**
casually	115
catch	**116**
categorize	116
category	**116**
cattle	**117**
cause	**117**
cave	118
cavity	**118**
cease	**118**, 195
ceasefire	118
celebrate	**119**
celebration	119
celebrity	119
cell	**119**
cell phone	119
cellar	119
center	**120**
centigrade	**120**
centimeter	120
centipede	120
central	120
century	120
ceremony	**121**
certain	**121**
certainly	121
certainty	121
chair	**122**
chairperson	122
challenge	**122**
challenging	122
chance	114, **123**
change	**123**, 270
changeable	123
channel	**124**
chaos	**124**
chaotic	124
character	**125**
characteristic	125
characterize	125
charge	**125**, 216
chase	**126**, 564
cheap	**126**
cheaply	126
cheat	**127**
check	**127**
cheer	**128**
cheerful	128
chef	**129**
chest	**128**
chicken	129
chief	9, **129**
chiefly	129
chill	**130**
chilly	130
chip	**130**
chirp	**131**
choice	132
choke	**131**
choose	**132**

Word	Page
clan	**132**
clap	**133**
clash	**133**
class	**134**
classic	134
classify	134
clean	**134**
cleaner	134
clear	**135**, 196
clearly	135
client	**135**
cliff	**136**
climate	**136**
climax	**137**
climb	**137**
cline	438
clod	138
close	**138**, 154
closed	138
closely	138
clot	**138**
cloth	**139**
cloud	**139**, 140
cloudy	139, **140**
clue	**140**
cohere	383
cold	**141**
coldly	141
collapse	**141**
colleague	**142**
collect	**142**
collection	142
collector	142
collide	**143**
collision	143
color-blind	76
come	**143**
comfort	144
comfortable	**144**
comfortably	144
command	**144**, 202
commander	144
commend	582
comment	**145**, 474
commentary	145
commentator	145
commerce	145
commercial	**145**
commit	**146**
commitment	146
committee	**146**
common	**147**
communicate	147
communication	147
communism	147
community	147
company	**147**
comparable	148
comparative	148
compare	**148**, 517
comparison	148
compel	151
compete	**148**
competent	148
competition	148
competitive	148
competitor	148
complain	**149**
complaint	149
complete	**149**
completely	149
complex	**150**
complexity	150
compose	**150**
composer	150
composition	150
composure	150
compromise	**151**, 557
compulsory	**151**
compute	221
concede	**152**
conceive	152
concept	**152**
conception	152
conceptual	152
concern	**153**
concerned	153
concession	152
concise	**153**, 196
concisely	153
conclude	138, **154**, 404
conclusion	154
concrete	318
concussion	218
condition	**154**
confess	**155**
confession	155
confidence	**155**
confident	155
confirm	**156**, 312
confirmation	156
conflict	**156**
confront	**157**
confrontation	157
confuse	**157**, 585
confusing	157
confusion	157
congratulate	158
congratulation	**158**
conifer	331
connect	**158**
connection	158
conscience	159
conscious	**159**
consciousness	159
consequence	159
consequently	159
conservation	160
conservative	**160**
conserve	160
consider	**160**, 206
considerable	160
considerate	160
consideration	160
consist	**161**
consistency	161
consistent	161
consistently	161
constant	**161**, 637
constantly	161
consult	**162**
consultant	162
consultation	162
consume	**162**
consumer	162
consumption	162
contact	**163**
contain	**163**
container	163
context	**164**, 659
continent	164
continual	164
continue	**164**
continuity	164
continuous	164
contract	**165**
contractor	165
contradict	165
contrary	**165**, 174
contrast	**166**, 637
contribute	**166**

contribution 166	couple **176**	custom **187**	decision 196
control **167**	courage **176**	customary 187	declaration 196
controller 167	courageous 176	customer 187	declare 135, **196**
controversial 167	course **177**	customize 187	decline **197**
controversy **167**	court **177**	customs 187	decrease 197, 404
convenience 168	cover **178**, 218	cut **187**	dedicate **198**
convenient **168**	crack **178**	cute **188**	dedication 198
convention 168	cracker 178	cycle 71	deed 224
conversation 168	crash 133, 143, **179**, 183		deep 192, **198**, 213
converse 168	create **179**, 404	**D**	deepen 198
convict 169	creation 179	daily 191	deeply 198
convince **169**	creative 179	damage **188**	defeat **199**
cook **169**	creature 179	damaging 188	defend **199**
cooker 169	crescendo 179	damn 188	defendant 199
cookie 169	crescent 179, 404	danger 189	defense 199
cool **170**	crest 179	dangerous **189**	defensive 199
cooler 170	crime **180**	dark **189**	define **200**, 311
coolly 170	criminal 180	darken 189	definitely 200
cope **170**	crisis **180**, 181	darkness 189	definition 200
copious 171	critic 181	data **190**	definitive 200
copulate 176	critical 180, **181**	database 190	defy **200**
copy **171**	criticism 181	date **190**	degree **201**, 360
copyright 171	criticize **181**	dawn **191**	delay **201**
cordial 176, 582	crop **182**, 366	day **191**, 265	deliver **202**
corner **171**	cross **182**	daze 192	delivery 202
correct **172**, 214	cross-examina-	dazzle **192**	demand 144, **202**
correction 172	tion 182	dead **192**, 193, 198, 211	demanding 202
correctly 172	crossing 182	deadline **193**	demonstrate **203**
corrupt 55, **172**	crowd **183**	deadly 192	demonstration 203
corruption 172	crowded 183	deaf 192, **193**	depend **203**
cost **173**	crush 133, 179, **183**	deal **194**	dependence 203
costly 173	cry **184**	dealer 194	dependent 203
cough **173**	cultural 184	death 211	depict 527
could **107**	culture **184**	debate 169	depress **204**, 545
count 8, **174**	cultured 184	debt 235, 237	depression 204
countable 174	cure 112, **185**	decay **194**	depth 198
counter 165, **174**, 175, 252	current **185**, 500	deceased 118, **195**	descend **204**
counterblow 252	currently 185	deceit 195	descendant 204
counterpart **175**	curse **186**	deceive **195**, 580	descent 204
country 174, **175**	curtail **186**	decide 153, **196**	describe **205**
coup 170	cuss 186		

description 205	digital 26	dislike 448	drawer 230
deserve **205**, 612	dim 189	dismiss **220**, 478	drawing 230
design **206**, 622	dip 198, **213**	dismissal 220	dream **230**
designer 206	dipper 213	display **221**	dreamy 230
desirable 206	direct 172, **214**	dispute **221**	dress 12, **231**
desire 160, **206**	direction 214	distance	dressing 231
desired 206	directly 214	222, 637	drill **231**
destination **207**	director 214	distant 222	drink
destine 207	dirt 214	distress 642	230, **232**, 234
destiny 207	dirty **214**	distribute 166	drinkable 232
destroy **207**	disagreement 19	district **222**	drinker 232
destruction 207	disappear **215**	disturb **223**	drip 233
destructive 207	disappearance	disturbance 223	drive 12, **232**
detail **208**	215	ditch 213	driver 232
detect **208**, 560	disappoint **215**	divert 224	driving 232
detective 208	disappointing	divide **223**, 405	droop 233
deteriorate 194	215	dividend 223	drop **233**
determination	disappointment	divisible 223	drought 229, 234
209	215	division 223	drove 232
determine	disarm 37	divorce **224**	drown **233**
209, 658	disarmament 37	do 10, **224**	drowning 233
determined 209	disaster **216**	doctor **225**	drug **234**
detour 667	disastrous 216	doctrine 225	dry 232, **234**
devastate 689	discern 153	document 225	dubious 227
develop **209**	discharge	dog **225**	due **235**
developing 209	125, **216**	doggie 225	dull **235**
development 209	disciple 217	dole 194	duly 235
devote 198	discipline **217**	dolt 235	duplicate 227
diagnose	disconnect 158	dome 226	durable 254
210, 398, 428	discourage	domestic **226**	during **236**
diagnosis 210	**217**, 253	door **226**	dust **236**
diameter **210**	discouragement	dot 190	duty **237**
diction 154	217	double **227**	dye **237**
die 192, **211**	discover	doubt **227**	
diet **211**	178, **218**	doubtful 227	E
dietary 211	discovery 218	down **228**	
differ 212	discuss **218**	download 454	each **238**
difference 212	discussion	draft **228**	eager **238**
different **212**	36, 218	drag **229**	eagerly 238
difficult **212**	disease **219**	drain **229**	early **239**
difficulty 212	disguise **219**	drainage 229	earn **239**
dig **213**	dish **220**	draw	earnings 239
digest 352	disk 220	229, **230**, 232	earth **240**

716

Word	Page
earthen	240
earthquake	240
ease	240
easily	240
easy	**240**
easygoing	240
eat	**241**
echo	**241**
ecological	242
ecology	**242**
economic	242
economics	242
economist	242
economize	242
economy	**242**
ecosystem	242
edge	**243**
educate	**243**
educated	243
education	243
educational	243
effect	15, **244**
effective	244
efficient	244
effort	**244**, 326
effortlessly	244
either	**245**
eject	498
elaborate	**245**, 429
elaboration	245
elbow	88
elder	246
elderly	**246**
elect	142, **246**
election	246
electric	247
electrical	247
electricity	**247**
electrify	247
element	**247**
elementary	247
eliminate	**248**, 450
elimination	248
else	**248**
elsewhere	248
email	461
embarrass	55, **249**
embarrassing	249
embarrassment	249
embrace	89
emerge	**249**
emergence	249
emergency	249
emotion	**250**, 485
emotional	250
emphasis	250
emphasize	**250**
employ	**251**
employees	251
employer	251
employment	251
empty	**251**
enable	2, **252**
encounter	174, **252**
encourage	217, **253**
encouragement	253
encouraging	253
encyclopedia	71
end	**253**
endless	253
endurance	254
endure	**254**
enemy	254
engage	**255**
engagement	255
enhance	**255**
enhancement	255
enjoy	**256**, 421
enjoyable	256
enjoyment	256
enormous	**256**
enough	**257**
ensure	**257**, 649
enter	**258**
entertain	**258**
entertainer	258
entertainment	258
entire	**259**
entirely	259
entrance	258
entry	258
envelope	209
environment	**259**
environmental	259
equal	**260**
equality	260
equally	260
equation	260
equinox	260
equip	**260**
equipment	260
equivalent	**261**, 681
escape	111, **261**
essence	**262**
essential	262
essentially	262
essentials	262
establish	**262**, 636
establishment	262
esteem	263
estimate	21, **263**
estimation	263
eternal	**263**
eternally	263
eternity	263
ethnic	**264**
ethnicity	264
evade	406
evaporate	**264**
evaporation	264
even	**265**
evening	**265**
evenly	265
event	**266**
eventual	266
eventually	266
ever	**266**
evergreen	266
every	**267**
evidence	**267**
evident	267
evolution	268
evolutionary	268
evolve	**268**, 415, 685
exact	**268**
exactly	268
examination	269
examine	**269**
excel	**269**
excellence	269
excellent	269
except	**270**
exception	270
exceptional	270
exchange	123, **270**
excite	**271**
excited	271
excitement	271
exciting	271
excuse	8, **271**
execute	**272**

execution	272
exercise	**272**
exhaust	**273**
exhausting	273
exhibit	**273**
exhibition	273
exist	**274**
existence	274
existing	274
expand	**274**, 280
expansion	274
expect	**275**
expectancy	275
expectation	275
expected	275
expend	**275**, 634
expenditure	275
expense	275
expensive	275
experience	**276**
experienced	276
experiment	276
expert	276
expiration	276
expire	**276**
expiry	276
expiry date	276
explain	**277**, 528
explanation	277
explicit	278
explode	**277**
exploit	**278**
exploitation	278
explore	**278**
explorer	278
explosion	277
explosive	277
export	**279**
exporter	279
expose	**279**
exposed	279
exposure	279
express	**280**, 402, 545
expression	280
extend	46, 274, **280**
extension	280
extensive	280
extent	280
exterior	282
extinct	**281**
extinction	281
extinguish	**281**
extinguisher	281
extra	282
extraordinary	510
extreme	**282**
extremely	282
eye	**282**
eyesight	622

F

fable	291, 298
fabric	**283**, 285
fabricate	283
fabrication	283
face	**283**
facial	283
facile	212, 284
facilitate	**284**
facilitation	284
facilitator	284
facilities	284
facility	286
fact	**284**, 285, 305
faction	285
factor	**285**, 296
factory	283, 284, **285**
factual	284
faculty	284, **286**
fade	**286**
fail	**287**, 291, 299
failure	**287**
faint	**288**
faintly	288
fair¹	**288**
fair²	**289**
fairly	288
faith	**289**
faithful	289
fake	**290**
fall	**290**
fallacy	291
false	287, **291**
falsely	291
falsify	291
fame	**291**, 298
famed	291
familiar	**292**
familiarity	292
familiarize	292
family	**292**
famine	**293**
famish	293
famous	291
fan	**293**
fanatic	293
fancy	**294**
fantastic	294
fantasy	**294**
far	**295**
fare	**295**
farm	**296**, 312
farmer	296
farming	296
fashion	285, **296**
fashionable	296
fast	**297**
fasten	297
fastener	297
fat	**297**
fatal	**298**
fatalitics	298
fatally	298
fate	291, **298**
fatigue	**299**
fatty	297
fault	287, **299**
favor	**300**, 304
favorable	300
favorably	300
favorite	**300**
favoritism	300
fear	**301**
fearful	301
feasible	301
feat	199, 301
feature	**301**
fed up	302
fee	**302**
feed	**302**, 324
feel	**303**
feelers	303
feeling	303
feign	288
female	**303**
feminine	303
feminism	303
feminist	303
fence	199
ferry	304, 331, 645
fertile	**304**
fertility	304
fertilize	304
fertilizer	304
festival	289
feudal	302
fever	300, **304**
feverish	304
few	**305**
fiction	284, **305**
fictional	305
fictitious	305
fidelity	200
field	**306**

fight **306**	flesh **316**	forbear 328	frank **334**
fighter 306	fleshly 316	forbid 328	frankly 334
figure **307**	fleshy 316	force 244, **326**	frankness 334
filament 307	flex **316**	forceful 326	fraud **335**, 339
file **307**	flexibility 316	fore 312, 325, 330	fraudulent 335
fill **308**, 341	flexible 316	forecast 97, **326**	free **335**
filling 308	flight 321	forecaster 326	freedom 335
final **308**, 311	float **317**, 319	foreign **327**	freely 335
finalize 308	flock **317**	foreigner 327	freeze **336**
finally 308	flood **318**, 319	forest **327**	freezer 336
finance **309**, 311	floor 315, **318**	forestry 327	freezing 336
financial 309	flooring 318	forget **328**	frequency 336
financially 309	flour **319**	forgetful 328	frequent **336**
find **309**	flourish 319	forgive **328**	frequently 336
finding 309	flow 317, 318, **319**	forgiveness 328	fresh **337**
fine **310**, 311	flower 319, **320**	forgiving 328	freshness 337
finger **310**	flowery 320	form **329**	friend **337**
finish 200, 308, 309, 310, **311**	flu 407	formal **329**	friendly 337
fire **311**, 340	fluctuate **320**	formality 329	friendship 337
firearms 311	fluctuation 320	formally **329**	from **338**
firefighter 306	fluent 320	formative **329**	front **338**
fireworks 311	fluid 320, 407	former 312, **330**	frontier 338
firm 156, 296, **312**	fly **321**	formerly 330	frost 336
firmly 312	flyer 321	forsake 328	fruit **339**
first **312**	focal 321	forswear 328	fruitful 339
fish **313**	focus **321**, 340	forth **330**	fruity 339
fisherman 313	fog **322**	forthcoming 330	frustrate 335, **339**
fishery 313	foggy 322	fortunate 331	frustrating 339
fishing 313	fold **322**	fortunately 331	frustration 339
fist 310	folder 322	fortune **331**	fry **340**
fit **313**	follow **323**	forward **331**	frying pan 340
fix **314**	follower 323	fossil **332**	fuel 311, 321, **340**
fixed 314	fond **323**	fossilize 332	fulfill 308, **341**
flabby 314	fondle 323	found **332**, 343	fulfillment 341
flag **314**	fondly 323	foundation 332	full 308, **341**
flame 311	food 302, **324**	founder 332	fully 341
flat **315**, 318	fool **324**	fraction **333**	fun **342**
flatten 315	foolish 324	fracture 333	function **342**
flavor **315**	foot **325**	fragile **333**	functional 342
flavoring 315	footnote 325	frail 333	fund 332, **343**
fleet 317	footstep 325	frame **334**	
	for **325**	framework 334	

fundamental 343	generation 351	graduate **361**	guardian 368
fundamentally 343	generic 350	graduation 361	gubernatorial 359
funeral **343**	generosity 351	grain **361**	
funeral director 343	generous 351, 352	granary 361	guess **368**
	genetic 350	grant **362**	guesswork 368
funeral home 343	gentle 351, **352**	grantee 362	guest **369**
funny 342	gently 352	grapple 362	guidance 369
furnish 344	gesture **352**	grasp **362**, 365	guide **369**
furnishings 344	get **353**	grasping 362	guilt 370
furniture **344**	gift **353**, 354	grass 363, 364, 367	guilty **370**
further **344**	give 353, **354**	grasshopper 363	guise 219
fuse 345	glad **354**	gratitude 158	
fuss **345**	gladly 354	grave **363**	## H
fussy 345	glass **355**	gravel 363	
futile **345**	glassful 355	gravity 363	habit **370**
futility 345	glassware 355	great **364**	habitat 370
future **346**	glassy 355	Great Dipper 213	habitual 370
	global **355**		hair **371**
## G	globalize 355	greatly 364	haircut 371
	globe 355	greedy 365	hairy 371
gain **346**	gloom 356	green 363, **364**	half **371**
gainful 346	gloomy **356**	green belt 364	halfway 371
gamble 347	glory 356	greenery 364	halve 371
game **347**	gloss 356	greenhouse 364	hand **372**
gap **347**	glow **356**	greet **365**	handful 372
gape 347	go 143, **357**	greeting 365	handle **372**
gaping 347	goal **357**	gregarious 349	handling 372
garbage **348**	god **358**	grief 586	handy 372
garden **348**	goddess 358	grip 362, **365**	hang **373**
gardener 348	godsend 358	ground 366, 367	hangover 373
gardening 348	gold **358**	grounder 366	happen **373**, 374
gas 124, **349**	golden 358	groundless 366	happening 373
gaseous 349	good **359**	group 182, 349, **366**	happiness 374
gasoline 349	goods 359	grove 366	happy 373, **374**
gather **349**	govern **359**	grow 363, 366, **367**	hard **374**
gender 350	governance 359	growth 367	harden 374
gene **350**	government 359	guarantee **367**	hardly **375**
general **350**	governor 359	guarantor 367	hardship 374
generally 350	gradation 360	guard **368**, 585	hardware 374
generate **351**	grade 201, **360**	guard dog 368	harm **375**
	gradual **360**		harmful 375
	gradually 360		harmless 375
			harvest **376**

haste **376**
hasten 376
hastily 376
hasty 376
hate **377**
hatred 377
have 63, **377**, 386
head **378**
headache 378
heading 378
headline 378
headlong 378
heal **378**
healer 378
health 378
healthcare 378
healthful 378
healthy 378
hear **379**
hearing 379
heart **379**, 477
heartfelt 379
heartwarming 379
heat **380**
heater 380
heating 380
heave 377, 381
heaven **380**
heavenly 380
heavily 381
heavy **381**
hectic **381**
height 384
heighten 384
help **382**, 604
helpful 382
helpless 382
herd 317
here **382**
hesitant 383
hesitate **383**
hesitation 383
hidden 383
hide **383**
hide-and-seek 383
high **384**, 654
highlight 384
highly 384
hind 384
hind leg 63
hinder 63, **384**
hindrance 384
hint **385**
historic 385
historical 385
history **385**, 642
hit **386**
hoist 372
hold 372, 377, **386**
holder 386
holding 386
hole **387**
holiday **387**
hollow 387
holy 387
home **388**
homeless 388
honest **388**, 389
honestly 388
honesty 388
honor 388, **389**
honorable 389
honorary 389
hope **389**
hopeful 389
hopefully 389
horizon **390**
horizontal 390
horizontally 390
horn 171
hospice 390
hospital **390**, 391
hospitalize 390
host 369, 390, **391**
hostage **391**
hostess 391
hostile 391
hot 380
hotel 390, 391
house 388
hug 372
human **392**
human being 392
human beings 392
humanism 392
humanity 392
humble **392**
humid 392
hundred **393**
hunger 393
hungrily 393
hungry **393**
hunt 372, **394**
hunter 394
hunting 394
hurry **394**
hurt **395**, 408
hurtful 395

I

ice **395**
ice cube 395
iced 395
icicle 395
idea **396**
ideal **396**
identical 397
identify 397
identity **397**
idle **397**
if **398**
ignorance 398
ignorant 398
ignore 210, **398**, 428
ill **399**
illegal 441
illness 219, 399
ill-starred 216
illustrate **399**
illustration 399
illustrious 399
image 400
imaginary 400
imagination 400
imagine **400**
imitate **400**
imitation 400
immediate **401**
immediately 401
immersion 249
impatient 522
import 279, 401
importance 401
important **401**
importantly 401
impossible 538
impress 280, **402**, 545
impression 402
impressive 402
imprisonment 550
improve **402**
improvement 402
improvise 562
in **403**
incidence 403
incident 7, **403**
incidental 403
incidentally 403
include 154, **404**
including 404

inclusive 404	interesting 411	journal **420**	knowledgeable 428
increase 179, 197, **404**	interfere **412**	journalism 420	knuckle 427
increasing 404	interference 412	journalist 420	
independence 203, 405	international **412**	journey **420**	**L**
independent **405**	internationally 412	joy 256, **421**	
independently 405	interrupt **413**	joyful 421	labor 245, **429**
individual 223, **405**	interruption 413	joyous 421	laborer 429
individualism 405	into **413**	judge **421**	laborious 429
individuality 405	introduce **414**, 583	judicature 421	lack **429**
individually 405	introduction 414	juice **422**	lacking 429
industrial 406	invent **414**	juicer 422	land **430**
industrialize 406	invention 414	juicy 422	landing 430
industrious 406	inventor 414	jump **422**	landlord 430
industry **406**	invitation 415	junior **423**	landscape **430**
inevitable **406**	invite **415**	juror 421	landscape gardener 430
infant 291	inviting 415	jury 421	language **431**
inflict 156	involve 268, **415**, 685	just 421, **423**	lap **431**
influence **407**	involvement 415	justice 423	laptop 431
inform **407**	iron **416**	justify 423	large 72, **432**
information 407	ironed 416	juvenile 423	largely 432
ingredient **408**	ironing 416		last¹ **432**
inhabit 370	issue **416**	**K**	last² **433**
inhabitant 370	it **417**		lasting 433
inject 587	item **417**	keep **424**	late **433**
injure **408**	itemize 417	keepsake 424	lately **434**
injury 408		key **424**	later 433
input **409**	**J**	keyboard 424	launch **434**
inspire 276		kick **425**	launder 435
instruct **409**	jealous **418**	kickoff 425	laundry **435**
instruction 409	jealousy 418	kill **425**	lavatory 435
instructor 409	jest 419	killer 425	law **435**
insult **410**, 596	jet 587	kind **426**	lawful 435
insurance 410	job **418**	kindly 426	lawsuit 435
insure **410**	jobless 418	kindness 426	lawyer 435
intend **411**	join **419**	kitchen **426**	lay 435, **436**, 445
intention 411	joint 419	knee **427**	lazily 436
interest 411	joke **419**	kneel 427	laziness 436
		knock **427**	lazy **436**
		know 210, 398, **428**	lead **437**
		knowingly 428	
		knowledge **428**	

722

leader	437	light²	**448**
leadership	437	lighten	447, 448
leading	437	lightly	448
leak	**437**	lightning	447
leakage	437	likable	448
leaky	437	like¹	**448**
lean	**438**	like²	**449**
learn	**438**	likelihood	449
learner	438	likely	**449**
least	**439**	liking	448
leave¹	**439**	limit	248, **450**
leave²	**440**	limitation	450
lecture	443	limited	450
left	**440**	limitless	450
left-handed	440	line	**450**
lefty	440	linear	450
leg	**441**	linguistics	431
legal	**441**	link	**451**
legally	441	linkage	451
lend	442, 454	list	**451**
less	**442**	listen	**452**
lessen	442	listener	452
lesser	442	listing	451
lesson	**443**	little	**452**
let	**443**	live	446
letter	**444**	live¹	**453**
level	**444**	live²	**453**
liar	446	lively	453
liberal	**445**	living	453
liberal arts	445	load	**454**
liberalism	445	loan	442, **454**
liberalization	445	local	**455**
liberate	202	local time	455
liberty	445	locally	455
lie¹	**445**	locate	**455**
lie²	**446**	location	455
life	**446**	lock	**456**
lifespan	446	locker	456
lifestyle	446	long	**456**
lift	**447**	look	**457**
lift-off	447	lookout	457
light¹	**447**	loose	**457**
		loosely	457
loosen	457		
lose	457, **458**		
loser	458		
loss	458		
lost	458		
lot	**458**		
lottery	458		
loud	**459**		
loudly	459		
lovable	459		
love	**459**		
lovely	459		
loving	459		
low	**460**		
lower	460		
luck	**460**		
luckily	460		
lucky	460		
luster	399		

M

mad	**461**
madly	461
madness	461
mail	**461**
mail order	461
main	**462**
mainly	462
maintain	258
major	**462**
majority	462
make	**463**
maker	463
makeup	463
making	463
malaise	219
manage	**463**
manageable	463
management	463
manager	463
manner	**464**
manual	464
manufacture	285, **464**
manufacturer	464
manufacturing	464
many	**465**, 482
march	**465**
mark	**466**
marked	466
markedly	466
marker	466
market	**466**
marketable	466
marketing	466
marriage	467
married	467
marry	**467**
mass	**467**
mass media	472
massive	467
master	**468**
mastermind	468
masterpiece	468
mastery	468
match	**468**
material	**469**
matter	469
may	462, **470**
maybe	**470**, 551
mean	**471**
meaning	471
meaningful	471
meaningless	471
measure	**471**
measurement	471
media	**472**
mediate	472
medical	472
medication	472
medicine	**472**

meet	**473**	modernization		multiplication		newcomer	493
meeting	473		480		486	newly	493
melt	**473**	modernize	480	multiply	**486**	news	493
memo	474	moment	**481**	murder	**486**	news media	472
memorable	474	momentarily	481	murderer	486	next	**493**
memorial	474	momentary	481	murmur	484	nice	**494**
memorize	474	monetary	481	muscle	**487**	nicely	494
memory	**474**	money	**481**	muscular	487	night	265, **494**
mental	145	money order		must	**487**	nightly	494
mention			510	mute	484	nightmare	494
	145, **474**	monster	203	mutter	484	no	**495**
merge	249	monument	203			nonprofit	555
message	**475**	moo	484	N		norm	256
method	**475**	mood	**482**			normal	256
methodical	475	moody	482	name	**488**	notable	495
methodology		more	**482**	namely	488	note	**495**
	475	morning	265	narrow	**488**	noteworthy	495
middle	**476**	mortal	486	narrowly	488	nothing	**496**
might	462, **470**	mortgage	255	nation	412, **489**	notice	**496**
mild	**476**	most	**483**	national	489	noticeable	496
mildly	476	mostly	483	nationalism	489	notify	496
mind	**477**	motivate		nationalist	489	notion	496
mindful	477		**483**, 485	nationality	489	now	**497**
mindless	477	motivation	483	nationally	489	number	**497**
mingle	349	motive	483	nationwide	489	numerous	497
mini	477	motorbike	71	native	**489**		
minute	**477**	mound	484	natural	490	O	
miss	**478**	mountain	**484**	naturally	490		
missing	478	mountain range		nature	**490**	object	**498**
mission			38	near	**490**	objection	498
	12, 220, **478**	mountaineer	484	nearby	490	objective	**498**
missionary	478	mountaineering		necessarily	491	objectively	498
mist	322		484	necessary	**491**	objectivity	498
mistake	**479**	mountainous		necessity	491	observation	499
mix	**479**		484	need	**491**	observatory	499
mixed	479	mouth	**484**	needy	491	observe	**499**
mixture	479	mouthful	484	negotiate	**492**	observer	499
moan	484	move		negotiation	492	obvious	
moderate	**480**		250, 483, **485**	neighbor	**492**		499, 547
moderately	480	movement	485	neighborhood		obviously	499
moderation	480	moving	485		492	occasion	
moderato	480	much	482, **485**	neighboring	492		114, **500**
modern	**480**	multiple	486	new	**493**	occasional	500

occasionally 500	origin 511	papyrus 518	period **525**
occur 185, **500**	original **511**	parent **518**	periodical 525
occurrence 500	originality 511	parental 518	periscope 525
odd **501**	originally 511	park **519**	person **526**
of **501**	originate 511	parking 519	personal 526
off **502**	other **512**	parking lot	personality 526
offend 199	otherwise **512**	458, 519	personally 526
offer **502**	ought 513, 515	part **519**	petition 148
office **503**	out **513**	partial 519	pick **526**
officer 503	outcome **514**	particle 520	pickpocket
official 503	outperform 524	particular **520**	526, 532
officially 503	output 409	particularly 520	picture **527**
often **503**	outside **514**	partly 519	picturesque 527
oil **504**	outsider 514	partner 519	piece **527**
oily 504	outsource 632	party **520**	place
old **504**	over **515**	pass **521**	528, 591, 625
old-fashioned	overeager 238	passable 521	plain 277, **528**
504	overly 515	passage 521	plainly 528
on **505**	overnight 494	passenger 521	plaintiff 199
once **505**	overrate 575	passport 521	plan **529**
one **506**	oversensitive	past **521**	plane 529
only **506**	610	patience 522	plant **529**
open **507**	owe	patient **522**	plantation 529
opening 507	513, **515**, 516	patiently 522	plaster 530
openly 507	owing 515	pay **522**	plastic **530**
opinion **507**, 509	own 515, **516**	payable 522	plate 529
opinion poll 507	owner 516	payment 522	play **530**
opinionated 507	ownership 516	peck 526	play ball 530
opportunity **508**		pendant 203	player 530
oppose 508, 649	P	people 523, 536	pleasant 531
opposite **508**		percent **523**	please **531**
opposition 508	pack 317	percentage 523	pleased 531
opt 509	pain **516**	percussion 218	pleasure 531
option 507, **509**	painful 516	perfect **524**	plural 33, 531
optional 509	painkiller 516	perfection 524	plus 33, **531**
or **509**	paint **517**	perfectionism	pocket **532**
order **510**	painter 517	524	poem **532**
orderly 510	painting 517	perfectly 524	poet 532
ordinary **510**	pair 148, **517**	perform **524**	poetic 532
organ 511	panacea 274	performance 524	poetry 532
organization 511	paper **518**	performer 524	point **533**
organize **511**	paperless 518	perhaps 470, **525**	pointed 533
organized 511	paperwork 518	peril 276	pointless 533

索 引 725

police **533**	praise **541**, 548, 551	prince 548	programming 555
police officer 533	praiseworthy 541	principle **548**	progress **556**
policeman 533	pray **542**	print **549**	progression 556
policewoman 533	prayer 542	printer 549	progressive 556
policy **534**	precise 153	printing 549	progressively 556
political 534	predict **542**	prior 549	project **556**, 644
politically 534	predictable 542	priority **549**	projection 556
politics 534	prediction 542	prison **550**	projector 556
poll **534**	prefer **543**	prisoner 550	promise 151, **557**
polling station 534	preferable 543	privacy 550	promising 557
pollutant 535	preferably 543	private **550**	promote **557**
pollute **535**	preference 543	privately 550	promoter 557
pollution 535	prefix 314	privatize 550	promotion 557
poor **535**	pregnancy 543	prize 541, 548, **551**	proof **558**, 562
poorly 535	pregnant **543**	probability 551	proofread 558
popular 523, **536**	preparation 544	probable 551	proper **558**, 559
popularity 536	prepare **544**	probably **551**	properly 558
populate 536	presence 262	probe 558	property 558, **559**
population **536**	present 4, **544**	problem **552**	proposal **559**
pose 150, 279	presentation 544	problematic 552	propose 559, 649
position **537**	presently 544	procedure 552	prospect **560**
positive **537**	preservation 545	proceed **552**, 553	prospective 560
positively 537	preservative 545	process 552, **553**	protect 208, **560**
possibility **538**	preserve **545**	procession 553	protection 560
possible **538**	press 204, 280, 402, **545**	processor 553	protective 560
possibly 538	press release 588	produce **553**	protector 208, 560
post **539**	pressure 545	producer 553	protest **561**
postage 539	presume 44	product **554**	Protestant 561
pound **539**	pretend **546**	production 554	protesters 561
poverty 535	pretense 546	productive 554	proud **561**
power 326, **540**	pretentious 546	profess 155	proudly 561
powered 540	pretty **546**	professional **554**	prove 558, **562**
powerful 540	prevent **547**	professionally 554	provide **562**
powerless 540	prevention 547	professor 155, 554	provided 562
practical **540**, 541	preventive 547	profit **555**	psychoanalysis 27
practically 540	previous 499, **547**	profitable 555	public **563**
practice 540, **541**	previously 547	profound 332	publication 563
practitioner 541	price 541, **548**	program **555**	
	pride 561	programmer 555	

publicity	563	racial	572	receipt	580	relatively	587
publicly	563	racing	571	receive	195, **580**	release	**588**
publish	**563**	racism	572	receiver	580	remain	**588**
publisher	563	racist	572	recent	**581**	remainder	588
pull	**564**	radius	210	recently	581	remaining	588
punish	516	rain	**572**	reception	580	remains	588
purchase	126, **564**	rainbow	88, 572	recipient	580	remember	**589**
purpose	**565**	rainfall	572	recline	197	remembrance	589
purposely	565	rainstorm	572	recognition	581	remind	**589**
pursue	**565**	rainy	140, 572	recognize	**581**	reminder	589
pursuit	565	raise	**573**, 599	recommend	**582**	removal	590
push	**566**	range	38, **573**	recommendation	582	remove	**590**
put	528, **566**	rapid	**574**	record	**582**	repeat	**590**
put out	281	rapidity	574	recover	**583**	repeatedly	590
		rapidly	574	recovery	583	repeater	590
		rare	**574**	rectangle	172	repetition	590
Q		rarely	574	rectum	172	replace	528, **591**
		rarity	574	reduce	414, **583**	replacement	591
qualification	567	rash	575	reduction	583	reply	33, **591**
qualify	**567**	rate	**575**	refer	**584**	report	**592**
quality	**567**	rather	**575**	reference	584	reportedly	592
quarter	**568**	rating	575	reflex	316	reporter	592
quarterly	568	ratio	575	reform	**584**	reputation	221
quartet	568	reach	39, **576**	reformation	584	request	568, **592**
quest	568	read	**576**	refusal	585	research	593, 605
question	**568**, 592	reader	576	refuse	157, **585**	researcher	593
questionnaire	568	readily	577	regard	368, **585**	reservation	593
quick	**569**	readiness	577	regarding	585	reserve	**593**
quicken	569	reading	576	regardless	585	resist	274
quickly	569	ready	**577**	regret	**586**	resource	**594**
quiet	**569**, 570	real	**577**, 578	regrettable	586	resourceful	594
quietly	569	realistic	577	regular	**586**	respect	**594**
quit	569, **570**	reality	577	regularly	586	respectable	594
quite	**570**	realization	578	regulate	586	respond	**595**
quotation	571	realize	577, **578**	regulation	586	response	595
quote	**571**	really	577, **578**	reject	**587**	responsibility	**595**
		reason	579	rejection	587		
R		reasonable	579	relate	**587**	responsible	595
		reasonably	579	related	587	responsive	595
race^1	**571**	rebel	**579**	relation	587	rest	**596**
race^2	572	rebellion	579	relationship	587	restaurant	641
		rebellious	579	relative	587	restful	596
		recall	**580**				

restless 596	sadness 603	sentence **611**	shop **619**
restore 641	safe **603**, 604	sentiment 611	shopping 619
result 410, **596**	safely 603	sentimental 611	short **619**
retail 208	safety 603	separate **611**	shortage 619
return **597**	same **604**, 624	separately 611	shortcut 187
returnable 597	satisfy 42, 603	separation 611	shorten 619
returnee 597	save 603, **604**	sequence 159, 606	shortly 619
review **597**, 682	saving 604	serious **612**	shot 618, **620**
revolve 415	say **605**	seriously 612	should **615**
rich **598**	saying 605	seriousness 612	show **620**
richly 598	script 205	serve 205, **612**	showy 620
richness 598	scurry 394	server 612	sick **621**
ride **598**	search 593, **605**, 608	service 612	sickness 219, 621
rider 598	second **606**	set **613**, 625	side **621**
right **599**	secondary 606	setting 613	sidewalk 621
righteous 599	secondhand 606	settle **613**	sideward 621
rightful 599	secrecy 606	settlement 613	sight **622**
rightly 599	secret **606**	settler 613	sightseeing 622
rise 573, **599**	secretary 606	sex **614**	sign 206, **622**
risk **600**	secretly 606	sexism 614	signal 622
risky 600	secure 112, **607**	sexual 614	signature 622
role **600**	security 607	sexuality 614	silence **623**
role model 600	see **607**	sexy 614	silent 623
roll 600	seed **608**	shade 614	silently 623
room **601**	seek 40, 605, **608**	shadow **614**	similar **623**, 624
roomy 601	seem **609**	shady 614	similarity 623
route **601**	seemingly 609	shake **615**, 618	similarly 623
routine 601	select 132, 246	shaky 615	simple 150, 604, **623**, **624**
rule **602**	self-conscious 159	shall **615**	simply 624
ruler 602	self-evident 267	shape **616**	simulate 623
run **602**	self-taught 656	shapeless 616	since **624**
runner 602	sell **609**	share **616**	sit 613, **625**
running 602	seller 609	shareholder 616	site **625**
running costs 602	semen 608	sharp **617**	situate 626
rupture 55, 172, 413	seminar 608	sharpen 617	situation 626
rush 394	send **610**	sharply 617	sit-ups 625
	sender 610	ship **617**	sleep **626**
S	sense **610**	shipment 617	sleepiness 626
sad **603**	sensible 610	shock 615, **618**	sleepy 626
sadden 603	sensitive 610	shocking 618	slow **627**
		shoot **618**, 620	slowly 627
		shooting 618	

slumber 626	speedy 634	studious 643	sure 121, 257, **649**
small **627**	spend 275, **634**	study **643**	surely 257, 649
smallness 627	spending 634	stuff 641, **644**	surface 283
smoke **628**	spot **635**	subject 556, **644**	surge 632
smoked 628	spotless 635	subjective 498, 644	surround 631, **650**
smoker 628	spread **635**	subliminal 248	surroundings 650
smoky 628	stability 636	succeed **645**	surveillance 650
snowy 140	stabilize 636	succeeding 645	survey **650**
sociability 628	stable 262, **636**, 637	success 645	survival 651
sociable 628	staff **636**	successful 645	survive **651**
socialize 628	stage **637**	successfully 645	survivor 651
society 43, **628**	stall 640	successive 645	suspect **651**
solution 629	stamp 640	suffer **645**	suspicion 651
solve **629**	stance 222	sufferer 645	suspicious 651
some **629**	stand 161, 166, 222, 596, 636, **637**, 638, 639	suffering 645	swallow 232
sonar 631		suffix 314	system **652**
soon **630**		suggest **646**	systematic 652
sore 630		suggestion 646	
sorry **630**	standard 637, **638**	suggestive 646	T
sort **631**	standardize 638	suit **646**	
sorter 631	start **638**	suitable 646	tact 163
sound 631, 650	startle 638	suitably 646	tailor 186, 208
soundly 631	state **639**	sum **647**	take **652**
source **632**	statement 639	summarize 647	tale 657
Southern Cross 182	statue 639	summary 647	talent **653**
sow 608	stay 637, **639**	summit 647	talented 653
soybean flour 319	step **640**	sun **647**	talk **653**, 657
space **632**	still **640**	sunlight 647	talkative 653
spacious 632	stillness 640	sunny 140, 647	tall 384, **654**
spare **633**	sting 281	sunrise 647	target **654**
spare key 633	stone 318	sunscreen 647	task **655**
spareribs 633	stop 641, 644	sunset 647	taste **655**
sparing 633	store **641**	sunshine 647	tasty 655
sparingly 633	story 385, **642**	supervise 650	tax 655
speak **633**, 653	strain 642	supplier 648	teach **656**
speaker 633	stress **642**	supply **648**	teacher 656
spectacular 560	stressful 642	support **648**	teaching 656
speech 633	strict 222	supporter 648	tear[1] **656**
speechless 633	structure 207, 406	supportive 648	tear[2] **657**
speed **634**	struggle **643**	suppose **649**	tell 653, **657**
speedily 634	student 643	supposed 649	
		supposedly 649	

teller	657	tire	**664**	troubleshoot		universe	**676**
tend	**658**	tired	664		618, 672	unlawful	435
tendency	658	tiring	664	troublesome	672	unless	**677**
term	209, **658**	to	**664**	true	**672**	unload	454
terminal	658	together	349	truly	672	unlock	456
terminate		tongue	**665**, 72	trust	**673**	unmarried	467
	209, 658	tongue twister		trustee	673	until	**677**
text	164, **659**		665	trustworthy	673	untreated	671
text message		top	**665**	truth	672	unusual	680
	659	total	**666**	try	**673**	unwanted	688
textbook	659	totally	666	trying	673	up	**678**
textile	164	touch	652, **666**	turbine	223, 674	update	190, **678**
textual	659	touchy	666	turbulent		upon	**679**
texture	659	tough	**667**		223, 672	upper	678, **679**
thank	**659**	toughness	667	turn	667, **674**	up-to-date	
thankful	659	tour	**667**, 674	twice	505		190, 678
thankfully	659	tourist	667	twofold	322	usable	680
thanks	659	towards	**668**			use	**680**
then	660	town	**668**	U		used	680
there	382	townspeople				useful	680
thing	**660**		668	unaided	20	useless	680
think	659, **661**	trace	669	unattended	46	usual	**680**
thinking	661	track	**669**	unavoidable	50	usually	680
thorough	662	tractor	47	unbelievable	64	utensil	680
thought	661	trade	**669**	under	**674**	utility	680
thoughtful	661	trader	669	understand	**675**	utilize	680
threat	**661**	trading	669	understandable			
threaten	661	train	**670**		675	V	
threatening	661	trained	670	understandably			
through	**662**	trainer	670		675	valuable	681
throughout	662	training	670	understanding		valuables	681
throw	**662**	traitor	69		675	value	
thundery	140	trap	671	unemployed	251		49, 261, **681**
tight	**663**	travel	**670**	unflagging	314	vapor	264
tighten	663	traveler	670	unhurried	394	variable	681
tightly	663	tread	669	unicycle	676	varied	681
tightness	663	treat	**671**	union	**675**	variety	681
tile	318	treatment	671	unique	**676**	vary	**681**
till	677	trek	669	uniqueness	676	via	547
time	**663**	trial	673	unit	675	victim	**682**
timely	663	tribute	166	unite	675	victimize	682
timing	663	trip	**671**	unity	675	video	267
tip	665	trouble	**672**	universal	676	view	597, **682**

viewer	682	wanted	688	whether	**697**	working	704
viewpoint	682	warm	**688**	which	**697**	workload	454
violate	683	warmth	688	while	**698**	workout	704
violence	**683**	warn	**689**, 690	whiskers	59	workshop	619, 704
violent	683	warning	689	who	**698**		
virtual	**683**	waste	**689**	whole	378, **699**	world	**705**
virtually	683	wasteful	689	wholesale	699	worldwide	705
visibility	684	watch	687, 689, **690**	why	**699**	worried	705
visible	**684**	watchful	690	wide	**700**	worry	**705**
vision	682, 684	water	**690**, 695	widely	700	worrying	705
visit	14, **684**	waterfall	690	widen	700	worth	**706**
visitation	684	watery	690	widespread	635, 700	worthwhile	706
visitor	684	wavelength	691	width	700	worthy	706
visual	684	wave	**691**	wild	**700**	would	**701**
vocal	685	waver	691	wildlife	700	wow	703
voice	**685**, 686	wavy	691	wildly	700	writ	706
volume	268, 415, **685**	way	**691**	wildness	700	write	**706**
vote	685, **686**	way of life	691	will	**701**	writer	706
voter	686	weak	**692**	win	169, **701**	writing	706
vow	686	weaken	692	wind	92	written	706
vowel	685	weakness	692	winner	701	wrong	**707**
		wear	**692**	winning	701	wrongly	707
W		weary	692	wish	**702**		
		weather	**693**	wishful	702	**Y**	
wage	255	week	**693**	with	**702**		
wait	**686**	week day	693	wither	693	year	**707**
waiter	686	weekend	693	wonder	**703**	yearly	707
waitress	686	weekly	693	wonderful	703	yet	**708**
wake	690	weigh	**694**	wood	318, **703**	yield	**708**
walk	**687**	weight	694	wooded	703	young	**709**
walker	687	welcome	**694**	wooden	703	youth	709
walking	687	wet	690, **695**	word	704	youthful	709
wall	**687**	what	**695**	wordy	704		
wander	687	when	**696**	work	**704**	**Z**	
want	**688**	where	**696**	worker	704	zero	**709**

[著者紹介]

政村秀實(まさむら ひでみ)

1944年，山口県周防大島町久賀に生まれる．
大阪教育大学，Temple University (Philadelphia), Central Washington University (Ellensburg) の各大学院で英語・英語教育学を学ぶ．
広島女子大学国際文化学科（現・県立広島大学）などで教鞭をとる．
2004年に教職を退き，現在に至る．
著書に『図解 英語基本語義辞典』（桐原書店），『英語語義イメージ辞典』（大修館書店），『イメージ活用英和辞典』（小学館），『イメージでつかむ英語基本動詞100』（くろしお出版）などがある．編著書・分担執筆に『ブライト和英辞典』（小学館），『ベーシックジーニアス英和辞典』（大修館書店）などがある．
E-mail: hidemi@kvision.ne.jp

イラスト　　ひろせさかえ
編集協力　　ランゲージアーツ言語教育研究所

[図解] 英単語イメージ辞典
©Hidemi MASAMURA, 2018　　　　　　　　NDC 833/ii, 731p/19cm

初版第1刷——2018年2月20日

著　者————政村秀實
発行者————鈴木一行
発行所————株式会社 大修館書店
　　　　　　〒113-8541　東京都文京区湯島2-1-1
　　　　　　電話 03-3868-2651(販売部)　03-3868-2292(編集部)
　　　　　　振替 00190-7-40504
　　　　　　[出版情報] https://www.taishukan.co.jp

装丁・本文デザイン——内藤創造
印刷所————壮光舎印刷
製本所————ブロケード

ISBN978-4-469-04184-2　Printed in Japan
Ⓡ本書のコピー、スキャン、デジタル化等の無断複製は著作権法上での例外を除き禁じられています。本書を代行業者等の第三者に依頼してスキャンやデジタル化することは、たとえ個人や家庭内での利用であっても著作権法上認められておりません。